Bridging the Gaps

Bridging the Gaps

Integrating Archaeology and History in Oaxaca, Mexico

A Volume in Memory of Bruce E. Byland

EDITED BY

DANNY ZBOROVER AND PETER C. KROEFGES

UNIVERSITY PRESS OF COLORADO
Boulder

© 2015 by University Press of Colorado

Published by University Press of Colorado
5589 Arapahoe Avenue, Suite 206C
Boulder, Colorado 80303

 The University Press of Colorado is a proud member of
The Association of American University Presses.

The University Press of Colorado is a cooperative publishing enterprise supported, in part, by Adams State University, Colorado State University, Fort Lewis College, Metropolitan State University of Denver, Regis University, University of Colorado, University of Northern Colorado, Utah State University, and Western State Colorado University.

∞ This paper meets the requirements of the ANSI/NISO Z39.48-1992 (Permanence of Paper).

ISBN: 978-1-60732-328-0 (cloth)
ISBN: 978-1-60732-329-7 (ebook)

Library of Congress Cataloging-in-Publication Data
Bridging the gaps : integrating archaeology and history in Oaxaca, Mexico : a volume in memory of Bruce E. Byland / edited by Danny Zborover and Peter C. Kroefges.
    pages cm
  Includes index.
  ISBN 978-1-60732-328-0 (cloth) — ISBN 978-1-60732-329-7 (ebook)
  1. Archaeology and history—Mexico—Oaxaca (State) 2. Oaxaca (Mexico : State)—Antiquities. I. Byland, Bruce E., 1950–2008. II. Zborover, Danny. III. Kroefges, Peter C.
  F1219.1.O11B74 2015
  972'.7401—dc23
                            2014028187

24   23   22   21   20   19   18   17   16   15   10   9   8   7   6   5   4   3   2   1

Cover photographs. The genealogy of the rulers of Ihualtepec, photograph by Vittorio D'Onofri (*top*); Carved human mandible from the Museo Rufino Tamayo, Oaxaca City, photograph by Danny Zborover (*bottom*).

DZ: To my parents, Anca and Yona Zborover, and to my Verónica.

PK: To my grandmother, Elisabeth A. Carlson, and in
memory of my grandfather, Conrad W. Carlson

Contents

Acknowledgments   ix

1. From "1-Eye" to Bruce Byland: Literate Societies and Integrative
   Approaches in Oaxaca
   Danny Zborover   1

2. The Convergence of History and Archaeology in Mesoamerica
   Ronald Spores   55

3. Bruce Edward Byland, PhD: 1950–2008
   John M.D. Pohl   75

4. Multidisciplinary Fieldwork in Oaxaca
   Viola König   83

5. Mythstory and Archaeology: Of Earth Goddesses, Weaving Tools, and
   Buccal Masks
   Geoffrey G. McCafferty and Sharisse D. McCafferty   97

6. Reconciling Disparate Evidence between the Mixtec Historical Codices
   and Archaeology: The Case of "Red and White Bundle" and "Hill of the Wasp"
   Bruce E. Byland   113

7. Mixteca-Puebla Polychromes and the Codices
   Michael D. Lind   *131*

8. Pluri-Ethnic Coixtlahuaca's Longue Durée
   Carlos Rincón Mautner   *157*

9. The Archaeology and History of Colonialism, Culture Contact, and Indigenous Cultural Development at Teozacoalco, Mixteca Alta
   Stephen L. Whittington and Andrew Workinger   *209*

10. Salt Production and Trade in the Mixteca Baja: The Case of the Tonalá-Atoyac-Ihualtepec Salt Works
    Bas van Doesburg and Ronald Spores   *231*

11. Integrating Oral Traditions and Archaeological Practice: The Case of San Miguel el Grande
    Liana I. Jiménez Osorio and Emmanuel Posselt Santoyo   *263*

12. Decolonizing Historical Archaeology in Southern Oaxaca, and Beyond
    Danny Zborover   *279*

13. Prehispanic and Colonial Chontal Communities on the Eastern Oaxaca Coast on the Eve of the Spanish Conquest
    Peter C. Kroefges   *333*

14. Locating the Hidden Transcripts of Colonialism: Archaeological and Historical Evidence from the Isthmus of Tehuantepec
    Judith Francis Zeitlin   *363*

15. Using Nineteenth-Century Data in Contemporary Archaeological Studies: The View from Oaxaca and Germany
    Viola König and Adam T. Sellen   *391*

   List of Contributors   *411*

   Index   *413*

Acknowledgments

Like its subject matter, this book is the physical materialization of oral presentations, written words, and visual images. The idea for putting it together sprang after an animated session titled "Integrating Archaeology and History in Oaxaca," held at the Society for American Archaeology Annual Meeting in April 2007. The editors would like to thank all the participants of the original session; the discussants Geoffrey G. McCafferty and Maarten E.R.G.N. Jansen; and Bruce Byland, who afterwards invited us for dinner and wine. We would like to express our deepest gratitude to the resulting volume contributors for their collaborative efforts (and patience) across several countries and continents; to Cara Tannenbaum for kindly providing photos and information about her late husband, Bruce Byland; and to John M.D. Pohl for preparing the codex illustrations. Danny Zborover would also like to acknowledge the support of the Department of Archaeology at the University of Calgary and the Center for U.S.-Mexican Studies at the University of California, San Diego. We thank the two anonymous reviewers who made this a better volume by providing their constructive criticisms and positive feedbacks. Finally, we express our sincere gratitude to Darrin Pratt and especially Jessica d'Arbonne of the University Press of Colorado for their enthusiastic support and professionalism throughout the editorial process.

Bridging the Gaps

I

From "1-Eye" to Bruce Byland

Literate Societies and Integrative Approaches in Oaxaca

DANNY ZBOROVER

A major problem has been to bridge the gap between the peoples who are identified by Spanish and Indian documentary records and those who are known to us only through the ruins of their buildings and the broken elements of their material culture which have survived. —Vaillant 1937:324

The would-be correlator faces the problem of a genuine "gap" between the emphasis in the native traditions on political and dynastic history and the sequent modifications in artifact form which are the chief concern of the excavator . . . The problem is to bridge this gap, to tie the two kinds of history together at key points, to integrate the two sets of data in a meaningful synthesis. —Nicholson 1955:596

Los avances que se han hecho y los que están por hacerse, descansan en la confluencia conciente y coordinadora de dos disciplinas . . . esta recreación del acercamiento antropológico unificado, que llena la brecha entre disciplinas, es la ola del futuro. En la medida en que nuestras tareas estén coordinadas, en esa medida podremos aprender. —Byland and Pohl 1990:385–386

SCOPE AND DEFINITIONS

It is safe to assume that all past human societies were both material and historical, in the sense that all created objects and had developed visual and rhetorical strategies to encode and transmit social memory. Yet of those, only a few societies ever

DOI: 10.5876/9781607323297.c001

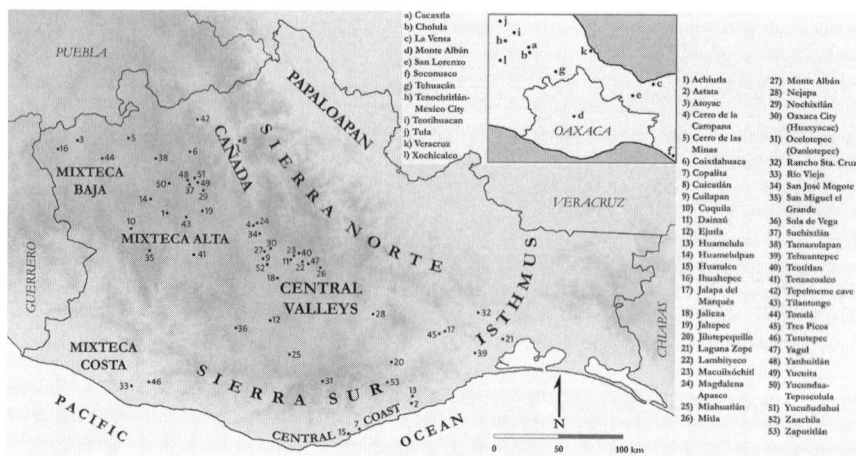

FIGURE 1.1. The state of Oaxaca and adjacent areas, with places and regions mentioned in the volume.

"materialized" their history to create durable record-keeping systems that would preserve their voices for future generations. Mesoamerican civilization was unified in the past, and defined in the present, by its shared material and intellectual achievements, most notably as expressed through art styles, iconography, architecture, ceramics, calendars, and writing systems (Kirchhoff 1952; R. Joyce 2004). The cultural area roughly corresponding to the modern state of Oaxaca has been long recognized as a focal point for these cultural manifestations, while serving as a crossroads of people, objects, and ideas within greater Mesoamerica. For the last 12,000 years or so people settled throughout the complex Oaxacan geography, which encompasses steep mountain ranges, ample valleys, lush lowlands, and coastal plains, creating in the process a remarkable cultural and ethnolinguistic tapestry. Today we recognize several subregions within Oaxaca, which largely correspond to these broad geographical zones (figure 1.1).

Bearing in mind that the modern state boundaries of Oaxaca are the abstraction of a long geopolitical process that began in the 1520s CE and was formalized in the mid-nineteenth century, it is remarkable that these still roughly correspond to the spatial extent of several artifactual types throughout prehispanic times, the known distribution of the Classic-period Zapotec script variants in southern Mexico, certain documentary traditions of the Postclassic and Colonial periods, as well as the historical and contemporary dispersion of most Otomanguean languages (Cline 1972; Gerhard 1993; Urcid 1993, 2001, 2005a, 2011b, 2011c; see also Chance 1986; Kowalewski et al. 1989; Paddock 1966a). Consequently, these subregions and the state boundaries themselves have played significant roles in the way integrative research has been defined and conducted in the region, and have shaped a scholarly tradition that for the most part is distinctively "Oaxacan" (see below). As such, this volume's spotlight on Oaxaca is firmly rooted in the idiosyncratic geographical, material, documentary, and cultural parameters that set the region apart from adjacent ones, yet without overlooking the region's mutual influences on neighboring states and the larger Mesoamerican picture.

The distinct practice of integrating the durable material and historical records so as to reflect upon the past can often be traced back to the same early scholars of those literate societies, through the beginning of archaeology as a modern discipline in the nineteenth century and down to modern-day scholarship. The recent and growing international literature on the subject of interdisciplinary integration of material culture, documentary, and oral sources in reconstructing the past clearly demonstrates that the topic is still highly relevant today, even as the goal continues to be extremely challenging.[1] Considering the long trajectory of literate societies and their respective academic research in the culture area under focus, it is surprising that despite the numerous publications on both Mesoamerican archaeology and ethnohistory, only one thematic volume on the subject of material and documentary source integration has been previously dedicated to Mesoamerica in general (Brambila Paz and Monjarás-Ruiz 1996), and none to Oaxaca in particular. This volume attempts to fill this gap, by taking an interdisciplinary and long-term perspective through several Oaxacan case studies that approach artifacts, documents, and oral traditions as distinct yet interrelated heuristic modes of inquiry about the past.[2]

There are frequently three assumptions at the heart of our enduring fascination with literate societies: (1) that these were intrinsically different from nonliterate or oral cultures; (2) that the interplay between the material and the documentary, conceived as distinct modes of cultural expression, substantially shapes our understanding of these societies; and (3) that our respective methods of studying such literate societies should be epistemologically distinctive. The first premise does not need to presuppose an evolutionary perspective of inevitable progress from oral-to-written, pictographic-to-alphabetic cultures, as historical cases throughout the world—including our own modern society—clearly show. It does however suggest that literacy—even if ultimately shared by a small minority within the society—played a significant role in shaping social, political, religious, and economic institutions, along with their material manifestations.[3] The second premise has to do with how and why one source of information directly shapes our understanding of the other, and of the society that created it. The third assumption reflects mostly on current disciplinary and departmental divisions. But whereas academic boundaries between archaeology, history, sociocultural anthropology, ethnology, art history, and other related fields might be better drawn through each discipline's respective set of methodologies and approaches, the lines are blurrier still when it comes to their subject matter.

To be sure, *archaeology* and *history* are conceptually loaded categories and are often taxonomically ambiguous. For the purpose of this volume, *material culture* and *artifacts* are generally associated with the disciplinary-derived construct of the *archaeological record*, which is broadly understood to encompass any category of human-modified objects and ecofacts, loosely ranging between ceramic sherds and burnt seeds to structures and landscapes.[4] On the other hand, *documents* and *writing* are generally associated with the disciplinary-derived construct of the *(ethno) historical record,* broadly understood as a suite of communication technologies that preserved and still convey specific thoughts and other codified information across time and space, and independently from its original author.

Obviously, documents are artifacts themselves and the study of their physical characteristics and context can reveal much about their meaning. Yet, it is not the medium that transforms an object into a document, but rather the presence or absence of writing. Although we can often include works of art and codified visual representations such as maps under the rubric of *historical documents*, all the cases in this volume explicitly draw from a variety and mixed array of conventionalized notational systems including semasiographic, pictographic, ideographic, glotto-graphic, logosyllabic, logographic, and alphabetic, all of which correspond broadly to the inclusive definition of *writing* as "the communication of relatively specific ideas in a conventional manner by means of permanent, visible marks" (Boone 1994:15). These written documents often demonstrate linear sequencing, reading order, and a certain interdependence with a spoken language, which further sets them apart from complex iconography (Marcus 1976). Even those seemingly simplified pictorial systems have recently started to unveil their true complex structure and logic, and an even greater dependence on phonetic signs and speech patterns, than suspected before (e.g., Doesburg 2008; Jansen and van Broekhoven 2008; Lacadena 2008; Taube 2011). An important point to stress is that when it comes to reading the past, we should always attempt to make a distinction between the clarity of the message in the social context in which it was created, and our ability (or inability) to understand the same message today.

Oral traditions and oral history[5] similarly fall here under the category of the historical record, and several case studies in this volume acknowledge and demonstrate the value of orality and social memory in reconstructing the past. There is little doubt that orality and written records were inextricably intertwined in Mesoamerican literate societies, even if the former is forever lost for us. At the same time, we have to recognize that contemporary oral knowledge, even if about the past, is created in the present and is usually not contemporaneous with the archaeological or documentary records under discussion (while the same also holds true for retrospective written accounts vis-à-vis the respective material culture). The act of recording oral knowledge, whether it is through writing or more recently through voice and video recorders, already transforms this communication medium into the realm of "fossilized speech" and thus imbues it with a certain permanency that orality lacks. At the same time, the contextual nature of oral traditions makes the practice of multisource integration even richer, while allowing us to better connect the past with the present.

Beyond things, glyphs, letters, and words, this volume further emphasizes the continuous cultural trajectory in Oaxacan literary traditions. There are indeed few scholars today who would seriously question that many indigenous Mesoamerican societies possessed full-fledged historiographic traditions and were much concerned, often to the point of singular obsession, with the systematic and premeditated recording of past, present, and even future events. The conventional signs for *who*, *when*, *where*, and *what*—the backbone of every historiographic tradition in the world—are precisely those that appear first and survive the longest among Oaxacan literate societies. As such, and despite the still widespread use of the term, the Oaxaca cultural area stepped out of its "prehistory" in the Middle Formative period, and by the Late Formative many of Mesoamerica's societies followed suit. Nor did the story of these Oaxacan literate societies end with the Spanish arrival in the early sixteenth century. Much of the indigenous historiography, before and after the Spanish conquest, is retrospective in content and exposes a deeply contemplative stance about the material and written past. The long genealogical lists, for example, are firmly tied to specific places in Oaxaca and collectively represent the longest continuous histories ever recorded in the Western Hemisphere. Equally pertinent for integrative studies, this volume recognizes the relevance of the various nonindigenous literate societies that started occupying the Oaxacan landscape from the sixteenth century onward. Framed by these guidelines, following is a selective diachronic survey that places the volume contributions and other relevant literature within these long-term historical and material traditions of the Oaxacan literate societies.[6]

TWENTY-SEVEN CENTURIES OF OAXACAN LITERATE SOCIETIES

Although the Archaic and Early Formative periods have set the stage for many of Oaxaca's enduring cultural traits, it is the Middle Formative that has witnessed some of the most significant cultural revolutions relevant to the theme of this volume (figure 1.2). A significant yet poorly understood intensification in agricultural

FIGURE 1.2. A chronological outline of major periods represented in the volume.[7]

Year	Period (Calibrated)	Valley of Oaxaca (Central Valleys)		Cuicatlán Cañada	Mixteca Baja	Nochixtlán Mixteca Alta	Huamelulpan	Mixteca Costa (Lower Río Verde)	Central Coast	Isthmus of Tehuantepec	Huaxyacac-Oaxaca	Period (Uncorrected)
2000	Modern										Complejo 6	
1900	Independence/Republican										Complejo 5	
1800	Late Colonial										Complejo 4	
1700	Middle Colonial			Convento							Complejo 3	
1600	Early Colonial			Convento							Complejo 2	
1500		Cuilapan	Monte Albán V								Complejo 1	
1400	Late Postclassic	Zaachila / Chila	Monte Albán V	Iglesia Vieja	Nuyoo	Late Natividad		Yucudzaa	Copalita VI / Haultulco III	Ulam / Lagarto Complex		Late Postclassic
1300												
1200	Early Postclassic	Quelatini	Late Llobaa			Early Natividad		Yugüe	Huatulco II / Huatulco I / Copalita V	Aguadas		Early Postclassic
1100		Tanipaa										
1030			Early Llobaa	Monte Albán IV								
900	Late Classic	Xoo	Monte Albán IIIB	Trujano	Ñuiñe	Late Las Flores	Late III	Yuta Tiyoo	Copalita IV	Tixum		Late Classic
800												
700		Peche	Monte Albán IIIB									
600	Early Classic	Pitao/Dxu Complex	Monte Albán IIIA			Early Las Flores	Early III	Coyuche	Copalita III	Xuku		Classic
500												
400		Tani										
300	Terminal Formative	Nisa	Monte Albán II	Lomas	Ñudée	Ramos	II	Chachahua	Copalita II	Niti		Terminal Formative
200												
100								Miniyua		Kuak		
CE 1 / BCE 1	Late Formative	Pe	Monte Albán Late I			Ramos	I					Late Formative
100												
200				Perdido	Yatiyuta/Yododea			Minizundo		Goma		
300		Danibaan	Monte Albán Early I			Yucuita			Copalita I	Bicunisa		
400												
500					Yutañiusavi							
600	Middle Formative	Rosario	Rosario			Cruz D		Charco		Ríos		Middle Formative
700				(Tecomaxtlahuaca)								
800		Guadalupe	Guadalupe			Cruz C						
900										Golfo		
1000		San José	San José		(Santa Teresa)							
1100	Early Formative											Early Formative
1200						Cruz B						
1300		Tierras Largas	Tierras Largas	(Ranco Dolores Ortíz)						Lagunita		
1400						Cruz A						
1500												

production and demographic rise during this period led to an unprecedented sociopolitical complexity and the subsequent development of the first urbanized centers and monumental public architecture in the Valley of Oaxaca, the Mixteca, the Oaxaca Coast, and the Isthmus of Tehuantepec. The emergent hereditary elite classes in these regions were connected through long-distance trade networks in which ideas, styles, and exotic goods, such as shell, jade, and obsidian, circulated in a sweeping pattern that would continue throughout much of Mesoamerican history. Such developments might have been further ushered in by economic and ideological contacts with the Olmecs on the Gulf Coast and the Maya in Chiapas and Guatemala, who shared much of the same early iconography with Oaxaca (Blomster 2004, 2010; Flannery 1976; Joyce 2013; Joyce et al. 1998; Marcus and Flannery 1996; Winter 1994a; Whittington and Workinger, chapter 9, this volume).

In the Central Valleys, the implied hierarchy between incipient autonomous chiefdoms created a violent competition, in which context we find the vestiges of the earliest known writing system in the Western Hemisphere,[8] dated to the early sixth century BCE. Thus far this is represented by a single carved monolith from San José Mogote, the largest Middle Formative site in the valley, which depicts a sacrificed individual named "1-Eye" in the 260-day Zapotec ritual calendar and is further marked with stylized glyphs standing for heart and blood (Flannery and Marcus 2003; Marcus and Flannery 1996; Urcid 2005a, 2011a; 2011c).[9] This mix of semasiographic and glottographic conventions had undoubtedly emerged out of the Early Formative complex iconography and temporal computations and, although still serving as imagery captions and labels at this early phase, would later characterize the development of the Zapotec writing system and its derivatives through time (Urcid 2001). The spatial context of the San José Mogote monolith further betrays the social rationale behind this early function of writing: this was positioned horizontally on a corridor's threshold or a temple entrance as if the sacrificial victim was meant to be continuously trampled, and likely it was the prominent identity of this vanquished rival ruler that made it necessary to convey a more specific and unequivocal message than before.[10] From this onset and throughout the prehispanic era, the fact that all written content explicitly dealt with themes exclusive to the nobility, whereas no primary inscriptions were found so far in commoners' contexts, strongly suggests that the art of writing and full literacy were restricted to the elite and to specialized scribes.[11] Nevertheless, this same early complementarity between text, image, and spatial context would become the distinguishing characteristic for all of Mesoamerican writing systems, and the message would thus have been potentially directed to and understood by other nonliterate members of the society.[12]

The latter part of the Middle Formative period saw the decline of regional centers and singled out the great mountaintop city and ceremonial center of Monte

Albán, which was built in the late sixth century BCE at the heart of the contested valley, where it ruled at the top of a four-tiered settlement hierarchy[13] (Blanton 1978; Joyce 2010; Kowalewski et al. 1989; Winter 2011). That such archaeological manifestations for primary state-formation appeared in tandem with the development of complex recordkeeping strategies was likely not coincidental (Urcid 2011b; see also Goody 1986; Houston 2004; Marcus 1992; and Sanders 2006 for similar examples). In response to the burgeoning political factionalism throughout the region, the ruling elite of this state-level polity took the earlier iconographic template to a new level: hundreds of stone monuments depicting individuals similar to the one on the San José Mogote monument were incorporated directly into the architecture of the public main plaza. Although all were erected and dismantled in a relatively short period of time, these so-called *danzantes* monoliths show different styles and themes and surely belonged to several "narrative programs," not all of which were contemporaneous (Urcid 2011a; Winter 2011). These sequential representations are often explained as intimidation propaganda featuring slain captives, although other plausible interpretations include ranked individuals in a warrior-priest sodality, or a procession of the city-founders and other mythical ancestors (Marcus 1992; Marcus and Flannery 1996; Urcid 2011a; Urcid and Joyce 2014; Winter 2011). Either way, the fact that many of these carved individuals carry a calendrical name and specific attributes is consistent with the fundamental need for constructing an enduring social memory for the local elite, their subjects, and potential rival rulers. The *danzantes* iconography is further tied to the widespread Mesoamerican theme of the blood of nobles as a symbol of the sacred covenant between humans and gods, and highlights the role of Monte Albán as a sacred space for religious rituals (A. Joyce 2004, 2010).

Additional composite inscriptions on accompanying monuments probably celebrated the feats of Monte Albán's rulers and reveal the already developed nature of the Zapotec logosyllabic writing during this period, while other isolated glyphs appear on ceramic representations of anthropomorphic and zoomorphic deities.[14] The ubiquitous dates recorded in the ritual calendar similarly reflect the necessity of the nobility to position themselves as society's "timekeepers" and chroniclers, and so to herald central social activities. Because the elite class relied heavily on the physical labor, economic support, and political sponsorship of the commoner population who lived around the ceremonial center, it is probable that the latter would occasionally have viewed, and partially understood, these politico-religious statements, especially when accompanied by oral recitation during public ceremonies and processions (A. Joyce 2004; Marcus 1992).

The first Oaxacan writing system thus flourished in an urban setting that could have supported such a novel scribal institution. In turn, since these visual and written historiographies were embedded in the monumental architecture from the very beginning, the urban layout of Monte Albán was in turn shaped and transformed through time by the growing need to display such narratives. The act of writing itself was likely considered to have been a sacred privilege and was monopolized almost exclusively by the Valley's capital and its elite for centuries to come (Urcid 2011b). Although other areas in Oaxaca experienced rapid episodes of urbanization throughout the Late Formative, concrete evidence for associated writing is still largely lacking: Monte Negro fast became one of the primary civic-ceremonial centers in the Mixteca[15] (Balkansky et al. 2004; Geurds 2007; Spores 1984), and the Isthmus saw the rapid rise and decline of Tres Picos, a pan-regional urban center that boasted several ballcourts and might have been ruled by Mixe speakers. The position of this city on a natural lowland passage allowed it to participate in, or even control, the interregional exchange of ceramics and other exotic goods from Soconusco to the Gulf of Veracruz (Winter 2008b).

During the Terminal Formative, many ceramic and architecture styles became more standardized and widely spread, following a regional pattern that is largely contained within the Oaxacan state boundaries and so heralds the formation of this culture era. Although technological innovations and exchange among the elite had surely continued to propel the economic, religious, and ideological interactions between the different groups and regions (Joyce 2010; Joyce et al. 1998; Zeitlin 1993), some of this ubiquitous material distribution probably reflects Monte Albán's territorial and political expansion during the first century BCE. Such an expansion is primarily inferred from the seventy stone slabs set in a unique arrow-shaped structure in the central plaza, Building J, in which were depicted distinct yet mostly unidentified conquered places, their defeated rulers, and other calendrical references (Caso 1947; Marcus 1983, 1992; Marcus and Flannery 1996; Whittaker 1980; but see also Buigues 1993; Carter 2008; Justeson 2012; and Urcid and Joyce 2014 for alternative interpretations).[16] These Zapotec hill signs were all qualified with specific anthropomorphic, zoomorphic, and other elements, which likely stood for names of individual communities, in a semantic format that would endure in Oaxaca for centuries to come and later spread throughout central Mesoamerica. Much as with the earliest recorded anthroponymic glyphs, the need for geographical specificity in commemorating victories and demarcating territory seems to have motivated the early development of Mesoamerican logographic toponomy and further helped to promote a place-based corporate identity. A more anthropomorphic variation on the theme of commemorating rulers' feats and defeated adversaries was carved on stone slabs at the regional center of Dainzú, focusing on the outcome of the ritualistic Mesoamerican ball game.

Regional variants of the Zapotec script first appear during this period in the Mixteca nucleated urban centers of Huamelulpan and Yucuita in the form of short commemorative, political, and religious statements (Joyce 2010; Spores 2007). This further suggests that the area was either dominated by Zapotec nobles most likely affiliated with Monte Albán, or that the script characters were appropriated ideographically or phonetically by the local Mixtec nobility.[17] Although diverse products and crafts circulated among these ecological regions through traveling merchants, tribute, or marketplaces, an unexplained wide-ranging systemic collapse toward the third century CE marked the end of the Formative period and disrupted the political structure in the Mixteca and the Coast.

Other urban centers such as Jalieza began to rise in the Central Valleys during the Early Classic period. Monte Albán continued to be a dominant power throughout the region, and inscribed monuments in Monte Albán along with Zapotec-style ceramics and glyphs in a Teotihuacan *barrio* seem to attest to economic and diplomatic ties between these powerful cities starting from the third or fourth century CE. Several glyphs of the little-known Teotihuacan script were found in Monte Albán's inscriptions, although the former system might have been partially derived from the latter (Joyce 2010; Marcus and Flannery 1996; Taube 2011). Teotihuacan might have further traded with, or even partially controlled, the Mixteca and the western Coast. In contrast to Teotihuacan's mostly glyph-less "corporate ideology," however, the new carved inscriptions and imagery in Monte Albán's public areas had "put a face" on the earlier theme of military conquests and captive-taking and focused on the declaration of individual rulers' earthly exploits and their kinship with the divine. In many cases a single stone monument had several inscribed surfaces, meant to be viewed from multiple perspectives, while sets of individual monuments were positioned together to form sequential narrative programs. As also occurred to the earlier *danzantes*, these were occasionally dismantled, recarved, and later reassembled to create different political programs by new rulers, who were likely motivated by the desire to appropriate or contest the material and documentary records of past rulership. One of the most ambitious remodeling programs took place around the sixth century, when the great Lord 13 Night succeeded Lord 5 Jaguar as the supreme sovereign of Monte Albán (Urcid 2001, 2005a, 2011b, 2011c; Winter 1994b). Much as in later Postclassic and Colonial times, it is quite probable that these multifaceted written and visual narratives would have been occasionally reenacted through theatrical performances with the purpose of legitimizing rulership and perpetuating individual and communal identities.

This political and ideological legitimization of the nobility had developed during the Late Classic into lineage-oriented genealogical registers and marriage scenes in Monte Albán and other centers such as Cerro de la Campana, and their profusion might further argue for the spread of literacy to lower elite circles. These family histories are mostly represented on lintels, jambs, modeled panels, murals, and freestanding stelae found within elite residences and tombs of restricted access that were periodically reopened (Lind and Urcid 2010; Miller 1995; Urcid 2001, 2005a). Such genealogies emphasized both male and female rulers, and already demonstrated the growing preoccupation with tracing noble lines of descent that would later become the hallmark of Postclassic and Early Colonial indigenous historiography. The transformation from publicly displayed inscribed monuments toward more exclusionary elite settings echoed earlier urban rearrangement programs that effectively restricted the access of commoners to the main plaza at Monte Albán (A. Joyce 2004). This restricted access seems to reflect a shift in concern from consolidating commoner allegiance to internal factional competition within elite interaction spheres, within which deified lineage ancestors played a legitimating role. Other inscribed slabs and portable effigy vessels were designed to carry the identity of the respective ancestor or owner more widely, as conceivably did other documents that have not been preserved, written as they likely were on organic materials such as bark-paper, animal hide, or cotton cloth.

Smaller city-states emerged during the Classic period along with new regional artistic styles, and variants of the Zapotec script and complex iconography began to spread throughout the Valley of Oaxaca and surrounding mountains, the Mixteca, the Ejutla and Sola Valleys, the Nejapa Valley, the Lower Río Verde, the Isthmus of Tehuantepec, and beyond Oaxaca's modern boundaries to Guerrero and Chiapas (Balkansky 2002; Gutiérrez 2008; Urcid 1993, 2001, 2005a). This fragmentary corpus is mostly represented by short "tagging" inscriptions of calendrical dates or names, personal monikers, and toponyms, probably referring to major accomplishments of self-aggrandizing local rulers or deified ancestors. The most elaborate of those is the highly stylized *Ñuiñe* variant in the western Mixteca, which was further affiliated with Central Mexican writing systems. This script began showing up on a variety of media such as carved stones, bone, shell, and pottery in Cerro de las Minas and other sites, as well as clusters of wall inscriptions such as in the Tepelmeme cave, locally known as the "Puente Colosal Ndaxagua" (Rivera Guzmán 2008; Urcid 2005b; Winter 2007; Doesburg and Spores, chapter 10, this volume; König, chapter 4, this volume; Rincón Mautner, chapter 8, this volume). Other narratives painted on tomb walls represented complex creation stories that transcend mythical and historical time and that might have further served to legitimize the foundation of particular lineages (Urcid 2008).

In the Mixteca Alta, Yucuñudahui became one of the most important political and religious centers in the Nochixtlán Valley and beyond, judging by the extensive size of the settlement, isolated *Ñuiñe* inscriptions, and the numerous retrospective references in the Postclassic codices (Byland and Pohl 1994; Hamann 2002; Pohl 2004a; Spores 1967). A new Late Classic state capital resurfaced in Río Viejo on the western Coast, where its rulers, probably Chatino speakers, were depicting and naming themselves on public stone monuments while asserting their hierarchical divine mandate over the commoner population in a fashion similar to that of the early rulers of Monte Albán (Urcid and Joyce 2001). Zapotec-style glyphs also appear on "Talun Carved" ceramics distributed mainly along the central Pacific littoral, and a yet-unidentified script and complex scenes were painted on natural boulders in the Isthmus of Tehuantepec (Matadamas Díaz and Ramírez Barrera 2010; Urcid 1993; Zárate Morán 2003). Taken together, the spread of literacy and the proliferation of localized historiographic traditions across the Valley of Oaxaca and beyond might have manifested a growing regional factionalism and anticipated the subsequent rise of Postclassic petty kingdoms. Perhaps for related reasons, communities in the Isthmus of Tehuantepec shifted their economic and religious ties during this period from the Valley of Oaxaca toward exchange networks with Totonac and Maya groups in the Gulf Coast and Campeche (Joyce 2010; Winter 2008b; Zeitlin 2005).

Echoing the pan-Mesoamerican systemic collapse brought by interrelated environmental and sociopolitical triggers, the end of the Classic period marked the rapid decline and abandonment of Monte Albán and other major cities in the Valley, the Mixteca, and the Coast during the eighth and ninth centuries (Blomster 2008b; Joyce 2010; Lind and Urcid 2010; Markens et al. 2008; Kroefges, chapter 13, this volume; Rincón Mautner, chapter 8, this volume). Still, many of these places continued to be used as burial grounds and came to be venerated as places of ancestral creation, where later people appropriated both these ruins and ancient artifacts in a form of "indigenous archaeology" (Hamann 2002, 2008). The dispersal of the nobility and associated scribal schools could probably account for the disappearance of the phonetic Zapotec script and the inscribed freestanding stelae tradition, with the exception of few late carved monuments from the Valley of Oaxaca and the Mixteca Alta (Urcid 2005a, 2011b). This period also marked the beginning of a new cycle of sweeping movements of peoples and ideas throughout Mesoamerica (Rincón Mautner, chapter 8, this volume). During the Epiclassic, the Central Mexican writing systems of Xochicalco and Cacaxtla showed influences from Zapotec script, and especially from the *Ñuiñe* variant. The Zapotec sacred calendar survived largely intact into this period but was realigned and adapted to accommodate Central Mexican conventions, suggesting a bilateral flow of ideas. Although the Central Mexican Toltecs were likely involved in the region during the eleventh century, the material evidence for their presence is still fragmentary and inferences are mostly drawn from Late Postclassic and Early Colonial documentation, which retrospectively references various Toltec culture heroes and lineage founders as active in the Oaxacan political landscape (Blomster 2008b, 2008c;

Jansen and Pérez Jiménez 2007, 2009a; Oudijk 2008; Pohl 1999, 2003a, 2003b; Rincón Mautner, chapter 8, this volume).

The urban and political reorientation of the Early Postclassic period brought about the simultaneous development of multiple minor city-states. The respective settlement pattern became more dispersed, and earlier monumental temples were replaced by modest, multipurposed palaces, showing a fusion of architectural styles and decorated with repetitive iconographical motifs (Byland 1980; Byland and Pohl 1994; Pohl 2004a; Jiménez Osorio and Posselt Santoyo, chapter 11, this volume; Kroefges, chapter 13, this volume). With the coastal Río Viejo polity largely decentralized, non-inscribed sculptures of deities or nobles were now placed on natural hills instead of in the public civic-ceremonial center; commoners or "impoverished elites" were reoccupying the site core and reutilizing the Classic-period inscribed monuments for the construction of their houses and to contest the earlier political regime (Joyce 2008; Joyce et al. 2001; Urcid and Joyce 2001).

Towards the end of the Early Postclassic period, centers in the Valley of Oaxaca such as Cuilapan, Mitla, Yagul, Teotitlán del Valle, and Macuilxóchitl grew in size and influence, while the Mixteca saw the dramatic rise of Coixtlahuaca and Yucundaa-Teposcolula (Markens et al. 2008; Rincón Mautner, chapter 8, this volume; Spores, chapter 2, this volume). In the wake of political collapse on the west Coast, an intrusive Mixtec settlement was founded in Tututepec during the twelfth century and—according to the retrospective accounts in the Late Postclassic Mixtec codices—fast became the largest expansionist city-state on the Pacific littoral with the support of important Tolteca-Chichimeca alliances (Joyce 2010; Joyce et al. 2004; Levine 2007; Matadamas Díaz and Ramírez Barrera 2010; Spores 1993; see also Kroefges, chapter 13, this volume; Zborover, chapter 12, this volume). The Isthmus of Tehuantepec material culture further points to interregional interactions with Maya groups in Chiapas, as well as with the Valley of Oaxaca and Central Mexico (Winter 2008a, 2008b; Zeitlin 2005).

The intense Late Postclassic population movements and the economic commercialization on a scale unprecedented in Mesoamerican history was accompanied by an equally substantial body of documentary and material records, including the introduction of new exotic goods such as precious metals from Central America and turquoise from the North American Southwest (Smith and Berdan 2003). The thirteenth and fourteenth centuries are often characterized by a constant flux between violent factionalism and confederacy building, and the creation of regional and interregional "alliance corridors" between royal dynasties through marital alliances and gift-giving. Such intense interaction between the Mixteca, the Valley of Oaxaca, and the Central Highlands brought new levels of standardization in material culture and writing, and an "international" symbol set of a shared elite identity and religious ideology. Phoneticism was downplayed in these communication networks so as to accommodate these polyglot and multiethnic social landscapes[18] (Boone and Smith 2003; Pohl 2003a, 2003b, 2003d; Rincón Mautner, chapter 8, this volume).

At the same time, the endemic factional competition had created numerous localized hero cults and conflicting documentary histories, the most remarkable examples being the surviving Mixtec codices[19]—screenfold books composed on gesso-covered deer hide using the new logographic Mixtec writing system.[20] The codices and other portable inscribed media, such as masterfully painted poly-chrome ceramics, precious stones, shell, gold and silver jewelry, and carved animal and human bones, were more suitable to this socially dynamic era and thus further explain the fading of the stationary stelae tradition (Pohl 2003c; König, chapter 4, this volume; McCafferty and McCafferty, chapter 5, this volume). Although sim-ply decorated polychrome vessels were also used by nonelites, the elaborate serving vessels depicting complex iconography and "snapshots" of heroic narratives were used in gift exchanges among the noble families, as well as in feasts where codices were publicly performed in song and oratory (Levine 2007; Monaghan 1990; Pohl 2003c, 2007; Lind, chapter 7, this volume). Similarly, murals painted on lintels of palace courtyards and carved stone slabs were now oriented toward more cosmo-politan narratives and associations (Blomster 2008c; Pohl 1999; Winter 2008a).

Most of the codices were likely composed for special occasions, such as the enthronement of a ruler or a royal marriage, and were later deposited in the town archives; others were surely sent to be read throughout the different realms for vari-ous political, economic, and religious purposes. Even if in different formats and media, such documents continued to emphasize those previously established liter-ary themes of mythological creation, the religious pantheon, dynastic origins, elite genealogy, heroic biography and conquests, marital alliances, territorial conflicts, and individual and collective rites of passage. Much as the Classic-period inscrip-tions, calendrical references were mostly employed in naming individuals and fixing events in mythical and historical time, while the long astronomical computations known from the Maya codices are absent in the surviving Oaxacan records.

One of the most intriguing leitmotifs is the retrospective creation account of a new world-era emerging out of the Formative- and Classic-period ruins during the tenth century, a "mythistorical" event that is further echoed in the abovementioned changes in material culture and settlement patterns during the Classic-Postclassic transition[21] (Boone 2000; Byland 2008; Byland and Pohl 1994; Hamann 2002, 2008; Jansen and Pérez Jiménez 2007; Oudijk 2008; Rabin 2003; Byland, chapter 6, this volume; König, chapter 4, this volume; Rincón Mautner, chapter 8, this volume; Whittington and Workinger, chapter 9, this volume). Elite kinship was literally embedded in this sacred landscape, as the founders of Mixtec dynasties were commonly depicted emerging from the natural and constructed ancestral environment (often abandoned Classic-period settlements), whereas in the documents many of the claims for political legitimacy are drawn from places distant in space and time such as Monte Albán, Zaachila, Cholula, and Tula (Jansen 1998; Jansen and Pérez Jiménez 2007; Pohl 2003a; Byland, chapter 6, this volume; McCafferty and McCafferty, chapter 5, this volume; Lind, chapter 7, this volume; Rincón Mautner, chapter 8, this volume). Some of the religious mantic manuscripts were also rooted in a Mixtec historical geography, although sharing Nahua iconographic conventions with the Borgia Group of the Puebla-Tlaxcala plains; the recently discovered fragments of the Yautepec Codex in southern Oaxaca suggest that these divinatory almanacs were probably quite widespread, while their divergent content could be reflective of regional "cults" (Doesburg and Urcid 2009; see also Pohl 2004b; Lind, chapter 7, this volume).

Several of these surviving retrospective narratives follow the life and times of the great Mixtec Lord 8-Deer and his adversary Lady 6-Monkey during the eleventh and twelfth centuries (Byland, chapter 6, this volume; McCafferty and McCafferty, chapter 5, this volume), which chronologically corresponds with the Early Postclassic foundation of the Tututepec polity on the Pacific coast. Together with the fifteenth century conquest of the Isthmus of Tehuantepec by the Zapotec king Cosijopí I from Zaachila, these two historical events had dramatically transformed southern Oaxaca's already complex multiethnic and demographic makeup and started a fierce interpolity conflict on the Coast (Joyce 2010; Matadamas Díaz and Ramírez Barrera 2010; Winter 2008a; Zeitlin 2005; Kroefges, chapter 13, this volume; Zborover, chapter 12, this volume).

Drawn by the region's economic resources, artistic legacy, and strategic position as a passage to the southern coastal plains, the Aztecs conquered large parts of the Mixteca, Central Valleys, Sierra Norte, and Sierra Sur through several expeditions starting in the mid-fifteenth century, and established a garrison in Huaxyacac (later "Oaxaca") at the foot of Monte Albán. Among these conquered places were the important pluri-ethnic trading center of Coixtlahuaca (Bernal 1948; Rincón Mautner, chapter 8, this volume), the powerful city-state of Cuilapan, and various other towns that often rebelled and were violently subdued. In many such cases the Aztecs further replaced the local rulers with their own governors and administrators, and populated regions with Central Mexican migrants. This period further established Nahuatl as the lingua franca among the polyglot and often factionalized nobility across Oaxaca (a process that might have started with the Tolteca-Chichimeca migrations), and Nahuatl was still widely used in Early Colonial documents as a sign for indigenous elite status. Although the Aztecs recorded their conquests and (often excessive) tribute extracted from these provinces in their own historical documents, they left only isolated inscriptions and scant material record throughout the Oaxacan landscape, and their presence is mostly alluded to by Nahuatl toponyms and local documentation (Berdan et al. 1996; Doesburg and Spores, chapter 10, this volume; Kroefges, chapter 13, this volume; Whittington and Workinger, chapter 9, this volume; Zborover, chapter 12, this volume). These Oaxacan accounts often contrast with the "official" histories from Tenochtitlán, as was the case with the competing perspectives on the subjugated status of Tehuantepec and Zaachila. Tututepec retained its political autonomy and vast territorial control, but continued to rely heavily on the Central Mexican and the coastal exchange networks (Levine 2007).

The Aztecs' ambitious plans to consolidate their military and economic foothold in Oaxaca were, however, short-lived. The early sixteenth century saw the intrusion of the Spanish to Oaxaca, and the creation of a new Colonial milieu in which indigenous and European negotiations and interpretations resulted in yet another stratum of cultural, material, and documentary hybridity. Much like the Classic-Postclassic transition and other erratic phases in Mesoamerica's history, the Contact and Early Colonial periods in Oaxaca are characterized by a complex interplay between material/documentary disjunctions and continuities. In addition to representing an intrusive literate society on the Mesoamerican soil, the European conquest and colonialism further connected Oaxaca textually and materially to the Americas and integrated Mesoamerica with the Spanish Habsburgian world economy. In fact, it is through the selective preservation of the indigenous documentary sources and the rich detail encapsulated in the newly introduced alphabetic writing system and literary traditions that we know today more about this transitional phase in Oaxacan history than of any phase that preceded it.

The Spanish brought with them numerous books, some mass-produced with the relatively new invention of the printing press. Although those included tomes of Old World history, geography, sciences, arts, and literature, many of these early works consisted of illustrated religious manuscripts perhaps not so different from the Mesoamericans' own traditions, and their templates, themes, and iconography in turn heavily influenced the books later printed in the New World. Along with Mesoamerican foodstuffs, precious metals, and works of art, several of the pictorial codices were shipped back to be admired as curiosities by the European nobility, thus taking indigenous writing systems for the first recorded time outside of Mesoamerica's cultural boundaries. The establishment of New Spain soon resulted in a wealth of bureaucratic literature, such as the *Suma de Visitas* census, the *Libro de las Tasaciones* tributary records, and the comprehensive *Relaciones Geográficas* questionnaires, that provided important details on the land and its people and often included indigenous and European maps (Gerhard 1993; Mundy 1996; Kroefges, chapter 13, this volume; Rincón Mautner, chapter 8, this volume; Whittington and Workinger, chapter 9, this volume; Zborover, chapter 12, this volume). Even if indirectly and impersonally, the larger indigenous population was referenced in the written record for the first time, most notably in the Spanish economic and parish records. West African and Caribbean slaves brought in as forced labor contributed to the already increasingly complex social and genetic makeup of Oaxaca and, consequently, to its material and literary traditions (Aguirre Beltrán 1989; Fournier and Charlton 2008; Gallaga Murrieta 2009).

The larger Mesoamerican society was restructured so that the Spanish Crown would have dispossessed the Late Postclassic imperial elite of its ruling power, although much of the social makeup within the lower echelons of the indigenous *cacicazgos'* (transformations of the Postclassic city-states) was kept relatively intact. The traditional Spanish administrative institutions were in turn shaped by the idiosyncratic sociopolitical matrix of Oaxaca. The conquistadors were quick to subdue the large militaristic kingdoms such as Tututepec and Tehuantepec, often with the help of antagonistic indigenous groups. However, and in contrast to Central Mexico, in many regions of Oaxaca this period can be seen as a gradual cultural transition rather than an abrupt rupture. Numerous *cacicazgos* endured and even prospered throughout the Colonial and even the Republican period, while adapting to the European religious, economic, and political hierarchy (Chance 1986, 1989; Frassani 2009; Jansen and Pérez Jiménez 2009a, 2009b; Spores 2007; Taylor 1972; Terraciano 2001; Doesburg and Spores, chapter 10, this volume; Zeitlin, chapter 14, this volume). For the most part the hispanicized *caciques* were able to preserve their hereditary statuses and lands, continue with the tradition of intrapolity marital alliances, and keep their positions as intermediaries between their commoner subjects and the hegemonic powers, now represented by the Spanish Crown (Yannakakis 2008). Tehuantepec's ruler Cosijopí II, for example, followed to assist in the Spanish exploration and conquest of the western and northern coasts of New Spain.

The local Spanish seat of power, Antequera, was founded close to the Aztec garrison of Huaxyacac, in a place that would later become the current state capital of Oaxaca City.[22] Soon after, the Spanish Crown started congregating the dispersed Postclassic settlement pattern into large towns whose territories fell under the institutional control of the *encomienda* and the *república de indios*, thus severing long-established native political alliances and further creating a disjunction with the loci of indigenous ancestral identity (Chance 1986, 1989; Gerhard 1993; Ruiz Medrano 2010; Jiménez Osorio and Posselt Santoyo, chapter 11, this volume; Spores, chapter 2, this volume; Whittington and Workinger, chapter 9, this volume). Several

Oaxacan towns and villages resisted these relocations and fiercely rebelled against the excessive labor and tribute demands of the Spanish, most notably in the Isthmus and Mixe region (Kroefges, chapter 13, this volume; Zborover, chapter 12, this volume; Zeitlin, chapter 14, this volume).

European flora, fauna, and production technologies were rapidly introduced to Mesoamerica, often causing major transformations to the rural and urban landscapes (Zeitlin, chapter 14, this volume). The Bay of Huatulco functioned through much of the sixteenth century as the main port to connect Pacific Mesoamerica with South America and, by way of Veracruz, to the Atlantic capitalist economies. English, Dutch, and French pirates followed suit and produced a wealth of manuscripts and maps; their attacks along the Pacific littoral had also affected the indigenous and Spanish settlements and the circulation of goods (Gerhard 2003; Matadamas Díaz and Ramírez Barrera 2010; Kroefges, chapter 13, this volume). The local industries of salt, hides, cloth (including textiles produced from the newly introduced silk), and most notably the native cochineal dyestuff were monopolized and exported to Asia and other international markets through the Manila Galleon trade network, providing much wealth to Spanish *encomenderos*, Dominican institutions, and indigenous *caciques* and merchants alike (Chance 1986, 1989; Romero Frizzi 1996; see also Doesburg and Spores, chapter 10, this volume; Zeitlin, chapter 14, this volume). Foreign goods, such as European *mayólica* (majolica) pottery and Chinese porcelain, were imported for prestige displays of Spaniards and selected mestizo and indigenous sectors; some of these ceramic types were later emulated locally by indigenous and other craftsmen under the tutelage of the Dominican order, and further included new stylistic and technological innovations (Blackman et al. 2006; Fernández Dávila and Gómez Serafín 1998; Gómez Serafín and Fernández Dávila 2007; Zeitlin, chapter 14, this volume). Nevertheless, much of the prehispanic subsistence patterns and material culture persisted relatively uninterrupted among the commoners and semiautonomous or specialized groups and is evident through the present-day with domestic ceramic traditions and architecture (Doesburg and Spores, Chapter 10, this volume; Kroefges, Chapter 13, this volume; Zborover, Chapter 12, this volume; Zeitlin, Chapter 14, this volume). The rotating indigenous market system—still ongoing today—continued to serve as the basis for the peasant economy throughout the urban centers and rural hinterlands, while slowly incorporating European-based goods and adapting to a cash economy (Murphy and Stepick 1991).

It was the European communicable diseases that eventually proved more devastating than any war, mining operations, or the *repartimiento* forced labor, and drastically decimated the native population throughout the sixteenth and seventeenth centuries, especially in the Isthmus and along the Coast (Zeitlin 2005; see also

Spores, chapter 2, this volume). The high mortality rate among the ruling nobility and the competition among the surviving *caciques*, together with the Spanish colonialists' new claims for land, brought about an intricate political and territorial reorganization. Hernán Cortés himself claimed large parts of Oaxaca as his own Marquesado del Valle, and much of the period's legal documentation produced by the Spanish and indigenous alike revolved around private, communal, and *hacienda* land tenure and claims (Chance 1986; Taylor 1972). This abundant Colonial documentation on territorial conflicts demonstrates that disputes commonly arose between different factions within Spanish society (such as *peninsulares* against *criollos*), between the ecclesiastical and civil institutions, between the indigenous *caciques* and their subjects, and most commonly between neighboring communities[23] (Romero Frizzi 1996; Ruiz Medrano 2010).

Whereas many of the accomplished indigenous scribes perished in the demographic collapse and most of the Postclassic documents were destroyed by zealous priests, several autochthonous literary traditions continued to be employed during the Early Colonial period within indigenous interaction spheres, while others flourished in tandem with the Spanish administration. In Colonial Oaxaca, pictorial documents appear in areas previously known for their literary traditions, such as the Mixteca and the Central Valleys (Doesburg and Spores, chapter 10, this volume; König, chapter 4, this volume; Whittington and Workinger, chapter 9, this volume), but subsequently emerged among other ethnic groups for which we have little or no such surviving prehispanic documents, such as the Mazatec, Chinantec, Mixe, Chochos, Isthmus Zapotec, and the Chontal coast and highlands (König and Sellen, chapter 15, this volume; Kroefges, chapter 13, this volume; Rincón Mautner, chapter 8, this volume; Zborover, chapter 12, this volume). This indigenous corpus, along with the Spanish documentation, further established many of the ethnonyms still in use today for the contemporary sixteen Oaxacan ethnolinguistic groups (Bartolomé 2008).

The traditional pictorial style, even if by now anachronistic and mostly devoid of its complex iconographic and phonetic subtleties, was still considered by both indigenous and Europeans to be a symbol of ancestral legitimacy and was often manipulated to such ends in the Colonial courts of law. In the Mixteca and the Cañada, codices continued to be painted and older ones "recycled" to demonstrate and negotiate ancestral claims over land and political power (Jansen and Pérez Jiménez 2009a, 2009b; Ruiz Medrano 2010; Yannakakis 2008; König, chapter 4, this volume). Numerous new documents were commissioned by the literate indigenous *caciques* for their geopolitical negotiations with the Spanish authorities and other competing villages, and reflect their intermediary role in the new Colonial and religious world order.

Most ubiquitous were the *lienzos*, composed on cloth sheets; the *amate* or European paper *mapas*; and the paper or hide rolls. In particular, the *lienzos'* wide geographical distribution and typical single-sided large format convincingly argue for more inclusive engagement and communal decision-making than do the elite-oriented codices. These documents emphasized clearly delimited territorial boundaries for individual communities and *cacicazgos*, while their pictorial narratives—accompanied and bolstered by oral traditions—followed local and interregional group migrations. Some Oaxacan *lienzos* even recorded the auxiliary indigenous expeditions together with the Spaniards in their sweeping conquests across Mesoamerica (Boone 2000; Romero Frizzi 1996; Ruiz Medrano 2010; Smith 1973; Yannakakis 2008; see also Asselbergs 2008). In general, the pictorial narratives and genealogies depicted in the *lienzos* tend to be more complex and retrospective than those of the indigenous paper *mapas*, which are often limited to territorial demarcations. Although the smaller scale of the latter could be partially behind this pattern, the intended audience surely played an important role here: the *mapas* of the *Relaciones Geográficas* were composed primarily for the Spanish administration, and the oral narratives of the indigenous informants were transcribed into the accompanying alphabetic documents; the *lienzos*, however, were often presented exclusively for indigenous audiences.

The pictographic content of these Early Colonial documents was commonly accompanied by interpretative glosses written with the Roman alphabet, but by the Late Colonial period the latter writing system generally replaced the former. Most of the early alphabetic documents produced in indigenous towns were authored by Spanish priests and notaries, but indigenous elites and their *cabildos* (councils) soon appropriated the writing system to advance their community needs and own political ambitions, producing a rich notarial literature in their own native language or in Spanish, which eventually took the place of Nahuatl as the lingua franca. Commoners, although mostly men affiliated with the town *cabildo* or ecclesiastical institutions, also started to read and write in the Roman alphabet. Among the most common alphabetic literary genres produced during the seventeenth and eighteenth centuries are the community-oriented *títulos primordiales* ("primordial titles"), which follow territorial themes similar to those of the *lienzos* and *mapas* albeit without the elite-focused narratives, and the numerous individual wills and testaments and deeds of sale that were introduced by the Spanish legal system (Ruiz Medrano 2010; Taylor 1972; Terraciano 2001).

Several of the long-established indigenous genres continued to be represented in these pictorial and alphabetic Colonial documents, and their narratives were often retrospective: long genealogical-territorial documents extended back to the Early Postclassic period so as to legitimize the Colonial *caciques*, and were commonly linked to dynasties and places represented in the prehispanic codices; village chronicles were often projected back to mythistorical origins; and account books and tribute lists continued to be produced for internal indigenous affairs and for the benefit of the new European administration (Boone 2000; Jansen and Pérez Jiménez 2009a, 2009b; Oudijk 2008; Whitecotton 1990; Doesburg and Spores, chapter 10, this volume; Kroefges, chapter 13, this volume). Interestingly, in many of these documents the Spanish conquest or even the Spaniards themselves are often underrepresented, suggesting internal circulation within indigenous interaction spheres, and it is indeed quite common to find those today in communities far removed from their places of origin (Zborover, chapter 12, this volume).

One notable literary lacuna was the native religion, which was actively suppressed by the Spanish priests, although rituals were often still practiced in secret and the 260-day divinatory calendars survived in some areas in a rather clandestine fashion throughout the Colonial period and even to this day (Tavárez 2010; Zeitlin, chapter 14, this volume). It is not surprising, then, that the proceedings of the idolatry trials add another informative, if often tragic, documentary genre to Oaxacan literature (Frassani 2009). The evangelization of the indigenous peoples was given largely to the mendicant orders that sent missionaries to all of the ranking noble houses. Acting as mediators between the Crown and the *caciques* who actually controlled the land, the Dominicans eventually succeeded in forming more productive partnerships than the Franciscans. Friars such as Francisco de Burgoa wrote detailed chronicles on indigenous and Spanish life in Oaxaca by weaving ethnographic observations, surviving native documents and oral traditions, and Judeo-Christian Biblical references (Spores, chapter 2, this volume; Zeitlin, chapter 14, this volume), whereas others, such as Juan de Córdova, Francisco de Alvarado, and Antonio de los Reyes, worked with indigenous intellectuals to produce dictionaries, grammars, *doctrinas*, and other hybrid pictorial-alphabetic catechisms to help convert the indigenous population (Jansen and Pérez Jiménez 2009a). The first printing press established in Oaxaca, in 1720, was the third in New Spain and was primarily used to mass-produce religious texts.

The imposing European religious structures replaced the prehispanic temples, often on the same location and commonly echoing the indigenous architectural layout such as with open chapels designed to preach to the masses. Similarly, indigenous deified imagery and sculpture were gradually replaced by portrayals of Catholic saints of similar attributes, and ceramic traditions imbued with overt native religious iconography became covert or rapidly fell out of use (Frassani 2009; Jiménez Osorio and Posselt Santoyo, chapter 11, this volume; Lind, chapter 7, this volume; Rincón Mautner, chapter 8, this volume; Zeitlin, chapter 14, this volume). The local production of these European forms by indigenous hands and perspectives created the unique *tequitqui* hybrid art and architecture, while the common practice of incorporating prehispanic inscribed monuments into the walls of Christian religious structures could have been viewed as a sign for either subjugation or perseverance, depending on the eye of the beholder.

Spain's Bourbon reforms of the eighteenth century introduced important territorial, political, and economic legislations that impacted both the material and the literary landscapes of Oaxaca, although actively promoting the acculturation of indigenous people and languages (Frassani 2009; Yannakakis 2008). Cochineal production continued to be a prime activity in the hinterland during this period, and the dye was exported to textile industries throughout Europe (Murphy and Stepick 1991). Oaxaca played an important role in the ensuing creation of the nascent Mexican nation following its independence from Spain in the early nineteenth century, and the nation was subsequently governed by famous Oaxacan figures of indigenous descent such as Benito Juárez (being the first Native American president) and later Porfirio Díaz. Throughout the Republican period, numerous statistical reports, census lists, and maps were prepared by the new independent government to assess the land and its people, and dispatches were periodically sent to many villages (Gerhard 1993; Zborover, chapter 12, this volume). The social upheaval of this transitional period is also reflected in stylistic changes to Mexican ceramic types and the overall deterioration of locally produced glaze wares, along with the growing import of new European wares by way of the United States (Gómez Serafín and Fernández Dávila 2007). The mid-nineteenth century French intervention in Mexico connected Oaxaca once again to a complex web of world politics and fomented the scientific exploration of archaeological sites by foreign scholars (Robles García and Juárez Osnaya 2004).

Despite the remarkable demographic recovery among the native population and the introduction of schools in rural areas in the decades following Independence, manuscripts written in indigenous languages seem largely to have faded from the historical record, perhaps as a result of the period's liberal ideals of a uniform Mexican culture and the eventual assimilation of the indigenous *caciques*. Yet, written and pictorial indigenous land titles—old and new—once again started to circulate between the communities and the state following the mid-nineteenth century reform laws, the dissolution of Church properties, and the later territorial redistribution brought by the early twentieth century agrarian reform (Ruiz Medrano 2010).

Albeit at the expense of the impoverished indigenous population and the alienation of their lands, the late nineteenth century Porfiriato also saw the proliferation of railroads and factories throughout the state, as well as the development of communication technologies and networks such as the telegraph and telephone, postal services, printing presses, and periodicals (Murphy and Stepick 1991). These were destined chiefly for the literate upper and middle classes, many of them foreign investors. The nationalist ideology of the Díaz government was balanced by European-oriented trade and cultural influences, and was materialized through both the industrial present and the monumental past; new ceramic and architectural forms blended patriotic-themed and neoclassic iconography; and the first excavations and restoration at Monte Albán and Mitla took place in this period (Gómez Serafín and Fernández Dávila 2007; Robles García and Juárez Osnaya 2004). Tehuantepec was connected through the trans-Isthmian railroad to the Atlantic Ocean, which brought a fleeting economic prosperity to this region. One of the prominent figures in Tehuantepec during this period was Juana Catarina Romero who, in addition to becoming an accomplished international businesswoman who shaped much of the region's economy and fashion styles, also built schools and strongly advocated literacy education for both men and women (Chassen-López 2008). This was also the time when the Isthmus and the Mixteca witnessed the formation of passionate literary movements in Zapotec, Mixtec, and Spanish—often inspired by ancient manuscripts and oral traditions to invoke indigenous resistance and foment cultural identity—and whose vibrant legacies are still ongoing today (Jansen 1990; Jansen and van Broekhoven 2008; Romero Frizzi 2003).

Following the Mexican Revolution of 1910, which ushered in the Modern era, Spanish-based literacy started to spread at an unprecedented rate to all sectors of society through the national education system. Literacy was no longer the sole privilege of selected elites. Lamentably, it was this same nationalistic ideology that has directly contributed to the ongoing extinction of many indigenous languages, building on the *indigenismo* philosophy formulated by the Oaxacan author and education minister, José Vasconcelos, and others. That ideology attempted to assimilate the indigenous population in order to create a more homogenized *mestizo* society (Kowalewski and Saindon 1992; Stephen 2005). Ironically, throughout the late nineteenth and early twentieth centuries, much of the indigenous archaeological and historical legacy was appropriated by *criollo* and *mestizo* intellectuals in the definition of a post-Independence national identity. This led to an explosion of interest in the Mesoamerican past by national and foreign scholars and travelers, many of whom explored the ancient sites and produced a plethora of related written, visual, and aural media. Historical documents in their own right, some of the ethnographies from this period are often the only available source today for reconstructing indigenous traditions (König and Sellen, chapter 15, this volume; Spores, chapter 2, this volume).

The resulting disparate and often conflicting interaction with the material and literary heritage of Oaxacan cultures continues to this day. With over 70 percent of Oaxaca's territorial expanse still under communal and *ejidal* ownership (more than of any other Mexican state), many indigenous people still occupy, cultivate, and worship the same lands and settlements of their ancestors. Zealously guarded historical documents are often brought to defend these ancestral lands, even if such territorial testimonies were originally produced for the exclusive benefit of the native nobility. Equally important, oral traditions continue to play a significant role in the construction of place-based social memory (Bartolomé 2008; Monaghan 1995; Ruiz Medrano 2010; Jiménez Osorio and Posselt Santoyo, chapter 11, this volume; König, chapter 4, this volume; Pohl, chapter 3, this volume; Zborover, chapter 12, this volume). Still others are rather uninterested or unaware of their indigenous intellectual property and cultural heritage, which is often left neglected. Conversely, many of the monumental prehispanic centers have been physically and conceptually converted into "archaeological zones" oriented toward academic research and national and international tourism, and are today one of Oaxaca's major economic resources. Despite the growing phenomenon of community museums (König, chapter 4, this volume; Kroefges, chapter 13, this volume; Zborover, chapter 12, this volume), the majority of the excavated artistic legacy of the ancient Oaxacans is found outside its place of origins in museums, storerooms, and private collections throughout the world, while most of the historical documentation is kept and studied in national and international archives (König and Sellen, chapter 15, this volume). Concomitantly, uncontrolled urban developments are destroying much of the prehispanic and Colonial cultural heritage at an alarming rate, as is the extensive looting motivated by greed and poverty (Whittington and Workinger, chapter 9, this volume).

Beginning in the 1940s, industrialization, increased urbanization, and a new road infrastructure literally reshaped the physical, economic, and social landscapes of Oaxaca, connecting many remote indigenous villages to the state capital and beyond. Several of the traditional crafts employing prehispanic and Colonial-period techniques, such as blackware and glazed ceramics, and colorful woven textiles, became oriented toward national and international tourism and markets (Stephen 2005), which in turn has fomented the introduction of new handicrafts such as the famous Oaxacan wood carvings. World-renowned Oaxacan authors and artists, such as Rufino Tamayo, Andrés Henestrosa, and more recently, Francisco Toledo, drew extensively from their own indigenous material and documentary heritage in their respective works. In recent decades literature and textbooks in indigenous languages have become more common, as are the governmental programs to fortify and to rescue these languages, however effective or ineffective they might be.

At the same time, severe soil erosion, climatic changes, neoliberalism, and continued economic marginalization have all contributed to the rapid disintegration of traditional lifeways and the state's endemic poverty (Oaxaca being the second poorest state in Mexico). Although violent sociopolitical factionalism still propels much of the literature and media within Oaxaca, the escalating phenomenon of indigenous and mestizo emigration has taken many Oaxacan people and their respective stories to the big Mexican and US cities, and then back again (Stephen 2007; Jiménez Osorio and Posselt Santoyo, chapter 11, this volume; König, chapter 4, this volume). In turn, the material and literary manifestations of a North American–oriented capitalism and globalization can be seen today in all levels of contemporary Oaxacan society. With the digital "post-literate" age heralding yet another major transformation in which the Internet and cell phones are fast becoming the new written, oral, aural, and pictorial communication networks, the Oaxacan soil will surely continue to inspire and bring together fascinating literary and material traditions through the twenty-first century, making this one of the richest and longest-surviving cultural legacies in the world.

INTEGRATIVE ACADEMIC RESEARCH IN OAXACA

Undoubtedly, it is the very presence of complex literate societies and their continuous trajectory up to the present that has shaped the way most archaeological and historical research has been conducted in Oaxaca. Accordingly, interdisciplinary integrative approaches have had a long legacy that can be traced back to the indigenous and Spanish chroniclers (Hamann 2008; Spores, chapter 2, this volume). The era of modern research began in the nineteenth century when early European and Mexican explorers and antiquarians were equally interested in collecting the material, documentary, and oral heritage of these ancient cultures (König, chapter 4, this volume; König and Sellen, chapter 15, this volume). In this era, then, scholars around the world worked in relative isolation and with decontextualized objects and documents, including those few codices that had arrived to Europe during the Colonial period. One of the most prolific scholars of the time was the Oaxacan-born Manuel Martínez Gracida who compiled volumes of archaeological site descriptions, ethnohistoric documents, oral traditions, and linguistic material, of which only a small portion is currently published (see summary in Martínez Gracida 1986; see also König and Sellen, chapter 15, this volume). However, and in accordance with the current literary canons of the time, his early forms of integrative studies, and those of most others, were characterized by a rather romanticized narrative that did not clearly distinguish between the different types of information sources.

Although descriptions of inscribed monuments and partial excavations of major Oaxacan sites already took place in the nineteenth to early twentieth centuries (Robles García and Juárez Osnaya 2004; König and Sellen, chapter 15, this volume), systematic field research truly commenced in the late 1920s with pioneer Mexican archaeologists Alfonso Caso and Ignacio Bernal in the Valley of Oaxaca and later in the Mixteca. Through careful stratigraphic excavations and documentary decipherment, these scholars laid the foundation for ceramic typologies and regional chronologies, and attempted to establish the temporal and spatial correlates between inscriptions, sites, and historical or contemporary ethnic groups. Caso (1928) correctly identified several inscribed stelae as Zapotec monuments based on their distributional correlation with funerary urns, reconstructed the calendrical system with the aid of Colonial-period dictionaries, and began a systematic excavation at Monte Albán. A major turning point was Caso and colleagues' discovery of Tomb 7 in 1932; other than the dazzling artifacts in gold and other precious materials that drew the world's attention to Oaxaca, Caso was able to demonstrate that these inscribed jewels could be best correlated stylistically and contextually with the Late Postclassic Mixtec codices, while the urns and an inscribed stela found in their vicinity correlated with the Zapotec culture (Caso 1932; McCafferty and McCafferty 1994; McCafferty and McCafferty, chapter 5, this volume). Another breakthrough came when Caso (1949) connected the Early Colonial *Mapa de Teozacoalco* and the accompanying *Relaciones Geográficas* to dynasties and toponyms in the Mixtec codices, thus setting the ground for future studies of the Mixteca historical geography[24] (see also Jansen 1990; Rabin 2003; Whittington and Workinger, chapter 9, this volume). In those early days before the advent of archaeometric dating techniques, relative archaeological sequences were often correlated with datable indigenous documentary chronologies in search for "tie-ins" (Nicholson 1955; Vaillant 1937; Wauchope 1947). The focus of archaeological research thus turned its attention to other sites identified in Oaxacan and Central Mexican documents (Bernal 1948; Paddock 1983)—including Classic-period settlements that were mostly abandoned at the time of the composition of the codices— revealing additional writing systems and inscriptions in the process.

After the mid-twentieth century, many of the regional syntheses written for Oaxaca incorporated archaeological and historical documentation (Bernal 1965; Dahlgren 1966; Dark 1958; Paddock 1966a, 1966b; Spores 1967; Whitecotton 1977), and it is no surprise then that it was Bernal who was among the first to approach the theme of archaeological and documentary integration in Mesoamerica methodologically (Bernal 1962; but see also Nicholson 1955). Most of these studies, nonetheless, operated within the prevailing "culture history" paradigm, often resulting in an uncritical integration of sources to create a chronologically seamless narrative of the past. The inscribed Zapotec stelae depicting rulers' feats and genealogies were still conceived as mostly religious and mythological, thus reflecting a similar ahistorical notion prevalent at the time within Maya studies in North America and earlier on in German scholarship (Bernal 1962, 1965; Caso 1965). Although bringing Oaxacan indigenous literate cultures out of their anonymity and offering an alternative to Aztec/Mayan-centric scholarship, these scholars further embraced nationalist and diffusionist ideologies that focused on the "glorious" prehispanic past and invoked monolithic ethnic identities to explain culture change in Oaxaca.

Framed by the paradigm of processual archaeology and an ecological-evolutionary framework, North American research in the Valley of Oaxaca during the mid-1960s and early 1970s largely rejected the prevailing methods of culture historians on the grounds that historical studies were descriptive rather than explanatory, and so the chronicles of individuals, ruling families, and petty kingdoms were to be considered particularistic and largely irrelevant to the nomothetic goals of the New Archaeology (Binford 1968). Further aided by newly introduced radiometric techniques such as carbon dating, these large-scale projects brought scientific rigor to archaeological research design, method, and theory in Oaxaca, largely drawing from anthropological thinking, geographical modeling, and statistics. Through regional surveys of settlement patterns combined with household archaeology, the early emphasis on the ceremonial historical sites was replaced with the exploration of the much neglected Archaic and Formative periods in order to explore the origins of agriculture, sedentism, socioeconomics networks, and the development of social complexity (Blanton 1978; Flannery 1976; Flannery and Marcus 1983; Kowalewski et al. 1989). It was this exploration of Formative-period sites that pushed the origins of writing in Oaxaca back in time, heralded by the discovery of the earliest known inscribed monument in the New World—the aforementioned San José Mogote monument. Nevertheless, for the most part the historical record was largely ignored, even when later periods were discussed and interpreted.

Concomitantly, the continuous discovery of other inscriptions in situ, such as in royal tombs in Zaachila and the detailed excavations of other Late Classic and Postclassic sites, stimulated more historically oriented archaeological research in the Valley of Oaxaca (Paddock 1966a, 1966b, 1983; Whitecotton 1977; see also Bernal and Gamio 1974), and in 1972 the regional center of the Instituto Nacional de Antropología e Historia (INAH) was established in Oaxaca City to accommodate such dynamic and interdisciplinary research (Robles García and Juárez Osnaya 2004). Throughout the 1970s and 1980s North American scholarship largely adjusted into a unique brand of documentary-aided anthropological archaeology, although still within a vague evolutionary perspective (Appel 1982; Flannery and Marcus 1983; Spores 1967; 1980). Building on the works of Caso and similar breakthroughs in Maya studies (e.g., Berlin 1958 and Proskouriakoff 1960), the Classic-period Zapotec inscriptions were now recognized to be historical rather than purely mythological, even if history, myth, and propaganda were often regarded as interchangeable concepts for the ruling elite[25] (Marcus 1976, 1980, 1992). Still, the correlations between writing, iconography, and the archaeological records were largely limited to the few deciphered Zapotec glyphs and so highlighted aspects of militarism and territorial expansion wherein the inscriptions primarily played a corroborative role (Marcus 1976, 1980, 1984; Spencer and Redmond 1997).

Other integrative studies in the Mixteca by archaeologists, ethnohistorians, and art historians often started with a thorough historical analysis of prehispanic and Colonial documents in libraries, archives, and communities, which then served as the basis for ground-truthing of archaeological and geographical features, occasionally complemented by ethnographic work emphasizing oral traditions (Byland 1980; Byland and Pohl 1994; Jansen 1979; Pohl and Byland 1990; Smith 1973; Spores 1967, 1972, 1984; Byland, chapter 6, this volume; König, chapter 4, this volume; McCafferty and McCafferty, chapter 5, this volume; Pohl, chapter 3, this volume). This early form of Oaxacan "landscape archaeology" was still heavily oriented toward site identifications, but with a regional perspective and a well-defined research design. Thus, by taking the middle ground between culture-historical and processual approaches, archaeologists were looking at particularistic histories of the indigenous elite as a way to approach generalizations regarding political, social, and economic processes. Caso's early documentary chronology for the Mixteca was drastically revised and so allowed better integration and comparisons with the known archaeological sequences (Byland and Pohl 1994; Jansen 1990; Rabin 2003; Troike 1978).

Scholars in both the Valley of Oaxaca and the Mixteca drew extensively from the "direct historical approach" for their research, in which the documentary and archaeological records are usually not contemporaneous[26] (Flannery and Marcus 1983; Marcus and Flannery 1994; Spores 1972; see also Kroefges, chapter 13, this volume). The basic premise behind the approach, which is still quite prevalent today, is that certain cultural aspects can be inferred from a "known" context, such as Colonial historical documentation or ethnographic observation, which then helps to explain "unknown" contexts such as the archaeological record. This approach is particularly applicable when there is a considerable cultural continuity between the analogous units, such as with the case of Oaxacan literate societies. However, the inherent emphasis on continuity has often involved a selective filtering between assumed "traditional" and "nontraditional" traits, while in some cases the researcher simply "time traveled" from the ethnographic present to the archaeological past without considering the historical transformation between the two (see also Charlton 1981; Stahl 1993).

The last two decades of integrative research in Oaxaca are particularly characterized by a variety of collaborative projects combined with a growing specialization in Oaxacan archaeology and history. In addition to the continuing refinement of the archaeological phases in the Valley of Oaxaca, the Mixteca, and the Coast, a plethora of surveys and excavations throughout Oaxaca led to a better understanding of regional chronologies and interregional interactions (Markens 2008; figure 1.2). Specific attention is given to the spatial context of inscriptions and their "biography" of reuse through time rather than their study in isolation (Lind and Urcid 2010; Romero Frizzi 2003; Urcid 2001, 2005a, 2005b, 2011a, 2011b; Winter 1994b; König and Sellen, chapter 15, this volume). The simplistic models previously based on mere presence or absence of certain artifact styles and their "ethnic" affiliations are now being developed into nuanced theoretical frameworks that encompass both the material and the historiographic legacies of indigenous Mesoamerica, in which the Oaxaca Valley-Mixteca culture area stands out as one of the main players in a web of multiethnic interregional interactions and rival alliance corridors with the Valley of Puebla and other regions (Jansen 1998; Joyce 2010; Pohl 2003a, 2003b, 2003d, 2004b; Smith and Berdan 2003; Lind, chapter 7, this volume; Rincón Mautner, chapter 8, this volume). The subdiscipline of historical archaeology began to be formalized in Oaxaca in the 1990s, taking the much-neglected Colonial-period material culture and documentation as its basic point of departure for integrative research (Blackman et al. 2006; Charlton and Fournier 2008; Fernández Dávila and Gómez Serafín 1998; Gómez Serafín and Fernández Dávila 2007; Spores, chapter 2, this volume; Zborover, chapter 12, this volume; Zeitlin, chapter 14, this volume).

Together with advances in the decipherment of Zapotec and Mixtec scripts in a diachronic perspective, documentary research has refocused on indigenous perspectives and linguistics and included diverse historical and literary approaches such as source criticism, ethno-iconology, semiotics, intertextuality, and (new-) philology (Doesburg 2008; Jansen 1988; Spores, chapter 2, this volume; Zeitlin, chapter 14, this volume). This furthered the approach to some of the documentary traditions, most notably the Mixtec codices, as true literary works complete with poetic devices and prose (Jansen and Pérez Jiménez 2007, 2009a; Monaghan 1990; Pohl 1994). The growing study of indigenous alphabetic documents, consulted in national archives as well as local community archives, has demonstrated that even "mundane" literature can open a new window on all levels and aspects of Colonial society (e.g., Terraciano 2001). The Oaxacan documentary corpus has been further used to reconstruct emic indigenous chronologies and typologies that can be compared and contrasted with etic archaeological ones, and so get closer to how these people understood and interacted with their own ancestral material past (Hamann 2002, 2008; Oudijk 2008; Kroefges, chapter 13, this volume; Lind, chapter 7, this volume; figure 1.2). Oral knowledge was incorporated more rigorously into research designs and enhanced our understanding of the archaeological and the historical records, as well as the relevance of these to the modern-day people of Oaxaca (Byland and Pohl 1994; Geurds 2007; Jansen and Pérez Jiménez 2007; Markens et al. 2008; Monaghan 1995; Pohl, chapter 3, this volume; König, chapter 4, this volume; Jiménez Osorio and Posselt Santoyo, chapter 11, this volume; Doesburg and Spores, chapter 10, this volume; Zborover, chapter 12, this volume). Finally, computers and other digital media practically revolutionized the ways we collect, process, and interpret our archaeological and historical data.

Since the 1990s, culture change in prehispanic Oaxaca is framed more explicitly in terms of social and political institutions than as evolutionary stages, while some call attention to the potential complementarity between actor-based history and long-term evolutionary trends as gleaned from both documentary and archaeological records (Balkansky 1998, 2002; Lind and Urcid 2010; Marcus and Flannery 1996; Marcus and Zeitlin 1994; Robles García 2004). The application of various temporal and spatial scales was also inspired by the French Annales social history school, through the integration of archaeological and historical documentation in the study of various themes and periods (Feinman 1994; Hamann 2002; Kowalewski 1997, 2003; Kowalewski et al. 1989; Kroefges, chapter 13, this volume; Rincón Mautner, chapter 8, this volume). In recent years, the historically minded "postprocessual" turn in archaeology has clearly influenced the way integrative research has been conducted in Oaxaca. Practice theory, agency, gender, and subaltern studies have all introduced more sophisticated frameworks of analysis, shifting the focus from earlier ecological determinism to the subtle interactions between human actors and the larger system, and toward place-specific contextual research (Blomster 2008a, 2008b, 2010; Geurds 2007; Hamann 2008; Joyce 2010; McCafferty and McCafferty 1994; Zeitlin 2005; Zeitlin, chapter 14, this volume). While the persona-oriented inscriptions had sparked interest in embodied "agents" since the beginning of integrative research in Oaxaca, a growing attention is now given to the active role of "commoners' agency" in the shaping of those literate societies (Joyce 2008, 2010; Joyce et al. 2001).

BRIDGING THE GAPS

While it stands to reason that scholars today may choose to include or exclude the material, documentary, or ethnographic records in their respective research, the above overview makes it equally clear that all post-Formative archaeological studies in Oaxaca could be framed within a general or a specific historical context, whereas any and all documentary studies should regard the material culture as an inseparable manifestation of history. It is within this dual context and dynamic academic environment that this volume's editors felt it was time to draw together a session titled "Integrating Archaeology and History in Oaxaca," held at the 72nd Annual Meeting of the Society for American Archaeology in Austin, April 2007. The rationale behind bringing together an interdisciplinary and international group of scholars was twofold: (1) there seems to be a critical number of researchers world-wide who apply integrative approaches to Oaxaca's past but whose studies are not necessarily known to each other or to the academic mainstream, and (2) despite the various approaches, there is an evident need for methodological and theoretical orientation that could potentially lead toward more productive research.

The resulting volume brings some of these presented case studies together with contributions from other interested scholars who were not able to attend the con-ference, and it clearly reflects the rich spectrum of integrative studies today. The broad themes represented here—often intertwined within each of the individual contributions—effectively cover most of those relevant within the participants' respective disciplines, including social organization, politics, economy, technol-ogy, religion, and ideology; they range from the study of a specific artifact type to the examination of a particular community, kingdom, or regional interaction spheres; some highlight a particular period, whereas others take a more diachronic approach; and all establish explicit ties across space, time, and sources in order to explore larger questions regarding kinship, migration, colonialism, resistance, iden-tity, ethnicity, and territoriality, among other themes.

Yet despite the rich cultural and historical heritage and the long trajectory of research presented above, integrative studies in Oaxaca are still wrought with pro-found gaps. Perhaps the most apparent is the one stated in this chapter's opening quotes by George Vaillant and H. B. Nicholson over half a century ago, but which is still very much pertinent today: how do we go about bridging the gap between seemingly different cultural manifestations, such as artifacts and documents, so as to create a meaningful reconstruction of the past? The answers in this volume are multiple and largely situational. Any research question and the inherent potential for an integrative approach are particular for each case study and ultimately depend on the strengths and limitations of the available archaeological, documentary, and oral records. This in turn is a factor of the specific cultural traditions and the preser-vation of the records; an integrative research theme will often have to be framed and modified to accommodate these parameters. Temporal resolution is also a reflec-tion of the available records and our respective research questions and methodolo-gies (Kroefges, chapter 13, this volume; Zborover, chapter 12, this volume). Surely, there are ontological differences between the records as each often reflects the pas-sage of time differently. While it is often true that documents tend to be event-oriented and the material record is likely to reflect the long-term, the distinction is not always straightforward. Written and oral narratives can and do represent long swaths of time in a condensed fashion (such as with the literary device of historical "telescoping"), while the archaeological record is in many cases event-specific (such as with destruction episodes, burials, caches, etc.).

A central starting point to the authors in this volume, therefore, lies primarily with the construction of strong spatial, temporal, and thematic correlates and analogous units for comparison and integration. Most often, though, such integrative prospects might be apparent only when one of the records has been sufficiently explored and understood, which would consequentially serve as a departure point for the inclusion of other records or the formulation of models and analogies. Although some authors in this volume begin with a thorough historical analysis that later frames archaeological work, others start from the archaeological record and move to the historical one in search for answers. For the most part, however, the procedure is not clear cut and there is vigorous dialectic interplay between the different lines of evidence throughout the research process (see Zborover, chapter 12, this volume, for further discussion).

Clearly, the aptitude for bridging the gap between different types of data lies with the training, interests, and often inherent biases of the researcher. Given that the SAA session and this resulting volume drew together archaeologists, anthropologists, ethnohistorians, and art historians who were educated and work in North America, Mexico, and Europe, one would equally expect a plethora of bridging approaches and methods. The evident divergence in how scholars integrate the archaeological and the historical often has to do with different methodological approaches and theoretical schools of thought (Byland, chapter 6, this volume; Kroefges, chapter 13, this volume), and sometimes—particularly in Oaxaca—personal squabbles. Beyond such disparate scholastic and national traditions, significant epistemological gaps are most often generated by current institutional parochialism. The disciplinary segmentation of knowledge is clearest within North American scholarship, where anthropology and its subfield archaeology are largely, if often artificially, divorced from the discipline of history and its respective method and theory. At the same time, indigenous and indigenous-related documentary sources are still largely ignored by historians and history departments (with few notable exceptions), and are mostly studied under the rubric of "ethnohistory" by archaeologists.[27] In that sense, scholars in Europe and to some extent in Mexico often practice a less dichotomous, integrative research.

Despite voices worldwide to abolish the disciplinary boundaries between archaeology and history (e.g., Sauer 2004), the diverse contributions in this volume suggest that the ever-growing body of data, techniques, and methods in each respective discipline, combined with the academic need for specialization, would make such a task impractical. A more viable alternative is becoming clear from this chapter's opening quote by Byland and Pohl, who call for a "conscious and coordinated confluence" to bridge those disciplinary gaps (Byland and Pohl 1990:385). Such a "conscious" exploration for multidisciplinary sources and interdisciplinary methods in approaching specific research questions, along with an awareness of each discipline's relative strengths and weaknesses, characterize all the volume contributions. Several of these case studies further demonstrate a "confluence" through collaborative work between archaeologists, ethnohistorians, and art historians (e.g., König, chapter 4; König and Sellen, chapter 15 ; Doesburg and Spores, chapter 10; Pohl, chapter 3; Spores, chapter 2), which, however, remains unfortunately all too rare in Oaxaca itself. Outside of the state boundaries there has been little constructive dialogue between Oaxacanists and specialists from other regions in Mesoamerica, and even less so with other integrative schools throughout the world; especially relevant would be the Maya region, where epigraphy has literally revolutionized archaeological practice, and many scholars now approach integrative studies in a structured fashion (see for example the long trajectory of methodological treatises such as Carmack and Weeks 1981; Chase et al. 2008; Fash and Sharer 1991; Houston 1989; Maca 2010; Rice and Rice 2004; Wauchope 1947, among many others).

Other debilitating gaps are manifested by the incomplete and selective nature of archaeological and historical studies across space and time. Although this may seem to be the inescapable nature of our research, the almost exclusive emphasis in early research on the Valley of Oaxaca and—to a lesser extent—the Mixteca, largely continues today and has neglected more circumscribed (but not marginal!) literate societies, creating in the process a rather distorted picture of internal dynamics within ancient Oaxaca and interregional interaction throughout Mesoamerica (Winter 2008a). Integrative studies on the literate societies of the southern Isthmus and Central Coast are steadily growing (Kroefges, chapter 13, this volume; Zborover, chapter 12, this volume; Zeitlin, chapter 14, this volume), but there is still much to be done in other parts of Oaxaca. Standing out in their lack of representation are the poorly explored Sierra Norte, Papaloapan, and the northeastern Isthmus, despite the probable linguistic, material, and historical affiliation of the Mixe and Zoque ethnic groups who inhabit these regions with the millennial literate cultures of Veracruz and Tabasco.

Equally revealing are the gaps in temporal coverage. The Formative period is still underrepresented in integrative studies, owing partially to the relative dearth of excavated inscriptions but also due to the ongoing scholarly tradition in Oaxaca that continues to gravitate toward the rich historical and archaeological records of the Classic and Postclassic periods. But whereas temporal specialization and periodization are inevitable aspects of academic practice and discourse, these largely subjective abstractions often tend to produce a rigid and dogmatic scholarship. Perhaps the most critical conceptual gap for integrative research is brought by the artificial polarization between the "prehispanic" vis-à-vis the "Colonial/post-Columbian" eras, and the increasingly inadequate "1519/1521 CE" chronological "boundary" as their respective end/start points (Kowalewski 1997; see also Zborover, chapter 12, this volume). It is quite telling that although chronological sequences for the former are still based largely on typological changes in the material culture that vary from one subregion to another, those of the latter are determined through key historical events recorded in the documentary record and are mostly represented as uniform across Oaxaca[28] (figure 1.2). Drawing from prehispanic and Colonial documentation, changes and continuities in the material culture before and after the Spanish conquest, and oral traditions that are rooted in the present but reflect the deep past, many contributions in this volume seamlessly bridge this gap and so add to the growing literature that attempts to dispel such artificial temporal dichotomies in Oaxaca and beyond[29] (Doesburg 2008; Jansen and van Broekhoven 2008; Kepecs and Alexander 2005; Romero Frizzi 2003; Scheiber and Mitchell 2010; Spores 2007; Tedlock 2010). Most case studies in this volume further reflect the recent growing interest in the study of Colonial-period transformations (Doesburg and Spores, chapter 10; Jiménez Osorio and Posselt Santoyo, chapter 11; Kroefges, chapter 13; Lind, chapter 7; Rincón Mautner, chapter 8; Spores, chapter 2; Whittington and Workinger, chapter 9; Zborover, chapter 12; Zeitlin, chapter 14), and even the Independence/Republican period (Jiménez Osorio and Posselt Santoyo, chapter 11; König and Sellen, chapter 15). In this regard, much complementary research remains to be done on the material culture of the recent yet equally fascinating Independence/Republican and Modern periods (see for example Gómez Serafín and Fernández Dávila 2007), and its association with the well-preserved documentation and contemporary oral records.

Bridging the temporal gaps also implies stronger affinities between the people of past and those of the present. Indeed, the practice of bringing the past to life through the combination of artifacts, documents, and oral knowledge is at the heart of public approaches throughout the world. In Oaxaca, however, the potential public is not just the national and international tourists who visit archaeological sites or museums but is foremost the indigenous Oaxacans whose past we explore in collaboration with them. Forty percent of Oaxaca's population self-ascribes to sixteen contemporary indigenous groups, who speak over 200 dialects. This makes Oaxaca the most ethnically and linguistically diverse state, with the largest indigenous population, in Mexico (Bartolomé 2008). Oaxaca was also the first Mexican state (in 1990) to legally recognize the "multicultural composition" and indigenous rights of its inhabitants, and to legitimize the highly prevalent *usos y costumbres* traditional governance in 1995. Although several authors in this volume do call for

FIGURE 1.3. Bruce Byland (right) in the 2007 SAA session, with Maarten Jansen (left) and Ronald Spores (middle). Photo by Marco Ortega.

community engagement and participatory approaches, there is still a marked chasm between institutions, academics, and the various public audiences. For that matter, there is also a notable lack of integrative research on nonindigenous groups such as Afro-Mexicans, *criollos, mestizos*, and other peoples who shaped and continue to form the social and ethnic fabric of Oaxaca. The mere fact that such multiethnic collaborative research is not just indispensable in our days but is still even possible in Oaxaca, once again highlights the richness and importance of the region and the great potential for future avenues of research.

One of the leading protagonists of bridging the disciplinary, temporal, geographical, and social gaps was Bruce E. Byland, whose interdisciplinary work in Oaxaca has either directly intersected with, or has inspired, several generations of Oaxacanists, including many of the authors in this volume. At the time the SAA session was organized, Bruce was already battling cancer but decided to join in at the last moment at the encouragement of Carlos Rincón Mautner. During the conference Bruce made an immediate impression on the session participants with his friendly nature, curiosity, humility, and generosity (figure 1.3). Once the plans to publish the session's proceedings were subsequently circulated, Bruce's last email to the editors concluded with the words, "count me in." Sadly, Bruce passed away before he was able to send in his article, and an extended draft of his conference paper was adapted and is published here. At the suggestion of Viola König, the editors and participants promptly decided to dedicate the volume to Bruce's memory and so honor his enduring legacy to Oaxacan integrative studies.[30]

NOTES

1. In addition to numerous articles and unpublished dissertations, some of the specialized edited volumes and monographs include Andrén 1998; Bartlett 1997; Beaudry 1993; Boyd et al. 2000; Brambila Paz and Monjarás-Ruiz 1996; Dymond 1974; Funari et al. 1999; Kepecs and Kolb 1997; Knapp 1992; Levy 2010; Little 1992; Martinón-Torres and Rehren 2008; Moreland 2001; Orser and Fagan 1995; Rogers and Wilson 1993; Sauer 2004; B. Schmidt 2007; P. Schmidt 2006; Schuyler 1978; Small 1995; Topic 2009; Wainwright 1962; and Yoffee and Crowell 2006, among others.

2. In Mesoamerica, this is sometimes referred to as the "convergent" (Spores, Chapter 2) or the "conjunctive" approach (Carmack and Weeks 1981; Chase et al. 2008; Fash and Sharer 1991; see also Joyce et al. 2004; Kroefges, chapter 14, this volume). For a detailed discussion on the origin and use of the term *conjunctive* in Maya integrative studies, see Maca 2010.

3. The broader impact of writing and literacy on social institutions remains beyond the scope of this article; for a general discussion on the subject see Goody 1986 and Ong 1982, among others.

4. Recent suggestions to view artifacts as "texts" further add to this conceptual ambiguity (e.g., Hodder 1991), but these are mostly limited to illustrative and interpretive analogies.

5. Following Vansina (1985), *oral history* refers to accounts directly witnessed by the informant or that have happened in his or her lifetime, whereas *oral tradition* has been passed down the generations and the narrated events are not contemporary with the informant (see also Jiménez Osorio and Posselt Santoyo, chapter 11, this volume).

6. It should be emphasized that this reconstruction is an approximation based on the fragmentary state of research in Oaxaca, conflicting interpretations, and the inevitable constrains brought by the perishable nature of both the artifactual and documentary records. It does not attempt to present an exhaustive overview of Oaxacan archaeology and ethnohistory, but only as much as is relevant to the theme of source integration.

7. The ceramic phases for the Valley of Oaxaca/Tierras Largas–Chila, Mixteca Baja, and Mixteca Costa are based on calibrated carbon dates and adapted from Joyce 2010. The Mixteca Alta/Nochixtlán prehispanic phases are based on calibrated dates and are adapted from Joyce 2010, and the Colonial phases from Spores 2007. The phases for the Valley of

Oaxaca/Tierras Largas–Monte Alban V., Mixteca Alta/Huamelulpan, Cuicatlan Cañada, and the Isthmus of Tehuantepec are based on uncorrected dates and are adapted from Markens 2008, Matadamas Díaz and Ramírez Barrera 2010 (Central Coast), and Spores 2007 (Mixteca Alta). The Tanipaa-Cuilapan sequence (Valley of Oaxaca) is based on indigenous documents and is adapted from Oudijk 2008. The Colonial-to-Modern periodization is largely based on European and Mexican documentation and is adapted from Charlton and Fournier 2008, Gómez Serafín and Fernández Dávila 2007 (Huaxyacac-Oaxaca phases), Palka 2009, and Spores 2007.

8. Recent discoveries in the Olmec heartland of Veracruz and Tabasco might challenge this title. The Cascajal block, an undeciphered sixty-two-glyph inscription, was found out of context but is tentatively dated to around 900 BCE, based on association with other archaeological material and contemporary iconographic parallels (Rodríguez Martínez et al. 2006). An inscribed ceramic seal and greenstone fragments excavated at the site of San Andrés were securely dated to about 650 BCE (Pohl et al. 2002), although these are fragmentary and might represent complex iconography rather than language-based writing.

9. Although the name glyph was previously identified as "1 Earthquake" (see, e.g., Marcus and Flannery 1996), I follow here Javier Urcid's (2005a, 2011a) reading of "1 Eye." The dating of the monument was also contested, but recently published carbon dates confirm that it was placed in the sixth century BCE (Flannery and Marcus 2003). See Cahn and Winter (1993) and Winter (2011) for alternative chronological, functional, and stylistic interpretations of the San José Mogote monument.

10. Another possible interpretation of this and the later *danzantes* monoliths is that the associated calendrical name was that of the captor rather than of the captive, although the principle of individual specificity would still apply in this case (Urcid 2011c; Winter 2011).

11. It should be emphasized here that the binary and often dichotomous characterization of Mesoamerican society into endogamous elite and commoner strata is probably overly simplistic, and glosses over intermediate social classes and specialized groups who might have had differential access to literacy in the past. At the same time, the archaeological manifestations for such social distinctions are notoriously hard to define. For a detailed description of Oaxacan indigenous social organization in the prehispanic and Colonial periods see Chance (1986), Dahlgren (1966), Murphy and Stepick (1991), Spores (1967), Terraciano (2001), and Whitecotton (1977).

12. In some cases inscribed monuments were appropriated and recycled after the abandonment of the primary elite contexts in possible acts of commoner resistance, although it is uncertain whether the original written messages could still have been fully understood (see for example Joyce et al. 2001).

13. The social reasons behind choosing this particular hilltop location are still debated; see Winter 2011 for a discussion of the different interpretations.

14. It should be emphasized that much of the Zapotec script still remains undeciphered, as is the nature of its dependence on the Zapotec language (Urcid 2001, 2005a).

15. A circle-and-triangle blood glyph was carved here on the risers of Temple T.S. (Joyce 2010:167), similar to the ones seen in Building L-sub in Monte Albán.

16. The territorial extent and nature of Monte Albán influence throughout Oaxaca is still unclear and has been hotly debated in the literature. For some of the most recent publications on the topic, compare Joyce (2013), Sherman et al. (2010), Spencer et al. (2008), Workinger and Joyce (2009), and see further discussion in Zborover, chapter 12, this volume.

17. The same also holds for the following Classic-period script variants in this and other "non-Zapotec" regions.

18. The role that the Oaxaca area played in the creation and diffusion of this Mixteca-Puebla style is still poorly understood; see further discussion in Blomster (2008b), Smith and Berdan (2003), and Lind, chapter 7, this volume.

19. There are four known Late Postclassic codices: Nuttall, Vienna, Bodley, and Colombino-Becker I; and three Early Colonial codices: Selden, Egerton, and Becker II. In addition to their pictorial narratives, all these codices show additional alphabetic glossing and numbering that were added on different occasions and for different reasons, from the Colonial period and up to modern times. See Jansen and Pérez Jiménez (2007) for the histories and alternative names of these codices.

20. Interestingly, the Mixtec deity 9 Wind Quetzalcoatl is shown in page 48 of the Codex Vienna as the inventor of written and oral literature. Such achievements are also attributed to the Toltec Quetzalcoatl of the Early Postclassic and probably refer to the introduction of this logographic script across Mesoamerica.

21. Another intriguing possibility is that the primordial "stone men" attributed to the pre-Postclassic times were a codical reference to the inscribed stone stelae of Classic-period rulers that surely still dotted the landscape.

22. It is not surprising that these key Aztec and later Spanish settlements were established at the foot of Monte Albán, considering the historical, symbolic, and religious roles that this ancestral site still played within Late Postclassic society.

23. It is likely that these factional circumstances, along with the fragmented topography, partially stand behind both Oaxaca's current political partition into 570 municipalities and the number of endemic territorial disputes between villages, both being the highest of any state in Mexico.

24. Caso's and his colleagues work was largely inspired by Jiménez Moreno's (1941) identification of Tula (Hidalgo) as the historical Toltec capital, based on a combination of documentary and archaeological evidence.

25. Marcus (1992) further suggested that the writing of such hybrid political propaganda would have been directed "horizontally" towards other nobility, and "vertically" towards the commoners.

26. It is interesting to note here that while Trigger places the "direct historical approach" within a "humanistic outlook" (Trigger 1989:377), Marcus and Flannery (1994:55) regard it as a "scientific method" distinct from the "humanistic" approach.

27. This research agenda had its roots in US anthropology departments during the 1950s, which partially explains why the majority of scholars who practice integrative research in Oaxaca and elsewhere are archaeologists. Another determining factor is that archaeologists can exclusively produce their own material database, in addition to being able to study documentary sources and collect ethnographic data. However, access to primary data does not necessarily entail the ability to analyze and interpret the data adequately, and lack of disciplinary training, combined with time and funding constraints, will usually limit one's research agenda and scope (see also Spores, chapter 2, this volume).

28. In this regard, the prehispanic documentary periodization in Oudijk 2008 and the Colonial-to-Modern ceramic/documentary periodization in Gómez Serafín and Fernández Dávila 2007 are welcome steps in the right direction.

29. The Latin American school of social archaeology, for example, suggests reconceptualizing history as a cultural continuum that unites the prehispanic and the Colonial periods (Vargas Arenas 1995).

30. I would like to thank Alessia Frassani, Arthur Joyce, Peter C. Kroefges, Geoffrey McCafferty, John M.D. Pohl, Ethelia Ruiz Medrano, Aaron Sonnenschein, the "Mezcal Papers" group at the Center for US-Mexican Studies, and two anonymous reviewers for reading earlier drafts of this article and providing helpful comments. The errors are all mine.

REFERENCES

Aguirre Beltrán, Gonzalo. 1989. *La Población Negra de México: Estudio Etnohistórico.* Veracruz, Mexico: Universidad Veracruzana.

Andrén, Anders. 1998. *Between Artifacts and Texts: Historical Archaeology in Global Perspective.* New York: Plenum Press.

Appel, Jill A. 1982. "A Summary of the Ethnohistoric Information Relevant to the Interpretation of Late Postclassic Settlement Pattern Data, the Central and Valle Grande Survey Zones." In *Monte Albán's Hinterland, Part I: The Prehistoric Settlement Patterns of the Central and Southern Parts of the Valley of Oaxaca, Mexico,* 139–148. Ann Arbor, MI: Museum of Anthropology, University of Michigan, Memoir 15.

Asselbergs, Florine. 2008. *Conquered Conquistadors: The Lienzo de Quauhquechollan, a Nahua Vision of the Conquest of Guatemala.* Boulder: University Press of Colorado.

Balkansky, Andrew K. 1998. "Origin and Collapse of Complex Societies in Oaxaca (Mexico): Evaluating the Era from 1965 to the Present." *Journal of World Prehistory* 12 (4):451–493.

Balkansky, Andrew K. 2002. *The Sola Valley and the Monte Albán State: A Study of Zapotec Imperial Expansion*. Ann Arbor: Museum of Anthropology, University of Michigan, Memoir 36.

Balkansky, Andrew K., Verónica Pérez Rodríguez, and Stephen A. Kowalewski. 2004. "Monte Negro and the Urban Revolution in Oaxaca, Mexico." *Latin American Antiquity* 15(1):33–60.

Bartlett, John R., ed. 1997. *Archaeology and Biblical Interpretation*. London: Routledge.

Bartolomé, Miguel Alberto. 2008. *La Tierra Plural: Sistemas Interculturales en Oaxaca*. Mexico City: INAH.

Beaudry, Mary C., ed. 1993. *Documentary Archaeology in the New World*. Cambridge: Cambridge University Press.

Berdan, Frances, Richard Blanton, Elizabeth Hill Boone, Mary G. Hodge, Michael E. Smith, and Emily Umberger, eds. 1996. *Aztec Imperial Strategies*. Washington, DC: Dumbarton Oaks.

Berlin, Heinrich. 1958. "El Glifo 'Emblema' en las Inscripciones Mayas." *Journal de la Société des Americanistes* 47:111–119.

Bernal, Ignacio. 1948. "Exploraciones en Coixtlahuaca, Oaxaca." *Revista Mexicana de Estudios Antropológicos* 10:5–76.

Bernal, Ignacio. 1962. "Archaeology and Written Sources." *Akten des 34 Internationalen Amerikanistenkongresses*, 219–225. Vienna: Verlag Ferdinand Berger.

Bernal, Ignacio. 1965. "Archaeological Synthesis of Oaxaca." In *Handbook of Middle American Indians*, vol. 3, part 2, ed. Gordon Willey, 788–813. Austin: University of Texas Press.

Bernal, Ignacio, and Lorenzo Gamio. 1974. *Yagul: el Palacio de los Seis Patios*. Mexico City: UNAM.

Binford, Lewis R. 1968. "Some Comments on Historical versus Processual Archaeology." *Southwestern Journal of Anthropology* 24 (3):267–275.

Blackman, M. James, Patricia Fournier, and Ronald L. Bishop. 2006. "Complejidad e Interacción Social en el México Colonial: Identidad, Producción, Intercambio y Consumo de Lozas de Tradición Ibérica, con Base en Análisis de Activación Neutrónica." *Cuicuilco* 13 (36):203–222.

Blanton, Richard E. 1978. *Monte Albán: Settlement Patterns at the Ancient Zapotec Capital*. New York: Academic Press.

Blomster, Jeffrey P. 2004. *Etlatongo: Social Complexity, Interaction, and Village Life in the Mixteca Alta of Oaxaca, Mexico*. Belmont: Wadsworth/Thompson Learning.

Blomster, Jeffrey P., ed. 2008a. *After Monte Albán: Transformation and Negotiation in Oaxaca, Mexico*. Boulder: University Press of Colorado.

Blomster, Jeffrey P. 2008b. "Changing Cloud Formations: The Sociopolitics of Oaxaca in Late Classic/Postclassic Mesoamerica." In *After Monte Albán: Transformation and Negotiation in Oaxaca, Mexico*, ed. Jeffrey Blomster, 3–46. Boulder: University Press of Colorado.

Blomster, Jeffrey P. 2008c. "Legitimization, Negotiation, and Appropriation in Postclassic Oaxaca: Mixtec Stone Codices." In *After Monte Albán: Transformation and Negotiation in Oaxaca, Mexico*, ed. Jeffrey Blomster, 295–330. Boulder: University Press of Colorado.

Blomster, Jeffrey P. 2010. "Complexity, Interaction, and Epistemology: Mixtecs, Zapotecs, and Olmecs in Early Formative Mesoamerica." *Ancient Mesoamerica* 21 (1):135–149.

Boone, Elizabeth Hill. 1994. "Introduction: Writing and Recording Knowledge." In *Writing without Words: Alternative Literacies in Mesoamerica and the Andes*, ed. Elizabeth Hill Boone and Walter Mignolo, 3–26. Durham: Duke University Press.

Boone, Elizabeth Hill. 2000. *Stories in Red and Black: Pictorial Histories of the Aztecs and Mixtecs*. Austin: University of Texas Press.

Boone, Elizabeth Hill, and Michael E. Smith. 2003. "Postclassic International Styles and Symbol Sets." In *The Postclassic Mesoamerican World*, ed. Michael E. Smith and Frances F. Berdan, 61–66. Salt Lake City: University of Utah Press.

Boyd, M., J. C. Edwin, and M. Hendrickson, eds. 2000. *The Entangled Past: Integrating History and Archaeology*. Calgary: Chacmool Archaeological Association.

Brambila Paz, Rosa, and Jesús Monjarás-Ruiz, eds. 1996. *Los Arqueólogos frente a las Fuentes*. Mexico City: INAH.

Buigues, Santiago Vicente. 1993. "The Archaeology and Iconography of Monte Albán's Building J." Unpublished MA Thesis, Department of Archaeology, University of Calgary, Calgary.

Byland, Bruce E. 1980. "Political and Economic Evaluation in the Tamazulapan Valley, Mixteca Alta, Oaxaca, Mexico: A Regional Approach." Unpublished PhD diss., Department of Anthropology, Pennsylvania State University.

Byland, Bruce E. 2008. "Tree Birth, the Solar Oracle, and Achiutla: Mixtec Sacred Geography and the Classic to Postclassic Transition." In *After Monte Albán: Transformation and Negotiation in Oaxaca, Mexico*, ed. Jeffrey Blomster, 331–364. Boulder: University Press of Colorado.

Byland, Bruce E., and John M.D. Pohl. 1990. "Alianza y Conflicto de los Estados Mixtecos: El Caso Tilantongo." In *Lecturas Históricas del Estado de Oaxaca*, vol. 1. ed. Marcus Winter, 379–389. Mexico: INAH/ Gobierno del Estado de Oaxaca.

Byland, Bruce E., and John M.D. Pohl. 1994. *In the Realm of Eight Deer: The Archaeology of the Mixtec Codices*. Norman: University of Oklahoma Press.

Cahn, Robert, and Marcus Winter. 1993. "The San José Mogote Danzante." *Indiana* 13:39–64.

Carmack, Robert M., and John M. Weeks. 1981. "The Archaeology and Ethnohistory of Utatlán: A Conjunctive Approach." *American Antiquity* 46 (2):323–341.

Carter, Nicholas Poole. 2008. "The 'Emblem' Monuments of Structure J at Monte Albán, Oaxaca, Mexico." Unpublished MA Thesis, University of Texas, Austin.

Caso, Alfonso. 1928. *Las Estelas Zapotecas*. Mexico: SEP and Talleres Gráficos de la Nación.

Caso, Alfonso. 1932. "Reading the Riddle of Ancient Jewels." *Natural History* 32 (5):464–480.

Caso, Alfonso. 1947. "Calendario y Escritura de las Antiguas Culturas de Monte Albán." In *Obras Completas de Miguel Othón de Mendizábal* vol. 1, 15–143. Mexico City.

Caso, Alfonso. 1949. "El Mapa de Teozacoalco." *Cuadernos Americanos* 8 (5):145–181.

Caso, Alfonso. 1965. "Zapotec Writing and Calendar." In *Handbook of Middle American Indians*, vol. 3, part 2, ed. Gordon Willey, 931–947. Austin: University of Texas Press.

Chance, John K. 1986. "Colonial Ethnohistory of Oaxaca." In *Supplement to the Handbook of Middle American Indians*, vol. 4. ed. Ronald Spores, 165–189. Austin: University of Texas Press.

Chance, John K. 1989. *Conquest of the Sierra: Spaniards and Indians in Colonial Oaxaca*. Norman: University of Oklahoma Press.

Charlton, Thomas. 1981. "Archaeology, Ethnohistory, and Ethnography: Interpretative Interfaces." In *Advances in Archaeological Method and Theory*, vol. 4. ed. Michael B. Schiffer, 129–176. New York: Academic Press.

Charlton, Thomas, and Patricia Fournier. 2008. "Historical Archaeology in Mexico." In *Encyclopedia of Archaeology*, ed. Deborah M. Pearsall, 182–192. San Diego: Academic Press.

Chase, Arlen F., Diane Z. Chase, and Rafael Cobos. 2008. "Jeroglíficos y Arqueología Maya: ¿Colusión o Colisión?" *Mayeb* 20:5–21.

Chassen-López, Francie R. 2008. "A Patron of Progress: Juana Catarina Romero, the Nineteenth-Century Cacica of Tehuantepec." *Hispanic American Historical Review* 88 (3):393–426.

Cline, Howard F. 1972. "Ethnohistorical Regions of Middle America." In *Handbook of Middle American Indians*, vol. 12. ed. Howard F. Cline, 166–182. Austin: University of Texas Press.

Dahlgren, Barbro. 1966. *La Mixteca: Su Cultura e Historia Prehispánicas*. Mexico City: UNAM.

Dark, Philip. 1958. "Speculations on the Course of Mixtec History prior to the Conquest." *Boletín de Estudios Oaxaqueños* 10:1–14.

Doesburg, Sebastian van, ed. 2008. *Pictografía y Escritura Alfabética en Oaxaca*. Oaxaca, Mexico: IEEPO.

Doesburg, Sebastian van, and Javier Urcid. 2009. *"Dos Fragmentos de un Nuevo Códice en San Bartolo Yautepec, Oaxaca."* Presentation given at the 7th International Festival of Organs and Ancient Music. Oaxaca, Mexico: Biblioteca Francisco de Burgoa.

Dymond, David P. 1974. *Archaeology and History: A Plea for Reconciliation.* London: Thames and Hudson.

Fash, William L., and Robert J. Sharer. 1991. "Sociopolitical Developments and Methodological Issues at Copan, Honduras: A Conjunctive Perspective." *Latin American Antiquity* 2 (2):166–187.

Feinman, Gary M. 1994. "Towards an Archaeology without Polarization." In *Caciques and Their People: A Volume in Honor of Ronald Spores*, ed. Joyce Marcus and Judith F. Zeitlin, 13–43. Ann Arbor: Museum of Anthropology, University of Michigan, Anthropological papers no. 89.

Fernández Dávila, Enrique, and Susana Gómez Serafín, eds. 1998. *Memoria del Primer Congreso Nacional de Arqueología Historia.* Mexico City: CONACULTA/INAH.

Flannery, Kent V., ed. 1976. *The Early Mesoamerican Village.* New York: Academic Press.

Flannery, Kent V., and Joyce Marcus. 2003. "The Origins of War: New C–14 Dates from Ancient Mexico." *Proceedings of the National Academy of Sciences of the United States of America* 100 (20):11801–11805.

Flannery, Kent V., and Joyce Marcus, eds. 1983. *The Cloud People: Divergent Evolution of the Zapotec and Mixtec Civilizations.* New York: Academic Press.

Fournier, Patricia, and Thomas H. Charlton. 2008. "Negritos y Pardos: Hacia una Arqueología Histórica de la Población de Origen Africano en la Nueva España." In *Perspectivas de la Investigación Arqueológica, Volumen 3*, ed. Fernando López Aguilar, Walburga Wiesheu, and Patricia Fournier, 201–234. Mexico City: PROMEP-CONACULTA-ENAH.

Frassani, Alessia. 2009. "The Church and Convento of Santo Domingo Yanhuitlán, Oaxaca: Art, Politics, and Religion in a Mixtec Village, Sixteenth through Eighteenth Centuries." Unpublished PhD diss., CUNY Graduate Center, New York.

Funari, Pedro Paulo A., Martin Hall, and Siân Jones, eds. 1999. *Historical Archaeology: Back from the Edge.* London: Routledge.

Gallaga Murrieta, Emiliano, ed. 2009. *¿Donde Están? Investigaciones sobre Afromexicanos.* Chiapas, Mexico: UNICACH.

Gerhard, Peter. 1993. *A Guide to the Historical Geography of New Spain.* Norman: University of Oklahoma Press.

Gerhard, Peter. 2003. *Pirates of New Spain, 1575–1742.* New York: Dover.

Geurds, Alexander. 2007. *Grounding the Past: The Praxis of Participatory Archaeology in the Mixteca Alta, Oaxaca, Mexico.* Leiden: CNWS.

Gómez Serafín, Susana, and Enrique Fernández Dávila. 2007. *Las Cerámicas Coloniales del ex Convento de Santo Domingo de Oaxaca: Pasado y Presente de una Tradición.* Mexico City: INAH.

Goody, Jack. 1986. *The Logic of Writing and the Organization of Society.* Cambridge: Cambridge University Press.

Gutiérrez, Gerardo. 2008. "Classic and Postclassic Archaeological Features of the Mixteca-Tlapaneca-Nahua Region of Guerrero: Why Didn't Anyone Tell Me the Classic Period Was Over?" In *After Monte Albán: Transformation and Negotiation in Oaxaca, Mexico,* ed. Jeffrey Blomster, 367–392. Boulder: University Press of Colorado.

Hamann, Byron Ellsworth. 2002. "The Social Life of Pre-Sunrise Things: Indigenous Mesoamerican Archaeology." *Current Anthropology* 43 (3):351–381.

Hamann, Byron Ellsworth. 2008. "Heirlooms and Ruins: High Culture, Mesoamerican Civilization, and the Postclassic Oaxacan Tradition." In *After Monte Albán: Transformation and Negotiation in Oaxaca, Mexico,* ed. Jeffrey Blomster, 119–168. Boulder: University Press of Colorado.

Hodder, Ian. 1991. *Reading the Past: Current Approaches to Interpretation in Archaeology.* Cambridge: Cambridge University Press.

Houston, Stephen D. 1989. "Archaeology and Maya Writing." *Journal of World Prehistory* 3 (1):1–32.

Houston, Stephen D., ed. 2004. *The First Writing: Script Invention as History and Process.* Cambridge: Cambridge University Press.

Jansen, Maarten E.R.G.N. 1979. "Apoala y su Importancia para la Interpretación de los Codices Vindobonensis y Nuttall." In *Actes du XLIIe Congrès International des Américanistes,* 161–172. Paris: Société des Américanistes.

Jansen, Maarten E.R.G.N. 1988. "The Art of Writing in Ancient Mexico: An Ethno-iconological Perspective." *Visible Religion* 4:86–113.

Jansen, Maarten E.R.G.N. 1990. "The Search for History in the Mixtec Codices." *Ancient Mesoamerica* 1 (1):99–112.

Jansen, Maarten E.R.G.N. 1998. "Monte Albán y Zaachila en los Códices Mixtecos." In *The Shadow of Monte Albán: Politics and Historiography in Postclassic Oaxaca, Mexico,* ed. Maarten Jansen, Peter Kroefges, and Michel R. Oudijk, 67–122. Leiden: CNWS.

Jansen, Maarten, and Gabina Aurora Pérez Jiménez. 2007. *Encounter with the Plumed Serpent: Drama and Power in the Heart of Mesoamerica.* Boulder: University Press of Colorado.

Jansen, Maarten, and Gabina Aurora Pérez Jiménez. 2009a. *La Lengua Señorial de Ñuu Dzaui: Cultura Literaria de los Antiguos Reinos y Transformación Colonial.* Mexico: CSEIIO.

Jansen, Maarten, and Gabina Aurora Pérez Jiménez. 2009b. "Mixtec Rulership in Early Colonial Times: The Codex of Yanhuitlán." In *Das Kulturelle Gedächtnis Mesoamerikas im Kulturvergleich zum Alten China*, ed. Daniel Graña-Behrens, 149–180. Berlin: Gebr. Mann Verlag.

Jansen, Maarten, and Laura van Broekhoven, eds. 2008. *Mixtec Writing and Society: Escritura de Ñuu Dzaui*. Amsterdam: KNAW Press.

Jiménez-Moreno, Wigberto. 1941. "Tula y los Toltecas Según las Fuentes Históricas." *Revista Mexicana de Estudios Antropológicos* 5:79–83.

Joyce, Arthur A. 2004. "Sacred Space and Social Relations in the Valley of Oaxaca." In *Mesoamerican Archaeology: Theory and Practice*, ed. Julia Hendon and Rosemary Joyce, 192–216. Cornwall, UK: Blackwell.

Joyce, Arthur A. 2008. "Domination, Negotiation, and Collapse: A History of Centralized Authority on the Oaxaca Coast before the Late Postclassic." In *After Monte Albán: Transformation and Negotiation in Oaxaca, Mexico*, ed. Jeffrey Blomster, 219–254. Boulder: University Press of Colorado.

Joyce, Arthur A. 2010. *Mixtecs, Zapotecs, and Chatinos: Ancient People of Southern Mexico*. Malaysia: Wiley-Blackwell.

Joyce, Arthur A., ed. 2013. *Polity and Ecology in Formative Period Coastal Oaxaca*. Boulder: University Press of Colorado.

Joyce, Arthur A., Andrew G. Workinger, Byron Hamann, Peter Kroefges, Maxine Oland, and Stacie M. King. 2004. "Lord 8 Deer 'Jaguar Claw' and the Land of the Sky: The Archaeology and History of Tututepec." *Latin American Antiquity* 15 (3):273–297.

Joyce, Arthur A., Laura Arnaud Bustamante, and Marc N. Levine. 2001. "Commoner Power: A Case Study from the Classic Period 'Collapse' on the Oaxaca Coast." *Journal of Archaeological Method and Theory* 8 (4):343–385.

Joyce, Arthur A., Marcus C. Winter, and Raymond G. Mueller. 1998. *Arqueología de la Costa de Oaxaca: Asentamientos del Periodo Formativo en el Valle de Río Verde Inferior*. Oaxaca, Mexico: Centro INAH Oaxaca.

Joyce, Rosemary. 2004. "Mesoamerica: A Working Model for Archaeology." In *Mesoamerican Archaeology: Theory and Practice*, ed. Julia Hendon and Rosemary Joyce, 1–42. Cornwall, UK: Blackwell.

Justeson, John. 2012. "Early Mesoamerican Writing Systems." In *The Oxford Handbook of Mesoamerican Archaeology*, ed. Deborah L. Nichols and Christopher A. Pool, 830–844. New York: Oxford University Press.

Kepecs, Susan, and Michael J. Kolb, eds. 1997. "New Approaches to Combining the Archaeological and Historical Records." *Journal of Archaeological Method and Theory* 4 (3/4):193–198.

Kepecs, Susan, and Rani T. Alexander, eds. 2005. *The Postclassic to Spanish-Era Transition in Mesoamerica: Archaeological Perspectives.* Albuquerque: University of New Mexico Press.

Kirchhoff, Paul. (1943) 1952. "Meso-America: Its Geographic Limits, Ethnic Composition and Cultural Characteristics." In *Heritage of Conquest: The Ethnology of Middle America,* ed. Sol Tax and members of the Viking Fund Seminar of Middle American Ethnology, 17–30. Glencoe, Illinois: The Free Press Publishers.

Knapp, Bernard A., ed. 1992. *Archaeology, Annales, and Ethnohistory.* Cambridge: Cambridge University Press.

Kowalewski, Stephen. 1997. "A Spatial Method for Integrating Data of Different Types." *Journal of Archaeological Method and Theory* 4 (3/4):287–306.

Kowalewski, Stephen. 2003. "Scale and the Explanation of Demographic Change: 3,500 Years in the Valley of Oaxaca." *American Anthropologist* 105:313–325.

Kowalewski, Stephen A., Gary M. Feinman, Laura Finsten, Richard E. Blanton, and Linda M. Nicholas. 1989. *Monte Albán Hinterland, Part II: Prehispanic Settlement Patterns in Tlacolula, Etla, and Ocotlan, the Valley of Oaxaca, Mexico.* Ann Arbor: Museum of Anthropology, University of Michigan, Memoir 23.

Kowalewski, Stephen A., and Jacqueline J. Saindon. 1992. "The Spread of Literacy in a Latin American Peasant Society: Oaxaca, Mexico, 1890 to 1980." *Comparative Studies in Society and History* 34 (1):110–140.

Lacadena, Alfonso. 2008. "Regional Scribal Traditions: Methodological Implications for the Decipherment of Nahuatl Writing." *PARI Journal* 8 (4):1–22.

Levine, Marc N. 2007. "Linking Household and Polity at Late Postclassic Yucu Dzaa (Tututepec), a Mixtec Capital on the Coast of Oaxaca, Mexico." Unpublished PhD diss., Department of Anthropology, University of Colorado, Boulder.

Levy, Thomas E., ed. 2010. *Historical Biblical Archaeology and the Future: the New Pragmatism.* London: Equinox.

Lind, Michael, and Javier Urcid. 2010. *The Lords of Lambityeco: Political Evolution in the Valley of Oaxaca During the Xoo Phase.* Boulder: University Press of Colorado.

Little, Barbara, ed. 1992. *Text-Aided Archaeology.* Boca Raton: CRC Press.

Maca, Allan L. 2010. "Walter Taylor's Conjunctive Approach in Maya Archaeology." In *Prophet, Pariah, and Pioneer: Walter W. Taylor and Dissension in American Archaeology,* ed. Allan Maca, William Folan, and Jonathan Reyman, 243–298. Boulder: University Press of Colorado.

Marcus, Joyce. 1976. "The Origins of Mesoamerican Writing." *Annual Review of Anthropology* 5:35–67.

Marcus, Joyce. 1980. "Zapotec Writing." *Scientific American* 242 (2):50–64.

Marcus, Joyce. 1983. "The Conquest Slabs of Building J, Monte Albán." In *The Cloud People: Divergent Evolution of the Zapotec and Mixtec Civilizations*, ed. Kent Flannery and Joyce Marcus, 106–108. New York: Academic Press.

Marcus, Joyce. 1984. "Mesoamerican Territorial Boundaries: Reconstructions from Archaeology and Hieroglyphic Writing." *Archaeological Review from Cambridge* 3 (2):48–62.

Marcus, Joyce. 1992. *Mesoamerican Writing Systems: Propaganda, Myth, and History in Four Ancient Civilizations*. Princeton: Princeton University Press.

Marcus, Joyce, and Judith Francis Zeitlin, eds. 1994. *Caciques and Their People: A Volume in Honor of Ronald Spores*. Ann Arbor: Museum of Anthropology, University of Michigan, Anthropological papers no. 89.

Marcus, Joyce, and Kent Flannery. 1994. "Ancient Zapotec Ritual and Religion: An Application of the Direct Historical Approach." In *The Ancient Mind: Elements of Cognitive Archaeology*, ed. Colin Renfrew and Ezra Zubrow, 55–74. New York: Cambridge University Press.

Marcus, Joyce, and Kent Flannery. 1996. *Zapotec Civilization: How Urban Society Evolved in Mexico's Oaxaca Valley*. London: Thames and Hudson.

Markens, Robert. 2008. "Advances in Defining the Classic-Postclassic Portion of the Valley of Oaxaca Ceramic Chronology." In *After Monte Albán: Transformation and Negotiation in Oaxaca, Mexico*, ed. Jeffrey Blomster, 49–94. Boulder: University Press of Colorado.

Markens, Robert, Marcus Winter, and Cira Martínez López. 2008. "Ethnohistory, Oral History, and Archaeology at Macuilxóchitl: Perspective on the Postclassic Period in the Valley of Oaxaca." In *After Monte Albán: Transformation and Negotiation in Oaxaca, Mexico*, ed. Jeffrey Blomster, 193–215. Boulder: University Press of Colorado.

Martínez Gracida, Manuel. (1910) 1986. *Los Indios Oaxaqueños y Sus Monumentos Arqueológicos*. Oaxaca, Mexico: Gobierno del Estado de Oaxaca.

Martinón-Torres, Marcos, and Thilo Rehren, eds. 2008. *Archaeology, History and Science: Integrating Approaches to Ancient Materials*. Walnut Creek, CA: Left Coast Press.

Matadamas Díaz, Raúl, and Sandra Liliana Ramírez Barrera. 2010. *Antes de Ocho Venado y Después de los Piratas: Arqueología e Historia de Huatulco*. Oaxaca City: CSEIIO-SAI.

McCafferty, Sharisse D., and Geoffrey G. McCafferty. 1994. "Engendering Tomb 7 at Monte Albán, Oaxaca: Respinning an Old Yarn." *Current Anthropology* 35 (2):143–166.

Miller, Arthur. 1995. *The Painted Tombs of Oaxaca, Mexico: Living with the Dead*. Cambridge: Cambridge University Press.

Monaghan, John. 1990. "Performance and the Structure of the Mixtec Codices." *Ancient Mesoamerica* 1 (1):133–140.

Monaghan, John. 1995. *The Covenants with Earth and Rain: Exchange, Sacrifice, and Revelation in Mixtec Sociality*. Norman: University of Oklahoma Press.

Moreland, John. 2001. *Archaeology and Text*. London: Duckworth.

Mundy, Barbara E. 1996. *The Mapping of New Spain: Indigenous Cartography and the Maps of the Relaciones Geográficas*. Chicago: The University of Chicago Press.

Murphy, Arthur D., and Alex Stepick. 1991. *Social Inequality in Oaxaca: A History of Resistance and Change*. Philadelphia: Temple University Press.

Nicholson, Henry B. 1955. "Native Historical Traditions of Nuclear America and the Problem of Their Archaeological Correlation." *American Anthropologist* 57 (3):594–613.

Ong, Walter J. 1982. *Orality and Literacy: The Technologizing of the Word*. New York: Methuen.

Orser, Charles E., and Brian M. Fagan. 1995. *Historical Archaeology*. New York: HarperCollins.

Oudijk, Michel R. 2008. "The Postclassic Period in the Valley of Oaxaca: The Archaeological and Ethnohistorical Records." In *After Monte Albán: Transformation and Negotiation in Oaxaca, Mexico*, ed. Jeffrey Blomster, 95–118. Boulder: University Press of Colorado.

Paddock, John. 1966a. "Oaxaca in Ancient Mesoamerica." In *Ancient Oaxaca: Discoveries in Mexican Archaeology and History*, ed. John Paddock, 83–242. Stanford: Stanford University Press.

Paddock, John. 1983. *Lord 5 Flower's Family: Rulers of Zaachila and Cuilapan*. Nashville: Vanderbilt University Publications in Anthropology, No. 29.

Paddock, John, ed. 1966b. *Ancient Oaxaca: Discoveries in Mexican Archaeology and History*. Stanford: Stanford University Press.

Palka, Joel W. 2009. "Historical Archaeology of Indigenous Culture Change in Mesoamerica." *Journal of Archaeological Research* 17 (4):297–346.

Pohl, John M.D. 1994. *The Politics of Symbolism in the Mixtec Codices*. Nashville: Vanderbilt University Publications in Anthropology, No. 46.

Pohl, John M.D. 1999. "The Lintel Paintings of Mitla and the Function of the Mitla Palaces." In *Mesoamerican Architecture as a Cultural Symbol*, ed. Jeff Karl Kowalski, 176–197. New York: Oxford University Press.

Pohl, John M.D. 2003a. "Creation Stories, Hero Cults, and Alliance Building." In *The Postclassic Mesoamerican World*, ed. Michael E. Smith and Frances F. Berdan, 61–66. Salt Lake City: University of Utah Press.

Pohl, John M.D. 2003b. "Ritual Ideology and Commerce in the Southern Mexican Highlands." In *The Postclassic Mesoamerican World*, ed. Michael E. Smith and Frances F. Berdan, 172–185. Salt Lake City: University of Utah Press.

Pohl, John M.D. 2003c. "Ritual and Iconographic Variability in Mixteca-Puebla Polychrome Pottery." In *The Postclassic Mesoamerican World*, ed. Michael E. Smith and Frances F. Berdan, 201–206. Salt Lake City: University of Utah Press.

Pohl, John M.D. 2003d. "Royal Marriages and Confederacy Building among the Eastern Nahuas, Mixtecs, and Zapotecs." In *The Postclassic Mesoamerican World*, ed. Michael E. Smith and Frances F. Berdan, 243–248. Salt Lake City: University of Utah Press.

Pohl, John M.D. 2004a. "The Archaeology of History in Postclassic Oaxaca." In *Mesoamerican Archaeology: Theory and Practice*, ed. Julia Hendon and Rosemary Joyce, 217–238. Cornwall, UK: Blackwell.

Pohl, John M.D. 2004b. "Screenfold Manuscripts of Highland Mexico and Their Possible Influence on Codex Madrid: A Summary." In *Codex Madrid: New Approaches to Understanding an Ancient Maya Manuscript*, ed. Gabrielle Vail and Anthony Aveni, 368–413. Boulder: University of Colorado Press.

Pohl, John M.D. 2007. *Narrative Mixtec Ceramics of Ancient Mexico*. Princeton: Princeton University Program of Latin American Studies.

Pohl, John M. D., and Bruce E. Byland. 1990. "Mixtec Landscape Perception and Archaeological Settlement Patterns." *Ancient Mesoamerica* 1 (1):113–131.

Pohl, Mary E.D., Kevin O. Pope, and Christopher von Nagy. 2002. "Olmec Origins of Mesoamerican Writing." *Science* 298 (5600):1984–1987.

Proskouriakoff, Tatiana. 1960. "Historical Implications of a Pattern of Dates at Piedras Negras, Guatemala." *American Antiquity* 25 (4):454–475.

Rabin, Emily. 2003. "Toward a Unified Chronology of the Historical Codices and Pictorial Manuscripts of the Mixteca Alta, Costa and Baja: An Overview." In *Homenaje a John Paddock*, ed. Patricia Plunket, 100–136. Puebla, Mexico: Universidad de las Américas.

Rice, Don. S., and Prudence M. Rice. 2004. "History in the Future: Historical Data and Investigations in Lowland Maya Studies." In *Continuities and Changes in Maya Archaeology: Perspectives at the Millennium*, ed. Charles W. Golden, and Greg Burgstede, 71–87. New York: Routledge.

Rivera Guzmán, Iván. 2008. "La Iconografía de las Piedras Grabadas de Cuquila y la Distribución de la Escritura Ñuiñe en la Mixteca Alta." In *Pictografía y Escritura Alfabética en Oaxaca*, ed. Sebastian van Doesburg, 53–72. Oaxaca, Mexico: IEEPO.

Robles García, Nelly M., and Alberto Juárez Osnaya. 2004. *Historia de la Arqueología en Oaxaca*. Oaxaca, Mexico: CONACULTA-INAH.

Robles García, Nelly M. 2004. *Estructuras Políticas en el Oaxaca Antiguo: Memoria de la Tercera Mesa Redonda de Monte Albán*. Mexico City: INAH.

Rodríguez Martínez, María del Carmen, Ponciano Ortíz Ceballos, Michael D. Coe, Richard A. Diehl, Stephen D. Houston, Karl A. Taube, and Alfredo Delgado Calderón. 2006. "Oldest Writing in the New World." *Science* 313 (5793):1610–1614.

Rogers, Daniel J., and Samuel M. Wilson, eds. 1993. *Ethnohistory and Archaeology: Approaches to Postcontact Change in the Americas*. New York: Plenum Press.

Romero Frizzi, María de los Ángeles. 1996. *El Sol y la Cruz: Los Pueblos Indios de Oaxaca Colonial*. Mexico City: CIESAS/INI.

Romero Frizzi, María de los Ángeles, ed. 2003. *Escritura Zapoteca: 2,500 Años de Historia*. Mexico City: CONACULTA/INAH.

Ruiz Medrano, Ethelia. 2010. *Mexico's Indigenous Communities: Their Land and Histories, 1500–2010*. Boulder: University Press of Colorado.

Sanders, Seth L., ed. 2006. *Margins of Writing, Origins of Cultures*. Chicago: The Oriental Institute, University of Chicago.

Sauer, Eberhard, ed. 2004. *Archaeology and Ancient History: Breaking Down the Boundaries*. New York: Routledge.

Scheiber, Laura L., and Mark D. Mitchell, eds. 2010. *Across a Great Divide: Continuity and Change in Native North American Societies, 1400–1900*. Tucson: University of Arizona Press.

Schmidt, Brian B., ed. 2007. *The Quest for the Historical Israel: Debating Archaeology and the History of Ancient Israel*. Leiden: E. J. Brill.

Schmidt, Peter. 2006. *Historical Archaeology in Africa: Representation, Social Memory, and Oral Traditions*. Oxford: AltaMira.

Schuyler, Robert L., ed. 1978. *Historical Archaeology: A Guide to Substantive and Theoretical Contributions*. New York: Baywood Publishing Company.

Sherman, Jason, Andrew K. Balkansky, Charles Spencer, and Brian D. Nicholls. 2010. "Expansionary Dynamics of the Nascent Monte Albán State." *Journal of Anthropological Archaeology* 29 (3):278–301.

Small, David B., ed. 1995. *Methods in the Mediterranean: Historical and Archaeological Views on Texts and Archaeology*. Leiden: E. J. Brill.

Smith, Mary Elizabeth. 1973. *Picture Writing from Ancient Southern Mexico: Mixtec Place Signs and Maps*. Norman: University of Oklahoma Press.

Smith, Michael E., and Frances F. Berdan, eds. 2003. *The Postclassic Mesoamerican World*. Salt Lake City: University of Utah Press.

Spencer, Charles S., and Elsa M. Redmond. 1997. *Archaeology of the Cañada de Cuicatlán, Oaxaca*. American Museum of Natural History, Anthropological Papers, No. 80.

Spencer, Charles S., Elsa M. Redmond, and Christina M. Elson. 2008. "Ceramic Microtypology and the Territorial Expansion of the Early Monte Alban State in Oaxaca, Mexico." *Journal of Field Archaeology* 33 (3):321–341.

Spores, Ronald. 1967. *The Mixtec Kings and Their People*. Norman: University of Oklahoma Press.

Spores, Ronald. 1972. *An Archaeological Settlement Survey of the Nochixtlán Valley, Oaxaca*. Nashville: Vanderbilt University Publications in Anthropology, No. 1.

Spores, Ronald. 1980. "New World Ethnohistory and Archaeology, 1970–1980." *Annual Review of Anthropology* 9:575–603.

Spores, Ronald. 1984. *The Mixtecs in Ancient and Colonial Times*. Norman: University of Oklahoma Press.

Spores, Ronald. 1993. "Tututepec: A Postclassic-Period Mixtec Conquest State." *Ancient Mesoamerica* 4 (1):167–174.

Spores, Ronald. 2007. *Ñuu Ñudzahui: La Mixteca de Oaxaca. La Evolución de la Cultura Mixteca desde los Primeros Pueblos Preclásicos hasta la Independencia*. Oaxaca: IEEPO.

Stahl, Ann B. 1993. "Concepts of Time and Approaches to Analogical Reasoning in Historical Perspective." *American Antiquity* 58 (2):235–260.

Stephen, Lynn. 2005. *Zapotec Women: Gender, Class, and Ethnicity in Globalized Oaxaca*. Durham: Duke University Press.

Stephen, Lynn. 2007. *Transborder Lives: Indigenous Oaxacans in Mexico, California, and Oregon*. Durham: Duke University Press.

Taube, Karl. 2011. "Teotihuacan and the Development of Writing in Early Classic Central Mexico." In *Their Way of Writing: Scripts, Signs, and Pictographies in Pre-Columbian America*, ed. Elizabeth Hill Boone and Gary Urton, 77–109. Washington, DC: Dumbarton Oaks.

Tavárez, David. 2010. "Zapotec Time, Alphabetic Writing, and the Public Sphere." *Ethnohistory* 57 (1):73–85.

Taylor, William B. 1972. *Landlord and Peasant in Colonial Oaxaca*. Stanford: Stanford University Press.

Tedlock, Dennis. 2010. *2000 Years of Mayan Literature*. Berkeley: University of California Press.

Terraciano, Kevin. 2001. *The Mixtecs of Colonial Oaxaca: Ñudzahui History, Sixteenth through Eighteenth Centuries*. Stanford: Stanford University Press.

Topic, John R., ed. 2009. *La Arqueología y la Etnohistoria: Un Encuentro Andino*. Lima: IEP/IAR.

Trigger, Bruce. 1989. "History and Contemporary American Archaeology: A Critical Analysis." In *Archaeological Thought in America*, ed. C. C. Lamberg-Karlovsky, 19–34. Cambridge: Cambridge University Press.

Troike, Nancy. 1978. "Fundamental Changes in the Interpretations of the Mixtec Codices." *American Antiquity* 43 (4):553–568.

Urcid, Javier. 1993. "The Pacific Coast of Oaxaca and Guerrero: The Westernmost Extent of Zapotec Script." *Ancient Mesoamerica* 4 (1):141–165.

Urcid, Javier. 2001. *Zapotec Hieroglyphic Writing*. Washington, DC: Dumbarton Oaks.

Urcid, Javier. 2005a. *Zapotec Writing: Knowledge, Power, and Memory in Ancient Oaxaca.* Report submitted to FAMSI. http://www.famsi.org/zapotecwriting/zapotec_text .pdf, accessed Jan. 2014.

Urcid, Javier. 2005b. *Sacred Landscapes and Social Memory: The Ñuiñe Inscriptions in the Ndaxagua Natural Tunnel, Tepelmeme, Oaxaca.* Report submitted to FAMSI. http://www .famsi.org/reports/03068/ndaxagua.pdf, accessed Jan. 2014.

Urcid, Javier. 2008. "An Ancient Story of Creation from San Pedro Jaltepetongo." In *Mixtec Writing and Society: Escritura de Ñuu Dzaui*, ed. Maarten E.R.G.N. Jansen and Laura N.K. van Broekhoven, 145–196. Amsterdam: KNAW Press.

Urcid, Javier. 2011a. "Los Oráculos y la Guerra: El Papel de las Narrativas Pictóricas en el Desarrollo Temprano de Monte Albán (500 a.C.–200 d.C.)." In *Monte Albán en la Encrucijada Regional y Disciplinaria: Memoria de la Quinta Mesa Redonda de Monte Albán*, ed. Nelly M. Robles García, and Ángel I. Rivera Guzmán, 163–237. Mexico City: INAH.

Urcid, Javier. 2011b. "En la Cima de la Montaña Sagrada: Escritura y Urbanismo en Monte Albán." In *Seis Ciudades Antiguas de Monte Albán*, ed. Eduardo Matos Moctezuma, 77–119. Mexico City: INAH.

Urcid, Javier. 2011c. "The Written Surface as a Cultural Code: A Comparative Perspective of Scribal Traditions from Southwestern Mesoamerica." In *Their Way of Writing: Scripts, Signs, and Pictrographies in Pre-Columbian America*, ed. Elizabeth Hill Boone and Gary Urton, 111–148. Washington, DC: Dumbarton Oaks.

Urcid, Javier, and Arthur Joyce. 2001. "Carved Monuments and Calendrical Names: The Rulers of Río Viejo, Oaxaca." *Ancient Mesoamerica* 12 (2):199–216.

Urcid, Javier, and Arthur Joyce. 2014. "Early Transformations of Monte Albán's Main Plaza and Their Political Implications, 500 BC–AD 200." In *Mesoamerican Plazas*, ed. K. Tsukamoto and T. Inomata, 149–167. Tucson: University of Arizona Press.

Vaillant, George. 1937. "History and Stratigraphy in the Valley of Mexico." *Scientific Monthly* 44 (4):307–324.

Vansina, Jan. 1985. *Oral Tradition as History.* Madison: University of Wisconsin Press.

Vargas Arenas, Iraida. 1995. "The Perception of History and Archaeology in Latin America: A Theoretical Approach." In *Making Alternative Histories: The Practice of Archaeology and History in Non-Western Settings*, ed. Peter R. Schmidt, and Thomas C. Patterson, 47–68. Santa Fe: School of American Research Press.

Wainwright, Fredrick T. 1962. *Archaeology and Place Names and History: An Essay on Problem of Co-ordination.* London: Routledge and Kegan Paul.

Wauchope, Robert. 1947. "An Approach to the Maya Correlation Problem through Guatemala Highland Archaeology and Native Annals." *American Antiquity* 13 (1):59–66.

Whitecotton, Joseph W. 1977. *The Zapotecs: Princes, Priests, and Peasants.* Norman: University of Oklahoma Press.

Whitecotton, Joseph W. 1990. *Zapotec Elite Ethnohistory: Pictorial Genealogies from Eastern Oaxaca*. Nashville: Vanderbilt University Publications in Anthropology, No. 39.

Whittaker, Gordon. 1980. "The Hieroglyphics of Monte Albán." Unpublished PhD diss., Yale University.

Winter, Marcus. 1994a. "Los Altos de Oaxaca y los Olmecas." In *Los Olmecas en Mesoamérica*, ed. J. E. Clark, 129–141. Mexico: El Equilibrista/Turner Libros.

Winter, Marcus. 2007. *Cerro de las Minas: Arqueología de la Mixteca Baja*. Oaxaca, Mexico: CONACULTA/INAH.

Winter, Marcus. 2008a. "Classic to Postclassic in Four Oaxaca Regions: The Mazateca, the Chinantla, the Mixe Region, and the Southern Isthmus." In *After Monte Albán: Transformation and Negotiation in Oaxaca, Mexico*, ed. Jeffrey Blomster, 393–426. Boulder: University Press of Colorado.

Winter, Marcus. 2008b. *"Informe Final Proyecto Salvamento Arqueológico Carretera Oaxaca-Istmo 2006–2007, Tramo Jalapa del Marqués Km. 177–190*. Oaxaca, Mexico." INAH Regional Center. *Report*.

Winter, Marcus. 2011. "Social Memory and the Origins of Monte Alban." *Ancient Mesoamerica* 22 (2):393–409.

Winter, Marcus, ed. 1994b. *Escritura Zapoteca Prehispánica: Nuevas Aportaciones*. Oaxaca: INAH.

Workinger, Andrew, and Arthur A. Joyce. 2009. "Reconsidering Warfare in Formative Period Oaxaca." In *Blood and Beauty: Organized Violence in the Art and Archaeology of Mesoamerica and Central America*, ed. Heather Orr and Rex Koontz, 3–38. Los Angeles: Cotsen Institute of Archaeology Press.

Yannakakis, Yanna. 2008. *The Art of Being In-Between: Native Intermediaries, Indian Identity, and Local Rule in Colonial Oaxaca*. Durham: Duke University Press.

Yoffee, Norman, and Bradley L. Crowell, eds. 2006. *Excavating Asian History: Interdisciplinary Studies in Archaeology and History*. Tucson: The University of Arizona Press.

Zárate Morán, Roberto. 2003. *Un Mito de Creación Zapoteca en las Pinturas Rupestres de Dani Guíaati, Asunción Ixtaltepec, Oaxaca*. Asunción Ixtaltepec, Mexico: CONACULTA/ INAH.

Zeitlin, Judith. 2005. *Cultural Politics in Colonial Tehuantepec: Community and State among the Isthmus Zapotec, 1500–1750*. Stanford: Stanford University Press.

Zeitlin, Robert. 1993. "Pacific Coastal Laguna Zope: A Regional Center in the Terminal Formative Hinterlands of Monte Albán." *Ancient Mesoamerica* 4 (1):85–101.

2

The Convergence of History and Archaeology in Mesoamerica

RONALD SPORES

It is a matter of consensus among Mesoamerican anthropologists that history, archaeology, ethnology and linguistics are inextricably linked. Investigators recognize that although their principal focus may be on a specific archaeological site or a component within that site, their study is incomplete without reference to historic, ethnographic, or linguistic materials. The integration of archaeology and historical documentation, as well as ethnological, biological, and linguistic research, has been of special significance in Mesoamerican studies for decades, but the roots of this convergent methodology run even deeper.

The marriage of these fields extends back to Colonial times in the work of numerous early ethnographers and observers of native life, including Bernardino de Sahagún, Fernando de Motolinía (Toribio de Benavente), Diego Durán, Diego de Landa, and many others, both Spaniards and natives.[1] In Oaxaca this is reflected in the sixteenth-century linguistic studies of friars Francisco de Alvarado (1962), Juan de Córdoba (1942), and Antonio de los Reyes (1976), and in the seventeenth-century works of Francisco de Burgoa (1934). As in the case of the mid-sixteenth-century chroniclers and linguists, Burgoa reported extensively on social, political, and economic life and beliefs in all of the major regions of Oaxaca, but also on the history, languages, and demography of each area, as well as acculturation matters, religious syncretism, and even on prehispanic remains, geography, and abandonment and/or relocation of native towns. This combining of sources and synchronic-diachronic concerns continued into the nineteenth and early twentieth centuries in

DOI: 10.5876/9781607323297.c002

Oaxaca in the perceptive writings of José Antonio Gay (1982), Luis García Pimentel (1904), León and Rojas (1933), Manuel Martínez Gracida (1883), Zelia Nuttall (1902), as well as in the great general works of Hubert H. Bancroft (1886–1888), Manuel Orozco y Berra (1960), Eduard Seler (1960–1961), and others.

This convergent approach is the creation of Mexican scholars and a notable group of like-minded foreigners who have followed in their footsteps to contribute significantly to the growth of Mexican ethnohistory. Twentieth-century scholars embraced the approach, and they and their intellectual offspring have built on this rich background. As a result, a significant expansion of ethnohistorical resources and methodology has occurred and that has stimulated continuing growth of ethnohistoric research and publication. This is directly reflected in the contributions to the current volume and in the many cited sources.

Ethnohistory as practiced in Mexico is *documentary ethnology*, a set of methods and techniques for consulting all classes of documentation with the view to reducing those materials to ethnographic data applicable to the study of human behavior within an anthropological theoretical framework. A document, whether written, drawn, or painted yesterday or a thousand years ago, is for the ethnohistorian what the live informant is for the ethnologist. Documentation is approached as one would approach a group of live informants. Information is sought from documentation just as one would seek information from living Mixtec, Zapotec, Ixcateca, Chochona, Tarascan, Nahua, or Otomí informants or from a series of stratigraphic tests. Problems can be formulated and research strategy can be planned much as for any other kind of ethnological study.

Information arising from historical documents can be interpreted, described, and explained within a structural-functional, evolutionary, ecological, or cultural-developmental theoretical framework, with the manner of utilization of written sources depending on the theoretical interests of the individual scholar. Although we may all seek common goals, what is distinctive for the ethnohistorian is the specific methodology we employ. We must know how and where to find, read, and interpret written documents. It is also our obligation to protect, preserve, restore, and catalog the very documents we utilize.

Since around 1940 there have been notable advances in collaborative efforts among ethnohistorians and archaeologists at such centers as Teotihuacan, Tula, and Tenochtitlán (Acosta 1940, 1983; Calnek 1976; Jiménez Moreno 1941, 1954; Mastache et al. 2002). The archaeological constructs have been brought to life through the integration of the ethnohistorical detail in a highly notable fashion. In addition, there have been rapid advances in historical archaeology, where archaeologists and historians converge in their attempts to elucidate developments in historic sites throughout México (Fernández Dávila and Gómez Serafín 1998). This body of research is remarkable in that the Instituto Nacional de Antropología e Historia (INAH) has paid relatively little attention to Mexico's thousands of historical sites or to the artifacts that they produce. Archaeological research in these important centers has depended far more on individual motivation and initiative than on institutional support. To date, there is no special branch, department, or agency within the INAH to focus attention on these rich resources in any systematic way, nor is there a significant area of specialization on historic site archaeology in the training program of the Escuela Nacional de Antropología e Historia (ENAH). This lack of attention has led to neglect of hundreds of important historic sites and a failure to advance significantly on a broad scale of research, study, conservation, and restoration.

There is no clearer requirement for collaborative efforts between archaeologists and historians than in the historical archaeology of Mexico. One such project was recently conducted at Yucundaa Pueblo Viejo de Teposcolula, Oaxaca, and others are underway or planned for other areas of Mesoamerica. The specific objectives of the Yucundaa project were to study a prehispanic and Early Colonial capital city as it underwent important transformations between 1000 and 1550 CE (Spores and Robles García 2007a, 2007b; Robles García and Spores 2008).

The Yucundaa project produced highly significant findings. The ancient city of Yucundaa was well known as the Pueblo Viejo de Teposcolula, but this slender body of knowledge was based on very limited, almost incidental, historical documents and oral traditions. Over the years a more substantial collection of historical documentation had accumulated for Teposcolula and the surrounding area. The initial challenge for the project was to take a fresh look at the documentary record relating specifically to Teposcolula, and, as well, several surrounding Postclassic and Early Colonial towns, such as Yanhuitlan, Tamazulapan, Tejupan, Coixtlahuaca, Tilantongo, and Tlaxiaco. Preliminary archaeological data were similarly few and problematical. Accordingly, the archaeological objectives of the Yucundaa project were to excavate and thoroughly study the ancient city in what would be the first and most ambitious such investigation of a major Mixtec city during this critical time of cultural-historical transformation. During the 1980s an intensive surface survey was conducted, and important segments of the settlement were delineated. Then, between 2004 and 2008 a large-scale program of excavations was carried out, which involved more than fifty professional investigators. As was intended, all major components of the settlement were described and analyzed. The results were astounding.

Among the important discoveries were a vast *tecpan*—or royal palace-civic/ceremonial center—located at the highest point of the site (figure 2.1); a second ruling-class residential-ceremonial complex at the southern end of the city; a ceremonial

FIGURE 2.1. The Late Postclassic *cacique*'s palace at Yucundaa; the darker patch in the center of the floor location indicates where the carved stone panels were found. Photo by Ronald Spores.

ballcourt complex; a noble-class residential zone; an extensive common-class residential zone; a 2.5-kilometer grand avenue with accompanying ritually significant caves surrounding the site at mid-slope; a system of agricultural (*coo-yuu*) terraces; and other elements. Carved stone monuments in the Postclassic lapidary and scribal traditions were found in the *cacique*'s palace, overturned and face down, which would surely account for their fortuitous survival (figure 2.2). Based on cognate scenes in the Codex Nuttall, John Pohl (personal communication, 2012) interprets these as representing an important meeting between the Mixtec hero Lord Eight Deer and the warlord Four Jaguar, shortly after the former is awarded a nose ornament making him a Toltec *tecuhtli* (Figure 2.3). All evidence therefore points to a well-populated, multicomponent urban settlement, fully deserving of being called a diversified urban political capital, which flourished on the Yucundaa mountain for at least three hundred years before the Spanish conquest.

By around 1525, the city, which quickly became known to the Spaniards, began to undergo a notable transition. The excavations revealed many important material and cultural transformations in Yucundaa between about 1528 and 1550, shortly before the city was relocated to the valley floor, where it remains to the present day. Notable new institutions were the impressive Dominican church-convent and an

FIGURE 2.2. José Luis Tenorio Rodríguez and assistant prepare the carved panels for transportation. Photo by Ronald Spores.

extensive atrium, one of the earliest in New Spain, constructed in the urban core of the site along with possibly the earliest native *cabildo* in Oaxaca. Novel architectural conventions included the European arch and swinging doors. Indigenous technologies adapted to new forms and materials, as expressed in European-style pottery, metalwork, mural painting, and the traditional high-relief lapidary that now also depicted Christian iconography and alphabetic writing (figure 2.4). Old World grains, fruits, and animals were first introduced into the diet, and cemeteries were laid out to accommodate the vast numbers of victims of the devastating epidemics that struck the area between about 1530 and 1550.

One exceedingly important discovery was a burial of a young woman in the atrium of the church, surrounded by a burned offering of more than 70,000 artifacts executed mostly in the Mixtec indigenous tradition but mixed with other European-style artifacts, and many thousands of small animal bones (mostly of birds) and sea shells. This was truly an archaeological discovery, but the interpretation of the find depended very heavily on inferences drawn from extended testimony in an inquisitorial process centered in Yanhuitlan in 1544–1545 (Archivo

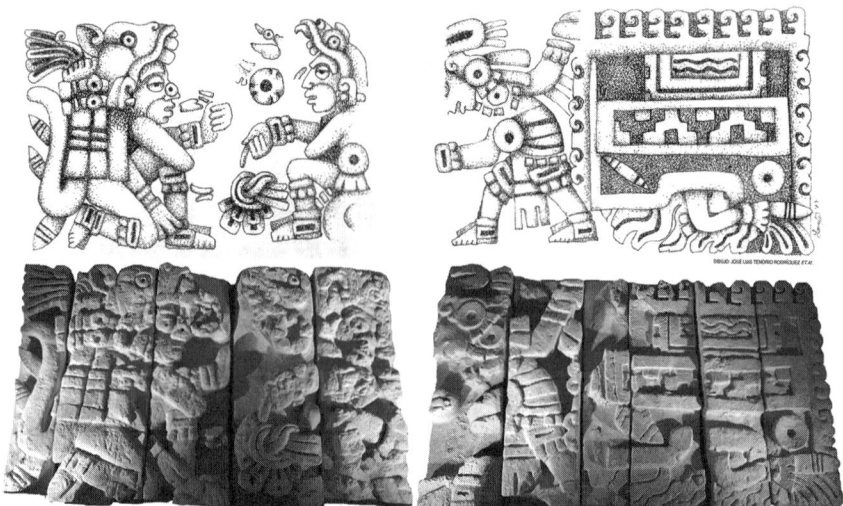

FIGURE 2.3. The carved panels after their restoration in the project's laboratory. Drawing by José Luis Tenorio Rodríguez et al.; composite photo by Danny Zborover.

General de la Nación, Ramo de Inquisición 37; Spores 2007:117–126). It was a perfect marriage of archaeological, biological, and historical evidence, and resulted in firmly based inferences regarding native life and cultural transformation during the earliest decades of the Colonial period. It was also exemplary of the methodological emphasis of the entire project, and a clear and convincing indication of the value of the convergent approach.

The value of this approach is evident in the collection of articles making up the present volume. A notable feature of these writings is the bottom-up approach of the anthropologist, who begins at the local level—the indigenous base, the towns and villages, individuals, households, kin groups, associations, and so on—eventually rising to higher levels of inclusion.[2] The conventional historian, on the other hand, tends to begin at the top with the great countries, institutions, and "men of action," but often reaches down to the regional and local levels.[3] Neither approach is inherently superior to the other. Obviously, they are quite complementary.

The ethnohistorian is in a position to search for solutions to anthropological problems and to engage in empirical research or test hypotheses as effectively as any other social scientist. Possible lines of inquiry might be as follows:

- What is the nature of the socioeconomic organization of a community and how may these patterns vary in relation to demographic fluctuation or technological innovation?

FIGURE 2.4. An architectural medallion depicting the Christian monogram of the Virgin Mary, which once adorned Yucundaa's church. Photo by Ronald Spores.

- How does a subject community (such as a *rancho, estancia, agencia,* or *sujeto*) relate to its head town (*cabecera*), province, or *municipio*, and what factors may contribute to changes in those relationships over time?
- How do communities in a given area interrelate socially and economically, and how do they function within a larger sociocultural context?
- How are internal economic systems linked into interregional economic networks, and how do political institutions facilitate those linkages and interrelationships?
- How are families and voluntary associations constituted, and how are family patterns, intergroup relations, or political structure related to demographic fluctuation, geographical limitation, or technological innovation?

- Who wields political power in the community; how is that power defined and delimited; how are political leaders recruited; how do they function; and how are they turned out of office?
- What is the nature of the belief system in a community or region and how might it serve to encourage social cohesion among clusters of communities or between regions?

Whether with reference to modern, colonial, or prehispanic Mexico, all of these problems are directly amenable to the documentary approach, and ethnohistorians have successfully pursued them. The value and reliability of ethnohistoric procedures is now firmly established. In terms of the kinds of problems that have been of interest to researchers over the past half-century, ethnohistory is the most productive and flexible of all methodologies available to the anthropologist. Our approach must always remain pragmatic. In many instances the investigator relies overwhelmingly on documentation. Certain problems may require the application of ethnological, archaeological, or linguistic methods. Others, as in the case of our studies of Mixtec culture over the past 3,500 years, require the application and integration of all four approaches.

It is useful to review the strengths and limitations of documentary ethnology, or ethnohistory, as practiced in Mexico. First, documentary ethnology allows for consideration of long developmental sequences, some covering decades, others much longer, as with the Mixteca of Oaxaca or the Valley of Mexico, each of which extends from before 1000 CE to modern times.[4] Although archaeology and historical linguistics can perhaps claim great temporal penetration, it has yet to be demonstrated that they alone can ever provide the wealth of cultural detail possible with ethnohistorical procedures. Moreover, ethnohistory allows for detailed synchronic functional analysis at any point in time for which documentation is available.[5]

Ethnohistory cannot provide all of the detail that an ethnographer can observe or elicit from live informants, but it can provide essential knowledge of forms of behavior that, because of their sensitive nature, or by intentional or unintended distortion or omission, might be concealed from the participant observer. Legal and administrative records or personal correspondence relating to such matters as interpersonal or intergroup conflict, wealth, demography, crime, economic productivity, marriage and family patterns, or political function often provide depth and insight that may not be forthcoming in a fieldwork situation. Divorce cases; investigations and trials for assault, murder, malfeasance, defamation, idolatry, blasphemy, and desertion; or suits over land and property all can afford access to information that might be extremely difficult to obtain from live informants. Thousands of such documents are available (but frequently ignored by social scientists) in such vast repositories as the Archivo General de la Nación de México or the Museo Nacional de Antropología (Glass 1964), the Archivo Histórico General del Estado de Oaxaca, the Archivo Histórico del Poder Judicial del Estado de Oaxaca, and similar such archives in every region of the Mexican Republic. It is curious that the armies of ethnologists, domestic and foreign, have made so little use of these resources.

Finally, documentary ethnology employs one of the most scientific methodologies in anthropology, in that its basic data are highly susceptible to verification and authentication. An ethnologist studies a community and writes a report, monograph, or book. Years later the community is restudied. The second ethnographer finds behavioral patterns that are substantially different from those perceived and presented in the original study. Have conditions changed? Did the first investigator present the true picture of life in the community, or was the second a wiser, more honest, more accurate observer? Are the differing presentations owing to different training, method, lack of application, too much reliance on the "man of action," limited sampling, dishonesty, fact merging into fiction, or is modernization to blame? Just what is, or was, the reality of life in Tepoztlan, Chan Kom, Tzintzuntzan, Mitla, or Zinacantan? We assume and accept the ethnographer's objectivity. The ethnologist's conclusions seem reasonable in terms of our experience, but can the work be checked, verified, or authenticated? Does *reasonable* mean "reliable"? Undoubtedly, the cultural reality will have changed, but the appearance of change could also result from differing theoretical and methodological orientations of the observers.

Documentary ethnology—ethnohistory—has advantages. As long as the documentation upon which a study is based is in existence, anyone can examine and reexamine that exact same documentation, retrace the investigator's steps, reevaluate the original data and the process of evidence and inference so vital to anthropological research, and draw conclusions regarding those inferences independently. In terms of replication, authentication, and scientific verifiability, documentary ethnology has advantages not found in observation-participation ethnography.

Our enthusiastic utilization of written documentation does not mean uncritical use of those materials. The context and purpose of every source is vitally pertinent to its proper interpretation. Who wrote it and why? What was the purpose for which the document was prepared? How did the objectives and personal qualities of the author(s) of the document color its content? As great though the writings of Sahagún, Motolinía, Durán, or Burgoa may be, their limitations and biases, as well as their great strengths, must be recognized. Why were the *Relaciones Geográficas* of 1579–1581 prepared? Who prepared them, and how do they vary in content and relative reliability? The same may be said for judicial and administrative sources, wills and contracts, dictionaries, personal correspondence, and so on. These are the lifeblood of ethnohistory, but anyone using sources uncritically runs the risk of introducing distortions, even errors, into the ethnohistorical record.

In order for our studies to be reliable and acceptable, we should understand the composition and operation of institutions such as the *Patrimonio Real*, the *Consejo de Indias*, the *Virreinato and Audiencia de Nueva España*, the *alcaldía mayor, corregimiento, cabildo, cacicazgo, cortes civiles y eclesiásticos,* the system of contracts, the *Inquisición*, *encomienda*, and the tributary system, or the *repartimiento* and system of labor. Such knowledge of Spanish colonial institutions is essential if we are to understand the context and interpret the meaning of the documents that they produced (Consejo de la Hispanidad 1943; Haring 1947; Puga 1945).

Priests, bishops, administrators, legalists, *visitadores generales* (whistle-blowers of the Colonial period), such as Diego Encinas (1596), Vasco de Puga (1945), or Jerónimo de Valderrama (1961), and soldiers or abused citizens have differing motives and perceptions. These biases, strengths, and limitations must be taken into consideration, just as an archaeologist must strictly observe and record the specific context of all cultural and physical remains if results are to be considered reliable.

Returning to archaeology, we may consider the relationship of archaeology to ethnohistory, while recognizing some limitations of historical documents and archaeological evidence, as well as the strength of a methodology that relies on both sorts of evidence. We should recognize that with respect to particular groups, areas of interest, or time periods, historical documents might be inadequate for pursuing or meeting research objectives. They may reach only so far, not far enough to answer the questions or provide the information we seek, or they may be vague or impossible to read. Documents may contain gaps, sometimes serious ones. When that occurs and there are no live informants, archaeology may furnish the best information available.

As discussed above, our recent primarily archaeological project regarding the evolution, operation, and prehispanic-Colonial transformation of the ancient city of Yucundaa-Pueblo Viejo de Teposcolula suffered from a serious shortage of specific historical documentation (Spores 2008b; Spores and Robles García 2007a, 2007b). We have known for many years that the earliest Spanish *encomienda* was established in Teposcolula around 1527 and that Dominican friars arrived in Yucundaa around 1528–1529. We knew virtually nothing more about Teposcolula until around 1540, and even that documentation is sparse until around 1560. We knew from the documents (Publicación Gubernamental Nacional 1867) that the first viceroy, Antonio de Mendoza, visited the city of Teposcolula, which had been relocated from its original mountain-top location two kilometers to the east-southeast. We knew furthermore that modern Teposcolula residents called this large mountain-top site "Pueblo Viejo de Teposcolula" and that one location within the site was called the "Iglesia Vieja." Although the site was thoroughly and admirably surveyed in the mid-1990s (Stiver 2001), the specifics of life in the big center were unknown. Only systematic excavation of the city could provide the desired information about its formation, growth, and function and the great cultural transformation that occurred there after 1520.

Not only does the project rely on a strong convergence of documentary history and archaeological excavation, but, from a methodological standpoint, it is concerned with the relative strengths and weaknesses of these lines of evidence and the complementary, as well as contradictory, nature of documentary evidence and material remains. We now know vastly more about processes of urbanization in the Mixteca and the city–political capital of Yucundaa and its great transformation—less from the documentation than from archaeological investigations—than we ever thought possible. The investigation of Yucundaa as an urban center required an extensive program of excavation reaching into every part of the city. In a very real sense, the site itself has become a document. Each day, as excavations advanced, we turned a new page. New knowledge was, and still is, constantly emerging regarding the structure, life, and great transformation of the site, and information is being disseminated in various publications and symposia (Spores and Robles Garcia 2007a, 2007b; Robles García and Spores 2008).

No better indication of the strength of a convergent ethnohistorical approach to the culture and history of Oaxaca in particular and Mesoamerica in general can be found than from the chapters that appear in this volume and from numerous other recent publications (Doesburg 2008; Hermann Lejarazu 2008; König 2008; Oudijk 2008; Swanton 2008; Urcid 2008; Zborover 2008; and others). Each results from the particular interests, objectives, and methodology of the author, but taken as a whole, the present collection represents a great leap forward in accumulated knowledge of the cultural-historical development of Oaxaca, as well as a demonstration of the effectiveness of this approach. The legacy of Fray Francisco de Burgoa, Manuel Martínez Gracida, Alfonso Caso, Wigberto Jiménez Moreno, Barbro Dahlgren, Ignacio Bernal, and John Paddock shines brightly through these contributions, and Oaxaca, along with the Central Valleys of Mexico, continues to thrive as a major center of development for the ethnohistorical methodology in Mesoamerica.

NOTES

1. Among others, see Fernando de Motolinía (Toribio de Benavente 1969), Diego Durán (1967), Alva Ixtlilxochitl (1952), Gonzalo Fernández de Oviedo y Valdés (1851), Juan B. Pomar (1941), the *Relación de Michoacán* (Alcalá and Gustave Le Clézio 2008) as

well as the *Relación de Tlaxcala* (Muñoz Camargo 1947), Bernardino de Sahagún (1956), Fernando Alvarado Tezozómoc (1944, 1949), Antonio de Herrera de Tordesillas (1947), Pablo Beaumont (1932), Francisco J. Clavijero (1958), and José F. Ramírez (1944).

2. Characteristic of this group of scholars are Barlow (1949), Berlin (1947, 1948), Broda (1978), Carrasco (1961, 1979, 1996); Carrasco and Broda (1976, 1978), Caso (1938, 1949, 1958, 1960, 1964, 1977), Dahlgren (1954, 1987), Gamio (1922), López Austin (1961), Monzón (1946, 1949), Moreno (1931), and Radin (1920).

3. Notable practitioners of this approach have been Bancroft (1886), Cook and Borah (1960, 1963, 1968), Gibson (1952, 1964), Millares Carlo and Mantecón (1955), Miranda (1952), Orozco y Berra (1959), Roys (1943), Scholes and Adams (1938), Scholes and Roys (1948), and Zavala (1984).

4. Examples include Barlow (1949), Broda (1978), Calnek (1976), Carrasco (1996), Caso (1949, 1960, 1964), Caso and Smith (1966), Chance (1978, 1989), Charlton (1969), Cook and Borah (1963), Gamio (1922), Gibson (1964), Gorenstein (1966), Gorenstein and Pollard (1983), Jansen (1982), Jansen and Pérez Jiménez (2000), Jiménez Moreno (1941, 1954), Jiménez Moreno and Mateos Higuera (1940), León Portilla (1959, 1961), López Austin (1961), López Sarrelangue (1965), Marcus (1992), Nicholson (1962), Parmenter (1982), Pohl (1994), Rabin (1982), Robertson (1959), Romero Frizzi (1990), Smith (1986, 1987), Spores (1967, 1984, 2007, 2008a, 2008b), and Wauchope (1964), among others.

5. See Bandelier (1879), Caso (1964), Dahlgren (1954), Gorenstein (1966), Hassig (1984), Hunt (1972), Katz (1966), López Austin (1961), Monzón (1946, 1949), Moreno (1931), Paddock (1966), Smith (1973), and Spores (1967, 2007).

REFERENCES

Acosta, Jorge R. 1940. "Exploraciones en Tula, Hidalgo, 1940." *Revista Mexicana de Estudios Antropológicos* 4:172–194.

Acosta, Jorge R. 1983. "Datos Arqueológicos de la Zona de Tula." In *Antología de Teotihuacan a los Aztecas: Fuentes e Interpretaciones Históricas*, ed. Miguel León-Portilla, 86–107. Mexico City: Universidad Nacional Autónoma de México/Instituto de Investigaciones Históricas.

Alcalá, Jerónimo de, and Jean-Marie Gustave Le Clézio, eds. 2008. *Relación de Michoacán*. Zamora, Spain: El Colegio de Michoacán.

Alvarado, Fray Francisco de. 1962. *Vocabulario en Lengua Mixteca. Reproducción Facsimilar con un Estudio de Wigberto Jiménez Moreno*. Mexico City: Instituto Nacional Indigenista/Instituto Nacional de Antropología e Historia.

Bancroft, Hubert H. 1886. *History of Mexico*. 6 vols. San Francisco: History Company.

Bandelier, Adolph E. 1879. "On the Social Organization and Mode of Government of the Ancient Mexicans." *Eleventh Annual Report of the Peabody Museum of Archaeology and Ethnology*, 385–448. Cambridge, MA: Harvard.

Barlow, Robert. 1949. *The Extent of the Empire of the Culhua-Mexica. Ibero-Americana 28*. Berkeley: University of California Press.

Beaumont, Pablo. 1932. *Crónica de Michoacán*. 3 vols. Mexico City: Talleres Gráficos de la Nación.

Berlin, Heinrich. 1947. *Fragmentos Desconocidos del Códice de Yanhuitlán y Otras Investigaciones Mixtecas*. Mexico City: Editorial Porrúa.

Berlin, Heinrich. 1948. *Anales de Tlatelolco: Unos Anales Históricos de la Nación Mexicana y Códice Tlatelolco*. Mexico City: Antigua Librería Robredo de José Porrúa e Hijos.

Broda, Johanna. 1978. "El Tributo en Trajes Guerreros y la Estructura del Sistema Tributario Mexica." In *Economía Política e Ideología en el México Prehispánico*, ed. Pedro Carrasco and Johanna Broda, 113–174. Mexico City: Editorial Nueva Imagen.

Burgoa, Fray Francisco de. 1934. *Geografía Descripción*, 2 volumes. Publicaciones del Archivo General de la Nación, 25–26. Mexico City: Talleres Gráficos de la Nación.

Calnek, Edward E. 1976. "The Internal Structure of Tenochtitlán." In *The Valley of Mexico: Studies in Pre-Hispanic Ecology and Society*, ed. Eric R. Wolf, 287–302. Albuquerque: University of New Mexico Press.

Carrasco, Pedro. 1961. "El Barrio y la Regulación del Matrimonio en un Pueblo del Valle de México en el Siglo XVI." *Revista Mexicana de Estudios Antropológicos* 17:7–26.

Carrasco, Pedro. 1979. *Los Otomíes: Cultura e Historia Prehispánica de los Pueblos Mesoamericanos de Habla Otomiana*. Mexico City: Gobierno del Estado de México.

Carrasco, Pedro. 1996. *Estructura Político-Territorial del Imperio Tenochca: La Triple Alianza de Tenochtitlán, Tezcoco y Tlacopan*. Mexico City: Colegio de México.

Carrasco, Pedro, and Johanna Broda. 1976. *Estratificación Social en la Mesoamérica Prehispánica*. Mexico City: Instituto Nacional de Antropología e Historia/Centro de Estudios Superiores.

Carrasco, Pedro, and Johanna Broda. 1978. *Economía Política e Ideología en el México Prehispánico*. Mexico City: Editorial Nueva Imagen.

Caso, Alfonso. 1938. *Exploraciones en Oaxaca: Quinta y Sexta Temporadas 1936–1937*. Mexico City: Instituto Panamericana de Geografía e Historia.

Caso, Alfonso. 1949. "El Mapa de Teozacoalco." *Cuadernos Americanos* 8 (5):145–181.

Caso, Alfonso. 1958. "La Tenencia de la Tierra Entre los Antiguos Mexicanos." *Memoria del Colegio Nacional* 4:29–54.

Caso, Alfonso. 1960. *Interpretación del Códice Bodley 2858*. Mexico City: Sociedad Mexicana de Antropología.

Caso, Alfonso. 1964. *Interpretación del Codex Selden 3135 (A.2)*. Mexico City: Sociedad Mexicana de Antropología.

Caso, Alfonso. 1977. *Reyes y Reinos de la Mixteca*. 2 vols. Mexico City: Fondo de Cultura Económica.

Caso, Alfonso, and Mary E. Smith. 1966. *Interpretación del Codex Colombino*. Mexico City: Sociedad Mexicana de Antropología.

Chance, John K. 1978. *Race and Class in Colonial Oaxaca*. Stanford: Stanford University Press.

Chance, John K. 1989. *Conquest of the Sierra: Spaniards and Indians in Colonial Oaxaca*. Norman: University of Oklahoma Press.

Charlton, Thomas H. 1969. "Ethnohistory and Archaeology: Post-Conquest Aztec Sites." *American Antiquity* 34 (3):286–294. http://dx.doi.org/10.2307/278411.

Clavijero, Francisco J. 1958. *Historia Antigua de México*. 4 vols. Mexico City: Editorial Porrúa.

Consejo de la Hispanidad. 1943. *Recopilación de Leyes de los Reynos de las Indias*. 3 vols. Madrid: Consejo de la Hispanidad.

Cook, Sherburne F., and Woodrow Borah. 1960. *The Indian Population of Central Mexico 1531–1610. Ibero-Americana 44*. Berkeley: University of California Press.

Cook, Sherburne F., and Woodrow Borah. 1963. *The Aboriginal Population of Central Mexico on the Eve of the Spanish Conquest. Ibero-Americana 45*. Berkeley: University of California Press.

Cook, Sherburne F., and Woodrow Borah. 1968. *The Population of the Mixteca Alta 1520– 1960. Ibero-Americana 50*. Berkeley: University of California Press.

Córdoba, Fray Juan de. 1942. *Vocabulario Castellano-Zapoteco*, ed. Wigberto Jiménez Moreno. Mexico City: Instituto Nacional de Antropología e Historia/Secretaría de Educación Pública.

Dahlgren, Barbro. 1954. *La Mixteca: Su Cultura e Historia Prehispánica*. Mexico City: Imprenta Universitaria.

Dahlgren, Barbro, ed. 1987. *Historia de la Religión en Mesoamérica y Áreas Afines*. Mexico City: Universidad Nacional Autónoma de México.

de los Reyes, Antonio. 1976. *Arte en Lengua Mixteca*. Nashville: Vanderbilt University Publications in Anthropology 14.

Doesburg, Sebastián van, ed. 2008. *Pictografía y Escritura Alfabética en Oaxaca*. Oaxaca, Mexico: Fondo Editorial del Instituto Estatal de Educación Pública de Oaxaca.

Durán, Diego. 1967. *Historia de las Indias de Nueva España e Islas de Tierra Firme*. 2 vols. Mexico: Editorial Porrúa.

Encinas, Diego, ed. 1596. *1945–1946. Cedulario Indiano*. 4 vols. Madrid: Ediciones Cultura Hispánica.

Fernández Dávila, Enrique, and Susana Gómez Serafín, eds. 1998. *Primer Congreso Nacional de Arqueología Histórica. Memoria.* Mexico City: CONACULTA / Instituto Nacional de Antropología e Historia.

Gamio, Manuel. 1922. *La Población del Valle de Teotihuacan.* 3 vols. Mexico City: Dirección de Talleres Gráficos.

García Pimentel, Luis, ed. 1904. *Relación de los Obispados de Tlaxcala, Michoacán, Oaxaca y Otros Lugares en el Siglo XVI.* Mexico: Published by the editor.

Gay, José Antonio. 1982. *Historia de Oaxaca.* Mexico City: Editorial Porrúa.

Gibson, Charles. 1952. *Tlaxcala in the Sixteenth Century.* New Haven: Yale University Press.

Glass, John B. 1964. *Catálogo de la Colección de Códices.* Mexico City: Museo Nacional de Antropología.

Gorenstein, Shirley. 1966. "The Differential Development of New World Empires." *Revista Mexicana de Estudios Antropológicos* 20:41–67.

Gorenstein, Shirley, and Helen P. Pollard. 1983. *The Tarascan Civilization: A Late Prehispanic Cultural System.* Nashville: Vanderbilt University Publications in Anthropology, No. 28.

Haring, Clarence H. 1947. *The Spanish Empire in America.* New York: Oxford University Press.

Hassig, Ross. 1984. *Aztec Warfare: Imperial Expansion and Political Control.* Norman: University of Oklahoma Press.

Hermann Lejarazu, Manuel. 2008. "Los Nombres Personales en los Códices Mixtecos: Un Análisis Lingüístico e Iconográfico." In *Pictografía y Escritura Alfabética en Oaxaca*, ed. Sebastián van Doesburg, 197–214. Oaxaca, Mexico: Fondo Editorial del IEPPO.

Hunt, Eva. 1972. "Irrigation and the Socio-Political Organization of Cuicatec Cacicazgos." In *The Prehistory of the Tehuacán Valley,* vol. 4: *Chronology and Irrigation,* ed. Frederick Johnson, 162–260. Austin: University of Texas Press.

Ixtlilxochitl, Fernando de Alva. 1952. *Obras Históricas,* 2 volumes. Mexico City; Editora Nacional.

Jansen, Maarten. 1982. *Huisi Tacu, Estudio Interpretativo de un Libro Mixteco Antiguo Codex Vindobonensis Mexicanus I.* 2 vols. Amsterdam: CEDLA.

Jansen, Maarten, and Gabina Aurora Pérez Jiménez. 2000. *La Dinastía de Añute.* Leiden: CNWS Publications.

Jiménez Moreno, Wigberto. 1941. "Tula y los Toltecas Según las Fuentes Históricas." *Revista Mexicana de Estudios Antropológicos* 5:79–83.

Jiménez Moreno, Wigberto. 1954. "Síntesis de la Historia Pretolteca de Mesoamérica." *Revista Mexicana de Estudios Antropológicos* 14:219–236.

Jiménez Moreno, Wigberto, and Salvador Mateos Higuera. 1940. *Códice de Yanhuitlán.* Mexico City: Instituto Nacional de Antropología e Historia/Secretaría de Educación Pública.

Katz, Friedrich. 1966. *Situación Social y Económica de los Aztecas Durante los Siglos XV y XVI,* translated from the German original by María Luisa Rodríguez Sala, and Elsa Brühler. Mexico: Universidad Nacional Autónoma de México/Instituto de Investigaciones Históricas.

König, Viola. 2008. "El Mapa de Teozacoalco y el Concepto de Mapamundi." In *Pictografía y Escritura Alfabética en Oaxaca*, ed. Sebastián van Doesburg, 215–232. Oaxaca, Mexico: Fondo Editorial del Instituto Estatal de Educación Pública de Oaxaca.

León, Nicolás, and Mariano Rojas. 1933. *Códice Sierra: Traducción al Español de su Texto Nahuatl y Explicación de sus Pinturas Jeroglíficas*. Mexico City: Imprenta del Museo Nacional de Arqueología, Historia y Etnografía.

León Portilla, Miguel. 1959. *La Filosofía Náhuatl, Estudiada en sus Fuentes*. Mexico City: Universidad Nacional Autónoma de México/Instituto de Investigaciones Históricas.

León Portilla, Miguel. 1961. *Los Antiguos Mexicanos a Través de sus Crónicas y Cantares*. Mexico City: Fondo de Cultura Económica.

López Austin, Alfredo. 1961. *La Constitución Real de México-Tenochtitlán*. Mexico City: Universidad Nacional Autónoma de México/Instituto de Investigaciones Históricas.

López Sarrelangue, Delfina E. 1965. *La Nobleza Indígena de Pátzcuaro en la Época Virreinal*. Mexico City: Universidad Nacional Autónoma de México/Instituto de Investigaciones Históricas.

Marcus, Joyce. 1992. *Mesoamerican Writing Systems: Propaganda, Myth and History in Four Ancient Civilizations*. Princeton: Princeton University Press.

Martínez Gracida, Manuel. 1883. *Colección de "Cuadros Sinópticos" de los Pueblos, Haciendas y Ranchos del Estado Libre y Soberano de Oaxaca*. Oaxaca, Mexico: Imprenta de Estado.

Mastache, Alba Guadalupe, Robert Cobean, and Dan Healan. 2002. *Ancient Tollan: Tula and the Toltec Heartland*. Boulder: University Press of Colorado.

Millares Carlo, Agustín, and José I. Mantecón. 1955. *Álbum de Paleografía Hispanoamericana de los Siglos XVI y XVII*. 3 vols. Mexico City: Instituto Panamericano de Geografía e Historia.

Miranda, José. 1952. *El Tributo Indígena en la Nueva España Durante el Siglo XVI*. Mexico City: El Colegio de México.

Monzón, Arturo. 1946. "La Organización Social de los Aztecas." In *México Prehispánico: Culturas, Deidades, Monumentos*, ed. Jorge A. Vivó, 791–803. Mexico City: Editorial Emma Hurtado.

Monzón, Arturo. 1949. *El Calpulli en la Organización Social de los Tenochca*. Mexico City: Universidad Nacional Autónoma de México/Instituto Nacional de Antropología e Historia.

Moreno, Manuel M. 1931. *La Organización Política y Social de los Aztecas*. Mexico City: Universidad Nacional Autónoma de México.

Motolinía (Toribio de Benavente). 1969. *Historia de los Indios de la Nueva España*. Mexico City: Editorial Porrúa.

Muñoz Camargo, Diego. 1947. *Historia de Tlaxcala*. Mexico City: Ateneo Nacional de Ciencias y Artes de México.

Nicholson, Henry B. 1962. "The Mesoamerican Pictorial Manuscripts: Research, Past and Present." In *Proceedings of the 34th International Congress of Americanists*, 199–215. Vienna: Verlag Ferdinand Berger.

Nuttall, Zelia. 1902. *Codex Nuttall: Facsimile of an Ancient Mexican Codex, with Introduction and Notes*. Cambridge, MA: Peabody Museum.

Orozco y Berra, Manuel. 1959. *Historia Antigua y de la Conquista de México*. 4 vols. Mexico City: Editorial Porrúa.

Oudijk, Michel. 2008. "Una Nueva Historia Zapoteca: La Importancia de Regresar a las Fuentes Primarias." In *Pictografía y Escritura Alfabética en Oaxaca*, ed. Sebastián van Doesburg, 89–116. Oaxaca, Mexico: Fondo Editorial del Instituto Estatal de Educación Pública de Oaxaca.

Oviedo y Valdés, Gonzalo Fernández de. 1851. *Historia General y Natural de las Indias, Islas y Tierra Firme del Mar Océano*, 4 volumes. Madrid: Academia de la Historia.

Paddock, John, ed. 1966. *Ancient Oaxaca*. Stanford: Stanford University Press.

Parmenter, Ross. 1982. *Four Lienzos of the Coixtlahuaca Valley*. Washington, DC: Dumbarton Oaks.

Pohl, John. 1994. *The Politics of Symbolism in the Mixtec Codices*. Nashville, TN: Vanderbilt University Publications in Anthropology.

Pomar, Juan B. 1941. *Relación de Tezcoco*. Mexico City: Editorial S. Chávez Hayhoe.

Publicación Gubernamental Nacional. 1867. *Instrucciones que los Virreyes de la Nueva España Dejaron a sus Sucesores: Añádense Algunas que los Mismos Trajeron de la Corte y Otros Documentos Semejantes a las Instrucciones*. Mexico City: Editorial Imperial.

Puga, Vasco de. 1945. *Provisiones, Cédulas, Instrucciones para el Gobierno de la Nueva España*. Madrid: Ediciones Cultura Hispánica.

Rabin, Emily. 1982. "Confluence in Zapotec and Mixtec Ethnohistories: The 1560 Genealogy of Macuilxóchitl." *University of Oklahoma Papers in Anthropology* 23 (2):360–368.

Radin, Paul. 1920. *The Sources and Authenticity of the History of the Ancient Mexicans*. Berkeley: University of California Publications in American Archaeology and Ethnology, no. 17.

Ramírez, José F. 1944. *Manuscrito del Siglo XVI Intitulado: Relación del Origen de los Indios que Habitan esta Nueva España, Según sus Historias (Códice Ramírez)*. Mexico City: Editorial Leyenda.

Robertson, Donald. 1959. *Mexican Manuscript Painting of the Early Colonial Period*. New Haven: Yale University Press.

Robles García, Nelly M., and Ronald Spores. 2008. "Teposcolula, Oaxaca." *Arqueología Mexicana* 15 (90):42–43.

Romero Frizzi, María de los Ángeles. 1990. *Economía y Vida de los Españoles en la Mixteca Alta, 1519–1740*. Mexico City: Instituto Nacional de Antropología e Historia/Gobierno del Estado de Oaxaca.

Roys, Ralph L. 1943. *The Indian Background of Colonial Yucatan*. Washington, DC: Carnegie Institution.

de Sahagún, Bernardino. 1956. *Historia General de las Cosas de Nueva España*. 4 vols. Mexico City: Editorial Porrúa.

Scholes, France V., and Eleanor Adams. 1938. *Don Diego Quijada, Alcalde Mayor de Yucatán, 1561–1565*. 2 vols. Mexico City: Antigua Librería Robredo de José Porrúa e Hijos.

Scholes, France V., and Ralph L. Roys. 1948. *The Maya Chontal Indians of Acalan-Tixchel: A Contribution to the History and Ethnography of the Yucatan Peninsula*. Washington, DC: Carnegie Institution.

Seler, Eduard. 1960–1961. *Gesammelte Abhandlungen zur Amerikanischen Sprach-und Alterthumskunde*, 5 volumes. Graz, Austria: Akademische Druck- und Verlagsanstalt.

Smith, Mary Elizabeth. 1973. *Picture Writing from Ancient Southern Mexico: Mixtec Place Signs and Names*. Norman: University of Oklahoma Press.

Smith, Michael E. 1986. "The Role of Social Stratification in the Aztec Empire: A View from the Provinces." *American Anthropologist* 88 (1): 70–91. http://dx.doi.org/10.1525/aa.1986.88.1.02a00050.

Smith, Michael E. 1987. "The Expansion of the Aztec Empire: A Case Study in the Correlation of Diachronic Archaeological and Ethnohistorical Data." *American Antiquity* 52 (1):37–54. http://dx.doi.org/10.2307/281059.

Spores, Ronald. 1967. *The Mixtec Kings and Their People*. Norman: University of Oklahoma Press.

Spores, Ronald. 1984. *The Mixtecs in Ancient and Colonial Times*. Norman: University of Oklahoma Press.

Spores, Ronald. 2007. *Ñuu Ñudzahui: La Mixteca de Oaxaca; La Evolución de la Cultura Mixteca Desde los Primeros Pueblos Preclásicos hasta la Independencia*. Oaxaca: Instituto Estatal de Educación Pública de Oaxaca.

Spores, Ronald. 2008a. "La Mixteca: Tres Mil Años de Cultura en Oaxaca, Puebla y Guerrero." *Arqueología Mexicana* 15 (90):28–33.

Spores, Ronald. 2008b. "Excavations at Yucundaa, Pueblo Viejo de Teposcolula." In *Mixtec Writing and Society: Escritura de Ñuu Dzahui*, ed. Maarten Jansen and Laura N.K. van Broekhoven, 253–289. Amsterdam: Kininklije Nederlandse Akademie van Wetenschapen.

Spores, Ronald, and Nelly Robles García. 2007a. "A Prehispanic (Postclassic) Capital Center in Colonial Transition: Excavations at Yucundaa Pueblo Viejo de Teposcolula, Oaxaca, Mexico." *Latin American Antiquity* 18 (3):333–353. http://dx.doi.org/10.2307/25478184.

Spores, Ronald, and Nelly Robles García. 2007b. *Informe Final al Consejo de Arqueología del Instituto Nacional de Antropología e Historia de la Cuarta Temporada del Proyecto Teposcolula Yucundaa*. Mexico City: Instituto Nacional de Antropología e Historia.

Stiver, Laura R. 2001. "Prehispanic Mixtec Settlement and State in the Teposcolula Valley of Oaxaca, Mexico." Unpublished PhD diss., Vanderbilt University, Nashville.

Swanton, Michael. 2008. "La Escritura Indígena como 'Material Lingüístico': Una Carta en Lengua Ixcateca al Presidente Lázaro Cárdenas." In *Pictografía y Escritura Alfabética en Oaxaca*, ed. Sebastián van Doesburg, 353–387. Oaxaca, Mexico: Fondo Editorial del Instituto Estatal de Educación Pública de Oaxaca.

Tezozómoc, Fernando Alvarado. 1944. *Crónica Mexicana*. Mexico City: Editorial Leyenda.

Tezozómoc, Fernando Alvarado. 1949. *Crónica Mexicayotl*. Mexico City: Universidad Nacional Autónoma de México.

Tordesillas, Antonio de Herrera. 1947. *Historia General de los Hechos de los Castellanos en las Islas y Tierra Firme del Mar Océano*, 15 volumes. Madrid: Real Academia de la Historia.

Urcid, Javier. 2008. "La Lápida Grabada de Santiago Matatlan." In *Pictografía y Escritura Alfabética en Oaxaca*, ed. Sebastián van Doesburg, 23–52. Oaxaca: Fondo Editorial del Instituto Estatal de Educación Pública de Oaxaca.

Valderrama, Jerónimo. 1961. *Cartas del Licenciado Jerónimo de Valderrama y Otros Documentos Sobre su Visita al Gobierno de la Nueva España, 1563–1565*. Ed. France V. Scholes and Eleanor B. Adams. Mexico City: Editorial Porrúa.

Wauchope, Robert. 1964. *Handbook of Middle American Indians*. 16 vols. Austin: University of Texas Press.

Zavala, Silvio. 1984. *Estudios Indianos*. Mexico City: Colegio Nacional.

Zborover, Danny. 2008. "Identidades 'Faccionales' en las Narraciones Territoriales de la Oaxaca Colonial: Un Enfoque de las Montañas Chontales." In *Pictografía y Escritura Alfabética en Oaxaca*, ed. Sebastián van Doesburg, 233–70. Oaxaca, Mexico: Fondo Editorial del Instituto Estatal de Educación Pública de Oaxaca.

3

Bruce Edward Byland, PhD

1950–2008

John M.D. Pohl

"*Oye! Saludos!*" the farmer called from the hillside. Bruce stopped and immediately told us to hold up. We were used to these interruptions. In fact we welcomed them. These were becoming the opportunities we looked for during survey because the men out plowing their fields throughout the day invariably recollected stories about the ancient ruins and terraces that surrounded the Tilantongo countryside. The farmer signaled to his wife and children to call off the dogs and then charged down the slope to confront Bruce. "I hear you're a doctor!" he called. Bruce was taken aback—there was no accounting for the rumors that proceeded us in the more remote areas of the valley. "Well, yes, in a manner of speaking. But what can I do for you?" replied Bruce. "Oh! The wife and kids and I are plagued with all kinds of disruptions up here. The doors and shutters of the house fly open and close all night long—we can't get any sleep. Listen doctor, what can we possibly do? What could be causing it?"

Bruce thought for a minute. We had heard many legends of ancient kings, queens, and saints associated with groves, caves, and canyons. They reminded us of the supernatural beings that appeared in the codices, spirit forces in the natural environment like the *ñuhu*, a small red anthropomorph with fanged teeth whose name could mean "earth," "spirit," or even "sun." We always thought it wise to think of courteous replies but, with tongue in cheek, Bruce couldn't resist a chance to try out his knowledge from the weekly classes I was conducting in deciphering the ancient pictographic books. He thought it would prompt a discussion about any

DOI: 10.5876/9781607323297.c003

FIGURE 3.1. Bruce Byland and Susan Snow surveying the Tilantongo Valley.

surviving legends of the earth lord. "Hmmm, well maybe it's a *ñuhu?*" replied Bruce. The farmer scratched his chin and looked back at the hillside. Suddenly, his face lit up, he slapped his hand on his thigh, and declared "You know, you might be right. I think I know exactly what to do, it just never occurred to me before. Thank so you very much, doctor!" I'll never forget the look of astonishment on Bruce's face as he watched the farmer hurry back up the hillside calling after his wife. The spirit forces in the natural environment might seem mythic to us, but they could be very real to the people who had been living on the Tilantongo Valley landscape for the past three millennia. It was this profound sense of reverence for this world endowed with spiritual beliefs that got us to start thinking of it as a kind of text built up over time that could be deciphered archaeologically (figure 3.1).

Bruce and I first met at the 1980 Society for American Archaeology Meetings in San Diego. A devoted student of William Sanders, I knew Byland had just finished his dissertation at Pennsylvania State University. At that time he was not only one of very few American archaeologists doing fieldwork in Mexico, but the first to apply a full-coverage survey methodology in the Mixteca Alta of Oaxaca. Bruce had first joined the Monte Albán site survey directed by Richard Blanton in 1972 and later worked on the household terrace excavations with Marcus Winter. In 1977, after doing some work in the southeastern United States, including excavations at Poverty Point, he conceived his own survey project at Tamazulapan and Tejupan, two adjacent *cacicazgos* in the Mixteca Alta. By 1978, he had become an expert on ceramic typology and therefore on the entire three-thousand-year cultural chronology for site occupation of the Mixteca Alta—a real feat, considering the cultural preference in ancient Oaxaca for plain grayware vessels.

I was eager to talk to Bruce about a theory I had developed in the course of my study of the Mixtec codices, namely that the depiction of so many distinct temples and palaces enclosed within broad geographical frames was indicative of an actual settlement pattern in which the Mixtec elite has distributed themselves into scores of dispersed palaces over relatively confined valley landscapes. "Something more like what you would see in a painting by Pieter Bruegel of these vast agricultural regions dotted with tiny churches and manors surrounded by steep mountains," I explained over lunch. Bruce leaned over, pulled his dissertation out of his briefcase, opened it up to the map of his Postclassic distribution of sites for the Tamazulapan Valley and said, "you mean something like this?" It looked like a paper target shattered by a shotgun blast, a hundred tiny black dots each representing a separate palace or associated farming community spread across the valley floor. "Why don't we test your theory for the Tilantongo Valley and survey it then?" Bruce continued.

That summer I assisted Bruce with his study of red-on-cream painted ceramic patterns from his Tamazulapan-Tejupan project. Then we traveled into the Mixteca and spent two days with the community authorities of Tilantongo discussing our ideas and performing some preliminary reconnaissance. It took Bruce a few more years to secure a permanent position at Lehman College and for me to finish my dissertation, but by June 1985 we found ourselves standing atop a large cone-shaped mound behind the church in the center of Tilantongo, listening to a farmer explain to us that the name for the location was *Vehe Andehui*, or "House of Heaven." We had discovered the remains of the Temple of Heaven, the legendary religious structure for which Tilantongo could be identified with a pictographic place sign in Codices Nuttall, Bodley, Colombino, and Becker. Below us stood the vestiges of the palace of the legendary warlord, Yya Nacuaa—Lord Eight Deer (figure 3.2).

Over the next six years Bruce and I worked very closely together. We were *compadres*. Although we had developed very different areas of specialization, we were trained in many of the same innovations in archaeological field research, had studied with some of the same people, and had much in common with our perspectives. Bruce was born in Battle Creek, Michigan, on March 17, 1950. His father was a career army officer and his mother a nurse. The family moved to Houston, Texas, where Bruce told me he was raised Baptist but, when his critical analysis of biblical chronology got him into trouble, he became fascinated with the relationship between religion, humanism, and science. Anthropology attracted him when he attended Rice University and studied with Frank Hole.

FIGURE 3.2: Bruce Byland excavating the Temple of Heaven.

A true individualist, Bruce also served as a US Army Reserve captain during the latter part of the Vietnam War. He was never sent overseas, but his extraordinary training as a ranger was obvious when we worked together. He had a unique combination of field savvy, physical ability, assertiveness when things got tough, and profound respect for the people we worked with that endeared him to everyone from the very poorest farmer we might meet in some remote canyon to the powerful *presidentes municipales* of both the Tilantongo and Jaltepec communities we worked with. Children adored him.

Bruce also liked food. Our favorite lunchtime conversation in Oaxaca, a city renowned for its restaurants, was usually where we were going to have dinner. No need to wonder why. Bruce met Cara Tannenbaum, a graduate student working in statistical archaeology with both Robert Carmack and Dean Snow at SUNY Albany, when he taught there between 1979 and 1980. By the time they married, Cara had become fascinated with haute cuisine and embarked on a career as a chef. Cara opened a restaurant in White Plains where one could not only be treated to one of the finest dining experiences in Westchester County but simultaneously receive a discourse on the latest theories on human origins from the maître d'. When Eduardo Matos Moctezuma, then head of the *Consejo* (the Mexican Council for Archaeology) and former chief of excavations at the Templo Mayor, asked if we could meet with him during a trip to New York, Bruce brought him to Cara's restaurant. We were applying to the *Consejo* to excavate a portion of the palace and the Temple of Heaven at Tilantongo that the community had exposed during the construction of a school. It would allow us to test some of our ideas from the two previous seasons of survey across the southern Nochixtlán Valley, during which we not only identified the palace of Lord Eight Deer but that of his rival Lady Six Monkey at Jaltepec as well.

When we demonstrated the case for the identification with a scale contour model of the Temple of Heaven precinct and showed Eduardo that the very structure in Tilantongo was actually named in the *Relación Geográfica de Tilantongo*, he expressed what a formidable challenge it was for an archaeologist trained in the survey archaeology of the ancient Toltec capital of Tula to confront the ethnohistory of the Aztecs. Cara's restaurant had become a symposium and Bruce and I began to understand why we were attracting so much interest among our Mexican colleagues. While we thought of ourselves as working in a remote part of Oaxaca, far from the excitement of the excavations of the Templo Mayor, it had become clear that we were all facing comparable challenges in trying to determine how to apply interdisciplinary approaches to the archaeology of the ritual behavior of the elite, when our training in spatial archaeology had been oriented to looking at the social evolution of entire populations.

The project was later approved by the *Consejo*, and we worked throughout the summer of 1989 until the end of August, when I had arranged permission from the municipal authorities and Padre Pacheco, a priest in Yodocono, to marry Georganne Deen in the church of Santiago at Tilantongo. Bruce, of course, was best man. Except for a brief reconnaissance of Mitlantongo that we carried out for a *National Geographic* article that we were working on with Ron Spores and John Monaghan, Bruce and I had to suspend our field research together due to the necessity of making a living on my part and the raising of a family on his.

After the publication of *In the Realm of Eight Deer* (1994), Bruce went on to use our research to write a commentary on Codex Borgia, while I became more interested in Late Postclassic political confederations in an effort to establish the Mixtecs, together with their eastern Nahua and Zapotec alliance partners, as the dominant culture of southern Mexico before the rise of the Aztec Empire. In 1998, Bruce was made full professor of anthropology at Lehman College as well as the Graduate School and University Center of the City University of New York. He also became involved in a number of significant projects, not the least of which was serving as an archaeologist with New York City's Metropolitan Forensic Anthropology Team (MFAT) performing crime scene investigations. Between 2002 and 2007, he directed archaeological investigations at the Jay Heritage Center, a National Historic Landmark and the site of a Colonial-period estate in Rye, New York. His research drew considerable attention for its focus on the slave quarters from such an early historical period of the northeastern United States.

In 2007, I was stunned when Bruce notified me at Princeton that he was very ill and that I should arrange to take over our research materials if something should happen to him. I believed Bruce to be almost invincible and told him there was no doubt in my mind that he would recover. In 2008 he succumbed, and the following year Cara called to let me know that she had managed to secure all of our survey research materials from Bruce's office and lab at Lehman College. I was very grateful and a few weeks later, as I found myself sitting in Cara's kitchen watching her work out the plan for an event at Lincoln Center, we talked about all that had unfolded over the years. And yet it was as if Bruce was with us, for the Byland girls were there. It is remarkable how much Bruce's eldest daughter, Leah, shares his stature while Sophie shares his features.

As I work in my studio, where I can lay out all the maps on drafting tables that Cara rescued, the events of the entire survey come flooding back to me. Every single site has a story. The Monte Negro cliff face that Bruce had fallen off of, twenty feet backward—protected by his pack, he had jumped right back to his feet, dusted himself off, and flashed his characteristically broad grin before starting right back up the mountain. Here, by the Río Labor, I remember what a formidable *tequio* team we made, rigging electrical wiring for the town of Tilantongo by standing on each other's shoulders to match the height of the twelve-foot precut poles that the government had delivered. That's where my wedding procession ended in front of the town store of our friend and patron, Don Crispín. There are a hundred stories to tell, as if Bruce and I had composed a personal landscape narrative of our own, an account of those exciting years of discovery when we walked the mountains with all those who had come before, from the powerful *caciques* and *cacicas* who ruled all that they surveyed, to the proud farmers who continue to plow the land and tell the legends of the spirit forces, gods, and heroes that still inhabit that Mixtec universe.

PRINCIPAL PUBLICATIONS OF BRUCE EDWARD BYLAND

Byland, Bruce Edward. 2008. "Tree Birth, The Solar Oracle, and Achiutla: Mixtec Sacred History and the Classic to Postclassic Transition." In *After Monte Albán: Transformation and Negotiation in Oaxaca, Mexico*, ed. Jeffrey P. Blomster, 331–366. Boulder: University Press of Colorado.

Byland, Bruce Edward. 2001. "Community Kingdoms: Oaxaca (Mixtec and Zapotec)." In *The Oxford Encyclopedia of Mesoamerican Cultures: The Civilizations of Mexico and Central America*, ed. David Carrasco, 239–241. Oxford: Oxford University Press.

Byland, Bruce Edward. 2000. "Introduction." In *An Aztec Herbal: The Classic Codex of 1552 by William Gates, iii–xxi*. New York: Dover Publications.

Byland, Bruce Edward. 1999. "Introduction." In *Ancient Civilizations of Mexico and Central America, By Herbert J. Spinden*. New York: Dover Publications.

Byland, Bruce Edward. 1997. "Places in the Mixtec Historical Codices: The Archaeology of Mixtec History." In *Códices y Documentos sobre México, Segundo Simposio, Volumen I*, ed. Salvador Rueda Smithers, Constanza Vega Sosa, and Rodrigo Martínez Baracs, 173–188. Mexico: Instituto Nacional de Antropología e Historia, CONACULTA.

Byland, Bruce Edward. 1993. "Introduction and Commentary." In *The Codex Borgia Full-Color Restoration of the Ancient Manuscript*, ed. Gisele Díaz and Alan Rodgers, xiii–xxxii. New York: Dover Publications.

Byland, Bruce Edward. 1988. "On the Origin and Nature of Cities." In *Urban Life: Readings in Urban Anthropology*, ed. George Gmelch and Walter Zenner, 9–17. Prospect Heights, IL: Waveland Press.

Byland, Bruce Edward. 1984. "Boundary Recognition in the Mixteca Alta, Oaxaca, Mexico." In *Essays in Otomanguean Culture History*, ed. Katherine Josserand, Marcus Winter, and Nicholas Hopkins, 109–140. Nashville: Vanderbilt University Publications in Anthropology 31.

Byland, Bruce Edward. 1980. "Political and Economic Evolution in the Tamazulapan Valley, Mixteca Alta, Oaxaca: A Regional Approach." Unpublished PhD diss., Department of Anthropology, Pennsylvania State University, State College.

Byland, Bruce Edward. 1979a. "Archaeological Site Survey in the Cannon Reservoir, a Bicultural Approach." *University of Nebraska Department of Anthropology Notebook Series* 5:29–41.

Byland, Bruce Edward. 1979b. "Controlled Surface Collection in a Regional Settlement Pattern Survey Framework." *Western Canadian Journal of Anthropology* 8 (2–4):114–120.

Byland, Bruce Edward, and John M.D. Pohl. 1994a. *In the Realm of 8 Deer: The Archaeology of the Mixtec Codices*. Norman: University of Oklahoma Press.

Byland, Bruce Edward, and John M.D. Pohl. 1994b. "Political Factions in the Transition from Classic to Postclassic in the Mixteca Alta." In *Factional Competition and Political Development in the New World*, ed. Elizabeth M. Brumfiel and John W. Fox, 117–126. Cambridge: Cambridge University Press. http://dx.doi.org/10.1017/CBO9780511 598401.012.

Byland, Bruce Edward, and John M.D. Pohl. 1990. "Alianza y Conflicto de los Estados Mixtecos: El Caso Tilantongo." In *Lecturas Históricas del Estado de Oaxaca, Volumen 1*, ed. Marcus C. Winter, 379–390. Mexico: Instituto Nacional de Antropología e Historia.

Pohl, John M. D., and Bruce Edward Byland. 1996. "The Identification of the Xipe Bundle-Red and White Bundle Place Sign in the Mixtec Codices." *Journal of Latin American Lore* 19 (1–2): 3–29.

Pohl, John M.D., and Bruce Edward Byland. 1994. "The Mixteca-Puebla Style and Early Postclassic Socio-Political Interaction." In *Mixteca-Puebla: Discoveries and Research in Mesoamerican Art and Archaeology*, ed. H. B. Nicholson, and Eloise Quiñones Keber, 189–199. Culver City: Labyrinthos.

Pohl, John M. D., and Bruce Edward Byland. 1990. "Mixtec Landscape Perception and Archaeological Settlement Patterns." *Ancient Mesoamerica* 1 (1):113–131. http://dx.doi.org/10.1017/S0956536100000134.

In addition, Bruce Byland was an enthusiastic contributor to encyclopedia projects including the *Encyclopedia of Human Evolution and Prehistory*, edited by Ian Tattersall, Eric Delson, and John Van Couvering (New York: Garland Publishing, 1988), and wrote reviews and numerous reports for the projects he directed for the Mexican Instituto Nacional de Antropología e Historia, the Jay Heritage Center, the City of New York, the Department of the Navy, and the US Army Corps of Engineers. He presented over sixty-five papers at professional conferences and served as seminar leader for the annual Mixtec Gateway meetings held in Las Vegas, Nevada, between 1995 and 2005.

4

Multidisciplinary Fieldwork in Oaxaca

Viola König

BRUCE BYLAND AND MULTIDISCIPLINARY FIELDWORK IN OAXACA

On May 17, 2008, our colleague Bruce Byland, an archaeologist and specialist in the Mixtec culture of Oaxaca, passed away. I am grateful that the editors promptly accepted my suggestion to dedicate this volume to Bruce. He had been an active representative in the "second generation" of the "Mixtec Codex Group" or "Mixtec Gang," as they called themselves, centered initially around the art historians Nancy Troike, Mary Elizabeth Smith, and Emily Rabin, and the journalist Ross Parmenter. Being strongly influenced by Alfonso Caso's work, the founding group concentrated on the decipherment and interpretation of the codices. At the same time, scholars such as ethnohistorian and archaeologist Ronald Spores and archaeologist Michael Lind conducted complementary research in their respective fields. All of them followed Ignacio Bernal, Wigberto Jiménez Moreno, John Paddock, and Cecil Welte, whose objectives were to reconstruct not only the Mixtec culture but all of ancient Oaxaca and its diverse cultures, from its beginning in the prehispanic era up to the Colonial period (Paddock 1966).

In Oaxaca, interdisciplinary field research has a long tradition. Since the arrival of the Spaniards, such different groups as Christian missionaries, local teachers, and doctors, as well as collectors and antiquarians, conducted "fieldwork" in some way or another, as did the early 'idol hunters' sent out by Carl Uhde in the 1820s. But the term "fieldwork" involves different modes of research in the field; ever since the very first archaeological surveys and excavations in the late nineteenth

DOI: 10.5876/9781607323297.c004

century, investigators in Oaxaca depended strongly on the active support of the locals. Systematic fieldwork that brought linguistics into focus, for example, started in the twentieth century, resulting in Schultze-Jena's (1938) linguistic records of the Nahua, Tlapanec, and Mixtec languages, whereas Schmieder (1930a, 1930b) recorded geographical knowledge in the Zapotec and Mixe languages.

One member of the "first generation" studying the Mixtec codices, Mary Elizabeth Smith, practiced a rather new method for her time: she combined linguistic and geographic research in order to identify place signs and to contextualize individuals, particularly the members of the Mixtec noble families shown in the pictorial manuscripts (Smith 1973). Smith conducted ethnohistorical and geohistorical fieldwork in coastal Mixteca, recording local knowledge of landscape toponyms for such features as mountains and rivers. She interviewed Mixtec-speakers, studied written and pictorial documents in local archives, and shared her knowledge with the people in the coastal communities. Supported by their feedback and assistance, she was able to locate places shown in the codices and to analyze them in their historical context. She compared different Mixtec variants kept in the records—such as the codices, *lienzos*, and other historical sources—with Mixtec dialects spoken at the present.

Since the mid-1970s, a second generation of scholars followed Smith and others in the field by applying an interdisciplinary approach from the onset, which integrated ethnohistory, ethnography, linguistics, archaeology, and epigraphy. Maarten Jansen spent a long time in the Mixteca Alta, repeatedly visiting selected communities. Jansen's (1982) work on the Mixtec codices certainly represents one of the most intensive applications of ethnohistorical analysis followed by fieldwork, through which he constantly emphasized the need to seriously consider local commentaries in the interpretation of native sources. Bruce Byland and John Pohl surveyed archaeological settlement patterns in the Tilantongo and Jaltepec valleys of the Mixteca Alta; they interviewed Mixtec people and compared the information to archaeological and ethnohistorical data (Byland and Pohl 1994). Among other aspects of his ethnographic and ethnohistorical work, John Monaghan's field trips added new information on the Mixtec society and, in particular, the local *caciques* during the Colonial period (Monaghan 1995).

Through my own research in the communities of the Mixteca Baja, I have focused on the geographical surveys that pioneers like Mühlenpfordt (1969) and Schmieder (1930a) initiated and Smith successfully continued, and localized previously unidentified place names in the codices (König 1979). Such place signs and glosses were the basic source for my questionnaires. Though my interviews focused on local geographical knowledge and toponymic terms in the native languages, data on ancient sites and sacred places, as well as local history, legends, and myths,

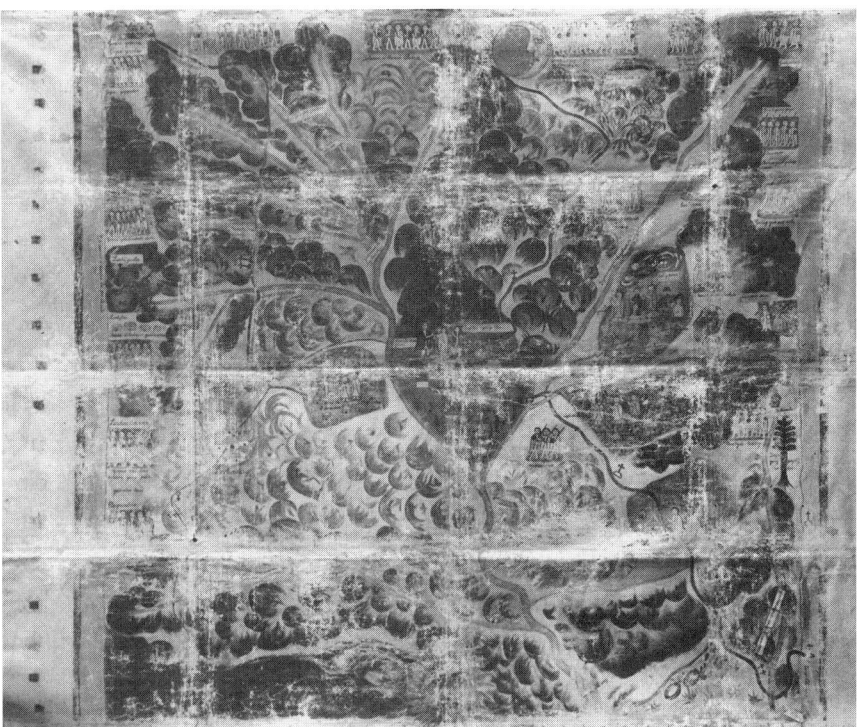

FIGURE 4.1. *Lienzo de San Juan Comaltepec,* Choapan (copy of 1819; found in the village on July 29, 1984). Photograph by Burkhard Brinker.

were recorded as by-products. I have extended my fieldwork to other ethnic groups of Oaxaca and to localized *lienzos* and *mapas* in Zapotec, Chinantec, and Mixe communities (König 1979, 1993) (figures 4.1 and 4.2). On my long hiking tours, some taking up to twelve hours, I experienced the old routes men and women once used to carry their local trade goods to the markets, bring a bride to her groom's hometown, or participate in festivities such as weddings, funerals, or a New Fire Ceremony in neighboring communities.

One platform for presenting and discussing the results of our multidisciplinary approach in Oaxaca was the so-called Mixtec Gateway, founded and chaired by Nancy Troike starting from the 1980s, and taking place every year in Las Vegas, Nevada. These Gateway events were also famous for their three-day workshops dedicated to the study of the Mixtec codices. During the last years the Gateway was co-chaired by Bruce Byland, who represented an attentive and inspiring critic to Troike's interpretations, and added innovative perspectives that advanced the

FIGURE 4.2. San Juan Comaltepec; the center around the church looks much the same as on the *Lienzo de Comaltepec*. Photograph by Burkhard Brinker.

interpretation of the codices. The Gateway was dissolved after Bruce got sick and a few months before he passed away.

MULTIDISCIPLINARY FIELDWORK AT SANTA MARÍA CUQUILA: A CASE STUDY

I first started thinking about the prehispanic importance of Santa María Cuquila (*ñuu cuiñi* or *ño cuy* in Mixtec), today a small village near the municipal town of Tlaxiaco in the western Mixteca Alta, when I realized that the place sign on page 5 of the Codex Egerton 2895 as "jaguar town," or more generally "feline town," most

FIGURE 4.3. Codex Egerton 2895, page 5, showing "jaguar town," circa fifteenth–sixteenth centuries. Illustration by John M.D. Pohl.

likely refers to this place (König 1979:54–59, 2005). This place sign in the Codex Egerton is most important because it represents the place of origin of the principal genealogical line shown in the codex (figure 4.3). However, there are several "feline places" to be found in the Mixteca, and some scholars believe that the small *agencia* of Cuyotepeji in the Mixteca Baja is the one appearing on page 5, arguing that the reverse of the codex focuses on places in the Mixteca Baja such as Acatlán and Tequixtepec del Rey (Mary Elizabeth Smith, Maarten Jansen, and Sebastián van Doesburg, personal communication).

In her later work, Smith (1998) had demonstrated the importance of several Mixtec towns in the western Mixteca Alta in prehispanic and Early Colonial times and, in particular, the importance of Cuquila. Moreover, she has shown the relationship between the Tlaxiaco area and the Mixteca Baja. In her line of argument she included important documents such as the Codex Tulane, the *Lienzos de Ocotepec* and *Córdova-Castellanos*, the *Genealogy of Tlazultepec*, and two Colonial maps from the Cuquila region southwest of Tlaxiaco (AGN Tierras 876-I and 3556–6; Smith 1998:180). Moreover, she argued that the lost Codex López Ruiz most probably came from either Ocotepec or Cuquila. However, she was noncommittal on the question of whether Egerton's "jaguar town" was either Cuyotepeji in the Mixteca Baja or Santa María Cuquila in Tlaxiaco.

In a recent publication, Maarten Jansen further comments:

> Codex Sanchez Solís or Egerton 2895 is now in the British Museum London, but originally belonged to the dynasty of Ñuu Ñaña (Cuyotepeji) in the Mixteca Baja. We therefore call it *'Codex Ñuu Ñaña.'* The individuals on the last page (p. 31),

representing the last rulers, are scratched out. Only the town of the person allied by marriage to the successor of the throne is still visible: Mountain of War, glossed Ñuu Yecu. Another gloss next to it reads *tnoho gui biyo,* 'lineage of 4 Reed'. From other documents we know that Lord 4 Reed *(Nahui Acatl* in Nahuatl) was the ruler of Ñuu Ñaña (Cuyotepeji) at the time of the conquest and was baptized as Don Francisco de Mendoza. He married two different wives, one (Ozomatzin from Camotlan) according to the ancient native law and one (Doña Catalina Cuetzpalin) according to the newly introduced Christian ritual. As was often the case, this provoked a lawsuit between the descendants of these two marriages as to who was the legitimate successor. According to the different testimonies Lord 4 Reed belonged to the line of rulers of Ñuu Ñaña. (Jansen and Pérez Jiménez 2011:89)

This is indeed a bold conclusion to be drawn from the pictorial place-sign on page 5 that shows a feline and the evidently manipulative gloss on page 31 that pretends to describe scratched-out name glyphs of a noble couple. Thus, the person responsible for the Colonial-period modifications of the pictorial contents achieved exactly the result he intended, to make the potential reader (in this case, Jansen) believe that the Codex Egerton supposedly presents the line of 4 Reed, or Francisco de Mendoza, from Cuyotepeji, a small community in the Mixteca Baja not mentioned in any other Mixtec codices we know about. Although Jansen might be right to argue that the combative *caciques* from that place might have used this codex for their own interests (as is perfectly documented in the Ramo Civil 669), I find it precarious to rename the document as "Codex Ñuu Ñaña."

My alternative argument for identifying the Egerton Codex place glyph with Cuquila is based on a number of reasons: there is an almost completely faded gloss on page 5 that I read as *cuy,* meaning "jaguar" in the Mixtec language. On the *Lienzo de Ocotepec* and the AGN Map of Cuquila (Ramo de Tierras 3556, exp. 6) the town's Mixtec name *Ñucuiñe,* meaning "jaguar town," is represented by a mountain glyph represented with a "jaguar" or "wild cat," in just the same way as in the Codex Egerton (Smith 1998:153, 182; Smith and Parmenter 1991:22). Earlier, a jaguar glyph is shown on monument 1 from Ñucuiñe, a site close to Cuquila, belonging to the *ñuiñe* style from the Classic period (Rivera Guzmán 2004:7). The obverse of the Codex Egerton shows places in the western part of the Mixteca Alta and Baja in the present-day states of Oaxaca and Guerrero that are much nearer to Cuquila than to Cuyotepeji. Furthermore, intermarriage between the caciques of "jaguar town" and Tilantongo, the important center in the Mixteca Alta, are shown three times on the obverse. On the reverse of the codex, however, Tilantongo is replaced by Cholula in Puebla. Obviously, the focus of the Codex Egerton genealogy had switched further north to the Mixteca Baja, where a strong relationship to the adjacent Puebla-Cholula area was established.

Quite unexpectedly, twenty-five years after the publication of my monograph on the Codex Egerton (König 1979), two studies from two different fields, archaeology and history, supported my thesis for Cuquila's being the first couple's home town. Iván Rivera Guzmán discussed several stone carvings from Santa María Cuquila/ Ñucuiñe, which reflect the Ñuiñe style (Rivera Guzmán 2004:1). He compared the iconography on these monuments with images from the Codex Egerton and associated the latter with carved stones from San Pedro/San Pablo Tequixtepec and Acatlán—both important places in the Mixteca Baja that appear several times in the Codex Egerton (Rivera Guzmán 2004:7–9, 11–13, 17). Rivera Guzmán also linked the stones from Tlaxiaco carved in the Mixteca-Puebla style of the Postclassic period with the iconography represented in the Mixtec codices. He concluded that the Ñuiñe style expanded from northwest Oaxaca—that is, the Puebla part of the Mixteca Baja—to the central Mixteca Alta and western Oaxaca. With the appearance of the Mixteca-Puebla style, which is represented in the codices and in the Postclassic imagery, we can see another strong connection between the Mixteca Baja and western Oaxaca. As such, the iconography of the Codex Egerton and the San Pedro/San Pablo Tequixtepec and Acatlán carved stones bear striking similarities to the Ñucuiñe stones near Cuquila. At the same time, we do not have such iconographical evidence from Cuyotepeji in the Mixteca Baja (König 2005:114).

The other confirmation for the identification of Cuquila as the place shown on page 5 in the Codex Egerton came from historian Ethelia Ruiz Medrano, who has studied the historical importance of Cuquila in collaboration with the community for more than four years (Ruiz Medrano 2009). Her work is based on written *expedientes* from the Colonial period, which show a very long and close relationship between the *caciques* from Cuquila and other places in the Mixteca Baja shown in the Codex Egerton (such as Acatlán and San Pedro/San Pablo Tequixtepec), starting from the Early Colonial period and up to Late Colonial times. Much as the Codex Tulane transited between the Mixteca Baja and Tlaxiaco (Smith and Parmenter 1991), other pre-Columbian codices, Ruiz Medrano has argued, might also have traveled. The Codex Egerton, for example, might have been taken by the *caciques* and *cacicas* from Cuquila to the Mixteca Baja, where they intermarried or inherited territories, while the documents continued to serve as important evidence in legal lawsuits. The Codex Egerton was kept in a local community for centuries before being acquired by Felipe Sánchez Solís (Jansen 1994:145). Although we currently do not know the biography of the codex before the mid-nineteenth century, there is little doubt regarding the document's relationship to Cuquila and its possible origin from this town.

FIGURE 4.4. The Museo Comunitario at Santa María Cuquila, Tlaxiaco. Photograph by Iván Rivera Guzmán.

A VISIT TO SANTA MARÍA CUQUILA

I visited Cuquila in August 2008 with the intention to study the Codex Egerton together with the people of the village.[1] The *síndico municipal*, Licenciado Germán Ortiz, had invited the authorities from all the *agencias* to participate in the lecture. Living in the shadows of the Classic-period site Ñucuiñe, the local people show a strong interest in their local history and founded a *Museo Comunitario* (figure 4.4). In front of the *ayuntamiento*, Ortiz and Rivera Guzmán started with a general introduction to the topic, followed by the display and a page-by-page study of the codex facsimile that Ethelia Ruiz had donated to the community (figure 4.5). The meeting was adjourned following a discussion concerning the Codex Egerton's contemporary custody in the British Museum in London. At the end of the debate, we concluded that the preservation and storage in the British Museum can be looked at from different standpoints, and that the museum should be informed of the present interpretation of the codex, publish it in their records, show the codex to the public and, last but not least, allow people from Cuquila to come and study the original any time. The audience postulated, however, that the payment of any such travel should be provided by the British Museum.

Because I also wanted to deepen our knowledge on the former role of Cuquila in the Mixteca, I was seeking for more arguments to support Cuquila's position as an important intersection between the Mixteca Alta, Baja, and Costa. Elsewhere I

FIGURE 4.5. Studying the Codex Egerton at Santa María Cuquila. Photograph by Iván Rivera Guzmán.

argued for a "western corridor" linking the Mixteca Baja and Costa via Cuquila in the Alta (König 2005), a thesis further confirmed by Ruiz Medrano's (2009) recent studies. Today, long and hard marches become less common as new paved roads link the most remote mountain communities. Geographical knowledge of landscape and familiarity with toponyms in the native languages will consequently get lost in the next generation. However, such information is fundamental for interpreting the pre-Columbian codices and Colonial *lienzos* and maps that feature numerous place signs, sometimes accompanied by their respective glosses. As I was looking for individuals with a specific knowledge of recent and ancient trails and routes, I was introduced to Don Camilo Coronel Sánchez, an expert who was able to specify all the names of intermediate stops on the way down to the Pacific coast. In addition, he drew a beautiful circular map with glosses describing the former territorial extensions of Cuquila, its old and new boundaries after this was reduced due to a "cholera" epidemic (more likely typhus), and the communities owning this land today (figure 4.6).

AN OUTLOOK FOR THE FUTURE

Multidisciplinary fieldwork goes on. However, unlike archaeological fieldwork, which has a promising future in Oaxaca considering the multiple sites and artifacts above and below the surface, linguistic fieldwork might no longer be possible in the next few generations, depending as it does on the survival of Mixtec as a spoken language in the communities. The same goes for ethnohistorical and ethnographical fieldwork. As places in Oaxaca increasingly become connected by signposted roads and motorways, the geographical knowledge of ancient sites, markers, trails, routes, and boundaries is becoming lost because it is no longer as necessary for orientation and communication.

Other important aspects are the *transformation* of native knowledge into internationally acknowledged contemporary art and the *transference* of native knowledge with the Mixtec immigration to the United States. As an illustration of the former aspect, I have recently learned that a film that documented a contemporary Oaxacan artist's work also presented an excellent ethnographic source that can aid our understanding of a pre-Columbian codex. In his film *Mit den Füßen im Himmel* (*Pisando en el Cielo: Pintores de Oaxaca*, or *Treading in Heaven: Painters of Oaxaca*), the German filmmaker Boris Penth interviews artist Filemón Santiago in his Mixtec home community of *San José Sosola* (Penth 1996/97). The artist presents his deer mask and explains the instructions and procedures for hunting a deer that he learned from his father. The same oral tradition was recorded in Guerrero by Schultze-Jena (1938) in the early 1900s and is further visualized in the pre-Columbian Codex Copsi.

FIGURE 4.6. Don Camilo Coronel Sánchez drawing a round map in Santa María Cuquila. Photograph by Iván Rivera Guzmán.

Although contemporary native artists from all over Oaxaca step deep into their history and mythology in order to construct fresh ideas from old traditions, others leave behind their country. However, many Mixtecs who live in the diaspora often feel more nostalgic about their *tierra* and the ancient customs and traditions they still remember from their parents and grandparents. In a Manhattan pizzeria I met two young Mixtec pizza makers from Guerrero. In addition to speaking Mixtec, they also knew Mixtec customs and traditions. Young Mixtecs from Guerrero who are living in California today participated at the last Mixtec Gateway in Las Vegas and contributed information that helped in the interpretation of the codices. Thus, fieldwork today is no longer limited to the Mixtec homeland. However, native knowledge is not based merely on oral tradition passed from parents to children but is also closely linked to the experience of life in a Mixtec village and its environment. If such a context is no longer available, native knowledge will fail to achieve its original function and meaning. It will consequently be lost.[2]

NOTES

1. The trip was organized in advance by Ethelia Ruiz Medrano and I was accompanied by Iván Rivera Guzmán.

2. I am grateful to Burkhard Brinker for permission to publish figures 4.1 and 4.2 and to Iván Rivera Guzmán for permission to publish figures 4.4, 4.5, and 4.6.

REFERENCES

Byland, Bruce E., and John M.D. Pohl. 1994. *In the Realm of 8 Deer: The Archaeology of the Mixtec Codices*. Norman: University of Oklahoma Press.

Jansen, Maarten E.R.G.N. 1982. *Huisi Tacu*. Amsterdam: CEDLA incidentele publicaties 24.

Jansen, Maarten E.R.G.N. 1994. *La Gran Familia de los Reyes Mixtecos: Libro Explicativo de los Códices Llamados Códices Egerton y Becker II*. Austria: Akademische Druck- und Verlagsanstalt/Fondo de la Cultura Económica.

Jansen, Maarten E.R.G.N., and Gabina Aurora Pérez Jiménez. 2011. *The Mixtec Pictorial Manuscripts: Time, Agency, and Memory in Ancient Mexico*. Leiden: Brill.

König, Viola. 1979. *Inhaltliche Analyse und Interpretation von Codex Egerton*. Hamburg: Beiträge zur mittelamerikanischen Völkerkunde 15, Hamburgischen Museum für Völkerkunde.

König, Viola. 1993. *Die Schlacht bei Sieben Blume: Konquistadoren, Kaziken und Konflikte auf alten Landkarten der Indianer Südmexikos*. Bremen, Germany: Edition Temmen.

König, Viola. 2005. "Mary E. Smith's Interpretation of the Codex Tulane, the Codex López Ruíz, and Other Documents: Some Conclusions on the Role of Tlaxiaco in the Western Part of the Mixteca Alta." *Mexicon* 27 (6):112–115.

Monaghan, John. 1995. *The Covenants with Earth and Rain: Exchange, Sacrifice, and Revelation in Mixtec Sociality*. Norman: University of Oklahoma Press.

Mühlenpfordt, Eduard. (Original work published 1844) 1969. *Versuch einer getreuen Schilderung der Republik Mexico*. Graz, Austria: Akademische Druck- und Verlagsanstalt Graz.

Paddock, John, ed. 1966. *Ancient Oaxaca: Discoveries in Mexican Archeology and History*. Stanford: Stanford University Press.

Penth, Boris. 1996/97. *Mit den Füßen im Himmel: Maler in Oaxaca/ Pisando en el Cielo: Pintores de Oaxaca* (documentary film). Mexico: Fundación Cultural Rodolfo Morales, A. C.

Rivera Guzmán, Iván. 2004. *La Iconografía de las Piedras Grabadas de Cuquila y la Distribución de la Escritura Ñuiñe en la Mixteca Alta, Oaxaca*. Mexico: Dirección de Registro Público de Monumentos y Zonas Arqueológicos, Instituto Nacional de Antropología e Historia.

Ruiz Medrano, Ethelia. 2009. "Mixteca Alta, un Lugar Llamado Santa María Cuquila y el Códice Egerton." *Mexicon* 31 (5):113–118.

Schmieder, Oscar. 1930a. *The Settlements of the Tzapotec and Mije Indians, State of Oaxaca, Mexico*. Berkeley: University of California Press.

Schmieder, Oscar. 1930b. "Der Einfluss des Agrarsystems der Tzapoteken, Azteken und Mije auf die Kulturentwicklung dieser Völker." In *Akten des XXIV Amerikanischen Kongresses*, 109–111. Hamburg.

Schultze-Jena, Leonhard. 1938. *Bei den Azteken, Mixteken und Tlapaneken der Sierra Madre del Sur von Mexiko*. Published under the auspices of El Sociedad México-Alemana Alejandro de Humboldt.

Smith, Mary Elizabeth. 1973. *Picture Writing from Ancient Southern Mexico: Mixtec Place Signs and Maps*. Norman: University of Oklahoma Press.

Smith, Mary Elizabeth. 1998. *The Codex López Ruiz: A Lost Mixtec Pictorial Manuscript*. Nashville: Vanderbilt University Publications in Anthropology, no. 15.

Smith, Mary Elizabeth, and Ross Parmenter. 1991. *The Codex Tulane*. New Orleans: Tulane University Middle American Research Institute.

5

Mythstory and Archaeology

Of Earth Goddesses, Weaving Tools, and Buccal Masks

Geoffrey G. McCafferty and Sharisse D. McCafferty

GEOFFREY'S MEMORIES OF BRUCE BYLAND
AND THE TAMAZULAPAN SURVEY

Shortly after publishing our "Engendering Tomb 7" paper (McCafferty and McCafferty 1994), I was accosted by a Real Oaxacan Archaeologist who demanded, "what gives you the authority to write about Oaxaca!?" Bruce Byland deserves much of the credit and blame. On a cold and dreary day in State College, Pennsylvania, way back in 1977, my former college roommate Dave Reed ran into eager grad-student Bruce posting notices in the Anthropology Department offering positions on his archaeological survey project in the Mixteca Alta. Always up for an adventure and looking to get out of the snow, my buddy Dave signed on and, in an act of altruism, signed me up, too. I promptly quit my job digging ditches in Los Angeles (the job for which my BA in ancient Near Eastern archaeology best qualified me) and flew south. Over the next eleven months I wandered the hills and valleys of the Tamazulapan Valley in Bruce's considerable shadow.

The Tamazulapan Valley survey was run on a shoestring, as exemplified on those weekends when we visited Richard Blanton's posh Valley of Oaxaca survey camp to splash in the pool, play volleyball with Oaxacan aristocracy, and revel in relative opulence. In Tamazulapan we shared a two-room house behind the church, awakened at dawn by the bell and loudspeaker (which played only Christmas carols), and with our lab in the pig pen that we shared with Henrietta until her untimely demise and consumption (figure 5.1). Shortly after that sad occasion, our numbers

DOI: 10.5876/9781607323297.c005

FIGURE 5.1. Bruce Byland with Carel McCafferty in the Tamazulapan ceramic laboratory. Photo by Geoffrey McCafferty.

swelled with the arrival of a summer team of Tennessee volunteers; we remodeled the Henrietta Suite for the newbies.

The Tamazulapan Valley is located on the western edge of the Mixteca Alta, adjacent to Teposcolula, Yanhuitlán, Coixtlahuaca, and Huajuapan de Leon further west. Bruce had originally planned a more comprehensive study that would have included a survey of the Teposcolula Valley as well as more intensive surveys of select sites encountered during the general reconnaissance. These plans were mostly abandoned due to time constraints, though the Pueblo Viejo site outside of Tamazulapan was subjected to more-intensive survey using a survey grid of the site center (figure 5.2). Another innovation that Bruce introduced was the use of 30- meter transects intervals, based on the typical size of a "household cluster"; thus the research design hoped for the identification of all site types at the house level or greater.

Before initiating the project, of course, it was necessary to obtain our INAH permit, and because of the recent election of the Echeverría government, the process was delayed. Consequently we spent a month or more in Oaxaca city, waiting. We stayed at the old Mansion Imperial hotel on the *Parque el Llano* near the current INAH offices. Among other things, we worked in the Cuilapan bodega to rebag artifacts from Ron Spores's Nochixtlán survey that had been scattered by a recent

FIGURE 5.2. Bruce Byland, Deb McCafferty, and Ken Jones survey the "Pueblo Viejo." Photo by Geoffrey McCafferty.

earthquake. Considering the rudimentary ceramic sequence of the time, this was a very useful task, and when we finally hit the field we were armed with the practical knowledge that: if painted, it's Postclassic; if incised, Preclassic; and if neither, Classic. Woefully, thirty-five years later the practical wisdom for field identification is not much more developed.

Byland's survey recognized 228 sites in the Tamazulapan Valley, ranging from isolated features such as a maguey roasting pit to fortified hilltop sites, and from a dry cave off the road toward Coixtlahuaca with Early Formative pottery to remains of the Colonial chapel at Pueblo Viejo. The major site of Yatachio, outside of the congregated town of Tamazulapan, the elite houses on the ridge above Tejupan, and the large obsidian-processing site at Yucuchicano are among other sites crying out for more investigation. One of the "aha!" moments came when Ron Spores brought us an image of Colonial Tejupan from the *Relaciones Geográficas* and we spent evenings comparing the map with the survey data, identifying roads, palaces, and defensive walls on the mountain citadel. This integration of ethnohistorical and archaeological data shaped both of our career paths and may have contributed in some small way to the conceptualization of this volume. Much of the Tamazulapan research was conducted by the three-person team of Bruce, Mike Fuentes, and myself, though for brief periods the group featured such notables as Chip Stanish and Larry Gorenflo. My sister Deb even joined us for a month and commemorated her experience by creating a Mixtec codex of the project.

Every time I revisit the Tamazulapan Valley and its generous people, I yearn to continue Bruce's program. And maybe one day I will set aside my other projects and do just that. Meanwhile, Sharisse and I continue to putter on the fringes of Oaxacan archaeology, using codices and other armchair resources to keep in touch with the field and its practitioners. Thanks, Bruce!

FEMALE EARTH/FERTILITY CULTS AND SACRED LANDSCAPES

Shared religious themes are one of the important linkages that support the idea of Mesoamerica as a common cultural area (Kirchhoff 1952). One particularly promi- nent characteristic is the representation of members of the female earth/fertility cults from across the region and through time. For example, aspects of the young goddess, affiliated with the moon, sexuality, and domestic crafts (especially spin- ning and weaving) are clearly parallel in the goddesses Xochiquetzal of the Aztecs, Ix Chel of the Maya, and 13 Flower of the Mixtecs (Nicholson 1971; Sullivan 1982; Tate 1999).

Another parallel is that aspect of the cult relating to the earth and the cycle of birth and death. The most detailed description of this goddess comes from the Aztecs, where Cihuacóatl (literally "woman-serpent") was described in the Florentine Codex and the *Primeros Memoriales* (Klein 1988). For example, the goddess Cihuacóatl was associated with both death and rebirth. When delivering a baby, the Aztec midwives would tell the laboring mother to "be like the brave war- riors, like Cihuacóatl and Quilaztli" to capture the baby (Sahagún 1950–1982, Book 6:167). Cihuacóatl was known to wear white face paint, like a skull, and obsidian earspools (Sahagún 1997). She carried a weaving batten, or *tzotzopaztli*, that in the hands of a female priestess could be used as a sacrificial knife. Small amaranth- dough effigies were ceremonially cut open with battens during mountain worship (Sahagún 1950–1982, Book 2:29).

A characteristic of Cihuacóatl, at least in the pictorial manuscripts such as the Codex Magliabechiano (1983) and Codex Borbonicus (1979), was the costume element of a skeletal buccal mask. In these scenes the goddess is shown with what appears to be a human mandible as her lower jaw, while carrying a batten as her diagnostic staff (figure 5.3). Cecelia Klein (1988) has written extensively about Cihuacóatl, especially of the multiple roles of the goddess and her priest- esses. While the goddess herself took on the attributes described above, relating to

FIGURE 5.3. Cihuacóatl, with characteristic skeletal mandible, in the Codex Magliabechiano (1983:45). Illustration by John M.D. Pohl.

death and childbirth, priestesses of her cult served as oracles and political advisors (see also Pohl 1984). In a third element of this complex, the military advisor to the Aztec *tlatoani* held the office of Cihuacóatl, as represented in the Durán Codex (1971) where the *tlatoani*, or first speaker, observes a sacrificial ritual while accompanied by his Cihuacóatl, as denoted by the small glyph of a female head and serpent. Tlacaelel was a prominent Cihuacóatl under several of the early Aztec rulers and received his title and insignias of office as a result of leading a victorious conquest of city-states in the southern Basin of Mexico where the goddess Cihuacóatl was revered (Klein 1988).

John Pohl (1984) has pointed out parallels between the Aztec goddess Cihuacóatl and the Mixtec Lady 9 Grass, a prominent character in several codices where she fills at least two of the prominent roles of Cihuacóatl. For example, in the "War of Heaven" depicted in the Codex Nuttall, Lady 9 Grass is shown with a skeletal head and axe as she battles the "Stone Men" along with the Mixtec culture hero Lord 9 Wind. In this scene from mythical time, she is portrayed as one of the primordial deities engaged in establishing the Mixtec world. In other scenes, however, the skeletal-jawed Lady 9 Grass is depicted at the Temple of Skull, perhaps Chalcatongo, where she acts as an oracle and political counsel to visiting mortals such as Lady 6 Monkey of Jaltepec. For example, after being insulted by the "flinty words" of her enemies in the Codex Selden (1964), Lady 6 Monkey is counseled by 9 Grass and then attacks, captures, and sacrifices her opponents (figure 5.4). In the Codex Nuttall, a dispute between Lady 6 Monkey and Lord 8 Deer is resolved at the Temple of Skull by Lady 9 Grass.

FIGURE 5.4. Lady 9 Grass giving council at the Temple of Skull (Codex Selden 1964:7). Illustration by John M.D. Pohl.

The goddess herself is characterized by the deity in full skeletal head, while the political office-holders are more simply depicted by the skeletal mandible. Possibly related to this symbol is the calendar sign for "grass," which in the Mixtec system of notation is represented as a tuft of long grass emerging from a skeletal jawbone. Skeletal jaws are also a prominent feature in Maya calendrics, representing a framing element in the head variants of numerals 14 through 19, though this may be a coincidental parallel between the two calendrical systems.

Spinning and weaving were other activities intimately related to female productivity, but metaphorically were also linked to sexual intercourse and reproduction (Sullivan 1982). If marriage was a necessary act for a woman to acquire *yee*, or reproductive power, could spinning and weaving be an alternative, or surrogate, method for a woman to charge her political powers? This could therefore relate to the codical representation and mortuary practice of interring spinning and weaving implements as symbolic testimony of female power.

An example of spinning and weaving tools as emblems symbolic of lineage and political power is presented in a story recorded in Mitla in the 1930s (Parsons 1936:222–223, 324–328). The characters include Sus Ley (an old female supernatural), her husband (the earth/fertility god), her brother (the rain god), and Sus Ley's adopted son and daughter. The adopted children killed Sus Ley's husband and then fled the widow's wrath, taking her weaving tools with them. Sus Ley and her brother followed in close pursuit. Whenever it seemed that Sus Ley and her brother were going to catch the two children, they threw down one of the weaving tools, which became mountains in the path of the pursuing kin. The children eventually escaped after creating a new cultural landscape, and they became transformed into the sun and the moon.

Several points are of interest. First, the story is about two competing lineages. The younger lineage steals the weaving tools of the rival matriarch—her symbols of power. The young usurpers use these tools to create their own landscape, which repels their political rivals. For the Mixtec, at least, geographic space was inextricably tied to the lineage that ruled it (Pohl and Byland 1990). In creating its own landscape, the younger lineage created its own domain and placed itself prominently in the cosmos as the sun and moon.

Similar interrelationships are found among the Mixtec and the Huichol. Landscape revelation as a prerequisite to the initiation of celestial movement is found in the Codex Vindobonensis Mexicanus (1974). This creation story is divided into two main sections. In the first, the culture hero Lord 9 Wind raises the waters from the surface of the earth to reveal the Mixtec landscape for the first time. Nine and a half pages of the codex list the place signs of the revealed geography. This revelation is concluded by a ritual featuring sixteen knotted cords, a "knot-bound" mountain and, finally, symbols of the three layers of the revealed Mixtec cosmos (Codex Vindobonensis Mexicanus 1974: 38). If the Mixtecs did conceive of the landscape as woven, then it would be consistent for a knotting ritual to formalize it, just as the warp threads of a cloth woven on a backstrap loom must be knotted to prevent unraveling. With the geography stabilized, the second half of the Mixtec creation story—the first rising of the sun and the initiation of *yee* circulation throughout the cosmos—could begin.

Another solar/weaving/landscape trope is found in contemporary Huichol cosmology (Schaefer 1990). Each unit of the Huichol loom is associated with a specific feature of the ritual landscape, with the various battens and heddle bars named after specific mountains or communities. These loom parts were ordered from east to west (top to bottom), and thus the loom becomes a veritable map of geographic space, recreating the path of the sun as it follows the peyote trail. The use of spinning and weaving tools as modifiers of both Mixtec and Zapotec place glyphs may be specific references to a "woven" landscape.

Could there be a deeper, supernatural significance as well, perhaps relating to an earth goddess who "wove" the earth's surface into a cultural landscape (cf. Klein 1982)? The characteristic association between the Aztec earth/fertility goddess Cihuacóatl and weaving battens, and Lady 9 Grass with a weaving pick (Codex Nuttall 1975:20-II), may parallel this theme. Were weaving tools necessary to ceremonially reconfigure the dynastic/geographical structures? By considering the possible ties between dynastic foundations, the landscape, and weaving tools, the actions of Lady 3 Flint (Shell Quechquemitl) on page 15 of the Codex Nuttall (1975) may be explained (figure 5.5). In the scene that fills two-thirds of the page, Lady 3 Flint and her husband have arrived for the first time at the Temple of the Ascending Serpent. This is to be the capital of their new kingdom. At the center of the scene, Lady 3 Flint and two priests stand at the foot of the Mountain of Sand

FIGURE 5.5. Lady 3 Flint (Shell Quechquemitl) "weaving" the cultural landscape of Ascending Serpent place (Codex Nuttall 1975:15). Illustration by John M.D. Pohl.

and present offerings to this focal point of the landscape. Lady 3 Flint holds an incense brazier in one hand and a decorated weaving pick in the other. Like the children in the legend of Sus Ley, she utilizes a weaving tool to transform the landscape into a home for her new lineage.

By interpreting the potential for weaving tools to function as symbols of gathering, consolidation, and transformation, women were identified as those members of the marriage unit who held the power to create a lineage, and symbolically to reconfigure the cultural landscape. As individual married women came into their own symbolically as powerful political players, their stereotypical tools of production functioned as material metaphors for the consolidation of lineage and landscape. Female power in ancient Oaxaca was conceived as a force that could quite literally weave the fabric of a new kingdom together or sever the cords of alliance between one polity and another.

ARCHAEOLOGICAL EVIDENCE

From an archaeological perspective, material correlates of spinning and weaving tools and buccal masks have been found in prominent ritual contexts and provide important insights into the possible roles of members of the earth/fertility deity complex. All were found together at Tomb 7 of Monte Albán by Alfonso Caso (1969), but other elements have been found in tombs from Zaachila and Mitla, as well as in other deposits. Bone weaving tools have been discussed in previous articles (McCafferty and McCafferty 1994, 2003) and include small battens and picks, sometimes elaborately carved with Mixtec codex–style imagery, but in other cases undecorated.

Skeletal jaws have been discovered and may offer some additional insights. Several buccal masks were uncovered in the famous Tomb 7 of Monte Albán, one of the richest burials known from the pre-Columbian world, which was excavated by Alfonso Caso in 1932 (Caso 1969). The principal skeleton of Tomb 7, Individual A, was interred in a flexed, seated position against the west wall of the two-chambered, east-west oriented tomb (Caso 1969; McCafferty and McCafferty 1994). Individual A has ambiguous sexable characteristics but was interpreted as male by Caso and his physical anthropologist Daniel Rubín de la Borbolla, though we have since suggested a possible female identification based in part on female grave goods (McCafferty and McCafferty 1994). An engendered interpretation of the associated objects, including numerous pieces identifiable as part of a spinning and weaving kit, is clear: these correspond well with characteristic traits of the Postclassic female earth/fertility deity complex (McCafferty and McCafferty 1991). Diagnostic artifacts include thirty-four carved bone tools resembling small weaving battens, as well as spindle whorls, onyx and crystal spinning bowls, and a carved bone comb. A large gold amulet depicts a spider, an animal that is closely related to spinning and weaving in Mesoamerican mythology (Taube 1983) and that is specifically mentioned in Mixtec lore as the inspiration used in primordial times to "invent" the spinning technique.

Two objects from Tomb 7 specifically relate to Sahagún's (1997) description of the Aztec goddess Cihuacóatl: turquoise mosaic inlays in a batten and weaving pick parallel his description of the goddess's tools from the *Primeros Memoriales*, and finely polished obsidian earspools are a costume element of Cihuacóatl. As noted previously, weaving battens are one of the central symbols of the goddess, and the intricately carved battens from Tomb 7 were likely powerful icons of the cult. One of the carved bones actually depicts a female, Lady 9 Reed, holding an object that Caso (1969:192) identified as a batten. Lady 13 Flower similarly holds a batten and spindle with whorl in the Codex Nuttall (1975:19), though the deity 9 Grass, most similar to Cihuacóatl, does not use this symbol.

Included among the scattered bones of nine individuals in Tomb 7 were five additional mandibles, described as being perforated and painted for ceremonial use (Caso 1969:61; Rubín de la Borbolla 1969). These were identified as belonging to adult male individuals, and all came from Region 6 of the tomb, farthest from Individual A (McCafferty and McCafferty 2003). These would be the physical manifestations of the buccal masks illustrated in the codices. Interestingly, one of the most famous of the gold objects from Tomb 7 depicts an individual with a

FIGURE 5.6. Golden pendant showing face with skeletal mandible from Tomb 7, Monte Albán. Museo de las Culturas de Oaxaca. Photo by Danny Zborover.

skeletal jaw (figure 5.6) and wearing a headdress similar to the one worn by Lady 3 Flint/Shell Quechquemitl (Codex Nuttall 1975:14), who wears spindle whorls in her headdress.

Another object found in Tomb 7 that ties in with the skeletal theme was an incense burner made out of a human skull with a hole cut out of the crown of the head. It was covered with an amaranth-dough paste, known as *tzoalli*, which acted as glue for small mosaic plaques of jade, turquoise, and shell. Notably, one of the perforated and painted mandibles was found in association with this skull incense

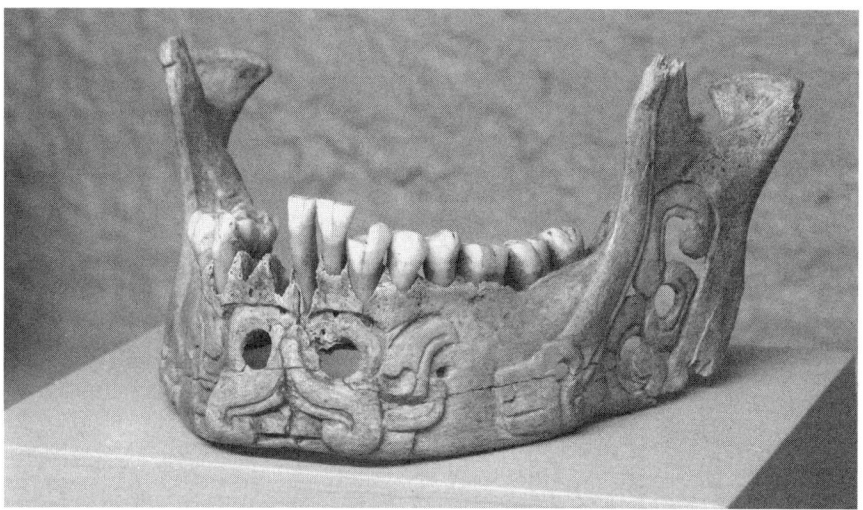

FIGURE 5.7. Carved human mandible. Museo Rufino Tamayo, Oaxaca City. Photo by Danny Zborover.

burner (Caso 1969:61). Similar skull idols are known from the Codex Nuttall (1975:6, 10), where they are associated with Lady 9 Monkey. Numerous extra pieces of shell were found that may have come from similar *incensarios*, perhaps of more perishable materials such as pure *tzoalli* or wood.

Other decorated mandibles are known archaeologically and may have served as buccal masks in ceremonial contexts, or perhaps as other costume elements. Winter and Urcid (1990) point out that one of the individuals depicted in a stucco relief from Lambityeco wears a human mandible on his forearm, while in other scenes human long bones are carried, perhaps as symbols of inheritance. An elaborately carved mandible was found at Eloxochitlan, in the Mazatec region of northern Oaxaca. It features a floral motif in a cartouche, identified as Glyph D from the *Ñuiñe* calendrical system, and also a numerical element of a single dot, indicating the number 1 (Winter and Urcid 1990). A similar carved mandible is on display at the Museo Rufino Tamayo in Oaxaca (figure 5.7).

In recent excavations at the site of Macuilxóchitl in the Valley of Oaxaca, another fragment of a carved human mandible was found. The project was part of highway expansion between Oaxaca and Mitla, and excavations took place at several mounds along the right of way (Markens et al. 2008). All of the mounds dated to the Late Classic Xoo phase (600–900 CE), but also featured Early Postclassic Liobaa phase (900–1200 CE) ritual activities, perhaps relating to ancestor veneration. For

FIGURE 5.8. Carved human mandible from Macuilxóchitl. Photo by Geoffrey McCafferty.

example, an adolescent was buried on the north-facing staircase of Mound 36 at the midpoint, suggesting ritual interment, and common artifacts found in the post-abandonment fill were long-handled incense burners, miniature vessels, and urn fragments. Mound 55 was probably a temple, based on its small size and steep sides. Ceremonial objects such as the aforementioned *sahumadores* and miniatures were common, and a large fragment of a hollow ceramic jaguar figure was found at the base of the staircase. Also found was a carved human mandible, featuring intricately carved bird images among volute designs (figure 5.8).

CONCLUSIONS

The combination of ethnohistorical and archaeological data can provide a richer perspective on the pre-Columbian past. Greater reliability can be gained for interpretations of the prehistoric or protohistoric past using the direct historical approach (Marcus and Flannery 1994). More typically, however, ambiguous or even contradictory evidence muddies what we generally hope to be clear insights.

Spinning and weaving tools used for the symbolic creation of the cultural landscape or modified human mandibles are examples of this. Was the metaphoric association of weaving with sexual reproduction invoked by members of the earth/fertility cult during other acts of creation? Were buccal masks worn as part of a ritual mask, as insignia for priestesses of the earth/fertility cult? Or as arm bands to signify lineage? Or were they part of complex icons of the deity herself? Did the association of the mandible with oracles, as in Codex Selden (1964), indicate that they could communicate with deified ancestors? The complexity of these possible interpretations is precisely what makes this an interesting exercise. Past cultures were varied, and finding simplistic solutions is just that: overly simplistic. We recognize and celebrate the diversity represented by this fascinating data set and offer the study of the mythstory and archaeology of buccal masks as an example of the wonderful potential for a multidisciplinary approach to Oaxacan archaeology.

REFERENCES

Caso, Alfonso. 1969. *El Tesoro de Monte Albán*. Mexico City: Instituto Nacional de Antropología e Historia.

Codex Borbonicus. 1979. *Códice Borbónico: Manuscrito Mexicano de la Biblioteca del Palais Bourbon*. Mexico City: Siglo Veintiuno.

Codex Magliabechiano. (Original work published 1903) 1983. *The Book of the Life of the Ancient Mexicans Containing an Account of their Rites and Superstitions,* translated and commentary by Zelia Nuttall. Berkeley: University of California Press.

Codex Nuttall. 1975. *The Codex Nuttall: A Picture Manuscript from Ancient Mexico*, ed. Zelia Nuttall, introduction by A. G. Miller. The Peabody Museum Facsimile. New York: Dover Publications.

Codex Selden. 1964. *Codex Selden,* facsimile with commentary by Alfonso Caso. Mexico City: Sociedad Mexicana de Antropología.

Codex Vindobonensis Mexicanus, I. 1974. *Codex Vindobonensis Mexicanus I, second facsimile edition*. Graz, Austria: Akademische Druck- und Verlaganstalt.

Durán, Diego. 1971. *The Book of the Gods and Rites and the Ancient Calendar*. Trans. F. Horcasitas and D. Heyden. Norman: University of Oklahoma Press.

Kirchhoff, Paul. (1943) 1952. "Meso-America: Its Geographic Limits, Ethnic Composition and Cultural Characteristics." In *Heritage of Conquest: The Ethnology of Middle America*, ed. Sol Tax, and members of the Viking fund seminar of Middle American ethnology, 17–30. Glencoe, IL: The Free Press Publishers.

Klein, Cecelia F. 1982. "Woven Heaven, Tangled Earth: A Weaver's Paradigm of the Mesoamerican Cosmos." In *Ethnoastronomy and Archaeoastronomy in the American*

Tropics, ed. Anthony F. Aveni, and Gary Urton, 1–35. New York: Annals of the New York Academy of Sciences, vol. 385. http://dx.doi.org/10.1111/j.1749-6632.1982.tb34257.x.

Klein, Cecelia F. 1988. "Re-Thinking Cihuacóatl: Aztec Political Imagery of the Conquered Woman." In *Smoke and Mist: Mesoamerican Studies in Memory of Thelma D. Sullivan*, ed. J. Kathryn Josserand and Karen Dakin, 237–277. Oxford: BAR International Series.

Marcus, Joyce, and Kent Flannery. 1994. "Ancient Zapotec Ritual and Religion: An Application of the Direct Historical Approach." In *The Ancient Mind: Elements of Cognitive Archaeology*, ed. Colin Renfrew and Ezra B. Zubrow, 55–74. New York: Cambridge University Press. http://dx.doi.org/10.1017/CBO9780511598388.008.

Markens, Robert, Marcus Winter, and Cira Martínez López. 2008. "Ethnohistory, Oral History, and Archaeology at Macuilxóchitl: Perspective on the Postclassic Period in the Valley of Oaxaca." In *After Monte Albán: Transformation and Negotiation in Oaxaca, Mexico*, ed. Jeffrey Blomster, 193–215. Boulder: University Press of Colorado.

McCafferty, Geoffrey G., and Sharisse D. McCafferty. 2003. "Questioning a Queen? A Gender-Informed Evaluation of Monte Albán's Tomb 7." In *Ancient Queens: Archaeological Explorations*, ed. Sarah Nelson, 41–58. Walnut Creek, CA: AltaMira Press.

McCafferty, Sharisse D., and Geoffrey G. McCafferty. 1991. "Spinning and Weaving as Female Gender Identity in Post-Classic Central Mexico." In *Textile Traditions of Mesoamerica and the Andes: An Anthology*, ed. M. Schevill, J. C. Berlo, and E. Dwyer, 19–44. New York: Garland Publishing.

McCafferty, Sharisse D., and Geoffrey G. McCafferty. 1994. "Engendering Tomb 7 at Monte Albán: Respinning an Old Yarn." *Current Anthropology* 35 (2):143–166. http://dx.doi.org/10.1086/204252.

Nicholson, Henry B. 1971. "Religion in Pre-Hispanic Central Mexico." In *Handbook of Middle American Indians*, Vol. 10: *Archaeology of Northern Mesoamerica, Part 1*, ed. R. Wauchope, G. F. Ekholm, and I. Bernal, 395–446. Austin: University of Texas Press.

Parsons, Elsie Clews. 1936. *Mitla: Town of the Souls and Other Zapotec-Speaking Pueblos of Oaxaca, Mexico*. Chicago: University of Chicago Press.

Pohl, John M.D. 1984. "The Earth Lords: Politics and Symbolism in the Mixtec Codices." Unpublished PhD diss., University of California, Los Angeles.

Pohl, John M.D., and Bruce E. Byland. 1990. "Mixtec Landscape Perception and Archaeological Settlement Patterns." *Ancient Mesoamerica* 1 (1):113–131. http://dx.doi.org/10.1017/S0956536100000134.

Rubín de la Borbolla, Daniel F. 1969. "Appendix: La Osamenta Humana Encontrada en la Tumba 7." In *El Tesoro de Monte Albán*, by Alfonso Caso, 275–324. Mexico City: Instituto Nacional de Antropología e Historia.

Sahagún, Bernardino de. (1547–1585) 1950–1982. *Florentine Codex: General History of the Things of New Spain*. 13 vols. ed. and trans. A.J.D. Anderson and C. E. Dibble. Salt Lake City: University of Utah Press.

Sahagún, Bernardino de. (1561) 1997. *Primeros Memoriales*. Palaeography of Nahuatl Text and English Translation by Thelma Sullivan. Norman: University of Oklahoma Press.

Schaefer, Stacy B. 1990. "The Loom and Time in the Huichol World." *Journal of Latin American Lore* 15 (2):179–194.

Sullivan, Thelma. 1982. "Tlazolteotl-Ixcuina: The Great Spinner and Weaver." In *The Art and Iconography of Late Post-Classic Central Mexico*, ed. Elizabeth Hill Boone, 7–36. Washington, DC: Dumbarton Oaks.

Tate, Carolyn E. 1999. "Writing on the Face of the Moon: Women's Products, Archetypes, and Power in Ancient Maya Civilization." In *Manifesting Power: Gender and the Interpretation of Power in Archaeology*, ed. Tracy L. Sweely, 81–102. New York: Routledge Press.

Taube, Karl A. 1983. "The Teotihuacan Spider Woman." *Journal of Latin American Lore* 9 (2):107–189.

Winter, Marcus, and Javier Urcid. 1990. "Una Mandíbula Humana de la Sierra Mazateca, Oaxaca." *Notas Mesoamericanas* 12:39–49.

6

Reconciling Disparate Evidence between the Mixtec Historical Codices and Archaeology

The Case of "Red and White Bundle" and "Hill of the Wasp"

BRUCE E. BYLAND[1]

INTRODUCTION

The Mixtec historical codices represent a remarkable documentary resource for the study of Postclassic political organizations in Oaxaca, Mexico and, indeed, for the study of pre-Columbian society in general. These documents are long screenfold manuscripts that relate genealogies of ruling families, narratives of warfare and alliance that often run for generations, and lists of communities that belonged to ancient polities. To make use of them in the quest for understanding political, social, and economic processes, we must be able to agree on basic interpretations of the meanings of the images that appear throughout the documents.

Often that agreement is simple. Many images are visually distinctive and are widely understood. The images of men and women are clearly separate, defined by their dress, their hair, and sometimes by their posture. Alfonso Caso (1960) and Mary Elizabeth Smith (1973) defined the images of hills, rocks, rivers, springs, buildings, and other geographic features long ago. Many objects are similarly evident. We have no disagreement over what a tripod vase is, or what a blanket or straw mat is. We all agree on the representation of various weapons, articles of clothing, animal images, and many other things.

At a higher level of abstraction that agreement is not always so simple. The meaning of an action depicted in the codices is not always obvious. We do not always understand why a particular passage is included in the narrative at a particular place, or is included at all. The identities of the people in the story or the places where

DOI: 10.5876/9781607323297.c006

things take place are not always apparent. We can often achieve a reading of the name of a place but we do not always agree on the location of that place. This particular problem is critical in trying to extend beyond the simple translation of the text to a reconstruction of the political and social dynamics that the text records, and it is this very problem that is the focus of this chapter. Nowhere is that more evident than in the disagreement in the literature about the scale of political dynamics in the Mixtec historical codices.

I have been accused of having too parochial a view (Brotherston 1996). Jansen observes that the important question here is "of the geographical dimensions of the Mixtec histories" (Jansen 1998:94, my translation). He commends John Pohl and me in our rejection of the pan-Mesoamerican range claimed by various scholars who see references in the historical action of the codices from Teotihuacan to the Maya sites of the Peten, but still challenges our place name identifications as too limited in scope; instead, he suggests that we need to look for a middle ground between the all-inclusive range and minute parochialism (Jansen 1998:95). I absolutely agree with that assessment though, and indeed deny the charge of excessive parochialism. I too have sought a middle ground, but have done so in my own way. This essay will explore our disagreement over one set of place sign identifications.

CONTESTED PLACES IN THE MIXTEC CODICES

One illustration of this problem is found in the differing identifications of a complex of place signs that includes "Red and White Bundle" and "Mountain That Is Opened/Hill of the Wasp"—places that are plainly and unequivocally depicted in the codices. Place of the "Red and White Bundle" is often shown as a hill or stone or platform, with a distinctive red and white cloth-bound bundle of sticks placed on it. The "Mountain That Is Opened/Hill of the Wasp" place sign is shown as a hill that has two hands reaching into it, pulling it open, and with an insect on its side (figure 6.1; see also Caso 1960). I have identified this qualifier as a bee or a wasp because of the bands of black and yellow on its abdomen (Byland and Pohl 1994), but Jansen has identified it as a fly (1998:109–111). Other place names that are found with it in various codical images include "Place of Reeds" and "Place of the Rain Deity Vessel." The images are clear; it is their geographic identification that is at issue. These places, wherever they are in physical geography, are very important in the early history of the Mixtec people. They figure prominently in the genealogies and in the alliances from the time before the historical event known to codex students as "The War of Heaven" (Rabin 1979). The ruling family of "Mountain That Is Opened/Hill of the Wasp" was destroyed during that conflict, and its daughters were married off to the victors. The site is rarely mentioned again in the long history related in the codices.

FIGURE 6.1. The southern Valley of Nochixtlán, looking north. To the right, "Place of the Red and White Bundle" in the Codex Nuttall (page 83) and the identified archaeological site of Huachino; at the center-left, "Mountain That Is Opened/Hill of the Wasp" in the Codex Nuttall (page 19) and its respective archaeological site. Illustration by John M.D. Pohl and Danny Zborover. Landscape image courtesy of GoogleEarth.

Its defeat was absolute. "Red and White Bundle" persisted for a while, until Lord 8 Deer "Jaguar Claw" destroyed it in the climactic battles surrounding his efforts to create a new dynasty at Tilantongo (Byland and Pohl 1994).

Alfonso Caso (1960) has already noted the place sign of "Xipe Bundle," our "Red and White Bundle," in his analysis of the Codex Bodley, but did not venture a proposal as to its location on the ground. He had little to say about the place, other than to describe its role in the marital alliance structure of the early history of the codices and its subsequent destruction by Lord 8 Deer "Jaguar Claw." He described the place sign of "Hill of the Bee" in the same study and again declined to offer a specific identification of it. Still, he referred to the place as a "metropolis" and described it as "preponderant" in the early years of Mixtec history, clearly implying that it was a large and important community.

So, what is the disagreement? During the 1990s two schools of thought emerged in Mixtec studies. The first hypothesis, proposed by John Pohl and myself during our survey of the southern Valley of Nochixtlán, proposed to identify these places as relatively small communities located somewhere between Tilantongo and Jaltepec (Byland and Pohl 1990, 1994; figure 6.1). The next effort to identify these places came in response to our suggestions. Maarten Jansen and colleagues (Jansen 1998; Jansen and Pérez Jiménez 2005) proposed that these sites were located at or near the major site of Monte Albán in the Valley of Oaxaca. These two competing interpretations lead inevitably to, or perhaps from, two very different views of the political scope of the codices and of the nature of interactions between people and communities in the Mixteca at this critical time. In Jansen's (1998) view, the Mixtec city-states in the Late Classic and Early Postclassic were intimately involved with major centers like Tula, Cholula, Monte Albán, Zaachila, and Chichen Itza. In my view, the Mixtec states were aware of these distant states and interacted with them sparingly, but were much more focused on local political concerns. The reading of the codices either as having pan-Mesoamerican scope or as being local documents recording local political concerns is at stake; in either frame, the importance of these documents and significance to our understanding of Mesoamerican cultures is unquestionable.

These competing interpretations lead us to two essential questions. First, how can one set of "facts" lead two scholarly teams to such different conclusions? And second, can we fairly examine these two identifications and identify the strengths and weaknesses of each of them? At a deeper level, the problem here is to recognize the cognitive processes involved in our respective research programs and to make transparent the pitfalls of reasoning, learning, and discovery that can waylay our quest for knowledge. I propose here to confront each of these questions head on. This, then, is a study about the process of learning, as much as it is about the history of the Mixtec people.

CONFIRMATION BIAS, PREMATURE CLOSURE, AND INADEQUATE SYNTHESIS

To better understand how we have managed to come to different conclusions when faced with the same evidence, I have turned to the literature of cognitive psychology. A subfield within cognitive psychology has emerged in the last several years that is concerned with high pressure decision-making in emergency medicine. Doctors in emergency rooms are routinely faced with unfamiliar patients who present them with very complex cases. The ER physician must rapidly evaluate an unknown patient, assimilate a lot of disparate information while determining what is relevant and what is not, and quickly diagnose the medical problems being experienced by the patient. This must be done accurately so that a treatment plan can be developed that will start the patient on the road to recovery. Errors in any step of the process can be costly in terms of the patient's well-being and long-term prognosis.

Our problems in codical interpretation are not so laden with issues of life and death, but they are in many ways similar. We too must consider a wide range of information about unfamiliar subjects, recognize which parts are relevant to the problem at hand, synthesize that information in the context of what we already know, and come to conclusions about the meaning of the images and the importance of the narrative that they relate. If we make errors the patient will not die, but the costs are real nevertheless. When we are wrong, scholarship may be led down a path that does not reflect the reality of the lives of our subjects. Our mistakes fail to honor the real accomplishments of the Mixtec people who lived so long ago and fail to honor their modern inheritors, the Mixtec people of today.

Doctors studying medical mistakes that happen in emergency rooms have identified a number of cognitive processes that can lead doctors into error (cf. Croskerry 2002; Groopman 2007; Kuhn 2002; Redelmeier and Shafir 1995). We can use their work to examine our own efforts to identify places in the Mixtec codices. In one important study, Pines (2006) examined the role of confirmation bias in medical error. *Confirmation bias* is the mistake that results from coming to a conclusion too early in the examination of the patient and then accentuating confirmatory information and ignoring or discounting contradictory or non-confirmatory information. Pines suggests that confirmation bias is the logical outcome of an effort to avoid cognitive dissonance, which might result from an ongoing effort to assess evidence that seems to disagree with one's early conclusions.

An examination of how one might arrive at an incorrect conclusion through confirmation bias can be instructive. Voytovich et al. (1985) identified three or four mechanisms that could lead to mistakes. If we may generalize from their medical categories, they suggest that confirmation bias errors can result from (1) "wrong synthesis" or "omission," resulting from a lack of adequate foundational knowledge about either the question or the evidence; (2) "premature closure," or failing to look for and discover all of the relevant information before coming to a conclusion; and (3) "inadequate synthesis," or using extraneous evidence that does not actually support the conclusions being reached. Voytovich et al. (1985) recognize that premature closure and the associated anchoring of one's early diagnosis, even in the face of later contradictory information, was by far the most significant of these mechanisms.

I think that these classes of errors are relevant to our discussion here. Both Jansen and I have clearly been victims of confirmation bias and premature closure. This bias has been proposed for my work (Brotherston 1996; Jansen 1998), but it can also be identified in the work of Jansen. Jansen and I have each anchored our interpretations and have been less than willing to fully consider non-confirmatory evidence. We can each correct that shortcoming by consciously adopting a method of analysis that is not dependent on forming an early conclusion, and looking for the supporting evidence. I submit that we should utilize a more scientific method in which we propose a variety of early hypotheses, and then look for evidence to exclude them (Croskerry 2002). In the end we will not be relieved of the responsibility of coming to a conclusion based on inadequate and incomplete data, but at least we will have done so while avoiding glaring cognitive error.

A quick review of the reasons given by each camp for their identifications will be useful in light of the cognitive pitfalls in the processes of discovery and learning raised here. I will review some of the arguments made by Jansen and his colleagues and by myself, and will point out moments when we are each guilty of confirmation bias, either through premature closure or inadequate synthesis. This analysis will also provide a basis for a more intellectually appropriate consideration of the problems at hand: just where did the events of the early sacred history of the Mixtec people take place? What is the appropriate scale of interaction in these documents? This analysis will help us to better understand the political and social context of the historical accounts recorded in the codices and in other pictorial documents.

THE ARGUMENT ABOUT IDENTIFICATION

Jansen's argument for the identification of "Hill of the Wasp" and "Red and White Bundle" in the Mixtec Codices is presented in the context of his identification of place signs associated with Monte Albán and Zaachila in the codices. Jansen's most thorough presentation of the argument is found in his article "Monte Albán y Zaachila en los Codices Mixtecos" (Jansen 1998:67–122). Jansen and Pérez Jiménez (2005) adopt these identifications in their study of the Codex Bodley and expanded the discussion somewhat. My argument is found in the context of the analysis of codical history and archaeological survey from the Tilantongo and Jaltepec regions (figure 6.1). Alternative identifications are best presented in my coauthored book, *In the Realm of 8 Deer* (Byland and Pohl 1994), and in the coauthored article, "The Identification of the 'Xipe Bundle'/'Red and White Bundle' Place Sign in the Mixtec Codices" (Pohl and Byland 1996).

Monte Albán

Jansen makes use of a wide variety of sources in his analysis of the locations of places in the Mixtec codices and other documents produced in the Mixtec pictorial tradition. In a strong rhetorical form he begins with identifications that are widely accepted. He builds a chain of interpretations beginning with the recognition, following Smith (1973) and Whittaker (1980), that the ridge of mountains depicted on the Mapa de Xoxocotlán represents Monte Albán. The images on the Mapa, the glosses in Nahuatl and Mixtec, and the physical shape of the row of hilltops all suggest that the intent of the map makers was to identify Monte Albán. Jansen notes a concordance between the depiction of two men armed with bows and arrows and one with a *macana* on the Mapa de Xoxocotlán, and a passage in the *Relación Geográfica de Teozapotlan* (Zaachila) in which the use of bows and arrows as well as *macanas* is mentioned during a discussion of ancient warfare (Jansen 1998:68). Both of these weapons were used in many parts of Mesoamerica, and their mention in these two documents does not constitute confirmation of the Monte Albán identification on the Mapa de Xoxocotlán image. This may be a case of inadequate synthesis. This is a small criticism, though, because Jansen's analysis is convincing without this extraneous support.

Another example of using extraneous evidence to bolster an argument follows in the discussion of the pictorial elements of the central mountaintop (Jansen 1998:70). It shows a man seated on a throne and encircled by an oval cartouche made of feathers, with a stone doorway above. Jansen mentions the Nahuatl gloss, *teuhtli tepeque*, and reads it as meaning "Hill of the Lord." That is consistent with the pictorial image and is completely reasonable. For support of this reading, Jansen then draws on the Nahuatl and Mixtec *difrasismo* that means "señorio" (*petlatl icpalli* and *yuvui tayu*, respectively, both mean "straw mat, throne" in English). This despite the absence of a *petate*, or straw mat, in the image or the mention of a *petate* in the glosses. This mention does not contribute in any way to the identification or interpretation of the image.

His complex reinterpretation of the Mixtec gloss for this place, on the other hand, is a perfectly appropriate and persuasive piece of work. Where Smith (1973:205) reads the gloss as *yucua niyyo doo ñomana* and translates it as "the hill where was now seated the purified one who is sleepy," Jansen proposes the more satisfactory reading of *yucu ani yya, dzoco nana*, a phrase that means "hill of the palaces of the lords and of the sepulchers" (Jansen 1998:72, my translation); this translation is indeed more consistent with the pictorial image and the Nahuatl gloss.

HILLS OF THE JAGUAR, MOON, REED, AND INSECT

Jansen then goes on to read the names of a series of other places that form parts of Monte Albán, including a "Hill of the Jaguar" that is also known as "Hill of the *Teponoztli* Drum"; a "Hill of the Jewels and of Gold" (which incidentally is interpreted as referring to the knowledge of Colonial-period artists about precious things in tombs at Monte Albán, rather than a remembered or traditional name of the place); an A-O year sign on a hill that is read as "Hill of the Rope," discounting the place sign because of the glosses associated with the hill; a "Hill of the Round Plain," or more metaphorically as "Hill of the Round Quetzal Feather"; and a "Hill of the Moon" or, by adding a missing syllable to the glossed Mixtec word for moon, "Hill of the Reed." In this reading the Mixtec *yoo*, or "moon," becomes the root for *tnuyoo*, or "reed." Note that the syllable *tnu* is not in the gloss at all but can be suggested because a different version of the Mapa shows a reed toponym for this hill. Jansen also finds support for this reading in a Codex Bodley scene, in which a "Place of Reeds" is found positioned in the story of Lady 6 Monkey where the Codex Selden has the "Hill of the Moon." To identify this place as "Reed," Jansen must discount the plain gloss "moon" that is written for the place on the Mapa, and the possibility that the "Place of Reeds" from the Codex Bodley and "Hill of the Moon" from the Codex Selden are different locations but are important to the respective authors of these codices because of their distinct regional points of view (Smith 1983). This alternative may be supported by the observation that the personages sacrificed in the two codices are different as well. It is at least possible to suggest that each author took note of only the places and sacrifices that were important to him and his story. Finally, Jansen lists a series of four other places whose names are glossed but that "do not support special mention" (Jansen 1998:75, my translation). These include, among others, a "Hill of the Insect" that will become important later on. It is interesting that this site, so important in the histories of the codices, is so minimally mentioned on this Mapa de Xoxocotlán.

Cacaxtli Hill

Jansen supports the identification of the "Hill of the Jaguar" part of this complex with a discussion of the Escudo de Armas de Cuilapan (Jansen 1998:76–83). This Colonial-period document shows a hill encircled by two stone walls and labeled with the image of a jaguar. It is connected to a group of three hilltops displayed in sequence, a tree with an eagle bearing a European style crown, a carrying frame (or *cacaxtli*), and a nopal cactus. Though Jansen had elsewhere argued that the "*Cacaxtli* Hill" place represented Cuilapan and that the other place names represented unknown parts of Cuilapan (Jansen 1992), he now persuasively identifies the *Cacaxtli* place sign as Zaachila.

Embedded in this discussion is an analysis of the two flanking images as if they were one. He sees the nopal place as representing the Aztec capital of Tenochtitlán and the crowned eagle as representing a Colonial reinterpretation of the Aztec eagle, though it is sitting on the tree instead of the cactus and does not have a serpent in its beak as it would have in an unambiguous representation of Tenochtitlán. I see this as an example of inadequate synthesis resulting from confirmation bias. The great power represented by the Aztec capital needs to be found here so that the power of Monte Albán, and later of Zaachila, can be compared to, or equated with, that of Tenochtitlán. Why else see two separate images attached to separate hills on either side of the prominent valley of Oaxaca, and concatenate them into one place sign ascribed to a site located some four hundred kilometers away?

A more parsimonious interpretation would be that all four place signs, the jaguar of Monte Albán, the *cacaxtli* of Zaachila, the adjacent nopal, and the adjacent crowned eagle on a tree, represent places in the central Valley of Oaxaca and that the last three of them are at or near Zaachila. Though I have never written about any of these places, I recognize the strength of Jansen's argument that "*Cacaxtli* Hill" is Zaachila and that this "Jaguar Hill" is part of Monte Albán. The effort to identify the other place signs on the Escudo de Armas de Cuilapan as the distant Aztec capital is tenuous at best and, indeed, is extraneous in any case.

Jansen now turns to the story of Lady 6 Monkey, a royal personage from Jaltepec, a community in the Mixteca Alta, and works to connect it to Monte Albán in the Valley of Oaxaca. About this story I have had a lot to say. In part of this well-known story, two men located on places containing a Moon and an Insect threaten Lady 6 Monkey with "flinty words." The men have calendrical names attached to their legs (Lord 6 Lizard and Lord 2 Alligator) and each has what appears to be a personal name attached to his legs ("Bent Hill with a Lock of Hair" and "*Cacaxtli* with a Lock of Hair"). Jansen chooses to interpret the personal names of these two figures in an unusual way: as representing two elements of the place name of Zaachila, their presumed place of origin, and their roles as priests. The priest reading comes from a Nahuatl word for priest, *papahuaque* or 'those with long hair,' and identifies the lock of hair as a symbol of that office even though no similar term is offered in Mixtec (Jansen 1998:86). Jansen then identifies their place signs in the Codex Selden as also representing the "Hill of the Moon" and "Hill of the Insect" found on the Mapa de Xoxocotlán in association with the hills of Monte Albán. Here he uses one identification to support another, and now we see the reason for the discussion of the Escudo de Armas de Cuilapan. There, Zaachila and Monte Albán are found together and so here, too, they must be. On the surface this seems reasonable, as indeed it may be, but it is not demonstrated conclusively.

Jansen argues that a second appearance in the Codex Selden of the concatenated place sign of "Hill of the Moon" and "Hill of the Insect" confirms their identification as representing Monte Albán. In this image on page 8, the two symbols are found together on one hill frame that is further modified with a human bottom and two feet that are all attached to the moon. Jansen correctly recognizes that this image is not the same as a simple pair of feet attached to a hill sign, which would be read as meaning "at the foot of the mountain." His interpretation is that they represent a "seated place," and simultaneously that they represent the position of the legs during birth and so indicate "origin" through original birth (1998:86). The "birth" reading appreciates a woman's posture during birth in the codices, but the "seated place" reading requires the simultaneous reading of the same image as meaning two entirely separate things and ignores the normal seated position of a woman with knees and feet together or with legs crossed. Jansen argues this so that the combined image of the moon, insect, and bottom with feet on a hill can be read metaphorically as "Monte Albán, the established or seated place, the place of origin," and that the two men found there can be priests of Zaachila, an inheritor of the power once seated at Monte Albán.

In another example of confirmation bias through premature closure, Jansen fails to mention that there is a fourth modifier of this place, the two flame symbols atop the moon. These images of flame are read elsewhere as an indicator of the site of Achiutla, *Ñuu Ndecu* or "Burning Town," when coupled with a frieze (Jansen and Pérez Jiménez 2005:45) or when found in other contexts (Byland 2008; Byland and Pohl 1994:169–170). Jansen also does not mention the presence of a hill called today "Hill of the Moon" near the "Hill of the Sun" at the actual site of Achiutla. I would suggest a possible alternative reading of this image as "hill where the moon was born," and that defining this place as part of Monte Albán is a stretch. The possibility that the flames might suggest that the place is actually near Achiutla in the Mixteca Alta is discounted, presumably because it is not consistent with the previously established conclusion. I have not made statements as to the locations of these place signs depicted in the Codex Selden previously.

This seems to me to be a running example of confirmation bias and, more specifically, the cognitive error of premature closure. Jansen seems determined to find the most powerful Classic-period state in Oaxaca in the codices and so reads images that are normally indicating personal names as very unusual statements about social roles and places of origin. He must assume that the bent hill is of necessity a part of the name of Zaachila, an assumption that is clearly not the case, as bent hills are found in many contexts throughout the pictorials. Similarly, the *cacaxtli* appears elsewhere for the Mixteca Alta as a title for lords on the Lienzo de Zacatepec (Smith 1973). Jansen must also assume that his untested identification of the lock of hair as an indication of a priestly role is correct. Only then can he read the concatenated personal names of these two men as "The Great Hill of Zaachila" and identify that in turn as a reference to Monte Albán.

One might look for alternate explanations. The mountain of Monte Albán is not particularly close to Zaachila (thirteen kilometers distant), and a closer candidate for its "great hill" is found in the large batholith under the central mounds of that site. Those mounds are the location of the important Late Postclassic tombs at Zaachila found by Gallegos (1978). The hill, the mounds, and the tombs were clearly important to the Postclassic residents of the site. Why were alternative explanations not explored?

Jansen also neglects the problems presented by the timing of Monte Albán's demise as a center of power in the Valley of Oaxaca. Monte Albán was a very powerful city during the Classic period in the Valley, during MA IIIb/IV. Its regional authority seems to have waned by about 800 CE, the date of the end of the Xoo phase as defined by Lind (1994). The memory of its power was certainly present, but other regional centers wielded actual political control by 1090 CE, like Zaachila, Mitla, Yagul, and Macuilxóchitl. To be convincing, Jansen will have to explain why these centers were not more directly involved in the conflict.

The timing of events and physical distances between places involved in this passage is also apparently discounted. In the Codex Selden, Lady 6 Monkey begins her journey at Jaltepec on the day 9 Serpent of the Year 13 Rabbit (1090 CE). She is insulted at "Hill of the Moon" and "Hill of the Insect" while being carried to her marriage and returns from these places to Chalcatongo to consult with the oracular figure Lady 9 Grass. She then gathers together warriors from two places and returns to the "Moon" and "Insect" places, where she engages and captures the two insulters on the days 3 Grass and 4 Reed, seven and eight days after the beginning of the story. She then returns to Jaltepec where one of them is sacrificed, and then journeys to the temple at "Red and White Bundle" where the other insulter is sacrificed. She receives a new personal name in honor of her military exploits, and on the day 6 Eagle the Lady 6 Monkey is married to Lord 11 Wind, the ruler of "Red and White Bundle." The total elapsed time is just ten or eleven days. In this time frame Jansen would have Lady 6 Monkey travel from Jaltepec to Monte Albán, to Chalcatongo, to two unidentified places, and then back to Monte Albán, back to Jaltepec, and to "Red and White Bundle" (which we will learn he thinks is located just east of Monte Albán [Jansen 1998:88, Jansen and Pérez Jiménez 2005:37]). This is a journey undertaken by a significant group of people of a total distance of well over 330 kilometers of mountainous terrain. In this time several major events had to take place, including a consultation with a powerful oracle, the raising of an army and equipping them for travel and battle, a two-day battle, two ceremonies of ritual human sacrifice, a naming ritual, and a wedding. Jansen obviously understands this sequence of events, but it is discounted in his argument because it would tend to disagree with the foregone conclusion that the Moon, Insect, and "Red and White Bundle" places are at or near Monte Albán. Jansen avoids cognitive dissonance by achieving premature closure.

A different and problematical sequence of events is recounted in the Codex Bodley (pages 36 iii–34 ii). The Bodley story starts on the day 8 Movement of the year 13 Rabbit (1090 CE), when Lord 11 Wind of "Red and White Bundle" sends a messenger with offerings to the parents of Lady 6 Monkey, apparently asking for her hand in marriage. This is two days after the day 6 Eagle, when the marriage is shown in the Codex Selden. Then, on a day that has been lost, Lady 6 Monkey and Lord 11 Wind travel to Chalcatongo to present or receive various gifts to Lady 9 Grass, the oracular priest of that community. After this in the painting sequence—but paradoxically eleven days before it, as given by the calendrical date 10 Death, year 13 Rabbit—Lady 6 Monkey takes a captive for sacrifice when she conquers a "Place of the Reeds, Breasts, and Crossed Legs." Jansen believes this place is interpositional with "Hill of the Moon." This day, 10 Death, is the day after Lady 6 Monkey began her expedition from Jaltepec to her wedding at "Red and White Bundle" in the Codex Selden. The captive here is named Lord 10 Movement and so is not the same as either of the two captives mentioned in the Codex Selden, Lord 6 Lizard and Lord 2 Alligator, who in any case were not captured until the day 4 Reed, or seven days after the capture of Lord 10 Movement. In the Codex Bodley sequence the marriage occurs on the day 11 Deer, one day after the capture and conquest of "Place of Reeds." It is difficult to put these events into an undisputable sequence, but the likelihood that the conquest at "Place of Reeds" and that at "Hill of the Moon and Insect" are two different events cannot be ruled out. Clearly the respective authors of the two books placed them on differing days and put differing sets of people into the action. On the other hand, each of these conquests happened shortly before the wedding day, variously one or two or three days before, and so could represent a sequence of related events. In any case, a third noble captive is indicated and his sacrifice must be added to the list of events in that ten-day period.

"Red and White Bundle"/ "Xipe Bundle"

Jansen next takes up the identification of "Red and White Bundle," the site called "Xipe Bundle" by Caso (Jansen 1998:91–95). He begins this discussion in the first paragraph with the conclusion that this important site is located just east of Monte Albán. This, on the face of it, seems a case of premature closure. The discussion then proceeds to a critique of my proposal with John Pohl (Byland and Pohl 1994) that the site of Huachino, located near Jaltepec and Tilantongo, is the actual location of "Red and White Bundle" (figure 6.1).

Jansen points out at length that the etymology of the name *Huachino* is incorrect (Jansen 1998:91). Priscilla Small, a noted Mixtec linguist, first questioned our interpretation of the place name *Huachino* in 1995 at the second Mixtec Gateway meeting in Las Vegas. Joining her in this critique were Aurora Pérez Jiménez, a native speaker of Chalcatongo Mixtec, and Maarten Jansen, the discussant of this session. I subsequently set the interpretation aside in favor of reporting only what local Jaltepec Mixtec people told me about the name with regard to a legendary *curandero* (Pohl and Byland 1996:16). The question remains, though, whether an interpretation of *Huachino* affects the identification of the "Red and White Bundle" place sign, because that identification depends little on the name and more on its interaction with surrounding places, including Jaltepec, Tilantongo, and Suchixtlán, both in the codices and in the archaeological record.

Accordingly, if the identification of "Red and White Bundle" as the site of Huachino near Jaltepec is correct, and if the "Hill of the Moon" and the "Hill of the Insect" are located near Achiutla in the Mixteca Alta, then the distances traveled during that ten-day sequence are only about 120 kilometers. No single leg of the trip is more than about 30 kilometers, a distance easily covered in a single day, leaving time during the day for a ceremony, a wedding, or a battle.

Another realm of criticism of the proposed identification of Huachino as "Red and White Bundle" is placed in the comparison of the archaeological chronology (cf. Drennan 1983) with the historical chronology derived from the codices (Rabin 2003). Jansen points out that the dates for the Las Flores phase, the Classic period in the Mixteca Alta, range from 300 to 1000 CE and that this is about a hundred years too early for the Lady 6 Monkey story (Jansen 1998:94). He also points out that "Red and White Bundle" appears in the Jaltepec genealogy in the fifteenth century, at about 1450 CE (Codex Selden, p. 16 iv). The critique here is that (1) the ninety-year gap between the end of the Las Flores phase and the events in the Lady 6 Monkey story is inexplicably long, and (2) the continued existence of "Red and White Bundle" as a powerful kingdom 350 years later means that Lord 8 Deer could not have destroyed it in 1102 CE.

The first of these arguments is based on an ethnohistorian having too much confidence in the dates published by archaeologists for the end of the Classic and the beginning of the Postclassic in the Mixteca Alta. The date of 1000 CE is often used because it rests neatly between earlier dates for the Las Flores phase and later dates for the Natividad phase. There are no good published dates for the Classic-Postclassic transition in the Mixteca Alta. Furthermore, the transition from one ceramic phase to another is always a fluid process; some ceramic types will persist while others will change. The chronological border is an intellectual construct and should not be taken to represent a moment of sudden cultural change. That is why an archaeological chronology based on ceramics is referred to as being "relative" in date. The destruction of a city can be a sudden event, or it can happen gradually. We know from the ceramics that the site of Huachino was largely abandoned at the end of the Classic Las Flores phase and that only a small portion of the site was inhabited by the Late Postclassic part of the Natividad phase. The evidence indicates continued occupation but by a much reduced population under the direction of a noble family of *toho*, or secondary, rank.

The appearance of "Red and White Bundle" in the genealogy at 1450 CE is similarly misconstrued. This community was clearly very important in the eleventh century, and the codices are unambiguous about its fate in the early twelfth century.

Lord 8 Deer "Jaguar Claw" destroyed the town and executed its rulers and many of their family members. The town disappeared from genealogical reckoning for about 350 years, as it was not an important kingdom during that time. The fact that the parents of one woman came from a site called "Red and White Bundle" after so long a time does not mean that it had been continuously occupied and an important town for all that time (cf. Hamann 2002).

So, where does Jansen think that "Xipe Bundle," the site we know as "Red and White Bundle," is to be found? He suggests that it must be located at the foot of Monte Albán near the town of Xoxocotlán, another part of the site of Monte Albán near the "Hill of the Moon" and the "Hill of the Insect." He carefully says that this is not a conclusive identification, in part because no specific site is proposed. I would point out that the Xipe Bundle does not appear on the Mapa de Xoxocotlán, though many other ancient places do.

This potential identification raises several contextual questions. If the sites of "Red and White Bundle," "Hill of the Moon," and "Hill of the Insect" are all found on, or near to, Monte Albán, then they collectively represent heirs to the power of that great city. They share that status with Zaachila, the "*Cacaxtli* Place." We are led to think of them as near one another physically, and with a shared political and familial heritage. How can we account for a Jaltepec princess's ability to conquer the "Moon" and "Insect" places and take their Zaachila connected leaders off to be sacrificed? Why would she sacrifice the first of them back at her hometown in the Mixteca Alta and then drag the second of them back down to the valley to sacrifice at "Red and White Bundle"? Why did they wait for her at these places when she went back up to the Mixteca Alta to consult with Lady 9 Grass at Chalcatongo? Wouldn't they have raised an army to protect themselves? Wouldn't their natural allies have been "*Cacaxtli*," or Zaachila, and "Red and White Bundle"? These political issues must be reconciled with the proposed location of "Red and White Bundle" before it can be seriously considered. Not considering them represents another case of confirmation bias.

"Mountain That Is Opened/Hill of the Wasp"

The place sign that we know as "Mountain That Is Opened/Hill of the Wasp," and the complex of associated names including "Enclosure," "Corn Plants or Reeds," and "Rain Deity Vessel," is the next main issue in this discussion. Jansen (1998) identifies this group of names as meaning Monte Albán. He sees the "Hill of the Insect" from the Mapa de Xoxocotlán as the same as the insect in this place name, and the corn plants or reeds here as isomorphic with the "Hill of the Moon (or Reeds)" from the Mapa. He reads the hands opening the hill as phonetically meaning *Yucu Cahnu* or "Large Mountain," and thus not as a separate place name that would distinguish this "Hill of the Insect" from others with the same basic name. He interprets the crenellations and the vessel with the rain deity face as descriptive names that refer to the foundations of buildings and to the funerary urns with images of *Cocijo* (the Zapotec rain deity) that are so characteristic of Monte Albán (Jansen 1998:111–112).

Ultimately, Jansen places all the place names from the scene on page 19 of the Nuttall Codex at Monte Albán. This includes the "Bent Hill," the "Rocky Cave with the *Yahui*," and the "White Hill of Flints." All must be part of the Valley of Oaxaca site because all are part of the same large mountain frame. This raises new questions about confirmation bias. The "Hill of Flints" and the *Yahui* flying into the cave were observed on a carved stone found at "Mogote del Cacique," a site located in Tilantongo and known locally as the "Hill of Flints," and which was reported by Jansen and Winter (1980). This carved stone was found about one kilometer from the site that Pohl and I have suggested is the actual location of "Mountain That Is Opened/Hill of the Wasp" (figure 6.1). Still, this is described by Jansen as a simple coincidence in another instance of discounting contradictory information.

Byland and Pohl Proposals

The Byland and Pohl hypothesis is quite different. We have proposed that "Red and White Bundle" is located at the site of Huachino near Jaltepec, a prominent Las Flores–period ceremonial center. We have proposed that the site of "Mountain That Is Opened/Hill of the Wasp" is located on the ridge between Jaltepec and Tilantongo (figure 6.1). We have suggested that each of these sites shows significant connections with the powers in the Valley of Oaxaca during the Late Classic Las Flores phase, around 1000 to 1100 CE and before. "Hill of the Wasp" has a mound group that follows the Temple-Patio-Adoratorio architectural plan found most prominently at Monte Albán, but also at various other Late Classic sites in the Valley of Oaxaca. The site of Huachino is heavily populated with Xoo phase (MA IIIb/IV) ceramics and has a two-chambered temple, again an architectural form known from the Valley of Oaxaca and found at Monte Albán, among other valley sites. At that time the powerful centers in the valley were Zaachila, Mitla, Macuilxóchitl, Jalieza, and others.

We have tried to link these place signs with many others that are widely seen as being in the southern Nochixtlán Valley in the Mixteca Alta. These sites include Jaltepec or *Añute/Vehe Ñuhu* (the "Place of Sand/House of the Ñuhu"), Tilantongo or *Ñuu Tnoo/Huahi Andehui* ("Black Town/Temple of Heaven"), and Suchixtlán or *Chiyo Yuhu* ("Platform of White Flowers"). In so doing it is possible that I have not sufficiently considered alternative identifications of the surrounding sites, and I may have been guilty of confirmation bias through premature closure. However, all efforts were made to correct for this bias by conducting a full-coverage survey of the southern end of the Nochixtlán Valley, with the intent to include all possible candidates for my identifications, given the sphere of social and political interaction that could be demonstrated by previous studies of place signs in the codices, including those of Jansen.

These identifications are built within the context of social interactions depicted in the Mixtec historical codices and with the aid of other pictorial artifacts such as the Nochixtlán Vase. I considered the marital alliances arranged by Lord 8 Wind of Suchixtlán between Tilantongo and Jaltepec; all three of these towns are within about fifteen kilometers of each other. When Lady 6 Monkey marries Lord 11 Wind from "Red and White Bundle" instead of the heir of Tilantongo, she breaks the alliance. I believe that the interloping site is also in the same ambit.

Conclusion

Jansen points out that "it is a methodological imperative that one must identify clusters or coherent conjunctions of toponyms, but one must always take into account that place names may be common and may be repeated in the region so that one can find what one wants when looking for it. We must add another criterion: the conjunction of toponyms must not only be coherent, it must also be *significant*" (Jansen 1998:93; my translation). Of course I agree with that assessment. I would only note that significance is not measured properly by concordance with one's own preconceived conclusions. Jansen suggests that we need to look for a middle ground between vast claims of pan-Mesoamerican scope and minute parochialism (Jansen 1998:95). Indeed, I agree with that assessment as well, though I would find the middle ground at a different place than he does. If I have been guilty of confirmation bias and premature closure, we must also recognize the same shortcoming in Jansen's work. If I found too limited a scope in the political reach of the Mixtec lords, Jansen seems determined to see too grand a scope for those same personages. Surely the middle ground must be found. I conclude that the authors of the codices and their royal patrons were aware of distant powers in Mesoamerica. They certainly interacted with them with some frequency, while building alliances by marrying brides from other ethnic groups and from distant capital towns. Nevertheless, it seems to me that most of the action in the codices is best understood as local, taking place in communities of approximately equal size and power.

NOTE

1. Editors' note: a version of this article was read by Bruce Byland in the session "Integrating Archaeology and History in Oaxaca," 72nd Annual Meeting of the Society for American Archaeology, Austin, Texas. The editors wish to thank Geoffrey McCafferty, who provided the original manuscript given to him by Byland at the SAA session; John M.D. Pohl, who helped prepare the manuscript for publication; and Cara Tennenbaum, who kindly gave permission to publish it here.

REFERENCES

Brotherston, Gordon. 1996. "Book Review of 'In the Realm of 8 Deer: The Archaeology of the Mixtec Codices.'" *Latin American Indian Literatures Journal* 12 (1):67–72.

Byland, Bruce. 2008. "Tree Birth, the Solar Oracle, and Achiutla: Mixtec Sacred History and the Classic to Postclassic Transition." In *After Monte Albán: Transformation and Negotiation in Oaxaca, Mexico*, ed. Jeffrey Blomster, 331–364. Boulder: University of Colorado Press.

Byland, Bruce, and John M.D. Pohl. 1990. "Alianza y Conflicto de los Estados Mixtecos: El Caso Tilantongo." In *Lecturas Históricas del Estado de Oaxaca*, vol. 1., ed. Marcus Winter, 379–389. Oaxaca, Mexico: INAH/Gobierno del Estado de Oaxaca.

Byland, Bruce, and John M.D. Pohl. 1994. *In the Realm of 8 Deer: The Archaeology of the Mixtec Codices*. Norman: University of Oklahoma Press.

Caso, Alfonso. 1960. *Interpretación del Códice Bodley 2858*. Mexico: Sociedad Mexicana de Antropología.

Croskerry, Pat. 2002. "Achieving Quality in Clinical Decision Making: Cognitive Strategies and Detection of Bias." *Academic Emergency Medicine* 9 (11):1184–1204. http://dx.doi.org/10.1111/j.1553-2712.2002.tb01574.x.

Drennan, Robert. 1983. "Appendix: Radiocarbon Dates from Oaxaca." In *The Cloud People: Divergent Evolution of the Zapotec and Mixtec Civilizations*, ed. Kent V. Flannery and Joyce Marcus, 363–370. New York: Academic Press.

Gallegos, R. Roberto. 1978. *El Señor 9 Flor en Zaachila*. Mexico City: Universidad Nacional Autónoma de Mexico.

Groopman, Jerome. 2007. *How Doctors Think*. New York: Houghton Mifflin.

Hamann, Byron. 2002. "The Social Life of Pre-Sunrise Things: Indigenous Mesoamerican Archaeology." *Current Anthropology* 43 (3):351–382. http://dx.doi.org/10.1086/339526.

Jansen, Maarten. 1992. "Mixtec Pictography: Conventions and Contents." In *Supplement to the Handbook of Middle American Indians: Epigraphy*, ed. Victoria R. Bricker, 20–33. Austin: University of Texas Press.

Jansen, Maarten. 1998. "Monte Albán y Zaachila en los Códices Mixtecos." In *The Shadow of Monte Albán: Politics and Historiography in Postclassic Oaxaca, Mexico*, ed. Maarten Jansen, Peter Kröfges, and Michel Oudijk, 67–122. Leiden: Research School CNWS.

Jansen, Maarten, and Gabina Aurora Pérez Jiménez. 2005. *Codex Bodley: Painted Chronicle from the Mixtec Highland, Mexico*. Oxford: Bodleian Library.

Jansen, Maarten, and Marcus Winter. 1980. "Un Relieve de Tilantongo, Oaxaca, del año 13 Búho." *Antropología e Historia, Época* III (30):3–19.

Kuhn, Gloria. 2002. "Diagnostic Errors." *Academic Emergency Medicine* 9 (7):740–750. http://dx.doi.org/10.1111/j.1553-2712.2002.tb02155.x.

Lind, Michael. 1994. "Monte Albán y el Valle de Oaxaca Durante la Fase Xoo." In *Monte Albán: Estudios Recientes*, ed. Marcus Winter, 99–111. Oaxaca, Mexico: Proyecto Especial Monte Albán 1992–1994, Contribución no. 2. Centro INAH Oaxaca.

Pines, Jesse M. 2006. "Profiles in Patient Safety: Confirmation Bias in Emergency Medicine." *Academic Emergency Medicine* 13 (1):90–94. http://dx.doi.org/10.1197/j.aem .2005.07.028.

Pohl, John M.D., and Bruce Byland. 1996. "The Identification of the 'Xipe Bundle'/'Red and White Bundle' Place Sign in the Mixtec Codices." *Journal of Latin American Lore* 19 (1):3–29.

Rabin, Emily. 1979. "The War of Heaven in Codices Zouche-Nuttall and Bodley Preliminary Study." In *42nd International Congress of Americanists*, Paris 1976, 7:171–182.

Rabin, Emily. 2003. "Toward a Unified Chronology of the Historical Codices and Pictorial Manuscripts of the Mixteca Alta, Costa and Baja: An Overview." In *Homenaje a John Paddock*, ed. Patricia Plunket, 100–136. Puebla: Universidad de las Américas.

Redelmeier, Donald, and Eldar Shafir. 1995. "Medical Decision Making in Situations That Offer Multiple Alternatives." *Journal of the American Medical Association* 273 (4):302–305. http://dx.doi.org/10.1001/jama.1995.03520280048038.

Smith, Mary Elizabeth. 1973. *Picture Writing from Ancient Southern Mexico: Mixtec Place Signs and Maps*. Norman: University of Oklahoma Press.

Smith, Mary Elizabeth. 1983. "Regional Points of View in the Mixtec Codices." In *The Cloud People*, ed. Kent Flannery and Joyce Marcus, 260–266. New York: Academic Press.

Voytovich, Anthony, Robert Rippey, and Anthony Suffredini. 1985. "Premature Conclusions in Diagnostic Reasoning." *Journal of Medical Education* 60:302–307.

Whittaker, Gordon. 1980. "The Hieroglyphics of Monte Albán." Unpublished PhD diss., Yale University.

7

Mixteca-Puebla Polychromes and the Codices

Michael D. Lind

MIXTECA-PUEBLA POLYCHROMES

At the time of the Spanish conquest, at least four different types of polychrome pottery were being produced and used in Central Mesoamerica, from the Valley of Mexico to the Valley of Oaxaca (figure 7.1). Collectively these polychromes are referred to as *Mixteca-Puebla polychrome*, and they include Cholula polychrome, Mixteca polychrome, Acatlán polychrome, and Chinantla polychrome (Lind 1967; Moser 1969). There are actually eight types of Cholula polychrome that occur during different phases or time periods at Cholula, beginning in 900 CE and ending around 1650 CE (table 7.1). The polychromes that date between 900 and 1150 CE include Marta, Estela, and Cristina. Those that date between 1150 and 1350 CE include Albina and Silvia (Lind 1994:81).

When archaeologists speak of Cholula polychrome, they are generally referring to Catalina and Nila polychromes, which date from 1350 to 1550 CE and were still being produced around the time of the Spanish conquest. Nila polychrome is sometimes referred to as the "poor man's" polychrome because of the simplicity of its decoration and the frequency of its occurrence in association with households of commoners. Catalina is Cholula's elite polychrome (figure 7.2). It manifests very elaborate decorations, was a relatively scarce commodity, and occurs in association with elite households. Polychrome in the Cholula Catalina style (not necessarily all of which was made in Cholula, but which follows the ceramic canons of Cholula) is found distributed throughout the Puebla-Tlaxcala Valley, the Tepeaca region, and

DOI: 10.5876/9781607323297.c007

FIGURE 7.1. The distribution of Mixteca-Puebla polychromes.

the Valley of Mexico. It is primarily associated with Nahua speakers. The Spanish conqueror Bernal Díaz del Castillo (1962:155) remarked upon the beauty of this polychrome and stated that the Aztec emperor Moctezuma dined from polychrome serving dishes produced in Cholula.

To date, it has been possible to identify two different types of Mixteca polychrome that were made at different time periods, one before and one after the Spanish conquest (Lind 1987:14). When archaeologists speak of Mixteca polychrome, they are usually referring to Pilitas polychrome, which was being produced before the Spanish conquest and dates between 1350 and 1550 CE (figure 7.3). Mixteca polychrome of the Pilitas type (not all of which was produced in the Mixteca, but which follows the ceramic canons of the Mixteca) is found distributed throughout the southern part of the Mixteca Baja beginning at Huajuapan de León and extending

TABLE 7.1 Chronological chart of Mixteca-Puebla polychromes

Absolute Dates(CE)	Cholula	Mixteca / Valley of Oaxaca	Acatlán	Chinantla
		Ceramic phases and Diagnostic Polychrome types		
1550–1650	Convento phase[1] Iglesia Polychrome	Convento phase[2] Iglesia Polychrome	Colonial?	Convento phase[3] Iglesia Polychrome
1350–1550	Mártir phase[4] Catalina / Nila Polychromes	Natividad / Chila phases[5] Pilitas Polychrome	Late Postclassic[6] Acatlán Polychrome	Late Postclassic Chinantla Polychrome
1150–1350	Tecama phase[7] Albina / Silvia Polychromes	Natividad / Chila phases?	Middle Postclassic?	Middle Postclassic?
900–1150	Aquiáhuac phase[8] Marta Polychrome Estela Polychrome Cristina Polychrome	Natividad / Liobaa phases?	Early Postclassic?	Early Postclassic?

 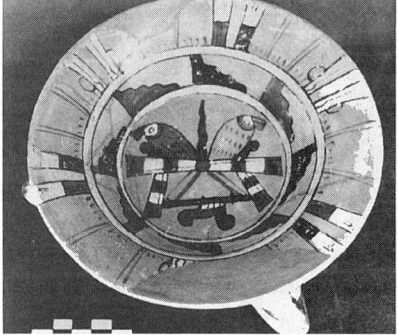

FIGURE 7.2. Cholula Mártir-phase polychrome: Catalina tripod bowls. (MCC; photo courtesy of Gilda Hernández; CRP)[9]

throughout the Mixteca Alta, Cuicatlán Cañada, Mixteca de la Costa, and Valley of Oaxaca. Mixteca polychrome is primarily, but not exclusively, associated with Mixtec speakers.

Acatlán and Chinantla polychromes are easily distinguished from one another and from the Cholula and Mixteca polychromes and will not concern us further here. However, the Cholula Catalina and Mixteca Pilitas polychromes, which are the focus of this study and which are the polychromes archaeologists generally

FIGURE 7.3. Mixteca Pilitas polychrome: (left) tripod bowl and (right) tripod *olla.* (CRO; MNAM; photos by Chris Moser)

think of as Mixteca-Puebla, are very similar, at least superficially. Both have a shiny orange painted ground that was placed over a white painted undercoating. Design motifs were executed on this ground in red, black, and white, with additional colors occurring less frequently. They share a large number of design motifs, including those that most frequently decorate them: feathers, grecas, flowers, cloud or smoke motifs, and stylized bird or serpent heads (Lind 1994:Table 7.4).

Because of their similarity, Cholula Catalina and Mixteca Pilitas polychromes have been referred to indiscriminately as "Mixtec" or "Cholula" polychrome. The literature is full of careless references and mislabeling of illustrations as "Cholula" or "Mixtec" polychrome. However, a careful comparison of vessel shapes, supports, and design motifs provides for a clear distinction between them, although it does take some expertise to distinguish them (Lind 1994:79–99). One factor that has exacerbated the problem of distinguishing between Mixteca and Cholula polychromes is that after the Spanish conquest, a Colonial version of Cholula polychrome was distributed throughout the Mixteca, Valley of Oaxaca, and even the Chinantla. This Colonial type is called Iglesia polychrome, and it is clearly derived from Cholula Catalina polychrome.

It should be noted that the prehispanic ceramic tradition continued on well beyond the Conquest. The first types to dramatically change were decorated wares, such as the polychromes, and ritual wares, such as incense burners. However, even Spanish priests were unable to change these types immediately, and it probably took them at least a generation (until about 1550 CE) to eradicate the religious symbols on the polychromes and eliminate ritual wares such as incense burners (Lind 1987).

FIGURE 7.4. Mixteca polychrome tripod *olla*. (MNAM)

Even then "sanitized" polychromes, like Iglesia polychrome, continued to be produced well into the seventeenth century.

INTERPRETING POLYCHROME POTTERY

What do we really know about the Cholula and Mixteca polychromes? Many people have probably seen illustrations of the polychrome vessel in figure 7.4 or of other vessels with similar decoration. It occupies its own case in the Museo Nacional de Antropología in Mexico City. It is decorated with codex-like figures that have been discussed by Seler (1993) and more recently by Byland and Pohl (1994:77–80). But what can an archaeologist tell about it? Like any curious person, archaeologists are interested in knowing: (1) What is it? (2) Where does it come from? (3) How old is it? and (4) What was it used for?

If an archaeologist is asked, "what is it?" chances are he or she will describe it. Archaeologists use a series of terms to describe pottery. A maxim of archaeology seems to be, "If you can't explain it, describe it." This vessel would be described as a tripod *olla* (jar) or, more properly, *olla* with a globular body and cylindrical neck with polychrome decoration and tripod supports.

If an archaeologist is asked, "where does it come from?" he or she would probably say that it is a vessel shape characteristic of the Mixteca Pilitas polychrome and probably comes from the Mixteca or the Valley of Oaxaca. The tripod *olla* vessel shape does not occur in Cholula Catalina polychrome. This particular tripod *olla*, in fact, is said to come from the Mixteca Alta. It was purportedly found in

Nochixtlán's Pueblo Viejo and was acquired by the Museo Nacional from avid collector Dr. Fernando Sologuren around 1905 (Paddock 1994:101–109).

If an archaeologist is asked, "how old is it?" he or she would probably say that vessels of the Pilitas type have been dated between 1350 and 1550 CE in the Mixteca. There is only one radiocarbon date associated with Pilitas polychrome from the Mixteca. While working with Ron Spores (1972) on the Nochixtlán Valley Project in 1970, I obtained an uncalibrated radiocarbon date of 1340 ± 90 CE in association with Pilitas polychrome at Yucuita in the Nochixtlán Valley. This does not mean that Pilitas polychrome was not being made before 1340, it just means that this is the oldest date we have at present. The date of 1550 comes from an archaeomagnetic date that Dan Wolfman took for me at Chachoapan in the Nochixtlán Valley. Pilitas polychrome was found mixed with Early Colonial remains at Chachoapan, which were dated to this time. Around 1550 Pilitas polychrome ceased to be produced and the "new" Colonial Iglesia polychrome appeared in the Mixteca. Therefore, this tripod *olla* probably dates between 1350 and 1550. At present we cannot be more specific, and we will probably never have a more precise date on this particular tripod *olla* because it was removed from any datable context before Sologuren purchased it for his collection.

If an archaeologist is asked, "what was it used for?" the response will likely be vague. This particular tripod *olla* was supposedly found in a "tomb" in Nochixtlán's Pueblo Viejo. Therefore, the archaeologist would probably state that it was a "burial offering," which is hardly a satisfactory response. It leaves one thinking that Mixteca polychromes were made for "burial offerings." For years archaeologists have avoided talking about vessel function because this information is hard to obtain. The primary indicators of a vessel's function are the vessel's shape and the context in which it is found.

Archaeologists working with Mixteca-Puebla polychromes are fortunate because they have access to the codices—native histories and ritual manuscripts prepared by the people who made and used the polychrome pottery. By studying the vessels depicted in the codices, we can observe their function. Of course, not all vessel shapes and probably not all the functions of a given vessel are depicted. However, the codices give us an insight into vessel function we would not otherwise have.

And it is to the function of Mixteca and Cholula polychromes that I will now turn. The focus is on Mixteca Pilitas and Cholula Catalina polychromes which were being produced and used in their respective regions at the same time, that is, between 1350 and 1550, which is also the time period during which the extant codices were produced. These are the polychromes the Spaniards observed and commented upon when they arrived in Mesoamerica. I will refer to the polychromes as Cholula and Mixteca polychromes with the understanding that they are of the

Catalina and Pilitas types, respectively. Space will not permit me to go into detail, so I will basically point out some of the salient differences between them, beginning with the Mixteca polychrome.

MIXTECA PILITAS POLYCHROME

Tripod *ollas* of the type we have been discussing are the most frequent vessel shape in Mixteca polychrome. In a sample of 135 complete Mixteca polychrome vessels from excavations and museum collections, tripod *ollas* accounted for 37 percent of all vessel shapes (Lind 1994:table 7.2). They occur in two varieties. The more frequent variety has a globular body and cylindrical neck and the less frequent variety has a simple cylindrical vase-like shape (figure 7.5). These two shape variants occur both in the codices (such as the Codex Nuttall) and the archaeological record (figure 7.6).

From her studies of the codices, Mary Elizabeth Smith (1973:31) has shown that these tripod *ollas* appear in royal wedding ceremonies where the bride presents the groom with a tripod *olla* filled with chocolate drink (figure 7.6, left). Furthermore, she has shown that this is an integral part of the marriage ceremony in Mixtec culture. Fray Antonio de los Reyes (1976), a Spanish priest who lived and worked in the Mixteca in the sixteenth century and compiled a Mixtec-Spanish dictionary, states that one phrase in Mixtec for royal marriage is *nisiñe saha ya*, which means "a royal vessel is placed before the nobleman." This idiom is somewhat analogous to our phrase "he placed a ring on her finger." Smith (1973:31) believes that the vessel of chocolate may represent or symbolize the bride's dowry because Reyes uses the Mixtec word for chocolate, *dzehua*, in a phrase he translates as meaning "royal dowry." This gives us a good understanding of at least one of the functions of these tripod *ollas* in Mixtec culture and helps explain why they are the most frequent vessel shape. Apart from tripod *ollas*, tripod bowls are also depicted in Mixtec marriage scenes (figure 7.7). They are shown filled with chocolate in the Codex Nuttall (1992; Anders, Jansen, and Pérez Jiménez 1992:97). These tripod bowls are the second most frequent Mixteca polychrome vessel shape found archaeologically and account for 33 percent of all Mixteca polychrome vessel shapes (Lind 1994:Table 7.2).

Apart from the wedding ceremonies, I suspect that the tripod *ollas* and most tripod bowls functioned as drinking vessels in other contexts. In a study of the Codex Vindobonensis, Jill Furst (1978:201–203) has discussed the Mixtec *pulque* ritual. On page 25 of the codex, an old priest named 2 Dog is shown ordering the creation of *pulque* or perhaps teaching its preparation at Apoala. A jar of *pulque* is depicted with a human head protruding from it and a serpent wrapped around its

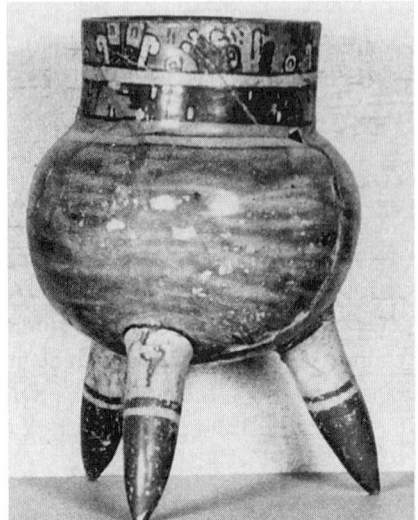

FIGURE 7.5. Mixteca polychrome (left) necked and (right) cylindrical tripod *ollas*. (MNAM; photos by Chris Moser)

FIGURE 7.6. (Left) Necked tripod olla (pages 27–28) and (right) cylindrical tripod *olla* (page 31) in the Codex Nuttall. (Illustrations by John M.D. Pohl)

base. Above are two females (2 Flower and 3 Alligator), the latter with a skeletal jaw associated with earth/fertility deities and a lunar nose ornament associated with *pulque*, serving *pulque* to 2 Dog and 9 Wind. Although the vessels depicted in the Codex Vindobonensis (1992) are hemispherical bowls (which are frequent non-polychrome vessel shapes in the Mixteca), many tripod *ollas* and tripod bowls were possibly used in the Mixtec *pulque* ritual. In the Codex Laud, a tripod *olla* filled with *pulque* occurs in association with Mayauel (3 Alligator?), the goddess of *pulque* (Anders and Jansen 1994:243).

FIGURE 7.7. (Left) Mixteca polychrome tripod bowl (MFM; photo by Chris Moser) and (right) a tripod bowl in the Codex Nuttall (page 5). (Illustration by John M.D. Pohl.)

Although 2 Dog and 9 Wind began the *pulque* ritual, the Codex Vindobonensis (Furst 1978:241–243) places the ritual under the patronage of Lord 7 Flower, who is a kind of Bacchus of *pulque* and whose Nahua counterpart is Xochipilli. An effigy *olla* from a tomb in Zaachila portrays the head of Lord 7 Flower (figure 7.8). The neck of this vessel is decorated with special flowers associated with *pulque*. Interestingly, these special flowers are not found on the Catalina polychrome from Cholula. Another tripod *olla* from Yagul has a flowing motif ending in a flower from which a human head emerges. Paddock (1966:Plate 31) identified this as Mixcóatl, the cloud serpent, but I think it relates to flowing *pulque* personified as Lord 7 Flower. In the Codex Laud, Xochipilli (Lord 7 Flower) is shown with a tripod *olla* filled with *pulque* (Anders and Jansen 1994:235).

A number of pitchers have U-shaped or omega-like moon symbols on them that relate to *pulque* (figure 7.9), and others have cacao beans that, of course, relate to chocolate. Of interest here is the fact that no polychrome pitchers occur at Cholula. However, polychrome pitchers are the third most frequent vessel shape in Mixteca polychrome and account for 11 percent of all vessel shapes (Lind 1994:Table 7.2). Many tripod *ollas*, tripod bowls, and pitchers with motifs relating to *pulque*, then, were probably used in the *pulque* ritual.

Taken together, tripod *ollas*, tripod bowls, and pitchers account for over 80 percent of all Mixteca polychrome vessel shapes. Because we know from the codices that tripod *ollas* and most tripod bowls were vessels from which chocolate and/or *pulque* were drunk, and because pitchers are fine dispensers for chocolate or *pulque*, we can say that over 80 percent of Mixteca polychrome vessels (*ollas*, bowls, and pitchers) were dedicated to the imbibing of chocolate or *pulque*—a tippling trinity, as it were. We know these vessels functioned as part of the Mixtec wedding ceremony. They probably also functioned in the *pulque* ritual. However, I also suspect

FIGURE 7.8. Mixteca polychrome effigy *olla* portraying Lord 7 Flower, patron of *pulque*. (MNAM; photo courtesy of John Paddock)

FIGURE 7.9. Mixteca polychrome pitcher. (MNAM; photo by Chris Moser)

FIGURE 7.10. (Left) Mixteca polychrome ladle censer (MFM; photo courtesy of Chris Moser) and (right) similar ladle censer in the Codex Borgia (page 67). (Illustration by John M.D. Pohl)

that the tripod *ollas* and most tripod bowls functioned as elaborate drinking vessels among the Mixtec, like fancy German beer steins. Every household in our excavations in the Nochixtlán Valley, including those of common people, had at least one or two polychrome tripod *ollas* (Lind 1987:90–93).

If over 80 percent of Mixteca polychrome vessels were related to drinking chocolate or *pulque*, what were the other 20 percent used for? Many were used as ritual incense burners, which are commonly found as elite household items. These include censer bowls, which were probably placed on household altars, and ladle censers, carried in public rituals like the one shown in the Codex Borgia (1963) (figure 7.10).

The polychrome effigy in figure 7.11 is in the form of a life-size human skull with a round hole in the top. The example depicted comes from the Templo Mayor of Tenochtitlán (Seler 1992:III, 184–185, figure 104). None of these effigies has yet been reported from the Mixteca, but effigy vessels similar to these do occur in Cholula. A problem with this is that we know the Aztecs placed offerings in the Templo Mayor from conquered regions (Matos Moctezuma 1987:37). Therefore, although possible, it is unlikely that this polychrome effigy skull is from Cholula because Cholula was never conquered by the Aztecs and never paid them tribute (Davies 1968; Hassig 1988:169–170; 263; Rojas 1927:160). The question remains, "what is it?"

In the Codex Vindobonensis (1992), known by its content to have come from the Mixteca, a skull like this is shown as a musical instrument used in the Mixtec hallucinogenic mushroom ceremony (figure 7.11). The Mixtec culture hero, Lord 9 Wind, is shown playing a bone rasp atop the skull, which functions as a resonator (Furst 1978:205). Polychrome effigy skulls, then, may occur in the Mixteca Pilitas polychrome and do occur in Cholula Catalina polychrome, to which we now turn.

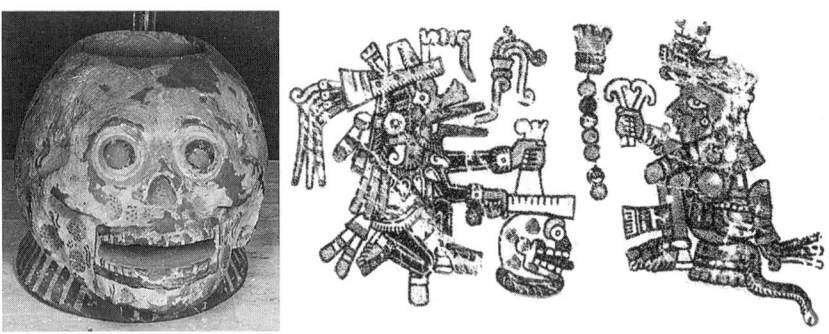

FIGURE 7.11. (Left) Polychrome effigy skull (MNAM; photo by Chris Moser) and (right) effigy skull resonator in the Codex Vindobonensis (page 24). (Illustration by John M.D. Pohl)

CHOLULA CATALINA POLYCHROME

Within Cholula Catalina polychrome, hemispherical bowls are the most frequent, accounting for 30 percent of all vessel shapes. Interestingly, no polychrome hemispherical bowls have been reported among the Mixteca Pilitas polychrome vessel shapes. Goblets are the second most frequent Cholula polychrome vessel shape, accounting for 17 percent of vessels (figure 7.12). Goblets are very uncommon vessel shapes in Mixteca polychrome. Only four examples (about 3%) are known and all come from a single tomb at Zaachila in the Valley of Oaxaca. Taken together, hemispherical bowls and goblets account for nearly half (47%) of all Cholula polychrome vessel shapes, but are either absent or exceedingly uncommon as Mixteca polychrome vessel shapes. What were all these hemispherical bowls and goblets used for by the Nahuas of Cholula? For the answer we can turn to the codices.

The Codex Borgia (1963) depicts both hemispherical bowls and goblets as drinking vessels for chocolate or *pulque* (figure 7.13). It seems likely, then, that while the Mixtec preferred drinking their chocolate and *pulque* from tripod *ollas* and tripod bowls, the Nahua of Cholula preferred hemispherical bowls and goblets as their drinking vessels. But no evidence exists that the hemispherical bowls and goblets functioned in Nahua marriage ceremonies in the manner in which tripod *ollas* and tripod bowls functioned in the Mixtec marriage ceremony. Nahua marriage ceremonies involved tying one end of the bride's blouse (*huipil*) to one end of the groom's cape (*tilmatl*), literally "tying the knot" (Vaillant 1950:118).

However, there is evidence that the hemispherical bowls and goblets functioned in ritualized *pulque* drinking at Cholula, where we meet an old friend. The only deity in human form portrayed on Catalina polychrome from Cholula is Xochipilli, the counterpart of Lord 7 Flower of the Mixteca, the patron deity of ritualized

FIGURE 7.12. (Left) Cholula polychrome hemispherical bowl and (right) goblet. (CRO; photos courtesy of Gilda Hernández)

FIGURE 7.13. Hemispherical bowls on (left) page 4 and (right) page 5 of the Codex Borgia. (Illustrations by John M.D. Pohl)

pulque drinking, whom we have seen portrayed in effigy in Mixteca polychromes. Xochipilli is only depicted on goblets and hemispherical bowls and has not been found portrayed on any other Cholula polychrome vessel shapes. However, depictions of deities in human form are very rare on Cholula polychrome and few hemispherical bowls or goblets contain depictions of Xochipilli. In the Codex Borgia (1963), Xochipilli is clearly shown with a goblet of *pulque* at his side. For archaeologists this is most interesting because it shows a case of how different vessel shapes may perform essentially the same function in different regions. Just as every excavated Mixteca household had its fancy polychrome tripod *olla* and tripod bowl, every household in our excavations at Cholula, including those of commoners, had its fancy drinking goblet and hemispherical bowl.

Tripod bowls, the third most frequent Cholula polychrome vessel shape (14%), present us with a case in which similar vessel shapes perform different functions in two different regions. Superficially, the Cholula tripod bowls are similar to the Mixteca tripod bowls, which, as we have seen, were used mostly as drinking vessels. However, a careful comparison reveals some important differences between them. Mixteca tripod bowls, such as the one shown in figure 7.7, generally have relatively thin vertical walls and are fairly deep. They have elongated tripod supports and carry their major decoration on the exterior vessel wall. In 75 percent of the examples, Mixteca tripod bowls totally lack decoration on the vessel interior center. This makes sense if the bowls were intended as drinking vessels and their interiors were filled with chocolate or *pulque*. The exterior designs would easily be visible, especially when raised high on the tall supports, whereas the interior would not.

Cholula tripod bowls generally have relatively thick out-flaring walls and are very shallow (figure 7.14). They have short splayed tripod supports and carry their major decoration on the interior center and interior wall, with the exterior wall left undecorated or with the simplest of decorations. These tripod bowls were not designed as drinking vessels. Instead, they must have served some other function, but what? Again, we can turn to the codices.

In the Codex Borgia (1963), tripod bowls of this type are shown as vessels in which offerings were placed, such as parts of sacrificed animals. The Codex Borgia depicts tripod bowls placed in temples with a bird diving down to feed on the offering within (figure 7.15). The Cholula tripod bowls, then, were probably used as receptacles for sacrificial offerings. The highly decorated interior about to receive the sacrificial offering would be highly visible, especially given the out-flaring walls and short splayed tripod supports.[10]

The design motifs that decorate the Cholula tripod bowls support the contention that they served principally as receptacles for offerings. The interior centers are frequently decorated with a bird head whose beak has a bloody tip. Furthermore, a highly standardized band of decoration occurs on the interior walls of the tripod bowls. Gilda Hernández (1995:29), who has completed a thorough study of the iconography of Cholula Catalina polychrome, calls this the "solar band." However,

FIGURE 7.14. Cholula polychrome tripod bowls with (left) jaguar and (right) opossum supports. (Left: CRP; photo courtesy of Gilda Hernández. Right: MNAM; photo by Chris Moser)

FIGURE 7.15. Tripod bowls as vessels for offerings in the Codex Borgia (page 8). (Illustration by John M.D. Pohl)

I prefer the term *sacrificial band* because the motifs are principally sacrificial blood-letting instruments: bone awls and maguey thorns (see figure 7.2).

Plates, which are the fourth most frequent vessel shape (9%) at Cholula, were also probably used as vessels for offerings because their decoration is almost identical to that of tripod bowls. The sacrificial band may be seen on two plates of Cholula polychrome (figure 7.16). In its simplest form, it consists of pairs of bone awls with blood trickling down them and maguey thorns. In its more elaborate form, the

FIGURE 7.16. Cholula polychrome plates. (CRP; photo courtesy of Gilda Hernández)

sacrificial band is composed of three bands of decoration. The first contains the pairs of bone awls and maguey thorns for bloodletting; the second contains feathers of alternating colors, which represent "preciousness" (Hernández 1995:46); and the third contains *xicalcoliuhquis* or grecas of alternating colors, which Hernández (1995:34) interprets as "nobility." Taken together they may read "this precious offering of noble blood." The central motif probably indicates the deity to which the offering is being made, in this instance the eagle, which represents the sun (Caso 1958:33). The eagle's beak is splotched with red from feeding on the blood offering. The sacrificial band almost never occurs on Cholula hemispherical bowls and goblets, which were used principally as drinking vessels. Likewise, the sacrificial band does not occur on Mixteca polychromes.

Although eagle heads with bloody beaks occur as central motifs on many tripod bowls and plates, other design motifs also occur. Jaguars, which represent the deity Tezcatlipoca (Caso 1958:14), are common central motifs on plates and also occur on tripod bowls with jaguar-head supports. Offerings placed in these vessels were probably dedicated to Tezcatlipoca. Plumed serpent heads, which represent Quetzalcóatl, also occur frequently as central motifs on plates and tripod bowls. Presumably, offerings placed in these vessels were dedicated to Quetzalcóatl, the plumed serpent and patron deity of Cholula. Other plates and tripod bowls have an eagle claw/tied double maize ear as a central motif, which Nicholson (1994:113) relates to the maize deity, Cintéotl, and earth/fertility deities such as Chantico or Cihuacóatl[11] (see Figure 7.2).

The tripod bowls decorated with eagle heads and jaguars consistently manifest jaguar head effigy supports, but those decorated with plumed serpent heads and the eagle claw/tied double maize ear motifs consistently feature opossum

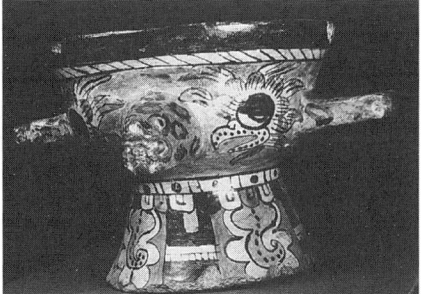

FIGURE 7.17. Cholula polychrome censer bowls. (Left: UDLA; photo courtesy of Gilda Hernández. Right: MANM; photo by Chris Moser)

head supports (see figures 7.2 and 7.14). The reason for this difference is unclear. Interestingly, vessels with jaguar head and opossum head supports do not occur in Mixteca polychrome. Apart from tripod bowls and plates, ritual ware in every excavated Cholula household included incense burners. Censer bowls are present in both commoner and elite households and nearly always include jaguar head effigies protruding from opposite sides (figure 7.17). Ladle censers also occur, but less frequently.

Finally, two other vessel shapes that occur in Cholula polychromes, but that have not been documented for Mixteca polychromes, are vases and basins. Although relatively common in museum collections, neither of these vessel shapes is of common occurrence in household middens or burial offerings at Cholula, which leads us to suspect that they functioned more in ceremonial contexts in temple precincts. Cholula polychrome vases are most frequently decorated with symbols of death and sacrifice. These include depictions of human skulls with holes punched in their temporal bones for mounting on skull racks (*tzompantli*), crossbones recognizable as human femora and tibiae, skeletal hands, human hearts, sacrificial knives, and stellar eyes (stars), which are symbols of human sacrifice. They are also decorated with either black or red vertical stripes, which was a common way to paint the body of a sacrificial victim. Although they have generally been considered *pulque* cups, they probably were used to drink *pulque* in ceremonies in temple precincts where human sacrifices took place. The Codex Borgia (1963) shows a vase, apparently containing *pulque*, associated with a human sacrifice. The vase is simply decorated with black stripes, but nearly identical vases have been found in excavations at Cholula (figure 7.18).

The large Cholula polychrome basins measure about one meter high and around sixty centimeters in diameter. They are frequently decorated with the standardized

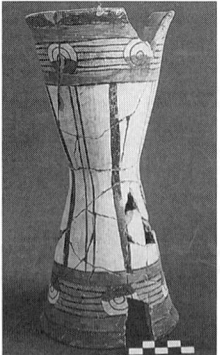

FIGURE 7.18. (Left and center) Cholula polychrome vases and (right) vase in the Codex Borgia (page 26). (Left: MNAM; photo by Chris Moser. Center: CRP; photo courtesy of Gilda Hernández. Right: illustration by John M.D. Pohl.)

sacrificial band, and many are decorated with depictions of human skulls, human crossbones, human hearts, sacrificial knives, and stellar eyes (stars), or other symbols of human sacrifice. What was the function of these large pots? In the Codex Borgia (1963) we see a fairly straightforward example of a human sacrificial victim being cooked with ears of corn in the large pot or basin (figure 7.19).

CONCLUSIONS

Over half of all Cholula Catalina polychromes appear to have been dedicated to religious purposes—offering vessels and ritual ware—while less than half represent fancy drinking vessels. This contrasts markedly with Mixteca Pilitas polychrome, about 80 percent of which appears to have been dedicated to drinking. These represent significant cultural differences or foci in the function of the polychrome despite their superficial similarities. Also, there are significant differences in the vessel shapes that distinguish Mixteca and Cholula polychromes. Are these differences apparent in the codices?

As demonstrated here, the codices provide us with invaluable information on the function of the polychrome pottery. They are books picturing how the polychromes were used. But, what, if anything, can the polychrome tell us about who wrote the books? Most archaeologists, of course, would like to be able to provide information on the proveniences of the codices. The late Don Robertson asked me a number of years ago if a study of the polychrome could reveal whether or not the Codex Borgia came from the Mixteca, as he believed (Robertson 1966:298–312), or from Cholula in the Valley of Puebla, as Henry Nicholson (1966:145–158) believed.

FIGURE 7.19. (Left) Cholula polychrome basin (MNAM; photo by Chris Moser) and (right) basin in the Codex Borgia (page 57). (Illustration by John M.D. Pohl.)

The problem of the provenience of the Codex Borgia, and other codices of the Borgia group—the Codices Laud, Fejérváry-Mayer, Vaticanus B, and Cospi—has concerned experts for years (Glass 1975:63–66).

Because we now know a great deal about the differences between Cholula and Mixteca polychromes, it is possible to make some pertinent observations about the Mixtec and Borgia group codices (table 7.2). As we have seen, tripod *ollas* are typical Mixteca polychrome vessel shapes that do not occur in Cholula Catalina polychrome. An examination of the Codex Borgia (1963) reveals depictions of some nineteen tripod *ollas*, which account for 10 percent of all vessel shapes in this codex. It cannot be a question here of a non-polychrome vessel shape depicted in Borgia because even if the tripod *ollas* in Borgia were not polychromes, tripod *ollas* do not occur as vessel shapes even among non-polychrome ceramic types at Mártir-phase Cholula. On the other hand, several vessel shapes typical of Cholula polychrome (hemispherical bowls, goblets,[12] vases, basins, and human skull resonators), but rare or absent in Mixteca polychrome, also occur in Borgia. However, hemispherical bowls, vases, basins, human skull resonators and, rarely, goblets are also depicted in codices known to be Mixtec (table 7.2).

Apart from Borgia, both Robertson and Nicholson have proposed a Mixtec origin for the Laud and Fejérváry-Mayer. An examination of the Codex Laud (1994) also revealed depictions of four tripod *ollas*, which account for over 6 percent

Table 7.2 Vessels in the Mixtec[13] and Borgia Group codices[14]

Vessel Shapes	Nuttall (1992)	Bodley (1960)	Selden (1964)	Colombino (1966)	Vindobonensis (1992)
Tripod Bowls	3 / 4.35[15]	1/3	0/0	0/0	5/4.67
Goblets	0 / 0	1/3	0/0	0/0	0/0
Tripod Ollas	24 / 34.79	6/18	0/0	0/0	12/11.21
Basins	1 / 1.45	4/12	2/15.4	0/0	0/0
Ladle Censers	9/13.05	8/24	5/38.5	2/50	12/11.21
Hemispherical Bowls	30/43.47	8/24	3/23.1	1/25	41/38.32
Censer Bowls	0/0	0/0	1/7.7	0/0	1/0.94
Pitchers	0/0	0/0	0/0	0/0	2/1.87
Bowls	1/1.45	4/12	1/7.7	1/25	23/21.50
Vases	1/1.45	1/3	1/7.7	0/0	0/0
Effigy Vessels	0/0	0/0	0/0	0/0	1/0.94
Small Ollas	0/0	0/0	0/0	0/0	2/1.87
Platters	0/0	0/0	0/0	0/0	1/0.94
Tecomates	0/0	0/0	0/0	0/0	1/0.94
Totals	69/100	33/100	13/100	4/100	107/100
Vessels per page	0.82	0.82	0.65	0.17	1.65

Borgia Groups Codices

Vessel Shapes	Borgia (1963)	Laud (1994)	Fejérváry-Mayer (1994)	Cospi (1994)	Vaticanus B (1992)
Tripod Bowls	110/57.59	44/68.75	19/47.50	14/48.28	64/62.13
Goblets	24/12.56	1/1.56	0/0	1/3.45	5/4.85
Tripod Ollas	19/9.94	4/6.25	3/7.50	0/0	5/4.85
Basins	16/8.37	0/0	8/20.00	0/0	4/3.88
Ladle Censers	9/4.71	3/4.68	1/2.50	4/13.79	0/0
Hemispherical Bowls	8/4.18	2/3.12	2/5.00	6/20.69	19/18.45
Censer Bowls	2/1.04	0/0	0/0	0/0	0/0
Pitchers	1/0.52	0/0	0/0	0/0	0/0
Bowls	1/0.52	14/21.87	5/12.50	3/10.34	3/2.92
Vases	1/0.52	0/0	2/5.00	1/3.45	3/2.92
Effigy Vessels	0/0	0/0	0/0	0/0	0/0

continued on next page

TABLE 7.2—*continued*

BORGIA GROUPS CODICES

Vessel Shapes	Borgia (1963)	Laud (1994)	Fejérváry-Mayer (1994)	Cospi (1994)	Vaticanus B (1992)
Small Ollas	0/0	0/0	0/0	0/0	0/0
Platters	0/0	0/0	0/0	0/0	0/0
Tecomates	0/0	0/0	0/0	0/0	0/0
Totals	191/100	64/100	64/100	29/100	103/100
Vessels per page	2.51	1.39	0.93	1.76	1.07

of all vessel shapes in this codex. The tripod *ollas* in Laud are associated with offerings related to deities including Mayauel (3 Earth?), goddess of *pulque*, and Xochipilli (Lord 7 Flower), a patron of *pulque* (Anders and Jansen 1994:235–243). In the Codex Fejérváry-Mayer (1994) there are three tripod *ollas*, which account for over 7 percent of all vessel shapes in this codex. These tripod *ollas* seem to be offerings containing chocolate or water for different pairs of deities, including Xochipilli (Lord 7 Flower) and Xochiquetzal (Lady 2 Flower?) (Anders, Jansen, and Pérez Jiménez 1994:284–286).

Codex Vaticanus B and Codex Cospi are considered non-Mixtec by Robertson, and Nicholson believes they come from the Puebla-Tlaxcala region where Cholula Catalina polychrome occurs. In Codex Vaticanus B (1992) five tripod *ollas* account for nearly 5 percent of all vessel shapes in the codex. These tripod *ollas* occur in marriage prognostication scenes (Anders and Jansen 1993:247–256). In the Codex Cospi (1994) there are no tripod *ollas* among the twenty-nine vessels depicted in the codex.

The presence of tripod *ollas* depicted in Codices Borgia, Laud, Fejérváry-Mayer, and Vaticanus B suggests that these codices come from the Mixteca, Valley of Oaxaca, or nearby regions.[16] The tripod *olla* is distinctive of the Mixteca and Valley of Oaxaca; it does not occur in the Cholula-Tlaxcala region or the Valley of Mexico. Furthermore, to my knowledge, the distinctive Oaxaca-style tripod jar does not occur in Late Postclassic contexts anywhere else in Mesoamerica outside Oaxaca and southern Puebla, that is, the Mixteca including the Acatlán region, the Chinantla, the Cuicatec Cañada, and the Valley of Oaxaca. Therefore, anyone proposing any origin for the Borgia group codices (except Cospi) other than Oaxaca or southern Puebla is going to have to explain why the tripod *ollas* are depicted in these codices. Furthermore, they are going to have to explain why these tripod *ollas* are shown in marriage or marriage prognostication scenes, typical of the Mixteca, or associated with deities related to *pulque* and probably the Mixtec *pulque* ritual.

This study has shown how integrating history and archaeology can illuminate both types of data. The documents (in this case the codices) have provided invaluable information on the function of polychrome vessels that otherwise could not be obtained from the archaeological record. The polychrome has offered an insight into the possible regions of provenience for the codices that, to date, has not been obtained from other sources. It is therefore incumbent upon both ethnohistorians and archaeologists to integrate their data to achieve a fuller understanding of past cultures.

NOTES

1. Uruñuela and Álvarez-Méndez (1989:70) obtained a radiocarbon date of 1640 ± 80 CE (I–14,613) on an ancient well from Cholula that contained polychrome.

2. Bernal and Gamio (1974:22, figures 2c, 2e) illustrate Iglesia polychrome from the north room of Patio A at Yagul associated with a radiocarbon date of 1593 ± 100 CE (M–1250). Lind (1987:9) obtained a radiocarbon date of 1660 ± 80 CE (GX–2093) on a colonial midden (F–10) at Yucuita in the Nochixtlán Valley of the Mixteca Alta that contained abundant Iglesia polychrome.

3. Delgado (1960:119) found Iglesia polychrome in Tomb 1 at Hondura Viejo, Yetla, in the Chinantla that also contained Spanish glass trade beads.

4. Uruñuela and Álvarez-Méndez (1989:70) obtained a radiocarbon date of 1450 ± 80 CE (I–14,614) from an ancient well at Cholula that contained diagnostic Mártir phase polychromes.

5. Lind (1987:7) obtained a radiocarbon date of 1340 ± 90 CE (GX–2185) on a Natividad midden (F–10A) at Yucuita that contained Pilitas polychrome.

6. Examples of both Acatlán and Chinantla polychromes occur in the offering of the Ex-Volador in Mexico City, which Noguera (1968) has dated to 1507 CE.

7. Mountjoy and Peterson (1973:30) obtained a radiocarbon date of 1250 ± 95 CE (GX–1815) on a midden at Cholula that contained Tecama phase polychromes.

8. Sergio Suárez Cruz (1995:110) obtained radiocarbon dates of 855 ± 55 CE (INAH–1102) and 990 ± 140 CE (INAH–1103) from an ancient well in Cholula that contained diagnostic Aquiáhuac-phase polychromes. In an earlier article (Lind 1994), the radiocarbon years of 960 and 1065 were mistakenly cited as dates for these samples.

9. Abbreviations used in the figures: CRO, Centro Regional Oaxaca; CRP, Centro Regional de Puebla; MCC, Museo de la Ciudad de Cholula; MFM, Museo Frissell de Mitla; MNAM, Museo Nacional de Antropología, Mexico City; UDLA, Universidad de las Américas, Cholula.

10. It should be noted, however, that up to 25% of Mixteca tripod bowls decorated on the interior center also probably functioned as receptacles for offerings in temples or on household altars, while the remaining 75% served as drinking vessels. On page 14 of the Codex Porfirio Díaz (Doesburg 2001), a bird is also shown diving down to feed off an offering placed in a tripod bowl. The Codex Porfirio Díaz is from the Cuicatec region, which also produced and used Mixteca style polychromes.

11. It is not the purpose of this chapter to offer a detailed iconographic study of Cholula polychrome. Gilda Hernández (2004a, 2004b, 2005, 2008) has presented an excellent iconographic analysis and interpretation of the symbolism of the design motifs on Cholula Catalina and Mixteca Pilitas polychrome.

12. Goblets are fairly common in Chinantla and Acatlán polychromes, but rare in Pilitas polychrome. It should also be noted that the sample of Cholula polychrome available to us far exceeds the sample of Mixteca polychrome by a margin of 10 to 1, if not more.

13. The Mixtec codices are known to come from the Mixteca because of their historical content.

14. Not all vessels depicted in the codices are necessarily polychromes. Certain vessel shapes known not to be polychromes, such as spiked braziers, were not counted.

15. The total number is followed by the percentage.

16. This does not mean that these codices are necessarily Mixtec because other ethnic groups occupying neighboring areas also used Mixteca-style polychromes. The Cuicatec Codex Porfirio Díaz has a religious section on pages 9–18, which is very similar to the Borgia group codices, and also has a separate historical section (Doesburg 2001). Nevertheless, it is interesting that all the codices known to be Mixtec are basically historical, while all the Borgia group codices are religious manuscripts that are most often arbitrarily assigned to the Puebla-Tlaxcala region because of their "differences" from the Mixtec historical codices.

REFERENCES

Anders, Ferdinand, and Maarten Jansen. 1993. *Libro Explicativo del Llamado Códice Vaticano B*. Austria: Akademische Druck- und Verlagsanstalt.

Anders, Ferdinand, and Maarten Jansen. 1994. *Libro Explicativo del Llamado Códice Laud*. Austria: Akademische Druck- und Verlagsanstalt.

Anders, Ferdinand, Maarten Jansen, and Gabina Aurora Pérez Jiménez. 1992. *Libro Explicativo del Llamado Códice Zouche-Nuttall*. Austria: Akademische Druck- und Verlagsanstalt.

Anders, Ferdinand, Maarten Jansen, and Gabina Aurora Pérez Jiménez. 1994. *Libro Explicativo del Llamado Códice Fejérváry Mayer*. Austria: Akademische Druck- und Verlagsanstalt.

Bernal, Ignacio, and Lorenzo Gamio. 1974. *Yagul: El Palacio de los Seis Patios*. Mexico: Universidad Nacional Autónoma de México.

Byland, Bruce, and John M.D. Pohl. 1994. *In the Realm of 8 Deer: Archaeology of the Mixtec Codices*. Norman: University of Oklahoma Press.

Caso, Alfonso. 1958. *The Aztecs: People of the Sun*. Norman: University of Oklahoma Press.

Codex Bodley. 1960. Facsimile. Mexico: Sociedad Mexicana de Antropología.

Codex Borgia. 1963. Facsimile. Mexico: Fondo de Cultura Económica.

Codex Colombino. 1966. Facsimile. Mexico: Sociedad Mexicana de Antropología.

Codex Cospi. 1994. Facsimile. Austria: Akademische Druck- und Verlagsanstalt.

Codex Fejérváry-Mayer. 1994. Facsimile. Austria: Akademische Druck- und Verlagsanstalt.

Codex Laud. 1994. Facsimile. Austria: Akademische Druck- und Verlagsanstalt.

Codex Nuttall. 1992. Facsimile. Austria: Akademische Druck- und Verlagsanstalt.

Codex Selden. 1964. Facsimile. Mexico: Sociedad Mexicana de Antropología.

Codex Vaticanus B. 1992. Facsimile. Austria: Akademische Druck- und Verlagsanstalt.

Codex Vindobonensis. 1992. Facsimile. Austria: Akademische Druck- und Verlagsanstalt.

Davies, Claude Nigel Byam. 1968. *Los Señoríos Independientes del Imperio Azteca*. Mexico: Instituto Nacional de Antropología e Historia.

Delgado, Agustín. 1960. "Arqueología de la Chinantla." *Revista Mexicana de Estudios Antropológicos* 16:105–123.

Díaz del Castillo, Bernal. 1962. *Historia Verdadera de la Conquista de la Nueva España*. Introducción y notas de Joaquín Ramírez Cabañas. Mexico: Editorial Porrúa.

Doesburg, Sebastian van. 2001. *Códices Cuicatecos Porfirio Díaz y Fernández Leal: Edición Facsimilar, Contexto Histórico e Interpretación*. Mexico City: Gobierno Constitucional de Oaxaca Secretaria de Asuntos Indígenas and Miguel Ángel Porrúa Grupo Editorial.

Furst, Jill Leslie. 1978. *Codex Vindobonensis Mexicanus I: A Commentary*. Institute for Mesoamerican Studies 4. Albany: State University of New York.

Glass, John B. 1975. "A Survey of Native Middle American Pictorial Manuscripts." In *Handbook of Middle American Indians*, vol. 14., vol. ed. Howard F. Kline, gen. ed. Robert Wachope, 3–80. Austin: University of Texas Press.

Hassig, Ross. 1988. *Aztec Warfare*. Norman: University of Oklahoma Press.

Hernández, Gilda. 1995. *Un Acercamiento a la Iconografía de la Cerámica Policroma Tipo Códice de Cholula*. Cholula, Mexico: Tesis de Licenciatura, Departamento de Antropología, Universidad de las Américas.

Hernández, Gilda. 2004a. "Las Vasijas Polícromas Tipo Códice con Banda Solar del Estilo Mixteca-Puebla." *Mexicon* 26 (3):56–61.

Hernández, Gilda. 2004b. "Temas Rituales en la Cerámica 'Tipo Códice' del Estilo Mixteca-Puebla." *Journal de la Société des Américanistes* 90 (2):7–34.

Hernández, Gilda. 2005. *Vasijas para Ceremonia: Iconografía de la Cerámica Tipo Códice del Estilo Mixteca-Puebla*. Leiden: CNWS Publication.

Hernández, Gilda. 2008. "Vasijas de Luz y de Oscuridad: La Cerámica Tipo Códice del Estilo Mixteca-Puebla." *Itinerarios* 8:113–127.

Lind, Michael. 1967. "Mixtec Polychrome Pottery: A Comparison of the Postclassic Polychrome Pottery from Cholula, Oaxaca, and the Chinantla." Unpublished Master's Thesis, Department of Anthropology, Universidad de las Américas, Cholula, Mexico.

Lind, Michael. 1987. *The Sociocultural Dimensions of Mixtec Ceramics*. Nashville: Vanderbilt University Publications in Anthropology, No. 33.

Lind, Michael. 1994. "Cholula and Mixteca Polychromes: Two Mixteca-Puebla Regional Sub-Styles." In *Mixteca-Puebla: Discoveries and Research in Mesoamerican Art and Archaeology*, ed. H. B. Nicholson and Eloise Quiñones-Keber, 79–99. Culver City, CA: Labyrinthos.

Matos Moctezuma, Eduardo. 1987. "The Templo Mayor of Tenochtitlán: History and Interpretation." In *The Great Temple of Tenochtitlán: Center and Periphery in the Aztec World,* ed. Johanna Broda, David Carrasco, and Eduardo Matos Moctezuma, 15–60. Berkeley: University of California Press.

Moser, Chris L. 1969. "Matching Polychrome Sets from Acatlán, Puebla." *American Antiquity* 34 (4):480–483. http://dx.doi.org/10.2307/277749.

Mountjoy, Joseph, and David Peterson. 1973. *Man and Land at Prehispanic Cholula*. Nashville: Vanderbilt University Publications in Anthropology, No. 4.

Nicholson, Henry B. 1966. "The Problem of the Provenience of the Members of the 'Codex Borgia Group': A Summary." In *Summa Anthropologica: Homenaje a Roberto J. Weitlaner*, ed. A. Pompa y Pompa, 145–158. Mexico: Instituto Nacional de Antropología e Historia.

Nicholson, Henry B. 1994. "The Eagle Claw/Tied Double Maize Ear Motif: The Cholula Polychrome Ceramic Tradition and Some Members of the Codex Borgia Group." In *Mixteca- Puebla: Discoveries and Research in Mesoamerican Art and Archaeology*, ed. H. B. Nicholson and Eloise Quiñones-Keber, 101–116. Culver City, CA: Labyrinthos.

Noguera, Eduardo. 1968. "Ceremonias del Fuego Nuevo." *Cuadernos Americanos* 27 (CLVIII):146–151.

Paddock, John. 1994. "A Codex Style Vessel from Nochixtlán, Oaxaca." In *Caciques and Their People: A Volume in Honor of Ronald Spores*, ed. Joyce Marcus and Judith Francis Zeitlin, 101–109. Ann Arbor: Anthropological Papers 89, Museum of Anthropology, University of Michigan.

Paddock, John, ed. 1966. *Ancient Oaxaca*. Stanford: Stanford University Press.

Reyes, Antonio de los. (1593) 1976. *Arte en Lengua Mixteca*. Nashville: Vanderbilt University Publications in Anthropology, No. 14.

Robertson, Donald. 1966. "The Mixtec Religious Manuscripts." In *Ancient Oaxaca*, ed. John Paddock, 298–312. Stanford: Stanford University Press.

Rojas, Gabriel. 1927. "Descripción de Cholula." *Revista Mexicana de Estudios Históricos* 1 (6):158–170.

Seler, Eduard. 1992. "Excavations at the Site of the Principal Temple in Mexico." In *Collected Works in Mesoamerican Linguistics and Archaeology*, vol. 3, translated by Charles P. Bowditch, and ed. J. Eric S. Thompson and Francis B. Richardson, 114–198. Culver City, CA: Labyrinthos.

Seler, Eduard. 1993. "Some Excellently Painted Old Pottery Vessels of the Sologuren Collection from Nochistlan and Cuicatlan in the State of Oaxaca." In *Collected Works in Mesoamerican Linguistics and Archaeology*, vol. 4, translated by Charles P. Bowditch, and ed. J. Eric S. Thompson and Francis B. Richardson, 285–290. Culver City, CA: Labyrinthos.

Smith, Mary Elizabeth. 1973. *Picture Writing from Ancient Southern Mexico*. Norman: University of Oklahoma Press.

Spores, Ronald. 1972. *An Archaeological Settlement Survey of the Nochixtlán Valley, Oaxaca*. Nashville: Vanderbilt University Publications in Anthropology, No. 1.

Suárez Cruz, Sergio. 1995. "La Cerámica Lisa Cholulteca." *Arqueología,* Segunda época, 13–14:109–120.

Uruñuela, Gabriela, and Raúl Álvarez-Méndez. 1989. "Un Caso de Síndromo de Klippel-Feil en Restas Prehispánicas de Cholula, Puebla." *Revista Mexicana de Reumatología* 4 (3):69–72.

Vaillant, George C. 1950. *The Aztecs of Mexico*. Middlesex, UK: Penguin.

8

Pluri-Ethnic Coixtlahuaca's Longue Durée

CARLOS RINCÓN MAUTNER

INTRODUCTION

An overview of scholarly efforts aimed at reconstructing the culture histories of indigenous groups inhabiting the vast area encompassing the Puebla-Tlaxcala Basin to Northwestern Oaxaca presents several paradoxes (figure 8.1). This region is considered the center for diversification of Otomanguean languages, and the proposed cultural foundations of its earliest inhabitants lie in the Tehuacán tradition (Winter et al. 1984). In Late Postclassic times, this same region became the heartland for the distinctive Mixteca-Puebla style. Although the historical trajectories of these groups eventually resulted in sociolinguistic differentiation and divergence from their common cultural roots, the timing, causative factors, and processes involved remain poorly understood. In spite of the linguistic divergence, during the Late Classic and Late Postclassic, the corresponding cultural assemblages for these periods seem remarkably homogeneous and convergent. Nevertheless, by using linguistic and archaeological data, a number of scholars have sought to attribute the cultural material from these time periods to specific linguistic groups in an attempt to present the people and their cultures as more ancient and as uniquely distinct from their neighbors, favoring the cultural achievements of one group or urban center over those of others.[1]

Native documentary sources refer to prehispanic migrations and settlement of this broad region by incoming ethnic groups and the conflicts that arose among rival factions as they accommodated these new arrivals (Kirchhoff 1940; Rincón

DOI: 10.5876/9781607323297.c008

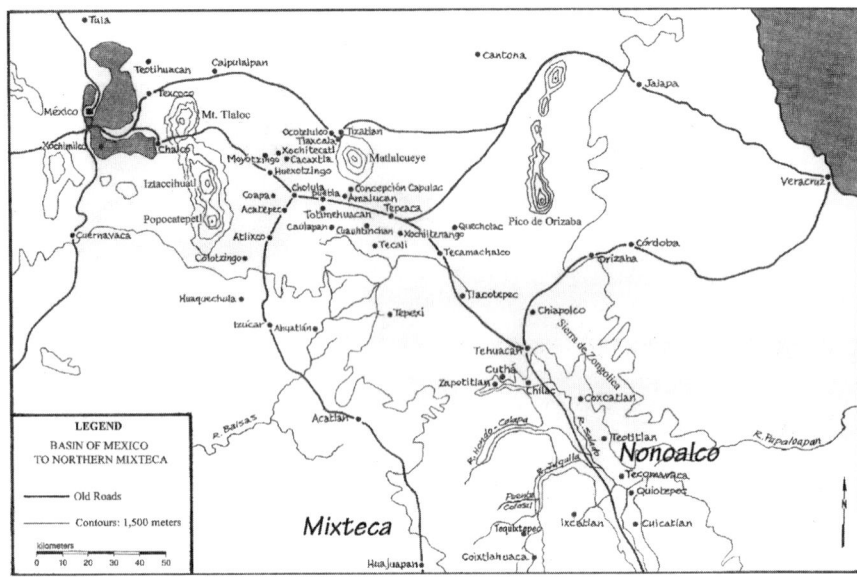

FIGURE 8.1. Area between Coixtlahuaca in the northern Mixteca, the Tehuacan Valley, Nonoalco, eastern Puebla, and the Basin of Mexico showing the location of old roads and settlements referred to in the text and in table 8.1.

Mautner 1999:309–312). Postconquest sixteenth-century accounts describe numerous ethnic groups who, although they spoke different languages and shared the same territory, interacted regularly with each other. The greatest diversification of peoples in historic times occurred following the Postclassic-period Chichimec migrations and settlement of the southeastern sector of this region, a territory known as Nonoalco (Kirchhoff 1940; Kirchhoff et al. 1989:map 4). This territory encompassed the Tehuacán Valley and extended north into the Sierra de Zongolica, southeast toward the Cuicatlán Cañada, and south into the highlands of the Mixteca Alta (figure 8.1). A major mercantile exchange thoroughfare passes through it, connecting the Gulf Coast and the Valley of Oaxaca. This region apparently takes its name from the specific Chichimeca group that settled there, the Nonoalca, an ethnonym that captures the essence of the experience this intrusive Nahua-speaking group had upon entering and settling what would become their new homeland. It is connoted as a foreign land "where one becomes mute"[2] due to the confluence of many ethnically distinct groups along the trade route who spoke different languages. Although pictographic writing has ancient roots, it seems logical to infer that the need for intelligibility among these groups would have spurred the expansion and widespread adoption of the reliable canon of symbol conventions that has come to be known as Mixteca-Puebla by means of which they could communicate and maintain records of different sorts.

Indigenous documentary sources refer to conquests and elite marriages between polities, as well as to Terminal Classic and Early Postclassic migrations (figure 1.2). However, it is generally assumed that each group occupied the territory of its ancestors and has done so since time immemorial.[3] This static view is reinforced by the premise that urbanism, as the hallmark of complex societies, results in isolation of populations that in turn contributes to linguistic differentiation. Yet, it is posited that once a group's subsistence is primarily dependent on agriculture and it is organized as a permanent village, an ethnic identity emerges that permeates the material culture.

When language areas are proposed—such as Mixtec, Nahua, Popoloca, Chocho (Southern Popoloca), Ixcatec, Zapotec, and so on—essentialist interpretations of the material culture as belonging to a particular group follow. These usually consider the diffusion of styles from major urban centers like Teotihuacan, Cholula, or Monte Albán. Yet they less often take into account the possibility of transculturation resulting from the influx of new people into an area. People acculturate, acquire new skills, learn a new language or become bi- or trilingual if their societal position and occupation require it. Merchants, specific ethnic enclaves, or pluri-ethnic polities de-emphasize or ignore their differences by participating in a shared culture and subscribing to a supra-identity. Although cultures and languages have historical associations that, like relationships to other populations, change through time, they are independent variables. In this chapter, I propose that when different groups with distinct languages and culture histories coincide and persist in an area, the resultant new culture is an amalgamation of cultural traits, transformed as they are adopted and accommodated to provide meaning to most or all of the region's inhabitants. Therefore, in the case of pluri-ethnic polities, it is inaccurate to attribute elements of the material culture, such as ceramics, exclusively to one specific ethnic or linguistic group.

Some of the following questions seem particularly germane to the topic of integrating archaeology and ethnohistory. Is it realistic to expect great differences in the cultures of people who speak different languages but live in close proximity and share the same technology and belief systems, within similar environments? What historical processes and sociopolitical developments could have contributed to homogeneity in the assemblage of material culture? The limitations of the archaeological record notwithstanding, can the study of a region's material culture, ethnohistory, and environmental and linguistic data explain shifts in the dynamics of sociopolitical developments during transitions between periods, such as from Terminal Classic to Early Postclassic, or Early Postclassic to Late Postclassic?

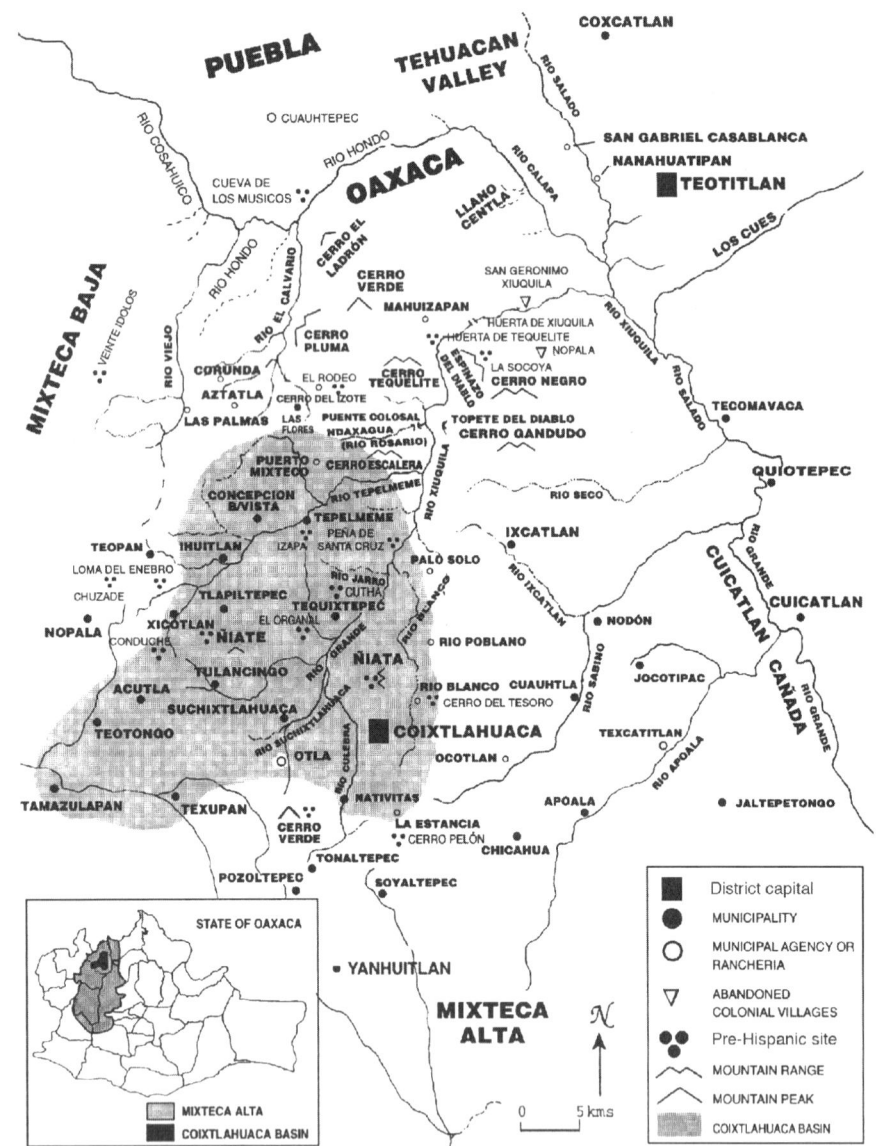

FIGURE 8.2. Principal sites and settlements of the Coixtlahuaca Basin and environs, State of Oaxaca, Mexico.

FIGURE 8.3. A high oblique panoramic view from above the Yanhuitlán-Nochixtlán Basin, looking northwards across the Coixtlahuaca Basin and the Tehuacán Valley. Photo by the author, January 1991.

I endeavor here to address these issues and provide answers by referring to my findings in the Coixtlahuaca Basin, which occupies the northern sector of the Mixteca Alta of Oaxaca (figures 8.1, 8.2, 8.3). Its rich assemblage of material culture and wealth of Colonial-period ethnohistorical sources allow for inferences to be made about the economic, religious, and political subsystems in the transitions from the Classic to the Postclassic and Colonial periods.

My interpretive approach aims to reconcile different types of records for the purpose of reconstructing a dynamic, richly textured regional history. It was first necessary to assemble a complete sequence of ruler succession from the numerous *lienzos* of Coixtlahuaca and compile all dates associated with certain rulers in the sequence (Rincón Mautner 1997, 1999:309–361, 2000). Despite certain anachronisms, cognate passages in the indigenous sources from Coixtlahuaca and the eastern Puebla Basin shed light on settlement histories and specific instances of interregional interaction and sociocultural change in these two regions. Radiocarbon dates from controlled excavations in the Mixteca Alta and the neighboring Tehuacán Valley are few in number, and the time period spanning the end of the Classic period to the Late Postclassic (650–1250 CE), which coincides with the greatest linguistic divergence in the Otomanguean family, is poorly documented for both regions

(Drennan 1983:363–370; Winter 1989b:127–128n2). Correlating the intercept probability ranges of radiocarbon dated cultural material and alluvial deposits with: (1) poorly defined archaeological phases, (2) the point dates provided by recent palaeoclimatic reconstruction, (3) the "faster paced," personage- and event-driven annals genre of indigenous sources, with (4) the dates inferred from linguistic data for the separation of languages and the displacement of language groups (Josserand 1983)—together creates an epistemological quandary. Events have different temporal rhythms and durations, operate at different scales (*sensu* Braudel 1972:20–21), and leave records that are incompletely preserved. Yet, despite these challenges and the immensity of the undertaking, the most appealing and logical objective of archaeological-ethnohistorical research is that it offers the possibility of reconstructing the most accurate coherent social history of a people through inference that results from the integration of different categories and hierarchies of data.

From the vantage point of the present, the past seems to consist of a tableau of regular long-term processes or periods of gradual change characterized by natural oscillations and successions that appear cyclical and resemble continuity. From such a perspective, the Mixteca's past is here inferred as a structured, historically expanded longue durée (Braudel 1958) consisting of deep regularities and cycles, perhaps several millennia in duration, that incorporates cultural adaptations resulting from the coupling of society and the environment. Human presence and its accompanying environmental impact can be inferred from stream deposits and in the fine lenses of sediment that have accumulated behind stone-faced terraces along natural drainages (Rincón Mautner 1999:634–741). Terracing is an agricultural adaptation to the drought and erosion to which this highland region is prone. Gradual, recurrent events with cumulative outcomes like seasonal sediment deposition—and in the cultural sphere, like the development of local ceramic traditions or writing or the establishment of trade networks—are interrupted by abrupt, high-energy episodic events of short duration that result in accelerated change, such as 100- or 500-year storm cycle floods, protracted drought resulting in famine, disease, and high mortality rates, and conquests and migrations of incoming people, all of which have significantly impacted the surrounding landscape affecting resident societies and their cultures.

Given its nature, the archaeological record is well-suited to account for cumulative patterns of gradual change that emerge at a locus, because the meaning of abrupt shifts or breaks in, say, the styles of the local ceramic tradition, while noticeable, are not easily interpreted. On the other hand, the historical record offers what seems an improved resolution about the past because it accounts for crises (the more extreme, unique, less patterned, vectorial, and relatively recent reference events) from which a conjunction with sociopolitical and economic implications can be posited, as in the case of the Aztec and Spanish conquests (Rincón Mautner 1999:80–82). While the archaeological record seemingly homogenizes or "flattens" events, the historical record portrays them as highlights. There is a growing recognition that while geological and environmental processes occur within human time scales or quicktime, a deep history or longue durée that preserves its chromatic heterogeneity requires bridging interdisciplinary gaps and learning to operate at multiple scales so that patterns do not take precedence and eclipse details (Smail 2012).

Smith (1992:65–68, table 4.2) presents areas of agreement, disagreement, and non-comparability between archaeology and ethnohistory for certain social categories or "factors" (demography, urbanism, economics, and political/military) within the Basin of Mexico. While his study showed non-comparable areas outnumbering the areas of agreement and disagreement, he found comparable areas for some Postclassic events and processes, including the Aztlan migrations and population increase (demography), the rise of primate cities (including Tula's chronology), and the extent of the Aztec empire. However, the archaeological and ethnohistorical record disagreed on the extent of the preceding Toltec empire and Late Postclassic warfare.

As to the reliability of local Colonial period *lienzos* as historical sources on events of the prehispanic era, concerns can be allayed and tempered by identifying the areas of agreement and disagreement regarding the data offered by these sources, whose primary intended purpose seems to have been to create a visual account once possession of native domains had been confirmed by the Crown (Rincón Mautner 2014:162) or to pursue the definition of contested jurisdictional territorial boundaries for each of the native states whose rulers commissioned them (Rincón Mautner 2012a, 2012b). Such pictorial sources not only provide an indigenous perspective but, if properly vetted through comparison to other documents and confronting their accounts with archaeological data, also contribute to the reconstruction of a local and regional history with a long-term view. If used judiciously, the *lienzos* provide unparalleled and valuable data that ground events in space and time and offer insights into otherwise unknown aspects of the sociopolitical and religious subsystems. Knapp (1992:2) postulates that historical documents in general, when used with archaeology, tend to eclipse material cultural findings. I allege that these pictographic historical sources help bridge the gap between historical and archaeological findings, although they are difficult to interpret individually; as historical sources they do not dominate sociocultural and historical interpretations.

Geoarchaeological studies and dating of local alluvial and agricultural terrace deposits (Rincón Mautner 1999:644–720, 2015) and palaeoclimatic reconstructions (Stahle et al. 2011) provide an environmental framework for the study of cultural change locally and across Mesoamerica. Although these approaches likewise exhibit either ranges of probability or precise point dates, respectively, knowing whether, how, and when environmental stressors acted as causative factors to elicit human response can be inferred only by studying well-documented historical records and present-day meteorological events, and by developing an understanding of their effects on populations. The inconsistencies and lacunae in the records may be overcome with new data from (1) controlled excavations in the Mixteca, Tehuacán Valley, and the Eastern Puebla Basin, (2) previously unknown documentary sources as they come to light, and (3) careful correlation of tree-ring and stalagmite-growth evidence with drought across different regions, as well as (4) the application of new interpretive approaches aimed at reconciling the different records.

There is a general tendency to create overly simplistic, exclusive classificatory categories in organizing information, so that certain attributes of material culture are used in formulating archaeological ethnic identities. Artifacts of material culture are usually the products of individual, enculturated craftsmen, rather than the result of group effort. Given the human ability to adopt and imitate ideas and styles, it is improbable that material artifacts are imprinted with the unique essence or quality of a culture that resides in them, so that they can then be attributed exclusively to a specific group and used as indicators that identify and distinguish that particular group from other groups of people.

In Mesoamerica, archaeologists routinely use distinctive ceramic forms with decorative elements (vessels, spindle whorls, representations of deities and figurines, etc.) and artifacts made of other materials, together with mortuary rituals and tomb construction forms, not only to establish chronologies, but as markers of ethnic self-identity within a geographic range. For Brumfiel (1994:96) *ethnic affiliation* involves the use of artifacts, whereas *ethnic attribution* refers to the manner in which others portray a distinct ethnic group by using symbolic pictographic conventions that subsume its distinctive character and serve to identify it. She is one of the few archaeologists to have tested with archaeological data the character of ethnicity suggested by documentary sources (Brumfiel 1994:96–101). However, I find that ethnic affiliation may also be portrayed from inside the ethnic group as a way of distinguishing itself from other groups. For example, a visual reference and metaphor for both the main ethnic group inhabiting the Coixtlahuaca Basin and the ancient, high rank of the nobility of the principal ruling lineage is represented by the apical ancestor, Lord 7 Reed, depicted on both the *Lienzo de Tequixtepec I* and the reverse of the Fragmento Gómez de Orozco as standing on a jade jewel within a river of reeds. Such a representation is not only a geographic reference to Tollan (Tula Xicocotitla) or to Tollan de Tamazolac (Tenayuca) as "places of reeds" (i.e., settlements), but the green color of the jade stone and reeds constitute visual references to the sixteenth-century Ñudzahui (Mixteco) expressions by which the people of the Coixtlahuaca Basin were known—*tocuijñuhu* or *tocuijñudzavui*—meaning "green, precious, or esteemed people," while their close relationship to the Ñudzahui was also recognized (de los Reyes 1976:i–ii). I have proposed that the name *Chocho* or *Chocholteco* commonly used in reference to these people is derived from the Hispanized Nahuatl expression *xoxouhqui* or *xoxo*, also meaning "green" and "precious" (Rincón Mautner 1999:184–187). The different Chichimec ethnic components of Coixtlahuaca, which arrived later than the Toltec nobility, were distinguished in the *lienzos* by means of "saw-toothed crowns" and black face paint as originating in the legendary Chicomoztoc, with references to their migration saga involving Itzpapalotl (Rincón Mautner 2012a:260).

In terms of dress and custom of body decoration, including the customary piercing of lips and nose, all seem to have wide distribution. Given that these are traits shared among different groups, the question is whether such attributes are reliable indicators of ethnicity or ethnic identity useful in interpreting the recorded incursions or arrival of different peoples into the Coixtlahuaca Basin as portrayed in the codices and *lienzos*. For instance, if the use of tau-shaped, ground obsidian labrets or lip-plugs were exclusive to Otomí self-identity as suggested by Brumfiel (1994:98), then I could conclude that this group was present in the Mixteca, based on similar type labrets I have seen in collections locally. Labrets used by several personages in the codices from the Mixteca, like the *Codex Selden* (11-III, 12-I, 13-I), are used to identify them as foreigners. It is difficult to ascertain from painted images of warriors wearing labrets the nature of the material from which they are made. More significant is that the presence of labrets appears to be more of a chronological marker for the Postclassic than it is a marker of ethnicity. A seated personage with a labret is depicted in the Early Postclassic period Panel 1 from the cave-tunnel on the Ndaxagua (Rincón Mautner 2012b:133, figure 4.10), and on Late Postclassic polychrome ceramic sherds. However, different groups, including the Nahuatl-speaking Tlaxcalans, also used labrets.

Traditional ceramic forms and styles change slowly, and their geographic distribution reflects both popular acceptance and adoption by the group based on some valuing characteristic: quality, usefulness, price, aesthetics, or even symbolic significance. However, I question whether ceramics alone can be assumed to be a reliable distinguishing marker or a generalized representation of ethnicity for one group as perceived by another. Do ceramics from the Mixteca Alta, for example, serve to distinguish among the different groups residing throughout that region or in the Tehuacan Valley, considered to be part of the same cultural region, especially during the Postclassic period? Systematic studies in which the plausible subtlety of intraregional variations in style between Late Postclassic polities might be recognized have yet to be performed.

Tehuacán Valley ceramic affiliations were correlated with the principal Meso-american archaeological sequences, but their relationships with the materials from the neighboring Mixteca, and more specifically the Coixtlahuaca Basin, were alluded to only in passing (Johnson and MacNeish 1972:32–37; MacNeish et al. 1970a:177, 186, 189). For instance, the Coxcatlan Brushed, and especially the Coxcatlan Gray stamped-bottom tripod vessels with different supports (MacNeish et al. 1970a:186–196), also known as *molcajetes de fondo sellado*, were considered an Early Venta Salada ware. These flat-bottomed tripod bowls may have become a trade ware during the Late Venta Salada, as they are found in great quantities at Late Natividad-phase sites in the Coixtlahuaca Basin, where Byland (1984) con-sidered them as one of the ceramic markers that demonstrate a boundary between Coixtlahuaca and Texupan. However, MacNeish et al. (1970a:196, 1970b:236) found the designs in the few published depictions of stamped-bottom bowls from Coixtlahuaca (Bernal 1949:42, Plate 4) to be simpler in appearance than those from the Tehuacán Valley. Although the existence of regional substyles is a possibility, the numerous *fondo sellado* sherds I have examined in the Coixtlahuaca area are vir-tually identical to the examples depicted in MacNeish et al. (1970a:figures 111–113, 115) and Seler-Sachs (1912:206–215).

There is an apparent recognition of both Toltec-style ceramics (MacNeish et al. 1970a:208) and the influence from the Valley of Mexico, but little is said of the influ-ence from that area during the Early Venta Salada phase of the Tehuacan Valley. For the Late Venta Salada phase, the findings were considered as "obviously connected with the spread of the Aztec Empire" (MacNeish et al. 1970b:237). Interestingly, the pan-regional or pan-Mesoamerican events occurring during the Terminal Classic to Postclassic transition had already been recognized (Litvak 1970a, 1970b; Sanders 1965; Sanders and Price 1968:29–34, 206, 208) and associated with Tula's rise to power. Tula's broad area of influence had been recognized quite early by ethnohis-torians (Jiménez Moreno 1941, 1966; Kirchhoff 1940, 1955). In addition, prior to the Tehuacán Valley Project, there had been an early attempt to establish an affilia-tion between the ceramics found in Tehuacán and Tula (Cook de Leonard 1957) or Cholula (Noguera 1954, 1960).

The end of the Palo Blanco phase, placed circa 700 CE, and the possibility that it may have actually taken place one or two centuries earlier, is problematic for those arguing for the continuous occupation of the area, especially because there are no Early Venta Salada dates (Johnson and MacNeish 1972:32–37, 49, 51). The earliest reported date for Venta Salada is 900 ± 110 CE. Although there were rather cau-tious explanations offered for the absence of dates within this phase, subsequent work in the Valley of Oaxaca and Mixteca Alta has led Winter (1989b:127; 1990:56) to propose the possibility of large-scale abandonment during the same time frame.

The Early Venta Salada (700–1100 CE) ceramic assemblage does not seem to be well-defined, and correlating the different Postclassic-period types chronologically presents some problems. Recent work on the assemblage from Cuthá (Site Tr 319) did not include any new radiocarbon dates and some of the ceramic types excavated, like the thin orange that would fit into Late Palo Blanco, were not distinguished from Early Venta Salada wares (Castellón Huerta 2006:109).

MacNeish et al. (1970a:209) also refer to the rise of Mixtec imperialism during the Postclassic period, "when towns in the [Tehuacán] valley were definitely ruled by Mixtec caciques." However, no specific evidence was provided or even alluded to in making the statement. Using the data compiled during the Tehuacán Valley survey, and referring to the abandonment of Tula about 1150 CE, Pohl and Byland (1994:194, map 1, map 2) have proposed that the shift in settlement pattern and abandonment of sites observed in the Tehuacán Valley at the end of the Classic period and the population explosion that occurs during the Late Venta Salada of the Postclassic, are the result of the arrival of a large intrusive group of Nahuatl-speaking Tolteca-Chichimeca. Pohl and Byland (1994:192, map 2) link the invasion "to the erosion of the authority of the Tr 319 site and the foundation of the Postclassic Popolocan city-state of Chilac." The problem with their proposal is that Postclassic Chilac (Tr 216) was actually Nahuatl-speaking and, although it was relocated to the site of present-day San Gabriel Chilac during early Colonial times, the Tr 319 site is not located on a promontory above this town. Its origins are described as a Toltec migration that involved relocation and warfare against the resident Popoloca (Gil Huerta 1972; Gil Huerta and Neely 1967). Its "pueblo viejo" is located northeast of the present town, not west at Cuthá (Tr 319). Furthermore, one of its extant hamlets was Popolocan-speaking San Juan Atzingo, relocated in Colonial times from a site to the south called Rinconada (Castellón Huerta 2006:30). Although the ethnic group that occupied Cuthá has not been identified archaeologically, extant documentation reveals that it was primarily Popolocan-speaking and its Postclassic-period population was settled below this hilltop site in the area by Zapotitlan (Castellón Huerta 2006:54, 218, 294, 309). Although Pohl and Byland (1994) attribute the Tehuacán Valley's transition to the Postclassic and its repopulation to incursions of Nahuatl-speaking groups, Castellón Huerta (2006:294) links the transition and this site's brusque population decline to political events in the Mixteca.

Unarguably, as long as one is cautious with oversimplifications, this approach of segregating and attributing artifacts on the basis of style may provide some benefit for distinguishing peoples who are geographically distant from one another—such as the Chinantec from the Mixtec (Lind 1967)—or that are circumscribed in their interactions—as appears to be the case with both the Mixe, who apparently had neither Classic-period stone carvings with glyphs or dates nor Postclassic poly-chrome ceramics (Winter 2008:407, 409), and the Tlapanec, who lacked the latter (Gerardo Gutierrez, personal communication 2004). For groups whose artifacts constitute a medium for maintaining their cultural identity, it may also be pos-sible in some rare cases to distinguish peoples on the basis of decorative style, in which case we might expect behaviors that are conservative. Combined with an assessment of "quality of manufacture," this approach has been used to propose the existence of boundary correspondence between ceramics and different linguistic groups inhabiting the Oaxaca Coast, suggestive of "functional interrelationships" that reflect sociopolitical hierarchical position and distance decay from the regional capital (Brockington 1982:12).

THE ARCHAEOLOGY OF THE COIXTLAHUACA BASIN AND ITS RETROSPECTIVE COLONIAL-PERIOD PAINTED HISTORIES

The very large Tehuacán Valley has been the subject of relatively intense archaeolog-ical study. As a result of its close proximity to many different regions, it functioned as a wide corridor for information flows in multiple directions. In contrast, access to the neighboring highland Coixtlahuaca Basin is relatively restricted. The Basin is not well known archaeologically for periods preceding the Late Postclassic, and what is known for that period is based on excavations conducted in the 1940s by Moedano and Ortega (Rincón Mautner 2015) and Ignacio Bernal (1949). Recent reconnoitering and assessments of environmental impacts have revealed older material culture and numerous settlements scattered throughout the Basin (Rincón Mautner 1999, 2015; Winter 1994:211, 213, figures 8, 12). Its geographic location, immediately south and perched high above the Tehuacán Valley, offers strategic advantages (figures 8.2, 8.3). High mountain ranges that rise to 2800 meters and the deep canyons of the Hondo-Calapa and Juquila Rivers protect the Coixtlahuaca Basin along the north side that borders the Tehuacán Valley. Ranges of similar elevation enclose this basin along its perimeter to the south and west. However, given its temperate, subhumid climate and high frequency of drought, maize culti-vation was and still is a precarious subsistence activity. Adaptive strategies to these conditions included the creation of fields within ravines, or *barrancas*, by building retaining walls and terraces that functioned as check dams in natural drainages,[4] expanding them periodically to capture sediments and concentrate run-off mois-ture from passing cold fronts. Planting early in the spring—months ahead of the summer rainy season—helped produce the highest corn yields. Consequently, once the population expanded, perhaps exceeding carrying capacity, the Basin's inhabit-ants could never really afford to isolate themselves or develop political and religious subsystems that were not inclusive of other communities and ethnicities. The year-round production of maize in the warm, well-irrigated neighboring Tehuacán Valley made interacting with that area not only desirable but necessary.

Aspects of the sociopolitical organization such as the antiquity and hierar-chical position of royal houses, territorial boundaries, and interactions between communities, as well as the significance of certain preeminent landscape features or sacred landforms, would be difficult to ascertain or interpret if archaeology were the sole source of information about the past. However, the great number of sixteenth-century native painted retrospective histories from the Coixtlahuaca Basin, known as codices and *lienzos*, provide complementary information on the region's prehispanic past.[5] These cartographic dynastic histories register events that supported the claims and defined the territorial and tributary domains of the royal lineages that ruled there. Linking the *lienzo* registers of ruler succession to associated dates and places allowed for the reconstruction of a regional settle-ment political history (Rincón Mautner 1997, 1999:312–349, 2012b), which can be correlated with the archaeological chronology. The accounts they record begin in the ninth century and document approximately seven hundred years of dynastic history that preceded the Spanish conquest. The record ends in the Early Colonial Period, after thirty-two generations of rulers. There are no recognizable references in these sources to Teotihuacan or to Monte Albán, the two anchoring sites for much of Oaxaca's Classic-period archaeology. Despite their strong emic perspec-tive, these richly textured retrospective accounts refer to a number of interactions that took place between Coixtlahuaca and areas located north and northwest of the Basin and provide a unique portrait of how simple kingdoms (*yuhuitayu* in Mixtec) were transformed into a complex state (Rincón Mautner 1994, 1997, 1999:27–55, 286–347, 2000).

INTEGRATING COIXTLAHUACA'S ARCHAEOLOGY AND HISTORY

Numerous sites found throughout the Coixtlahuaca Basin of the northern Mixteca predate Ngüiteri, Coixtlahuaca's elite western *barrio* excavated by Bernal (1949) in the 1940s, by as much as 1500 years. Some of these archaeological sites are associated with prominent landforms, like the Nudo Mixteco, a mountain complex dominated by the Cerro Verde (figures 8.2, 8.3, and 8.4D–F), with a platform on its summit and stone-faced contour terraces along its windward slopes; as the name indicates, the surrounding relics of oak forest receive abundant moisture so that the mountain retains its green color even during the dry season. Adjacent and to the east of the Cerro Verde is a large-terraced Classic-period ridge site (figures 8.4G–H; Rincón Mautner 1999:673). This ridge site is represented on the *Lienzo de Otla* and the

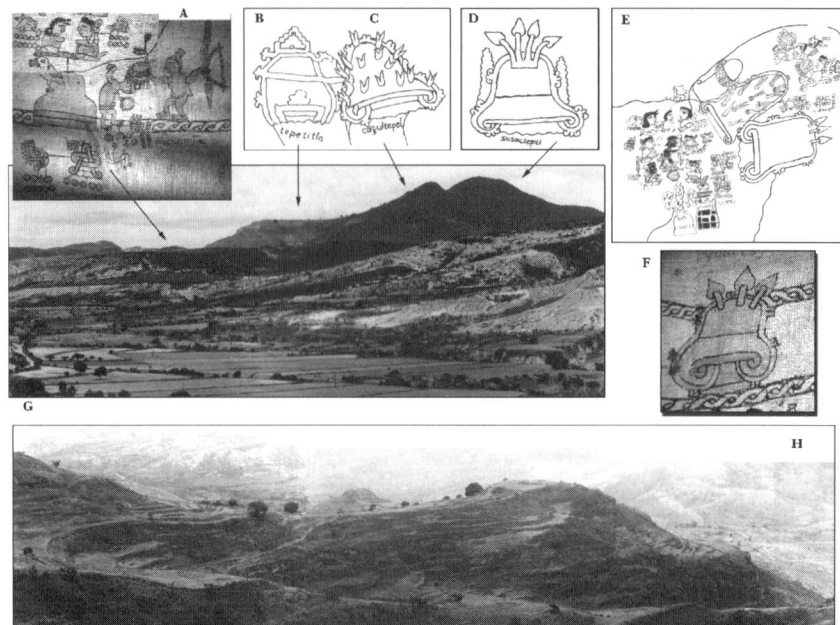

FIGURE 8.4. The Nudo Mixteco mountain complex and its major promontory, Cerro Verde, defines the southern boundary of the Coixtlahuaca Basin and is depicted in Early Colonial documents. (A) The conquest of Cerro de la Paloma on the *Lienzo de Nativitas* and the approximate location of the battle indicated by the arrow pointing to figure 8.4G. (B) and (C) The promontories of Tepetitla and the Cerro Verde Chico as depicted on the *Lienzo de Otla*. Cerro Verde as depicted on (D) the *Lienzo de Otla*, (E) the *Lienzo de Tlalpitepec*, and (F) the *Lienzo de Nativitas*. (G) General view of the northern slopes of the Nudo Mixteco. (H) Terraces along the southern slopes or back side of Tepetitla (8.4B). Photos and drawings by the author.

Lienzo de Tlalpitepec as a stepped-pyramid-on-a-hill glyph (figure 8.4B) and as a mountain summit surrounded by a wall (figure 8.4E), respectively. Landforms with recognizable, surficial evidence of earlier settlement served as points of reference in the landscape to demonstrate antiquity of land claims and foster group cohesion. Their representations were incorporated in the *lienzos*. Such landforms were frequently represented in the *lienzos* as defended or conquered by certain warrior leaders and as boundary markers delimiting the territorial possessions of the native polity. The detail taken from the *Lienzo de Nativitas* (figure 8.4A) illustrates the defeat and conquest of the lands and subjects of the lord of the Cerro de la Paloma by Lord 4 Ocelot. The arrow from figure 8.4A points to the approximate location in figure 8.4G where this battle took place.

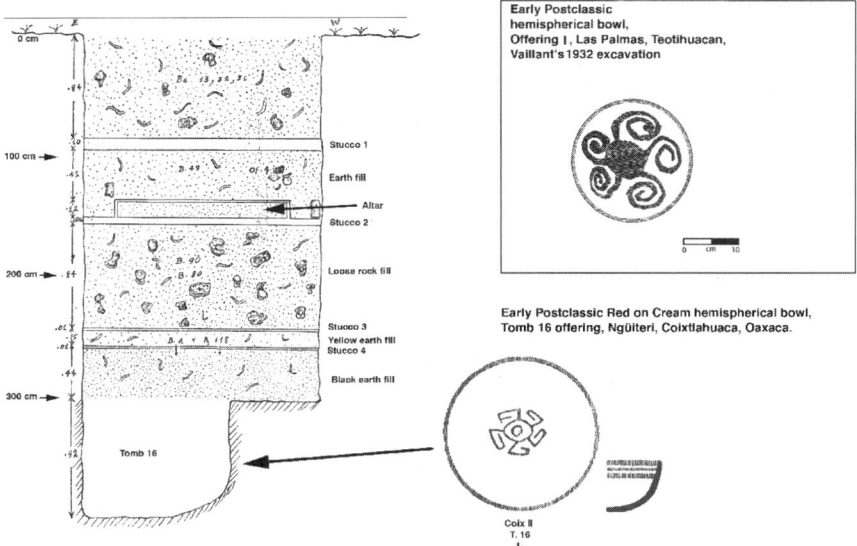

FIGURE 8.5. (*Left*) Pit 10 cross section, Patio C, Ngüiteri, Coixtlahuaca. (*Bottom right*) Early Postclassic red-on-cream bowl found in Ngüiteri, Coixtlahuaca, compared with (*top right*) Toltec red-on-buff bowl from Las Palmas, Teotihuacan. Adapted and modified by the author from Bernal (1949:17, plan 6; 69, plate 12) and Elson and Mowbray (2005:200, figure 2a).

Following his excavations at Ngüiteri, Bernal concluded that it was a late site dating to about two hundred years before the Spanish conquest (Bernal 1949:72). Dating of sediments associated with check dams along the natural drainage that runs along the south side of this site suggests that Ngüiteri was inhabited earlier than Bernal proposed. Coarse sands and gravels rapidly buried a stable surface consisting of a thin palaeosol that dates to 780–960 CE (Rincón Mautner 1999:685– 686). A thick layer of Early Postclassic ceramic sherds embedded in a matrix of calcium carbonate stripped from the denuded hill slopes above Ngüiteri was subsequently deposited over the sandy gravel deposit; check dams were later built at different points along the entire drainage in what appears to have been a major effort to curb erosion and hedge against drought conditions.

A close reinterpretation and comparison of Bernal's (1949) published excavation report with recently published material excavated by Vaillant in 1932 in the Teotihuacan region (Elson and Mowbray 2005) further leads me to conclude that Ngüiteri also has an Early Postclassic component. A cross-sectional diagram (figure 8.5) of Pit 10, excavated in Patio C, presents Tomb 16, which contained an offering of two identical unburnished red-on-cream hemispherical bowls, and above it four stucco floors, an altar, and Offering 4 (Bernal 1949:plan 6, 17, 33). Bernal's unpublished 1948 field report (Bernal 1948:47, photo 67) describes another Early Postclassic ceramic type, which he calls a "cajete con decoración incisa," of which he found only fragments in the lowest levels. This is a well-burnished, flat-bottomed bowl with an angular, everted rim that opens upwards from the base, with globular rattle tripod supports. It is made of thin to semi-fine brown or orange pastes and may present an orange interior and a slipped black or brown exterior. On the outer face, long and relatively wide incisions run almost the length of the support. The external incised decoration consists of two parallel lines that run along the vessel's entire circumference, one just below the rim and the other along the base. Between these lines and between supports along the bowl's horizontal axis are two incised rectangles; one enclosed a long capsule shape and the other enclosed five circles, with smaller interior circles next to each other. It has a stamped decoration in its interior identical to the polished gray type. Lind (personal communication, 2010) considers this type similar to the "Marta incised" bichrome, diagnostic of the early part of Cholula's Aquiahuac Phase (900–1150 CE; Lind 1994:81, table 1), based on two dated samples: INAH 1102 and 1103. The published dates for these samples are incorrect. The correct dates are 885 ± 55 and 990 ± 140 CE, respectively (Lind, personal communication, 2010). Referring to it as "false plumbate" because the dark slip appears vitrified, Noguera (1954:212–213) considered the type "foreign," possibly a tradeware, that appears early at Cholula and is also reported in more recent deposits. Sherds of a similar type were identified by Paddock and Bernal as "Cholula Inciso," a tradeware allegedly from the late part of the Venta Salada ceramic phase of the Tehuacan Valley (MacNeish et al. 1970b:227, fig. 13.7).

According to the *Lienzo Coixtlahuaca I* (*Seler II*), Lord 12 Lizard of the primary lineage came to Coixtlahuaca from neighboring Tequixtepec in the twelfth century CE and established himself as its ruler through a second marriage to a local princess, Lady 3 Ocelot (Rincón Mautner 1994, 1997, 1999:309–322, 2000, 2012b, 2015). This primary lineage distinguished itself as ancient, most noble, and descendant from Toltecs because its members traced their ancestry to the aforementioned Lord 7 Reed, who had emerged from the place of the river of reeds (Tollan). Interestingly, the nominative glyph below an open mortuary bundle of pictogram Panel 2 in the cave-tunnel at the Colossal Bridge coincides with the name *7 Reed* and may constitute a Late Classic or Epiclassic reference to this lord (Rincón Mautner 2005b: 62–63, figures 24 and 73). These are instances in which archaeology and ethnohistory complement each other, and it becomes possible to better understand the shifts in power relations and elucidate the circumstances that contributed to the emergence of Coixtlahuaca as the regional capital with a double seat of government.

At Coixtlahuaca, Bernal (1949:72) found materials similar to those reported at other sites in the Mixteca and concluded that Coixtlahuaca was the typical Mixtec site. Yet he was informed that the people were Chocho, so he surmised that the Chocho had a Mixtec culture. Already, in the sixteenth century, de los Reyes (1976:i–ii) described the relationship between the Chocho and Mixtec speakers at Coixtlahuaca as involving joint participation and communication and as having a great deal of kinship. I favor de los Reyes's sixteenth-century understanding of the social milieu since the local culture is the result of synergistic information flows within pluri-ethnic polities and between neighboring groups. As I will demonstrate, Coixtlahuaca offers the possibility to understand the complex nature of culture that stems from the interaction of different resident groups within a polity. Elsewhere, I have questioned and discussed the "material culture-ethnicity link"—that is, attributing ethnic authorship to one of the two main resident linguistic groups on the basis of pictographic ethnohistorical sources from Coixtlahuaca (Rincón Mautner 1996b) and/or artifacts (Rincón Mautner 1999:55–74). The historical events recorded in the *lienzos* can contribute to a better understanding of the archaeology. Given that I have recently found evidence for the presence of a third resident group within the bounds of this pluri-ethnic kingdom, I would like to take the argument further and propose that Coixtlahuaca shared in a wider sphere of interactions than has been previously recognized, and that the Postclassic "Mixtec" culture is more accurately to be considered the product of multigroup interactions over a wide area rather than solely the product of Mixtec speakers or restricted to the inhabitants of the Mixteca.

THE CLASSIC PERIOD (200–650 CE)

Although the proposed ceramic phases for this period in the Mixteca Alta are not well supported by an adequate number of consistent dates,[6] after the Early Urban period (300 BCE–200 CE) and until the beginning of the Late Postclassic period (circa 1250 CE), the Mixteca Alta is believed to have remained a cultural backwater and its peoples are often characterized as followers of cultural developments occurring elsewhere rather than as pioneers. On the basis of small artifactual assemblages, their culture is viewed as derivative, lacking in light or luster of its own, and as reflecting influences from the more powerful sites in Mesoamerica such as Teotihuacan or Monte Albán.

My findings for the Coixtlahuaca Basin are in sharp contrast with the characterization of the Late Classic-period Mixteca Alta as a region that was poor in terms of glyphic writing, symbols, and deities (Winter 1992:160) or, according to both Nicholson (1961:432) and Spores (1984:57), a "recipient" society more under northern influences than a functioning center of creativity in its own right. I find

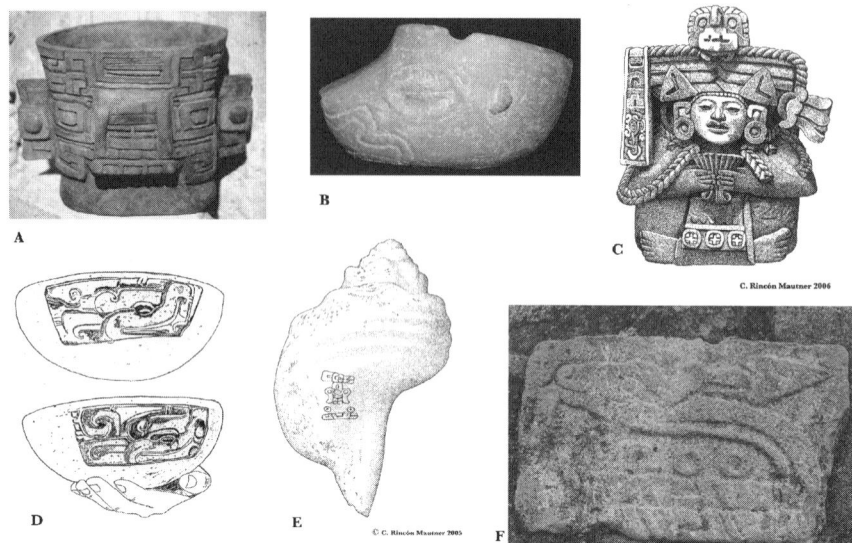

FIGURE 8.6. Classic-period materials from the Coixtlahuaca Basin. (A) Large "café" clay polychrome brazier, representing the "Wide-Billed Bird Deity," Las Flores, Tepelmeme. (B) Thin-orange opossum effigy vessel, Aztatla. (C) Polychrome effigy urn of a priest or ruler holding offering, Cerro Conduche, Xicotlan. (D) Imitation thin-orange paste with excised decoration of distinct serpents, Cuthá by San Miguel Tequixtepec. (E) Glyph 7A "Knot" personalizing a trumpet made of a horse conch shell, Las Flores, Tepelmeme. (F) Sculpted stone glyph 13 "Snake-Deer-Projectile," Ñiatexa-Tlalpitepec. Photos and drawings by the author. Figures C and E by Mr. David Smee.

evidence that strongly suggests that the Basin's inhabitants were engaged in dynamic interactions with Teotihuacan, the Central Valleys of Oaxaca, the Puebla Basin, and the Gulf Coast, as illustrated by the architecture, stone and shell carvings, ceramic effigy urns, and braziers found throughout this area (figure 8.6).

Although the literature abounds with references to the generally held view of one territory per ethnic group, during the Classic period cities like Teotihuacan were pluri-ethnic, and enclaves of different ethnicities—including groups from Oaxaca's Central Valley—have been recognized through their material culture. Beginning in the Late Miccaotli/Early Tlamimilolpa (200 CE) through Xolalpan (300–500 CE) phases, Oaxacans were identified as constituting a "barrio" at Teotihuacan (Spence 1992, 2002; Spence and White 2005), although ties between it and the Valley of Oaxaca do not appear to have been strong or continuous (Rattray 1993). Yet, the fact that a number of sites across a broad region, some of which are stable and transgenerational, present Oaxacan-style ceramics has led Spence (2005) to propose the existence of a Zapotec diaspora network and to consider its economic role vis-à-vis the Teotihuacan state. During the Xoo phase (600–800 CE), Zapotec merchant colonies were possibly present in the Toluca Valley as well (Smith and Lind 2005:169, 174–175).

Reconnaissance of the Coixtlahuaca Basin has revealed a number of Classic-period mountaintop sites, some of them surrounded by steep natural rock walls and man-made terraces (figure 8.4H). Buried stone and stucco platforms can be observed along the exposed banks of the Middle Río Culebra, at what appears to be a site of moderate size that includes a mounded stone platform, terraces, and house foundations on the nearby Cerro Ñiaxugue, 3.5 kilometers south of Coixtlahuaca (Rincón Mautner 1999:694–703, figures 111, 119). Ceramics from superimposed structures along this perennial stream correspond to the Yucuita, Ramos, and Las Flores phases of the chronological sequence. This site of Ñiaxugue is significant because it indicates continuous occupation for at least a thousand years. It appears to have been abandoned during the Late Classic period prior to the end of Las Flores phase, and was partially reoccupied during the Late Postclassic Natividad phase.

During the Late Classic period when Teotihuacan's influence was waning, the northern half of the Coixtlahuaca Basin seems to have had closer ties to Monte Albán and the Mixteca Baja. Mica as tempering material is more prevalent in ceramics from Tehuacán and the Mixteca Baja (Winter 1994:210) and is also present in sherds examined from Cerro del Tesoro in the Río Blanco Valley to the east and from the Colossal Bridge on the Ndaxagua to the north.

On the basis of the currently available information, it is not possible to ascertain whether the population of the Coixtlahuaca Basin during the Classic period was pluri-ethnic. However, one could conclude this to have been the case on the basis of the style of the material culture. In fact, were I to apply the same criteria used to establish that the use of certain glyphic conventions are tied to language, as in the arguments made for the emergence of an ethnic identity for the Zapotec (Marcus and Flannery 1996:160–161, 242), then I would logically conclude that perhaps the northern half of the Basin and the Mixteca Baja had Zapotec-speaking inhabitants (ethnic enclaves?), or that at least the elites may have understood Zapotec. Alternatively, perhaps the glyphs are not truly language-specific and are ultimately poor indicators for attribution to a particular ethnic group. In a recent paper, Rivera Guzmán (2008) proposes that the Classic-period writing style of the Mixteca Alta was similar enough to that of the Mixteca Baja to be likewise termed Ñuiñe. Although some glyphs from the Colossal Bridge resemble those found at Teotihuacan, Ñuiñe script is believed by some to be derived from Zapotec writing of the Valley of Oaxaca.

The Classic-Postclassic Transition (700–900 CE)

The end of the Classic period brought about significant changes to both upland and lowland regions throughout Mesoamerica. Site abandonment is reported across a widespread area and evidence for social upheaval is found throughout the Central Mexican Highlands. It is likely that a natural phenomenon like prolonged drought lasting from the sixth to the eleventh centuries CE, accompanied by famine and an outbreak of epidemic hemorrhagic fevers resulting in extremely high mortalities, could have led to the eventual collapse of Classic-period settlements in the Mixteca (Acuña-Soto et al. 2005; Smith and Berdan 2003:6; Winter 1989a:70, 125).[7] Recent tree-ring data have revealed the occurrence of drought that lasted twenty-five years (897–922 CE) in the Querétaro region, not far from Tula or Tenochtitlán (Stahle et al. 2011). The timing of the drought appears to coincide with events contained in the narratives of pre-Columbian codices and the Colonial period *lienzos*.

In all likelihood, the effects of this drought differed from region to region, affecting nomadic groups of the arid interior basins differently than sedentary agriculturalists, whose ability to cope with such a phenomenon depended on the abundance of water and the population density. The resulting collapses were probably multicausal and occurred at different rates interregionally. The codices depict the social upheaval that is to have characterized those times as an epic "War of Heaven," in which terrifying female supernaturals known as *tzitzimime* descended from the celestial realm, auguring conflict (Byland 2008:346–350).

Extreme population decline resulting from drought-induced famine, starvation, disease, warfare, and the migrations of uprooted groups could have prompted rulers to actively seek recruits for the purpose of replacing those who had died or fled, and to provide necessary labor, defense, and tribute. Subhumid areas to semi-arid areas like the southern Tehuacán Valley and the relatively dry northern Mixteca Alta where Coixtlahuaca is situated would have been most vulnerable. Elsewhere I have used the framework of drought to explain the construction and subsequent abandonment of stone-faced check dams in natural drainages and the cultivation of bowl maize (*maíz cajete*) in the Mixteca (Rincón Mautner 1999:241–249, 678–687; 2015); the interpretation of rituals involving rulers and priests depicted in the *lienzos* (Rincón Mautner 2000); the ritual use of caves (Rincón Mautner 2005a, 2005b); and political instability and the expansion of the Chocho into the Tejupan-Tamazulapan Valleys (Rincón Mautner 1999:322–324, 338–340).

Population decline and widespread regional abandonment can be inferred by dating the massively bedded floodplain deposits, indicating that a rapid process of sedimentation was underway that buried stoned-faced, cross-drainage check dams and other features. The dams were no longer used, maintained, or enlarged from one year to the next, as would have been necessary to continue using them and prevent them from becoming buried or breached. Several centuries would pass until sedimentation decreased and soil development on slopes once again ensued. Stone-faced check dams were built anew in the natural drainages on the most recent stable surface and over older buried water and soil management features (Rincón Mautner 1999:678–687, 704). Additional evidence of abandonment can be found among the painted panels on the walls of the cave-tunnel at the Colossal Bridge on the Ndaxagua. The carefully executed paintings of the Early and Middle Classic period, which suggest a period of exclusive use and possibly restricted access, were subsequently scribbled upon. The deliberate defacement of Panel 2 and the graffiti on Panel 3 that is unrelated to the subject matter of the original paintings represent a relaxation of access to the cave-tunnel interior by possibly unrelated people during the transition to the Postclassic, potentially indicating a lack of continuity between these two periods (Rincón Mautner 2005b:28–29, 58–59). The fact that no graffiti or new paintings were added during the Late Postclassic and instead rich ritual offerings were deposited in the cave-tunnel's interior, suggests a recontextualization and the assignment of new meanings. Such possible meanings include that it was the preeminent sacred place made by a xiucoatl, or fire serpent, to which the two male deities involved in the creation of the world, Mixcoatl-Tezcatlipoca and Quetzalcoatl, descended from the sky and from which their mortuary bundles were brought forth and through which the ancestor of the principal lineage entered the Coixtlahuaca Basin (Rincón Mautner 1995, 2005a, 2005b).

A new and distinct ceramic assemblage consisting of bichrome orange/red-on-brown or brown-on-cream designs replaced the Classic-period ceramics. Although it is as of yet undated, this new type of ceramic assemblage resembles the Coyotlatelco-horizon ceramics of Central Mexico in design and appears to be a precursor for the red-on-cream ceramics of later times (figure 8.7). Common decorative designs on hemispherical bowl exteriors strongly resemble Corral-phase examples from Tula (Cobean 1990:92–104, 130–147, plates 25–27, 29, 52–57, 63, 73–74, 85). Until now, this type of decorated ceramics has been recorded in the northern sector of the Coixtlahuaca Basin and could indicate the arrival and settlement of the area by outsiders with a different cultural tradition. One of the most common forms appears to be a hemispherical bowl decorated with an interior tri-spiral or scroll motif (figure 8.7).

Groups intrusive into the Mixteca, such as the Ixcatec and the Chocho-popoloca, separated at different times from Popoloca (*Nguiwa*)—their linguistic precursor spoken in the Tehuacán Valley—possibly as a result of increasing conflict and displacement by incoming Nahua or "Chichimeca" groups.[8] The split between the Ixcatec and the Popoloca occurred in about 700 CE, after which the Ixcatec

FIGURE 8.7. (*Bottom left*) Epiclassic (?) Coyotlatelco-style decoration of ceramic sherds of hemispherical bowls from Cumbre Alta and Torrecillas, Central Coixtlahuaca Basin: (A) black on cream; (B–C) brown on cream; and (D) red on cream. (*Upper left and center right*) Hemispherical bowl decorated with orange on cream tri-spiral spatula motif. (*Far right*) Hemispherical bowl with extended vertical sides decorated with black and orange on cream alternating hook and thorn motifs. Drawings and photos by the author.

migrated and settled in the Mixteca Alta, northeast of Coixtlahuaca. The Chocho split from the latter circa 1200 CE (Hopkins 1984; Winter et al. 1984:84, 90–91, 95), ending up in the Coixtlahuaca Basin and separated from the Popoloca by the Nahua settlements of Chilacatla (San Gabriel Chilac), Nextepec (San Gabriel Casablanca), and Nanacoatipac (San Antonio Nanahuatipac).

While Nahua speakers entered Mesoamerica around 500 CE (Kaufman 2001a), it is generally believed that non-Nahua speaking "barbarian" Chichimeca groups began migrating in the eighth century (if not earlier) from areas northwest of the Basin of Mexico (Campbell 1988:277–278). Wright-Carr (2010) posits that three Proto-Nahuatl-speaking groups split and migrated to the Sierra de Puebla; Guatemala; and Veracruz and El Salvador, respectively, between 800 and 1250 CE. Eastern Nahua separated from Proto-Nahua by the end of the Classic to Early Postclassic in a second migration or series of migrations (500–1100 CE) before the last Nahua migration from Western Mexico to Central Mexico ensued between the Epiclassic and the Early Postclassic (850–1300 CE) and the Late Postclassic (1200–1520 CE). These migration events preceded the internal branching of

Central Mexican Nahua (1135–1475 CE). Migrants from Western Mexico appear to have contributed to an "intense gene exchange" that transformed the physiognomies of the original Central Mexican population at the Classic-Postclassic transition (González-José et al. 2006). Until the Nahua migrations, the Popoloca had constituted the majority of population throughout the vast region encompassing the Puebla Basin and Tehuacán Valley. Popoloca kingdoms were overtaken first by the Acolhua and then by the Mexica who married Popoloca royalty. However, a number of Popoloca royal houses still remained in the sixteenth century, ruling over the kingdoms of Cuauhtinchan, Tepexic, and Zapotitlán (table 8.1).

Between 500 and 700 CE, Nahua migrations into southern Puebla seem to have displaced/replaced a number of groups, including the Mangue-speaking inhabitants of Cholula, who left and eventually settled in the Soconusco, Honduras, and Nicaragua, where they became known as Chorotega (Kaufman 2001a:3, 12, 2001b). These migrations also created a corridor of independent kingdoms whose people brought with them different traditions and new ideas, some of which were subsequently incorporated into local traditions over a wide area that stretched from the western Chichimec hinterland east to Nicaragua (Kirchhoff 1940). Their presence in other areas of the Mixteca and coastal Oaxaca is likewise documented in the Codex Selden (1964:11-III, 12-I, 13-I) and in the *Relación de Guatulco*. In this latter source, the people refer to themselves as Chichimeca and to the fact that they speak a "corrupt and disguised" form of Nahuatl (in all likelihood an early form Nahuat) (Vargas 1984:188). Like Coixtlahuaca, they, too, had a Coatepec or Snake Mountain (Vargas 1984:189) and had worshipped Itzpapalotl at Pochutla (Vargas 1984:193).

It is apparent from Josserand's (1983) numerous maps of lexical isoglosses that the Chocho-popoloca are intrusive into the Coixtlahuaca Basin. Josserand (1983:108) identified a Mixtec dialect in an area east of the Coixtlahuaca Basin, which she considered to have resulted from the displacement of Mixtec speakers from the Basin by the arrival of the Chocho-popoloca. She further identified Coixtlahuaca's Mixteco and that of Cuilapan as corresponding to the northeastern Mixteca Alta (Kathryn Josserand, personal communication, 1994; Mata 1984; Salazar 1984).

The *lienzo* accounts refer to the initial arrival and settlement of migrating groups in the more arid and sparsely populated northern end of the Basin, perhaps as early as 800 CE (Rincón Mautner 1999:182). These groups eventually pushed south and displaced the Basin's resident Mixtec-speaking inhabitants in historic times, which supports the linguistic findings. The pictographic accounts also reveal how warfare and conquest contributed to Coixtlahuaca's complex ethnic constituency.

Early Postclassic Period Repopulation (950–1250 CE):
Changing the Balance of Power

By the Early Postclassic period, broad areas of Mesoamerica had experienced changes in settlement distribution and nucleation. In areas where the population appears to have declined significantly, competition to recruit commoners as warriors, laborers, and tribute providers would have been intense. Alliances and social prestige appear to have been offered even to hunter-gatherers, when generally such were reserved for equals. The most usual enticements to forge the alliance were to offer lands, women, and social position. This form of recruitment appears to have been widespread and it is recorded in the *Historia Tolteca-Chichimeca* (folio 16r, Kirchhoff et al. 1989), where Toltec lords can be seen coaxing the Chichimeca to emerge from Chicomoztoc. Once they emerge, they are given names and wives. The making of lords from the ranks of hunter-gatherers would also appear to contradict current thinking on class exclusivity and absence of upward social mobility.

The *Selden Roll* refers to the arrival of priests and warriors, some of whom wear the *xihuitzolli* diadem and others "saw-tooth" crowns. Their distinct headdresses and the paint around the warriors' eyes suggest they belong to a different ethnic group. The priests carry the sacred mortuary bundles of two deities or ancestors and other ritual objects. Such a depiction suggests that they are leading a group of people (*calpolli*), who are not portrayed, on a migration. Upon entering the Basin from the northeast, they request permission to settle in the northern area of the Coixtlahuaca Basin from the local Lord 2 Dog[9] (Rincón Mautner 1999:311–312; 2012a:258). This event appears to have occurred perhaps as early as the tenth century.

Subsequently, the reigning Lord 13 Rain, tenth ruler of the first dynasty of the primary lineage, was challenged, perhaps by these very same people who had sought refuge among the Basin's inhabitants or by their immediate descendants, leading to his abdication and forced migration from Tequixtepec, north of Coixtlahuaca to the Eastern Puebla Basin (Rincón Mautner 1997, 1999:314–319). Although there is a discrepancy in the sources as to when this migration occurred (Reyes García 1998:67, 71), in keeping with custom, Lord 13 Rain and his retinue were welcomed and given lands and wives at Zacahuilotlan by Tecamachalco. The Toltec lineage's eventual return to Coixtlahuaca is depicted most explicitly in the *Lienzo of Ihuitlan* and the *Lienzo de Tequixtepec I* upon the arrival of Lord 9 Alligator and his family, who begin the second dynasty in the mid- to late-eleventh century. His children become established as rulers at Tequixtepec and Tulancingo and eventually, through a grandson named Lord 12 Lizard, the Toltec lineage is seated at Coixtlahuaca (Rincón Mautner 2012b:151).

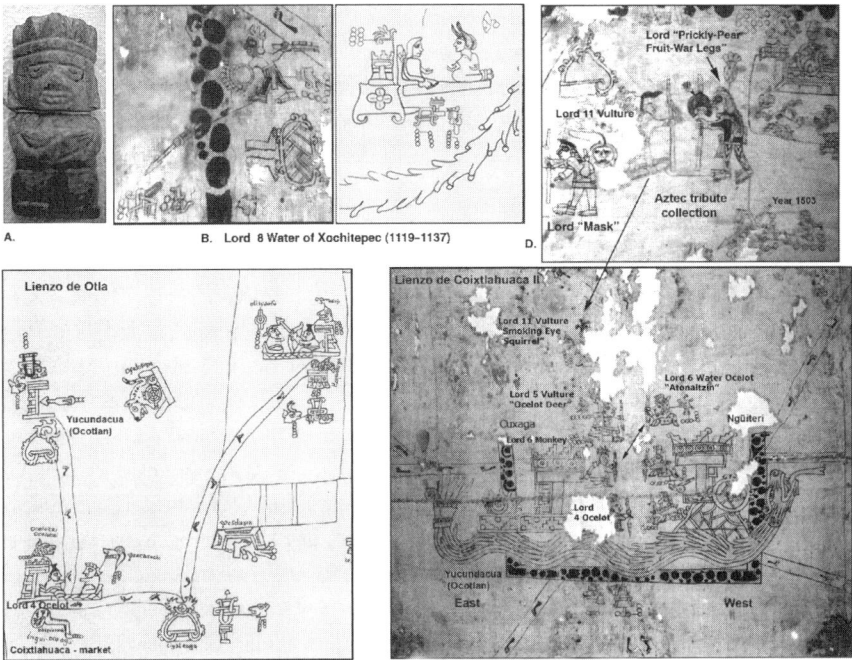

FIGURE 8.8. (A) Saw-toothed crown on a green stone *penate* (an anthropomorphic figure representing an ancestor); (B–C) Colonial period depictions of warfare, conquests, and fiefdoms of Lords 8 Water (*left, Lienzo de Coixtlahuaca II* [Ixtlan] and *right, Lienzo de Coixtlahuaca I* [Seler II]) and 4 Ocelot (*Lienzo de Otla*); (D) the Mexica presence at Coixtlahuaca (*Lienzo de Coixtlahuaca II* [Ixtlan]); (E) Royal houses on Coixtlahuaca's place sign and rulers at the time of the Aztec Conquest identified by line with double arrow points. Arrow between D and E identifies the second Aztec imposed Lord 11 Vulture who reigned in 1503. Drawings and photos by the author.

LORD 4 OCELOT AND THE CHICHIMECA AT COIXTLAHUACA

A generation after the second dynasty had been established at Tequixtepec and Tulancingo, Chichimec warriors who shared in the cultural spheres of the Popoloca and Eastern Nahua were invited by a group of lords from the Coixtlahuaca Basin and its vicinity to participate in war campaigns against several Mixtec-speaking *yuhuitayu* located along the southern end of the Basin (Rincón Mautner 1997:139, 2012b:152). Four documents, the *Lienzo de Nativitas* (figure 8.4A), *Lienzo of San Jerónimo Otla* (figure 8.8c), *Lienzo de Coixtlahuaca I* (*Seler II*) and the *Lienzo Tlalpitepec,* depict these Chichimec warriors bearing bows and arrows[10] (Rincón Mautner 2007b). With their aid, Lords 12 Lizard and 11 Flower established their lineages at Coixtlahuaca, which became the new seat of the realm: a complex *alte-petl* or double *yuhuitayu* ruled by two royal houses, one with Toltec and the other with Chichimec ancestries. I propose that these campaigns displaced the original Mixtec-speaking residents of the Basin, which serves to explain the diaspora of Mixtec speakers from the area, as Josserand (1983:108) discovered. Coixtlahuaca's new rulers paid their Chichimec warrior allies with the lands and women of the vanquished, as was customary. They settled in areas southeast (Ocotlan), west (Otla), and north (Xochitepec) (figure 8.8B and 8.8C) of Coixtlahuaca.

One of the protagonists of these campaigns was a Lord Ocelotzin "Tiger Claw" (4 Ocelot) who, according to the *Lienzo de Otla*, came from a place called *Tizaltoya* or *Tizalcoya*, consisting of a flaming mountain with a white disk on its summit, perhaps meaning "the place where lime is made." This place seems to have been located north and outside the Coixtlahuaca Basin (figure 8.8C). This lord and his accompanying retinue of warriors armed with bows and arrows, the signature weapon of the Chichimec, had departed their mountain home for Coixtlahuaca in the year 1 House, day 7 Dog, equivalent to 1065 or 1117 CE. Lord 4 Ocelot married Lord 11 Flower's daughter and became the first Chichimec ruler of Coixtlahuaca's secondary lineage. He is shown in the lower left of figure 8.8C, seated above the Coixtlahuaca place sign consisting of a coiled rattlesnake that presents a circular form.

However, it is the footprints within the snake's body and the faint gloss below it that reads *tia qui zco togo* (*tianquiztonco,* meaning "small place of the market" in Nahuatl), which confirms this lord's preeminent association with Coixtlahuaca's market[11] (Rincón Mautner 2007b:88). The *Lienzo de Tlalpitepec* also associates Lord 4 Ocelot with the market by representing him above a circular stone shield that encloses crude footprints and insignia of his rank: a tiger claw, and ocelot and coyote pelts with tails. The special placement of this lord relative to other lords upon the snake place sign on the *Lienzo de Otla* and on Coixtlahuaca's large *lien-zos*, together with the references to a market place, identify him and possibly his lineage descendants as having extraordinary privileges and a significant function in Coixtlahuaca's great market (Rincón Mautner 2012b:152–53, figures 4.21–4.23). Lord 4 Ocelot and his lineage were perhaps entrusted with overseeing the orderly functioning of the market, enforcing the collection of tribute, and maintaining constructive relations with merchants from distant lands (Rincón Mautner 2012b:157, 163). Furthermore, the placement of this lord's spouse and palace on the left side of the lines representing the Río Culebra, the perennial stream that divides this settlement, indicate that both his seat of government and the market were located in the eastern sector of the settlement, which coincidentally was Mixtec-speaking (Rincón Mautner 1999:189). From this capital, Lord 4 Ocelot (ca. 1087–1142 CE or 1139–1194 CE) launched a great number of war campaigns, including a major incursion into the Tehuacán Valley and the eastern Puebla Basin. According to the *lienzo* accounts, this lord greatly expanded Coixtlahuaca's dominion over territory to the east and south, including Yucundacua (Ocotlán), represented as a hill with a blood spiral (figure 8.8C) and by a spiral on a platform extension (figure 8.8E, Rincón Mautner 1997:142n32, 1999:334n94, 2000:39–41). The memory of the outcome of some of these campaigns is preserved in the extant 1579–1580 *Relaciones Geográficas* from villages east of Coixtlahuaca, which contain references to the payment of tribute to this great conqueror (Suárez 1984:143). He is also immortalized conquering Cuauhtla (Nahuatl) or Yucuyaha (Mixtec), the "place of eagles" on the *Lienzos Coixtlahuaca II* and *III*. Lord 4 Ocelot is the only Coixtlahuaca ruler depicted in the prehispanic codices as Lord 8 Deer's companion in arms (Rincón Mautner 1999:332–334, 2000:40).

In addition to identifying the Chichimeca by their predilection for the bow and arrow, several scholars refer to face paint as an indicator of ethnic/deity affiliation (Burland 1955:26; Seler 1904:179–180) which, like language, does not leave a physical record that can be detected archaeologically. Black face paint is usually associated with Chichimec custom or with the Mixcoatl/Tezcatlipoca cult (Rincón Mautner 1999:323–324, 2000:31). It is also considered a hallmark characteristic used in identifying "outsiders," who are represented in the codices as having blackened faces or black circles around the eyes—that is, speakers of Mexican (Nahuatl), who are called *sami nuu* in Mixtec, which means "burnt eye" or "burnt face" (Smith 1973:209).

One such "burnt face" personage is the Chichimeca Lord 8 Water (figure 8.8B), a companion in arms of Coixtlahuaca's aforementioned famous ruler *Ocelotzin* (Lord 4 Ocelot). He is depicted on Coixtlahuaca's *lienzos*, sporting the red stripes of the deity Camaxtli on his face and body, while carrying out campaigns along the eastern frontier. According to the *Lienzo de Coixtlahuaca I* (*Seler II*), he too was given a fiefdom, which appears to have been located in the northern end of the Basin at Xochitepec ("Hill of the White Flower"). Like the priests and warriors on the *Selden Roll* and the mortuary bundles on the *Lienzo of Ihuitlan*, he also wears a crown similar to that of an anthropomorphic greenstone *penate* that was found at Coixtlahuaca (figure 8.8A).

The active recruiting of either single men or *calpolli* as laborers and as warriors for defense and/or territorial expansion would have undoubtedly shifted the regional power balance. Once a ruler resorted to this strategy of recruiting or retaining ascribed warriors and/or tribute providers, other rulers from neighboring kingdoms would have had little choice but to follow suit in order to protect themselves, increasing the complexity of the cultural system. Such groups would constitute an example of collective specialization. This process of "social infilling" by recruiting warriors and *calpollaque* (name for members of the collective known as *calpolli*) from different ethnic groups who are initially welcomed but then vanquish the original residents and take over their lands (Martínez 1984; Olivera 1978:61–88, figure 7; Reyes García 1988) could explain the myriad tiny ethnic enclaves arranged in a pattern of pluri-ethnic kingdoms throughout the broad area from the Basin of Mexico eastwards to the Puebla Basin and the Northern Mixteca, constituting the foundation for Late Postclassic states (figure 8.1 and table 8.1). Given its resilience, a social unit like the *calpolli* would have survived the widespread Classic-period collapses because its cohesion appears to have been based on having a common patron deity, history, and ethnic affiliation (Rincón Mautner 2012b:123).

Demographic recovery and social infilling were also accomplished through marriage alliances. Migration and settlement of Mixtec speakers among the Zapotec during the Middle and Late Postclassic periods is particularly well described in the *Relaciones Geográficas* of Cuilapan and Teozapotlan (Zaachila). In both instances, we learn that Mixtecs had arrived from the Almoloyas region of the Mixteca Alta near the Cuicatlán Cañada due to certain marriages among noble families, the first of which had taken place more than three hundred years earlier (ca. 1280 CE). As part of the dowry on the occasion of his daughter's marriage, the Lord of Zaachila gave the lands near Cuilapan to his son-in-law and new wife. The nobleman brought his *terrazguerros*, or landless peasants, with him to work these new lands (Salazar 1984:178–179). A larger retinue of Mixtecs is said to have accompanied the husband-to-be of the sister of the lord of Teozapotlan's spouse, in preparation for a second marriage that took place shortly before the Spanish conquest (Mata 1984:157–158). The groom was a lord from Yanhuitlan who settled in Cuilapan, which was given to the newlyweds as a gift. For this reason Cuilapan and other communities in the Valley of Oaxaca like Xoxocotlán were predominantly Mixtec-speaking towns as recently as the twentieth century.

THE LATE POSTCLASSIC EMERGENCE OF A SUPRA-IDENTITY (1250–1461 CE): THE TOLTECA CHICHIMECA COIXTLAHUAQUE

Following custom, the newcomers to the Coixtlahuaca Basin renamed certain places with the place names of their homeland (Rojas 1985:128–129), supplanting old names with those familiar to them, embellishing the perceived environment and special landforms with additional layers of meaning. At least two Basin toponyms refer to places in the Tula region: Tulancingo (*Tollantzinco*, meaning "New Tollan") and Tepelmeme (*Tepenenec*). The legendary Tepenenec was the staging point for Chichimec migrants from Chicomoztoc into the Basin of Mexico and Cholula (Davies 1980:43). Tepelmeme de Morelos is a village north of Coixtlahuaca whose name is derived from *Tepenenec* ("Hill of the Echo") which, according to Muñoz

Camargo (1984:147), was the name of the province where the hero Mimich, one of the Mimixcoa, shot the Chichimec Goddess Itzpapalotl with arrows.

Owing to its pluri-ethnic character, it is not surprising to find mixed attributes in deity representations, conflations, and evidence of the coexistence of what may have constituted different ideologies and/or traditions at Coixtlahuaca. The *Selden Roll* depicts a "mixed" allegorical epic story that combines the culture hero/deity Ehecatl-Quetzalcóatl's descent to earth with the creation cycle involving this deity and his counterpart Mixcoatl/Tezcatlipoca, who both transformed themselves into giant serpents and together tied the Earth Goddess upon the water at the beginning of the Fifth Sun (i.e., the Postclassic period). However, the account also records the journey in which Quetzalcóatl's mortuary bundle is taken back to the place where the Earth Goddess was tied, to the summit of Coatepec—the legendary Snake Mountain and the Place of Creation and Mountain of Sustenance—depicted in the *lienzos* as a mountain surmounted by knotted serpents (Rincón Mautner 2007a; 2012a:259–261). Part of the inauguration rituals for taking legitimate possession of the territory from this mountain's summit seems to have included a reenactment of Creation in which the enthroned mortuary bundles of the patron deities "participated." Fire was lit in their presence. The account is further conflated by including references to the migration accounts of the Chichimeca. The scene of the beheaded warriors whose heads are atop the cacti in the *Selden Roll* is similar to the Aztec migration accounts in the codices *Aubin* and *Boturini* (Burland 1955:18; Graulich 1974:345). My interpretation is that these beheaded warriors in the *Roll* were the legendary Mimixcoa ("cloud serpents" in Nahuatl), who were among the first sacrificed to feed the Earth because she could no longer feed herself and had to be fed by humans, which conforms to a creation tradition recorded in Texcoco (Garibay 1985:108). Perhaps owing to the coexistence of different ethnic groups and their traditions in this area, the identity of the Earth Goddess and Itzpapalotl appear to have been conflated (Rincón Mautner 2007a; 2012a:260). Itzpapalotl was the leader and teacher of the Chichimecs who, upon her death, became their deified ancestor. The goddess was also one of the *tzitzimime*, female deities who presaged destruction and whose appearance was generally feared. The warrior heads have lip-plugs, but they lack the black face paint because at the time of their death, Itzpapalotl was still alive. Only after her cremation did it become customary for Chichimec warriors to memorialize her by smearing ashes around their eyes.

Its historical interactions with other areas and numerous movements of detachments of nobles and commoners during the first and second dynasties contributed to Coixtlahuaca's becoming an ethnic mosaic. Yet, the most fascinating part of its history is how the surprisingly fluid political situation that developed would be steadied. In view of these comings and goings, and in order to guarantee community longevity, all groups would have had to subscribe to a superorder or organizing strategy, beginning with the allocation of lands to newcomers and continuing with the embellishing and sharing of their unique origin traditions, sacred beliefs, and political histories. Part of the answer can be found in the administrative arrangement between two royal houses, which I have earlier proposed as reflecting the major ethnic composition of the kingdom and complementary functions each had (Rincón Mautner 2012b:154–57, 163). The rest of the answer rests on the emphasis placed on the Creation tradition, Coixtlahuaca's two origin myths, its patron deities, the exaltation of its lineages and worship of ancestors, the production of handicrafts, participation in Coixtlahuaca's famous market, and in religious rituals. Under these circumstances, elites and commoners had every reason to be interdependent rather than exclusive, and it would have required the development of a canon of symbols and the production of portable artifacts that could be recognized by all. These promoted cohesion through the adoption of a cosmopolitan Tolteca-Chichimeca supra identity and a tradition in which the people of the Coixtlahuaca Basin and the inhabitants of the broad Mixteca-Puebla region participated.

As mentioned, Bernal (1949) compared Coixtlahuaca's archaeological assemblage with that of the Mixteca and concluded that Coixtlahuaca had a Mixtec culture. In turn, Noguera (1950) compared Late Postclassic materials from the Mixteca to the Tolteca-Chichimeca of Cholula and Tepeaca, and recognized that a close relationship had existed between Mixtec culture and the Tolteca-Chichimeca, which he subsumed as a Tolteca-Chichimeca Horizon. Although Early Postclassic materials for the Mixteca had not been described at the time, he observed that Late Postclassic Mixteca polychrome wares resembled early Cholula types more so than late ones, which may reflect a shared early history (Lind 1994:98).

It seems remarkable that the relatively homogeneous Postclassic material assemblage known as Mixteca-Puebla (Nicholson 1982; Nicholson and Quiñones Keber 1994) would have been achieved during a time period characterized as one of "balkanization" (Dumond and Muller 1972:1215; Marcus and Flannery 1983:217), when there was not one single or pair of dominant centers but rather numerous, warring small polities in the Central Mexican Highlands, Oaxaca, and the Tehuacán Valley. While intraregional variation in the style of the artifacts from this time period has been recognized, explanations as to what it represents or how it relates to cultural processes have not been forthcoming.[12] Sociopolitical forces driving the creation of this assemblage appear to have promoted the development of a collective supra-identity that would have greater permanence and cut across the divisiveness of factionalism and warfare. The role played by religion in fostering cohesion offers one possible explanation.

The rapid spread of the unifying Quetzalcóatl religion throughout Mesoamerica during the Epiclassic (Ringle et al. 1998) is evident by the broad distribution of "feathered serpent" motifs and religious symbols associated with this religion, which follows the prescribed requirement for a horizon. Notwithstanding the incomplete status of regional and site chronologies, the codices place the appearance of Ehecatl-Quetzalcóatl at about this time, which also happens to coincide with, or follow closely, the appearance and wide geographical distribution of the oldest component of the Mixteca-Puebla tradition, the so-called Religious Style of the Early Postclassic (Smith and Heath-Smith 1980:18). Despite Nicholson and Quiñones Keber's (1994:x–xi) disavowal of the existence of this early component of the tradition, Diehl (1993:267) considers it to have been initially a true horizon, which later evolved into a generalized elite religious system.

The fast spread of the religion and its accompanying symbol system was achieved among peoples participating in established market networks through the manufacture and use of ceramic stamps and molds and the circulation of paper with printed designs, which would have required only a few workshops and markets for mass production and dissemination of uniform designs. In addition to the elite, commoners participated actively in the development of this Postclassic cultural tradition by producing, exchanging, and transporting the artifacts.

Concomitant with the thriving market and vast trade networks in which Coixtlahuaca was involved, there was a notable expansion of the pantheon of deities during the Late Postclassic period. Religion and ritual not only became seemingly more complex, but there is a clear increase in the number of participants in religious ritual at different levels: domestic, corporate (*calpolli*), and community. Although the name *Coixtlahuaca* appears to be quite ancient, in all likelihood it was during the transition to the Early Postclassic that the seat of the kingdom adopted the "feathered serpent-on-a-plain motif" as its topogram (figure 8.8E). Thus Coixtlahuaca, Cholula, and Tula were united symbolically through the Quetzalcóatl religion with the earlier Classic and Epiclassic centers where plumed serpents, emblems of cosmic unity, and rulership had also been represented. During the Late Postclassic, both Cholula and Coixtlahuaca became major market and pilgrimage centers that attracted commoners and rulers alike from far and wide. In addition, Cholula would become a paramount religious center where rituals of accession were performed to memorialize what seems to have been the Toltec ceremony of anointing a king under the patronage of the elite's deity, Quetzalcóatl. The prevalence of blood sacrifice themes in the diagnostic Late Postclassic polychrome assemblage from Cholula noted by Lind (1994:87) contrasts with that of the chocolate serving/drinking vessel assemblage of the Mixteca, and probably reflects the custom of making sacrificial offerings that included blood sacrifice during at least three types of ritual ceremonies: ruler accession, the yearly feast to the patron deity 9 Rain, and in times of drought (Rojas 1985:131–132; Zorita 1963:15–19).

By the Late Postclassic, Coixtlahuaca had risen to prominence as a center that both produced and traded exquisite Mixteca-Puebla handicrafts. The role of a state like Coixtlahuaca in directing religious participation is not completely clear, although in all likelihood the governing elite would have encouraged participation of the representatives of all constituencies in ritual ceremonies, for the purpose of reducing social tension and promoting a sense of community.

Pohl (2003a–d) considers that Late Postclassic Mixteca-Puebla-styled arti-facts exhibit ethnicity and reflect political and elite marriage alliances, whereby the nobility directed religion and the commercial production and circulation of luxury items. Although recognizing the different emphases of rituals and the use of Mixteca-Puebla symbols in Cholula and Oaxaca, Pohl (2003c:202) attributes the homogeneity over such a broad geographic area as the result of "so many four-teenth century court artisans" painting the same set of icons with similar stylis-tic precision as "a testament to the tremendous degree of elite integration that Nahua, Mixtec and Zapotec royal houses achieved through their feast networks." In the first place this leaves the Popoloca, including the Chocho or Southern Popoloca, who were also present as elites throughout this area and Coixtlahuaca, unaccounted for in Pohl's scheme. In the second place, I argue that the manu-facture and use of ceramic stamps and molds and the circulation of paper with stamped designs would have required only a few workshops and markets for mass production and dissemination of a canon of motifs with uniform designs among peoples living far and wide. Moreover, Pohl appears to posit that commoners were excluded from exchanges and participation in the development of Postclassic cul-ture. Prior to being conquered by the Mexica, Coixtlahuaca distinguished itself from other Mixteca kingdoms by having a specialized class of merchants that thrived on the commerce between the Mixteca, Tehuacan, Eastern Puebla, the Cuicatlan Cañada, and the lower Papaloapan Basin. I propose that what perhaps contributed most significantly to the spread of the Mixteca-Puebla artistic style is the presence of Nahuatl-speaking Chichimecs throughout this broad area. As latecomers, the Chichimeca warriors would have first devoted themselves to aid-ing the Chocho-Popoloca lords as mercenaries. In time, given that cultivable lands for distribution would have been scarce, they eventually carved out a socio-economic niche for themselves by participating in trade and markets scheduled according to the widely observed ritual calendar of feasts shared by different eth-nic groups with Nahuatl as the lingua franca.

The Aztec Period (1461–1521 CE)

By 1326 CE, Coixtlahuaca had expanded into the neighboring Texupan and Tamazulapan valleys to the west. However, the maximum expansion and integration of the kingdom was achieved during the reign of Lord 10 Serpent (1413–1436 CE). Although integration of the kingdom may have resulted in further acculturation, assimilation, and the development of a coherent ideology among the Coixtlahuaca Basin peoples, another tendency toward homogenization occurred with the rise of Tenochtitlán. The presence of Aztec-style materials is generally assumed to have occurred after the Aztec conquest at several locations, reflecting the shared experience and history of conquest and transculturation.

Coixtlahuaca fell to the Aztecs in 1461 CE, thus ending the joint rulership of the kingdom as rulers selected by the Aztec supplanted the legitimate heirs. Regional integration appears to have continued following the Aztec conquest. Interestingly, according to the *Lienzo de Ihuitlan,* it is only after 1467 that Tulancingo's royal house with its Toltec lineage established kinship ties with the royal houses of Coxcatlan, Tehuacán, and Zacatlán or Acatlán, in what is now the Mexican state of Puebla (Rincón Mautner 1999:369). Therefore, the evidence provided by this document does not support Pohl and Byland's (1994:193) proposal for a preexisting confederation, factional allegiances, or the establishment of alliance corridors with the Nonoalca, with whom Popoloca kingdoms had been waging war prior to the Aztecs' intrusion.

During the early Postclassic, the social landscape extending from the Basin of Mexico eastward and southward was a configuration of a multitude of Nahua-speaking enclaves interspersed among other ethnic groups, including Popoloca and Mixtec speakers. In fact, Coixtlahuaca's emergence as a major market center must be viewed as a result of cooperation between the enterprising Nahua-speaking Chichimec and the Chocho-Popoloca.

In the fifteenth century, the Aztecs' arrival changed the geopolitical landscape of the Tehuacan Valley and the Mixteca. They aimed to destabilize existing polities by appealing to and enlisting the aid of Nahua speakers settled in pluri-ethnic polities like Coixtlahuaca. Their strategy would have aimed to continue the pattern of intermarriage with local elites, while at the same time bolstering internal dissension and factionalism that would switch allegiances in their favor. This led to uprisings that facilitated conquest and regime change (Rincón Mautner 1999:350–353). It was also part of their strategy to subdue some groups while leaving their neighbors free, in essence playing one group against the other.

The Aztec domination of the kingdom is recorded on two of Coixtlahuaca's *lienzos: Coixtlahuaca II (Ixtlan)* and *Coixtlahuaca III (Meixuiero),* as well as on the *Lienzo de Ihuitlan* (Rincón Mautner 2012b:158–61, figures 4.6, 4.20, and 4.24). Two of the lords who ruled after the Aztecs conquered Coixtlahuaca are depicted in figure 8.8E, seated above Lord 6 Monkey of the secondary lineage represented on the left and tail end of the Coixtlahuaca place sign. Lord 6 Monkey was a contemporary of Lord 6 Water of the first lineage, as indicated by the line with double arrows pointing to these figures. Both of these rulers were deposed and sacrificed in 1461 CE. In 1503, the subsequent reigning Lord 11 Vulture "Smoking Eye Squirrel" (figure 8.8D and 8.8E) is shown interacting with the Aztec *calpizque*, or tribute collectors, who lack calendar names but who are identified by their blackened faces and personal names: Xoconotzin (Lord "Prickly-Pear-Fruit War Legs") who is facing Lord 11 Vulture, and another one possibly named Xayacatzin or Lord "Mask," who carries a load on his back and walks away from Coixtlahuaca's reigning king[13] (figure 8.8D). The fact that the Aztec period rulers were depicted above the secondary (Chichimec) lineage rather than over the primary (Toltec) lineage, whose role had been political and religious, supports my interpretation that the secondary lineage had been in charge of tribute collection and Coixtlahuaca's market, a role now taken over by the most recent Chichimec arrivals (figure 8.8E).

Because they constituted a technological innovation for mass production of identical materials, the most intriguing items for sale in markets throughout this broad area may have been highly portable clay molds and stamps (figure 8.9A–B), and mold-made and hand painted red-on-cream hemispherical bowls or *cajetes* (figure 8.9C). Mold-made figurines appear during the Early Postclassic period and continued to be made in Late Postclassic times (figure 8.9D–F). Although these figures representing dead nobles and people participating in daily activities characterize a large part of the assemblage, they have not been recognized as constituting a significant regional cultural expression (see Ramsey 1975). The fact that some of these stamps from Ngüiteri are almost exact copies of those from the Basin of Mexico suggests that the elites may have controlled the production of certain objects that bore these symbols (Seler 1990–1998:III:172). The mold-made figures include an older "Toltec style" (figure 8.9D; see Parsons 1972:plate 46E), while the new Aztec style is evident in the female clay figurine fragments (figure 8.9H) and the locally made variety of black-on-orange "Aztecoid" (figure 8.9G). These figurines and black-on-orange wares may be considered examples of Coixtlahuaca's continued participation in long-distance trade in Aztec times. Similar figurines have been reported from other areas that the Aztecs conquered (Parsons 1972:83–86, plate 19E; Seler 1990–1998:III:165; Smith 2002:105–106, figure 9.4).

FIGURE 8.9. Postclassic ceramics from local collections, Coixtlahuaca. (A) Stamps and mold of a lord with plaster impression; (B) stamp, spindle whorl and obsidian point; (C) red on cream decorated hemispherical bowls; (D) mold-made "Toltec" style solid figurines; (E) mold-made solid musician figurines; (F) mold-made solid figurines representing dead lords (rictus); (G) "Aztecoid," a local rendition of graphite (black) on orange Aztec III; the sherd with double asterisks (*upper left*) is from Yucundaa (Teposcolula Viejo); (H) Aztec-type maternity figures.

THE EARLY COLONIAL PERIOD (1530–1580 CE)

The resident population's familiarity with the set of symbols developed during Coixtlahuaca's pre-Columbian past served to maintain the cohesion of its peoples during the transition to the Colonial period (Rincón Mautner 2007a; 2012a). Decorating the church at Coixtlahuaca, and consistent with native iconography, was the use of a spotted pelt motif (figure 8.10). This spotted pelt appears to be derived from two types of terrestrial animals: spotted cats (jaguars and ocelots) and a large constrictor snake (Rincón Mautner 1996a). Both types of animals were admired by native peoples because of their beauty, strength, and stealth as predators. Jaguar pelts were a luxury trade item reserved for use by the highest-ranking nobles. In the codices, the spotted-pelt motif of jaguars and ocelots connotes the preciousness of the nobility and adorns their thrones and dress, and even decorates their polychrome ceramics. Conflated

FIGURE 8.10. The use of the jaguar/ocelot pelt motif as a decorative ribbon unites the interior vaulting of Coixtlahuaca's sixteenth-century church. Drawing by the author.

with the serpent pelt to become the jaguar-serpent (as occurs in the Epiclassic murals of Cacaxtla), this motif was employed to define and enclose the kingdom's boundaries and the plain of Coixtlahuaca's place sign (figure 8.8E). Its use in the church underscores the idea of nobility because this was the house of the supreme lord who ruled in the celestial realm but had such power that he owned many such houses.

The polysemic value ascribed to ocelot/snake pelts serves as a fitting point on which to conclude this essay, in which I have emphasized the great time-depth of Coixtlahuaca's culture history and pluri-ethnic coexistence. The pelt symbol likewise has a long historical trajectory to which multiple uses and meanings were ascribed. Like a ribbon, it links the nobility to their ancestors represented in the *lienzos*, binds the lands of the kingdom, and serves as a symbol that generated cohesion for its pluri-ethnic population in prehispanic times. During the Early Colonial period it was employed to attract the people to the new faith by imbuing the house of the Christian god with the ancient insignia of royalty.

CONCLUSIONS

The lacunae in Coixtlahuaca's archaeological record notwithstanding, this study provides a more comprehensive understanding of cultural developments for a key

TABLE 8.1. Pluri-ethnic composition, supra-identity, and form of government of native kingdoms in the Eastern Basin of Mexico, Puebla Basin, Tehuacán Valley, and the northern sector of the Mixteca Alta and Mixteca Baja.

Region	Indigenous Señorío	Major Language	Minor language	Supra-identity, internal organization, form of government
Eastern Basin of Mexico	Texcoco	Nahuatl	Otomí	Chichimeca; governed by 7 tlahtoque (Gerhard 1986:321). Fifteen different groups incorporated into Texcocan realm (Offner 1983)
Tlaxcala	Tlaxcallan; Ocotelulco, Quiyahuiztlan; Tepeticpac, Tizatlan	Nahuatl	Otomí, Popoloca	Chichimeca; four kingdoms (Gerhard 1986:333-334; Muñoz Camargo 1984)
Puebla Basin	Cholula	Nahuatl	Popoloca, Mixtec (?)	Tolteca-Chichimeca; governed by co-rulers and noble council (Gerhard 1986:116; González-Hermosillo 2005:13, n. 8; Noguera 1950; Olivera 1978:69)
	Cuauhtinchan,	Popoloca	Nahuatl	Tolteca-Chichimeca (Gerhard 1986:220)
	Quecholac and Tecamachalco	Popoloca	Nahuatl, Mixtec	Tolteca-Chichimeca? (Gerhard 1986:286).
	Tecali	Nahuatl	Popoloca (S–SE) Otomí (NW)	Tolteca-Chichimeca (Gerhard 1986:262; Olivera 1978:133-134)
	Tepeaca	Nahuatl	Popoloca (E), Otomí (N)	Tolteca-Chichimeca government shared between three related tlahtoque (Gerhard 1986:286; Martínez 1984:43-44)
	Tepexic	Popoloca	Nahuatl, Mixtec	Tolteca-Chichimeca (Gerhard 1986:290)
Tehuacán Valley	Coxcatlan	Nahuatl	Popoloca (W), Mazatec (E)	Tolteca-Chichimeca (Gerhard 1986:268)
	Chiapolco	Popoloca		Gerhard (1986:268)
	Chilac	Nahuatl	Popoloca (SW)	Tolteca (Gil Huerta 1972)
	Tehuacán	Nahuatl	Popoloca (NW)	Tolteca-Chichimeca (Gerhard 1986:268)

continued on next page

TABLE 8.1.—*continued*

Region	Indigenous Señorío	Major Language	Minor language	Supra-identity, internal organization, form of government
	Teotitlan	Nahuatl	Popoloca, Mazatec	Nonoalca-Chichimeca (Gerhard 1986:315)
	Zapotitlan	Popoloca	Nahuatl	Tolteca?
Mixteca	Acatlan and Piastla; Chila?	Mixtec	Nahuatl	Tolteca-Chichimeca; Piastla (W) in Totollan had co-rulers (Gerhard 1986:42); Smith and Parmenter (1991) suggested that Acatlan and Chila constituted a joint polity with co-rulers.
	Coixtlahuaca	Chocho-Popoloca	Mixtec, Nahuatl	Tolteca-Chichimeca; co-rulers from 12th century until 1461.
	Huajuapan	Mixtec		Gerhard (1986:128)
	Ixcatlan	Ixcatec		Gerhard (1986:315)
Cañada	Quiotepec	Mazatec		Gerhard (1986:315)
	Cuicatlan	Cuicatec		Gerhard (1986:315)
	Tecomahuaca	Mazatec		Gerhard (1986:315)

area of Mesoamerica with a long historical trajectory. The Late Classic relocation of Nahua speakers contributed to the displacement of peoples and the emergence of Postclassic pluri-ethnic polities like Coixtlahuaca, setting the stage for the rise of merchant warriors who operated vast exchange networks across the breadth of Mesoamerica to Central America. Current available evidence supports the ideas proposed by Price (1977) about how technological and structural innovations (forms of organization/administration) emerge at about the same time within and between regions. Furthermore, by considering the pictographic sources together with the material culture, new insights can be gained regarding Northern Mixteca's Postclassic period spheres of interaction in terms of economic, political, and religious subsystems that were probably preceded by similar patterns of interaction in Classic times. Studying Coixtlahuaca's archaeological assemblage from a perspective of regional interaction derived from its historical links to other neighboring peer-polities (Renfrew 1986) has helped elucidate the trade and political networks in which Coixtlahuaca was enmeshed and the roles these played in directing cultural developments.

My findings at Coixtlahuaca echo what Stark (2008:44) describes as the strategy of successful Postclassic states, which had "incentives to incorporate groups of clients, settle them on lands internally, or pacify new holdings by settling loyal enclaves in distant areas." To these incentives I would add the need for the mass production of wares like clay stamps and mold-made figurines to help promote a sense of community and participation by reinforcing inclusiveness, solidarity, and the strengthening of individual and sodality affiliations such as Tolteca-Chichimeca Coixtlahuaque. The similarities in the assemblage of material culture of the Late Postclassic reflect the pluri-ethnic character of the entire region, the dynamic interactions between peoples and historical events over a protracted period of time, and the need to develop cultural consonance that promoted group cohesion.[14]

NOTES

1. These identifiable cultural achievements are referred to as *stylistic-iconographic syntheses*, which become hallmark traditions. During the Classic period it is Teotihuacan and Monte Albán, and in the Postclassic it is Cholula and Tula, that become centers for these syntheses or traditions (Nicholson 1982:230). During the Late Postclassic, the center is no longer located in an urban setting but rather in a region—for example, the Mixteca or Mixteca-Puebla—inhabited by a number of different linguistic groups. Although Nicholson (1961, 1982:232–238) cautions against reducing Mixteca-Puebla to "a simple, easy to remember, disyllabic gentilitial," a number of scholars call attention to the superior abilities in craftsmanship of the Mixtec, so they are in essence the new "Toltec." This prominent role ascribed to the Mixtec appears to be based on the surviving pre-Columbian codices, all of which are attributed to the Mixteca Alta. Their influence on artistic expression is summed up by Kubler (1993:185) as "all Mixtec figural art is derived from the workshops of manuscript illuminators."

2. "Land wo man stumm (nontli) wird, 'das fremdsprachliche land' bezeichnete insbesondere das fremdsprachliche Land an der Karavanenstrasse, die von Cozcatlan und Teotitlan del Camino nach der GolfKüste führte . . ." (Seler 1908:49).

3. In contrast to this view, Jiménez Moreno (1970:62) recognized that the Nahua, Chocho-popoloca, and Mixtec lived intermingled in sixteenth-century southern Puebla and created the cultural tradition that he called the *Mixteca-Cholula culture*. Furthermore, he proposed that Teotihuacan influenced Mixtec culture upon its collapse, possibly by an elite group of Nahua and Mazatec who transferred Teotihuacan's culture to the Mixteca. On the other hand, based on Jiménez Moreno's idea, Paddock posits that Teotihuacan was a Mixtec capital, as was Cholula after its abandonment by Mangue speakers, and that Mixtecs moved from there into the Mixteca in the tenth century CE (Paddock 1970:195–200, 1994:3–4).

4. Almost all *barrancas* present breached stone walls at several locations along their lengths. These stone walls are prehispanic and Early Colonial in age and serve to demarcate individual plots for cultivation.

5. Unlike their prehispanic counterparts, the provenance communities of most Coixtlahuaca codices are known.

6. For the phases of occupation and the associated cultural material from Coixtlahuaca, I follow the correlations of cultural sequences for Oaxaca and the Tehuacán Valley, Puebla (Winter 2006a, 2006b). Winter (1989b:127) has commented on how the Classic Period for the Mixteca Alta, Las Flores phase, is securely dated between 200 and 550 CE, and that the ceramic sequence and the lack of radiocarbon dates present a gap in the record that spans 600–1300 CE.

7. Moreover, palaeolimnological evidence from the eastern Puebla Basin also points to a centennial-scale interval of increasing aridity and changes in the summer monsoonal precipitation patterns between 500 and 1050 CE (Bhattacharya et al. 2015).

8. *Nguiwa* (Chocho or Southern Popoloca) refers to both the people of *ngĕchĕ* (Coixtlahuaca, "the plain of the snake") and to "those of the plain," a plausible gentilitial employed by the people of the Tehuacán Valley and eastern Puebla Basin, the homeland of the Popolocan-speaking tribes. The name *ngiwa* is based on the reduced form of *nkĕ*, meaning "plain," and a demonstrative morpheme, *-a*, still in use in Popoloca (Annette Veerman, personal communication, 2007). Prior to the linguistic classification of Chocho as a distinct language from Popoloca, an unpublished elementary school geography course booklet written by the local teacher for the students of the District of Coixtlahuaca states that the languages spoken in this region were Popoloca and Castillian Spanish (Ramírez 1889:3).

9. An interesting parallel in which a *calpolli* of outsiders was allowed to settle within the boundaries of a polity can be found in the request made and the permission granted the Aztec by the lord of Culhuacan (Alvarado Tezozómoc 1992:49–50). The Aztec were allowed to settle at Tizapan, the rugged, infertile volcanic malpaís (badlands) of extensive lava flows known today as the Pedregal de San Angel, where they could subsist from hunting and gathering while serving him as mercenaries to fight the Xochimilca (Townsend 1992:61). Eventually they would come to dominate their neighbors and far-flung Coixtlahuaca.

10. The Chichimec were dedicated to a life of hunting with the bow and arrow, in which "they excelled more than any other nation" (Muñoz Camargo 1984:142).

11. Footprints arranged within a circle constitute the pictographic convention for market place.

12. Kubler (1993:184–185) recognized the regional variation in materials from the area between Cholula and Mixteca, and Lind (1994:87) posited two substyles in the polychrome ceramic assemblage that reflect different cultural foci. In reference to the elite Catalina polychrome ceramics, these appear at Cholula during the Mártir phase (1350–1500 CE) and about the same time in the Mixteca, where it is referred to as Pilitas Polychrome. Furthermore, in reference to the settings in which certain vessel forms appear in the codices, Lind (1994) proposes a different emphasis in ritual use between the two areas.

13. The name of Lord "Mask," which is lost on this section of the *Lienzo de Coixtlahuaca II* (left), was drawn and Photoshop® edited by the author based on the same personage who is depicted on the *Lienzo de Coixtlahuaca III* in the Latin American Library, Tulane University, New Orleans.

14. Acknowledgments: over the course of several decades of fieldwork and research, friends in Coixtlahuaca, Tequixtepec, Tepelmeme, Nativitas, Aztatla, and Tlalpitepec have graciously shared their homes, food, and knowledge with me. They have shown me their collections of artifacts, assembled from what has been unearthed by plowing their fields or by the undercutting of streams during many rainy seasons, or when, as children, their herding of goats and sheep led them to find tools and figurines where the ancients once lived. I have photographed some of these artifacts and have used some of them to illustrate this essay. I am especially grateful to Gustavo Salazar and his wife Josefina in Coixtlahuaca; Conrado Guzmán and Juan Cruz and their families in Tequixtepec; Don Constantino Sampedro, Doña Elena Hernández Cruz, Dr. Edgar Mendoza, and their families in Tepelmeme; and Antonio Hernández Altamirano and his family in Aztatla. I am indebted to them for their hospitality. I also acknowledge the support of the municipal authorities in these villages, who permitted me to reconnoiter the lands of their municipalities and arranged for members of the Ayuntamiento to accompany me on these excursions. *Lienzo* details photographed by the author with permission: figures 8.4A and 8.4F from the *Lienzo de Nativitas*, courtesy of the Honorable Ayuntamiento of the Municipality of Santa María Nativitas; figures 8.9B(left), 8.9D, and 8.9E from the *Lienzo de Coixtlahuaca II (Ixtlan)*, courtesy of the Biblioteca Nacional de Antropología e Historia, Mexico City; figure 8.9B(right) from the *Lienzo de Coixtlahuaca I (Seler II)*, courtesy of the Ethnologisches Museum, Staatliche Museen zu Berlin. The Teotihuacan bowl reproduced in figure 8.5 is used with permission from Christina Elson. I also thank my friends and colleagues for their input regarding the identification of ceramics, especially Marcus C. Winter, James A. Neely, Mickey Lind, Robert Markens, and Cira Martínez López. I am especially grateful to the late Kathrynn Josserand and her husband, Nick Hopkins, Mickey Lind, and Michael Spence for copies of their unpublished documents. Robert Markens, Ruth Gubler, and Robert Ricklis have spent many hours discussing many of the ideas I have presented in this essay.

REFERENCES

Acuña-Soto, Rodolfo, David W. Stahle, Matthew D. Therrell, Sergio Gomez Chavez, and Malcolm K. Cleaveland. 2005. "Drought, Epidemic Disease, and the Fall of Classic Period Cultures in Mesoamerica (AD 750–950): Hemorrhagic Fevers as a Cause of Massive Population Loss." *Medical Hypotheses* 65 (2):405–409. http://dx.doi.org/10.1016/j.mehy.2005.02.025.

Bhattacharya, Tripti, Roger Byrne, Harald Böhnel, Kurt Wogau, Ulrike Kienel, B. Lynn Ingram, and Susan Zimmerman. 2015. "Cultural Implications of Late Holocene Climate Change in the Cuenca Oriental, Mexico." *Proceedings of the National Academy of Sciences* 112 (6): 1693–1698.

Bernal, Ignacio. 1948. *Excavaciones en Ngüiteria, Coixtlahuaca: Informe Inédito*. Mexico City: Archivo de la Dirección de Arqueología, Instituto Nacional de Antropología e Historia.

Bernal, Ignacio. 1949. "Exploraciones en Coixtlahuaca, Oaxaca." *Revista Mexicana de Estudios Antropológicos* 10:5–76.

Braudel, Fernand. 1958. "Histoire et sciences sociales: La longue durée." In *Annales, Economies, Sociétés, Civilisations*. XIII/4: 725–753.

Braudel, Fernand. 1972. *The Mediterranean and the Mediterranean World in the Age of Philip II*. New York: Harper and Row.

Brockington, Donald L. 1982. "Spatial and Temporal Variations of the Mixtec-Style Ceramics in Southern Oaxaca." In *Aspects of the Mixteca-Puebla Style and Mixtec and Central Mexican Culture in Southern Mesoamerica*, ed. Jennifer S. H. Brown and E. Wyllys Andrews, 7–13. New Orleans: Middle American Research Institute, Occasional Paper No. 4, Tulane University.

Brumfiel, Elizabeth M. 1994. "Ethnic Groups and Political Development in Ancient Mexico." In *Factional Competition and Political Development in the New World*, ed. Elizabeth M. Brumfiel and John W. Fox, 89–102. Cambridge: Cambridge University Press. http://dx.doi.org/10.1017/CBO9780511598401.009.

Burland, Cottie. 1955. *The Selden Roll: An Ancient Mexican Picture Manuscript in the Bodleian Library at Oxford*. Monumenta Americana II. Verlag Gebr. Berlin: Mann.

Byland, Bruce E. 1984. "Boundary Recognition in the Mixteca Alta." In *Essays in Otomanguean Culture History*, ed. Kathryn J. Josserand, Marcus Winter, and Nicholas Hopkins, 109–140. Nashville: Publications in Anthropology 31, Vanderbilt University.

Byland, Bruce E. 2008. "Tree Birth, the Solar Oracle and Achiutla: Mixtec Sacred History and the Classic to Postclassic Transition." In *After Monte Albán: Transformation and Negotiation in Oaxaca, Mexico*, ed. Jeffrey P. Blomster, 331–364. Boulder: University Press of Colorado.

Campbell, Lyle Richard. 1988. *The Linguistics of Southeastern Chiapas, Mexico*. Provo, UT: Brigham Young University.

Castellón Huerta, Blas Román. 2006. *Cuthá: El Cerro de la Mascara, Arqueología y Etnicidad en el sur de Puebla*. Mexico City: Colección Científica 490, Serie Arqueología. Instituto Nacional de Antropología e Historia.

Cobean, Robert H. 1990. *La Cerámica de Tula, Hidalgo*. Colección Científica 215. Mexico City: Instituto Nacional de Antropología e Historia.

Codex Selden. 1964. Facsimile. Mexico City: Sociedad Mexicana de Antropología.

Cook de Leonard, Carmen. 1957. "Algunos Antecedentes de la Cerámica Tolteca." *Revista Mexicana de Estudios Antropológicos* 14:37–43.

Davies, Nigel. 1980. *The Toltec Heritage, from the Fall of Tula to the Rise of Tenochtitlán.* Norman: University of Oklahoma Press.

de los Reyes, Antonio. (1593) 1976. *Arte en Lengua Mixteca.* Nashville: Vanderbilt University Publications in Anthropology, No. 14.

Diehl, Richard A. 1993. "The Toltec Horizon in Mesoamerica: New Perspectives on an Old Issue." In *Latin American Horizons*, ed. Don Stephen Rice, 263–294. Washington, DC: Dumbarton Oaks.

Drennan, Robert. 1983. "Appendix: Radiocarbon dates from Oaxaca." In *The Cloud People: Divergent Evolution of the Zapotec and Mixtec Civilizations*, ed. Kent V. Flannery and Joyce Marcus, 363–370. New York: Academic Press.

Dumond, Donald E., and Florencia Muller. 1972. "Classic to Postclassic in Highland Central Mexico." *Science* 175 (4027):1208–1215. http://dx.doi.org/10.1126/science.175 .4027.1208.

Elson, Christina M., and Kenneth Mowbray. 2005. "Burial Practices at Teotihuacan in the Early Postclassic Period in the Vaillant and Linné Excavations (1931–1932)." *Ancient Mesoamerica* 16 (02): 195–211. http://dx.doi.org/10.1017/S0956536105050224.

Garibay, K. Ángel María. 1985. Teogonía e Historia de los Mexicanos: Tres Opúsculos del Siglo XVI. Mexico City: Editorial Porrúa.

Gerhard, Peter. 1986. *Geografía Histórica de la Nueva España 1519–1821.* Mexico City: UNAM-IIH.

Gil Huerta, Gorgonio. 1972. "History of the Foundation of the Town of San Gabriel Chilacatla." In *The Prehistory of the Tehuacan Valley*, vol. 4, ed. Frederick Johnson, 154–161. Austin: University of Texas Press.

Gil Huerta, Gorgonio, and James A. Neely. 1967. "Historia del al Fundación del Pueblo de San Gabriel Chilacatla." *Tlalocan* 5 (3):198–219.

González-Hermosillo Adams, Francisco. 2005. "De Tecpan a Cabecera: Cholula o la Metamorfosis de un Reino Soberano Naua en Ayuntamiento Indio del rey de España Durante el Siglo XVI." *Dimensión Antropológica* 12 (33):7–67.

González-José, Rolando, Neus Martínez-Abadías, Antonio González Martín, Josefina Baustista Martínez, Jorge Gómez Valdés, Mirsha Quinto, and Miguel Hernández. 2006. "Detection of a Population Replacement at the Classic-Postclassic Transition in Mexico." Proceedings of Biological Sciences, the Royal Society. doi.:10.1098/rspb 2006.0151.

Graulich, Michel. 1974. "Las Peregrinaciones Aztecas y el Ciclo de Mixcoatl." *Estudios de Cultura Nahuatl* 11:311–354.

Hopkins, Nicholas A. 1984. "Otomanguean Linguistic Prehistory." In *Essays in Otomanguean Culture History*, ed. Kathryn J. Josserand, Marcus C. Winter, and Nicholas A. Hopkins, 25–65. Nashville: Publications in Anthropology 31, Vanderbilt University.

Jiménez Moreno, Wigberto. 1941. "Tula y los Toltecas Según las Fuentes Históricas." *Revista Mexicana de Estudios Antropológicos* 5:79–83.

Jiménez Moreno, Wigberto. 1966. "Los Imperios Prehispánicos de Mesoamérica." *Revista Mexicana de Estudios Antropológicos* 20:179–195.

Jiménez Moreno, Wigberto. 1970. "Mesoamerica before the Toltecs." In *Ancient Oaxaca: Discoveries in Mexican Archaeology and History*, ed. John Paddock, 3–82. Stanford: Stanford University Press.

Johnson, Frederick, and Richard S. MacNeish. 1972. "Chronometric Dating." In *The Prehistory of the Tehuacan Valley*, vol. 4. ed. Frederick Johnson, 3–55. Austin: University of Texas Press.

Josserand, J. Kathryn. 1983. "Mixtec Dialect History (Proto-Mixtec and Modern Mixtec Text)." Unpublished PhD diss., Tulane University, New Orleans. Ann Arbor, MI: University Microfilms.

Kaufman, Terrence. 2001a. "The History of the Nawa Language Group from the Earliest Times to the Sixteenth Century: Some Initial Results." http://www.albany.edu/anthro/maldp/Nawa.pdf, accessed May 2011.

Kaufman, Terrence. 2001b. "Language History and Language Contact in Southern Meso-America." Unpublished manuscript in possession of the author.

Kirchhoff, Paul. 1940. "Los Pueblos de la Historia Tolteca-Chichimeca: Sus Migraciones y su Parentesco." *Revista Mexicana de Estudios Antropológicos* 4 (1–2):77–104.

Kirchhoff, Paul. 1955. "Quetzalcóatl, Huémac, y el Fin de Tula." *Cuadernos Americanos* 14:169–196.

Kirchhoff, Paul, Lina Odena Güemes, and Luis Reyes García. 1989. *Historia Tolteca-Chichimeca*. Mexico City: Fondo de Cultura Económica.

Knapp, A. Bernard. 1992. "Archaeology and *Annales*: Time, Space and Change." In *Archaeology, Annales and Ethnohistory*, ed. A. Bernard Knapp, 1–21. Cambridge: Cambridge University Press.

Kubler, George. 1993. *The Art and Architecture of Ancient America: The Mexican, Maya, and Andean Peoples*. New Haven: Yale University Press.

Lind, Michael. 1967. "Mixtec Polychrome Pottery: A Comparison of the Late Preconquest Polychrome Pottery from Cholula, Oaxaca, and the Chinantla." Unpublished MA thesis, Graduate School University of the Americas, Puebla, Mexico.

Lind, Michael. 1994. "Cholula and Mixteca Polychromes: Two Mixteca-Puebla Regional Sub-Styles." In *Mixteca-Puebla: Discoveries and Research in Mesoamerican Art and*

Archaeology, ed. H. B. Nicholson and Eloise Quiñones Keber, 79–99. Culver City, CA: Labyrinthos.

Litvak, Jaime. 1970a. "Xochicalco en la Caída del Clásico: Una Hipótesis." *Anales de Antropologia* 7:131–145.

Litvak, Jaime. 1970b. *El Valle de Xochicalco, Formación y Análisis de un Modelo Estadístico para la Arqueología Regional*. Mexico City: Universidad Nacional Autónoma de México.

MacNeish, Richard S., Frederick A. Peterson, and Kent V. Flannery. 1970a. "The Early Part of the Venta Salada Phase." In *The Prehistory of the Tehuacan Valley*, vol. 3. ed. Douglas S. Byers, 177–210. Austin: University of Texas Press.

MacNeish, Richard S., Frederick A. Peterson, and Kent V. Flannery. 1970b. "The Late Part of the Venta Salada Phase." In *The Prehistory of the Tehuacan Valley*, vol. 3. ed. Douglas S. Byers, 211–237. Austin: University of Texas Press.

Marcus, Joyce, and Kent V. Flannery. 1983. "An Introduction to the Late Postclassic." In *The Cloud People: Divergent Evolution of the Zapotec and Mixtec Civilizations*, ed. Kent V. Flannery and Joyce Marcus, 217–226. New York: Academic Press.

Marcus, Joyce, and Kent V. Flannery. 1996. *Zapotec Civilization: How Urban Society Evolved in Mexico's Oaxaca Valley*. London: Thames and Hudson.

Martínez, Hildeberto. 1984. *Tepeaca en el Siglo XVI: Tenencia de la Tierra y Organización de un Señorío*. Mexico City: CIESAS, Ediciones Casa Chata.

Mata, Fray Juan de. 1984. "Relación de Teozapotlan." In *Relaciones Geográficas del Siglo XVI: Antequera*, vol. 2: 3, ed. René Acuña, 153–164. Mexico City: Universidad Nacional Autónoma de México.

Muñoz Camargo, Diego. 1984. "Descripción de la Ciudad y Provincia de Tlaxcala." In *Relaciones Geográficas del Siglo XVI: Tlaxcala*, vol. 1, ed. René Acuña, 34–285. Mexico City: Universidad Nacional Autónoma de México.

Nicholson, Henry B. 1961. "The Use of the Term 'Mixtec' in Mesoamerican Archaeology." *American Antiquity* 26 (3):431–433. http://dx.doi.org/10.2307/277413.

Nicholson, Henry B. 1982. "The Mixteca-Puebla Concept Revisited." In *The Art and Iconography of Late Postclassic Central Mexico*, ed. Elizabeth H. Boone, 227–254. Washington, DC: Dumbarton Oaks.

Nicholson, Henry B., and Eloise Quiñones Keber. 1994. "Introduction." In *Mixteca-Puebla: Discoveries and Research in Mesoamerican Art and Archaeology*, ed. Henry B. Nicholson and Eloise Quiñones Keber, vii–xv. Culver City, CA: Labyrinthos.

Noguera, Eduardo. 1950. "El Horizonte Tolteca-Chichimeca." In *Enciclopedia Mexicana de Arte 4*. Mexico City: Ediciones Mexicanas.

Noguera, Eduardo. 1954. *La Cerámica Arqueológica de Cholula*. México: Editorial Guaranía.

Noguera, Eduardo. 1960. "Relaciones de Oaxaca con Puebla y Tlaxcala: Culturas Cholulteca, Mixteca y Zapoteca." *Revista Mexicana de Estudios Antropológicos* 16:129–135.

Offner, Jerome A. 1983. *Law and Politics in Aztec Texcoco.* Cambridge Latin American Studies 44. Cambridge: Cambridge University Press.

Olivera, Mercedes. 1978. *Pillis y Macehuales: Las Formaciones Sociales y los Modos de Producción de Tecali del Siglo XII al XVI.* Mexico City: CIESAS, Ediciones Casa Chata.

Paddock, John. 1970. "Oaxaca in Ancient Mesoamerica." In *Ancient Oaxaca: Discoveries in Mexican Archeology and History*, ed. John Paddock, 83–242. Stanford: Stanford University Press.

Paddock, John. 1994. "Mixteca-Puebla in Its Times." In *Mixteca-Puebla: Discoveries and Research in Mesoamerican Art and Archaeology*, ed. H. B. Nicholson and Eloise Quiñones Keber, 1–6. Culver City, CA: Labyrinthos.

Parsons, Mary H. 1972. "Aztec Figurines from the Teotihuacan Valley, Mexico." In *Miscellaneous Studies in Mexican Prehistory,* Museum of Anthropology Anthropological Papers 45, ed. Michael W. Spence, Jeffrey Parsons, and Mary H. Parsons, 81–164. Ann Arbor: University of Michigan.

Pohl, John M.D. 2003a. "Creation Stories, Hero Cults, and Alliance Building: Confederacies of Central and Southern Mexico." In *The Postclassic Mesoamerican World*, ed. Michael E. Smith and Frances F. Berdan, 61–66. Salt Lake City: The University of Utah Press.

Pohl, John M.D. 2003b. "Ritual Ideology and Commerce in the Southern Mexican Highlands." In *The Postclassic Mesoamerican World*, ed. Michael E. Smith and Frances F. Berdan, 172–177. Salt Lake City: The University of Utah Press.

Pohl, John M.D. 2003c. "Ritual and Iconographic Variability in Mixteca-Puebla Polychrome Pottery." In *The Postclassic Mesoamerican World*, ed. Michael E. Smith and Frances F. Berdan, 201–206. Salt Lake City: University of Utah Press.

Pohl, John M.D. 2003d. "Royal Marriage and Confederacy Building among the Eastern Nahuas, Mixtecs and Zapotecs." In *The Postclassic Mesoamerican World*, ed. Michael E. Smith and Frances F. Berdan, 243–248. Salt Lake City: University of Utah Press.

Pohl, John M.D., and Bruce E. Byland. 1994. "The Mixteca-Puebla Style and Early Post-Classic Socio-Political Interaction." In *Mixteca-Puebla: Discoveries and Research in Mesoamerican Art and Archaeology*, ed. H. B. Nicholson and Eloise Quiñones Keber, 189–199. Culver City, CA: Labyrinthos.

Price, Barbara J. 1977. "Shifts in Production and Organization: A Cluster Interaction Model." *Current Anthropology* 18 (2):209–234. http://dx.doi.org/10.1086/201885.

Ramírez, Juan Francisco. 1889. *Elementos de geografía descriptiva para los alumnos de las escuelas de los pueblos del distrito de Coixtlahuaca formada por . . .* Oaxaca: Biblioteca Francisco Burgoa, unpublished.

Ramsey, James Robert. 1975. "An Analysis of Mixtec Minor Art, with a Catalogue."
    Unpublished PhD diss., Tulane University. Ann Arbor, MI: University Microfilms.

Rattray, Evelyn. 1993. "The Oaxaca Barrio at Teotihuacan." In *Monografías mesoamericanas*
    1. Cholula, Mexico: Universidad de las Américas-Puebla.

Renfrew, Colin. 1986. "Introduction: Peer Polity Interaction and Sociopolitical Change."
    In *Peer Polity Interaction and Sociopolitical Change,* ed. Colin Renfrew and John F.
    Cherry, 1–18. London: Cambridge University Press.

Reyes García, Luis. 1988. *Cuauhtinchan del Siglo XII al XVI: Formación y Desarrollo*
    Histórico de un Señorío Prehispánico. Mexico City: Fondo de Cultura Económica.

Reyes García, Luis. 1998. "Documentos Pictográficos del Señorío Popoloca de
    Tecamachalco." *Indiana Journal of Hispanic Literatures* 13:67–74.

Rincón Mautner, Carlos. 1994. "A Reconstruction of the History of San Miguel
    Tulancingo, Coixtlahuaca, Mexico, from Indigenous Painted Sources." *Texas Notes*
    on Precolumbian Art, Writing and Culture, 64. Austin: CHAAAC Art Department,
    University of Texas.

Rincón Mautner, Carlos. 1995. "The Ñuiñe Codex from the Colossal Natural Bridge on
    the Ndaxagua: An Early Pictographic Text from the Coixtlahuaca Basin." *Institute of*
    Maya Studies Journal 1 (2):39–66.

Rincón Mautner, Carlos. 1996a. "The 1580 'Plan Topographique de Santa Maria Ixcatlan':
    Description and Commentary." *Latin American Indian Literatures Journal: A Review of*
    American Indian Texts and Studies 12(1):43–66.

Rincón Mautner, Carlos. 1996b. "The Notes and Sketch of 'Lienzo Seler I' or 'Mapa de
    Santa Maria Ixcatlan', Oaxaca: Description and Commentary." *Latin American Indian*
    Literatures Journal: A Review of American Indian Texts and Studies 12 (2):146–177.

Rincón Mautner, Carlos. 1997. "Reading the History of Place-Becoming in the Codices
    from the Coixtlahuaca Basin." In *Messages and Meanings*, ed. M. Preuss, 129–148.
    Lancaster, CA: Labyrinthos.

Rincón Mautner, Carlos. 1999. "Man and the Environment in the Coixtlahuaca Basin
    of Northwestern Oaxaca, Mexico: Two-Thousand Years of Historical Ecology."
    Unpublished PhD diss., University of Texas, Austin. Ann Arbor, MI: University
    Microfilms.

Rincón Mautner, Carlos. 2000. "La Reconstrucción Cronológica del Linaje Principal de
    Coixtlahuaca." In *Códices y Documentos Sobre México,* Tercer Simposio, ed. Constanza
    Vega, 25–43. Mexico City: Instituto Nacional de Antropología e Historia.

Rincón Mautner, Carlos. 2005a. "Sacred Caves and Rituals from the Northern Mixteca of
    Oaxaca: New Revelations." In *In the Maw of the Earth Monster: Studies of Mesoamerican*
    Ritual Cave Use, ed. James E. Brady and Keith M. Prufer, 117–152. Austin: University of
    Texas Press.

Rincón Mautner, Carlos. 2005b. "The Pictographic Assemblage from the Colossal Natural Bridge on the Ndaxagua, Coixtlahuaca Basin, Northwestern Mixteca Alta of Oaxaca, Mexico." *Ketzalcalli* 2 (2):2–69.

Rincón Mautner, Carlos. 2007a. "Donde Ataron a Nuestra Madre: La Diosa de la Tierra y el Coatepec de la Mixteca." In *Iconografía Mexicana,* Volumen VII: *Atributos de las Deidades Femeninas, Homenaje a la Maestra Noemí Castillo Tejero*, ed. Beatriz Barba Ahuatzin and Alicia Blanco Padilla, 155–171. Mexico City: Instituto Nacional de Antropología e Historia.

Rincón Mautner, Carlos. 2007b. "A Study of the 'Lienzo of San Jerónimo Otla' from the Coixtlahuaca Basin of Oaxaca, Mexico." *Latin American Indian Literatures Journal: A Review of American Indian Texts and Studies* 23(1):74–95.

Rincón Mautner, Carlos. 2012a. "Cave, Mountain and Ancestors: History and Cartography in the Preservation of Native Dominions of the Early Colonial Mixteca of Oaxaca, Mexico." In *Comparative Studies in Mesoamerican Systems of Remembrance,* ed. Amos Megged and Stephanie Wood. Norman: University of Oklahoma Press.

Rincón Mautner, Carlos. 2012b. "Linajes y Casas señoriales de los Tolteca-Chichimeca de Coixtlahuaca en la Mixteca de Oaxaca." In *El Poder Compartido: Ensayos Sobre la Arqueología de Organizaciones Políticas Segmentarias y Oligárquicas de Mesoamérica,* ed. Annick Daneels and Gerardo Gutiérrez. Mexico: CIESAS.

Rincón Mautner, Carlos. 2014. "Colonial Period Pictographic Dedicatory Inscriptions from the Mixteca Popoloca Nahua Region: The Tehuacan Valley and Coixtlahuaca Basin." *Mexicon* 36 (6):161–166.

Rincón Mautner, Carlos. 2015. *Investigaciones Arqueológico-Ambientales y Etnohistóricas Sobre la Sociedad y Cultura en la Cuenca de Coixtlahuaca, Mixteca Alta, Oaxaca: Contexto y Significados.* Oaxaca, Mexico: Carteles Editores.

Ringle, William M., Tomás Gallareta Begrón, and George J. Bey III. 1998. "The Return of Quetzalcoatl: Evidence for the Spread of a World Religion during the Epiclassic Period." *Ancient Mesoamerica* 9 (02):183–232. http://dx.doi.org/10.1017/S0956536 100001954.

Rivera Guzmán, Iván. 2008. "La Iconografía de las Piedras Grabadas de Cuquila y la Distribución de la Escritura Ñuiñe en la Mixteca Alta." In *Pictografía y Escritura Alfabética en Oaxaca,* ed. Sebastian van Doesburg, 53–72. Oaxaca, Mexico: IEEPO.

Rojas, Gabriel. 1985. "Relación de Cholula." In *Relaciones Geográficas del Siglo XVI: Tlaxcala,* ed. René Acuña, 121–145. Mexico City: Instituto de Investigaciones Antropológicas, Universidad Nacional Autónoma de México.

Salazar, Fray Agustín de. 1984. "Relación de Cuilapa." In *Relaciones Geográficas del Siglo XVI: Antequera,* vol. 1: 2, ed. René Acuña, 173–182. Mexico City: Universidad Nacional Autónoma de México.

Sanders, William T. 1965. *The Cultural Ecology of the Teotihuacan Valley: A Preliminary Report of the Results of the Teotihuacan Valley Project*. University Park: Department of Sociology and Anthropology, Pennsylvania State University.

Sanders, William T., and Barbara Price. 1968. *Mesoamerica: The Evolution of a Civilization*. New York: Random House.

Seler, Eduard. 1904. *Mexican Picture Writings of Alexander von Humboldt in the Royal Library at Berlin, Fragments III and IV*. Bureau of American Ethnology Bulletin 28. Washington, DC: Bureau of American Ethnology:123–229.

Seler, Eduard. 1908. "Die alten Bewohner der Landschaft Michuacan." In *Gesammelte Abhandlungen zur amerikanischen Sprach und Alterthumskunde*, vol. 3. Berlin.

Seler, Eduard. 1990–98. In *Collected Works in Mesoamerican Linguistics and Archaeology*. 6 vols. ed. Frank E. Comparato. Culver City, CA: Labyrinthos.

Seler-Sachs, Cecilie. 1912. "Die Reliefscherben von Cuicatlan und Teotitlan del Camino." *Proceedings of the International Congress of Americanists* 12:206–215.

Smail, Daniel. 2012. "Beyond the Longue Durée: Human History in Deep Time." *Perspectives on History* (2012):59–60.

Smith, Mary Elizabeth. 1973. *Picture Writing from Ancient Southern Mexico: Mixtec Place Signs and Maps*. Norman: University of Oklahoma Press.

Smith, Mary Elizabeth, and Ross Parmenter. 1991. *The Codex Tulane*. New Orleans: Middle American Research Institute, Tulane University.

Smith, Michael E. 1992. "Rhythms of Change in Postclassic Central Mexico: Archaeology, Ethnohistory, and the Braudelian Model." In *Archaeology, Annales and Ethnohistory*, ed. A. Bernard Knapp, 51–74. Cambridge: Cambridge University Press.

Smith, Michael E. 2002. "Domestic Ritual at Aztec Provincial Sites in Morelos." In *Domestic Ritual in Ancient Mesoamerica*, ed. Patricia Plunket, 93–114. Los Angeles: Cotsen Institute of Archaeology, University of California.

Smith, Michael E., and Cynthia M. Heath-Smith. 1980. "Waves of Influence in Postclassic Mesoamerica? A Critique of the Mixteca-Puebla Concept." *Anthropology* 4 (2):15–50.

Smith, Michael E., and Frances F. Berdan. 2003. "Postclassic Mesoamerica." In *The Postclassic Mesoamerican World*, ed. Michael E. Smith and Frances F. Berdan, 3–13. Salt Lake City: University of Utah Press.

Smith, Michael E., and Michael D. Lind. 2005. "Xoo-Phase Ceramics from Oaxaca Found at Calixtlahuaca in Central Mexico." *Ancient Mesoamerica* 16 (02):169–177. http://dx.doi.org/10.1017/S095653610505011X.

Spence, Michael W. 1992. "Tlailotlacan, a Zapotec Enclave in Teotihuacan." In *Art, Ideology, and the City of Teotihuacan*, ed. Janet C. Berlo, 59–88. Washington, DC: Dumbarton Oaks.

Spence, Michael W. 2002. "Domestic Ritual in Tlailotlacan, Teotihuacan." In *Domestic Ritual in Ancient Mesoamerica*, ed. Patricia Plunket, 53–66. Los Angeles: Cotsen Institute of Archaeology, University of California.

Spence, Michael W. 2005. "A Zapotec Diaspora Network in Classic Period Central Mexico." In *The Archaeology of Colonial Encounters: Comparative Perspectives*, ed. Gil Stein, 173–205. Santa Fe: School of American Research.

Spence, Michael W., and Christine D. White. 2005. "Cronología y Continuidad en Estructura 6 de Tlailotlacan." Unpublished manuscript in possession of the author.

Spores, Ronald. 1984. *The Mixtecs in Ancient and Colonial Times*. Norman: University of Oklahoma Press.

Stahle, D. W., J. V. Diaz, D. J. Burnette, J. C. Paredes, R. R. Heim, Jr., F. K. Fye, R. Acuna Soto, M. D. Therrell, M. K. Cleaveland, and D. K. Stahle. 2011. "Major Mesoamerican Droughts of the Past Millennium." *Geophysical Research Letters* 38 (5):1–4. http://dx.doi.org/10.1029/2010GL046472.

Stark, Barbara L. 2008. "Archaeology and Ethnicity in Postclassic Mesoamerica." In *Ethnic Identity in Nahua Mesoamerica: The View from Archaeology, Art History, Ethnohistory, and Contemporary Ethnography*, ed. Frances F. Berdan, John K. Chance, Alan R. Sandstrom, Barbara L. Stark, James M. Taggart, and Emily Umberger, 38–63. Salt Lake City: University of Utah Press.

Suárez, Melchor. 1984. "Relación de Cuautla." In *Relaciones Geográficas del Siglo XVI: Antequera*, vol. 2(1), ed. René Acuña, 137–159. Mexico City: Instituto de Investigaciones Antropológicas, Universidad Nacional Autónoma de México.

Tezozómoc, Fernando de Alvarado. 1992. *Crónica Mexicáyotl*, translated from Nahuatl by Adrián León. Mexico: Universidad Nacional Autónoma de México.

Townsend, Richard. 1992. *The Aztecs*. London: Thames and Hudson.

Vargas, Gaspar de. 1984. "Relación de Guatulco y su Partido." In *Relaciones Geográficas del Siglo XVI: Antequera*, vol. 2(1), ed. René Acuña, 183–206. Mexico City: Instituto de Investigaciones Antropológicas, Universidad Nacional Autónoma de México.

Winter, Marcus C. 1989a. *Oaxaca: the Archaeological Record*. Mexico City: Minutiae Mexicana.

Winter, Marcus C. 1989b. "From Classic to Post-Classic in Prehispanic Oaxaca." In *Mesoamerica after the Decline of Teotihuacan: A.D. 700–900*, ed. Richard A. Diehl and Janet C. Berlo, 123–130. Washington, DC: Dumbarton Oaks Research Library and Collection.

Winter, Marcus C. 1990. "El Clásico en Oaxaca." In *La época clásica*, ed. Amalia Cardos de Méndez, 55–59. Mexico City: Universidad Nacional Autónoma de México.

Winter, Marcus C. 1992. "Ñuiñe: Estilo y Etnicidad." *Notas Mesoamericanas* 13:147–162.

Winter, Marcus C. 1994. "The Mixteca Prior to the Late Postclassic." In *Mixteca-Puebla: Discoveries and Research in Mesoamerican Art and Archaeology*, ed. H. B. Nicholson and E. Quiñones Keber, 201–221. Culver City, CA: Labyrinthos.

Winter, Marcus C. 2006a. "La Cerámica el Clásico de la Mixteca Alta y la Mixteca Baja de Oaxaca." In *La Producción Alfarera en el México Antiguo,* Vol. II: *La Alfarería durante el Clásico (100–700 d.C.)*, ed. Beatriz Leonor Merino Carrión and Ángel García Cook, 91–118. Mexico City: Instituto Nacional de Antropología e Historia.

Winter, Marcus C. 2006b. "La Cerámica del Posclásico de Oaxaca." In *La Producción Alfarera en el México Antiguo,* Vol. V: *La Alfarería en el Posclásico (1200–1521 d.C.)*, ed. Beatriz Leonor Merino Carrión and Ángel García Cook, 79–191. Mexico City: Instituto Nacional de Antropología e Historia.

Winter, Marcus C. 2008. "Classic to Postclassic in Four Oaxaca Regions: The Mazateca, the Chinantla, the Mixe Region and the Southern Isthmus." In *After Monte Albán: Transformation and Negotiation in Oaxaca, Mexico*, ed. Jeffrey P. Blomster, 393–426. Boulder: University Press of Colorado.

Winter, Marcus, Margarita Gaxiola, and Gilberto Hernández. 1984. "Archaeology of the Otomanguean Area." In *Essays in Otomanguean Culture History*, ed. J. Kathryn Josserand, Marcus C. Winter, and Nicholas Hopkins, 65–108. Nashville: Vanderbilt University Publications in Anthropology, No. 31.

Wright-Carr, David. 2010. "Las migraciones nahuas de la época prehispánica: una perspectiva lingüística." Paper presented at the II Congreso Internacional de Historia e Historiografía Guanajuatenses, 6 de septiembre de 2007. Updated 2010. Guanajuato: Centro de Investigaciones Humanísticas, Universidad de Guanajuato.

Zorita, Alonso de. 1963. *Breve y Sumaria Relación de los Señores de la Nueva España*. Mexico City: Universidad Nacional Autónoma de México.

9

The Archaeology and History of Colonialism, Culture Contact, and Indigenous Cultural Development at Teozacoalco, Mixteca Alta

Stephen L. Whittington and Andrew Workinger

Anthropology has been criticized for lacking the comprehensive theories of colonialism and culture contact needed to explain the full range of encounters and their behavioral impact for all time periods (Bartel 1985; Schortman and Urban 1998). This is significant because colonialism and contact are fundamentally related to cultural interactions and change, and their understanding can contribute to developing social theory (Rogers 2005). In this chapter we explore the issues of colonialism and culture contact in regards to recent investigations of Teozacoalco in the Mixteca Alta region of Oaxaca. Teozacoalco participated in at least four major episodes of contact with foreign cultures and therefore represents a particularly rich area of study.

Culture contact is a "general term used by archaeologists to refer to groups coming into or staying in contact for days, years, decades, centuries, or even millennia" (Silliman 2005:58). Schortman and Urban (1998:102) suggest it involves "protracted, direct interchanges among members of social units who do not share the same identity." Whether or not one insists that contact continue for an extended period of time, its terminology is only appropriate to situations where autonomous groups meet and neither has political power over the other (Silliman 2005). Colonialism has recently been defined as:

> the dual process (1) of attempted domination by a colonial/settler population based on perceptions and actions of inequality, racism, oppression, labor control, economic marginalization, and dispossession and (2) of resistance, acquiescence, and living

DOI: 10.5876/9781607323297.c009

through these by indigenous people who never permit these processes to become final and complete and who frequently retain or remake identities and traditions in the face of often brutal conditions. (Silliman 2005:59)

No single definition of colonialism is universally accepted, but it is generally agreed that any definition must extend beyond European colonialism in the modern era to encompass earlier cultural encounters. Domination is something attempted and resisted, but never complete. Colonialism has specific characteristics that make it a subset of culture contact, but not fundamentally different from it. It is primarily the power differential between colonizer and colonized that separates colonialism from other kinds of culture contact (Gosden 2004). A comprehensive anthropological theory of culture contact will integrate colonialism in all its variations into the continuum of cultural interactions.

Scholars increasingly see the archaeological record as the key to developing a comparative anthropological theory of social power and control (Bartel 1985). Archaeology provides a wide range of case studies that differ from common views of colonial expansion (Stein 2005). A prehistoric perspective is necessary to analyze the cultural transformations of colonialism (Lyons and Papadopoulos 2002) and provide a much broader view of colonialism beyond that based on historical Europe.

Archaeology generates material data independent of the textual records that are the basis of most colonial theory (Stein 2005). It can provide insights and interpretations that complement, challenge, and expand upon those obtained from documents (Bartel 1985; Lyons and Papadopoulos 2002; Rogers 2005; Schortman and Urban 1998). It provides the way to overcome the inherent bias of authors of colonial texts and to study people who did not write their own historic narratives (Bartel 1985; Lyons and Papadopoulos 2002). It can test hypotheses and build theory about indigenous societies' responses to colonial encounters (Bartel 1985; Rogers 2005).

The Teozacoalco Archaeological Project is undertaking a cross-cultural comparison of colonialism and culture contact in the Mixteca Alta region of Oaxaca, Mexico. The project compares the archaeological implications and social impact for Teozacoalco of European colonialism in the modern era, precapitalist Aztec colonialism, contact with the Zapotec culture, and contact with the nearby Mixtec polity of Tilantongo. It also explores the indigenous development of Mixtec culture at Teozacoalco. The project evaluates the social, political, and economic implications of multiple episodes of colonialism and culture contact on a single indigenous society and the landscape where it developed, using data collected from surface survey, mapping, and test-pitting.

The Teozacoalco Archaeological Project uses the *Mapa de Teozacoalco* (Anders et al. 1992a) and the *Relaciones Geográficas* (Acuña 1984) as points of departure (Shoemaker 2000; Whittington 2002, 2003). The *Relaciones* are responses to fifty questions sent to the municipalities of New Spain following the Spanish conquest (figure 9.1). As part of its responses, in 1580 San Pedro Teozacoalco submitted a famous map (figure 9.2) illustrating its territory and many of its rulers. Apparently the *Mapa* was drawn prior to 1580 (Jansen and Pérez Jiménez 2005) by a native artist who blended traditional Mixtec and European conventions. Glosses written in Spanish help to identify some of its features.

COLONIALISM AT TEOZACOALCO

Evidence of European colonialism starting in the 1520s at Teozacoalco is clear. Books and tribute lists are one source of data. *El Libro de las Tasaciones de Pueblos de la Nueva España* (Cossío 1952) indicates that Teozacoalco was assessed tribute payments by the Spanish Crown early in the Colonial period. "Están tasados que den cada día dos pesos de oro en polvo y una carga de ají y otra de frisoles, de cuarenta en cuarenta días" (Cossío 1952:462). Descriptions of tribute show it consisted of quantitative objects, a trait of modern-era colonialism (Gosden 2004). Such objects have value because they can be counted or weighed and can be subdivided without changing their intrinsic characteristics.

More evidence of European colonialism appears in Teozacoalco's *Mapa* and *Relación*. The documents' existence, the written words, the Spanish names of signatories of the *Relación* and of the last rulers of Teozacoalco, and the saints' names connected to each settlement are all pieces of evidence. The circular map shares characteristics with the European *mappa mundi* (Harvey 1996), including having east at the top. The layout of the *cabecera* (capital) of Teozacoalco is typical of Spanish colonial towns formed by *congregación* and centered on a plaza bordered by a Catholic church on one side and the seat of government on another (Spores 1967). *Congregación* was the policy of congregating scattered indigenous populations into more compact and permanent settlements (Lockhart 1992). Thirteen subject *estancias* (ranches) are marked by Christian churches, while the roads connecting them are marked by the prints of Spanish horseshoes.

Physical evidence of European colonialism is ubiquitous in the territory of the municipality today. The foundation of the ruler's palace shown on the *Mapa* still exists in the center of San Pedro Teozacoalco as a 50-centimeter high, 28-by-26-meter platform with a small stairway at one corner (figure 9.3). The town's Catholic church is located precisely where the *Mapa* shows a church adjacent to the palace, although the current church does not date to the Colonial period. Deep sewer trenches dug around the town's central plaza during 2002 uncovered only a few artifacts, including Formative and Postclassic ceramics, and did not reveal any buried buildings. Terraces and stone walls of uncertain antiquity exist throughout the

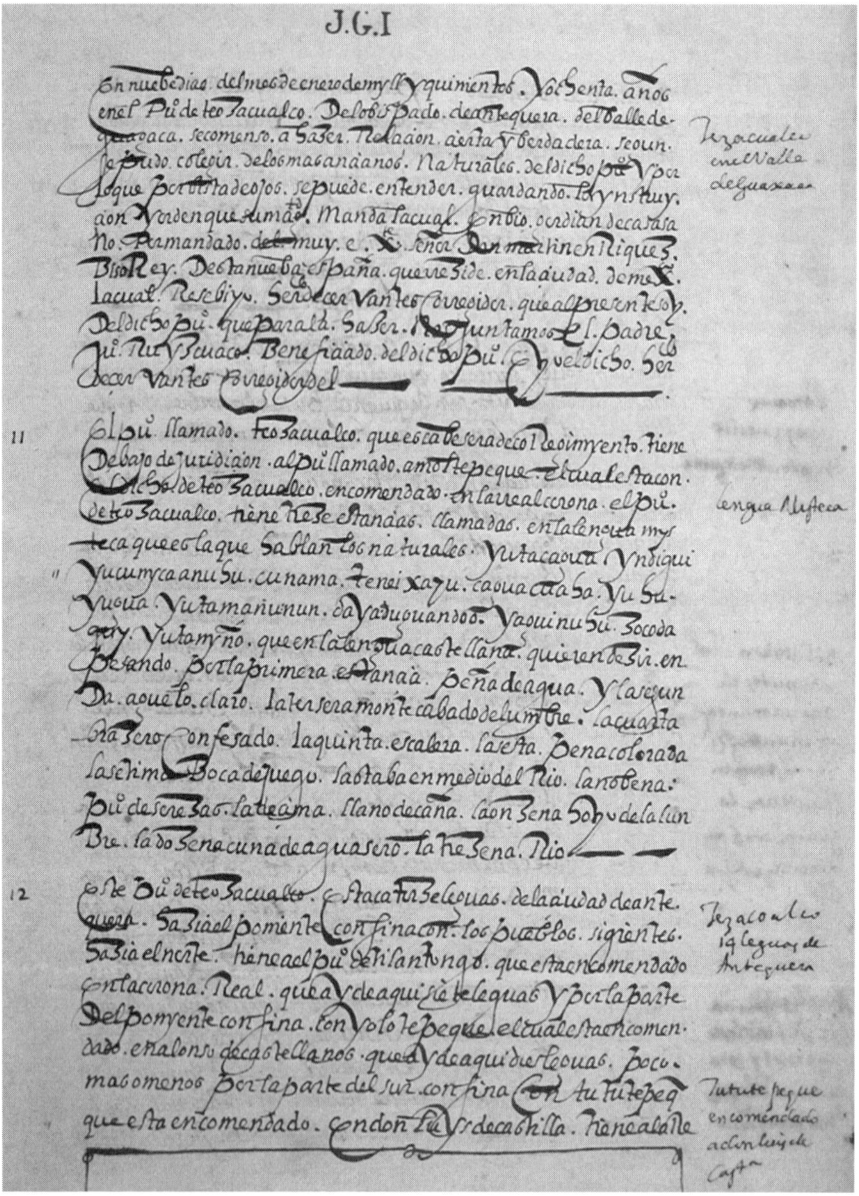

FIGURE 9.1. The *Relación Geográfica* of Teozacualco and Amoltepeque. Benson Latin American Collection, University of Texas at Austin.

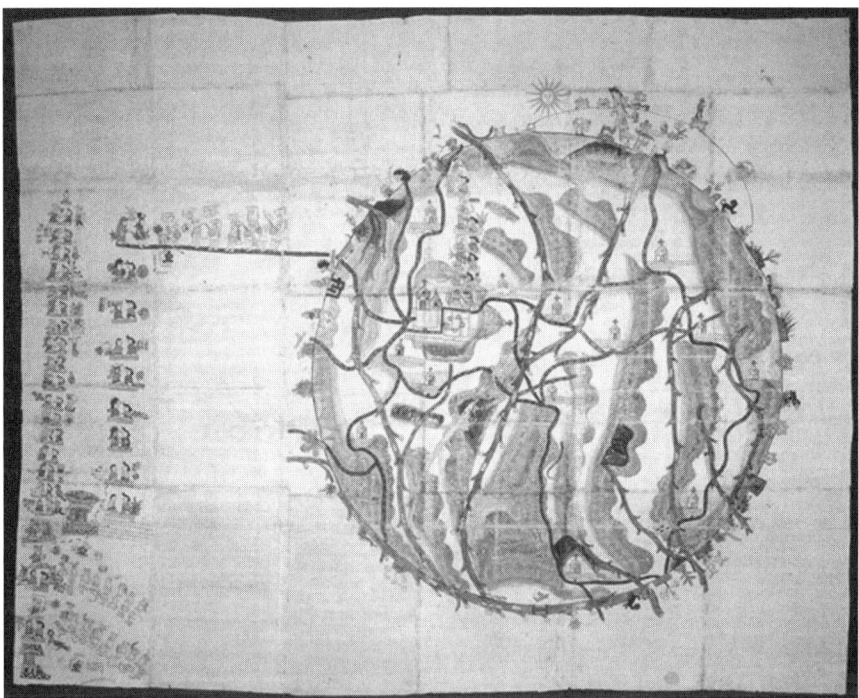

FIGURE 9.2. The *Mapa de Teozacoalco*. Benson Latin American Collection, University of Texas at Austin.

modern town. Some Colonial-period ceramics have been found near the town as well. Overall, evidence suggests the town was founded in its current location during the period of *congregación*.

Ruins that date to the Colonial period appear where the map shows *estancias* existed around 1580 (figure 9.4). San Jerónimo is an abandoned *estancia* on the slope of a piedmont spur reaching down from a mountain. This 454-by-50-meter site overlooks the modern town of Zapotitlán del Río, to which the population of San Jerónimo reportedly moved in the nineteenth century. The site has ruins identified as a church, two mounds, many terraces, and a cistern. The larger, 2.5-meter-high mound probably was the seat of local political power. Another abandoned *estancia* is San Juan, where stone, brick, and mortar ruins of walls, a floor, columns, and a vaulted roof lie in an alluvial pocket formed by the Río Minas. Eighteen abandoned gold mines (not appearing on the *Mapa*) are situated on a hillside near the Río Minas. These are probably the source of both the river's name and the gold paid as tribute to the Spanish Crown.

FIGURE 9.3. The foundation of the ruler's palace in San Pedro Teozacoalco has modern houses on top. The edge of the structure is to the right of the truck. (Inset) The depiction of the *cabecera* of San Pedro Teozacoalco on the *Mapa* shows a church on the east side of a central plaza and the palace on the south side.

Gosden (2004) argues that Aztec imperialism was colonialism, and we agree with that assessment. The Aztecs infrequently settled colonists in newly conquered areas, but it is possible to have colonialism without colonization and the two concepts should not be conflated (Domínguez 2002; Silliman 2005); *colonization* is simply a manifestation of colonialism by which settlements are established and maintained (Lyons and Papadopoulos 2002).

Evidence of Aztec colonialism at Teozacoalco starting during the reign of Motecuhzoma II (Xocoyotzin) exists in the *Mapa* and the *Relación*. The latter states, "pocos tiempos antes que los españoles viniesen, los sujetó Montezuma...al cual dicho Montezuma tributaban piedras (que entre ellos se dicen chalchihuites) y plumería, y mantas de algodón y [de he]nequén; y que le hacían sementeras de maíz, frijoles, y chian y algodón, todo lo cual se gastaban entre los soldados que en este dicho pu[ebl]o tenían de guarnición" (Acuña 1984:143). The *cabecera* and *estancias* all have associated Nahuatl names, and we read that Teozacoalco is a corruption of *Huezacualco*, meaning "gran solar o sitio" (Acuña 1984:143).

Early Colonial-period documents such as the Codex Mendoza (Berdan and Anawalt 1997) demonstrate that Aztec colonialism was precapitalist. We see graphic

FIGURE 9.4. (Upper right) Ruins identified by residents of Zapotitlán del Río as the church of San Jerónimo. (Left) Probable Colonial-period ruins of San Juan on alluvium adjacent to the Río Minas. (Lower right) Portion of the *Mapa* depicting the *estancias* of San Juan and San Jerónimo

depictions of tribute as both quantitative objects and qualitative things in groups, such as warriors' regalia. The latter are associated with meanings that give them an aggregate value greater than the intrinsic value of the materials comprising them (Gosden 2004).

Barlow (1949) places Teozacoalco (Teotzacualco) within the Aztec tributary province of Coyolapan, yet early Colonial-period tribute lists do not confirm this from the perspective of Tenochtitlán. The *Matrícula de Tributos* (Berdan and Durand-Forest 1980; Sepúlveda y Herrera, León Portilla, and Castillo Farreras 2003) places neighboring Mitlatongo (Mictlan) within the tributary province of Coayxtlahuacan but does not indicate that Teozacoalco was part of Coyolapan. Smith (1996) and Smith and Berdan (1996) resolve this problem by placing the city-state of Teozacoalco and twenty-three subject towns within one of the empire's strategic provinces, created as part of a frontier strategy to buffer tributary provinces from enemy polities, in this case coastal Tututepec. Tribute offered by strategic provinces emphasized military service, was often categorized as a gift, and was not necessarily paid at regular intervals. Unfortunately, strategic provinces also were not included in documents such as the Codex Mendoza and

Matrícula de Tributos. Because military service and material goods were considered gifts to the empire given out of friendship, Teozacoalco would have been under "political subjection," rather than "tributary subjection," where service and goods were considered obligatory (Hicks 1984:242). Even so, Smith and Berdan (1996) feel Teozacoalco was significant enough to have a *tlatoque,* a governor imposed by the empire, and Smith (1996) argues that the garrison reported in the town's *Relación* was a real entity.

An armed Aztec colony, such as existed at Oaxaca or Tuxtepec, should exhibit nonlocal architecture and artifacts. Quauhtochco, an Aztec garrison center and capital of a tributary province on the Gulf Coast, has a central structure resembling an Aztec temple, fortifying walls, and unusually high frequencies of Aztec ceramics. A provincial capital significant enough to have a *tlatoque* might also be expected to have a palace similar to the *tecpan* at Cihuatecpan (Evans 1991). However, Davies (1987) argues such colonies were rare and the status of the garrison at Teozacoalco is uncertain. The meaning of *guarnición* in sixteenth-century Spanish did not necessarily imply a standing military force, but rather "soldiers guarding or protecting a place where they were" or "a squadron of soldiers" (Davies 1987:326–327). Berdan and Anawalt (1997:30) "use the term 'garrison' with the understanding that the degree of permanence and strength of the forces is a matter of empirical discovery and could be quite different in each case."

In light of the competing interpretations of *guarnición*, it is hard to predict what archaeological evidence of Aztec colonialism might appear at Teozacoalco. In the Mixteca Alta, Bernal (1949) uncovered evidence of an Aztec presence in Coixtlahuaca, including Late Postclassic ceramics imported from the Basin of Mexico and a possible Aztec burial. Kowalewski et al. (2008) confirmed the presence of Aztec ceramics at Inguiteria, the Late Postclassic capital of Coixtlahuaca. Elsewhere in the Mixteca, a few Aztec III ceramics have been found (Byland 1984; Byland and Pohl 1994; Spores 1984) incidental to projects that did not specifically address the archaeological repercussions of Aztec conquest. To date, no Aztec-style structures or ceramics have been encountered in the area around Teozacoalco.

CULTURE CONTACT AT TEOZACOALCO

Evidence of Zapotec culture contact, starting no later than 1321 and emanating from Zaachila in the Valley of Oaxaca, is less visible than Spanish or Aztec colonialism. Apparently there was no colonization. The relationship between Zaachila and Teozacoalco involved unstable and changeable power relations mediated by kin and marriage alliances. The *Relación* does not refer to Zapotec contact, but evidence appears on the *Mapa* (figure 9.5). Lord 2 Dog of Zaachila married Lady 6 Reed

FIGURE 9.5. Nobles from Teozacoalco greet Lord 2 Dog of Zaachila and Lady 6 Reed of Tilantongo on the road from Tilantongo, *Mapa de Teozacoalco*.

of Tilantongo, and they traveled the road from Tilantongo to found Teozacoalco Dynasty 3 (Anders et al. 1992a).

The Codex Nuttall provides a more nuanced picture of the unstable power relations between Zaachila and Teozacoalco. Lady 4 Rabbit was a daughter of Lord 9 Movement, the last king of Teozacoalco Dynasty 2. She married into the ruling house of Zaachila and produced a son, the same Lord 2 Dog who returned to found the new dynasty at Teozacoalco (Anders et al. 1992a). Historical documents do not show or describe tribute Teozacoalco either paid to or received from Zaachila, and we do not know what form it may have taken, if it was paid at all.

No archaeological evidence of Zapotec contact at Teozacoalco has been discovered. The similarity between Zapotec and Mixtec material culture during this period and apparent lack of colonization suggest it will be difficult to find. Even if distinctive Zapotec artifacts are found, it will be hard to decide whether they represent intensive culture contact or simply trade.

Evidence of Teozacoalco's contact with the Mixtec polity of Tilantongo, starting no later than the first half of the 1100s, is more apparent than that with Zaachila. The polities again had unstable power relations mediated by kin and marriage alliances. The imprint of Tilantongo on Teozacoalco is overwhelming on the *Mapa* (figure 9.6). A Spanish gloss reads, "Éstos son los principales y señores que, antiguamente, salieron del pu[ebl]o de Tilanton[go] para éste de Teozacualco" (Acuña 1984:138). Graphically, we see Tilantongo's toponym, its dynasty, and the road connecting it to Teozacoalco. We see the footprints and portraits of Tilantongo lords and ladies who married into the ruling house of Teozacoalco and founded new dynasties.

FIGURE 9.6. Tilantongo's toponym appears at the lower-left corner of the *Mapa de Teozacoalco.*

The *Relación* states, "reconocían a su señor natural, [al] que habían traído del pu[ebl]o de Tilantongo, que se llamaba en lengua mixteca Occo Ñaña . . . al cual tributaban como a señor y le daban, en tributo, todos géneros de caza, y mantas de algodón y de [he]nequén" (Acuña 1984:143). There is no indication that the quantities of materials given were important. Depictions of possible tribute in the Codex Nuttall (Anders et al. 1992a) show bundles that often consist of qualitative things in sacred contexts. Evidence of complex marital and kin relationships in the codices means it was a two-way road between Teozacoalco and Tilantongo: daughters of Teozacoalco went to Tilantongo; sons and daughters of Tilantongo returned to Teozacoalco. The same lords and ladies appear in both the Teozacoalco and Tilantongo dynasties (Anders et al. 1992b).

Archaeological evidence of Tilantongo contact will be difficult to discern at Teozacoalco because the two Mixtec polities should share much material culture, such as ceramics, with each other and with other areas of the Mixteca Alta. So far, the only material evidence pertaining to the relationship between the polities consists of stone piles still used as municipal boundary markers that an informant identified as defining the old territorial boundary (figure 9.7).

INDIGENOUS CULTURE AT TEOZACOALCO

Beneath the layers of colonialism and culture contact evident in the historical documents, archaeological remains, and landscape is the underlying Teozacoalco Mixtec culture independent of outside influence. Analysis of documents, archaeology, and

FIGURE 9.7. A pile of stacked stones known locally as Cruz de Llegalán marks the old border between Teozacoalco and Tilantongo. The inset shows the probable representation of a similar marker from the northern border of the *Mapa*.

landscape allows us to understand indigenous Teozacoalco. People have inhabited the landscape embodied by the *Mapa* since at least 1000 BCE, according to our surveys and excavations. This has permitted development of unique local cultural traits such as indigenous ceramics. For more than three millennia, the landscape has structured the lives of the inhabitants, while their activities have also been sedimented into the landscape's features (Given 2004).

The translation of Teozacoalco's toponym on the *Mapa* (figure 9.8) gives its Mixtec name, *Chiyo Cahnu*, meaning "Large Altar or Pyramid" (Jansen and Pérez Jiménez 2005). Each of the communities subject to Teozacoalco also had a Mixtec name on the *Mapa*, and the *Relación* states that "El pu[ebl]o de Teozacualco tiene trece estancias llamadas en lengua mixteca, que es la que hablan los naturales" (Acuña 1984:141). The *Mapa* shows the portraits and glyphic names of Teozacoalco's ruling elite, many of whom were indigenous to Teozacoalco.

Striking features of landscapes have local religious, mythic, political, and/or historic meanings. Related to colonialism is development of a "landscape of resistance,"

FIGURE 9.8. Teozacoalco's toponym on the *Mapa* translates as "large or great altar or foundation."

in which indigenous knowledge of landscape is deliberately hidden from colonizers (Given 2004). Prominent natural and cultural features identifying Teozacoalco's boundaries are marked by symbols and glyphs on the *Mapa*, but all lack Spanish glosses. The native artist apparently did not share their significance with the colonist given the task of writing glosses. One example is an area on the eastern border marked by serpents. This corresponds to a cliff bearing a natural likeness of a snake's head with an extended tongue (figure 9.9).

Another aspect of a landscape of resistance is that natives co-opt symbols used by the colonizers. Cerro Amole, the mountain south of Teozacoalco, is marked by a red Christian cross on the *Mapa*, but no gloss explains why. The mountaintop most likely had ritual significance for the indigenous people similar to a church for the colonists. On top of Cerro Amole is the site known locally as Iglesia Gentil, with the largest concentration of monumental architecture encountered to date within the territory of Teozacoalco (figure 9.10). Characteristics of Iglesia Gentil suggest that it may have been founded during the Classic period, although the sparse ceramics on the ground surface have not confirmed this so far. The extent of the site core is 260 by 225 meters, and there are more than thirty-eight structures, including a 5-meter-high mound. A major feature of the mountaintop is a large I-shaped ball court. Other important constructions are an acropolis-like area at the north

FIGURE 9.9. A cliff marked by a serpent's head, a natural feature of the landscape, corresponds to (inset) a serpent symbol and a toponym on the eastern border of Teozacoalco's territory on the *Mapa*.

end of the site core and a large pyramid and palace-like structure in the south. The steep slopes of the upper third of the mountain are densely covered with structures, including concentrations of architectural features and almost continuous areas of terraces. An ancient road extends at least two kilometers around the mountain at the bottom of the densely settled area; below this, the slope of the middle third of the mountain is too steep for habitation. If Iglesia Gentil corresponds to the pattern reported for similar sites in the Nochixtlán Valley (Spores 1972), then evidence of Postclassic habitation should be light and mostly restricted to the periphery, suggesting people during that period used the mountaintop primarily as a shrine. Numerous structures encountered during survey on the gentler slopes of the mountain's lower third may represent the location of Teozacoalco's Postclassic population.

We have encountered archaeological evidence of considerable time depth within the area shown on the *Mapa*. Two petroglyphs of four-legged animals high on an overhanging cliff ("perritos") could be very old, although there is no proof of this. One of the numerous caves in cliffs adjacent to rivers and in mountainsides ("Cueva de los Huesos Perdidos") is associated with Formative ceramics. A ceramic sherd

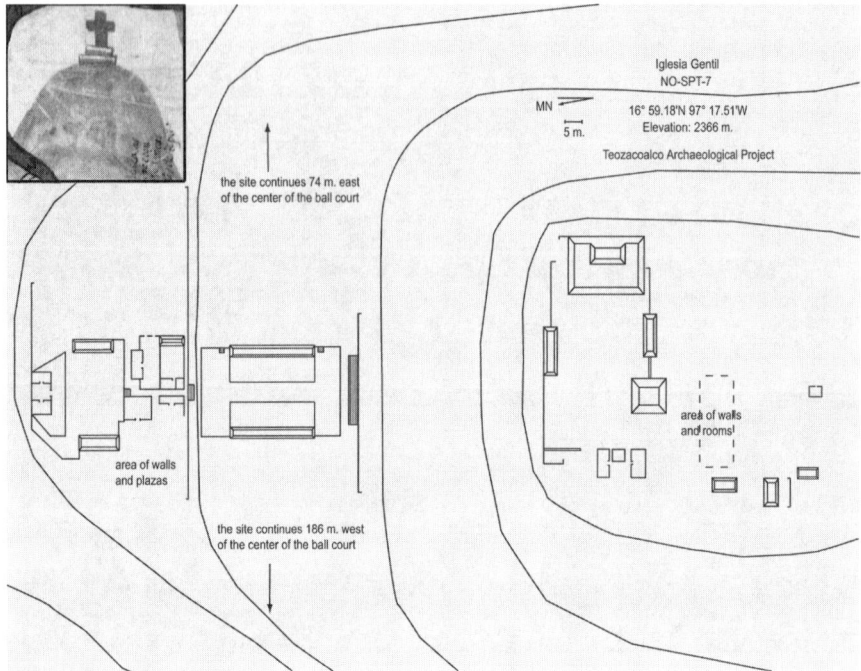

FIGURE 9.10. A sketch map of Iglesia Gentil, located on top of Cerro Amole, the most complex archaeological site found to date. (Inset) Iglesia Gentil is depicted on the *Mapa* by a red cross on a stepped construction.

from a G-12 vessel, typical of the Central Valley of Oaxaca, was found at "Mama 1," a hilltop site, signaling a Late Formative Ramos-phase (300 BCE–300 CE) component. At this site, hilltop architecture consists only of foundation walls flush with the ground surface, although the slopes around the hilltop are covered by extensive terracing. Local farmers have collected other G-12 sherds from unidentified sites around Teozacoalco, a clear indication of a sizeable Ramos population.

Analysis of ceramics from six sites test-pitted during 2008 to learn more about the regional ceramic sequence revealed an Early Formative Cruz B (1200–900 BCE) component at Cerro del Fortín, near the town of Zapotitlán del Río (figure 9.11). The site consists of a single 7.5-meter-high, 42.5-by-41.5-meter flat-topped mound. Terraces flank the southern and western sides, and a 1-meter-high, 21.3-by-7-meter superstructure with a stairway once traversed the top of the mound on the west. Two radiocarbon dates from one of the test pits confirmed the site's early component (Beta Analytic Inc., "Report of Radiocarbon Dating Analyses," June 11, 2009) sample from level 13 (Beta-260246) dated to 2690 ±40 BP, with a 2-sigma

FIGURE 9.11. Cerro del Fortín near Zapotitlán del Río is a large mound built on a hilltop near the lower end of a piedmont spur.

calibrated result of 910–800 BCE. The sample from level 14 (Beta-260247) dated to 2810 ± 40 B.P., or 1050–890 BCE and 870–850 BCE (Multiple probability ranges, as in this case, are due to short-term fluctuations in the atmospheric C-14 contents at certain time periods.) Date ranges for both samples were Late Cruz B–Early Cruz C and corresponded well with what the ceramics indicated.

Cerro del Fortín is located nearly eighty meters above the Río Grande on an artificially modified hilltop near the end of a piedmont spur jutting southward from the mountains. Spores's survey in and around Yanhuitlán, Yucuita, and Nochixtlán revealed that two of eighteen Cruz sites were on piedmont spurs and that the majority of the remaining sites were located in similarly elevated areas up off valley floors (Spores 1972:171–173). Balkansky et al. (2000:369) reported fifty-five Early Cruz sites within the combined Central Mixteca Alta Settlement Pattern Project, Huamelulpan, and Teposcolula archaeological survey areas and implied that all were "on low piedmont and piedmont spurs close to stream channels on productive valley floor lands." Cerro del Fortín's location therefore appears to be unexceptional for this period.

According to Spores (1972), polities of the Cruz A phase (1400–1200 BCE) had a two-tiered settlement hierarchy, with larger centers like Yucuita surrounded by smaller satellite villages. A similar settlement pattern has been documented for the Valley of Oaxaca, where San José Mogote grew to dominate the Etla arm of the valley (Winter 1994). It was in the subsequent Cruz B phase that centers in the Mixteca Alta began to participate in "the pan-Mesoamerican Early Formative style of carved and incised ceramics" (Balkansky et al. 2000:369), most often referred to as the *Olmec horizon*.

Excavations have occurred at only three Mixteca Alta sites with Cruz B components: Yucuita (Winter 1982; 1992), Etlatongo (Blomster 2004), and Tayata (Balkansky et al. 2008; Duncan et al. 2008). Recent excavations at Tayata, located near Huamelulpan, have revealed that the site was inhabited for at least one thousand years beginning as early as 1300 BCE. Based on those excavations, Balkansky et al. (2008) and Duncan et al. (2008) argue that the Cruz B phase was a particularly important time for the initial growth of social complexity and the emergence of characteristic features that define Mixtec civilization, making it unnecessary to posit importation of technology and political structures from elsewhere. Tayata was part of extensive Formative exchange networks including obsidian, ceramics, greenstone, mica, and marine shell ornaments, although it is unclear from published reports the degree to which the site interacted with the Gulf Coast. Balkansky et al. (2008) and Duncan et al. (2008) interpret two human cremations and evidence that dogs were eaten at Tayata as signaling the existence of differences in ideology and identity between the Mixteca Alta and other regions and the emergence of social hierarchy.

Not all researchers believe that changes in the Alta's sociopolitical organization were entirely autochthonous. The Cruz B phase falls within the Olmec horizon, a time when influences appear to have spread from the Olmec culture on the Gulf Coast to areas such as the highlands of Oaxaca and Mexico. Winter (1994) goes so far as to suggest that Olmec influences coupled with a disruption in settlement in the Oaxacan highlands could be linked to invading groups from the Gulf Coast, just a few days' walk away. Blomster (2004) offers an alternative explanation, believing that interaction with the Olmec, and particularly the adoption of their ritual paraphernalia, "jump-started" an already emerging social complexity.

Small, secondary sites like Cerro del Fortín probably did not participate directly with the Gulf Coast but may have received carved and incised ceramics (if at all) from larger centers (Jeffrey Blomster, personal communication 2008). Results of obsidian source analysis showed that Cerro del Fortín, like Tayata, participated in Formative exchange networks. Obsidian from test-pit levels containing Cruz B ceramics and/or Late Cruz B–Early Cruz C radiocarbon dates originated at Ucareo, Michoacán, Pico de Orizaba, Veracruz, and Paredón, Puebla (Archaeometry Laboratory, Research Reactor Center, University of Missouri, "X-ray Fluorescence Analysis of Obsidian Artifacts from Cerro del Fortín, Oaxaca, Mexico," June 17, 2009).

Much of the problem associated with the emergence of social inequality in the Alta stems from a dearth of data, not only at regional centers but at the secondary sites as well. It is at the latter that the control by the first-order centers would be demonstrated. At this point it would be interesting to see if any of the Olmec horizon materials were being redistributed to sites like Cerro del Fortín by regional elite.

Far removed from both Tayata (50 kilometers) and Etlatongo (45 kilometers), the Teozacoalco region has only recently been the subject of archaeological study. Data from the region may eventually help to test current interpretations of the transition from egalitarian to ranked society. This appears to have taken place between the Tierras Largas and San José phases in the Valley of Oaxaca, and between the roughly contemporaneous Cruz A and B phases in the Alta. Cerro del Fortín, for example, may reflect indigenous development of social complexity during the Early Formative period, not from the perspective of larger, primary sites such as Etlatongo that participated directly in the Olmec horizon (Blomster et al. 2005), but rather from a secondary site, a class overlooked to date in the Mixteca Alta.

CONCLUSIONS

One can think of culture contact as a spectrum, rather than as a single phenomenon. At Teozacoalco, this spectrum begins with indigenous cultural development influenced by trade, extends through Tilantongo contact and rule, Zapotec contact and rule, and Aztec colonialism, and ends with Spanish conquest and colonization. In reality, the spectrum does not end there but extends into the present with integration into the Republic of Mexico. The archaeological evidence of culture contact becomes increasingly easier to discern, both because archaeological processes cause it to be generally better preserved and less deeply buried, and because the cultures are less closely related and their material culture is stylistically more divergent. Simultaneously, the corpus of associated historical documentation becomes increasingly rich and unambiguous.

Archaeology can help to correct deficiencies in documentary record, but the converse is also true: historical records may provide the first clue that archaeologists should look for evidence of culture contact. Culture contact may be difficult to discern archaeologically in the absence of historical records if the surviving artifacts are nearly identical for the cultures involved, as at Teozacoalco. However, as we have seen, stratigraphic excavations and application of techniques, such as radiocarbon dating, obsidian source analysis, and ceramic source analysis (as has been done at Tayata and Etlatongo), can help archaeologists tease out patterns of trade and influence. Thus, the integration of historical and archaeological data permits a far more nuanced approach to understanding culture contact than either data set does alone.

Teozacoalco is an important place to study because the integration of historical and archaeological data is producing insights into the implications and social impact of four episodes of colonialism and culture contact, as well as indigenous development of Mixtec culture. Cross-cultural comparisons based on Teozacoalco's evolving society and landscape, with physical boundaries defined by the natives themselves, is permitting researchers to begin developing robust models of colonialism, culture contact, and the emergence of cultural complexity for the Mixteca Alta and greater Mesoamerica[1].

NOTE

1. We would like to acknowledge the Foundation for the Advancement of Mesoamerican Studies, Inc. (FAMSI); the Mudge Foundation; an anonymous foundation; and the Social, Behavioral, and Economic Sciences Research Fund and the Pro Humanitate Fund at Wake Forest University that funded fieldwork in Teozacoalco. The late David Shoemaker was the driving force behind the first year of fieldwork, upon which subsequent years have been based. Crews have included Nancy Anchors, Jamie Forde, Nancy Gonlin, Jessica Hedgepeth, Ronald Harvey of Tuckerbrook Conservation, Taylor and the late Dale Mudge, and Christine and Daniel Whittington, with special help from Joseph Whittington. We are grateful for John M.D. Pohl's encouragement and guidance of David Shoemaker, Nancy Troike's encouragement and advice, and help with ceramics from Jeffrey Blomster, Arthur Joyce, Michael Lind, and Marcus Winter. Work has been possible only with support of the Consejo de Arqueología of the Instituto Nacional de Antropología e Historia and authorities of the present-day municipalities within the territory of Colonial Teozacoalco.

REFERENCES

Acuña, René, ed. 1984. *"Relación de Teozacualco y Amoltepeque."* *Relaciones Geográficas del siglo XVI: Antequera II.* vol. 3., 129–151. Mexico: UNAM, Instituto de Investigaciones Antropológicas.

Anders, Ferdinand, Maarten Jansen, and Aurora Gabina Pérez Jiménez. 1992a. *Crónica Mixteca: El Rey 8 Venado, Garra de Jaguar, y la Dinastía de Teozacualco-Zaachila.* Mexico: Fondo de Cultura Económica.

Anders, Ferdinand, Maarten Jansen, and Aurora Gabina Pérez Jiménez. 1992b. *Origen e Historia de los Reyes Mixtecos.* Mexico: Fondo de Cultura Económica.

Balkansky, Andrew K., Stephen A. Kowalewski, Verónica Pérez Rodríguez, Thomas J. Pluckhahn, Charlotte A. Smith, Laura R. Stiver, Dimitri Beliaev, John F. Chamblee, Verenice Y. Heredia Espinoza, and Roberto Santos Pérez. 2000. "Archaeological Survey in the Mixteca Alta of Oaxaca, Mexico." *Journal of Field Archaeology* 27 (4):365–389. http://dx.doi.org/10.1179/jfa.2000.27.4.365.

Balkansky, Andrew K., Nava Rivera Felipe de Jesús, and Teresa Palomares Rodríguez. 2008. "Huamelulpan y Tayata, Oaxaca." *Arqueología Mexicana* 15 (90):36–37.

Barlow, R. H. 1949. *The Extent of the Empire of the Culhua Mexica. Ibero-Americana 28.* Berkeley: University of California Press.

Bartel, Brad. 1985. "Comparative Historical Archaeology and Archaeological Theory." In *Comparative Studies in the Archaeology of Colonialism,* ed. Stephen L. Dyson, 8–37. BAR International Series 233. Oxford: BAR.

Berdan, Francis F., and Patricia R. Anawalt. 1997. *The Essential Codex Mendoza.* Berkeley: University of California Press.

Berdan, Frances F., and Jacqueline de Durand-Forest. 1980. *Matrícula de Tributos: (Códice de Moctezuma): Museo Nacional de Antropología, México (Cod. 35–52).* Graz, Austria: Akademische Druck- und Verlagsanstalt.

Bernal, Ignacio. 1949. "Exploraciones en Coixtlahuaca, Oaxaca." *Revista Mexicana de Estudios Antropológicos* 10:5–76.

Blomster, Jeffrey P. 2004. *Etlatongo: Social Complexity, Interaction, and Village Life in the Mixteca Alta of Oaxaca, Mexico.* Belmont: Wadsworth/Thompson Learning.

Blomster, Jeffrey P., Hector Neff, and Michael D. Glascock. 2005. "Olmec Pottery Production and Export in Ancient Mexico Determined through Elemental Analysis." *Science* 307 (5712):1068–1072. http://dx.doi.org/10.1126/science.1107599.

Byland, Bruce E. 1984. "Boundary Recognition in the Mixteca Alta, Oaxaca, Mexico." In *Essays in Otomanguean Culture History,* ed. J. Kathryn Josserand, Marcus Winter, and Nicholas Hopkins, 109–140. Nashville: Publications in Anthropology, vol. 31.

Byland, Bruce E., and John M.D. Pohl. 1994. *In the Realm of 8 Deer: The Archaeology of the Mixtec Codices.* Norman: University of Oklahoma Press.

Cossío, Francisco González de. 1952. *El Libro de las Tasaciones de Pueblos de la Nueva España, Siglo XVI.* Mexico: Archivo General de la Nación.

Davies, Nigel. 1987. *The Aztec Empire: The Toltec Resurgence.* Norman: University of Oklahoma Press.

Domínguez, Adolfo J. 2002. "Greeks in Iberia: Colonialism without Colonization." In *The Archaeology of Colonialism*, ed. Claire L. Lyons and John K. Papadopoulos, 65–95. Los Angeles: Getty Research Institute.

Duncan, William N., Andrew K. Balkansky, Kimberly Crawford, Heather A. Lapham, and Nathan J. Meissner. 2008. "Human Cremation in Mexico 3,000 Years Ago." *Proceedings of the National Academy of Sciences of the United States of America* 105 (14):5315–5320. http://dx.doi.org/10.1073/pnas.0710696105.

Evans, Susan Toby. 1991. "Architecture and Authority in an Aztec Village: Form and Function of the Tecpan." In *Land and Politics in the Valley of Mexico*, ed. Herbert Harvey, 62–93. Albuquerque: University of New Mexico Press.

Given, Michael. 2004. *The Archaeology of the Colonized*. London: Routledge.

Gosden, Chris. 2004. *Archaeology and Colonialism*. Cambridge: Cambridge University Press.

Harvey, P.D.A. 1996. *Mappa Mundi: The Hereford World Map*. Toronto: University of Toronto Press.

Hicks, Frederic. 1984. "La Posición de Temascalapan en la Triple Alianza." *Estudios de Cultura Nahuatl* 17:235–260.

Jansen, Maarten, and Aurora Gabina Pérez Jiménez. 2005. *Codex Bodley*. Oxford: Bodleian Library, University of Oxford.

Kowalewski, Stephen A., Luis A. Barba Pingarrón, Jorge Blancas, Marisol Yadira Cortés Vilchis, Gabriela García Ayala, Leonardo López Zárate, Agustín Ortiz, Thomas J. Pluckhahn, Benjamin A. Steere, and Blanca Vilchis Flores. 2008. "Proyecto Urbanismo Temprano y Tardío en Coixtlahuaca, Oaxaca: Informe Técnico Final." Report submitted to Consejo de Arqueología, Instituto Nacional de Antropología e Historia, Mexico City.

Lockhart, James. 1992. *The Nahuas after the Conquest*. Stanford: Stanford University Press.

Lyons, Claire L., and John K. Papadopoulos. 2002. "Archaeology and Colonialism." In *The Archaeology of Colonialism*, ed. Claire L. Lyons and John K. Papadopoulos, 1–23. Los Angeles: Getty Research Institute.

Rogers, J. Daniel. 2005. "Archaeology and the Interpretation of Colonial Encounters." In *The Archaeology of Colonial Encounters: Comparative Perspectives*, ed. Gil J. Stein, 331–354. Santa Fe: School of American Research Press.

Schortman, Edward, and Patricia A. Urban. 1998. "Culture Contact Structure and Process." In *Studies in Culture Contact: Interaction, Culture Change, and Archaeology*, ed. James G. Cusick, 102–125. Center for Archaeological Investigations, Occasional Paper No. 25. Carbondale: Southern Illinois University.

Sepúlveda y Herrera, Maria Teresa, Miguel León Portilla, and Víctor M. Castillo Farreras. 2003. *La Matrícula de Tributos*. Arqueología Mexicana, Edición Especial no. 14. México, DF.: Editorial Raíces: Instituto Nacional de Antropología e Historia.

Shoemaker, David E. 2000. "El Mapa de Teozacoalco." Report submitted to FAMSI. http://www.famsi.org/reports/98032/index.html; accessed 06/2007.

Silliman, Stephen W. 2005. "Culture Contact or Colonialism? Challenges in the Archaeology of Native North America." *American Antiquity* 70 (1):55–74. http://dx.doi.org/10.2307/40035268.

Spores, Ronald. 1967. *The Mixtec Kings and Their People*. Norman: University of Oklahoma Press.

Spores, Ronald. 1972. *An Archaeological Settlement Survey of the Nochixtlán Valley, Oaxaca.* Nashville: Vanderbilt University Publications in Anthropology, vol. 1.

Spores, Ronald. 1984. *The Mixtecs in Ancient and Colonial Times.* Norman: University of Oklahoma Press.

Smith, Michael E. 1996. "The Strategic Provinces." In *Aztec Imperial Strategies*, ed. Frances F. Berdan, Richard E. Blanton, Elizabeth Hill Boone, Mary G. Hodge, Michael E. Smith, and Emily Umberger, 137–150. Washington, DC: Dumbarton Oaks Research Library and Collection.

Smith, Michael E., and Frances F. Berdan. 1996. "Appendix 4. Province Descriptions." In *Aztec Imperial Strategies*, ed. Frances F. Berdan, Richard E. Blanton, Elizabeth Hill Boone, Mary G. Hodge, Michael E. Smith, and Emily Umberger, 265–323. Washington, DC: Dumbarton Oaks Research Library and Collection.

Stein, Gil J. 2005. "Introduction: The Comparative Archaeology of Colonial Encounters." In *The Archaeology of Colonial Encounters: Comparative Perspectives*, ed. Gil J. Stein, 3–31. Santa Fe: School of American Research Press.

Whittington, Stephen L. 2002. "El Mapa de Teozacoalco: An Early Colonial Guide to Cultural Transformations." Report submitted to FAMSI. http://www.famsi.org/reports /01032/index.html; accessed 06/2007.

Whittington, Stephen L. 2003. "El Mapa de Teozacoalco: An Early Colonial Guide to a Municipality in Oaxaca." *The SAA Archaeological Record* 3 (4):20–22, 25.

Winter, Marcus. 1982. *Guía Zona Arqueológica de Yucuita.* Oaxaca, Mexico: Centro INAH Oaxaca.

Winter, Marcus. 1992. *Oaxaca: The Archaeological Record.* Mexico: Minutiae Mexicana.

Winter, Marcus. 1994. "Los Altos de Oaxaca y las Olmecas." In *Las Olmecas en Mesoamérica*, ed. J. E. Clark, 129–141. Mexico: El Equilibrista/Turner Libros.

Salt Production and Trade in the Mixteca Baja

The Case of the Tonalá-Atoyac-Ihualtepec Salt Works

BAS VAN DOESBURG AND RONALD SPORES

INTRODUCTION

In 1982, Mary Elizabeth Smith reported on the existence of a pictographic map in the village of San Vicente del Palmar, a small community located in the heart of the Mixteca Baja. Unfortunately, Smith's discussion of the document at the American Society for Ethnohistory annual meeting was never published, and the large sheet of *amate* (bark) paper received little attention thereafter, in spite of its beauty and traditional style. In 2000, Laura Rodríguez returned to the village with an interest in the topography painted on the document and was able to convince the village authorities to have the manuscript restored. In the course of the restoration it was discovered that the document dealt with the distribution of important brine springs in the Tonalá-Atoyac-Ihualtepec area (Doesburg 2008a, 2008b). In the present chapter we describe the document and attempt to place it in a broader context by using historical documentation from Mexican archives, as well as ethnographic and archaeological observations in the region.[1] We believe that the vast archaeological record, the rich historical sources of indigenous Oaxaca, and the notable cultural continuities until the present need to be studied not in isolation from each other but rather in a holistic manner.[2] This methodological approach is especially rewarding in controlled case studies, which can then be compared and contrasted with other case studies at a later stage. In this contribution we do not claim to present a finished project, but mainly to express our hope that our efforts will stimulate more intensive study of the history and archaeology of this little known region in the future.

DOI: 10.5876/9781607323297.c010

THE *MAPA DE SAN VICENTE DEL PALMAR*: GENERAL
DESCRIPTION AND PROVENIENCE

The Mixteca Baja is located in the area where the contemporary states of Oaxaca, Puebla, and Guerrero converge. The average altitude of the region varies between 1,200 and 1,800 meters above sea level, with almost half of the territory between 1,400 and 1,600 meters. Today, the Mixteca Baja, and especially its western portion, is a highly marginalized and geographically isolated region, where poverty and related problems are conspicuous and still unresolved. Although in prehispanic and early colonial times this area was socially and economically well articulated with the rest of central Mesoamerica, and—as far as the few known historical sources show—seems to have been relatively prosperous, almost no substantial archaeological and/or ethnohistorical research has been carried out in the region. The notable exception is some work on the distinctive symbolism expressed in the archaeological materials from the Classic period, the so-called *Ñuiñe* style that flourished from 250 to 800 CE (Moser 1972, 1977; Paddock 1965, 1966, 1968, 1970a, 1970b; Rivera Guzmán 1999; Rodríguez Cano 1995; Urcid 2005; Winter 1989, 1996; Winter et al. 1976).

The *Mapa de San Vicente del Palmar* was first seen by scholars in 1982 in the village of San Vicente del Palmar, located in the heart of the Mixteca Baja, but no in-depth study was undertaken at that time, and the document was largely forgotten[3]. Laura Rodríguez called attention to this document when, in 2000, she started her study of Mixteca Baja documents[4]. The document is painted on *amate* paper and is quite damaged, which makes its interpretation considerably more difficult (figure 10.1). The size of this extraordinary document, after restoration, is 214 by 121 centimeters. The map consists of two layers of *amate* paper, but it may originally have had more layers. The upper layer, which contained the painting, consists of twenty-two pieces of *amate* arranged and glued together to form the larger sheet. The base preparation of this sheet was made with gypsum, possibly mixed with cornstarch. The reds are composed of cochineal, and indigo was used to make the blues and greens.[5] Fortunately, the overall composition is still clear. Its general style and script indicate it was probably painted sometime in the sixteenth century. As we will try to show, the document is probably about a dispute or an agreement related to the control of salt-producing communities in the former Tonalá-Atoyac-Ihualtepec *señoríos*.

At first glance, it is clear that the document is a typical sixteenth-century map of the so-called Mixteca-Puebla tradition: topographs, churches, and personages (here only represented by their heads) are the usual elements composing the highly stylized and geometrical representation of a real landscape in the Mixteca Baja. Because the document is kept in San Vicente del Palmar, it may be assumed that the document represents that area. Mary Elizabeth Smith suggested the document

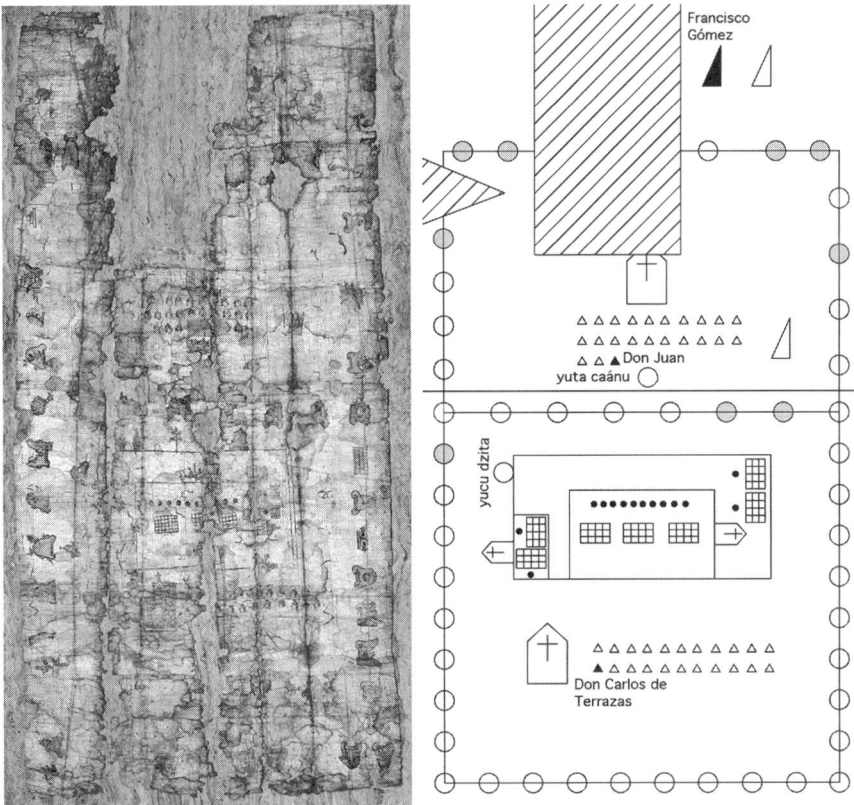

FIGURE 10.1. (Left) *The Mapa de San Vicente del Palmar.* (Right) A schematized outline of the *mapa*, with some of the features mentioned in the text; the circles represent topographs and the triangles stand for persons.

might represent San Vicente by "establishing its relationship to its larger and more important neighbors (Huajuapan at the top of the map, and possibly Tonalá below)" (in Smith and Parmenter 1991:95). This, however, seems unlikely as there is no indication that San Vicente was of any importance on the regional level at the time that the map was made.[6] To resolve the problem of the document's provenience, it is necessary to search for additional evidence.

THE IDENTIFICATION OF THE MAIN POLITY

On the lower half of the sheet, one distinguishes a large rectangle made up of a series of topographs, a typical representation of a community's territory and its boundaries;[7] in this case, there are thirty-four boundary markers (figure 10.1). Within this territory, a church represents the principal settlement. The drawing shows an attempt at rendering a "Renaissance-style" perspective, but this should not be taken as an indication that an actual existing church was depicted. Although new to the repertoire of Mixtec writing, the drawings of new building forms and objects were immediately conventionalized into the graphic system. In this case the drawing seems to represent the generic idea of the small chapels that were built in many places in the Mixteca: square buildings with a big central door and no nave (naves being added later on in front of the door).[8] In front of the building, one observes a group of 22 human heads (ordered in two rows of eleven), representing a group of Mixtec men (figure 10.1 and 10.2). Each figure wears a royal diadem (*dzite* in Mixtec) and is glossed in Latin characters. These glosses begin with the word *ya*, meaning "governing lord," followed by Mixtec calendrical names.[9] The series of heads, therefore, must form some kind of genealogy of the settlement's rulers, because it is unlikely that this community had so many contemporaneous rulers.[10] The man in front of the group of heads has a damaged gloss above his head, which can be read as *don car(llos) de terrazas*, who must have been an early colonial ruler of the depicted community. This man is well known from the documentary record; Don Carlos was the hereditary ruler of Ihualtepec during the late sixteenth century, according to documents in Mexico's National Archives. He was the son of Don Juan de Aguilar, the first known colonial lord of Ihualtepec.[11] Don Carlos appears as the ruler of Ihualtepec from 1578 onwards,[12] while his father was still alive. Only ten years later, Don Carlos died and a younger brother, Don Felipe de Terrazas, inherited the *cacicazgo*. In 1592, just a few years after his death, the youngest brother, Don Diego, became the *cacique* of Ihualtepec.[13] Documents from this period relate something of the troubled times in the family: in 1561, Don Juan was subject to an audit;[14] in 1575–1576, Don Juan was accused of murdering his wife;[15] in 1580, Don Juan accused his own son Carlos— maybe impatient to replace his father—of stealing objects from his home;[16] in 1588, Don Carlos—already the ruling lord for ten years—was accused of "*agravios, excesos, malos tratamientos, molestias, vejaciones y derramas*"[17]; in 1592, Don Diego's position as governor was seriously challenged by Don Francisco Pacheco de Alvarado, his niece's husband;[18] in the same year Don Diego was accused of having a mistress, who had also been the mistress of his late brother Carlos.[19] Most of these accusations seem to have related to the ongoing power struggle in the ruling family.

THE IHUALTEPEC POLITY DURING THE SIXTEENTH CENTURY

Having identified Don Carlos (which suggests that the map may have been made between 1578 and 1589), it follows that the church probably represents the community

FIGURE 10.2. The genealogy of the rulers of Ihualtepec. (Detail of figure 10.1.)

of Ihualtepec (the name derives from Yoaltepec, "on the mountain of the night"[20]), an important *cacicazgo* on the northwestern border of the modern-day state of Oaxaca. According to some sources, it was conquered by the Aztecs during the reign of Moctezuma I (1440–1464 CE), although Ixtlilxochitl ascribed this conquest to Nezahualcoyotl.[21] In the Late Postclassic period, and according to the *Matrícula de Tributos*, Ihualtepec was the tributary capital with Calihuala,[22] Silacayoapan,[23] Patlanala, Jicayán de Tovar, and Iscatoyac (merged with Jicayán in 1608) forming this tributary province located in the higher Balsas Basin.[24] According to some sources—especially the recently rediscovered *Genealogía de Igualtepec*—Yoaltepec formed a sort of double *señorío* with Suchiquilazala (or Ayoxochiquilazala), further to the south. The Aztecs established a garrison in Yoaltepec, but one document states that that garrison was stationed in Suchiquilazala.[25] The products paid in tribute to the Aztec capital consisted of military clothing, textiles, honey, gold, and lapidary products of greenstone. Very early in the colonial period, the area (Tecomaxtlahuaca, Ihualtepec, Juxtlahuaca, and maybe Mixtepec) rebelled against the Spanish presence, attacking Spaniards and burning crosses. Bernardino Vázquez de Tapia (1972:52) headed an expedition into the area.[26] During the reign of the Terrazas *caciques*, Ihualtepec was still a large *señorío*. In 1598, twenty-six villages were said to be *sujetos* or *estancias* of Ihualtepec.

THE IDENTIFICATION OF THE SECOND POLITY

Returning to the *Mapa de San Vicente del Palmar*, the topographs along the upper side of the rectangle of boundaries of Ihualtepec also make up the lower side of a second rectangle of border glyphs in the upper part of the document (much like a digital number 8), apparently representing a neighboring community of Ihualtepec. In this second rectangle of twenty-four boundaries (holes in the document account for possibly three missing topographs), there is also a church and again a group of twenty-three human heads with royal crowns, forming the royal genealogy of the neighboring community. Again, most men have names starting with the *ya* prefix, followed by Mixtec calendrical names. And just as in the lower section of the document, the man in front has a Christian name of "Don Juan"[27] (figure 10.1). The absence of a last name complicates his identification in other sources. There is, however, an additional clue. Below the row of men, a topograph seems to represent the community they and the church belong to. This central glyph consists of a green valley from which springs a stream of water. Nearby, to the side, is a Mixtec language gloss which reads "[. . .] *tayu yuta caāno.*" Although *tayu* is possibly the second part of *yuhui tayu* (*señorío*), *Yuta ca'no* ("big river") is the name of San Pedro Atoyac ("at the river"), today a very small community on the banks of the Río Mixteco, and Ihualtepec's neighbor immediately to the east.[28] In the sixteenth century, Atoyac was a *señorío* under the influence of Tonalá.[29] In fact, the lords of Atoyac are looking at a man seated on a throne to the right, who may represent a Tonalá authority. Unfortunately, his name gloss is unreadable. Little is known about the *señorío* of Atoyac, and there is no Don Juan recorded as a late sixteenth-century ruler of this place.[30] We will have to turn to other evidence to secure the identifications made so far.

THE *MAPA DE SAN VICENTE DEL PALMAR* AND THE PRODUCTION OF SALT

Within the rectangle formed by the borders of Ihualtepec, a smaller separate region is set apart by a red line. This region is divided into three even smaller areas by other red lines (figure 10.1 and figure 10.3). Two of these areas have a chapel depicted, suggesting they represent subject communities of Ihualtepec. The third area has no chapel. In each of these smaller areas we find black rectangular shapes subdivided into small squares. In several places, especially on their corners, the red division lines are accompanied by plants, trees, and cactuses, apparently functioning as borders. However, the general character of the flora is not very helpful in locating the area on a modern map. Fortunately, among the flora, one single topograph is more specific and represents a hill with a number of tortillas in its interior. A Mixtec gloss added to the drawing names this hill as *yucu dzita* ("tortilla hill").[31] Today Cerro de Tortilla is a prominent mountain just north of the present-day village of San Ildefonso, a small community up in the mountains halfway between Atoyac and Ihualtepec. Interestingly, San Ildefonso is one of four communities that produce salt in this area. The wells in this area—near present-day Mariscala de Juárez— have produced fine salt since prehispanic times in the villages called Santa María, San Ildefonso, San Pedro, and San Bartolo (figures 10.4 and 10.5). According to a document of 1598, San Pedro and San Bartolo—both to the north of Cerro de

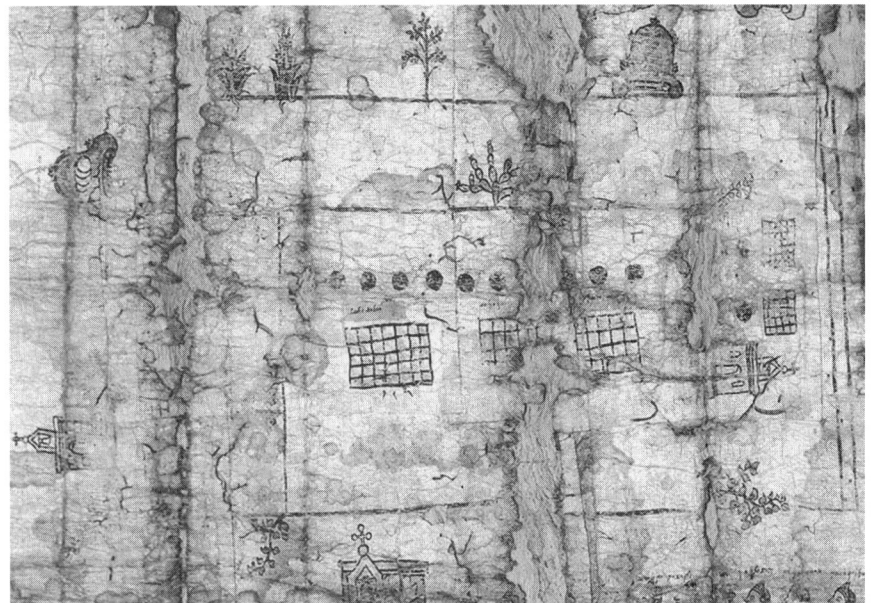

FIGURE 10.3. Delimited area and salt fincas; "tortilla hill" is to the upper left.

FIGURE 10.4. The contemporary village of Santa María, with salt *fincas* in the foreground.

Tortilla—belonged to Ihualtepec; in a list of twenty-six dependent communities, written by the *cacique* of Ihualtepec, these villages are at the top of the list:

> *Memoria de las estanscias de Yoaltepec. Primeramente Yohualtepeque, ra [sic] tierra fria, tiene sesenta y dos tributarios. [2] San P[edr]o Cuezcomayztapa*[32] *salinas, tiene dos caserias: Xaliyztapa y Caxiyztapa;*[33] *tierra callente, tributarios con sus dos caserias trei[n]ta y tres. [3] Sa[n] Bartolome Xoxouhquiyztapa,*[34] *tiene ona caserias que se llama Huiloyztapa;*[35] *tierra callente, tiene tributarios con sus caserias trei[n]ta y iocho.*[36]

Another document mentions the same salt works of Xoxouqui Yztapan (together with the unidentified Guitzo Ystatapan [sic] and Noexcaxaiztapan [sic][37]) as bordering a cattle ranch of the community of Ihualtepec.[38] Santa María and San Ildefonso—both south of Cerro de Tortilla—are not mentioned in this document, but they may have been the *caserías* Xaliyztapa and Caxiyztapa mentioned in the list and belonging to San Pedro. The same 1598 document, which includes a short description of a visit to the salt villages, suggests San Ildefonso was called Santiago during the sixteenth century.[39]

All this suggests that the rectangles subdivided into smaller units seen in the *Mapa de San Vicente* south of Cerro de Tortilla represent "salt farms," or *fincas de sal*,[40] and that the two associated chapels south of Cerro de Tortilla may represent Santa María and San Ildefonso or Santiago.[41] The document very likely represents an agreement between the two *cacicazgos*—Ihualtepec and Atoyac—regarding the distribution of the depicted salt works. We know indeed of marriage arrangements between nobles of Ihualtepec and Atoyac that involved salt (Appendix 10.1).

THE CONFLICT OF 1556–1585

It is now essential to introduce additional documentation to confirm our identifications. At the top of the document, outside the borders, on what would be the eastern extreme, a man is seated on a royal throne. According to the gloss above his head, his name is Don Francisco Gómez (figure 10.1 and figure 10.5). Other possible paintings surrounding Don Francisco have been lost due to severe damage in this part of the document. However, traces of painted lines behind his back suggest that a woman sat to his right; one can just barely discern her bent knees under her *huipil* and her left hand resting on the cloth[42] (figure 10.5). Don Francisco Gómez appears in a very helpful document preserved in Mexico's National Archives, and which explains the relations that existed between the persons discussed.[43] The file is about a prolonged court case over the rights to certain lands and salt works between Don Carlos de Terrazas of Ihualtepec and Don Juan de Santiago of Tonalá—possibly the Don Juan of Atoyac in the *mapa*—covering the years from 1556 to 1585. The two

FIGURE 10.5. Don Francisco Gómez.

men were married to two sisters, Doña María and Doña Inés, daughters of Don Francisco Gómez of Tonalá, who is seen sitting at the top of the document.[44] Don Francisco did not leave any male heirs. Inés Gómez, the wife of Don Carlos, died in 1559 and, according to a testament presented years later, had left her part of her father's heritage to her husband. However, according to Don Carlos in his complaint of 1585, Doña María, the eldest sister, and her husband Don Juan had taken possession of all that Don Francisco left, claiming it as an entailed *cacicazgo*. Among these were the salt works in the above-mentioned Jaliztapa (one of the *caserías* of San Pedro), described as "many plots of small basins in which salt sets," producing around 400 *fanegas* a year.[45] Half of these were awarded to Don Carlos in 1585, when several witnesses indicated that the salt works were not part of the Tonalá *cacicazgo*, because Don Francisco Gómez had bought them from Ihualtepec nobles around 1540. During the possession ceremony in Jaliztapan, Don Carlos "took salt water from the wells where it springs, and threw it from one place to the other, and he walked and went among the basins where the salt sets and is made."[46] In later documents, the descendants of Don Carlos are said to own three *fincas* in San Ildefonso, equating this village with Jaliztapan.[47] The other half of the heritage went to the descendants of Doña María Gómez.[48]

The pictographic *Mapa de San Vicente* was possibly a document used in this conflict between Ihualtepec and Atoyac-Tonalá over the distribution of the brine springs in Santa María and San Ildefonso. The fact that each salt-community had its own chapel suggests that these were *macehual* settlements, meaning villages of free commoners who were supposed to pay tribute to the lord of the polity and—through him—to the Aztec or Spanish administration. According to the pictorial, Santa María and San Ildefonso each received two *fincas* (each with one black dot[49]), while another group of three *fincas* (perhaps the ones later owned by the Terrazas family), with ten black dots, were reserved for nobles. Glosses above the *fincas* contain the word *toho* ("noble, foreigner").[50] In their community *fincas*, Santa María and San Ildefonso probably produced salt for the regional markets. With the gains, they acquired the items necessary to pay their tribute. On the other hand, the salt works of the nobles were possibly worked by *terrazgueros*, or land-bound commoners, who only gave tribute to their lord but not to the community. This salt was probably sold to provide the noble's palaces with luxury goods. The existence of salt works exclusively owned by the elite is confirmed by the *Relación Geográfica de Acatlán* (1985), which states that some of the *fincas* were of the ruler Don Gregorio and of another nobleman from town. Based on the surviving *Relaciones Geográficas*, the distribution pattern of the salt from the Tonalá-Atoyac-Ihualtepec *fincas* can be traced approximately (figure 10.6).

CORRELATIONS WITH OTHER PICTORIAL DOCUMENTS

The identifications presented here have implications for other documents as well. As Mary Elizabeth Smith showed without knowledge of the documents' provenience, the boundaries of Atoyac on the *Mapa de San Vicente del Palmar* coincide with the boundaries of the *Mapa Número 36* (figure 10.7) in the Mexico's Museo Nacional de Antropología and of the so-called *Lienzo Mixteco III* (figure 10.8), a copy of which is kept in Geneva[51] (the grayed-out topoglyphs in figure 10.1 coincide with topoglyphs in these two documents). This means that these two documents also represent Atoyac. The prominent river in both documents must then represent the Río Mixteco. Both documents show salt works of Atoyac to the west of the Río Mixteco, although the *Mapa Número 36* seems to deal mainly with a dispute over

FIGURE 10.6. The distribution pattern of the salt from the Tonalá-Atoyac-Ihualtepec *fincas* according to the *Relaciones Geográficas*.

the distribution of the fertile lands on the banks of the Río Mixteco between Don Juan—surely the same Don Juan that appears on the *Mapa de San Vicente*—and Doña Margarita. In the next part of our contribution, we will try to place the salt production of this region in a broader context, using ethnographic and archaeological observations in the region itself.

SALT PRODUCTION IN MESOAMERICA

The production and trade of salt has a long history in Mesoamerica. It has been the object of a series of studies. Besides general studies (Ewald 1985; Flores Clair

FIGURE 10.7. *Mapa Número 36.* Museo Nacional de Antropología, Mexico City.

1992; Mendizábal 1946; Reyes Garza 1995, 1998; Saravia Viejo 1994; among others), several production areas have been studied in some detail (e.g., Andrews 1983 for Yucatán; Good 1995 for the Guerrero coast; Machuca Gallegos 2007 for Tehuantepec; Menegus Bornemann 1994 for Taxco; Parsons 2001 for Nexquipayac; Williams 1999; 2002 for Michoacán; etc.).[52] Salt was obtained in a great variety of ways. As has been noted by several authors, three distinct origins of natural salt can be distinguished in Mesoamerica, all of which were heavily exploited: the coastal estuaries, the soil banks and beaches of inland saline lakes and rivers, and the brine springs in the mountains. In Tehuantepec white salt forms naturally in the shallow estuaries; in most other areas artificial processing was necessary in the form of boiling down the brine or exposing the brine or sea water to solar evaporation to crystallize the salt. In saline soil banks, leaching the soil was a common method to obtain *tequisquite*, low-sodium-chloride mixtures containing high amounts of sodas and

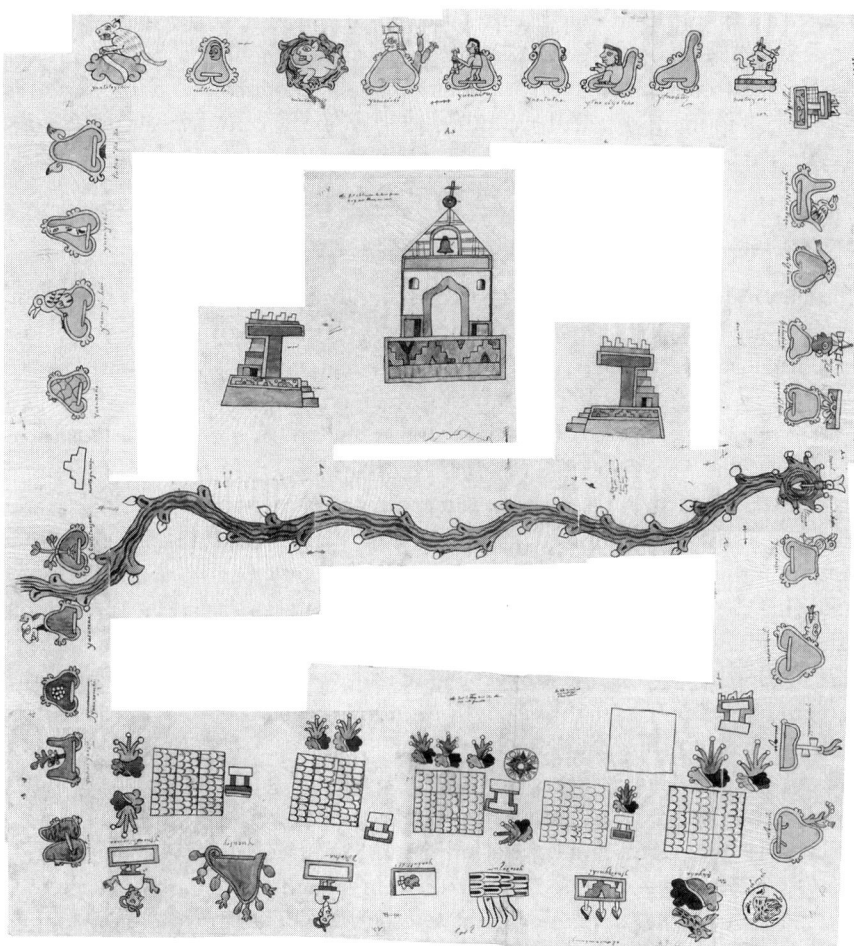

FIGURE 10.8. *Lienzo Mixteco III.* Bibliotheque Publique et Universitaire, Geneva.

clay. As for its use, besides the physiological need and the culinary aspect in human consumption, it was used to preserve foods (fish), to fix dyes in cotton and, in very small quantities, to tan leather (deer). Prehispanic use of salt was thus relatively limited. In the Colonial period, however, great amounts of salt were required for new industries (glass, glazing, and soap), the growing cattle economy (feeding sheep and goats and salting bacon), and for the so-called patio process in silver mining (i.e., the extraction through amalgamation with quicksilver)[53]. Because these industries—and especially the silver industry—used far greater amounts of salt than ever before, the production of salt intensified many times during the Colonial period.

The increasing demand may have resulted in significant changes in the management and exploitation of salt. Accordingly, great care should be taken in projecting Colonial and contemporary information on salt production into the past. It is therefore important that we have information from the early years of the Colony, like the data discussed above from the Tonalá-Atoyac-Ihualtepec salt works.

SALT PRODUCTION IN THE MIXTECA BAJA

The salt production of the Mixteca Baja and the neighboring Tehuacán valley to the east is relatively well known. Zapotitlán Salinas and surrounding villages to the east have been studied on several occasions by different authors (Ewald 1985; Paredes Colín 1960; Sisson 1973; and recently by Castellón 1998 [in Reyes Garza 1998] and Castellón Huerta 2006). Salt production was and still is practiced in Coxcatlán, Nanahuatipan, San Gabriel Casas Blancas (Nextepec), Texcala, and Zapotitlán itself. Ewald (1985:44) related these salt springs with the springs near Piaxtla and Chiautla to the west, in the Puebla part of the Mixteca Baja.[54] It seems that brine springs in this region form a "salt-belt" that runs roughly east-west, approximately following the modern political state border between Oaxaca and Puebla. Subsoil salt deposits of the Cretaceous era feed the brine springs that occur all along this line and apparently coincide with geological faults.[55] The earliest description of the salt production process in this belt is by Motolinia from the 1540s; referring to the valley of Tehuacán and the village of Coxcatlán, he noted: "there are also wells of live salt (*sal viva*), and it is very worthwhile to see the white springs, which always produce very white veins and when you take the water and put it in small lime-coated threshing floors and leave it in the sun, in a short while it becomes salt."[56] The *Relación Geográfica de Acatlán* of 1581, from the other extreme of the belt, tells us: "in the said village of Piaztla they have salt works in their district, in four or five parts and places, from which they extract a great quantity of salt, with which they sustain themselves and pay their tribute."[57]

SALT PRODUCTION TECHNIQUES IN THE STUDY AREA

However, the salt production of the Santa María, San Ildefonso, San Pedro, and San Bartolome salt works in this belt of saline springs has been hardly noticed, with the exception of the excellent studies by Viramontes (1993; and in Reyes Garza 1995). The brine springs are located in narrow valleys of small tributaries of the Río Mixteco, itself a major tributary in the Río Balsas system. The brine springs in the valleys are artificially widened to allow the brine to collect in ponds (*pozos*). On the slopes of the valleys, the villagers have built, and continue to build, terraces that support the *fincas de sal* (figure 10.4). Occasionally the brine is conducted through a network of channels (or plastic hoses), and in other instances it has to be extracted by hand or by pump and carried to the *fincas*. Each *finca* consists of several *cajetes*, square or rectangular shallow drying-basins (figure 10.9). In general the *cajetes* are organized in an orderly manner, in parallel rows, each *cajete* measuring approximately two to three meters. All are interconnected by small sluices to allow the brine to distribute through the *finca*. Between the rows of *cajetes*, constructed *trojas* or *coscomates* consist of plastered depressions about half a meter to a meter deep, which are used to collect and purify the brine by sedimentation. They also serve to protect the brine in case of unexpected rain. The oldest *fincas* show an organic build-up with *cajetes* of varying size and shape, while the new ones tend to be more regular and square. Once cleaned, the brine is poured in the first *cajete*; while new salt water is added every once in a while to concentrate the brine, the solution is moved from one *cajete* to the next in order to work several production cycles at a time. The instrument used to move the brine is called a *carreta* or *palangana* and consists of a piece of dried squash rind. The process is most productive in the dry season (from January to April) when it requires almost daily maintenance for full productivity, but production may go on in other months, although with a lower yield. In general, the production process can yield 60 liters of salt per *cajete*. In a *finca* of six *cajetes*, one can produce 360 liters of salt in two weeks. In the area of the four villages, the total production might reach 70,000 liters of salt per season if the whole system were to be used to maximum capacity (Viramontes 1993:15). Analysis of *sal de grano* (salt produced for human consumption, in greater crystals, made by not removing the saline solution while crystallizing[58]) obtained in San Bartolo from Filiberto Espinosa and his wife Gloria Reyes proved to consist of almost pure sodium chloride (96.36%), with a small amount of calcium oxide (1.32%).[59]

SUPPORTING ARCHAEOLOGICAL AND ETHNOARCHAEOLOGICAL EVIDENCE

An obvious concern with respect to salt production in the area is the history and evolution of the industry in prehispanic times. Although our major emphasis has been on the ethnohistorical evidence, it is obvious that archaeological evidence can play a critical role in this enquiry. In June 2008 a short visit was made to San Bartolo Salinas, the most remote of the four salt villages. Surface survey in and around the system of salt-works along the eastern boundaries of the community center of San Bartolo indicate that the system has been active for centuries, if not millennia. Some 500 meters east and approximately 100–150 meters above the town is the archaeological site of "Iglesia Vieja" (figure 10.10). The site is situated on the

FIGURE 10.9. Salt *fincas* in the Mixteca Baja.

gently undulating crest of a ridge, which extends approximately 400 meters from the higher mountains on the north to the steep canyon walls along the river to the south. It measures approximately 300 meters east to west by approximately 375 meters north to south. There are five mounded areas, two quite extensive, as well as numerous alignments scattered about the ridge. The relatively light deposits of ceramics found on the site clearly relate to the Middle and Late Classic Periods of the Mixteca Baja, with an estimated temporal range of perhaps 350 to 800 CE. No clear representation of the Preclassic or Postclassic period was found.

Moving southward from the site proper and down the terraced canyon walls, there are two large caves, the entrances of which are abundantly strewn with ceramics. Some of the area near the caves is covered over with salt deposits formed over hundreds of years of draining from springs just beneath the archaeological site. Other areas are open as a result of having been slightly beyond the margins of the main flow, or because the overlying cap has been intentionally removed or has eroded away. Both caves provide evidence of centuries of use and occupation, but clear temporal and cultural delineation awaits future investigation. The zones around the caves and their entrances, and all of the terraced lands to the west, south,

FIGURE 10.10. The archaeological site of "Iglesia Vieja."

and east of the caves, as well as areas to the north, are occupied by quite clearly ancient salt works that have remained operational to the present day. Both fossilized and active salt production terraces extend in all directions from the caves. Ceramic sherds are large and well preserved, and they provide clear indications of Middle to Late Classic–period use of the site. There is also evidence of possible Late Preclassic use, although this cannot be ascertained until further intensive survey of the zone is completed. We did not find any heaps of discarded ceramics, fabric-marked pottery, or ceramic cylinders—all typical for the Zapotitlán-Calapan region—further suggesting the absence of intensive boiling and the existence of a different "drying and packaging" process, possibly using basketry to dry and transport the salt. In the Tehuacán area, the boiling process seems to be present in Classic times and to continue during the Postclassic (Castellón Huerta 2006; Parsons 2001:270), but this technique apparently was not introduced to the western Mixteca Baja.

It is noteworthy that due to the apparent lack of Postclassic ceramics (e.g., polychrome, red-on-cream, or fine graywares), the use of the system during this period could not be ascertained. One confounding circumstance is that the types of thick, heavy, plain-ware ceramic that has been used since prehispanic times has continued in use until the present, not only in San Bartolo, but in the adjoining communities of San Pedro, San Ildefonso, and Santa María. This implies persistence in form, composition, and function of this class of ceramics from ancient prehispanic times to the present. Although sourcing studies have not been conducted, the people of San Bartolo and Santa María told us that the ceramics used to transport the brine until the 1940s, before the introduction of plastic containers, were acquired from Santiago Tamazola, located to the south of the salt communities. However, we were not able to receive a clear description of any particular type or shape used in salt production. It is to be noted that probably a majority of the ceramics used in these villages (for kitchen use, etc.) were acquired in Tamazola, but it is very likely that at least some ancient ceramics originated in the community of Ayuquila to the northeast. Both communities continue to produce ceramics.

In terms of the overall complex of ceramics, it is quite likely that various types and varieties of ceramics were produced in Silacayoapilla and in Acatlán, Puebla. In December 2008 we visited Tamazola[60] and Santa María Salinas. In Tamazola, ceramics are still made by several families in the Guadalupe *barrio* (figure 10.11). Black clay is extracted from hill slopes outside town and put to dry in the sun. The clumps are then soaked in water and mixed with fine white powder to form the paste. The white powder is produced by hammering and sifting light-colored soil extracted from another site close to the *barrio* itself. The clay pieces are formed without a turntable, but molds (primarily old pots and *cajetes*) are used as both inner and outer forms for shaping vessels. Most families are dedicated to making *comales, cajetes*, tripod *molcajetes, cántaros, cazuelas*, tripod *sahumerios*, and *ollas* of different sizes, though it seems that individual families have a tendency to specialize in one form or another. When dried after several days, the finished pieces are coated with a red earth slip (extracted from yet another site close to the Guadalupe *barrio*) on the outside and polished in and out with a smooth-surfaced quartz stone. Then they are fired in the open air during the weekends. To fire the *comales*, a little "wall" is formed with stacks of old pots or bricks. Next, the unbaked pieces are placed against the central wall and the whole structure is covered with firewood and old *comales*. Pots are carefully stacked one on top of another over a bed of coals and covered with firewood. Care is taken to avoid smoking wood that would blacken the ware. Baked ware shows an uneven orange-red color, a polished finish, and an almost shiny aspect (tiny glitters, probably mica inclusions, can be seen in the slip). The process is virtually identical to production procedures at other towns in the region (Mezontla, Ayuquilla, etc.).

In Santa María, a partially collapsed *cajete* in the biggest *finca* ("La Salina Grande") revealed an underlying fill that consisted of abundant ceramics. Among

FIGURE 10.11. Contemporary pottery-making in Tamazola.

the sherds, Tamazola ware was easily recognized, but the majority represented coarse ware with high mica content. Because mica is abundantly present in the rocks and stones around the Santa María *fincas* and seemingly less in the vicinity of

Tamazola, this may indicate local production, of which there is no current memory. Viramontes (1993:8) mentions a small site near Santa María, also called Iglesia Vieja, which he claims to be Ñuiñe. Although the ceramics we have seen do not seem to support such an identification, clearer classification of the ceramic complex must await future study. Moreover, delineation of modern and prehispanic use patterns and the sources of clays used in the heavy, undecorated utilitarian wares must be completed before clear inferences can be drawn. That being said, it is illogical and contrary to the ethnohistorical evidence to assume that after centuries of utilization during the Middle and Late Classic, salt production would have ceased during the Postclassic period. In fact, salt production likely increased during the Postclassic. Certainly all available ethnohistoric evidence points clearly in the direction of a continued use throughout the Classic and Postclassic periods, through Colonial times, and on to the present.

CONCLUSIONS

The pictographic and ethnohistorical sources of the Ihualtepec-Atoyac-Tonalá region offer the opportunity to study salt production in the Mixteca Baja in the Early Colonial period, that is, during the time before silver mining substantially increased the demand for salt. During the sixteenth century, salt production in this region was still controlled by indigenous rulers and was part of the intricate web of marital alliances and the related control of natural resources. The documentation has helped to better understand the way in which the brine springs and related *fincas* were distributed between communities, lords, and nobles. If ever there was a convincing case for a convergent archaeological, ethnohistorical, and ethnographic methodology, it can be found in the proper study of salt and its impact on local culture and development in the Mixteca Baja. This is an ideal testing ground that promises to provide abundant new data and insights on the culture and cultural processes of the region. The extant documentation, the well-preserved salt works, the continuity of production to the present day, the continuing production of pottery in Tamazola, and the well-preserved archaeological materials provide an ideal anthropological context.[61]

APPENDIX 10.1: DOCUMENTO 1. AGN, TIERRAS, VOL. 2988, EXP. 114, 1583.

Para que f[ec]ha la averiguaçion en esta/ carta contenida si por ella consta aber fallecido/ dona M[ari]a yndia se meta a dona M[ari]a de San Miguel su/ madre en la poss[esi]on de çiertos b[iene]s.

S[ecretari]o S[anch]o Lopez.

Don Phelippe etc. a uos/ el n[uest]ro correg[id]or del pu[ebl]o/ de Tonala
o v[uest]ro lugartheni[en]te/ salud y gr[aci]a sepades que ante el pres[ident]e
e oidores/ de la n[uest]ra audi[enci]a y chançilleria que rresside en la/ çibdad de
Mex[i]co de la Nueva Esp[añ]a paresçio/ la parte de doña María de San Migel yndia/
prinçipal del d[ic]ho pu[ebl]o, muger que ffue de/ don P[edr]o de San Migel dif-
funto y por pet[ici]on q[ue] pres[en]to/ nos hizo rrel[aci]on diziendo que siendo
su p[ar]te caçica/ natural del d[ic]ho pu[ebl]o de Atoyaque por lo aver/ heredado
de sus padres y antepasados y perte/neçiendo como le perteneçia la p[ar]te del d[ic]
ho casicasgo/ y los posos de agua donde se hazia sal y cantidad de/ quarenta yndios
maçeguales que estavan/ y rresidian en las d[ic]has salinas y tierras que/ todo era
de el d[ic]ho su patrimonio y erençia/ y que para casar una hyja suya con un don
Ju[an]/ de Terrazas prinçipal del pu[ebl]o de Ygual/tepeque que se llamava doña
M[ari]a la avia pro/metido el d[ic]ho caçicasgo y p[ar]te del con todos/ los d[ic]
hos poços de agua e yndios y mas çien caueças/ de yeguas y cavallos y que podia
aber/ un mes poco mas o m[en]os que la d[ic]ha doña M[ari]a/ su hyja abia muerto
y pasado desta press[en]te/ vida y que segun uso y costunbre usada y guardada, le
perteneçia el d[ic]h]o casicasgo y los poços de agua/ y maçeguales, yeguas y abia
de bolber/ al d[ic]ho patrimonio de donde proçedian/ y nos pidio y supp[li]co le
mandasemos dar/ e diesemos n[uest]ra/ c[art]a provi[cio]n rreal p[ar]a/ que vos el
d[ic]ho n[uest]ro correg[id]or/ auida ynform[aci]on de lo susod[ic]ho y despues
de/ muerta la d[ic]ha su hyja le anparasedes y me/tiesedes en la poss[esi]on del d[ic]
ho casicasgo y los/ maçeguales, yeguas a el perteneçientes/ o que sobre ello probeye-
semos lo que/ la n[uest]ra m[erce]d fuese lo qual visto por los/ d[ic]hos n[uest]ro
p[resident]e e oidores fue acordado que deviamos mandar dar esta n[uest]ra carta
en la d[ic]ha/ rrazon y nos tovimoslo por bien porque vos/ que luego que vos fuere
mostrada hagais yn/form[aci]on de lo susod[ic]ho aberigueis/ lo que serca de cada
una cosa y p[ar]te dello/ a pasado y pasa y si por ella constare/ aber falleçido y pasado de esta presente vida/ la d[ic]ha doña maria sin dexar hyjo ni eredero/ metereis
y areis meter a la d[ic]ha doña M[ari]a/ de San Migel su madre en la poss[esi]on del/
d[ic]ho casicasgo,/ poços de agua, maçeguales, yeguas e todos los demas b[iene]s/
que a la susod[ic]ha su hyja en docte y casami[ent]o/ uuiere dado anparandole y de/
fendiendole en ella de la qual no/ consintireis sea desposeydo en m[aner]a algu[n]
a/ y non fagades en deal por alg[un]a ma[ner]a so p[en]a/ de la n[uest]ra m[erce]
d y de çien p[es]os de oro para la/ n[uest]ra cam[ar]a. Dada en la çibdad de Mex[i]
co a/ v[ein]te y siete dias del mes de jullio/ de mill y qui[nient]os y ochenta/ e tres
años. El doctor V[ill]an[uev]a,/ el doctor P[edr]o Farfan,/ el doctor Fran[cis]co
de Sande, el lic[encia]do S[anche]s Paredes, el doctor Rrobles. Rr[efrenda]do de
s[ecretari]o S[anch]o Lopez de Ag[ur]to. Correg[i]do Juan Ser[ra]no.

NOTES

1. Abbreviations used for archives and other documentary sources: AGN, *Archivo General de la Nación*; GdP, *General de Parte*; LC, *Library of Congress*; NL, *Newberry Library*.

2. Interesting arguments for breaking down the boundaries between history and archaeology in Old World Classic studies were recently presented in the volume edited by Sauer (2004).

3. Mary Elizabeth Smith (in Smith and Parmenter 1991:94) reported that she, Mr. and Mrs. Welte, and Ross Parmenter saw the document in San Vicente in 1982. Smith published a short description and some observations in the 1991 study of the Codex Tulane.

4. We would like to thank Laura Rodríguez Cano for facilitating the study of the document. It was first brought to Doesburg's attention in March of 2005 during a short meeting in the offices of the Instituto del Patrimonio Cultural (INPAC) of Oaxaca, organized by Verónica Arredondo, in which the authorities of San Vicente expressed their desire to have the document restored.

5. Information supplied by María del Refugio Gutiérrez, responsible for the restoration of the document.

6. The village—or an antecedent—may have been known as Tianguistepec during the sixteenth century. A small map from 1594 that accompanies a request for a cattle ranch by Tonalá's *cacique* represents the Tonalá *cabecera* church and four other settlements. Three of these—Tianguistepec, Tianguistepec el Viejo, and Maqualtepec—are located to the south of Tonalá. Of these, Tianguistepec was located three leagues from Tonalá, which is approximately the location of the present-day San Vicente (AGN, Mercedes, vol. 19, f. 183v (*acordado*) and 264 (*merced*); and AGN, Tierras, vol. 2726, exp. 1 (1594): *merced a don Miguel de Guzmán II de un sitio de estancia para ganado menor en el sitio llamado Tianquiztepec 'el Viejo'*). *Tianguistepec* means "on the mountain of the market." In the *merced* the Mixtec name is given as *Yutacuhnu*. Interestingly, in one document (AGN, Vínculos 69, f. 202), the name of San Vicente el Viejo is given as *Saimdagui*. This name may contain the Mixtec word *yahui*, which means "market" or "plaza." The mountain above San Vicente is known today as *Loma la Plaza* ("the Market").

7. Numerous *lienzos* and maps show this format, e.g., the *Lienzo de Ocotepec*, the *Lienzo Abraham Castellanos*, and the *Lienzo de Tequixtepec*, among others.

8. These chapel-churches are preserved in many Mixtec communities, e.g., Tejupan, San Andrés Lagunas, Santa María Nduayacu, San Miguel Tixa, San Juan Teposcolula, etc., where one can still recognize the naves added later in front of the chapels.

9. Many of the glosses are heavily damaged, but enough remain legible to reconfirm the pattern. Reading from the top right to the left and then the second row (so as to end with Don Carlos as the last generation) are: *ya(..)ho, yacaquihui* (Lord 2 or 12 Alligator), *ya(qhi) quau* (Lord 4 House), *ya(q)hoxico* (Lord ?), [illegible], *yaxaqhi* (Lord 7 Movement), *[ya]xihuiçu* (Lord 10 or 13 Ocelote), [4 illegible names], *yañoquaa* (Lord 6 Deer), *[ya](ño)ñoho*

(Lord 6 Monkey), *yaqhoyo* (Lord 5 or 9 Snake), *yanaqhi* (Lord 8 Movement), *yacâuiçu* (Lord 1 Ocelote), *[ya](xi)uaco* (Lord 10 or 13 Flower), *yaqhiñoo* (Lord 4 Monkey), *yadzi(ni)(ta)* (Lord ?), [2 illegible names], *don car(llos) de terrazas.*

10. A more extensive form of a similar "horizontal" genealogy can be seen on the *Mapa de Xochitepec*, where twenty male figures, glossed with Mixtec calendar names, sit in a row.

11. Both last names, Aguilar and de Terrazas, were taken from the two *encomenderos* of Ihualtepec, García de Aguilar and Francisco de Terrazas.

12. He applied for personal service in his house and *milpa* (a privilege of the *caciques*) in 1579 (AGN, GdP, vol. 2, exp. 278, f. 59). A very interesting account of the dire relations between Don Carlos de Terrazas and Viceroy Alvaro Manrique, which apparently led to the death of Don Carlos, is presented in Hanke 1977:32–34.

13. AGN, Indios, vol. 6, exp. 177 (1592).

14. AGN, Mercedes, vol. 5, f. 290v/315v (1561).

15. AGN, GdP, vol. 1, exp. 73 (1575).

16. AGN, GdP, vol. 2, exp. 735, f. 152 (1580).

17. AGN, Jesuitas, Caja I–14, exp. 448, f. 2081 (1588). Also AGN, GdP, vol. 3, f. 207v (1587).

18. AGN, Indios, vol. 6, exp. 120/28 (I), 155 (II) y 176 (III) (1592): (I) *"[Dice] don Francisco Pacheco, cacique y principal de Ygualtepec, [. . .] que fue cacique y gobernador don Carlos de Terrazas y por su fin y muerte sucedió un hermano suyo llamado don Felipe de Terrazas, el cual asimismo había muerto de cuya causa el susodicho había dejado el dicho cacicazgo y gobierno y dos hijas suyas y toda su hacienda encomendado a un don Diego de Terrazas, el cual se había quedado con el señorío y cacicazgo y con unas salinas, tierras y joyas [. . .]; ahora el dicho don Francisco Pacheco había casado legítimamente con una de las dichas dos hijas que el dicho don Felipe de Terrazas había dejado, por cuyo respecto le venía y pertenecía a él el dicho cacicazgo. [. . .] La elección que ahora últimamente se había hecho en el dicho pueblo, había hecho el dicho don Diego de Terrazas de su autoridad, y con este mando y gobierno había hecho y cada día hace así al dicho don Francisco como a los demás naturales muchos agravios, molestias y vejaciones, echando muchas derramas [. . .]."*

(II) *"Los naturales del pueblo de Ygualtepec y Ayozochicalaçala se me ha[n] hecho relación que el año pasado de noventa y uno fue gobernador de allí don Diego de Terraças indio principal del dicho pueblo y por negociación que hizo fue también nombrado este año, contra la ordenanza, y que de su nombramiento se siguen muchos daños e inconvenientes en la república y me pidieron mandase que se abstuviese del uso de su oficio y nombrase en su lugar a don Francisco de Albarrado indio a quien todos eligían y era conveniente para la quietud [. . .]."*

(III) *"Don Diego de Terrazas, yndio cacique del pueblo de Ygualtepeque, me ha hecho relación que estando quieto en el dicho pueblo en las casas de su morada, fray Christobal*

Martel, vicario del monesterio de Tonala de la orden de Santo Domingo, sin causa nin-
guna, había mandado que no residiese en el dicho pueblo y se fuese a vivir fuera del, so
pena de descomunión, sin haber hecho ni cometido delito, solo por contemplación de un
don Francisco Pacheco, principal forastero, y que por estar casado con sobrina del dicho don
Diego de Terrazas el dicho religioso decía no había de haber en el dicho pueblo más de un
cacique y había de ser el dicho don Francisco Pacheco, y que pues era señor natural y de tres
hermanos varones que eran hijos de don Joan de Aguilar, su padre, había quedado él solo
y en el señorío y cacicazgo".

19. AGN, Indios, vol. 6, exp. 296 (1592).

20. Antonio de los Reyes (1976) records the Mixtec name as *Yucunicana*, "mountain that came out." In Tamazola, Eulalio Barragán told us the current Mixtec name is *Ndikana*.

21. *Codex Mendoza* 1980[1925]: f. 8, together with Tlalcoçauhtitla and Quiyauhteopan; *Anales de Cuauhtitlán* 1975: paragraph 238; Ixtlilxochitl 1975:I:446.

22. The gloss in the *Codex Mendoza* (1980) reads *Ehuacalco* < eua(tl)=cal(li)-co ('in the house of the skin'), but this is clearly a mistake for *Calihuala* <cal(li)=eua(tl)-la. The meaning of the name is curious, and the name may be related to the verb *eua*, "to leave, part." Calihuala is mentioned as a subject village of the *cacicazgo* of Atoyac (NL, Ayer 1121, ff. 114v–115 (1552); AGN, Tierras, 2809, 2a parte, exp. 2, f. 323, (1598)). Calihuala bordered with Ihualtepec in a place called *Telistlauaca* ("plain of stones") and *Acaystlauaca* ("plain of reeds") (NL, Ayer 1121, ff. 114v–115; AGN, Mercedes, vol. 23, f. 13v (1599)).

23. Silacayoapan ("in the squash water") formed a double *señorío* with Tonalá, as is evident both from the Mixtec codices (e.g., Codex Vindobonensis 1992: pp. 3 and 43, where the topographs "Village of Blood" (Tonalá) and "Wooden Rack" (Silacayoapan) are combined in one, as from other historical records (LdT, p. 524: "los indios de Tonalá y Cilacayoapa y las demás estancias y barrios a él [Tonalá] sujetos, sobre la tasación de tributos"). See also AGN, Tierras, vol. 2729, exp. 6.

24. *Jicayán* is translated as "where [water] leaks." The Codex Mendoza (1980) gives *Ych-caatoyac* as the name of the last village in the list. This village appears in the *Suma de Visitas* (Paso y Troncoso 1905), where it is said to share borders with Zacatepec and Xicayán. In AGN, Tierras, vol. 2959, exp. 65 (1608), it is mentioned as the site where Xicayán was to be congregated (see also AGI, Justicia, 110, N. 3 [1531–1542]: Juan de Tovar vs. Pierre Gómez over one half of the town of Yscatoyaque). This Jicayán should not be confused with San Pedro Jicayán, which is located in the coastal area of Oaxaca.

25. The dual organization is suggested by several sources: Francisco de Terrazas and García de Aguilar received the *encomienda* of Ihualtepec-Suchiquilazala as a shared grant. The *Genealogía de Igualtepec* (Doesburg, forthcoming) indicates the rulers of both places were closely related. The garrison is mentioned in the *Relación Geográfica de Suchiquilazala* (1984:300). It is not clear why the Aztecs would have preferred Suchiquilazala over Ihual-tepec, but they followed the same practice in the double *cacicazgo* Tonalá-Silacayoapan and

Atoyac-Calihuala, since only the secondary centers of these *señoríos* appear in the Codex Mendoza (1980).

26. This conqueror was *encomendero* of Huamuxtitlán, a *señorío* to the west of Ihualtepec.

27. Mary Elizabeth Smith (in Smith and Parmenter 1991:95) already mentioned this name.

28. The name appears in Antonio de los Reyes's (1976) Mixtec grammar and in a short letter written in Mixtec by Don Pedro de San Miguel in 1584 (AGN, Civil, 2303, exp. 3). This San Pedro Atoyac should not be confused with the village of the same name located towards the coast, near Jicayán.

29. It is mentioned together with Tonalá in the LdT, p. 525: *"los indios del pueblo de Tonalá y Atoyaque, sobre la tasación de tributos"*.

30. The earliest documents from Atoyac are: AGN, Tierras, vol. 2988, exp. 114 (1583) which talks about Doña María de San Miguel, Cacica of Atoyac, widow of Don Pedro de San Miguel I (see Appendix 10.1). Interestingly, Don Pedro de San Miguel I appears to have been a lord of Tonalá: AGN, Mercedes, vol. 9, f. 196v (1567): *merced a don Pedro de San Miguel I, indio principal de Tonalá, 'cacique del barrio de Tepexi', de un sitio de estancia entre los cerros Çoyatlaçala y Michiatlaçitli Ocamatli*. Don Pedro de San Miguel I is possibly the same as Don Pedro, governor of Tonalá in 1551 (LC, Kraus 140, ff. 287–288). Other early documents are: AGN, Tierras, vol. 5, exp. 1 (1589): *merced a la comunidad de Atoyaque de un sitio de estancia para ganado menor en el sitio llamado Ychcatengo* (the present-day Tacachi); AGN, Mercedes, vol. 15, f. 16 (1589): *merced a don Pedro de San Miguel II, cacique de Atoyaque, de un sitio de estancia para ganado menor en el sitio llamado Teymamatlalystlauaca*; AGN, Mercedes, vol. 15, f. 19v (1589): *merced a don Felipe de Guzmán, cacique de Atoyaque, de un sitio de estancia para ganado menor en el sitio llamado Tilantongo*.

31. Curious is the use of the *dz-*, which in the Mixteca Baja normally turns into *s-*. The *dz-* does appear also in other glosses on the Mapa, as in *yadzi(ni)(ta),* the name of one of the rulers of Ihualtepec.

32. Cuezcomayztapa, 'granary salt works'. The small pits built to clean and preserve the brine are also called *coscomate* (see below).

33. *Xaliyztapa,* "sand salt works"; *Caxiyztapa,* "bowl salt works."

34. *Xoxouhquiyztapa,* "green salt works."

35. *Huiloyztapa,* "dove salt works."

36. The list is found in AGN, Tierras, vol. 2809, 2a parte, exp. 22.

37. Both names possibly represent miswriting of Nahuatl names.

38. AGN, Mercedes, vol. 23, f. 14 (1599).

39. AGN, Tierras, vol. 2809, 2a parte, exp. 22, f. 324r and v.: *"Visita de las salinas. En el pueblo de S[an] P[edr]o Cuezcomayztapa, en ocho dias del mes de diz[iembr]e de mill y qui[nient]os e noventa e ocho años, Rrui Dias Çeron, juez comiss[ari]o por el rrey n[uest]ro señor, abiendo benido a este pu[ebl]o q[ue] son salinas de la cabeçera de Ygualtepec y estan en quattro puestos, que ottro se llama San Bar[tolo]me y Santiago e Santa Maria que dizen estan a*

legua e a media legua; quel pueblo de San Bar[tolo]me el dicho comissario bio de passada, yendo bisitando la cabeçera de Atoyac, y los ottros dos puestos dixeron se an de ber quando el d[ic]ho comiss[ari]o baya a el d[ic]ho pueblo de Ygualtepec q[ue]s ffuerça, e que todos estan asentados enttre çerros e cuestas a los quales m[an]do pareçer en este pueblo a todos los d[ic]hos yndios de todas las salinas que dizen son setenta y bn ttributarios y m[an]do a Baltassar de Balladolid, su alg[uaci]l, le (junte) los d[ic]hos yndios e los ttraiga ante el d[ic]ho comiss[ari]o e abiendolos ttraido, mediante Ju[an] de Alfaro, ynterpete, se les dio a entender lo q[onteni]do en la d[ic]ha ystrucss[i]on e comiss[i]on e que en cumplimi[en]to della benia a bysitarlos, los quales dixeron que tienen por granjeria la d[ic]ha sal e que la hazen todo el año donde beneffisian mas de seisçientas hanegas y se la vienen a conprar de la Misteca alta e baxa y de la costa y minas y de otras p[ar]tes donde se proveen y ellos parten toda la sal que hazen con su casique don Ger[oni]mo de la Cruz e que hazen algunas sementeras en las laderas de los çerros aunq[ue] son pocas porque su prinçipal granjería es la sal [. . .]." "[. . .] Salieron de las d[ic]has salinas p[ar]a el pueblo de Ygualtepec e biniendo por el d[ic]ho camino le mosttraron a el d[ic]ho comissario los çitios de los pueblos de Santiago e Santa Maria donde están las d[ic]has salinas que desde el camino par[eci]o quel açiento de los d[ic]hos pueblos estava enttre los d[ic]hos çerros e desbiados como media legua poco mas o menos del d[ic]ho camino [. . .]."

40. The rectangles we have identified as *fincas de sal* also appear in other documents from the sixteenth century, making it possible to recognize salt production in the pictographic record. Good examples are the salt works shown on the *Lienzo Seler II*, near the Río Calapa, where salt is still produced today. Interestingly, the salt-works are associated with two friars of the Coixtlahuaca convent who, according to Dominican sources, lived there in 1556. Again, the salt may have been an important commodity in sustaining the friars' life in Coixtlahuaca. Finally, confirmation for the identification of the subdivided rectangles as *fincas de sal* comes from an eighteenth-century unpublished map from Chila de la Sal.

41. In Tamazola, Eulalio Barragán told us that the Mixtec name for Santa María is *Nàndóho* and for San Ildefonso *Nàndóho yákà*.

42. The woman seated behind Don Francisco Gómez may be his daughter Doña Ana Gómez, wife of Don Miguel de Guzmán I, *caciques* de Tonalá after the death of Don Francisco (Fernández de Recas 1961:203). In 1552, a Don Miguel—possibly Don Miguel de Guzmán I—was appointed governor of Tonalá for three years (NL, Ayer 1121, f. 130). In 1565, Doña Ana was already a widow.

43. AGN, Vínculos 69, f. 63v.

44. The document contains contradictory information as to the rank of Don Francisco Gómez and Don Juan de Santiago. Both are called sometimes *principales* and sometimes *caciques*. On p. 112, Don Juan calls himself—not surprisingly—a *cacique*, and Don Francisco Gómez a *cacique* and *señor natural* of Tonalá.

45. AGN, Vínculos 69, f. 60. In Inés's testament, the salt works are described as *"salinas que se nombran Xaliztlapan y las otras salinas Yztapan"* (AGN, Vínculos 69, f. 59v). Since this

testament was translated from Náhuatl, it is possible that the original just stated "and the other salinas," since *yztapan* just means "salt works."

46. AGN, Vínculos 69, f. 48v.

47. AGN, Vínculos 69, f. 161–169: *"las salinas que están en el pueblo de San Ildefonso, sujeto a esta cabecera [de Ihualtepec] [. . .] se componen de dos pozos de agua-sal, el uno de blanca y el otro parda, en que hay doscientos y seis cajetes que es en que se beneficia dicha sal."* These were equally divided in 1703 between the lord of Ihualtepec and the lord of Tonalá to avoid conflict, with the condition that the Tonalá lord and his wife had to pay a yearly mass in memory of Doña Inés Gómez and Don Carlos de Terrazas and their descendants. However, in 1725 they were reclaimed by Doña Luisa de Terrazas of Ihualtepec. She claims to possess *"tres caletas [sic pro: cajetas] donde se hace sal en el pueblo de San Ildefonso Salinas"* (documents in the village of San Vicente del Palmar).

48. A Don Miguel de Guzmán II appears as *cacique* of Tonalá in the decade 1580–1590, for example AGN, Tierras, vol. 2726, exp. 1 (1594). This same Don Miguel inherited from Doña María de Sosa (also called de Villagómez or Gómez), *"mujer de don Juan de Santiago, cacica que fue de esta provincia"*, the *cacicazgo* in Tonalá and *"salinas que se llaman Doquichi-doo, quisi, Doyo, quende* [Doquichi, Dooquisi and Doyoquende?] *y demás ojos de agua sal"* (AGN, Vínculos, 69, f. 159). In another text (AGN, Indiferente Virreinal, caja 6596, exp. 39 (1584)) it is said that *"don Miguel de Guzman, gobernador, cacique y natural de ese dicho pueblo de Tonalá [. . .] me hizo relación diciendo que al tiempo que doña María Gómez, su tia, cacica que había sido del dicho pueblo, había pasado de esta presente vida le había dejado por su universal heredero en todos sus bienes muebles y raíces, ojos de agua salada que se nom-braban Talistacapan* [maybe an error for Xalistacapan] *y en otros declarados y nombrados en su testamento de su patrimonio y mayorazgo."* For this same lord, see also AGN, Mercedes, vol. 15, f. 21 y 48–48v (1589): *merced para don Miguel de Guzmán II, cacique de Tonalá, de un sitio de estancia para ganado menor en el sitio llamado Ytzonteconatlauaco;* AGN, Tierras, vol. 85, exp. 2 (1589), *merced a don Miguel de Guzmán II de un sitio de estancia para ganado menor en el sitio llamado Suchiteupa;* AGN, Mercedes, vol. 19, f. 183v y 264 y AGN, Tierras, vol. 2726, exp. 1 (1594), *merced a don Miguel de Guzmán II de de un sitio de estancia para ganado menor en el sitio llamado Tianquiztepec 'el Viejo'.*

49. The meaning of the black dots accompanying the *fincas* is not clear. They may represent the brine wells.

50. The first of the three *fincas* is called *toho tulua*, the second *toho ç(u/a)h(..)*, and the third has an unreadable gloss.

51. The whereabouts of the original *lienzo* are unknown. The copy was made by Saussure during his trip to Mexico in 1855 and 1856. The only known copy is a tracing on several pieces of transparent paper. The copy was discovered and published by Joaquín Galarza (1986), who already noted the similarities with the *Mapa Número 36*. The document is kept in the "Bibliotheque Publique et Universitaire" of Geneva, in the collection

Henri de Saussure. See Roguin and Weber (1993) for the letters written by Saussure during his trip through Mexico.

52. After the text of this chapter was completed, we learned of the publication by Lind and Urcid (2010) in which they argue that Late Classic Lambityeco rulers increased their power in part through the control of salt production revenues.

53. Salt is used to convert the silver minerals into silver chlorides, which can then be amalgamated with quicksilver. This process was invented in 1557.

54. Ewald (1985:51–54) cites the extensive historical information on salt in the Acatlán, Piaxtla, and Chiautla region.

55. Intermediate villages such as San Miguel Ixtapa and Santa Gertrudis Salitrillo reveal the presence of salt by their names alone.

56. Motolinia (1971), Primera Parte, capítulo 56, pár. 357; translation is ours. A similar technique was reported for Nextepec, near Teotitlán (*Relación Geográfica de Teutitlán* 1984:211).

57. *Relación Geográfica de Acatlán*, 60; see also the description on 41.

58. This is sometimes done to prohibit the heavier sulfates to mix with the sodium chloride, but this does not seem to be the case here.

59. Analysis conducted by Cedibac Laboratories, Oaxaca City.

60. Salt from the salt villages is still sold in the region, for example on the Sunday market of Tamazola. There, Eulalio Barragán told us that the *sal de grano* is called *ñìì yíhí* in Mixtec, while *sal blanca* (the fine powdery type of salt) is called *ñìì àdjà*.

61. The authors would like to thank Rubén Luengas, Patricia García, and Luis Octavio Castro from Tezoatlán for their company in the visits to San Ildefonso and San Bartolo. We are also in debt to Irma Urraga Rivera from San Ildefonso; to Filiberto Espinosa, his wife Gloria Reyes, and Andrea Sánchez from San Bartolo; and to Hugo and Gabriel Jiménez and Don Tranquilino Méndez in Santa María. Nicholas Johnson and Upe van Leeuwen also assisted us in the fieldwork. In Tamazola, we received the kind help of Doña Paty, who sells chiles at the market, Señora Marta Sánchez Chávez, and the "ancianos" Eulalio Barragán Galindo and Feliciano Espinosa. Michel Oudijk helped us with some references in the AGN.

REFERENCES

Anales de Cuauhtitlán. 1975. In *Códice Chimalpopoca*, trans. Primo Feliciano Velázquez. Mexico: Universidad Nacional Autónoma de México.

Andrews, Anthony. 1983. *Maya Salt Production and Trade*. Tucson: The University of Arizona Press.

Castellón Huerta, Blas. 2006. *Cuthá: El Cerro de la Máscara. Arqueología y Etnicidad en el Sur de Puebla*. Mexico: Instituto Nacional de Antropología e Historia.

Codex Mendoza. (1925) 1980. *Colección de Mendoza o Códice Mendocino: Documento Mexicano del Siglo XVI*. Mexico: Editorial Innovación.

Codex Vindobonensis. 1992. *Origen e Historia de los Reyes Mixtecos: Libro Explicativo del Llamado Códice Vindobonensis, Codex Vindobonensis Mexicanus 1, Österreichische Nationalbibliothek, Viena*. Facsimile reproduction with commentary by Ferdinand Anders, Maarten Jansen, and Aurora Pérez Jiménez. Spain: Sociedad Estatal Quinto Centenario.

Doesburg, Sebastián van. 2008a. "Documentos Pictográficos de la Mixteca Baja." *Arqueología Mexicana* 90:53–57.

Doesburg, Sebastián van. 2008b. "Documentos Pictográficos de la Mixteca Baja de Oaxaca: El Lienzo de San Vicente del Palmar, el Mapa No. 36 y el Lienzo Mixteco III." *Desacatos* 27:95–122.

Doesburg, Sebastián van. forthcoming. "La Genealogía de Igualtepec." Article prepared for *Mexicon*.

Ewald, Ursula. 1985. *The Mexican Salt Industry 1560–1980: A Study in Change*. Stuttgart, Germany: Gustav Fischer Verlag.

Fernández de Recas, Guillermo. 1961. *Cacicazgos y Nobiliario de la Nueva España*. Mexico: Universidad Nacional Autónoma de México.

Flores Clair, Eduardo. 1992. "Fuentes para el Estudio de la Renta de la Sal." *Boletín de Fuentes para la Historia Económica de México* 7:17–24.

Galarza, Joaquín. 1986. "Découverte de Codex Mexicains à Genève: La Collection Henri de Saussure de 1855." *Bulletin de la Société Suisse des Américanistes* 50:7–41.

Good, Catherine. 1995. "Salt Production and Commerce in Guerrero, Mexico: An Ethnographic Contribution to Historical Reconstruction." *Ancient Mesoamerica* 6 (1):1–13. http://dx.doi.org/10.1017/S0956536100002066.

Hanke, Lewis, ed., *with the collaboration of Celso Rodríguez*. 1977. *Los Virreyes Españoles en América durante el Gobierno de la Casa de Austria: México*, vol. 2. Madrid: Biblioteca de Autores Españoles, Atlas.

Ixtlilxochitl, Fernando de Alva. 1975. *Obras Históricas*, 2 vols. Edition by Edmundo O'Gorman. Mexico: Universidad Nacional Autónoma de México.

Lind, Michael, and Javier Urcid. 2010. *Lords of Lambityeco: Political Evolution in the Valley of Oaxaca during the Xoo Phase*. Boulder: University Press of Colorado.

Machuca Gallegos, Laura. 2007. *Comercio de Sal y Redes de Poder en Tehuantepec durante la Época Colonial*. Mexico City: CIESAS.

Mendizábal, Miguel Othón de. (1929) 1946. "La Influencia de la Sal en la Distribución Geográfica de los Grupos Indígenas de México." In *Obras Completas,* vol. 2, 181–340. Mexico: Carmen H. Viuda de Mendizábal.

Menegus Bornemann, Margarita. 1994. "Las Comunidades Productoras de Sal y los Mercados Mineros: Los casos de Taxco y Temascaltepec." In *Minería Regional Mexicana*, Primera Reunión de Historiadores de la Minería Latinoamericana, Zacatecas, 1990, vol. 4, ed. Carlos Contreras, Dolores Ávila Herrera, Inés Herrera Canales, and Rina Ortiz, 21–31. Mexico: Instituto Nacional de Antropología e Historia.

Moser, Christopher. 1972. "Ñuiñe Hieroglyphics of the Mixteca Baja." In *Religión en Mesoamérica: Memorias de la XII Mesa Redonda de la Sociedad Mexicana de Antropología*, ed. Jaime Litvak King and Noemí Castillo Tejero, 269–274. Mexico: Sociedad Mexicana de Antropología.

Moser, Christopher. 1977. *Ñuiñe Writing and Iconography of the Mixteca Baja*. Nashville: Vanderbilt University Publications in Anthropology, No. 19.

Motolinia, o Fray Toribio de Benavente. (1541) 1971. *Memoriales o Libro de las cosas de la Nueva España y de los Naturales de Ella*. Edition by Edmundo O'Gorman. Mexico: Universidad Nacional Autónoma de México.

Paddock, John. 1965. "Current Research: Western Mesoamerica." *American Antiquity* 31 (1):133–136.

Paddock, John. 1966. "Oaxaca in Ancient Mesoamerica." In *Ancient Oaxaca: Discoveries in Mexican Archaeology and History*, ed. John Paddock, 83–242. Stanford: Stanford University Press.

Paddock, John. 1968. "Una Tumba en Ñuyoo, Huajuapan de León, Oaxaca." *Boletín del Instituto Nacional de Antropología e Historia* 1 (33):51–54.

Paddock, John. 1970a. "A Beginning in the Ñuiñe: Salvage Excavations at Ñuyoo, Huajuapan." *Boletín de Estudios Oaxaqueños* 26:12.

Paddock, John. 1970b. "More Ñuiñe Materials." *Boletín de Estudios Oaxaqueños* 28.

Paredes Colín, Joaquín. 1960. *El Distrito de Tehuacán: Breve Relación de su Historia, Censo, Monumentos Arqueológicos, Datos Estadísticos, Geológicos, Etnográficos y Otros*. Tipografía Comercial "Don Bosco," Tehuacán.

Parsons, Jeffrey. 2001. *The Last Saltmakers of Nexquipayac, Mexico: an Archaeological Ethnography*. Ann Arbor: University of Michigan Anthropological Papers No. 92.

Paso y Troncoso. Francisco del, ed. 1905. *Papeles de la Nueva España*. Segunda Série: Geografía e Estadística, vol. 1. Madrid: Sucesor de Rivadeneyra.

Relación Geográfica de Acatlán. (1581) 1985. *Relaciones Geográficas del Siglo XVI*, vol. 5, *Tlaxcala*, book 2. Edition by René Acuña. Mexico: Universidad Nacional Autónoma de México.

Relación Geográfica de Suchiquilazala. (1580) 1984. *Relaciones Geográficas del Siglo XVI*, vol. 2, *Antequera*, book 1. Edition by René Acuña. Mexico: Universidad Nacional Autónoma de México.

Relación Geográfica de Teutitlán. (1581) 1984. *Relaciones Geográficas del Siglo XVI,* vol. 3, *Antequera,* book 2. Edition by René Acuña. Mexico: Universidad Nacional Autónoma de México.

Reyes, Antonio de los. (1593) 1976. *Arte en Lengua Mixteca.* Nashville: Vanderbilt University Publications in Anthropology, No. 14.

Reyes Garza, Juan Carlos. 1995. *La Sal en México.* vol. 1. Colima, Mexico: CNCA, Universidad de Colima.

Reyes Garza, Juan Carlos. 1998. *La Sal en México.* vol. 2. Colima, Mexico: CNCA, Universidad de Colima.

Rivera Guzmán, Ángel Iván. 1999. "El Patrón de Asentamiento en la Mixteca Baja de Oaxaca: Análisis del Área de Tequixtepec-Chazumba. Unpublished Master's Thesis, Escuela Nacional de Antropología e Historia, Mexico.

Rodríguez Cano, Laura. 1995. *El Sistema de Escritura Ñuiñe en la Mixteca Baja de Oaxaca, México.* Report submitted to FAMSI. http://www.famsi.org/reports/94013es, accessed June 2010.

Roguin, Louis de, and Claude Weber. 1993. *Henri de Saussure: Voyage aux Antilles et au Mexique, 1854–1856.* Geneva, Switzerland: Editions Olizane.

Saravia Viejo, María Justina. 1994. "La Sal en la Minería Mexicana: Su Evolución en el Siglo XVI." In *Minería y Metalurgia: Intercambio Tecnológico y Cultural Entre América y Europa durante el Periodo Colonial Español,* ed. Manuel Castillo Martos, 245–266. Sevilla: Munōz Moya Montraveta editores.

Sauer, Eberhard, ed. 2004. *Archaeology and Ancient History: Breaking Down the Boundaries.* New York: Routledge.

Sisson, Edward. 1973. *First Annual Report of the Coxcatlán Project.* Tehuacán Project Reports no. 3. Andover, MA: Peabody Foundation for Archaeology.

Smith, Mary Elizabeth, and Ross Parmenter. 1991. *The Codex Tulane.* New Orleans: Middle American Research Institute, Tulane University.

Urcid, Javier. 2005. *Sacred Landscapes and Social Memory: The Ñuiñe Inscriptions in the Ndaxagua Natural Tunnel, Tepelmeme, Oaxaca.* Report submitted to FAMSI. http://www.famsi.org/reports/03068/ndaxagua.pdf, accessed June 2010.

Vázquez de Tapia, Bernardino. (1939) 1972. *Relación de Méritos y Servicios del Conquistador Bernardino Vázquez de Tapia.* Mexico: Universidad Nacional Autónoma de México.

Viramontes, Carlos. 1993. "La Producción Tradicional de Sal en un Sitio de la Mixteca Baja, Oaxaca: Un Estudio Comparativo." *Cuadernos del Sur* 4:5–25.

Williams, Eduardo. 1999. "The Ethnoarchaeology of Salt Production at Lake Cuitzeo, Michoacán, Mexico." *Latin American Antiquity* 10 (4):400–414. http://dx.doi.org /10.2307/971964.

Williams, Eduardo. 2002. "Salt Production in the Coastal Area of Michoacan, Mexico: An Ethnoarchaeological Study." *Ancient Mesoamerica* 13 (02):237–253. http://dx.doi.org /10.1017/S0956536102132020.

Winter, Marcus. 1989. "Exploraciones en Cerro de las Minas, 1987." *Notas Mesoamericanas* 11:304–17.

Winter, Marcus. 1996. *Cerro de las Minas. Arqueología de la Mixteca Baja*. Oaxaca, Mexico: Casa de la Cultura de Huajuapan de León.

Winter, Marcus, Daría Degara, and Rodolfo Fernández. 1976. "Cerro de la Codorniz: Una Zona Arqueológica Ñuiñe en Santiago Chilixtlahuaca, Huajuapan, Oaxaca." *Boletín del Instituto Nacional de Antropología e Historia* 2 (17):29–40.

II

Integrating Oral Traditions and Archaeological Practice

The Case of San Miguel el Grande

Liana I. Jiménez Osorio and Emmanuel Posselt Santoyo

INTRODUCTION

The state of Oaxaca is characterized by its ethnic diversity and rich archaeological record.[1] It is divided into eight geographic regions, among which the Mixteca is further subdivided into the Alta, Baja, and Costa regions. These, in turn, show pronounced differences in microclimates due to the varying topography and altitude, which have provided a large spectrum of natural resources to its occupants and directly contributed to the formation of cultural identities on the regional and subregional levels. The Mixteca Alta, the focus of the present study, is distinguished by a historical trajectory that we nowadays perceive through the archaeological remains, historical documents, and the preserved collective memory and oral traditions of its inhabitants.

Every group shares a history of its past, although this is most often not recognized as such because it does not form part of the official state/national historiographic narrative. It is nonetheless relevant to the members of that community as well as to the investigators who study that group's past. Archaeologists can thus often gain access to a kind of history that complements and/or contrasts with the archaeological data.

The aim of this chapter is to highlight the importance of oral tradition in studying the past, by analyzing it as a historical record that may generate a data set not obtainable through other sources. We present the case of the municipality of San Miguel el Grande, located approximately six kilometers west of Chalcatongo de

DOI: 10.5876/9781607323297.c011

FIGURE 11.1. The contemporary community of San Miguel el Grande.

Hidalgo, and demonstrate how archaeology can utilize oral traditions to learn about the foundation of the village and other aspects of its history (Figure 11.1).

ARCHAEOLOGY AND ORAL TRADITIONS

Archaeology and the study of oral traditions constitute two approaches through which we can understand the human past, although in different ways: the former examines material remains and the latter is concerned with the spoken word. Both approaches provide distinct data that, when combined, offer a more profound understanding of the studied culture. To achieve this is a difficult task but, at the same time, a fascinating one. In order to conduct research of this nature, some aspects of the disciplines of archaeology and oral tradition first need to be considered.

Archaeology is a social and historical science that examines processes of social change in the past through its material remains. Due to the diversity and complexity of its subject of study (humans), archaeology needs to build bridges to other disciplines that can help expose different aspects of human history, including ideology, social organization, politics, customs, and interaction with other groups, for example. In Oaxaca, archaeologists occasionally have the opportunity to study ancient sites associated with a contemporary community that can trace its past to those remains; although these retrospective narratives change through time, such communities have consciously or unconsciously preserved part of their history by passing it down the generations orally. Thus, these traditions are useful to acquire relevant data on historical events and fill in certain gaps that are difficult to achieve through material culture alone.

A relevant point to consider is that these oral traditions form part of the linguistic and cultural heritage of these autochthonous communities and, as such, serve as a reference point when we go about reading the ancient pictography and when interpreting archaeological contexts. Such connections through time highlight cultural continuities while fomenting social memory and communal identity (Jansen and Pérez Jiménez 2010).

Oral tradition constitutes a narrative that is based ultimately on statements from people who experienced certain events either as protagonists or witnesses and which, by verbal transmission through time and space, make it possible for us in the present to perceive these past events (Olivera de Bonfil 1978:157; Vansina 1968:34). Oral traditions can be manifested at the individual or the collective level, yet they all include three components: referent, witness, and testimony (Vansina 1968:36). Understanding and analyzing these elements and their transmission are important for the study of every oral tradition, because they determine its change and/or permanency process and its function and meaning. These factors are delimited principally by the mode of transmission, in which the principal witness who determines the testimony is influenced directly by the society in which he or she is immersed. Since it is expected that the oral tradition will differ principally from other oral sources—such as rumor and folktales—due to its intrinsic historical content and value, some rules need to be followed in order to analyze the structure and the external factors involved in its formation.

A *testimony* covers different cultural aspects of the group from which it originated; in the present study, the focus is on the historical event *per se*. As testimony can be quite complex, it needs to be analyzed thoroughly in order to understand how the historical event relates to the different components of the narrative. In San Miguel el Grande, the diverse testimonies intertwine divine beings, extraordinary acts, and aspects of everyday life, all of which play their part in the historical events. It is important to point out that a testimony comprises not only the narrated traditions, but also the reminiscences of the narrators and their personalities and interests, as well as the cultural values of their society (Vansina 1968:58, 93). At the same time, these testimonies or memories form solely through social communication and interaction, which implies that the individual can remember only what conforms to his or her social framework in the present. When combined with an emotive connection as well as deliberate references to the past, then we are dealing with "cultural memory" (Assmann 2003:155).

As the oral traditions recovered from the San Miguel el Grande show, aside from historical events, other cultural and social aspects such as religious beliefs and customs are reflected by the worship of *ndoso*[2] as well as by the rivalry and conflicts over lands among municipalities. Although such traditions are well known in the community, the ones in charge of their communication are the elders who relate not merely the narrative but also the different feelings, emotions, and a sense of belonging to this town, which is often visually evident in their body language and gestures.

In addition to looking at the testimony, we need to analyze the chain of transmission, where we may encounter two basic types of distortion: (1) omissions due to "failure of memory," and (2) explanatory interpolations (Vansina 1968:56). To distinguish these types of distortion in our case study, different people were asked about a certain oral tradition. We later compared the results and selected the narratives that describe the events in a more detailed and coherent way. In several instances the narrators did not remember place names, locations, or other parts of the account, and it is notable that such distortions were more frequently made by the young storytellers. Such general lack of interest in oral traditions among the new generations is further intensified through frequent emigrations to other states within the Mexican Republic and to the United States, as well as new ideologies implemented through the different religious sects.

In regards to this "distorted" quality of oral traditions, we should also keep in mind that retelling these narratives is not a simple exercise of exact reproduction, such as copying a text, but rather the cumulative result of numerous versions that would always generate variations. Although there will always be a level of abstraction that permits us to recognize the principal structure, the narratives cannot be considered as static, fixed, or homogenous entities, but rather as a reflection of the multiple narrators' creativity (Goody 2010:63, 66).

Although it is probably true that this distinctive nature of an oral tradition—its mode of transmission—is at the same time its biggest restriction, we can assign to it certain validity if scientific rigor is applied, just as to any other type of data set. In addition, we can obtain data from other disciplines—archaeology in this case—to confirm, complement, and sometimes contradict our oral record and obtain an integrative view of the events under study.

THE ARCHAEOLOGICAL RECORD OF SAN MIGUEL EL GRANDE

The topography of the San Miguel el Grande municipality consists of two valleys surrounded by mountains, one of which is located northwest of the municipal head town and is part of a valley that belongs to Chalcatongo. The second valley, which is our main area of interest here, is located to the south and is named *Nduavee* ("Low

Plain," in Mixtec). The river *Shauacano* ("Big River") flows through it from north to south, giving the valley an elongated shape of approximately six kilometers long and between five hundred and twelve hundred meters in length. Two mountain ranges run parallel on the eastern and western sides of the river. Together with several springs throughout the area, these resources give the valley a high agricultural potential that is intensified through irrigation.

This area was studied as part of the archaeological project *Línea de Transmisión Tlaxiaco-Itundujia* in 2006 and 2007. The study was carried out in two phases: a surface survey (Jiménez Osorio et al. 2006) followed by the excavation of selected sites (Jiménez Osorio et al. 2007). At the end of this project, a total of fourteen archaeological sites were recorded on the hills that surround the *Nduavee* Valley: five sites on the east side of the mountain range, seven to the west, and the remaining two sites on the north and south sides of the valley (figure 11.2 and figure 11.3).

These sites demonstrate different dimensions, organization, and complexity, and we can further distinguish sites of the first, second, and third order (figure 11.2). *Nuvixi* (site 6) and Chalcatongo Viejo or Mogote (site 9) are sites of the first order; *Yukuyu'u* (site 3), *Nutanda'a* (site 10), and *Ñusa'a* (site 12) are sites of the second order; whereas *Shinicuno* or *Ñujatu* (site 1), *Ñurusio* (site 2), *Shinitikiki* (site 13), and *Ñuusii* (site 14) belong to the third order, including three additional sites whose names were not possible to recover in the field (sites 4, 5, and 11). Finally, a scatter of sherds (site 7) and a cave named *Yuyao* (site 8) were recorded.

The archaeological record in this area further demonstrates different occupation periods, with sites from the Late Formative/Ramos phase (400 BCE–300 CE), the Classic/Las Flores phase (300–900 CE), and the Postclassic/Natividad phase (900–1521 CE) (after Spores 2007:12). The archaeological sites dating to the Postclassic period, our main concern here, are *Shinicuno/Ñujatu* (1), *Yukuyu'u* (3), *Nuvixi* (6), Chalcatongo Viejo (9), *Nutanda'a* (10), *Ñusa'a* (12), *Shinitikiki* (13) and site 7 (figure 11.2 and figure 11.3; see also Spores 1995, 2007:466).

All recorded sites have access to fertile soil in the valley and to natural resources in the highlands. Moreover, they have numerous agricultural and residential terraces located at the piedmont. It is noteworthy that during the survey we did not observe any defensive features that might indicate hostile relationships between those sites. In fact, some sites are located in vulnerable areas such as the piedmont and at low hills, which would have made it difficult to defend them in the case of an attack; such examples include *Nujatu* and Chalcatongo, located on the tops of low hills at the north and south ends of the valley, and *Nuvixi* which is located on the piedmont.

It is also likely that most of these sites served as habitational and civic-administrative functions. *Yukuyu'u* probably had a more strategic/ceremonial purpose, due to its location on one of the highest elevations, with a privileged view over the valley

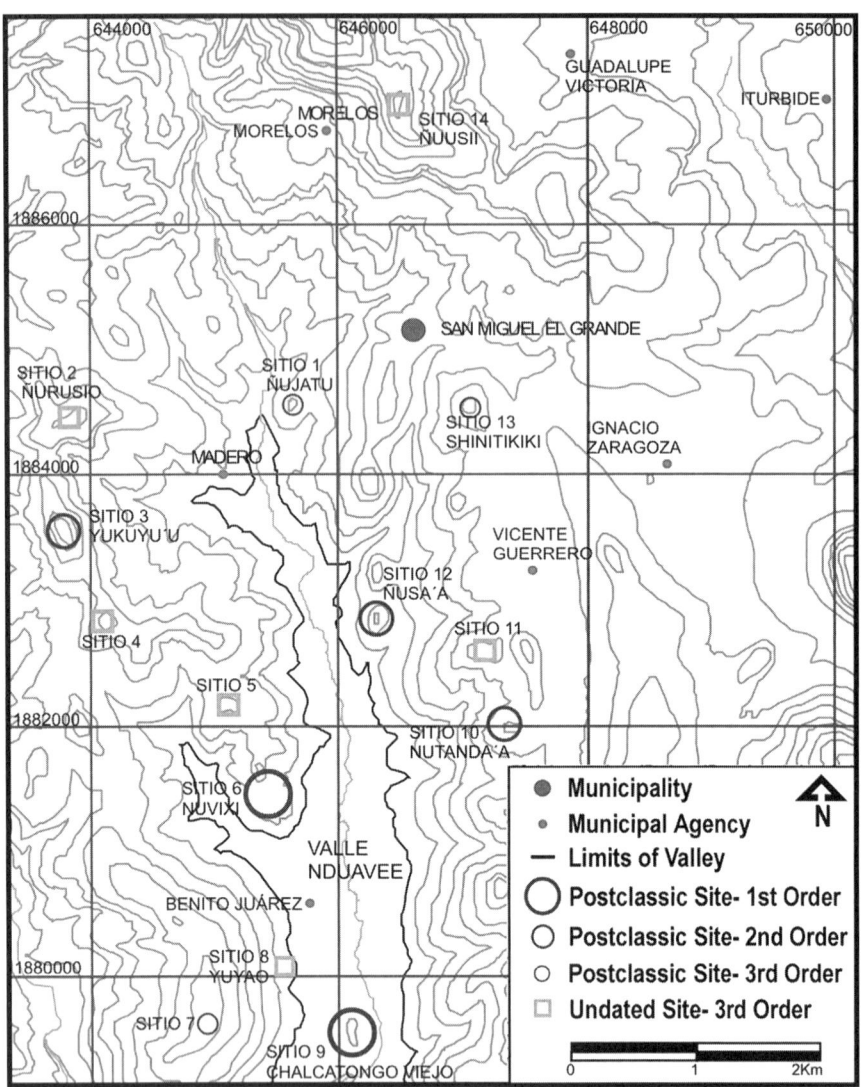

FIGURE 11.2. Archaeological sites surveyed in the municipality of San Miguel el Grande.

and neighboring areas and the monumental architecture that effectively restricts the access. Moreover, the cult of the *Señor de la Columna*—the patron saint of the village of Santa Catarina Yosonotu—is nowadays practiced in that site. According to the local inhabitants, this is a very old tradition that had widely spread among other villages in the Mixteca.

FIGURE 11.3. View of the *Nduavee* Valley and several of its archaeological sites.

ORAL NARRATIVES OF VILLAGE FOUNDATION
AND SETTLEMENT PATTERNS

Throughout our archaeological fieldwork we had informal conversations with inhabitants of this municipality in order to gather relevant data regarding the area. To that effect, our focus was to query in general about the Mixtec names of the sites and their translation into Spanish, as well as some aspects of the regional history and traditions. This activity started with interviewing two locally well-known elders, Sr. Isidro Aparicio Acuña and Sr. Felipe Sánchez Ramírez, who were recommended by the locals as the most suitable to provide answers to our queries. Both have lived in San Miguel el Grande all their lives and served as the town "municipal presidents," and so possess an ample knowledge of its territory and different places. Likewise, both were merchants who used to trade products from the Mixteca in Oaxaca City and the coast (Pinotepa and Jamiltepec), often carrying them by foot and on their backs; this way, they got to know the different routes and towns within the Mixteca. In addition we had the support of the municipal authorities Sr. Tereso Soria Cuevas, Sr. Alfredo Cruz Cruz, and Sr. Felipe Aparicio, who kindly agreed to show us some places in San Miguel and informed us about events relevant to those places; and Nicodemo Ortíz, an engineer from the Universidad Tecnológica de San Miguel, who further supported our research.

The oral tradition gathered from the first two expert storytellers is related to the foundation of San Miguel el Grande and is similar to the one reported by Alavez Chávez (2006), whose work comprises a compilation of oral traditions from the Mixteca Alta. In addition to the principal foundation narratives, we recorded other "secondary" accounts in the collective memory of San Miguel el Grande that can offer a more nuanced narrative of the town history and traditions. The principal tradition narrates that the town was founded in 1400 CE when its founders named it *Itun Yuku Ndaku,* Mixtec for "a hill where a powerful or enchanted herb sprouts" (Alavez Chávez 2006:106–108). The origin of this name relates to the growth of a mysterious plant on a hill where the current town church is located. The lifespan of this plant was remarkably short: it appeared on midnight of April 30 and lasted about five or six hours before disappearing under the ground on May 1. During this time, it made sounds resembling several people conversing. Its seeds were powerful: people who owned them were granted the wish of having their absent loved ones brought back home.

In addition, we were told that besides the principal location for the town of *Itun Yuku Ndaku,* there were seven additional "wards" that composed San Miguel in the past. In this regard, it is worth mentioning that there are some differences between what is stated by Alavez Chávez (2006) and the information recovered in this study. Although both share the notion of eight wards, some of these places have a different name, and it is not clear if Alavez Chávez was referring to different locations or if he simply recorded different names for the same places we documented (table 11.1, places 7 and 8).

In continuation to the narrative, the Spanish conquerors arrived and brought along an image of San Miguel, who became the patron saint of the town. Thus, all places had the saint name added to their Mixtec one, such as "San Miguel *Nuvixi.*" Finally, the tradition holds that around 1800 CE, a man named Rafael Pérez talked the inhabitants into moving from the eight wards to form the unified town of San Miguel el Grande (see also Alavez Chávez 2006:108).

INTEGRATING THE RECORDS

Table 11.1 compares the list of place-names published by Alavez Chávez (2006) and those collected from our informants in 2007. The last column to the right presents the correspondence to the archaeological sites recorded in our survey (see also figure 11.2 and figure 11.3).

As mentioned, the different experts consulted by Alavez Chávez and in this study agree that the town was originally divided into eight wards. The Mixtec names for places 1–5 are similar, although the translations can differ. For place 6 we can observe some similarity in the morphology of the names, and the difference between them may lie in the fact that these come from different narrators. We, however, believe that they refer to the same place because Alavez Chávez (2006:110) mentions that this is located to the northwest of town, and the place we visited is also situated in that general direction. Finally, places 7 and 8 differ entirely in each version, and with the data we have it is impossible to tell if they refer to the same location. However,

TABLE 11.1 Wards of San Miguel el Grande

Alavez Chávez (2006)	This Study (Sr. Aparicio and Sr. Sánchez 2007)	Archaeological Site
1 Yuku Ndaku ("hill of powerful herb")	Yuku Ndaku ("hill of powerful herb")	San Miguel el Grande (modern town)
2 Nujatu ("small place")	Ñuujatu ("spicy land")	Site 1
3 Nuvixi ("place of cold")	Nuvixi ("temperate land")	Site 6
4 Nutanda'a ("wedding place")	Nutanda'a ("wedding place")	Site 10
5 Ñusa'a ("place of gueza or cooperation")	Duañusa'a ("place where people eat" or "place of gueza")	Site 12
6 Nundii ("bare place")	Ñuusii ("joyful town")	Site 14 (2007 list)
7 Nuvi'ncha ("place of nopal cactus")	Ñunu ituyuku ("place where a green cornfield is sown")	
8 Nuka'mu ("warm place")	Chalcatongo Viejo or Ñuundeya3 (now translated as "town where people multiply" or "abundant town")	Site 9 (2007 list)

it is worth noting that the latter ward, Chalcatongo Viejo, does correspond to an archaeological site.

We visited six of the eight places listed by the two experts we consulted and it was possible to confirm that they correspond to archaeological sites (although Alavez Chávez had only referred to them as "locations"). Of Alavez Chávez's list, four or perhaps five places correspond to archaeological sites, if we regard *Nundii* and *Ñuusii* as the same place. The first place (*Yuku Ndaku*) mentioned in both versions corresponds to the current location of San Miguel el Grande. Although there are currently no mounds visible in the vicinity, the existence of ancient terraces and an ancient *ndoso* (see below) suggests a prehispanic occupation underlying the modern town, as is common in other communities throughout the Mixteca.

Upon further comparing the oral traditions regarding the foundation of San Miguel el Grande with the archaeological record and other documentary sources, we can recognize a historical narrative that forms a fundamental part of this community identity and that connects three important episodes in a coherent manner: the prehispanic period, the Early Colonial periods, and the posterior establishments of the municipality of San Miguel el Grande.[4] Although the principal narrative is brief, we can complement it with the "secondary" traditions to demonstrate that it has a clear internal structure with a well-defined sequence of historical episodes that are relevant for the town foundation.

The Prehispanic Period

During the Postclassic period Oaxaca and adjacent areas experienced a process of fragmentation of the sociopolitical landscape into numerous small and antagonistic city-states, each with a stratified and complex society controlled by an aristocratic elite (Marcus and Flannery 1983; Spores 1983:255). In the Mixteca Alta, such *cacicazgos* (or *yuvui tayu* in Mixtec) were mostly demographically limited polities that were circumscribed geographically to one or two valleys and bordering hills (Caso 1996:30; Spores 2007:103; Terraciano 2001:103). It is estimated that the prehispanic population reached its demographic peak during this period (Balkansky et al. 2000:380; Spores 1984:48). The settlement pattern recorded for these Postclassic polities is characterized by a capital town and its subject villages, and places for ceremonial activities and agricultural lands (Balkansky et al. 2000:380; Dahlgren 1990:142; Spores 1984:57, 2007:83).

Although this settlement distribution further corresponds to a centralized (or primary) sociopolitical organization, there are nevertheless other possible categories such as "convex," "primo-convex," and "double convex" (Falconer and Savage 1995; Johnson 1977, 1980), in which a decentralized pattern contains two or more "head" towns. For the Mixteca Alta this organizational type could be applicable to the Valley of Tlaxiaco from the Late Formative to the Postclassic, and it is notable that in the present several communities in this region do conform to such a pattern (Jiménez Osorio and Posselt 2012a, 2012b). This decentralized model also corresponds well to the observed settlement pattern and types recorded for the *Nduavee* Valley during the Natividad phase which, as mentioned, consists of two settlements of the first order (sites 6 and 9). Thus, we can argue for the existence of an important *cacicazgo* for this region during the Late Postclassic and contact period. It is worth mentioning that the ancient polity of Chalcatongo (*Ñuu Ndaya*) mentioned in the Mixtec codices could have indeed encompassed the *Nduavee* Valley, as might be further reflected in the toponym of site 9 (*Ñuu Ndaya*).

Interestingly, one of the "secondary" traditions we recorded mentions the various stages once required for a wedding, and involves four archaeological sites. It is reported that before getting married, a couple needed to converse with a priest who gave them advice about married life; this first stage was held at *Nuvixi* (Site 6). Then, the wedding ritual was performed at *Nutanda'a* (Site 10), and subsequently the procession headed toward *Duañusa'a* (site 12), where the reception party was celebrated and food was shared. A final celebration was held at *Ñuusii* (site 14). It is important to highlight that the three last sites' place names explicitly express the actions described in the account ("wedding place," the "place where people eat," and "joyful town," respectively). It is hard to ascertain if this complex ritual has had its roots in prehispanic times, but the fact that it is tied to a series of three Natividad-phase sites (and one undetermined) is intriguing and further demonstrates how contemporary oral narratives link and interact with the ancient landscape.

The Colonial Period

The second episode considered in the oral tradition takes us back to the Spaniards' arrival and narrates how the *ndoso* ("sacred ruler") of this prehispanic village was renamed after San Miguel, who then helped to place the bells in the church towers when this was being built. This *ndoso* continues to be a sacred element in the landscape today, in the form of a rocky outcrop with elongated shape. This account emphasizes the changes the inhabitants of San Miguel experienced through this transition period, how they adapted their ideology to the new religion by fusing elements from both, and which nowadays can be observed in some rituals and beliefs. A similar case was noted in the oral traditions of the neighboring community of Yosondúa, in which the *toho ndoso* eventually lost its influence to the new patron of the town, Santiago; until recently, however, this *ndoso* was still alive according to the local people (Sánchez Sánchez 2004:43–44).

An Early Colonial document in the Archivo General de la Nación mentions San Miguel in relation to the congregation efforts of the Spaniards in the Mixteca (*Comisión a Don Antonio de Cuenca y Contreras para la demarcación de los pueblos aquí contenidos de la Mizteca*; AGN, Congregaciones, volumen 1, expediente 36, Fs. 22–23v, 1603). The document states that during the first attempt to congregate the town in Almoloya, San Miguel el Grande had already had several subjects or *estancias*. However, the towns being considered for congregation opposed, and it was suggested instead to implement this policy in Chalcatongo and Santa Cruz Itundujia. This second attempt also failed, and it was therefore decided to merely demarcate the head towns and subject villages in 1603 (Sánchez Sánchez 2004:51). This further corresponds to Gerhard's (1977:385) observation that the congregation of indigenous towns in New Spain—with some regional variations—occurred in two stages: from 1550 to 1564 and from 1593 to 1605. It is possible that the *estancias* of San Miguel mentioned in the document correspond to the eight wards mentioned in the oral narrative and further recorded archaeologically.

THE FOUNDATION OF THE MUNICIPALITY

For the third and final episode, the oral tradition refers to the foundation of San Miguel el Grande as a municipality, because it points out that by 1800 CE an inhabitant brought the eight wards together and the current town was formed. It is important to stress that by the eighteenth century several communities in this region had survived the Spanish dominion and reemerged as independent towns (Gerhard 1986:97). Such is the case of Santiago Yosondúa, located to the southeast of San Miguel, which in 1767 requested to choose its own government and to be separated from Chalcatongo; the first time that a mayor is mentioned there is in 1861 (Sánchez Sánchez 2004:57, 76). We believe that a similar process took place in San Miguel el Grande and that the municipality foundation could have occurred at the beginning of the nineteenth century.

It is worth mentioning that at present this municipality is made up of a head town and eight municipal agencies, which are named after important figures of the Mexican Independence in addition to their Mixtec names. This pattern seems to echo that of the eight sites/wards mentioned above for the previous episodes of the oral tradition. Although these modern-day agencies are not located in the same locations as the ancient settlements, some are still found quite close to them and might reflect a possible continuity in the political unity of the municipality (figure 11.2).

CONCLUSION

A study that has as its objective to understand the past has to stem from an integrated vision that not only centers on the archaeological remains but also accommodates other cultural elements such as rituals, writing, calendars, sacred narratives, and oral traditions (Florescano 2002:95, 110). In the Mixteca Alta, such narratives continue to serve as a recurring mechanism to preserve the collective memory, a practice that dates back to the Colonial and prehispanic periods when the concept of "history" coupled the written and spoken word and was considered as the account of "what has been told" (Terraciano 2001:18, 407). Such an approach permits us to transcend the fragmented quality of the material remains and the temporally limited nature of the documentary record. Although this further implies keen awareness of cultural continuities, at the same time these should not be approached simply as illustrative data but rather as a way to consider the contemporary lives of people today (Jansen and Pérez Jiménez 2010:77).

To understand the oral tradition regarding the origin and development of San Miguel el Grande, it is essential to situate oneself in their landscape, which indeed becomes meaningless if approached from an isolated perspective.[5] The oral narrative thus revitalizes the landscape and vice versa, producing a contextual sense of identity and reinforcing the cultural memory of its inhabitants. In this sense, when an oral tradition is written down it often becomes static and canonized, ceases to be "lived," and so loses its profound symbolic vitality.

As the consciousness of a group is based on historical knowledge and heritage, the survival of collective memory of different communities stems from their need to prevail through space and time (Bonfil Batalla 2000:237). It is in this context that we perceive how the inhabitants of San Miguel claim their legitimate role as protagonists in this deep history, which is further supported by archaeological and documentary finds. The dynamic nature of these narratives corresponds to the proper character of these autochthonous communities which, from their present position, still possess a strong connection to the past and a prospect for the future. This latter point is clear in the principal narrative presented here, where the ending of the tradition remains open and without a fixed conclusion. We conclude, then, that we can approach history more holistically by listening to those people who consider the surrounding landscape and archaeological remains as their own past and heritage.

NOTES

1. This chapter was translated from Spanish by Leticia Karina Hernández Velázquez and Peter C. Kroefges.

2. This Mixtec term signifies "sacred ruler" and today can refer to an ancient ruler, god, saints, or natural phenomena (Jansen 1978:6).

3. It is interesting to note that this modern-day Mixtec name derives from the ancient tern Ñuu Ndaya ("City of Death"), the place where the Mixtec kings were buried (Jansen and Pérez Jiménez 2009:9).

4. For the purpose of this study, we highlight only those aspects of the principal narrative that make reference to past events, although there are other allusions to present and even future incidents.

5. We refer to the concept of "landscape" as it is understood by those who inhabit it, occupy its places, and travel along its roads, and which consists of a permanent register of past generations. It is perpetually in construction, and through our experiences we become part of it as it becomes part of us (Ingold 1993).

REFERENCES

Alavez Chávez, Raúl Gabriel. 2006. *Toponimia Mixteca II: Mixteca Alta, Comunidades del Distrito de Tlaxiaco*. Mexico City: CIESAS.

Assmann, Jan. 2003. "Cultural Memory: Script, Recollection and Political Identity in Early Civilizations." *Historiography East and West* 1 (2): 154–177. http://dx.doi.org/10.1163/15701860377400485.

Balkansky, Andrew K., Stephen A. Kowalewski, Verónica Pérez Rodríguez, Thomas J. Pluckhahn, Charlotte A. Smith, Laura R. Stiver, Dimitri Beliaev, John F. Chamblee,

Verenice Y. Heredia Espinoza, and Roberto Santos Pérez. 2000. "Archaeological Survey in the Mixteca Alta of Oaxaca, Mexico." *Journal of Field Archaeology* 27 (4):365–389. http://dx.doi.org/10.1179/jfa.2000.27.4.365.

Bonfil Batalla, Guillermo. 2000. "Historias que no Son Todavía Historia." In *Historia ¿para qué?* ed. L. V. Pereyra Carlos, Luis González, José Blanco, Enrique Florescano, Arnaldo Córdova, Héctor Aguilar, Carlos Monsiváis, Adolfo Gilly, and Guillermo Bonfil Batalla, 227–245. Mexico City: Siglo Veintiuno.

Caso, Alfonso. 1996. *Reyes y Reinos de la Mixteca*. vol. 1 and 2. Mexico City: Fondo de Cultura Económica.

Dahlgren, Barbro. 1990. *La Mixteca: Su Cultura e Historia Prehispánicas*. Mexico City: UNAM.

Falconer, Steven E., and Stephen H. Savage. 1995. "Heartlands and Hinterlands: Alternative Trajectories of Early Urbanization in Mesopotamia and the Southern Levant." *American Antiquity* 60 (1):37–58. http://dx.doi.org/10.2307/282075.

Florescano, Enrique. 2002. "Memoria Indígena: Un Nuevo Enfoque Sobre la Reconstrucción del Pasado." In *Sociedad y Patrimonio Arqueológico en el Valle de Oaxaca: Memoria de la Segunda Mesa Redonda de Monte Albán*, ed. Nelly Robles García, 93–111. Oaxaca, Mexico: CONACULTA-INAH.

Gerhard, Peter. 1977. "Congregaciones de Indios en la Nueva España antes de 1570." *Historia Mexicana* 103:347–395.

Gerhard, Peter. 1986. *Geografía Histórica de la Nueva España 1519–1821*. Mexico City: UNAM-IIH.

Goody, Jack. 2010. *Myth, Ritual and the Oral*. Cambridge: Cambridge University Press.

Ingold, Tim. 1993. "The Temporality of the Landscape." *World Archaeology* 25 (2):152–174. http://dx.doi.org/10.1080/00438243.1993.9980235.

Jansen, Maarten E.R.G.N. 1978. "Los Señores de la Mixteca, su Estatus y Orígen, Oaxaca." In *Primera Mesa Redonda de Estudios Mixtecos: Síntesis de las Ponencias*, ed. Maarten Jansen and Margarita Gaxiola, 5–6. Oaxaca, Mexico: INAH.

Jansen, Maarten, and Aurora Gabina Pérez Jiménez. 2009. *La Lengua Señorial de Ñuu Dzaui: Cultura Literaria de los Antiguos Reinos y Transformación Colonial*. Mexico: CSEIIO.

Jansen, Maarten, and Aurora Gabina Pérez Jiménez. 2010. "Mixtec Cultural Vocabulary and Pictorial Writing." In *Linguistics and Archaeology in the Americas: The Historization of Language and Society*, ed. Eithne B. Carlin and Simon van de Kerke, 45–82. Leiden: Brill. http://dx.doi.org/10.1163/9789047427087_005.

Jiménez Osorio, Liana Ivette, and Emmanuel Posselt. 2012a. "El Paisaje Arqueológico en el Valle de Tlaxiaco y su Organización Social durante el Preclásico Tardío." Unpublished BA thesis, Escuela Nacional de Antropología e Historia, Mexico City.

Jiménez Osorio, Liana Ivette, and Emmanuel Posselt. 2012b. "Organizaciones Políticas Descentralizadas del Preclásico Tardío en la Mixteca Alta de Oaxaca, México." Presentation given at the 54th International Congress of Americanists, Vienna.

Jiménez Osorio, Liana Ivette, Emmanuel Posselt, and Enrique Fernández. 2006. "Informe Técnico del Proyecto Arqueológico Línea de Transmisión Tlaxiaco-Itundujia. Primera Fase: Recorrido de Superficie." INAH-Oaxaca, CONACULTA, Consejo de Arqueología. *Report*.

Jiménez Osorio, Liana Ivette, Emmanuel Posselt, and Enrique Fernández. 2007. "Informe Técnico del Proyecto Arqueológico Línea de Transmisión Tlaxiaco-Itundujia. Segunda Fase: Excavación." INAH-Oaxaca, CONACULTA, Consejo de Arqueología. *Report*.

Johnson, Gregory A. 1977. "Aspects of Regional Analysis in Archaeology." *Annual Review of Anthropology* 6 (1):479–508. http://dx.doi.org/10.1146/annurev.an.06.100177.002403.

Johnson, Gregory A. 1980. "Rank-Size Convexity and System Integration: A View from Archaeology." *Economic Geography* 56 (3):234–247. http://dx.doi.org/10.2307/142715.

Marcus, Joyce, and Kent V. Flannery. 1983. "An Introduction to the Late Postclassic." In *The Cloud People: Divergent Evolution of the Zapotec and Mixtec Civilizations*, ed. Kent V. Flannery and Joyce Marcus, 217–226. New York: Academic Press.

Olivera de Bonfil, Alicia. 1978. "La Historia y la Tradición Oral." In *Jornadas de Historia de Occidente*, 157–159. Mexico: Centro de Estudios de la Revolución.

Sánchez Sánchez, Ernesto L. 2004. *Santiago Yosondúa, Oaxaca: Historia y Rescate de Tradiciones*. Mexico: CIESAS-IEEPO.

Spores, Ronald. 1983. "Ramos Phase Urbanization in the Mixteca Alta." In *The Cloud People: Divergent Evolution of the Zapotec and Mixtec Civilizations*, ed. Kent V. Flannery and Joyce Marcus, 120–122. New York: Academic Press.

Spores, Ronald. 1984. *The Mixtecs in Ancient and Colonial Times*. Norman: University of Oklahoma Press.

Spores, Ronald. 1995. "Informe Final al Consejo de Arqueología del INAH del Proyecto: Recorrido Arqueológico de la Región Mixteca Central y Oeste 1993–1995." Centro INAH Oaxaca, Oaxaca, Mexico. *Report*.

Spores, Ronald. 2007. *Ñuu Ñudzahui: La Mixteca de Oaxaca. La Evolución de la Cultura Mixteca desde los Primeros Pueblos Preclásicos hasta la Independencia*. Oaxaca: IEEPO.

Terraciano, Kevin. 2001. *The Mixtecs of Colonial Oaxaca: Ñudzahui History, Sixteenth through Eighteenth Centuries*. Stanford: Stanford University Press.

Vansina, Jan. 1968. *La Tradición Oral*. Trans. Miguel M. Llongueras. Barcelona: Edición Labor.

12

Decolonizing Historical Archaeology in Southern Oaxaca, and Beyond

Danny Zborover

It seems to me that more adequate progress demands the utilization—in areas and periods where it is possible—of both written sources and excavation. I therefore believe that we should train in Mesoamerica a new type of investigator who is not only an archaeologist, an ethnologist or a historian, but a new type for whom we eventually could perhaps find a shorter term than ethnoarcheohistorian. (Bernal 1962:225)

Digging in the documents and in the earth must be understood to be part of the same research and that one cannot do without the other. (Noël Hume 1969:19)

INTRODUCTION

The integration of archaeological and historical data has taken many shapes and forms throughout the centuries, but never achieved such a recognized status among scholars as it did with the current field of historical archaeology. With a rather humble beginning in the United States during the late 1960s, historical archaeology has now grown to become one of the most institutionalized subdisciplines worldwide, resulting in numerous volumes, peer-reviewed journals, professional societies, specialized conferences, and academic programs. The allure of the field to archaeologists can partially be explained with its promise to challenge the conceptual limits of our discipline, and encourage us to raise our heads from the narrow trenches to creatively engage with "things" and ideas beyond our traditional trade. Kathleen

DOI: 10.5876/9781607323297.c012

Deagan captured this notion well by stating:

> By definition, historical archaeology offers perhaps the only multidisciplinary articulation and integration of evidence from the material-cultural, natural, intellectual, and social worlds, both in the present and the past. When all these lines of evidence are integrated in historical archaeology, they should add up to more than the sum of their parts, and they often do. (Deagan 1991:102)

Indeed, from its very infancy the field has been explicitly defined by the method of archaeological-historical integration by its North American founding fathers (Cleland 2001; Jelks 1968; Pilling 1967), while Ivor Noël Hume (1969:12) even suggested that archaeology as a discipline should be redefined as "the study of the material remains of both the remote and recent past in relationship to documentary history and the stratigraphy of the ground in which they are found." More specifically, Robert Schuyler proposed in an early programmatic article that historical archaeology should be understood as

> *the study of the material remains from any historic period* . . . "Historic Period" means a period in which the cultures in question have a documentary record and that writing is having a full impact both on the cultures being studied and the scholarship of the investigation. When records are capable of altering the basic methods and techniques of studying past societies then we are dealing with Historical Archaeology. (Schuyler 1970:84, italics his)

In turn, James Deetz—one of the field's leading figures—saw historical archaeology as a practice that "studies the cultural remains of literate societies that were capable of recording their own history" (Deetz 1977:5), thus putting the emphasis on the culture's own literacy.

Accordingly, and as so defined, historical archaeology seems like a highly fitting framework for those Mesoamericanists who work within the context of indigenous literate societies in general, and with the integration of their material and documentary traditions from the Formative period and onwards. Not only have such indigenous "historical annals and maps" defined and delimited prehispanic Mesoamerica as a culture area (Kirchhoff 1952:25), but these documentary traditions have continued to transform and adapt throughout the Colonial period and up to the present. Still, despite the great potential for integrative research in Mexico or worldwide, there has been little scholarly exchange that could advance methodological and theoretical concerns. The purpose of this chapter is therefore twofold: (1) to argue that such disengagement is largely based on early misconceived precepts of historical archaeology, which can be bridged by an inclusive framework, and (2) to demonstrate this mutual relevance to Mesoamericanists and historical archaeologists alike by applying such an inclusive approach to the Chontalpa Historical Archaeology Project, which takes a long-term approach to southern Oaxacan territorial-narratives and focuses on indigenous interregional interaction, colonialism, domination, and resistance before, during, and after the Spanish conquest.

HISTORICAL ARCHAEOLOGY AND HISTORICAL MESOAMERICA

Why has historical archaeology as a field failed to impact integrative studies of Mesoamerican indigenous literate societies, and vice versa? Within North American scholarship, the answer seems to do with the specific intellectual roots of the field. Following the nationalistic interests of its Anglo-American founders, historical archaeology developed a concomitant definition that focused on the study of the European expansion, exploration, and colonization of the New World, starting from the fifteenth century onwards (Deetz 1977:5; Fontana 1965; Noël Hume 1969; Pilling 1967; Schuyler 1970). This methodological-temporal juxtaposition seemed quite valid for the early North American practitioners, because they regarded *history* and the *documentary record* to mean exclusively the "alphabetically written documents" that were first introduced to this region by the European explorers and settlers.[1] Historical archaeologists have consequentially directed their attention to the so-called historic-period sites of the Colonial period, not necessarily because these were emphasized in the documentary record, but rather because these were either founded by Europeans or were otherwise considered important to the European-based foundation of the United States. As such, indigenous sites in North America were mostly relegated to the realm of "prehistoric archaeology" and were considered relevant to historical archaeology only as much as these were impacted by the Colonial enterprise (Deetz 1977:5; Fontana 1965; see also Lightfoot 1995; Mitchell and Scheiber 2010; Rubertone 1996, 2000). Similarly, the postcontact history written by or about the indigenous people—*ethnohistory*—was considered qualitatively different from European conventional history and was studied mostly by anthropologists rather than historians (Krech 1991; Spores 1980; Trigger 1978, 1982).

Although formulating their newfound field within the specific sociocultural parameters of the United States, the declared geographical scope of North American historical archaeology pertained to effectively encompass the entire New World (Fontana 1965; Pilling 1967). Thus, in their eagerness to validate their epistemic distinctiveness as being both historical *and* post-Columbian, these pioneer historical archaeologists were fast to deny the place of Mesoamerica's literate societies in this historical New World.[2] Early on, and despite his excellent methodological definition above, Schuyler went on to exclude "all pre-contact New World civilizations," including the Maya, as being relevant to historical archaeology on the basis that their writing systems would contain only "scanty data" (Schuyler 1970:84; and see also Fontana 1965:61). Perhaps reflective of the time—only a decade or so after Berlin's (1958) and Proskouriakoff's (1960) key articles that started to fix Maya inscriptions in factual space and time—the prevailing misconceptions about Mesoamerican indigenous historiography hindered any productive exchange (Houston 1989). Similarly, the systematic study of Zapotec, Mixtec, and Aztec writing systems was only starting to gain momentum in the mid-twentieth century but was still not well known to the larger archaeological community outside of Mexico. In addition, although in its early years North American historical archaeology was still tied to the historical discipline and to fields such as Classical archaeology (Deetz 1987, 1993; Noël Hume 1969), the parallel development and strong processual influence of the New Archaeology had effectively severed these ties and made the literate indigenous societies of Mesoamerica even less pertinent to the growing circle of historical archaeologists who were now concerned with nomothetic anthropology rather than with 'historical particularism'[3] (Binford 1977; South 1977; see also Spores 1980:579–580).

Although in the last three decades North American historical archaeology has diversified its scope to produce a stimulating blend of "processual/scientific" and "postprocessual/contextual" approaches (Shackel and Little 1992), an unfortunate outcome of the early anthropological overemphasis in the field has been a slow drift away from *methodological* concerns (such as "integration of sources") and into an enduring *temporal* emphasis. In his quite popular redefinition of the field, Charles Orser proposed that "historical archaeologists should not be interested in all literate cultures, but only those that inhabited the time I broadly term 'modern times'... This period began sometimes around 1492 and extends until today"[4] (Orser 1996:27). Even though most historical archaeologists who follow this temporal definition and its topical extensions (such as "colonialism," "capitalism," "Eurocentrism," "modernity," "the recent past," etc.) continue to hold that the presence of the historical record and its methodological integration with the archaeological data is still at their modus operandi, it seems that the persistent legacy of exclusion within the field had already created a blind spot for Mesoamerican literate societies. Indigenous historiography is still largely overlooked or often misrepresented in the field's anthologies and textbooks (e.g., Orser and Fagan 1995:9–10, 15, 75), while the prehispanic cultures are often seen as a source of material evidence to be compared to the Colonial-period documentation (Orser 1996:34–35). Since its launch in 1967, articles on Mesoamerican case studies have played a minimal role in the *Journal of Historical Archaeology*, whose mission statement is that of the "post–1400

A.D. modern world," and even less so in the more recent *International Journal of Historical Archaeology* and the multivolume series, Historical Archaeology in Latin America, edited by Stanley South. In all these Mesoamerican cases, the temporal emphasis is on the Colonial and Republican periods, while none consider indigenous historical sources to any extent.[5] The Society for Historical Archaeology's position on the subject seems to be particularly ambiguous; while acknowledging that other pre–fifteenth century CE world civilizations had writing—including the Olmec and the Maya—the integrative study of those are left for "specialists in other fields" (Veit n.d.).

Perhaps not surprising, the same exclusionary temporal, geographical, and topical biases further extended to other seemingly methodological alternatives proposed by North American historical archaeologists, such as "historic sites archaeology" (Fontana 1965), "documentary archaeology" (Beaudry 1993; Wilkie 2006), and "text-aided archaeology"[6] (Little 1992). These cases further demonstrate that the "historical" nomenclature is not merely a descriptive prefix but rather implies conceptual baggage that directly influences the way North American historical archaeology is being practiced today.[7] Therefore, as long as "a focus on people with history highlights Europeans' history in relation to that of other peoples', creating an archaeology of the Age of Discovery, colonization, and the development of the modern world system" (Little 1994:5–6), the neocolonial agendas that perpetuate the "people without history" master narrative will continue to dominate historical archaeology rather than being dispelled by it (see also Funari et al. 1999b; Johnson 1999; Reid and Lane 2004; Schmidt 2006; Silliman 2010; Trigger 1989; Wolf 1982).

THE CURRENT MEXICAN PARADIGM

The Mesoamericanists, on their part, seem to have largely fallen into two extremes: those who either ignore or are unaware of historical archaeology's scope and methods, and those who largely subscribe to its North American exclusive parameters.[8] As institutionally defined and practiced in Mexico in the last decades, historical archaeology largely follows those same temporal and topical definitions by focusing on the archaeology of post-Columbian New Spain (broadly the sixteenth to the nineteenth century, or to the present), while still acknowledging the methodological importance of integrating (Colonial/European) documents with (Colonial/European) material culture (Charlton and Fournier 2008; Charlton, Fournier and Charlton 2009; Farnsworth and Williams 1992; Fournier 2003; Fournier-García and Miranda-Flores 1992; Gasco et al. 1997; Hernández Pons 1998; Pérez Castro 1990). As such, much of Mexico's historical archaeology is being practiced in urban centers rather than in federally declared "archaeological zones," and is often directly associated with salvage excavations or the restoration of Colonial- and Republican-period structures (Fernández Dávila and Gómez Serafín 1998; Gómez Serafín and Fernández Dávila 2007).

As often noted by its growing circle of practitioners, the post-Columbian temporal emphasis was first considered as a rejoinder to the Mexican institutionalized dichotomous tendencies to leave the pre-Columbian period to the archaeologists and the Colonial period to the historians, thus creating a fundamental lacuna in our archaeological knowledge of the last five hundred years. Although this proposal is much to be hailed, by continuing to adhere to the narrow Federal definitions of "archaeological" and "historical" patrimony on the one hand,[9] while adopting North American frameworks on the other, historical archaeology in Mexico has only helped perpetuate the Eurocentric bias and further contributed to false temporal divides between indigenous historical literatures and materialities before and after the Spanish conquest.

Even though studies that integrate indigenous archaeological and documentary records abound in Mesoamerica,[10] so far only a few have loosely framed their research within the framework of historical archaeology (Brambila and Avilez 1998; Charlton 2002, 2003; Charlton and Charlton 1998; Gasco 1992a, 1992b, 1993, 1997a, 1997b; Houston 1989; Matadamas Díaz 1998; Mondragon et al. 1997; Moreno Cabrera 2000; Palka 2009; Rice 2002; Rice and Rice 2004; Spores 1998; Whittington 2003). In most cases historical archaeology is brought into the discussion only parenthetically, and with little if any relation to the principal field's method and theory. At the same time, there is still a pervasive emphasis on indigenous material culture vis-à-vis European historical documents, while the explicit or implicit temporal emphasis continues to be post-Columbian to the point of dichotomizing the prehispanic period as "prehistoric" or "protohistoric" vis-à-vis the so-called historic Colonial period[11] (see also Fabian 1983 for an excellent discussion on "typological time"). This is even more perplexing if we consider that most historical archaeology projects in Mexico have focused on regions with enduring indigenous literary traditions: the Basin of Mexico, the Valley of Oaxaca, Chiapas, and the Yucatan Peninsula.[12] Practiced as such, archaeology of the European culture that is contextualized within the post-Columbian world, even though lacking a methodological inclusion of documentary evidence, is still considered by many to be historical by definition, whereas the archaeology of the prehispanic period that does integrate historical indigenous documents, would, by default, not be recognized as historical (see also Funari 1999:43). In this regard, I can only echo Ron Spores's assertion that "una arqueología historica sin documentos históricos no es aceptable en nuestra era" (1998:72).

RECONFIGURING HISTORICAL ARCHAEOLOGY

Historical archaeology of European colonialism and the modern world continues to be adopted and adapted uncritically in other parts of the world (Majewski and Gaimster 2009:xvii; Orser 2002), guided by the false reasoning that because post-conquest archaeology is (often) historical, then historical archaeology *is* postconquest archaeology. Other emerging schools, however, have largely rejected these exclusionary definitions and have attempted to refocus the field on its methodological aspects, namely integration of the archaeological and the documentary. In Europe, the long humanistic legacy stemming from Biblical, Classical, and Medieval archaeologies has been recently reframed under the rubric of historical archaeology in Sweden (Andrén 1998) and Britain (Carver 2002; Driscoll 2010; Halsall 1997; Moreland 2001). Although arguably less theoretically oriented than the North American school, European historical archaeology tends to be more reflexive and temporally unrestricted. Dedicating a few pages to the Classic Maya, Andrén (1998:83–91) indeed considered pre-Columbian Mesoamerica as a valid contribution to world historical archaeology (see also Moreland 2001:109, 111). The growing school of Africanist historical archaeology forcefully argues against the North American paradigm and further demonstrates the enormous potential of integrating oral traditions and material culture (Connah 2007; Posnansky and Decorse 1986; Reid and Lane 2004; Robertshaw 2004; Schmidt 2006; Schmidt and Walz 2007; Stahl 2001). Similar critical voices are coming from South America and other parts of the world (Funari et al. 1999a, 1999b; Levy 2010; Pedrotta and Gómez Romero 1998; Schmidt and Patterson 1995; Yoffee and Crowell 2006). Even so, these critiques "from the edge" still tend to have a narrow geographical focus and so far have had little impact on mainstream historical archaeology in general and Mesoamerican scholarship in particular.

It thus seems that the claims in North American literature about finally settling the field's early identity crisis were somewhat premature (Deagan 1982; Orser 1996, 2010); wherever historical archaeology may be headed as a field, its future may eventually bear on the question on what "historical" would mean to its practitioners and what makes it different from other archaeologies out there. In the most general sense of the term, all archaeologies can be considered as situated within a certain historical context regardless of time or place (Hodder 1987; Mitchell and Scheiber 2010; Silliman 2010; Trigger 1978), although this does not necessarily make them "historical archaeologies"; nor does the fact that the culture under study, or a selected segment within the population, was literate, if this historical legacy does not reflect directly on our research[13] (as defined by Deetz [1977] and Schuyler [1970] above). Historical archaeology must therefore return to the crux on which all of its world variants converge: the methodological integration of archaeological and historical data. Contrary to what some historical archaeologists may believe, this would not weaken or dissipate the field (Orser 1996; Robertshaw 2004; Schuyler 1999) but, if anything, could unify it across the globe (see also Andrén 1998:183).

Considering the current rifts between Mesoamerican studies and historical archaeology, a valid question may be raised: are these two fields even relevant to each other? After all, Mesoamericanists had so far successfully integrated indigenous archaeological and historical sources without turning to historical archaeology, whereas historical archaeology managed to thrive as a field without including Mesoamerican indigenous literate societies. However, and as the overview above demonstrates, the current exclusionary framework of historical archaeology does not stem from any heuristic or epistemological relevance but rather is due to misconceived temporal and geographical criteria. At the same time, Mesoamericanists would be equally mistaken to deny or turn their back to the field's breadth and advancements in the last five decades, and particularly those methodological and theoretical aspects that could bear on our particular sources, region, and time period. Formulating any methodological frameworks in isolation from historical archaeology (or any other formalized integrative method) may only lead to tautology and will discourage any potential disciplinary and interdisciplinary collaboration. For that matter, instead of coming up with redundant concepts such as "ethnoarchaeohistory" (Bernal 1962) or "arqueohistoria" (Corona Sánchez 2001; see also Hodder 1987:2, 8), or creating sub-subentities by adding various prefixes to historical archaeology (such as *ethno-*, *indigenous*, *Mesoamerican*, etc.), we may better draw and expand on those that are applicable and are already widely used. This would further allow us to communicate across regional and cultural particularities, and make our integrative research more approachable to other practitioners of historical archaeology worldwide.[14] In the following discussion I will demonstrate the relevance of historical archaeology to Mesoamerican studies and vice versa, by drawing from the Chontalpa Historical Archaeology Project conducted by the author in the Chontal highlands of southern Oaxaca.

THE CHONTALPA HISTORICAL ARCHAEOLOGY
PROJECT: SOURCES AND METHODS

Recent archaeological explorations in the southeastern Oaxacan highlands, lowlands, and coast show the region to have been heavily populated since the Formative period, and large residential and ceremonial centers are documented for the Classic and Postclassic periods (Brockington et al. 1974; Fernández Dávila and Gómez Serafín 1988; Kroefges 2004, 2006; Matadamas Díaz and Ramírez Barrera 2007, 2010; Wallrath 1967; Zborover 2007, 2014; R. Zeitlin 1990, 1993). The indigenous population declined dramatically during the Early Colonial period, as with the rest of New Spain, although native rulership was maintained on the local level and several towns flourished and further attracted the Spanish *encomenderos* (Bartolomé and Barabas 2006a; Gerhard 1993; Zeitlin 2005).

Today the region is still home to the Chontal-speaking people, a linguistic isolate whose origins, migration route, and arrival period to Oaxaca continue to be highly speculative (Kroefges 2006; Zárate Morán 1995; Zborover 2006, 2014). Despite the ethnographic complexity documented in the present (Carrasco 1960; Munch 1992; Oseguera 2003, 2004; Turner 1973), early Spanish officials who relied on testimonies of antagonistic ethnic groups described the Chontal people as "dumb," "dirty" (Acuña 1984a:348), and "brute as deer" (Acuña 1984b:62). Writing in the seventeenth century, Fray Francisco de Burgoa (1934:276–277) portrayed the Chontal as "scary-looking" animal-like cave dwellers who failed to found proper villages, a harsh image that has endured well into the recent literature (see also Gay 1986).

In contrast, historians and archaeologists are now beginning to get familiar with the remarkably rich corpus of indigenous documents pertaining to the region, most of which still goes unpublished[15] (Bartolomé and Barabas 2006a; Kroefges 1998; Oseguera 2003; Zborover 2002a, 2006, 2008a, 2009b, 2014). These documents are pictorial, alphabetic, or, most often in the Early Colonial period, a combination of complex iconography with phonetic complements and explicative glosses, and they were composed by indigenous hands in Chontal, Nahuatl, or Spanish.[16] With their emphasis on autochthonous historical narratives, these documents make it abundantly clear that the Chontal people recorded their own history, and the history of others, for the last five hundred years and more. Perhaps not too surprising for this rather circumscribed region, this rich historical legacy was further preserved in the form of ancestral oral knowledge systems among the contemporary Chontal (Bartolomé and Barabas 2006b; Carrasco 1960; Martínez Grácida 1910; O'Connor and Kroefges 2007; Turner 1973; Zborover 2007, 2009a, 2014).

In the formulation of a research design aimed at systematically comparing and contrasting these rich sources, I drew method and theory from various integrative approaches in Mesoamerica and elsewhere, and most particularly from North American, Mexican, European, and African historical archaeologies (figure 12.1). Despite the different and sometimes conflicting approaches within these variants, the basic premise was that all share the integration of archaeological and documentary data as their prime method. In addition, historical archaeologists throughout the world have placed special emphasis on the usefulness of oral histories and traditions to reconstruct the recent or the more distant past (Andrén 1998; Beck and Somerville 2005; Funari et al. 1999a, 1999b; Orser and Fagan 1995; Purser 1992; Schmidt 2006; Wilkie 2006; and see Henige 1985 and Vansina 1985 for methodological discussions). Borrowing from these anthropologically and humanistically oriented historical archaeologies can further permit us to bridge disciplinary gaps caused by distinct epistemologies, namely the ongoing "anthropology versus history" debate (Andrén 1998; Binford 1977; Deagan 1988; Deetz 1987, 1988, 1993; Feinman 1997; Funari et al. 1999a; Hodder 1987; Orser and Fagan 1995; Paynter 2000; Sauer 2004; Silliman 2010; Stahl 2001; Stahl, Mann, and Loren 2004; Trigger 1978, 1982, 1989).

In the Chontalpa Historical Archaeology Project (CHAP), a detailed source criticism of several indigenous historical documents from southern Oaxaca served as the initial incentive for the subsequent archaeological and ethnographic work (Zborover 2002a, 2002b, 2005, 2007, 2014; figures 12.1, 12.2, and 12.3). Various scholars have already commented on the enormous potential of documents as generators for models and hypotheses in historical archaeology (Alexander 1997; Andrén 1998; Beaudry 1993; Charlton 1969, 1981, 1991; Little 1992; Orser and Fagan 1995; Spores 1998). At the same time, while historical archaeologists have now mostly moved beyond the early inferiority complex that had grown from the "tyranny of the text" (Moreland 2001; Small 1999), they have been slow to accept historical documents as reliable testimonies of the past; even when integration is the goal, the documentary record is often viewed with suspicion and as misleading. This is often caused by lack of familiarity with critical historical methods, such as internal and external criticism as applied to the documentary and oral records (Howell and Prevenier 2001; Purser 1992; Shafer 1980; Vansina 1985), and it further creates approaches that render irrelevant the agency of the indigenous historians.[17] Perhaps the most common stumbling block among Mesoamericanists is the failure to distinguish between narratives that are *contemporaneous* with the time of composition and those with a *retrospective* account—which further implies two distinct temporal levels that can be integrated with the archaeological record (see also Smith 1992). Consequently, any historical narrative—pictorial, written, or oral—is best used to inform us about the conditions and predispositions of the people at the time of the account composition, before taking any of its "historical" content at face value (Beaudry et al. 1996; Galloway 2006; Purser 1992; Vansina 1985).

INTEGRATIVE THEME: INDIGENOUS TERRITORIAL-NARRATIVES

Considering the available documentation from southern Oaxaca, I was particularly interested in exploring the intersection of historical and archaeological epistemologies at the literary genre of *territorial-narratives*, understood as geopolitical constructs concerning place-making that structure indigenous corporate and factional identities through time (Zborover 2008a, 2009a, 2014). Through retrospective

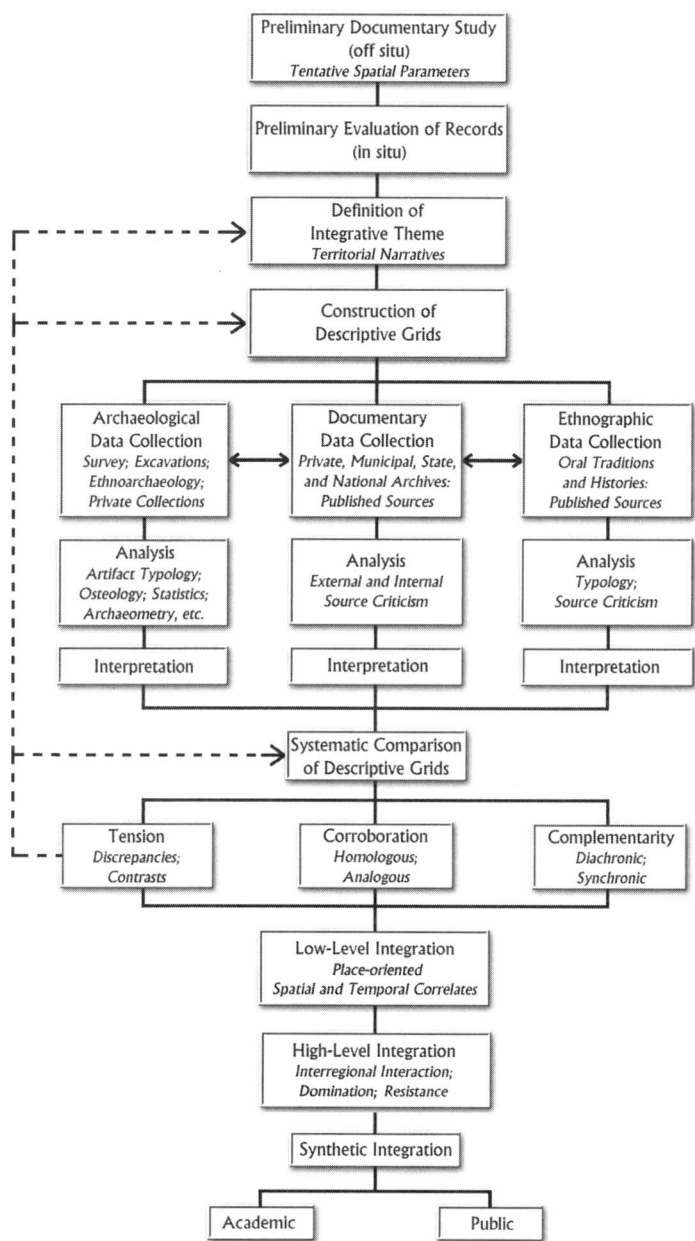

FIGURE 12.1. Flowchart of the methodological procedures used in the Chontalpa Historical Archaeology Project.

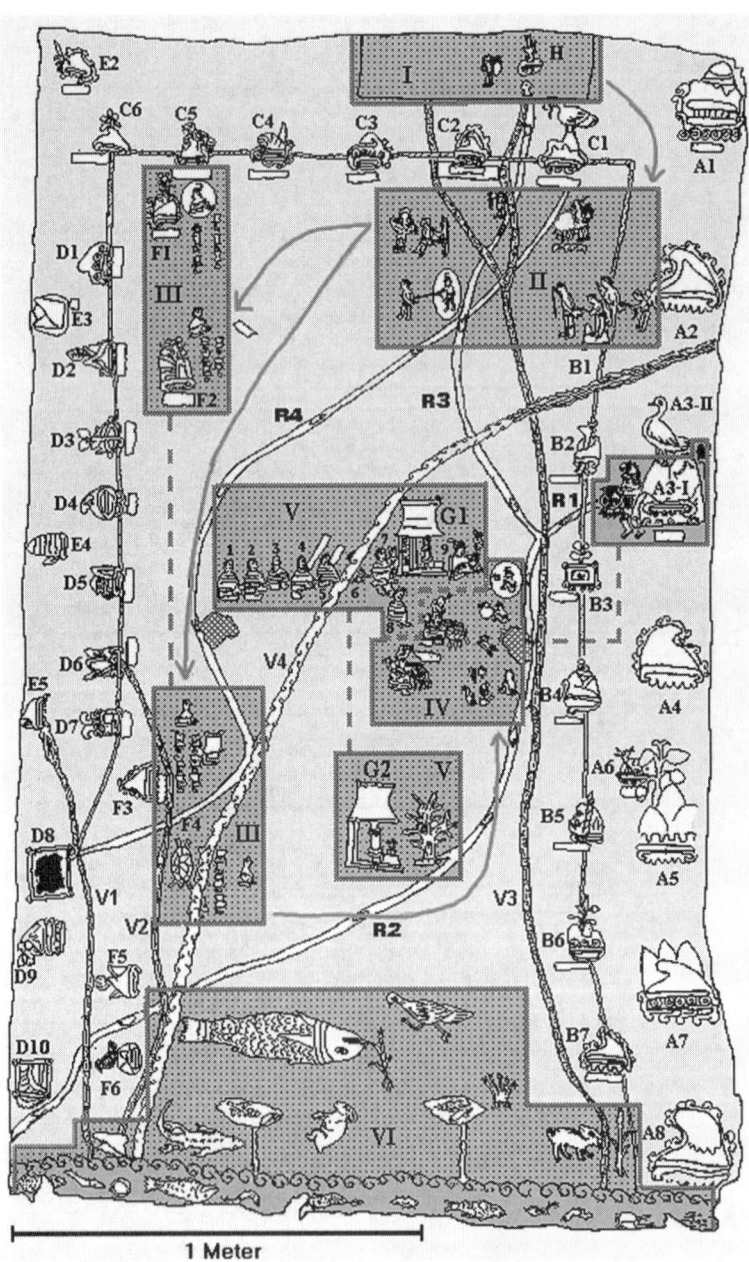

FIGURE 12.2. Content and narrative analysis of the *Lienzo de Tecciztlan y Tequatepec*, which contains three superimposed documentary strata.

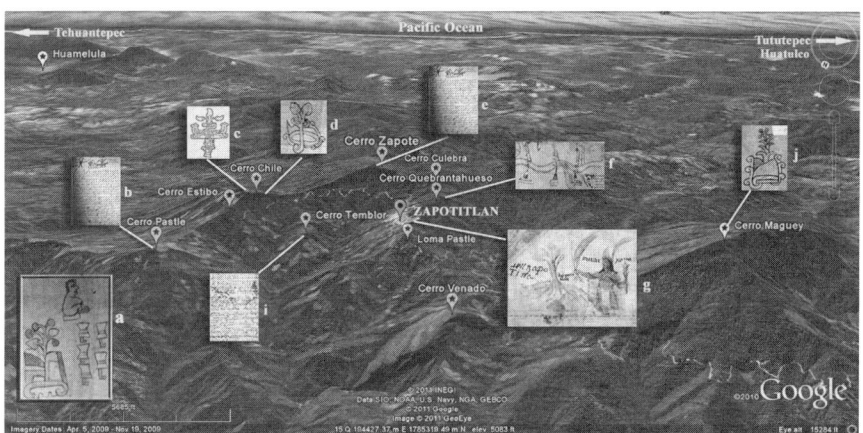

FIGURE 12.3. Archaeological sites in and around Santa María Zapotitlán, with some of the respective documentary territorial-narratives. (Landscape image courtesy of GoogleEarth.)

testimonies firmly tied to themes of land tenure and legitimation, indigenous elite were able to manipulate and reshape space, time, and collective memory and create "contracts" to be negotiated with their diverse audiences (Boone 2000; Joyce et al. 2004; Leibsohn 2004; Pohl 2004). The usefulness of such an overarching thematic category is that it transcends narrow classifications based on supporting media or Western-derived concepts, and focuses on a conceptual framework of indigenous territoriality and identity-building. Because the southern Oaxacan territorial-narratives can illuminate indigenous points of view and internal affairs before and after the Spanish conquest, within the CHAP framework I focused mostly on four interaction spheres: *Cacique-Cabecera*, *Cabecera-Sujeto*, *Cacicazgo-Cacicazgo*, and Indigenous-European (Zborover 2002a, 2008a, 2009a, 2014).

Territorial-narratives in Oaxaca can be traced back from the Formative period "conquest slabs" at Monte Albán, the carved topo-genealogical registers of the Classic period, the historical codices of the Postclassic period, the Early Colonial pictorial cloth *lienzos* and paper *mapas*, the Late Colonial alphabetic "primordial titles," and up to the modern-day performative oral traditions. Unlike decontextualized manuscripts in state and national archives, however, the documents we recorded in the Chontal communities are still rooted in an ancestral landscape, which is materialized through the surrounding vestiges of the past, while their palimpsest quality is often manifested through the retrospective interpretations by the same indigenous people who created and preserved them. As such, these stratigraphic testimonies further require a hermeneutic "excavation" of their multilayered pictorial content, *pentimenti, scholia* glosses, and contemporary oral readings.[18] Therefore, the inherent spatiotemporal structure of these territorial-narratives can be studied in conjunction with the associated archaeological record within diachronic yet interrelated "discursive contexts" (Andrén 1998:149ff; see also Galloway 2006; Purser 1992). Such a contextual approach brings us a step closer to John Moreland's definition of the field, in which "historical archaeology is a practice which recognises that artifacts and texts are more than just sources of evidence about the past; that they had efficacy in the past; and which seeks to determine the ways in which they were used in the construction of social relationships and identities in historically specific circumstances" (Moreland 2001:111).

DESCRIPTIVE GRIDS: CORROBORATIVE, COMPLEMENTARY, AND CONTRASTIVE

The first necessary step in any integrative research is the construction of independent archaeological, documentary, and oral "descriptive grids" (Leone 2007; Leone and Potter 1988; figure 12.1), which are then analyzed and interpreted in an "epistemic independence"[19] (Kosso 1995; see also Cleland 2001; Funari et al. 1999b; Kepecs 1997; Levy 2010; Small 1999; Smith 1987, 1992). This procedure ensures that each of the records is reconstructed as fully as possible without a selective manipulation of the data (conscious or not), and further sidesteps circular reasoning in which one uses assumptions from one data sets as "proof" in another.

However, although it was suggested that documentary and archaeological evidence are "epistemologically separate" because these "were made by different individuals, at different times, for different purposes . . . by two different sets of formation processes and dynamics" (Leone and Crosby 1987:399, see also Leone and Potter 1988:14), such a dichotomous position can be usually counteracted with a well-defined integrative theme and tight temporal and spatial correlates, as described above. It seems that similar statements in the historical archaeology literature often stem from current disciplinary divisions rather than from past realities, and it is questionable whether the producers of documents indeed segregated those from their material surroundings (Hamann 2002; Johnson 1999:30; Moreland 2001), especially when we consider the multiple media and contexts in which Oaxacan territorial-narratives were recorded. Instead, I maintain that it is the technical analysis and interpretation that should be epistemically separate, as these stem from different scholarly traditions (Galloway 2006; Halsall 1997; Sauer 2004; Wilson 1993). For that matter most historical archaeologists require a strong methodological background in more than one discipline and, whenever possible, collaborative projects between archaeologists, historians, and ethnologists should be encouraged.[20]

Once such independent descriptive grids have been created, these need to be compared against each other (Leone 2007; Leone and Potter 1988). Deetz (1993:158–159) has proposed a "multidirectional approach," in which one moves back and forth between the records in order to refine and reformulate research questions and assumptions. As the literature further shows, the most successful cases of integrating historical and archaeological records are those with a tight temporal and spatial "classificatory similarity" (Andrén 1998:158ff; see also Deetz 1991; Kowalewski 1997; Pedrotta and Gómez Romero 1998; Stahl 1993). It is necessary then to determine whether we are comparing analogous spatial and temporal entities, a procedure that often entails a clear understanding of the document's narrative structure and a comparable archaeological sample. Analogous spatial units might be a structure, a settlement, or a region, and further associations should be sought between functional (e.g., religious or economic) or sociocultural contexts (e.g., elite contexts). The same goes for comparable temporal scale and resolution, and although it is often argued that documents will be event-specific and the archaeological record will reflect larger swaths of time (Andrén 1998:157–168; Feinman 1997; Kowalewski 1997; Lucas 2006; Smith 1992; Wilson 1993), the opposite is also often true.

If done systematically rather than selectively, such comparisons between the archaeological, documentary, and oral descriptive grids should result in *corroborative*, *complementary*, and *contrastive* frameworks (Andrén 1998; Baerreis 1961; Little 1992; Smith 1992; figure 12.1). The first category is the one most commonly found in the literature, where either the archaeological or the historical (documentary and oral) record serves as a source of "positive correspondence" to the other (Stahl 1993:250–251). Such corroborations can be homologous and direct where data sets are taken from the same cultural context, or general and analogous when similar contexts are used to support each other (see also Charlton 1981; Deetz 1993). In the CHAP, as in other integrative studies, the most basic form of corroboration was site identification; although not always an easy and straightforward task, this is often an essential first step for any subsequent higher-level integration (Andrén 1998:157ff; Byland and Pohl 1994; Charlton 1969; Gasco 1997b; Jansen 1979; Kowalewski 1997; Orser and Fagan 1995:121ff; Rubertone 2000). Although corroborations from two or more independent sources can surely strengthen our arguments, the approach has often been criticized in historical archaeology as tautological, or as "the most expensive way in the world to learn something we already know" (Deetz 1991:1), especially in cases in which the archaeological data corroborate the documentary data.

Whereas corroborations are often synchronic in nature, complementary integration is often employed diachronically, where one record fills in temporal gaps in the other so to present a more holistic picture of the past. Typically, the archaeological record is followed by the documentary which is followed by the ethnographic, although the chain of inferences often proceed backward from the "known" present into the "unknown" past. As with the direct historical approach (Baerreis 1961; Charlton 1981; Marcus and Flannery 1994; Trigger 1989), this approach functions best in societies with strong cultural continuities and, as such, has proved useful in the CHAP public strategies (see below). Quite often, though, we might complement the sources synchronically in order to fill in thematic lacunas that are not covered in the other respective records (see also Smith 1992). At the same time, we should be wary of such additive integrations, because these often mask important conceptual and temporal differences between the sources and may create a contrived and homogenized reconstruction of the past (Stahl 1993, 2001).

To avoid such pitfalls, a systematic comparison should also demonstrate tensions between our interpretations of the material, documentary, and oral records. Although in Mesoamerica most archaeologists and historians have focused on the corroboration and complementarity of sources, historical archaeologists worldwide have started to emphasize and problematize intersource incongruities instead of simply discarding data as biased or equivocal (Charlton 1981:154ff; Gasco 1993; Stahl 1993, 2001). Stahl calls on archaeologists to "be attentive to the tensions and incompatibilities between sources, allowing different types of sources to destabilize the insight drawn from others" (Stahl 2001:33), while Andrén notes that "the difference between artifact and text is unique to the historical archaeologies, since this negative correspondence is an opportunity to create new and different images of the past" (Andrén 1998:175). Based on Binford's "middle range theory," Mark Leone and others (Leone 2007; Leone and Crosby 1987; Leone and Potter 1988) suggested highlighting such ambiguities between the descriptive grids and turning these into new research questions (see also Cleland's [2001:6–8] "method of alternate oppositions"). Similarly, inconsistencies between oral traditions and the archaeological/documentary record have often led to new understandings of the past (Beck and Somerville 2005; Henige 1985; Purser 1992; Schmidt 2006; Schmidt and Walz 2007).

Such a historical archaeology of "dissonance" can expose silences within the process of historical production and consumption (Hall 1999; Levy 2010; Moreland 2001; Orser 2002; Schmidt 2006; Schmidt and Walz 2007; Stahl 2001) and the limitations of culture material manifestations (Kosso 1995; Leone and Crosby 1987), and contribute to reevaluating our own archaeological and historical assumptions and their derivative dialectic significance (Charlton 1972, 1981, 2003; Smith 1992). For that matter, we should discard the still-prevailing notion that such tensions often arise because the documentary and oral records are subjective whereas the archaeological record is objective (Beaudry et al. 1996; Deagan 1988; Deetz 1987; South 1977), because both are conceptual constructs that are dependent on our contemporary hermeneutics. Accordingly, in the CHAP methodological procedure I have further distinguished between intersource *discrepancies*, where the tensions are often the result of our external research procedures, and *contrasts*, which are contextual and intrinsic. Under such framework, a contrast becomes significant and can further lead to new research questions only once we have reasonably eliminated discrepancies due to incomplete data, faulty analysis and interpretation, mismatched temporal and spatial correlates, or an unfocused integrative theme (see also Byland and Pohl 1994:16–17, 24–25). In the following sections I demonstrate how these frameworks were specifically applied in "low-level" and "high-level" integration (figure 12.1), and I further consider future avenues of research for solving some of the tensions arising from the data.

LOW-LEVEL INTEGRATION: ZAPOTITLÁN
DOCUMENTARY AND ORAL DATA

Rather than simply being an attempt to fill in one of the many blank spots on the Oaxacan archaeological map, the Chontalpa Historical Archaeology Project (CHAP) has focused on Santa María Zapotitlán, a Chontal community that is referenced in several of the most important pictorial and alphabetic territorial-narratives for the region: the *Lienzo de Tecciztlan y Tequatepec* (LTT; figures 12.2F2 and 12.3a), the *Zapotitlán Manuscript* (ZM), the *Lienzo de Jilotepequillo* (LJ; figure 12.3g), the *Jilotepequillo Manuscript* (JM; figure 12.3b,e), and the Chontecomatlan *titulos primordiales* (CTP), as well as other previously published Colonial documents (González de Cossío 1952; Paso y Troncoso 1905). Other primary documents pertinent to the town history were consulted in the town municipal archive and the Archivo General de la Nación in Mexico City. In these documents Zapotitlán is often attributed the status of an "origin place" for the Chontal people (JM, ZM, CTP), and it is further referenced as a key place involving the Aztec intervention in the region (ZM, LJ, LTT, and perhaps JM). Furthermore, Zapotitlán is shown in the LTT as one of the four Chontal subject towns that paid tribute to an indigenous *cabecera* during the sixteenth century, although the identity of this head town is still debated.[21]

To augment the historical research we systematically collected oral knowledge from both men and women in their private homes, public spaces, and the surrounding landscape. These formal sessions further ensured that we covered much of the variability and variants of the Chontal oral knowledge systems in Zapotitlán. These can be broadly divided into five themes: (1) toponyms and locations, (2) personal biographies, (3) settlement histories (villages and archaeological sites), (4) regional histories, and (5) "mythistorical" didactic narratives (Zborover 2007, 2014). None of these themes is entirely independent, as several can manifest within a single narrative, and all were found to be relevant to our integrative theme of territorial-narratives. For example, the named landscape often linked the historical documents to the archaeological sites, and stories about these places and the region showed a remarkable correspondence with those in the documentary record. Further attention was given to the intertextuality of Mesoamerican sources, as oral traditions occasionally originate from historical readings while documents are often the fossilized manifestations of orality[22] (Boone and Mignolo 1994; Hamann 2002; Henige 1985; Marcus 1992a; Moreland 2001; Purser 1992; Schmidt 2006; Stahl 2001; Vansina 1985).

Archaeological Data

Altogether twelve adjacent archaeological sites were identified and surveyed in an area of about four square kilometers within and around the contemporary community of Zapotitlán (figure 12.3). We mapped visible architecture and features and collected artifacts from the overall surface of these sites. At the same time, we attempted to differentiate elite from commoner contexts based on location and associated architecture, because our respective documents were most likely produced by, and primarily directed to, the former social sphere. Contemporary Chontal shrines and associated ritual paraphernalia were also documented on several of the sites. Eleven test units excavated in four of the sites further provided contextual and chronological data, and the subsequent artifactual and archaeometric analysis resulted in a preliminary ceramic typology and seven C-14 dates for the region (figure 12.4). Osteological, zooarchaeological, and paleobotanical analysis has provided important information regarding the Chontal diet, subsistence, and health, while visual and LA-ICP-MS obsidian sourcing helped to reconstruct trade and exchange networks. We further documented private collections of artifacts—found by residents of the community in cornfields located in archaeological sites—which mostly consisted of figurines and complete vessels.[23] Because Chontal pottery-making still follows traditional canons that can help illuminate the archaeological record, several ethnoarchaeological sessions were conducted with three of the last potters in the village, whereas in various households we also recorded ceramic folk taxonomies, form-to-function correlations, and vessel life-cycle of use and discard. In addition we recorded traditional construction techniques, principally of adobe and wattle-and-daub structures and residential stone terraces (Zborover 2014).

FIGURE 12.4. Eleut Sánchez standing beside the stratigraphic profile and corresponding chronology of a test pit excavated in Santa María Zapotitlán.

SPATIAL AND TEMPORAL CORRELATES

Although the modest size of the highland sites and associated architecture could probably be attributed to the rugged topography and the relatively scarce agricultural land, this further proved to be most favorable for documentary-oriented research as smaller sites further represented more manageable units for analysis and comparisons. Consistent with the depicted retrospective events and time-of-composition of most territorial-narratives under study, the radiometric dates and artifactual cross-ties indeed concentrated around the Late Postclassic and Early Colonial periods, thus providing us with strong temporal and spatial correlates on which to base any subsequent comparisons. In fact, the documented settlement pattern of a large site, Cerro Zapote, surrounded by smaller satellites is homologous to the topoglyph of Zapotitlán in the *Lienzo de Tecciztlan y Tequatepec* (figures 12.2F2 and 12.3a), where the five house-like icons, interpreted as *barrios* or wards, formed together a major tributary unit during the sixteenth century. The human figure appearing above these was most likely the Chontal ruler and tribute-collector of Zapotitlán,[24] while the document narrative suggests that this individual lived during the Postclassic to Colonial transition (Zborover 2002a, 2006).

The archaeologically recorded settlement pattern shift, which consisted of the abandonment of the dispersed hilltop sites in the Early Colonial period in favor of an amalgamated lower location, is further analogous to the documented congregation of villages in other parts of Oaxaca and Mesoamerica for this period. At the same time, surface collections and a deep test pit excavated in the heart of the Colonial-to-contemporary village revealed an occupational continuity starting from the Late Classic period and with a substantial occupation during the Postclassic period (figure 12.4). This seems to suggest that the selection of the Colonial-period congregation site might have had to do with indigenous preferences rather than merely reflecting Spanish relocation policies. The uppermost levels of the test pit were accumulated during the construction and modifications of the elementary school during the twentieth century, and their chronological position could be inferred mostly from discussions with elder informants and from modern artifacts such as coins and plastic.

As Andrén correctly points out, "an identification becomes interesting only when it can serve as a link between artifacts and text and hence be a means to create a new context that is unique to historical archaeology" (Andrén 1998:163). The long chronological sequence of the village provided us with the unique opportunity to anchor a specific archaeological site to the contemporaneous and historical Chontal people, and further study Republican- and Colonial-period material culture, but it also poses a problem as to the exact location referred to in the historical documents: were "Cerro Zapote" and "Zapotitlán" one and the same in the Early Colonial references, or two separate sites as we recorded them (figure 12.3)? In this regard the incongruity between the five pictorial *barrios* in the LTT and the seven or more Late Postclassic-Early Colonial sites identified around Zapotitlán is notable and could be the result of either an unfocused survey design or a conceptual emic-etic distinction in what constitutes such a habitational unit. The picture gets even more convoluted if we consider one of the most common oral traditions in Zapotitlán regarding the origins of the village. In most versions we heard, the village was founded in its current location after one of two factional groups abandoned an earlier settlement, Cerro Maguey, a prominent mountain with an associated archaeological "pueblo viejo" some 3.5 kilometers away[25] (figures 12.2F1 and 12.3j). Nevertheless, Zapotitlán (or Cerro Zapote) and Cerro Maguey are referenced in the historical documents as contemporaneous individual settlements in the sixteenth century, whereas in the territorial-narrative of the LTT, Zapotitlán even seems to have claimed the lead from Cerro Maguey in the regional politics (Zborover 2002a, 2008a; figure 12.2: III, IV). When was Cerro Maguey abandoned and how was it related, if at all, to the foundation of Zapotitlán? Raising such new research questions to resolve earlier discrepancies and contrasts will help guide future integrative research in the area.

Moreover, the different records complement each other to present a more holistic reconstruction of the life of people in Zapotitlán in ancient times. The most apparent synchronic complementarity is with the certain types of information gleaned through one record but not the other, such as archaeological data pertaining to economic and subsistence patterns that are largely absent in the southern Oaxacan documentary records. In addition, the detailed osteological and isotopic bone analysis of the first and only human skeleton found so far in controlled excavations in the Chontalpa has revealed much new information regarding the health conditions, diet, and occupational activities of the Chontal people during the Late Postclassic or Early Colonial periods, a time when most of our consulted documents were composed, or refer to retrospectively.

HIGH-LEVEL INTEGRATION: INTERACTION, COLONIALISM, AND RESISTANCE

Although studying particular sites is an important first step in low-level integration, historical archaeologists have long argued for a multiscalar approach that proceeds from historical sites to regional perspectives and broader questions (Cleland 2001; Deetz 1993; Lucas 2006; Orser 1996; South 1977). Beyond microhistories, the territorial-narratives of southern Oaxaca are particularly suitable for exploring interregional and pluri-ethnic themes and, by their very nature as indigenous territorial charters, further demonstrate that the mechanisms of conquest, colonialism, domination, and resistance were quite prevalent among indigenous interaction spheres in prehispanic and Colonial times, with the Spanish conquest representing yet another transformation in this long-term process (Zborover 2009a, 2014; see also Kepecs and Alexander 2005). Although these themes have been understandably highlighted in the post-Columbian-oriented historical archaeology in North America (Deagan 1991; Deetz 1977; Lawrence and Shepherd 2006; Orser 1996), this singular focus on European colonialism has recently been criticized as ethnocentric and of limited potential to any useful cross-cultural comparisons (Bartel 1985; Funari et al. 1999b; Jordan 2009; Little 1992; Mitchell and Scheiber 2010; Posnansky and Decorse 1986; Reid and Lane 2004; Rubertone 1996, 2000; Silliman 2010; see also Stein 2005). Arguing against the "flattening" social effect of the "Georgian Order" thesis (cf. Deetz 1977), Matthew Johnson has aptly summarized the point: "if an archaeology of the colonial encounter is to be part of a world historical archaeology, let us give historical and cultural depth to all parties in that encounter" (Johnson 1999:29).

THE FORMATIVE AND CLASSIC PERIODS

The historical archaeology of indigenous colonialism in southern Oaxaca might begin as early as the first century BCE. In what could be considered Mesoamerica's earliest known territorial-narrative, the so-called conquest slabs on Monte Albán's Building J were suggested to depict about seventy communities or other places that fell under the influence sphere of this polity during the Late and Terminal Formative periods (Caso 1947; Marcus 1983, 1992a, 1992b; Marcus and Flannery 1996; Spencer et al. 2008; Whittaker 1980). One of those depicted places was first interpreted by Alfonso Caso (1947:27, 97) as "Hill of the Chile Plant" (figure 12.3c). This was later tentatively identified by Joyce Marcus with Chiltepec in the Chontal highlands, further marking this region as a "suspected outlying province" of Monte Albán (Marcus 1992b:400–401; see also Marcus 1976:129–130). The accompanying inverted head of a defeated ruler further suggested to these authors that this place, as well as others, were subjugated through military coercion.[26]

Although Marcus's original toponymic correlation might have referred to San José Chiltepec, a neighboring community of Zapotitlán that appears on most topographic maps for the region, we did not identify an archaeological site at the current location of this village nor did its local inhabitants know of any other place in the vicinity by that name. In the *Lienzo de Tecciztlan y Tequatepec*, however, a topoglyph of a hill with chile plants and glossed *chitepetl* is depicted adjacent to Zapotitlán (figures 12.2D3 and 12.3d), while a pictorial *mapa* found in Zapotitlán's municipal archive and dated to 1935 includes the gloss "Serro [*sic*] de palo de Chile" for a hill at the same general area.

One of the major sites surveyed in the CHAP is known today in Zapotitlán's toponymic lore as Cerro Chile and, together with an offshoot named Cerro Estibo, forms an archaeological complex whose geographical position corresponds well to locations appearing in the *mapa* and the *lienzo* (figure 12.3). While a few finds from mixed deposits suggest that the area was occupied from the Late Formative period onward, so far, however, we did not identify any of the particular ceramics or features that are considered by some authors to be typical of Monte Albán's controlled sites during this period, such as incised G-12 bowls or creamware ceramics, Zapotec-style administrative or military structures, or fortifications and other evidence for violent conflict (Balkansky 2002; Feinman and Nicholas 1993; Spencer and Redmond 1997; Spencer et al. 2008). The surface ceramics at the site did include plain graywares at higher frequencies from those surrounding sites, but these were poorly fired and their dating remains uncertain.

The nature of corroborations and tensions in this case study raise some interesting methodological questions regarding the adequacy of our sample size, temporal disjunctions, and the expected visibility of the studied phenomena. Monte Albán clearly interacted during the Late Formative with the adjacent Isthmian region in a nuanced ebb and flow of lowland-highland exchange and emulation (R. Zeitlin 1990, 1993), and it is notable that Cerro Chile-Estibo's strategic hilltop position overlooking the Pacific coastal routes is quite consistent with other sites previously suggested to be under its influence (Balkansky 2002; Feinman and Nicholas 1993; Sherman et al. 2010). For the Late Classic, when Monte Albán had long lost its grip on its former territory, several unique artifacts point to an exchange corridor with the Valley of Oaxaca while Cerro Chile-Estibo's importance is attested by its relative size and the only ballcourt identified so far around Zapotitlán, with associated paraphernalia that suggest connections with Veracruz and the spread of the ballgame cult (see also J. Zeitlin 1993).

Such an increase in population during the Late Classic is also reflected in the earliest recorded occupation level of the Zapotitlán-Village site (figure 12.4) and perhaps can be associated with the Chontal first arrival to the area. In this regard it is interesting to note that Zapotitlán and Cerro Zapote are specifically mentioned in three of the Chontal documents as the place of a mythical creation (JM), the place where the Chontal language "was first born" (ZM), and one of two stops in the migration route of the Chontecomatlan ancestors (CTP).

Future surveys and excavations in the region should therefore aim to better define the nature of such Late Classic occupation in Zapotitlán vis-à-vis other communities and further search for the existence of primary Formative period contexts that could tie this region to other regional and interregional developments. Whether or not the Chontalpa should prove to have any relationship to Monte Albán, further iconographic and epigraphic work is also necessary on this capital's territorial statements from the Formative though the Classic periods, while critically reevaluating earlier toponymic identifications and suggesting alternative readings and meanings for these monuments.[27] By framing such inquiries within an historical archaeology of the Formative period, research in southern Oaxaca could directly contribute to larger debates on primary state formation in Mesoamerica and the nature of Monte Albán's influence on the Pacific coast and elsewhere.

THE POSTCLASSIC PERIOD

Clearer allusions to the Chontal ethnic group and their interactions with other ethnicities and polities are found in the retrospective territorial-narratives and other documents of the Early Colonial period. These appear mostly in reference to the complex Postclassic factional politics that further involved the Zapotecs of Tehuantepec, the Pochutec of Huatulco, the Mixtecs of Tututepec, and the Central Mexican Aztecs.

Although Spores (1993) and others have included the Chontal highlands and coast within the territorial extent of Tututepec, the area has not yet been identified in the Postclassic Mixtec codices as part of 8 Deer's conquest campaigns, whereas the Early Colonial local documentation only suggests an indirect Mixtec rule through Huatulco[28] (Fernández Dávila and Gómez Serafín 1988; Matadamas Díaz and Ramírez Barrera 2007, 2010; Zborover 2002a, 2006). The ceramic assemblage of Zapotitlán indeed shares similarities with the serving vessels and some decorated wares of Huatulco. This possibly suggests that both belonged to the same interaction and exchange sphere, if not even a direct political rule of the latter over the Chontal highlands during the Late Postclassic and Early Colonial period, as hinted at by the *Lienzo de Tecciztlan y Tequatepec* and other documents (Zborover 2002a, 2006, 2014; figure 12.2: III and IV). Since Tututepec's state of warfare with the Zapotecs of Tehuantepec and Coatlan/Miahuatlan (and later with the Aztecs) would have impeded secure passage through the Isthmus or the Copalita River to the Valley of Oaxaca, an alternative route for Tututepec's economic and military expansion might have been sought through its subject port of Huatulco and northeast towards the Chontal highlands. Still, the presence of "Codex style" polychrome ceramics in Huatulco stands in contrast to their almost virtual lack in both the Chontalpa highland and coastal sites, and seems to indicate that the Chontal rulers were not playing an active role in the circulation of this particular prestige commodity and its implied shared identity during the Late Postclassic, either by choice or as a result of their lower position in the Mixtec geopolitical hierarchy (Fernández Dávila and Gómez Serafín 1988; Kroefges 2004, 2006; Spores 1993; Zborover 2007, 2014). In tandem, the Postclassic fine grayware ceramics mostly associated with the Zapotec kingdom of Tehuantepec show a marked differential distribution in the Chontalpa, being relatively abundant on the coast (Kroefges 2004) but quite scarce in the highlands. This pattern corresponds well with the available indigenous territorial-narratives and other nineteenth-century historical reconstructions, in which the coastal Chontal sided with the Isthmus Zapotecs while the highland communities sided with the Aztecs.

It is precisely this latter case of colonial encounter—with the Aztecs—that presents us with another interesting case of tension between the records. According to indigenous and Spanish accounts, the Triple Alliance extent in southeastern Oaxaca during the reign of Motecuhzoma Xocoyotzin (1502–1520 CE) had reached only as far as Ozolotepec (Ocelotepec) in the strategic province of Miahuatlán (Smith and Berdan 1996:279), and the Aztecs were quite active in the Isthmus of Tehuantepec (Zeitlin 2005:80–86) and possibly in Huatulco (Matadamas Díaz and Ramírez Barrera 2010; Codice Ramírez 1979:89). Although the Chontal region is not mentioned in any known Central Mexican sources, several of the southern Oaxacan territorial-narratives are quite explicit about the Aztec intervention in the Chontal highlands' internal politics in general and of Zapotitlán in particular, and even specify a Chontal-Aztec marital alliance[29] (figure 12.2:II and figure 12.3g). Linguistic data such as Nahuatl toponyms, glosses on documents, and loan words further support such an influence in the region, as do the oral traditions recorded in Zapotitlán of an unnamed king who came from "Mexico City" (Tenochtitlán?) in ancient times to found a new capital in the region (Zborover 2007, 2014). Certainly, establishing a secure corridor through the Chontal highlands, perhaps as a preamble for an ensuing imperial conquest and domination, would have also allowed the Aztecs to access the coastal buffer zone between the competing kingdoms of Tehuantepec and Tututepec, both of which were antagonistic to the Aztecs. Such a strategy could have been motivated by economic control over coastal natural resources such as salt, dried fish, cacao, cotton, feathers, and marine shell and, perhaps more specific to the Chontal region, *purpura* shell dye, cochineal dye, and gold.[30]

Nevertheless, throughout our surveys and excavations in and around Zapotitlán, we have not identified clear material correlates for such an Aztec presence. Possible discrepancies might include a biased collection strategy and taphonomic processes; for example, if the Aztecs traded or exchanged gifts with the Chontal nobility, these might have consisted of perishable items such as textiles or feathers. Still, such contrasts between the documentary and archaeological data pertaining to the Aztec presence in the distant provinces are well documented from other places in Mexico and particularly from Oaxaca, and illustrate that even an imperial conquest and long-term domination can often be archaeologically invisible (Berdan et al. 1996; Hodge 1998). Similarly, perhaps we can explain the apparent absence of Aztec material culture with the possibility that their ephemeral presence was either exercised through the local Chontal elite or that the Aztec representatives were using local material culture.

The archaeological record, however, does show that other non-perishable exotic goods did find their way up the highlands during this period, and adds yet another dimension of interregional interaction that is absent in the documents: the analyzed obsidian found in Postclassic levels in Zapotitlán shows a near-exclusive reliance on the Oyameles-Zaragoza source in northern Puebla (Neff 2008), further complemented by smaller quantities of green Pachuca obsidian. Although the latter could have been acquired from the Aztec *pochteca* or through intermediate lowland distribution centers, the fact that the Oyameles-Zaragoza source is not common in other sites in the Isthmus and the western coast for this period seems to suggest a more exclusive route or even a direct contact with groups in northern Puebla and southern Veracruz.[31] Such contacts were already demonstrated by the Late Classic assemblage, and these might have continued well into the Postclassic and perhaps even the Colonial period. It is interesting to note that these "exclusive" Late Postclassic local ceramic traditions and obsidian patterns largely repeat for the coastal Chontal sites (Kroefges 2004, 2006), despite their strategic position on the inland and maritime travel-trade routes between the kingdoms of Tehuantepec and Tututepec.

THE SPANISH COLONIAL PERIOD

As noted above, any temporal comparison between the records must also take the retrospective nature of the documents into account: a critical comparison of the Chontal highlands' territorial-narratives further reveals that the Aztec intervention is mostly referenced in the specific context of conflicting heroic traditions, where the Aztec emperor Motecuhzoma or his emissary are diametrically presented vis-à-vis the Chontal culture-hero *Fane Kantsini* ("3 Hummingbird"). This seems to reflect an Early Colonial factional competition, where rival leaders competed for territorial resources while drawing their legitimating narratives from similar Postclassic symbolic figures (Zborover 2008a, 2009a, 2014). Accordingly, by further looking for material correlates to such factional competition, we have to start with the "heroic" representations as adopted and adapted by opposed agents during the Early Colonial period (compare also to Joyce et al. 2004:281–287; McCafferty 2000; Pohl 2003), followed by a detailed comparison of the respective archaeological records in the competing communities—both in the Early Colonial and Late Postclassic periods—in a search for material manifestations of dissonance and differentiation.[32] Because the documented factionalism and identity-building operated along supra-ethnic political divides, material differentials might manifest between neighboring antagonistic Chontal communities while nonetheless showing similarities at the polity level.[33] Such a comparison is, however, beyond the scope of the current project and would have to wait for future regional surveys.

A final illustrative episode of colonialism might help bring some of these aspects into perspective—the Spanish conquest. As undeniable a historical event as this was, the Spaniards appear only parenthetically (if at all) in the Early Colonial territorial-narratives, further supporting the notion that these documents were mostly created for, and circulated within, indigenous interaction spheres (Zborover 2002a, 2008a, 2009a, 2014). At the same time, official documents sent by the Spanish crown and recently found in Zapotitlán's municipal archive clearly show that even the smallest town was connected to the European hegemonic political economy.[34] As noted above, the abandonment of the dispersed settlement pattern in favor of a lower congregated community during the Early Colonial period is evident both in the documentary and the archaeological record. However, such a transition was not reflected in the traditional material culture of the Chontal, which seems to have continued uninterrupted well into the postconquest period. Very few examples of Early

Colonial wheel-thrown, glazed, or *mayólica* pottery were found so far in Zapotitlán, while roof tiles, porcelain, glass, metal objects, and European-introduced animals start to appear only in the Late Colonial and Republican period strata (figure 12.4). Household construction techniques continued using traditional materials and templates, as in fact they did until recently. A survey of the Catholic church grounds (now in ruins) has revealed mostly indigenous wares and a surprising amount of obsidian prismatic blades in the adobe wall matrix.[35]

Such continuities in the local material culture are again paralleled in the coastal Chontal communities (Kroefges 2004) and, as such, further set the Chontalpa apart from contemporaneous indigenous communities in the Isthmus of Tehuantepec and the Soconusco where European artifacts are clearly present in the Early Colonial period (Gasco 1992a, 1993, 1997a; Zeitlin 2005; Zeitlin and Thomas 1997). As with the other cases presented above, however, the absence of material evidence for contact does not necessarily translate to an evidence of absence. Taken together with the dynamic interactions as gleaned through the documents for the Late Postclassic and Early Colonial period, the similarities and differences in the material patterns between the highlands and coastal Chontal communities, as compared to those of neighboring regions, paint a complex picture that, further, makes it hard to dismiss the region as simply geographically marginal or of low socioeconomic status. Instead, the idiosyncratic material traditions of the Chontal might be better explained as a conscious resistance to symbols of foreign influence and a selective control over the rules of engagement (King and Zborover 2010; see also Stein 2002). Indeed, the Chontal rebelled and had to be reconquered several times during the Colonial period (Gerhard 1993:123, 195; Munch 1992), and the Spanish political and religious officials kept complaining about the difficulty of pacifying the highlands.[36]

Such cases of resistance to the materiality of colonial domination have concerned historical archaeologists around the world (Funari et al. 1999a; Hall 1999; Lawrence and Shepherd 2006; Reid and Lane 2004; Schmidt 2006; Stahl 2001). For the New World, several authors (Jordan 2009; Palka 2009; Rubertone 1989, 1996, 2000) have convincingly demonstrated how postconquest indigenous societies were not drawn inevitably toward acculturation through a passive consumption of the material culture of the ostensibly dominant society, but rather actively resisted hegemonic control through selective trade and cultural continuities (see also Joyce et al. 2001 for a prehispanic example). Similarly, although the sparingly decorated Chontal wares may seem today unremarkable in comparison to the surrounding regional and international styles,[37] this in itself made their material tradition distinctive and eventually more enduring than others. Such tensions in the historical archaeology of southern Oaxaca thus reveal a dual narrative of selective interaction and resistance; it challenges derogatory colonialist perspectives of the Chontal as "isolated cave dwellers," and exposes the intricate dialectics between indigenous historiographies and their respective material traditions.

TOWARD AN INCLUSIVE HISTORICAL ARCHAEOLOGY

Although *historical archaeology* is not necessarily a shorter term than *ethnoarchaeo-history* (to paraphrase Bernal's opening quote), it can definitely offer a useful methodological and theoretical canopy for Mesoamerican integrative studies in general and the study of Oaxacan literate societies in particular. As applied here, the starting point for a historical archaeology of southern Oaxaca, as in many other places in Mesoamerica, may be found in the Late Formative period some fifteen hundred years before the Spanish conquest. By focusing on prehispanic and Colonial indigenous territorial-narratives in conjunction with material continuities and change, we are able to move away from the restrictive binary oppositions such as "prehispanic versus historical" and place a new emphasis on indigenous agency and long-term historical trajectory before, during, and after the Spanish conquest (Kepecs and Alexander 2005; Lightfoot 1995; Mitchell and Scheiber 2010; Rubertone 1996, 2000; Silliman 2010; Trigger 1989; Wilson 1993; Zeitlin 2005). Furthermore, the deep roots of indigenous colonialism as gleaned through the southern Oaxacan territorial-narratives is enough to dispel the restrictive definition of a global, post–1500 CE historical archaeology based exclusively on the European colonial encounter (Deetz 1991; Falk 1991; Orser 1996; but see also Funari et al. 1999b; Robertshaw 2004). Even though the eventual impact of the Spanish conquest on the Chontal highlands and its people cannot be denied, so were the colonialist effects of other indigenous hegemonies in the region.

With the field of historical archaeology going "global" (Deetz 1991, 1993:163ff; Falk 1991; Orser 1996), its practitioners can no longer afford to ignore the multitude of subaltern and alternative histories (Orser 2010; Rubertone 1996; Schmidt 2006; Schmidt and Patterson 1995). As demonstrated here and elsewhere, the unique methodology of integrating the past makes historical archaeology particularly suitable for debunking myths derived from the "Colonial library" (Little 1992, 1994; Schmidt 2006; Schmidt and Walz 2007), be they European or indigenous in origin. One of these debunked modern myths should be precisely the monolithic "European-colonizer versus Indigenous-colonized" dichotomy, as we can no longer treat the indigenous as a passive, subdued, homogeneous entity, especially when we consider interregional interactions and factional competition with other indigenous groups and polities (Matthew and Oudijk 2007; McCafferty 2000; Mitchell and Scheiber 2010; Schmidt 2006; Silliman 2010; Stein 2002, 2005; Zborover

2009a, 2014). The Oaxacan indigenous history-makers were equally entangled in ideological power plays and manipulative "historytelling" as any other literary tradition in the world, and this fact alone qualifies historical archaeology to be considered as "one of the most democratic of the social sciences" (Deagan 1991:110).

As such, Mesoamerica has the potential to present us with the most comprehensive instance of historical archaeology in the American continent, through both the archaeological study of its indigenous literate societies and the archaeology of historically documented processes of colonialism, capitalism, and the "global world." Still, historical archaeology in Mexico has been often characterized as descriptive rather than explanatory (Fournier 2003; Gasco et al. 1997), which can be largely explained by its self-imposed temporal and topical confines. Accordingly, instead of using historical archaeology to simply "extend" the prehispanic past (Charlton, Fournier, and Charlton 2009:422), we now need to extend historical archaeology back into that prehispanic past. It is only then that historical archaeologists who work in the area could take advantage of the unique Mesoamerican characteristics of historical indigenous societies, and eventually be able to shape the field's method and theory. By the same token, those investigators of indigenous literate societies should heed historical archaeology's potential for their own research, even if not subscribing to its paradigmatic label.

But the unique integration of material, documentary, and oral narratives appeals not just to us academics. Historical archaeology has recently gone public through the application of critical theory and other applied anthropological approaches that often serve to engage and empower descendent and marginalized communities (Leone 1995, 2007, 2009; Leone and Crosby 1987; Little 1992; Orser 2010; Orser and Fagan 1995; Schmidt 2006; Zborover 2008c, 2014). In Zapotitlán, community-based participatory approaches within the CHAP had resulted in the training of indigenous committees in documentation and management of cultural heritage, the restoration of the historical archive and conservation of several important pictorial and alphabetic documents, and the creation of the first community museum and educational center in the Chontal highlands (figure 12.5). Still, although scholars may continue to argue about the role of historical archaeology as a "laboratory" for anthropological method and theory or its potential for untangling the articulation of materiality and textuality, we found that such academic debates were ultimately of little interest to the Chontal people who collaborated in the project. Because the local audiences were mostly interested in "the (hi)story of the village from its foundation to the present day," in the community museum many of the integrative nuances and open questions presented here had to be glossed over in favor of a coherent culture-historical narrative that is sensitive to indigenous concerns, interests, and benefits, yet is adaptable to accommodate new findings[38] (figure 12.1;

FIGURE 12.5. Elder and young Chontal visitors inspect the archaeological and documentary exhibits at the Community Museum and Educational Center of Zapotitlán.

see also Joyce 2006; Stahl, Mann, and Loren 2004; Trigger 1982; Zborover 2008c, 2014). In such public contexts the diachronic and synchronic complementarity of sources has played its most important role, as the archaeological data filled in temporal and thematic gaps in the historical record and vice versa. Such a particularistic historical archaeology (Deetz 1987:369–370) can further help prevent academic paternalism and dogmatism, and archaeology might yet serve as a "handmaiden to history" as it aids in decolonizing biased historical representations and in generating contextualized local histories (Joyce 2006; Leone 1995; Little 1994; Mitchell and Scheiber 2010; Reid and Lane 2004; Rubertone 1989, 2000; Schmidt and Patterson 1995; Schmidt and Walz 2007).

Although the Chontal presence in the region is not attested for the Formative and Classic periods, the local museumgoers were equally fascinated by these early documentary and material records, as these formed an integral part of their ancestral landscape and contemporary communal territory. Yet another showcase exhibits an important document recently uncovered in the municipal archive, sent to Zapotitlán in 1859 by the then newly elected president Benito Juárez and his cabinet during the turbulent years of the Reform War (1857–1861).[39] This document in turn sparked a heated exchange of post–1910 Revolution oral histories and traditions, shared by the elders with the younger audience. Most interestingly, these stories often pointed to the surrounding archaeological sites as places of temporary refuge from the "invading *carrancistas*" army, adding yet another dimension of hegemonic domination, conflict, and selective resistance that is unlikely to leave many material traces. As such, the community museum represents a space where the emic is actively integrated with the etic, as both are added to the perpetually building corpus of the Chontalpa territorial-narratives in object, text, and voice.[40]

NOTES

1. While apparently not considered relevant in the early days of historical archaeology, it is obvious that historical traditions were recorded and transmitted orally as well as in mnemonic and pictorial devices long before the European arrival to North America. Even now, however, the validity of integrating these with the archaeological record is still being debated by scholars (see Anyon et al. 1997).

2. Moreland (2001:21, 109) has identified these "text-free zones" as artificial constructs where archaeologists are "free" to practice their trade without contradictions from the historical record.

3. See the various articles in Schuyler 1978 as a reflection of this transition from "humanistic" to "scientific" oriented historical archaeology.

4. Orser further insisted that the potential inclusion of archaeologists who work with literate societies in "Central Mexico" within his brand of historical archaeology "does the field a disservice" (Orser 1996:25), and further added that "I have argued in the clearest possible terms why I do not believe Mayanists are historical archaeologists" (194). Nevertheless, Orser seems to have recently taken a more moderate approach to his own restrictive criteria (Orser 2002:xvi, 2004:274, 2010:112).

5. Of those, Janine Gasco's project in Colonial Soconusco (Gasco 1992a) is the one most cited in the North American historical archaeology literature (for example, Gasco 1992b, 1997a; see also Orser and Fagan 1995); however, and as Gasco herself acknowledges, there is little indigenous documentation for the town of Ocelocalco, the focus of her research.

6. The latter's geographical and temporal scope does encompass Colonial-period Mexico (Gasco 1992b) and several Old World pre-Colonial and non-Eurocentric case studies. However, Mesoamerica's indigenous literate societies are still absent from the discussion.

7. Orser and Fagan clearly illustrate this point by stating that "the use of the term *post-prehistoric* [in the field's definition] signifies that historical archaeology finds much of its subject matter in those places that Europeans visited and colonized. Thus, the term *post-prehistoric* stands in contrast to *prehistoric*, and is meant to suggest that the world was a different place after Europeans took Western culture to various places of the globe" (Orser and Fagan 1995:19, italics theirs).

8. The reasons for the latter are multiple, but partly have to do with the general influence of North American method and theory on Mexican scholarship, as well as the fact that many of the early archaeologists working on Colonial archaeology in Mexico were North Americans (Charlton and Fournier 2008). Although the oft-cited B.A. thesis "Arqueología Historica: Un Paradigma de Investigacion" (Besso-Oberto 1977) is considered as one of the early systematic uses of the term in Mexican archaeology, the author was drawing his definition of historical archaeology from North American scholars, Ivor Noël Hume (1969) and Stanley South (1977). And although Besso-Oberto still considered the Middle and Late Postclassic periods as part of the "Período Histórico de México," his research still focused primarily on Colonial-period archaeology and documentation.

9. Mexican Federal law (Cámara de Diputados 2014) defines *archaeological monuments* as ones that "predate the establishment of the Hispanic culture in the national territory"; and *historical monuments* and *documents* as those that postdate it, specifically from the sixteenth to the nineteenth centuries (articles 28, 35, and 36, my translation). This might also explain why so little historical and industrial archaeologies have been carried out so far for the Mexican Republican period (1821–present), which is completely excluded under these narrow definitions.

10. *Contra* Schuyler (1970:84, see above), the most rigorous integrative research to date is being conducted in the Maya area, both due to the abundance of available hieroglyphic texts as well as the long trajectory of academic interest in the region (see for example Carmack and Weeks 1981; Chase et al. 2008; Fash and Sharer 1991; Houston 1989; Rice and Rice 2004).

11. As far as I know, the Mexican ethnohistorian Eduardo Corona Sánchez (1998, 2001) is unique in distinguishing between *arqueología histórica*, *arqueología novohispana*, and *arqueohistoria*, while advocating the study of indigenous cultural continuities between the prehispanic and Colonial periods. Unfortunately, this interesting categorization was not developed much further and has so far made little impact on the field of historical archaeology.

12. For an overview of the field's history and key projects in Mexico, see Charlton, Fournier, and Charlton 2009; Charlton and Fournier 2008; Fernández Dávila and Gómez Serafín 1998; Fowler 2009; Hernández Pons 1998; and Palka 2009.

13. As such, the material study of the so-called post-1500 modern world should be considered *a branch* of historical archaeology only if it systematically involves the integration of sources. Other alternatives are to qualify or relabel the existing approaches according to temporal and topical categories, such as with "historical archaeology of capitalism" (Leone 1995; and see Funari 1999). By the same token, it is hard to see why the archaeology of "disenfranchised" people and others who are "invisible" or "silent" in the documentary record, regardless of how recently they lived, should be considered "historical" if only their material culture is being considered (Hicks and Beaudry 2006:2-3; Majewski and Gaimster 2009:xvii).

14. In this regard, the "fatherly counsel" of Edward Jelks, the first president of the North American Society for Historical Archaeology, still echoes true after almost half a century: "Historical archaeology has much to gain in the long run from encouraging a spirit of concerted, interdisciplinary, international cooperation; it stands to lose much if partisan competition for franchise rights to the field become overly biased or aggressive" (Jelks 1968:3).

15. The recently reported divinatory codex from San Bartolo Yautepec (Doesburg and Urcid 2009), which might have been composed in the nearby town of Nejapa during the Late Postclassic, demonstrates the presence of this literary tradition in an area traditionally occupied by Zapotec, Chontal, and Mixe people.

16. The most common use of phonetic complements in the pictorial documents is with homonyms in the construction of topoglyphs, or pictorial place names. The *Lienzo de Tecciztlan y Tequatepec* topoglyphs, for example, incorporated Nahuatl phonetic elements in the topoglyphs (Zborover 2002a). The longest Colonial alphabetic text in Chontal currently known, the *Jilotepequillo Manuscript*, is a thirty-five-page manuscript relating retrospectively to the formation of the highlands sociopolitical landscape in prehispanic times (Zborover 2008a).

17. Among others, Galloway (2006), Lightfoot (1995), Navarrete (1997), Stahl (1993), Trigger (1978, 1982), and Wood (1990) have already stressed the importance of using source criticism in the analysis of historical documents for archaeological purposes.

18. The *Lienzo de Jilotepequillo*, for example, has three distinct phases of explanatory glosses on the primary pictorial content, while the ongoing and shifting oral interpretations of the town people have added yet another annotative stratum. Perhaps the most striking example of a contemporary pictorial-oral juxtaposition we encountered in the CHAP is the territorial-narrative of the late Florencio Aparicio Hernandez, the *linnoyáhaba cuento* (chronicler/storyteller) of San Matias Petacaltepec (Zborover 2006, 2008a, 2009a, 2014).

19. In the "living culture" context of the CHAP, the collection of data sets often overlapped; for example, oral traditions were recorded during archaeological surveys and documents were often revealed to us while analyzing artifacts in the communities. However, I have attempted to keep the subsequent analytical and interpretative procedures as independent as possible.

20. In the CHAP, most of the oral traditions were collected by students trained in ethnographic fieldwork, Gabriela González (ENAH) and Veronica Pacheco (UCLA). The archaeological and historical data collection and analysis were primarily conducted by the author in frequent consultation with fellow archaeologists and historians, while the interpretation of all three data sets was conducted by the author. Since my primary training is as an archaeologist, this record has been inevitably studied more thoroughly than the others and further introduces a heuristic imbalance to this research.

21. Compare de La Cruz (2008), Kroefges (1998, 2004), Odena Güemes (1997), and Zborover (2002a, 2006, 2014) for further discussion. Although some of these interpretations differ in the identification of the *cabecera* depicted in the center of the document, they all seem to agree on identifying the "Zapote-tree hill" topoglyph and its accompanying *tçanpotitla* gloss with the Chontal village of Santa María Zapotitlán, municipality of S.M. Ecatepec, district of S.C. Yautepec.

22. One of the most instructive examples is the toponyms that appear on the contemporary INEGI topographic maps, which often serve as the basis for scholarly reconstruction of documents. Although these were recorded by INEGI officials in the 1980s from oral information in the village, the highly selective toponyms often reflect the biases and limitations of the original survey strategy; in several toponymic surveys conducted around Zapotitlán, we found a 1:8 ratio between the toponyms on the 1:50,000 maps and other orally preserved names still known for the same area (Zborover 2007, 2014).

23. Although decontextualized artifacts are often criticized as inadequate for the purposes of archaeological interpretation, the number and variety of these "unique" artifacts as compared to similar ones collected during the archaeological project was enough to justify their study, especially for the purpose of establishing cross-ties and external contacts. Though the artifacts are decontextualized, the people we interviewed were often able to remember the exact collected provenience of these artifacts.

24. In the *Relaciones Geográficas de Guatulco* we read that "y éste que era gobernador nombraba, para cada pueblo y barrio, un principal que les mandase, y un tequitato que recogiese los tributos; porque cada pueblo estaba repartido en barrios, y cada barrio tenía su recogedor de los tributos, al que llamaban tequitlato" (Acuña 1984a:189).

25. The second group founded the neighboring community of San José Chiltepec, where we recorded parallel foundation narratives.

26. For a detailed discussion of the "predatory state model" debate, compare Balkansky 1998, 2002; Feinman and Nicholas 1990; Joyce 2014; Joyce et al. 1998; Sherman et al. 2010; Spencer and Redmond 1997; Spencer et al. 2008; Workinger 2002; Workinger and Joyce 2009; R. Zeitlin 1990, 1993; and Zeitlin and Joyce 1999, among others.

27. There are other "Chiltepecs" in Oaxaca, and locally collected toponyms might reveal additional "hill of chile plants." Whittaker (1980:129), for example, suggested identifying the "chile plant" topoglyph with the town of Chilateca in the southern Oaxaca Valley (see also Marcus 1976:129–130). Based on similarities to plants depicted on other monuments in Monte Albán, Javier Urcid (personal communication, January 2014) further doubts that the "conquest slab" in fact depicts a chili pepper. Most recently, Urcid and Joyce (2014:157–166) proposed that the slabs represented named individuals from Monte Albán rather than distinct communities under its influence.

28. The Mixtec conquest of the Central Coast might have dated to the Early Postclassic, because Jansen (1998:102) tentatively identified the "Hill of the Raven" topoglyph

in page 48-II of the Codex Nuttall with Cacalotepec, close to Huatulco. As I argued elsewhere (Zborover 2002a, 2005, 2006), this same Postclassic island site might also be represented as a subject town to Huatulco in the *Lienzo de Tecciztlan y Tequatepec* (figure 12.2F6).

29. In addition to the documents mentioned above with regards to Zapotitlán, other references to the Aztec presence in the region are found in the *títulos primordiales* of Santa María Ecatepec dated to 1613 (S. M. Ecatepec Archivo Municipal, Expediente Agrario Número 43/95) and associated documents, as well as a 1941 copy of a "colonial codex" from San Miguel Ecatepec (Ruiz Medrano 2010:1, 197–199).

30. The Chontal were quite renowned for the procurement of these natural dyes up until recent times (Bartolomé and Barabas 2006a; Alejandro de Ávila Blomberg, personal communication, 2012). As for precious metals, the Pochutec of Huatulco reported in the *Relaciones Geográficas* that they obtained the gold dust paid as tribute to Tututepec in prehispanic times from the highland Chontal (Acuña 1984a:191), and the Colonial records further indicate tribute paid in gold to the Spanish crown (Paso y Troncoso 1905). In the village of Zapotitlán, we have recorded a cross-shaped petroglyph quite similar to the Aztec glyph for gold.

31. Tehuantepec and Tututepec received their obsidian from the closer Orizaba source as well as from Pachuca (Levine 2007; Workinger 2002; Zeitlin 1982).

32. It further seems that several of the contemporary intercommunity territorial conflicts in the Chontal highlands are a direct transformation of this Early Colonial factionalism as, for example, the land litigation between Zapotitlán and Jilotepequillo (Zborover 2008b). Interestingly, the respective oral traditions regarding Fane Kantsini in these villages are similarly conflicting: although he is "remembered" in Jilotepequillo as the hero king who saved the Chontal people from their enemies (Bartolomé and Barabas 2006b), in Zapotitlán (the Aztec faction) he is often portrayed as an evil sorcerer who kidnapped and ate children.

33. In the historical archaeology literature, Jones (1999), McGuire (1982), and Orser and Fagan (1995) indeed caution against taking claims of ethnicity in the documents at face value, but rather question the dynamic processes in the construction of such identities through further comparisons and contrasts with the archaeological record (see also King and Zborover 2010).

34. The earliest preserved document is "Carta de 1706 que envía el virrey al gobernador, alcaldes, rectores, principales común y naturales del pueblo sobre impuestos y obligaciones" (Santa María Zapotitlán Archivo Municipal, Gobierno: Cartas, Caja 1, Vol. 6).

35. This immense adobe structure finally collapsed in the 1950s, although its purpose and dating could have been determined from oral histories, old photographs, and the salvaged religious paraphernalia such as the altar, icons, and the church bells. It is interesting that this and other Early Colonial churches in the highlands are positioned in locations

where the prominent sacred mountain *juala lixcomoh* ("Cerro Señorita") was clearly visible to the worshipers. This might reflect the familiar Colonial pattern of superimposing Catholic churches over indigenous temples.

36. In the *Libro de las Tasaciones*, the sixteenth century *corregidor* for the highlands informed his superiors that "[Los] Chontales en la Provincia de Oaxaca, no han estado hasta aquí tan pacíficos y de asiento como convenía y que viven en tierra áspera y estéril y no están industriados en las cosas de Nuestra Fe Católica, como conviene que lo estén para que sean cristianos" (González de Cossío 1952:351).

37. Although surface and plastic decorations are rare, the technological skill of the ancient Chontal potters is evident in the varieties of fine pastes, thin-walled vessels, and controlled differential firing.

38. Hodder similarly notes that "subordinate groups who wish to be involved in archaeological interpretation need to be provided with the means and mechanisms for interacting with the archaeological past in different ways. This is not a matter of popularising the past, but of transforming the relations of production of archaeological knowledge into more democratic structures" (Hodder 1995:161).

39. The dispatch further references the famous Reform Laws and the bloody war that followed them: "el suelo de ese estado manchado con la sangre de los mexicanos, profusamente derramada en casi todo el territorio nacional a caso no hay un solo pueblo a donde la reacción no haya sacrificado alguna víctima" (Santa María Zapotitlán Archivo Municipal, Gobierno: Oficios y circulares, Caja 5, Vol. 55).

40. I would like to thank all of our Chontal collaborators and friends in Santa María Zapotitlán, San Lorenzo Jilotepequillo, San Matias Petacaltepec, and Santo Domingo Chontecomatlan, and especially to Mateo Cruz Ramos and family, Natán Martínez Sánchez, Florencio Aparicio, and Paul Turner; the INAH Consejo de Arqueología in Mexico City and the Centro INAH Oaxaca helped with permits and other support; FAMSI and the University of Calgary provided the funding for the project; the construction of the communitary museum was funded by the Mexican PACMYC program; the Biblioteca Burgoa, Oaxaca, and ADABI, Mexico performed the document restoration and organization in Zapotitlán; the osteological analysis was conducted by Martha Elena Alfaro Castro (INAH Oaxaca Center), and the stable isotope analysis was conducted by Stephen Taylor and Andrea Waters-Rist (University of Calgary, Canada) and Michael Joachimski (University of Erlangen, Germany); Verónica Pacheco, Juan Jarquín, Gabriela González, Peter C. Kroefges, Ulises Chávez, Ryan Espersen, and Marco Ortega participated in various seasons of the project; I would finally like to thank Geoffrey McCafferty, Arthur Joyce, my colleagues at the Center for U.S.-Mexican Studies, UCSD, as well as two anonymous reviewers, who all read earlier versions of this chapter and helped improve it.

REFERENCES

Acuña, René, ed. 1984a. *Relaciones Geograficas del Siglo XVI: Antequera*. vol. 1. Mexico City: Universidad Nacional Autónoma de Mexico.

Acuña, René, ed. 1984b. *Relaciones Geograficas del Siglo XVI: Antequera*. vol. 2. Mexico City: Universidad Nacional Autónoma de Mexico.

Alexander, Rani T. 1997. "Haciendas and Economic Change in Yucatán: Entrepreneurial Strategies in the Parroquia de Yaxcabá, 1775–1850." *Journal of Archaeological Method and Theory* 4 (3/4):331–351. http://dx.doi.org/10.1007/BF02428067.

Andrén, Anders. 1998. *Between Artifacts and Texts: Historical Archaeology in Global Perspective*. New York: Plenum Press. http://dx.doi.org/10.1007/978-1-4757-9409-0.

Anyon, R., T. J. Ferguson, L. Jackson, L. Lane, and P. Vicenti. 1997. "Native American Oral Tradition and Archaeology: Issues of Structure, Relevance and Respect." In *Native Americans and Archaeologists: Stepping Stones to Common Ground*, ed. N. Swidler, K. E. Dongoske, R. Anyon, and A. S. Downer, 77–87. Walnut Creek, CA: AltaMira Press.

Baerreis, David A. 1961. "The Ethnohistoric Approach and Archaeology." *Ethnohistory* 8 (1):49–77. http://dx.doi.org/10.2307/480348.

Balkansky, Andrew K. 1998. "Origin and Collapse of Complex Societies in Oaxaca (Mexico): Evaluating the Era from 1965 to the Present." *Journal of World Prehistory* 12 (4):451–493. http://dx.doi.org/10.1023/A:1022870516264.

Balkansky, Andrew K. 2002. *The Sola Valley and the Monte Albán State: A Study of Zapotec Imperial Expansion*. Memoir 36. Ann Arbor: Museum of Anthropology, University of Michigan.

Bartel, Brad. 1985. "Comparative Historical Archaeology and Archaeology Theory." In *Comparative Studies in the Archaeology of Colonialism*, ed. Stephen L. Dyson, 8–28. Oxford: BAR International Series 233.

Bartolomé, Miguel, and Alicia Barabas. 2006a. "Historia Chontal." In *Historia y Etnografía entre los Chontales de Oaxaca*, ed. Andrés Oseguera, 17–39. Mexico City: INAH.

Bartolomé, Miguel, and Alicia Barabas. 2006b. "Narrativa Chontal: La Leyenda del Rey Fane Kantsini." In *Historia y Etnografía entre los Chontales de Oaxaca*, ed. Andrés Oseguera, 175–181. Mexico City: INAH.

Beaudry, Mary C., ed. 1993. *Documentary Archaeology in the New World*. Cambridge: Cambridge University Press.

Beaudry, Mary, Lauren J. Cook, and Stephen Mrozowski. 1996. "Artifacts and Active Voices: Material Culture as Social Discourse." In *Images of the Recent Past: Readings in Historical Archaeology*, ed. Charles Orser, 273–310. Walnut Creek, CA: AltaMira Press.

Beck, Wendy, and Margaret Somerville. 2005. "Conversations between Disciplines: Historical Archaeology and Oral History at Yarrawarra." *World Archaeology* 37 (3):468–483. http://dx.doi.org/10.1080/00438240500204403.

Berdan, Frances, Richard Blanton, Elizabeth Hill Boone, Mary G. Hodge, Michael E. Smith, and Emily Umberger, eds. 1996. *Aztec Imperial Strategies*. Washington, DC: Dumbarton Oaks.

Berlin, Heinrich. 1958. "El Glifo 'Emblema' En Las Inscripciones Mayas." *Journal de la Société des Americanistes* 47 (1):111–119. http://dx.doi.org/10.3406/jsa.1958.1153.

Bernal, Ignacio. 1962. "Archaeology and Written Sources." In *Akten des 34 Internationalen Amerikanistenkongresses*, 18–25. Vienna: Verlag Ferdinand Berger.

Besso-Oberto, Humberto. 1977. "Arqueología Histórica: Una Paradigma de Investigación." Unpublished BA Thesis, Escuela Nacional de Antropología e Historia, Mexico City.

Binford, Lewis. 1977. "Historical Archaeology: Is It Historical or Archaeological?" In *Historical Archaeology and the Importance of Material Things*, ed. L. Ferguson, 13–22. Tucson, AZ: Society for Historical Archaeology.

Boone, Elizabeth Hill. 2000. *Stories in Red and Black: Pictorial Histories of the Aztecs and Mixtecs*. Austin: University of Texas Press.

Boone, Elizabeth Hill, and Walter D. Mignolo, eds. 1994. *Writing without Words: Alternative Literacies in Mesoamerica and the Andes*. Durham, NC: Duke University Press.

Brambila, Rosa, and María Rosa Avilez. 1998. "Testimonios Documentales y Materiales del Uso Continúo del Territorio en Jilotepec Durante el Siglo XVI." In *Memoria del Primer Congreso Nacional de Arqueología Historica*, ed. Enrique Fernández Dávila and Susana Gómez Serafín, 381–388. Mexico City: CONACULTA/INAH.

Brockington, Donald L., María Jorrin, and Robert Long. 1974. *The Oaxaca Coast Project Reports: Parts I and II*. Nashville: Vanderbilt University Publications in Anthropology, No. 8.

Burgoa, Francisco de. (Original work published 1674) 1934. *Geográfica Descripción, tomo II*. Mexico: Archivo General de la Nación.

Byland, Bruce E., and John M.D. Pohl. 1994. *In the Realm of Eight Deer: The Archaeology of the Mixtec Codices*. Norman: University of Oklahoma Press.

Cámara de Diputados del H. Congreso de la Unión. (1972) 2014. "Ley Federal Sobre Monumentos y Zonas Arqueológicos, Artísticos e Históricos." http://www.diputados.gob.mx/LeyesBiblio/pdf/131_130614.pdf, accessed June 2014.

Carmack, Robert M., and John M. Weeks. 1981. "The Archaeology and Ethnohistory of Utatlán: A Conjunctive Approach." *American Antiquity* 46 (2):323–341. http://dx.doi.org/10.2307/280211.

Carrasco, Pedro. 1960. *Pagan Rituals and Beliefs among the Chontal Indians of Oaxaca, Mexico*. University of California Anthropological Records, 87–117. Berkeley: University of California Press.

Carver, Martin. 2002. "Marriage of True Minds: Archaeology with Texts." In *Archaeology: The Widening Debate*, ed. Barry Cunliffe, Wendy Davies, and Colin Renfrew, 465–496. Oxford: Oxford University Press.

Caso, Alfonso. 1947. "Calendario y Escritura de las Antiguas Culturas de Monte Albán." In *Obras Completas de Miguel Othón de Mendizábal*, vol. 1, 15–143. Mexico City.

Charlton, Thomas. 1969. "Ethnohistory and Archaeology: Post-Conquest Aztec Sites." *American Antiquity* 34 (3):286–294. http://dx.doi.org/10.2307/278411.

Charlton, Thomas. 1972. "Population Trends in the Teotihuacan Valley, A.D. 1400–1969." *World Archaeology* 4 (1):106–123. http://dx.doi.org/10.1080/00438243.1972.9 979523.

Charlton, Thomas. 1981. "Archaeology, Ethnohistory, and Ethnography: Interpretive Interfaces." In *Advances in Archaeological Method and Theory*, vol. 4. ed. Michael B. Schiffer, 129–176. New York: Academic Press.

Charlton, Thomas. 1991. "Land Tenure and Agricultural Production in the Otumba Region, 1785–1803." In *Land and Politics in the Valley of Mexico: A Two Thousand Year Perspective*, ed. H. R. Harvey, 223–263. Albuquerque: University of New Mexico Press.

Charlton, Thomas. 2002. "Aztec Archaeology." In *Encyclopedia of Historical Archaeology*, ed. Charles E. Orser, 47–49. New York: Routledge.

Charlton, Thomas. 2003. "On Agrarian Landholdings in Post-Conquest Rural Mesoamerica." *Ethnohistory* 50 (1):221–230. http://dx.doi.org/10.1215/00141801-50-1-221.

Charlton, Thomas H., and Cynthia L. Otis Charlton. 1998. "Continuidad y Cambio Después de la Conquista: Hallazgos Recientes en la Ciudad-Estado Azteca de Otumba, Estado de Mexico." In *Memoria del Primer Congreso Nacional de Arqueología Historica*, ed. Enrique Fernández Dávila and Susana Gómez Serafín, 458–467. Mexico City: CONACULTA/INAH.

Charlton, Thomas, and Patricia Fournier. 2008. "Historical Archaeology in Mexico." In *Encyclopedia of Archaeology*, ed. Deborah M. Pearsall, 182–192. San Diego: Academic Press. http://dx.doi.org/10.1016/B978-012373962-9.00141-2.

Charlton, Thomas H., Patricia Fournier, and Cynthia L. Otis Charlton. 2009. "Historical Archaeology in Central and Northern Mesoamerica: Development and Current Status." In *International Handbook of Historical Archaeology*, ed. Teresita Majewski and David Gaimster, 409–428. New York: Springer.

Chase, Arlen F., Diane Z. Chase, and Rafael Cobos. 2008. "Jeroglíficos y Arqueología Maya: ¿Colusión o Colisión?" *Mayeb* 20:5–21.

Cleland, Charles E. 2001. "Historical Archaeology Adrift?" *Historical Archaeology* 35 (2):1–8.

Códice Ramírez. 1979. *Relación del Origen de los Indios que Habitan esta Nueva España Según sus Historias. Manuscrito del Siglo XVI Intitulado*. Mexico: Editorial Innovación.

Connah, Graham. 2007. "Historical Archaeology in Africa: An Appropriate Concept?" *African Archaeological Review* 24 (1-2):35–40. http://dx.doi.org/10.1007/s10437 -007-9014-9.

Corona Sánchez, Eduardo. 1998. "Arqueología Novohispana: La Arqueología Colonial." In *Memoria del Primer Congreso Nacional de Arqueología Histórica*, ed. Enrique Fernández Dávila and Susana Gómez Serafín, 85–92. Mexico City: CONACULTA/INAH.

Corona Sánchez, Eduardo. 2001. "Arqueología Histórica, Arqueología Novohispana y Arqueohistoria." In *Antología de Pasado: Una Mirada a la Memoria del Futuro*, ed. Jesús Nava Rivero, 27–39. Mexico City: INAH.

de La Cruz, Víctor. 2008. *Mapas Genealógicos del Istmo Oaxaqueño*. Oaxaca, Mexico: Coleccion Diálogos.

Deagan, Kathleen. 1982. "Avenues of Inquiry in Historical Archaeology." In *Advances in Archaeological Method and Theory*, vol. 5. ed. Michael B. Schiffer, 151–177. New York: Academic Press.

Deagan, Kathleen. 1988. "Neither History nor Prehistory: The Questions That Count in Historical Archaeology." *Historical Archaeology* 22 (1): 7–12.

Deagan, Kathleen. 1991. "Historical Archaeology's Contribution to Our Understanding of Early America." In *Historical Archaeology in Global Perspective*, ed. Lisa Falk, 97–112. Washington, DC: Smithsonian Institution Press.

Deetz, James. 1977. *In Small Things Forgotten*. New York: Anchor Press.

Deetz, James. 1987. "Scientific Humanism and Humanistic Science: A Plea for Paradigmatic Pluralism in Historical Archaeology." In *Mirror and Metaphor: Material and Social Constructions of Reality*, ed. Daniel W. Ingersoll, Jr., and Gordon Bronitski, 367–380. Lanham, MD: University Press of America.

Deetz, James. 1988. "American Historical Archeology: Methods and Results." *Science* 239 (4838):362–367. http://dx.doi.org/10.1126/science.239.4838.362.

Deetz, James. 1991. "Archaeological Evidence of Sixteenth- and Seventeenth-Century Encounters." In *Historical Archaeology in Global Perspective*, ed. Lisa Falk, 1–9. Washington, DC: Smithsonian Institution Press.

Deetz, James. 1993. *Flowerdew Hundred: The Archaeology of a Virginia Plantation, 1619–1864*. Charlottesville: University Press of Virginia.

Doesburg, Sebastián van, and Javier Urcid. 2009. "Dos Fragmentos de un Nuevo Códice en San Bartolo Yautepec, Oaxaca." Presentation given at the 7th International Festival of Organs and Ancient Music. Oaxaca: Biblioteca Francisco de Burgoa.

Driscoll, Stephen T. 2010. "Scottish Historical Archaeology: International Agendas and Local Politics." *International Journal of Historical Archaeology* 14 (3):442–462. http://dx.doi.org/10.1007/s10761-010-0115-9.

Fabian, Johannes. 1983. *Time and the Other: How Anthropology Makes its Object*. New York: Columbia University Press.

Falk, Lisa, ed. 1991. *Historical Archaeology in Global Perspective*. Washington, DC: Smithsonian Institution Press.

Farnsworth, Paul, and Jack S. Williams, eds. 1992. "The Archaeology of the Spanish Colonial and Mexican Republican Periods." *Historical Archaeology* Columbian Quincentenary Issue 26(1).

Fash, William L., and Robert J. Sharer. 1991. "Sociopolitical Developments and Methodological Issues at Copan, Honduras: A Conjunctive Perspective." *Latin American Antiquity* 2 (2):166–187. http://dx.doi.org/10.2307/972276.

Feinman, Gary. 1997. "Thoughts on New Approaches to Combining the Archaeological and Historical Records." *Journal of Archaeological Method and Theory* 4 (3/4):367–377. http://dx.doi.org/10.1007/BF02428069.

Feinman, Gary, and Linda Nicholas. 1993. "Shell-Ornament Production in Ejutla: Implications for Highland-Coastal Interaction in Ancient Oaxaca." *Ancient Mesoamerica* 4 (01):103–119. http://dx.doi.org/10.1017/S095653610000081X.

Fernández Dávila, Enrique, and Susana Gómez Serafín. 1988. *Arqueología de Huatulco*. Mexico City: INAH.

Fernández Dávila, Enrique, and Susana Gómez Serafín, eds. 1998. *Memoria del Primer Congreso Nacional de Arqueología Historica*. Mexico City: CONACULTA/INAH.

Fontana, Bernard. 1965. "On the Meaning of Historic Sites Archaeology." *American Antiquity* 31 (1):61–65. http://dx.doi.org/10.2307/2694022.

Fournier, Patricia. 2003. "Historical Archaeology in Mexico: A Reappraisal." *SAA Archaeological Record, Special Issue on Latin American Historical Archaeology* 3 (4):18–19.

Fournier-García, Patricia, and Fernando A. Miranda-Flores. 1992. "Historic Sites Archaeology in Mexico." *Historical Archaeology* 26 (1):75–83.

Fowler, William. 2009. "Historical Archaeology in Yucatan and Central America." In *International Handbook of Historical Archaeology*, ed. Teresita Majewski and David Gaimster, 429–447. New York: Springer. http://dx.doi.org/10.1007/978-0-387-72071-5_25.

Funari, Pedro Paulo A. 1999. "Historical Archaeology from a World Perspective." In *Historical Archaeology: Back from the Edge*, ed. Pedro Paulo A. Funari, Martin Hall, and Siân Jones, 37–66. London: Routledge.

Funari, Pedro Paulo A., Martin Hall, and Siân Jones, eds. 1999a. *Historical Archaeology: Back from the Edge*. London: Routledge.

Funari, Pedro Paulo A., Siân Jones, and Martin Hall. 1999b. "Introduction: Archaeology in History." In *Historical Archaeology: Back from the Edge*, ed. Pedro Paulo A. Funari, Martin Hall, and Siân Jones, 1–20. London: Routledge.

Galloway, Patricia. 2006. "Material Culture and Text: Exploring the Spaces Within and Between." In *Historical Archaeology*, ed. Martin Hall and Stephen W. Silliman, 42–64. Malden, MA: Blackwell Publishing.

Gasco, Janine. 1992a. "Material Culture and Colonial Indian Society in Southern Mesoamerica: The View from Coastal Chiapas, Mexico." *Historical Archaeology* 26 (1):67–74.

Gasco, Janine. 1992b. "Documentary and Archaeological Evidence for Household Differentiation." In *Text-Aided Archaeology*, ed. Barbara J. Little, 83–94. Boca Raton: CRC Press.

Gasco, Janine. 1993. "Socioeconomic Change within Native Society in Colonial Soconusco, New Spain." In *Ethnohistory and Archaeology: Approaches to Postcontact Change in the Americas*, ed. J. Daniel Rogers and Samuel M. Wilson, 163–180. New York: Plenum Press. http://dx.doi.org/10.1007/978-1-4899-1115-5_10.

Gasco, Janine. 1997a. "Consolidation of the Colonial Regime: Native Society in Western Central America." *Historical Archaeology* 31 (1):55–63.

Gasco, Janine. 1997b. "Survey and Excavation of Invisible Sites in the Mesoamerican Lowlands." In *Approaches to the Historical Archaeology of Mexico, Central & South America*, ed. Janine Gasco, Greg Charles Smith, and Patricia Fournier García, 41–48. Los Angeles: The Institute of Archaeology, UCLA.

Gasco, Janine, Greg Charles Smith, and Patricia Fournier-García. 1997. "Introduction." In *Approaches to the Historical Archaeology of Mexico, Central & South America*, ed. Janine Gasco, Greg Charles Smith, and Patricia Fournier García, 1–4. Los Angeles: The Institute of Archaeology, UCLA.

Gay, José Antonio. (Original work published 1881) 1986. *Historia de Oaxaca*. *"Colección 'Sepan cuantos,' No. 373*. Mexico City: Editorial Porrúa.

Gerhard, Peter. 1993. *A Guide to the Historical Geography of New Spain*. Norman: University of Oklahoma Press.

Gómez Serafín, Susana, and Enrique Fernández Dávila. 2007. *Las Cerámicas Coloniales del ex Convento de Santo Domingo de Oaxaca: Pasado y Presente de una Tradición*. Mexico City: INAH.

González de Cossío, Francisco, ed. 1952. *Libro de las Tasaciones de Pueblos de la Nueva España, Siglo XVI*. Mexico City: Archivo General de la Nación.

Halsall, Guy. 1997. "Archaeology and Historiography." In *Companion to Historiography*, ed. Michael Bentley, 807–829. London: Routledge.

Hall, Martin. 1999. "Subaltern Voices? Finding the Spaces between Things and Words." In *Historical Archaeology: Back from the Edge*, ed. Pedro Paulo A. Funari, Martin Hall, and Siân Jones, 193–203. London: Routledge.

Hamann, Byron. 2002. "Writing." In *Encyclopedia of Historical Archaeology*, ed. Charles E. Orser, 651–654. New York: Routledge.

Henige, David. 1985. *Oral Historiography*. New York: Longman.

Hernández Pons, Elsa. 1998. "Arqueología Histórica en México: Antecedentes y Propuestas." In *Memoria del Primer Congreso Nacional de Arqueología Historica*, ed. Enrique Fernández Dávila and Susana Gómez Serafín, 1–26. Mexico City: CONACULTA/INAH.

Hicks, Dan, and Mary C. Beaudry. 2006. "Introduction: The Place of Historical Archaeology." In *The Cambridge Companion to Historical Archaeology*, ed. Dan Hicks and Mary C. Beaudry, 1–9. New York: Cambridge University Press.

Hodder, Ian. 1987. *Archaeology as Long-Term History*. Cambridge: Cambridge University Press.

Hodder, Ian. 1995. *Theory and Practice in Archaeology*. London: Routledge.

Hodge, Mary G. 1998. "Archaeological Views of Aztec Culture." *Journal of Archaeological Research* 6 (3): 197–238. http://dx.doi.org/10.1023/A:1022876304931.

Houston, Stephen D. 1989. "Archaeology and Maya Writing." *Journal of World Prehistory* 3 (1):1–32. http://dx.doi.org/10.1007/BF00996244.

Howell, Martha, and Walter Prevenier, eds. 2001. *From Reliable Sources: An Introduction to Historical Methods*. Ithaca: Cornell University Press.

Jansen, Maarten. 1979. "Apoala y su Importancia para la Interpretación de los Códices Vindobonensis y Nuttall." In *Actes du XLII Congres International des Americanistes, Vol. VII*, 161–172. Paris: Société des Américanistes.

Jansen, Maarten. 1990. "The Search for History in the Mixtec Codices." *Ancient Mesoamerica* 1 (1):99–112. http://dx.doi.org/10.1017/S0956536100000122.

Jansen, Maarten. 1998. "Monte Albán y Zaachila en los Códices Mixtecos." In *The Shadow of Monte Albán: Politics and Historiography in Postclassic Oaxaca, Mexico*, ed. Maarten Jansen, Michel Oudijk, and Peter Kröfges, 67–122. Leiden: CNWS.

Jelks, Edward. 1968. "Observations of the Scope of Historical Archaeology." *Historical Archaeology* 2:1–3.

Johnson, Matthew H. 1999. "Rethinking Historical Archaeology." In *Historical Archaeology: Back from the Edge*, ed. Pedro Paulo A. Funari, Martin Hall, and Siân Jones, 23–36. London: Routledge.

Jones, Siân. 1999. "Historical Categories and the Praxis of Identity: The Interpretation of Ethnicity in Historical Archaeology." In *Historical Archaeology: Back from the Edge*, ed. Pedro Paulo A. Funari, Martin Hall, and Siân Jones, 219–232. London: Routledge.

Jordan, Kurt A. 2009. "Colonies, Colonialism, and Cultural Entanglement: The Archaeology of Postcolumbian Intercultural Relations." In *International Handbook of Historical Archaeology*, ed. Teresita Majewski and David Gaimster, 31–49. New York: Springer. http://dx.doi.org/10.1007/978-0-387-72071-5_3.

Joyce, Arthur A., Marcus Winter, and Raymond G. Mueller. 1998. *Arqueología de la Costa de Oaxaca: Asentamientos del Periodo Formativo en el Valle del Río Verde Inferior*. Oaxaca, Mexico: Centro INAH Oaxaca.

Joyce, Arthur A., Andrew G. Workinger, Byron Hamann, Peter Kroefges, Maxine Oland, and Stacie M. King. 2004. "Lord 8 Deer 'Jaguar Claw' and the Land of the Sky: The Archaeology and History of Tututepec." *Latin American Antiquity* 15 (3):273–297. http://dx.doi.org/10.2307/4141575.

Joyce, Arthur A., Laura Arnaud Bustamante, and Marc N. Levine. 2001. "Commoner Power: A Case Study from the Classic Period 'Collapse' on the Oaxaca Coast." *Journal of Archaeological Method and Theory* 8 (4):343–385. http://dx.doi.org/10.1023/A:101378 6700137.

Joyce, Rosemary. 2006. "Writing Historical Archaeology." In *The Cambridge Companion to Historical Archaeology*, ed. Dan Hicks and Mary C. Beaudry, 48–65. New York: Cambridge University Press.

Kepecs, Susan. 1997. "Introduction to New Approaches to Combining the Archaeological and Historical Records." *Journal of Archaeological Method and Theory* 4 (3/4):193–198. http://dx.doi.org/10.1007/BF02428060.

Kepecs, Susan, and Rani T. Alexander, eds. 2005. *The Postclassic to Spanish-Era Transition in Mesoamerica: Archaeological Perspectives*. Albuquerque: University of New Mexico Press.

King, Stacie, and Danny Zborover. 2010. "Garrisons, Forts, Hideouts, Rancherías, or Shrines? Interdisciplinary Research on Zapotec, Mixe, and Chontal Sites in the Sierra Sur of Oaxaca, Mexico." Presentation given at the Society for American Archaeology 75th Anniversary Meeting, St. Louis, Missouri.

Kirchhoff, Paul. (1943) 1952. "Mesoamerica: Its Geographic Limits, Ethnic Composition and Cultural Characteristics." In *Heritage of Conquest: the Ethnology of Middle America*, ed. Sol Tax and members of the Viking fund seminar of Middle American ethnology, 17–30. IL: The Free Press Publishers.

Kosso, Peter. 1995. "Epistemic Independence between Textual and Material Evidence." In *Methods in the Mediterranean: Historical and Archaeological Views on Texts and Archaeology*, ed. David B. Small, 177–196. Brill: E. J. Leiden.

Kowalewski, Stephen A. 1997. "A Spatial Method for Integrating Data of Different Types." *Journal of Archaeological Method and Theory* 4 (3/4):287–306. http://dx.doi.org/10.1007/BF02428065.

Krech, Shepard, III. 1991. "The State of Ethnohistory." *Annual Review of Anthropology* 20 (1):345–375. http://dx.doi.org/10.1146/annurev.an.20.100191.002021.

Kroefges, Peter C. 1998. "El Lienzo de Tecciztlan y Tequatepec: Un Documento Histórico-Cartográfico de la Chontalpa de Oaxaca." In *The Shadow of Monte Albán: Politics and Historiography in Postclassic Oaxaca, Mexico*, ed. Maarten Jansen, Peter C. Kroefges, and Michel R. Oudijk, 45–66. Leiden: Research School CNWS.

Kroefges, Peter C. 2004. "Sociopolitical Organization in the Prehispanic Chontalpa de Oaxaca, Mexico: Ethnohistorical and Archaeological Perspectives." Unpublished PhD diss., University at Albany-SUNY.

Kroefges, Peter C. 2006. "¿Arqueología de la Cultura Chontal o Arqueología de la Chontalpa?" In *Historia y Etnografía entre los Chontales de Oaxaca*, ed. Andrés Oseguera, 41–60. Mexico City: INAH.

Lawrence, Susan, and Nick Shepherd. 2006. "Historical Archaeology and Colonialism." In *The Cambridge Companion to Historical Archaeology*, ed. Dan Hicks and Mary C. Beaudry, 69–86. New York: Cambridge University Press.

Leibsohn, Dana. 2004. "Primers for Memory: Cartographic Histories and Nahua Identity." In *Writing without Words: Alternative Literacies in Mesoamerica and the Andes*, ed. Elizabeth Hill Boone and Walter D. Mignolo, 161–187. Durham, NC: Duke University Press.

Leone, Mark P. 1995. "A Historical Archaeology of Capitalism." *American Anthropologist* 97 (2):251–268. http://dx.doi.org/10.1525/aa.1995.97.2.02a00050.

Leone, Mark P. 2007. "Middle Range Theory in Historical Archaeology." In *Archaeological Anthropology: Perspectives on Method and Theory*, ed. James M. Skibo, Michael Graves, and Miriam T. Stark, 21–39. Tucson: The University of Arizona Press.

Leone, Mark P. 2009. "Making Historical Archaeology Postcolonial." In *International Handbook of Historical Archaeology*, ed. Teresita Majewski and David Gaimster, 159–168. New York: Springer. http://dx.doi.org/10.1007/978-0-387-72071-5_9.

Leone, Mark P., and Constance A. Crosby. 1987. "Middle-Range Theory in Historical Archaeology." In *Consumer Choice in Historical Archaeology*, ed. Suzanne M. Spencer-Wood, 397–410. New York: Plenum Press. http://dx.doi.org/10.1007/978-1-4757 -9817-3_17.

Leone, Mark P., and Parker B. Potter. 1988. "Introduction: Issues in Historical Archaeology." In *The Recovery of Meaning: Historical Archaeology in the Eastern United States*, ed. Mark P. Leone and Parker B. Potter, Jr., 1–22. Washington, DC: Smithsonian Institution Press.

Levine, Marc. 2007. "Linking Household and Polity at Late Postclassic Yucu Dzaa (Tututepec), a Mixtec Capital on the Coast of Oaxaca, Mexico." Unpublished PhD diss., Department of Anthropology, University of Colorado, Boulder.

Levy, Thomas E., ed. 2010. *Historical Biblical Archaeology and the Future: The New Pragmatism*. London: Equinox.

Lightfoot, Kent G. 1995. "Culture Contact Studies: Redefining the Relationship between Prehistoric and Historic Archaeology." *American Antiquity* 60 (2):199–217. http://dx.doi.org/10.2307/282137.

Little, Barbara. 1994. "People with History: An Update on Historical Archaeology in the United States." *Journal of Archaeological Method and Theory* 1 (1):5–40. http://dx.doi.org/10.1007/BF02229422.

Little, Barbara, ed. 1992. *Text-Aided Archaeology*. Boca Raton: CRC Press.

Lucas, Gavin. 2006. "Historical Archaeology and Time." In *The Cambridge Companion to Historical Archaeology*, ed. Dan Hicks and Mary C. Beaudry, 34–47. New York: Cambridge University Press.

Majewski, Teresita, and David Gaimster. 2009. "Introduction." In *International Handbook of Historical Archaeology*, ed. Teresita Majewski and David Gaimster, xvii–xx. New York: Springer.

Marcus, Joyce. 1976. "The Iconography of Militarism at Monte Albán and Neighboring Sites in the Valley of Oaxaca." In *Origins of Religious Art and Iconography in Preclassic Mesoamerica*, ed. H. B. Nicholson, 123–139. Los Angeles: UCLA Latin American Center Publications.

Marcus, Joyce. 1983. "The Conquest Slabs of Building J, Monte Albán." In *The Cloud People: Divergent Evolution of the Zapotec and Mixtec Civilizations*, ed. Kent Flannery and Joyce Marcus, 106–108. New York: Academic Press.

Marcus, Joyce. 1992a. *Mesoamerican Writing Systems: Propaganda, Myth, and History in Four Ancient Civilizations*. Princeton: Princeton University Press.

Marcus, Joyce. 1992b. "Political Fluctuations in Mesoamerica: Dynamic Cycles of Mesoamerican States." *National Geographic Research & Exploration* 8 (4):392–411.

Marcus, Joyce, and Kent Flannery. 1994. "Ancient Zapotec Ritual and Religion: An Application of the Direct Historical Approach." In *The Ancient Mind: Elements of Cognitive Archaeology*, ed. Colin Renfrew and Ezra Zubrow, 55–74. New York: Cambridge University Press. http://dx.doi.org/10.1017/CBO9780511598388.008.

Marcus, Joyce, and Kent Flannery. 1996. *Zapotec Civilization: How Urban Society Evolved in Mexico's Oaxaca Valley*. London: Thames and Hudson.

Martínez Grácida, Manuel. 1910. *Historia Antigua de la Chontalpa Oaxaqueña*. Mexico: Imprenta del Gobierno Federal.

Matadamas Díaz, Raúl. 1998. "Arqueología historica de Teotitlan del Valle, Tlacolula, Oaxaca." In *Memoria del Primer Congreso Nacional de Arqueología Historica*, ed. Enrique Fernández Dávila and Susana Gómez Serafín, 214–220. Mexico City: CONACULTA/INAH.

Matadamas Díaz, Raúl, and Sandra Liliana Ramírez Barrera. 2007. "Proyecto Arqueológico Bocana del Río Copalita, Huatulco, Tercera Temporada 2006–2007: Informe de Clasificación de Materiales Arqueológicos (Cerámica)." Unpublished report submitted to Centro INAH-Oaxaca, Oaxaca City.

Matadamas Díaz, Raúl, and Sandra Liliana Ramírez Barrera. 2010. Antes de Ocho Venado y Después de los Piratas: Arqueología e Historia de Huatulco. Oaxaca City: CSEIIO-SAI.

Matthew, Laura E., and Michel R. Oudijk, eds. 2007. *Indian Conquistadors: Indian Allies in the Conquest of Mesoamerica*. Norman: University of Oklahoma Press.

McCafferty, Geoffrey. 2000. "The Cholula Massacre: Factional Histories and Archaeology of the Spanish Conquest." In *The Entangled Past: Integrating History and Archaeology*, ed. M. Boyd, J. C. Erwin, and M. Hendrickson, 347–359. Calgary: Chacmool.

McGuire, Randall H. 1982. "The Study of Ethnicity in Historical Archaeology." *Journal of Anthropological Archaeology* 1 (2):159–178. http://dx.doi.org/10.1016/0278-4165 (82)90019-8.

Mitchell, Mark D., and Laura L. Scheiber. 2010. "Crossing Divides: Archaeology as Long-Term History." In *Across a Great Divide: Continuity and Change in Native North American Societies, 1400–1900*, ed. Laura L. Scheiber and Mark D. Mitchell, 1–22. Tucson: University of Arizona Press.

Mondragon, Lourdes, Patricia Fournier-García, and Nahum Noguera. 1997. "Arqueología Histórica y Etnoarqueologia de la Comunidad Alfarera Otomí de Santa María del Pino, Mexico." In *Approaches to the Historical Archaeology of Mexico, Central & South America*, ed. Janine Gasco, Greg Charles Smith, and Patricia Fournier-García, 17–28. Los Angeles: Institute of Archaeology, UCLA.

Moreland, John. 2001. *Archaeology and Text*. London: Duckworth.

Moreno Cabrera, María de la Luz. 2000. "El Castillo de Chapultepec: Arqueología e Historia." *Arqueología Mexicana* 8 (46):26–33.

Munch, Guido. 1992. "Los Chontales de Oaxaca." In *El Fuego de la Inobediencia: Autonomía y Rebelión India en el Obispado de Oaxaca*, ed. Héctor Díaz-Polanco, 133–150. Mexico City: CIESAS.

Navarrete, Federico. 1997. "Las Fuentes Indígenas más Allá de la Dicotomía entre Historia y Mito." *Estudios de Cultura Nahuatl* 30:231–256.

Neff, Hector. 2008. "Results of LA-ICP-MS Chemical Sourcing of CHAP Obsidian." Manuscript in the possession of the author.

Noël Hume, Ivor. 1969. *Historical Archaeology*. New York: Alfred A. Knopf.

O'Connor, Loretta, and Peter C. Kroefges. 2007. "The Land Remembers: Landscape Terms and Place Names in Lowland Chontal of Oaxaca, Mexico." *Language Sciences* 30 (2–3):291–315.

Odena Güemes, Lina. 1997. "El Lienzo de Astata: Una Nueva Posibilidad de Interpretación." In *Códices y Documentos sobre México: Segundo Simposio*, ed. Salvador Rueda Smithers, Constanza Vega Sosa, and Rodrigo Martínez Baracs, 305–318. Colección Científica, vol. 1. Mexico City: Instituto Nacional de Antropología e Historia.

Orser, Charles E. 1996. *A Historical Archaeology of the Modern World*. New York: Plenum Press. http://dx.doi.org/10.1007/978-1-4757-8988-1.

Orser, Charles E. 2004. "The Archaeologies of Recent History: Historical, Post Medieval, and Modern World." In *A Companion to Archaeology*, ed. John Bintliff, 272–290. Oxford: Blackwell.

Orser, Charles E. 2010. "Twenty-First-Century Historical Archaeology." *Journal of Archaeological Research* 18 (2):111–150. http://dx.doi.org/10.1007/s10814-009-9035-9.

Orser, Charles E., ed. 2002. *Encyclopedia of Historical Archaeology*. New York: Routledge.

Orser, Charles E., and Brian M. Fagan. 1995. *Historical Archaeology*. New York: HarperCollins.

Oseguera, Andrés. 2003. "Los Signos de un Territorio Oculto: Geografía Social de la Región Chontal Oaxaqueña." In *Diálogos con el Territorio: Simbolizaciones sobre el Espacio en las Culturas Indígenas de México*, ed. Alicia M. Barabas, 225–248. Mexico City: INAH.

Oseguera, Andrés. 2004. *Chontales de Oaxaca: Pueblos Indígenas de México Contemporáneo*. Mexico City: CDI.

Palka, Joel W. 2009. "Historical Archaeology of Indigenous Culture Change in Mesoamerica." *Journal of Archaeological Research* 17 (4):297–346. http://dx.doi.org/10.1007/s10814-009-9031-0.

Paso y Troncoso, Francisco del, ed. 1905. *Papeles de la Nueva España.* Segunda Série: Geografía e Estadística, vol. 1. Madrid: Sucesor de Rivadeneyra.

Paynter, Robert. 2000. "Historical and Anthropological Archaeology: Forging Alliances." *Journal of Archaeological Research* 8 (1):1–37. http://dx.doi.org/10.1023/A:1009429525703.

Pedrotta, Victoria, and Facundo Gómez Romero. 1998. "Historical Archaeology: An Outlook from the Argentinean Pampas." *International Journal of Historical Archaeology* 2 (2):113–131. http://dx.doi.org/10.1023/A:1022666314752.

Pérez Castro, Guillermo. 1990. "La Arqueología Histórica en México." *Revista Mexicana de Estudios Antropológicos* 36:229–244.

Pilling, Arnold R. 1967. "Beginnings." *Historical Archaeology* 1:1–22.

Pohl, John M.D. 2003. "Creation Stories, Hero Cults, and Alliance Building: Postclassic Confederacies of Central and Southern Mexico from A.D. 1150–1458." In *The Postclassic Mesoamerican World*, ed. Michael E. Smith and Frances F. Berdan, 61–66. Salt Lake City: University of Utah Press.

Pohl, John M.D. 2004. "Mexican Codices, Maps, and Lienzos as Social Contracts." In *Writing without Words: Alternative Literacies in Mesoamerica and the Andes*, ed. Elizabeth Hill Boone and Walter D. Mignolo, 137–160. Durham, NC: Duke University Press.

Posnansky, Merrick, and Christopher R. Decorse. 1986. "Historical Archaeology in Sub-Saharan Africa: A Review." *Historical Archaeology* 20 (1):1–14.

Proskouriakoff, Tatiana. 1960. "Historical Implications of a Pattern of Dates at Piedras Negras, Guatemala." *American Antiquity* 25 (4):454–475. http://dx.doi.org/10.2307/276633.

Purser, Margaret. 1992. "Oral History and Historical Archaeology." In *Text-Aided Archaeology*, ed. Barbara Little, 25–35. Boca Raton: CRC Press.

Rice, Prudence M. 2002. "Maya Archaeology." In *Encyclopedia of Historical Archaeology*, ed. Charles E. Orser, 384–387. New York: Routledge.

Rice, Don. S., and Prudence M. Rice. 2004. "History in the Future: Historical Data and Investigations in Lowland Maya Studies." In *Continuities and Changes in Maya Archaeology: Perspectives at the Millennium*, ed. Charles W. Golden and Greg Burgstede, 71–87. New York: Routledge.

Reid, Andrew M., and Paul J. Lane. 2004. "African Historical Archaeologies: An Introductory Consideration of Scope and Potential." In *African Historical Archaeologies*, ed. Andrew M. Reid and Paul J. Lane, 1–32. New York: Kluwer Academic/Plenum Publishers. http://dx.doi.org/10.1007/978-1-4419-8863-8_1.

Robertshaw, Peter. 2004. "African Historical Archaeology(ies): Past, Present, and a Possible Future." In *African Historical Archaeologies*, ed. Andrew M. Reid and Paul J. Lane, 375–391. New York: Kluwer Academic/Plenum Publishers. http://dx.doi.org/10.1007/978-1-4419-8863-8_14.

Rubertone, Patricia E. 1989. "Archaeology, Colonialism and 17th Century Native America: Towards an Alternative Interpretation." In *Conflict in the Archaeology of Living Cultures*, ed. Robert Layton, 32–45. London: Routledge.

Rubertone, Patricia E. 1996. "Matters of Inclusion: Historical Archaeology and Native Americans." *World Archaeological Bulletin* 7:77–86.

Rubertone, Patricia E. 2000. "The Historical Archeology of Native Americans." *Annual Review of Anthropology* 29 (1):425–446. http://dx.doi.org/10.1146/annurev.anthro.29.1.425.

Ruiz Medrano, Ethelia. 2010. *Mexico's Indigenous Communities: Their Land and Histories, 1500–2010*. Boulder: University Press of Colorado.

Sauer, Eberhard, ed. 2004. *Archaeology and Ancient History: Breaking Down the Boundaries*. New York: Routledge.

Schmidt, Peter. 2006. *Historical Archaeology in Africa: Representation, Social Memory, and Oral Traditions*. Oxford: AltaMira.

Schmidt, Peter, and Thomas C. Patterson, eds. 1995. *Making Alternative Histories: The Practice of Archaeology and History in Non-Western Settings*. Santa Fe: School of American Research Press.

Schmidt, Peter, and Jonathan R. Walz. 2007. "Re-representing African Pasts through Historical Archaeology." *American Antiquity* 72 (1):53–70. http://dx.doi.org/10.2307/40035298.

Schuyler, Robert L. 1970. "Historical and Historic Sites Archaeology as Anthropology: Basic Definitions and Relationships." *Historical Archaeology* 4:83–9.

Schuyler, Robert L. 1999. "Comments on 'Historical Archaeology in the Next Millennium: A Forum.'" *Historical Archaeology* 33 (2):66–70.

Schuyler, Robert L., ed. 1978. *Historical Archaeology: A Guide to Substantive and Theoretical Contributions*. New York: Baywood Publishing Company.

Shackel, Paul A., and Barbara J. Little. 1992. "Post-Processual Approaches to Meanings and Uses of Material Culture in Historical Archaeology." *Historical Archaeology* 26 (3):5–11.

Shafer, Robert Jones, ed. 1980. *A Guide to Historical Method*. Homewood, CA: Dorsey Press.

Sherman, Jason, Andrew K. Balkansky, Charles Spencer, and Brian D. Nicholls. 2010. "Expansionary Dynamics of the Nascent Monte Albán State." *Journal of Anthropological Archaeology* 29 (3):278–301. http://dx.doi.org/10.1016/j.jaa.2010.04.001.

Silliman, Stephen W. 2010. "Crossing, Bridging, and Transgressing Divides in the Study of Native North America." In *Across A Great Divide: Continuity and Change in Native North American Societies, 1400–1900*, ed. Laura L. Scheiber and Mark D. Mitchell, 258–276. Tucson: The University of Arizona Press.

Small, David B. 1999. "The Tyranny of the Text: Lost Social Strategies in Current Historical Period Archaeology in the Classical Mediterranean." In *Historical Archaeology: Back from the Edge*, ed. Pedro Paulo A. Funari, Martin Hall, and Siân Jones, 122–136. London: Routledge.

Smith, Michael E. 1987. "The Expansion of the Aztec Empire: A Case Study in the Correlation of Diachronic Archaeological and Ethnohistorical Data." *American Antiquity* 52 (1):37–54. http://dx.doi.org/10.2307/281059.

Smith, Michael E. 1992. "Rhythms of Change in Postclassic Central Mexico: Archaeology, Ethnohistory, and the Braudelian Model." In *Archaeology, Annales, and Ethnohistory*, ed. A. Bernard Knapp, 51–74. Cambridge: Cambridge University Press. http://dx.doi.org/10.1017/CBO9780511759949.005.

Smith, Michael E., and Frances Berdan. 1996. "Province Descriptions." In *Aztec Imperial Strategies*, ed. Frances F. Berdan, Richard Blanton, Elizabeth Hill Boone, Mary G. Hodge, Michael E. Smith, and Emily Umberger, 265–349. Washington, DC: Dumbarton Oaks.

South, Stanley. 1977. *Method and Theory in Historical Archaeology*. New York: Academic Press.

Spencer, Charles S., and Elsa M. Redmond. 1997. *Archaeology of the Cañada de Cuicatlán, Oaxaca*. New York: American Museum of Natural History Anthropological Papers, No. 80.

Spencer, Charles S., Elsa M. Redmond, and Christina M. Elson. 2008. "Ceramic Microtypology and the Territorial Expansion of the Early Monte Albán State in Oaxaca, Mexico." *Journal of Field Archaeology* 33 (3):321–341. http://dx.doi.org/10.1179/009346 908791071222.

Spores, Ronald. 1980. "New World Ethnohistory and Archaeology, 1970–1980." *Annual Review of Anthropology* 9 (1):575–603. http://dx.doi.org/10.1146/annurev.an.09.100180 .003043.

Spores, Ronald. 1993. "Tututepec: A Postclassic Mixtec Conquest State." *Ancient Mesoamerica* 4 (1):167–174. http://dx.doi.org/10.1017/S0956536100000845.

Spores, Ronald. 1998. "Documentos de Archivo como Auxiliares de la Arqueología Histórica." In *Memoria del Primer Congreso Nacional de Arqueología Historica*, ed. Enrique Fernández Dávila and Susana Gómez Serafín, 69–72. Mexico City: CONACULTA/INAH.

Stahl, Ann B. 1993. "Concepts of Time and Approaches to Analogical Reasoning in Historical Perspective." *American Antiquity* 58 (2):235–260. http://dx.doi.org/10.2307 /281967.

Stahl, Ann B. 2001. *Making History in Banda: Anthropological Visions of Africa's Past*. Cambridge: Cambridge University Press. http://dx.doi.org/10.1017/CBO97805114 89600.

Stahl, Ann, Rob Mann, and Diana DiPaolo Loren. 2004. "Writing for Many: Interdisciplinary Communication, Constructionism, and the Practices of Writing." *Historical Archaeology* 38 (2):83–102.

Stein, Gil J. 2002. "From Passive Periphery to Active Agents: Emerging Perspectives in the Archaeology of Interregional Interaction." *American Anthropologist* 104 (3):903–916. http://dx.doi.org/10.1525/aa.2002.104.3.903.

Stein, Gil J., ed. 2005. *The Archaeology of Colonial Encounters*. Santa Fe: School of American Research Press.

Trigger, Bruce. 1978. "Ethnohistory and Archaeology." *Ontario Archaeology* 30:17–24.

Trigger, Bruce. 1982. "Ethnohistory: Problems and Prospects." *Ethnohistory* 29 (1):1–19. http://dx.doi.org/10.2307/481006.

Trigger, Bruce. 1989. "History and Contemporary American Archaeology: A Critical Analysis." In *Archaeological Thought in America*, ed. C. C. Lamberg-Karlovsky, 19–34. Cambridge: Cambridge University Press. http://dx.doi.org/10.1017/ CBO9780511558221.002.

Turner, Paul. 1973. *Los Chontales de los Altos*. Mexico City: SepSetentas.

Urcid, Javier. 2001. *Zapotec Hieroglyphic Writing*. Washington, DC: Dumbarton Oaks.

Urcid, Javier, and Arthur Joyce. 2014. "Early Transformations of Monte Albán's Main Plaza and their Political Implications, 500 BC–AD 200." In *Mesoamerican Plazas*, ed. K. Tsukamoto and T. Inomata, 149–167. Tucson: University of Arizona Press.

Vansina, Jan. 1985. *Oral Tradition as History*. Madison: The University of Wisconsin Press.

Veit, Richard. n.d. "A Brief History of the Society for Historical Archaeology." http://www.sha.org/index.php/view/page/history; accessed 01/2014, accessed Oct 2010.

Wallrath, Matthew. 1967. *Excavations in the Tehuantepec Region, Mexico. Transactions of the American Philosophical Society-New Series 57(2)*. Philadelphia: The American Philosophical Society.

Whittaker, Gordon. 1980. "The Hieroglyphics of Monte Albán." Unpublished PhD diss., Yale University.

Whittington, Stephen L. 2003. "El Mapa de Teozacoalco: An Early Colonial Guide to a Municipality in Oaxaca." *The SAA Archaeological Record* 3:20–22, 25.

Wilkie, Laurie A. 2006. "Documentary Archaeology." In *The Cambridge Companion to Historical Archaeology*, ed. Dan Hicks and Mary C. Beaudry, 13–33. New York: Cambridge University Press.

Wilson, Samuel M. 1993. "Structure and History: Combining Archaeology and Ethnohistory in the Contact Period Caribbean." In *Ethnohistory and Archaeology: Approaches to Postcontact Change in the Americas*, ed. J. Daniel Rogers and Samuel M. Wilson, 19–30. New York: Plenum Press.

Wolf, Eric. 1982. *Europe and the People without History*. Berkeley: University of California Press.

Wood, W. Raymond. 1990. "Ethnohistory and Historical Method." *Archaeological Method and Theory*, vol. 2, ed. Michael B. Schiffer, 81–109. Tucson: University of Arizona Press.

Workinger, Andrew. 2002. "Coastal/Highland Interaction in Prehispanic Oaxaca, Mexico: The Perspective from San Francisco de Arriba." Unpublished PhD diss., Department of Anthropology, Vanderbilt University, Nashville.

Workinger, Andrew, and Arthur A. Joyce. 2009. "Reconsidering Warfare in Formative Period Oaxaca." In *Blood and Beauty: Organized Violence in the Art and Archaeology of Mesoamerica and Central America*, ed. Heather Orr and Rex Koontz, 3–38. Los Angeles: Cotsen Institute of Archaeology Press.

Yoffee, Norman, and Bradley L. Crowell, eds. 2006. *Excavating Asian History: Interdisciplinary Studies in Archaeology and History*. Tucson: The University of Arizona Press.

Zárate Morán, Roberto. 1995. "Los Chontales y el Patrimonio Cultural." In *El Patrimonio Sitiado: El Punto de Vista de los Trabajadores*, ed. Trabajadores Académicos del Instituto Nacional de Antropología e Historia, Delegación D-II-I-A–1, Sección X, 311–322. Mexico City: INAH.

Zborover, Danny. 2002a. "Kingdom on Cloth: Cartographic-Histories and the Curious Case of the Lienzo de Tecciztlan y Tequatepec." Unpublished Masters Thesis, Faculty of Archaeology, University of Leiden, Leiden.

Zborover, Danny. 2002b. "A Methodological and Stylistic Look at a Native Mexican Lienzo." In *Arte y Ciencia: Memoria del XXIV Coloquio Internacional de Historia del Arte*, ed. Peter Kreiger, 509–529. Mexico: UNAM.

Zborover, Danny. 2005. "Putting Mesoamerica on the Map: Exploring Art and Archaeology in the Lienzo de Tecciztlan y Tequatepec." In *Art for Archaeology's Sake: Material Culture and Style Across the Disciplines*, ed. Andrea Waters-Rist, Christine Cluney, Calla McNamee, and Larry Steinbrenner, 89–103. Calgary: Chacmool Archaeological Association.

Zborover, Danny. 2006. "Narrativas Históricas y Territoriales de la Chontalpa Oaxaqueña." In *Historia y Etnografía entre los Chontales de Oaxaca*, ed. Andrés Oseguera, 61–108. Mexico City: INAH.

Zborover, Danny. 2007. *The Chontalpa Historical Archaeology Project, Oaxaca.* Report submitted to FAMSI. http://www.famsi.org/reports/05038/index.html, accessed Aug 2010.

Zborover, Danny. 2008a. "Identidades Faccionales en 'Narrativas Territoriales' de la Oaxaca Colonial: Un Enfoque desde las Montañas Chontales." In *Pictografía y Escritura Alfabética en Oaxaca*, ed. Sebastian van Doesburg, 233–270. Oaxaca, Mexico: IEEPO.

Zborover, Danny. 2008b. "Territorial Narratives and Factional Competitions: The Deep Roots of Inter-Community Conflicts in Southeastern Oaxaca, Mexico." Paper presented at the American Anthropological Association 107th Annual Meeting, San Francisco.

Zborover, Danny. 2008c. "Public Historical Archaeology among the Chontal of Oaxaca." Presentation given at the Society for American Archaeology 73rd Annual Conference, Vancouver.

Zborover, Danny. 2009a. "'In those times . . . the mountains talked': Indigenous 'Territorial-Narratives' as Tools of Propaganda, Power, and Identity." In *Post-Colonial Perspectives in Archaeology: Proceedings of the 39th Annual Chacmool Archaeological Conference*, ed. Peter Bikoulis, Dominic Lacroix, and Meaghan Peuramaki-Brown, 169–182. Calgary: The University of Calgary.

Zborover, Danny. 2009b. Entries "Lienzo de San Lorenzo Jilotepequillo" and "Lienzo de Santo Domingo Chontecomatlan." Published online on Wiki-Filología: Pictografia. http://132.248.101.214/wikfil/index.php/Portada, accessed Aug 2010.

Zborover, Danny. 2014. "Decolonizing Historical Archaeology in Southern Oaxaca, Mexico: Late Formative to Republican Periods." Unpublished PhD diss., Department of Archaeology, University of Calgary.

Zeitlin, Judith. 1993. "The Politics of Classic-Period Ritual Interaction: Iconography of the Ballgame Cult in Coastal Oaxaca." *Ancient Mesoamerica* 4 (1): 121–140. http://dx.doi.org/10.1017/S0956536100000821.

Zeitlin, Judith. 2005. *Cultural Politics in Colonial Tehuantepec: Community and State among the Isthmus Zapotec, 1500–1750*. Stanford: Stanford University Press.

Zeitlin, Judith, and Lillian Thomas. 1997. "Indian Consumers on the Periphery of the Colonial Market System: Tracing Domestic Economic Behavior in a Tehuantepec Hamlet." In *Approaches to the Historical Archaeology of Middle, Central and South America*, ed. Janine Gasco, Greg Charles Smith, and Patricia Fournier-García, 5–16. Los Angeles: The Institute of Archaeology, UCLA.

Zeitlin, Robert. 1982. "Towards a more Comprehensive Model of Interregional Commodity Distribution: Political Variables and Prehistoric Obsidian Procurement in Mesoamerica." *American Antiquity* 47 (2):260–275. http://dx.doi.org/10.2307/279900.

Zeitlin, Robert. 1990. "The Isthmus and the Valley of Oaxaca: Questions about Zapotec Imperialism in Formative Period Mesoamerica." *American Antiquity* 55 (2):250–261. http://dx.doi.org/10.2307/281646.

Zeitlin, Robert. 1993. "Pacific Coastal Laguna Zope: A Regional Center in the Terminal Formative Hinterlands of Monte Albán." *Ancient Mesoamerica* 4 (1):85–101. http://dx.doi.org/10.1017/S0956536100000808.

Zeitlin, Robert, and Arthur Joyce. 1999. "The Zapotec-Imperialism Argument: Insights from the Oaxaca Coast." *Current Anthropology* 40 (3):383–391. http://dx.doi.org/10.1086/200029.

13

Prehispanic and Colonial Chontal Communities on the Eastern Oaxaca Coast on the Eve of the Spanish Conquest

PETER C. KROEFGES

INTRODUCTION

This chapter presents some considerations on the combined use of historical documents and archaeological materials for the study of the two most prominent prehispanic Chontal communities on the coast of Oaxaca: Huamelula and Astata. The focus is on changes in the sociopolitical integration, community organization, and economic activities of these two neighboring coastal Chontal communities, from their prehispanic beginnings into the Colonial period, around 1700 CE. Historical and archaeological evidence inform on these aspects at different degrees of depth, breadth, and detail. The focus is on how documentary sources and archaeological remains can serve to complement, confirm, or contradict each other. Such a conjunctive approach seems the most profitable, given the incomplete nature of the archaeological record and the selective and biased character of the historical sources (see Byland and Pohl 1994a, 1994b; Marcus and Flannery 1983).

By the end of the fifteenth century, the Chontalpa, set in the Sierra Madre del Sur and the coastal plain to the south, had been surrounded by expansive conquest states of the Mixtec kingdom of Tututepec and the Zapotec exile-kingdom of Tehuantepec, while Aztec military campaigns against these polities entered the Sierra Madre del Sur and the adjacent Isthmus, establishing garrisons and demanding staples and services from the local populations.

The *Relaciones Geográficas* (abbreviated here RGs, see Acuña 1984a, 1984b), a series of geographical reports that included the written responses to a questionnaire

DOI: 10.5876/9781607323297.c013

commissioned by the Spanish court from around 1579–1580 CE, can serve to map the dynamics and limits of these polities' geopolitics and political economy on the eve of the Spanish conquest. Frequently, the RGs include the natives' statements about who the overlord of a specific community before the Conquest was, and what kind of tribute was paid. The RGs also provide important information on settlement location and size, economic productivity, and other aspects of communal life. Lamentably, the corresponding reports have disappeared for large parts of the Chontalpa and adjacent regions, or perhaps had never reached their destination (e.g., in the case of Huamelula and Astata; see Cline 1972). Thus, our map of the geopolitical constellations in southern Oaxaca at the time of the Spaniards' arrival is incomplete.

HISTORICAL SOURCES

My initial interest in the prehispanic and Colonial Chontal societies was triggered by a sixteenth-century map painted on cloth and currently kept in the Biblioteca Nacional de Antropología e Historia in Mexico City, and which, according to Glass's (1964) catalog, originated in the Isthmus region of Oaxaca. This pictographic document—the *Lienzo de Tecciztlan y Tequatepec* (LTT) or *Lienzo de Astata*, as Glass had labeled it (see figure 12.2 for a line drawing)—is the oldest known pictorial document for the region, and it has served to contradict the long-lasting stereotype of the Colonial Chontal as cave-dwelling barbarians who perpetually lacked any centralized political organization or established settlements (see Kroefges 1998).

Any gloss that might have identified the central place's name has vanished, and so the most crucial issue was to identify its name and location. Following Maarten Jansen's reading of the logographic place glyph in the LTT (Jansen, personal communication, 1996), and according to the geographical location and a few short references of depicted subject towns, I suggested Quamimilollan (today San Pedro Huamelula; see Kroefges 1998) as the presumable kingdom's capital. Other authors have suggested its neighbor, Aztatlan (modern-day Santiago Astata, see Odena Güemes 1997), or both—Huamelula and Astata—as the central places of the LTT (de la Cruz 2008). Cuautulco (modern-day Huatulco; see Zborover 2002), which actually lies outside the area confined by the LTT, or even an unidentified "Cabecera X" (Zborover 2002) have also been nominated.

At a later point in time, the LTT was modified by the addition of place glyphs at the right or eastern edge, which partially erased earlier drawings and thus distorted the cartographic integrity of the earlier draft. A possibility is that this modification happened in the context of later Colonial rearrangements in the political geography and settlement location in the coastal Chontalpa, especially concerning

Astata's relocation further inland after a series of pirate attacks (see Kroefges 2004). Because Astata was the place where the LTT was photographed by Teobert Maler in the early twentieth century, and from where it was taken to finally end up in the Biblioteca Nacional de Antropología e Historia, I wanted to learn more about the prehispanic and Colonial past of the two towns involved in its creation, Huamelula and Astata. That started a series of subsequent historical investigations in archives and archaeological fieldwork in the study area along the Río Huamelula.

To obtain additional references that could illuminate the LTT's provenience and the identity of the central place and its ruling dynasty, other documentary evidence had to be consulted. The source selection had to be ample enough to include information about surrounding polities as well, in order to narrow down the localization of the LTT through exclusion—that is, the absence of contradicting information on outside territories and neighbor polities. That, of course, is one of biggest problems in historical inquiry, because confrontational territorial interests are long known to produce opposing views on the matters of possession. Hermeneutical source criticism can be a complicated procedure of connecting and contrasting arguments (compare the divergent paths followed by de la Cruz 2008; Kroefges 1998; Zborover 2002, 2006).

The selection of sources is the result of screening through secondary literature references: printed and electronic catalogs of primary sources stored in municipal, national, and international archives (AGN, AGI), and internet pages. Search criteria were place names, ethnonyms, regional specifications, and personal names of individuals mentioned in primary and secondary sources. Misclassified documents, alternatively spelled entries, or records that do not correspond to those search criteria thus may have been involuntarily excluded.

These sources can be grouped into three broad categories: (1) Colonial Spanish/*mestizo* chronicles (published editions), (2) Colonial written administrative records (table 13.1), and (3) indigenous cartographic documents (table 13.2). Oral traditions were opportunistically recorded without any systematic procedure during four field seasons between 1995 and 2005 and are not of concern for the present study.

The category of Spanish/*mestizo* chronicles comprises a small number of retrospective accounts of prehispanic or Colonial-period events. Fray Agustín Dávila Padilla's (1955) account is the first to emphasize the general impression of Chontal barbarism: "Es la tierra de los Chontales desabrida y la lengua muy bárbara ... como eran los más bárbaros en lenguaje, lo mostraban también en su trato" (Dávila Padilla 1955:521). The most extensive account on Chontal society is that of Friar Burgoa (1989). Burgoa focused on Dominican missionary efforts in the sixteenth century in the Chontal highlands. He did not report on coastal Chontal communities, but

TABLE 13.1 Alphabetic administrative sources pertaining to the eastern Oaxaca coast, c. 1530–1700 CE

Source Category	Document Name (Abbreviation) or Archive Section, Date	Edited Publication: (a) Catalogue Entry or (b) Published Excerpts
Spanish census and taxation reports	Suma de Visita de Pueblos (SVP), c. 1548 Libro de Tasaciones (LdT), c. 1531–1561	Paso y Troncoso 1905 González de Cossío 1952
Synthetic clerical descriptions	Relación del Obispado de Antequera (ROA), 1570	García Pimentel 1904:II:5–6
Spanish geographic reports (Relaciones Geográficas)	Relación de Guatulco (RdG), c. 1580; Relación de Suchitepec (RdS), c. 1579; Relación de Teguantepec (RdT), c. 1580	Acuña 1984a, 1984b; Cline 1972 (see also Esparza 1994 for late eighteenth century RGs)
Vice regal grants (licencias, mercedes, títulos)	AGN, ramo de mercedes; AGN, ramo de indios; AGN, ramo de tributos	(a) Spores and Saldaña 1973; (a) Spores and Saldaña 1975; (a) Spores and Saldaña 1976
Decrees (mandamientos)	AGN, ramo de tierras; AGI, Justicia, 113	(a) Méndez Martínez 1979; (b) Gerhard 1972
Orders (órdenes)	AGN, ramo de congregaciones; AGI, Indiferente General, ést. 145, caj. 7, leg. 8	(b) Paso y Troncoso 1939–1942; (b) Gerhard 1995
Commissions (comisiones)	AGI Patronato, Papeles de Simancas, ést. 1, caj. 1, leg. 1/20, No. 5, R. 24	(b) Paso y Troncoso 1939–1942
Land inspection reports (diligencias)	AGN, ramo de tierras; Archivo Municipal de Huamelula (AMPAL); Archivo Municipal de Huatulco (AMH)	(a) Méndez Martínez 1979; (b) Gerhard 1972; (b) de León Chávez 1995; (b) González 2002
Lawsuit documentation (incl. testimonies [autos])	AGI Escribanía 160 bis.	Machuca Gallegos 2007; Oudijk 2000; Zeitlin 2005

Note: AGI, Archivo General de las Indias; AGN, Archivo General de la Nación; RGs, Relaciones Geográficas.

his limited account initiated a pejorative stereotype on "the Chontal" in general that was adopted by many subsequent ethnographies and historiographies of the twentieth century (Basauri 1940; Bradomín 1987; Taracena 1941).

Although the available documentary sources were drafted after the Spanish conquest, several of them refer to people and events in preconquest times. Of these, statements in Spanish/mestizo chronicles and administrative records about the Aztec intrusion into the Chontal region and the Oaxacan coast under Axayacatl and Motecuhzoma II are the most common, providing an approximate time depth back to 1480 CE.

The historical document with perhaps the deepest reach into the prehispanic past is the LTT, because it lists nine predecessors of the Early Colonial cacique of the

TABLE 13.2 Indigenous pictorial documents pertaining to the eastern Oaxaca coast

Source Category	Document Name/Title (Abbreviation), Date, Location and Provenience	Reproduction and Descriptions
Historical-Cartographic; Genealogical pictorials	*Lienzo de Tecciztlan y Tequatepec* (LTT), early sixteenth century (?), Biblioteca Nacional de Antropología e Historia, Santiago Astata (?)	Photographs by Maler, late nineteenth–early twentieth century; Glass 1964; Kroefges 1998; Odena Güemes 1997; Zborover 2002
	Lienzo de Jilotepequillo (LSLJ), seventeenth century?, San Lorenzo Jilotepequillo	Schematic drawing in Oseguera 2003; photographs and line drawing in Zborover 2006, 2008.
	Maps of the *Relación Geográfica de Suchitepec*, 1579	Acuña 1984b

Chontal head town. A series of eight male figures and one female figure is connected through a line that indicates direct, biological descent from the earliest ancestor to the latest offspring. Only the latest figure wears Spanish-style clothing, whereas all predecessors wear indigenous garments and all appear to have been of prehispanic birth. Using estimates of an average generational change rate of 15 years minimum and 25 years maximum, the LTT's dynastic list would cover a time span of 135 years at a minimum and 225 years, maximum. For convenience, an average generational change rate of 20 years is used in figure 13.1, which would result in a time span of 180 years. If the last and Europeanized figure represents the first local *cacique* to have been baptized after the Spanish conquest around 1525 CE, his birthday should fall between 1500 CE and 1520 CE. Based on the value of around 180 years covered by the LTT's dynasty, the life of the earliest ruler of the central place and thus the time depth of the LTT's content could reach well into the early fourteenth century, or well within what Mesoamericanists call the Late Postclassic period (1200–1521 CE). However, it is not uncommon that dynastic lists, especially the earliest ones, are filled with fictive or mythical ancestors, and in that case the dynastic list in the LTT cannot be taken to perform such chronological estimates.

ARCHAEOLOGICAL SOURCES

Archaeological fieldwork at the Río Huamelula was not specifically designed to find material evidence for accepting or rejecting any of the interpretations of the LTT, but to obtain knowledge about the development and characteristics of the indigenous communities. Obtaining primary archaeological data for a specific research

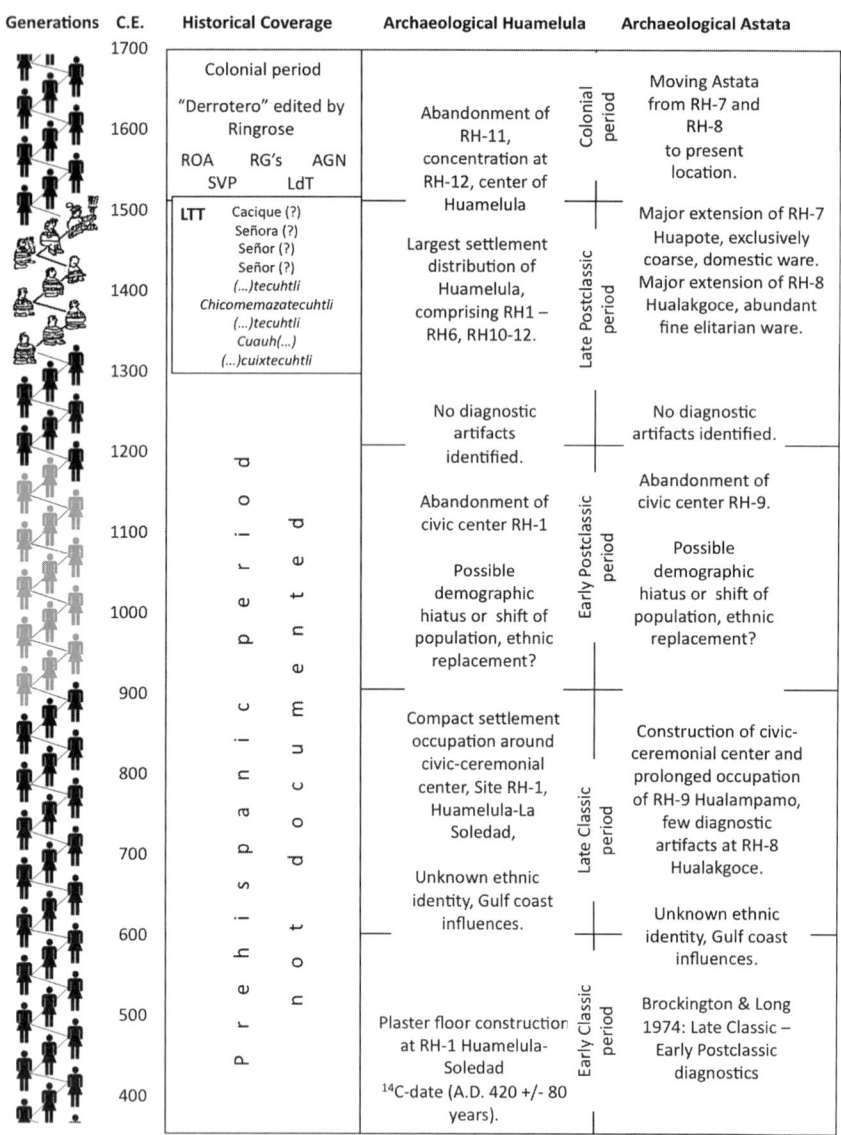

FIGURE 13.1. Time spans of historical and archaeological data on the eastern Oaxaca coast.

question is commonly achieved in situ in the field; in the present case, the only off-site collections were consulted in the small village museum hosted by the CDI (formerly the Instituto Nacional Indigenista) agency at San Pedro Huamelula. The research design to obtain archaeological data pertinent to the objectives usually focuses on fieldwork (survey and excavation), and is frequently restricted by cost factors (i.e., time and funding). It is to be expected that a totally complete register of archaeological remains is impossible, and thus a sort of systematic or unsystematic sampling seems unavoidable.

The Oaxaca Coast Project (OCP) of Brockington et al. (1974) conducted an opportunistic reconnaissance along the Oaxacan coast in 1969 and 1970 that included the sketch maps of two sites in our study area, diagnostic artifact collections, and some judgmentally placed test pits at Hualampamo. The Proyecto Arqueológico Río Huamelula (PARH), conducted by the author in 2001, focused on a much smaller survey area, about fourteen square kilometers along the Huamelula River. Surface coverage and intensity varied largely due to environmental and territorial conditions, but the aim was to register every archaeological structure visible on the surface and collect diagnostic artifacts associated with them. GPS device provided UTM coordinates for these with a range of about four to ten meters of error. Only eight test pits (1-by-1 m^2 or 2-by-1 m^2) were dug for stratigraphic purposes until reaching bedrock, in and around the civic-ceremonial compound of site RH01 in Huamelula.

Secondary archaeological sources directly informing on finds in the coastal Chontal study area are very limited and are included in the two published volumes on the OCP by Brockington et al. (1974) and Brockington and Long (1974). Posterior interpretations of their results are published in two articles (Brockington 1982, 1987). However, for the purpose of cross-dating and comparing archaeological observations in the study area with those of neighboring areas, a large number of field reports, catalogs, and synthetic studies had to be consulted; here I refer only to the geographically closest or thematically most relevant ones (Fernández Dávila and Gómez Serafín 1988, 1990; Joyce et al. 2009; Zeitlin 1978; Zeitlin and Zeitlin 1990).

Relative dating served as the basis for the stratigraphic observations made in the test pits of the PARH excavations at RH01 Huamelula; occurrence seriation performed on diagnostic pottery from stratigraphically excavated deposits provided some control of the chronological distinction between the pottery types. Together with two calibrated radiocarbon dates obtained from two excavated charcoal samples, the PARH chronology is not exhaustive for all sampled units but rather provides an internally consistent framework for reference and cross-dating.

The archaeological chronology for the coastal Chontalpa is largely based on cross-comparisons between diagnostic pottery traits found along that section of the Oaxacan coast and those studied in adjacent and distant areas; strongest resemblances were found with southern Isthmus assemblages published by Wallrath (1967) and Zeitlin (1978) (see detailed discussions in Brockington and Long 1974;

Kroefges 2006b). As a result, the chronological framework consists of periods—that is, blocks of time to which specific ceramic diagnostics have been assigned: Terminal Formative period (1–300 CE), Early Classic period (300–600 CE), Late Classic period (600–900 CE), Early Postclassic period (900–1200 CE), Late Postclassic period (1200–1521 CE), and Early Colonial period (1521–1700 CE).

Brockington and Long (1974) combined the materials with the same traits as pertaining to a single Late Classic/Early Postclassic assemblage, but they do not give precise start and end dates for this block of time. In my ceramic analysis, materials with these traits are exclusively regarded as Late Classic, whereas for the Early Postclassic period no diagnostic attributes were recognizable when compared to Isthmian ceramics (Zeitlin 1978) or to those from the western Oaxacan Coast (Joyce et al. 2009). This observation, together with the surface record of a predominant single-component settlement site distribution along the eastern coast, leads to the tentative reconstruction of a settlement history in the study region that shows a rupture between Classic and Postclassic population—that is, a hiatus between 900 and 1200 CE. Following this period, populations reoccupied some abandoned areas but frequently shifted their settlement centers by a hundred meters or more. Architecture and settlement patterns of Classic and Postclassic communities are quite different: The Classic-period sites are compact and include monumental architecture with ballgame courts and high platforms, whereas the Postclassic settlements are less monumental and more dispersed (Kroefges 2006b). Such a difference was also noted in the Isthmus (see Zeitlin and Zeitlin 1990) and in the western coast of Oaxaca (see Joyce et al. 2004).

The results of PARH and Brockington's OCP allow for the generation of maps of the prehispanic settlement distribution for the eastern Oaxaca coast. Portions further inland and distant to the riverbeds on these maps remain empty, largely due to the limited survey coverage.

COMBINING HISTORICAL AND ARCHAEOLOGICAL DATA

Three approaches to the conjunctive use of historical and archaeological data may be distinguished: (1) the correlation of historical events, dates, and processes with archaeological remains, (2) the direct-historical approach, and (3) the construction of hypotheses for archaeological testing.

At the same time, combining these two different disciplines and sources also constituted a methodologically problematic issue, as several studies on that issue have revealed (Andrén 1998; Bintliff and Gaffney 1986; Knapp 1992; Ramenofsky 1991a, 1991b). One problem can be that practitioners of one discipline selectively use source material from the other discipline without employing the appropriate source criticism according to that discipline. Or similarly, scholars of either discipline tend to follow only its corresponding strand of evidence systematically and merely illustrate them with selected "affirmative" data of the other discipline (as criticized by Brown 1983; Feinman 1997:372). Table 13.3 summarizes the specific research target and sources at each spatial level of archaeological and historical inquiry.

The Correlation of Historical Events and Processes with Archaeological Materials

Diachronic studies require chronologically correlating long-term temporal intervals of archaeological phases and periods with historical processes, episodes, and events (see Smith 1992). Braudel's (1972) tripartite hierarchical time scale, the concerns of a socioeconomically oriented history, and the Annales School's openness to interdisciplinary inquiry invited many archaeologists and historians to reconcile their opposing conceptual and methodological positions (see contributions in Knapp 1992; Wilson 1993).

Archaeologists considered Braudel's emphasis on the *longue durée* and on the cyclic societal progress to correspond particularly well with the long-term sociocultural developments identifiable in the material evidence. Sudden social events in the past, or *microprocesses* (Wilson 1993:22), which may be documented in historical sources are rarely identifiable in the archaeological record or cannot be considered as reflecting a patterned behavior. Wilson suggested that ephemeral microprocesses, such as marital alliances and warfare recorded in the texts, could be linked to long-term *macroprocesses* of population growth, polity formation, and increasing social differentiation as recorded in the archaeological record. Archaeology thus adds a temporal depth to historically fixed situations, whereas history provides "invisible components" to the archaeological interpretation, including such factors as named individuals, their personal motivations, and involvement in short-term events or life-long developments.

In figure 13.1, the documentary and archaeological sources are plotted along a vertical time line that includes a succession of human generations at twenty-year intervals. This diagram shows the temporal coverage of either discipline's sources, and the societal coverage of the past actors, individuals, and communities of Huamelula and Astata. According to the documentary sources, major sociopolitical changes and territorial developments happened within a time of four hundred years, between the early fourteenth century and 1700 CE, which included the founding of a Chontal dynasty, the Zapotec and Aztec intrusions in the late fifteenth century, and the Spanish conquest. Afterward, social and ideological changes brought by conversion, taxation, population shifts, and land disputes are in the center of historical recording.

TABLE 13.3 Historical and archaeological information on the Postclassic coastal Chontal region (source abbreviations in tables 13.1 and 13.2)

Behavioral Criterion	Textual Sources	Pictorial Sources	Archaeological Correlates
Ethno-linguistic identity	Ethnonyms, "ethnographic" details: SVP, ROA, RdG, RdS, RdT, AGI Escribanía 160 bis.	Different costumes in the LTT	Mortuary traditions, inscriptions, style of artifact production and architecture: no sufficient data
Demographic pattern	Census data (tributaries), number of settlements and houses for 1548/1570: SVP, ROA	Community distribution and ward counts in the LTT, AGN Tierras, Ringrose's map	Regional settlement patterns, site densities and distribution: Brockington 1974, Kroefges 2004, 2006b: limited data
Territorial divisions (size of polities)	Cabecera-sujeto relationships, boundary demarcations: SVP, RdG, RdS, RdT, Archived juridical documents	Boundary demarcations, distribution of subject towns: LTT	Boundary markers, settlement hierarchies, "empty" buffer zones: limited data in Kroefges 2006b.
Social differentiation	Hereditary nobility, commoners: RGs, AGI Escribanía 160 bis., AGN Indios	Iconography of status distinction, terms of native social categories	Wealth differences in domestic remains and burials, no data in Kroefges 2006b
Resource exploitation and subsistence	Resource exploitation, agricultural productivity and intensification: SVP	Resources and products	Food processing implements, terracing, irrigation, fishing net sinkers.
Staple and luxury goods production and exchange	Trade of salt and gold: RdG, RdS, RdT, cotton and paper production SVP.	Trade of salted fish, shrimp, animals in the LTT	Distribution of exotic goods and resources: obsidian imports, tools for textile and paper production and exports: limited data: Kroefges 2006b
Belief systems	Details on religion, deities, ancestor worship: No data available	Depiction of Christian church: LTT.	Figurine production, temple constructions, mortuary practices, offerings, rock carvings. Limited data available: Kroefges 2004

continued on next page

TABLE 13.3—continued

Behavioral Criterion	Textual Sources	Pictorial Sources	Archaeological Correlates
Civic-ceremonial institutions and rulership	Political and religious offices, administrative hierarchy among communities: AGN Mercedes, Indios AGI Escribanía 160 bis.	Palace depiction: LTT insignia of power and authority, dynastic ties and genealogical sequences	Number and monumentality of public buildings and plazas, limited data in Brockington et al. 1974, Kroefges 2006b. Public display of rulers and ancestor worship: insufficient data.
Political dominance and alliances	Conquest, regional overlords, administrative hierarchies, tribute obligations: LdT, RdG, RdS, RdT, Codex Ramírez, AGI Escribanía 160 bis.	Conquest, tribute payments of natural resources, products, military services: LTT	Site hierarchies in terms of size, architectural complexity (monumentality), distribution of artistic expressions: limited data in Brockington 1982
Warfare and conflict	Battles between communities: RdG, RdS, Codex Ramírez, AGI Escribanía 160 bis.	Depictions of warriors and battles: LTT	Fortification, defensive places, traces of destruction and abandonment: insufficient data

The archaeological record along the eastern Oaxaca coast includes material remains that span a period of over a thousand years. It registered settlement growth and decline in intervals of centuries packed into artificial periods, which for the Late Postclassic and Early Colonial periods confirm or at least illustrate the general dynamics referred to in the documentary sources.

The Direct Historical Approach and the Problem of the Chontal Arrival to the Eastern Oaxaca Coast

In archaeology, documentary information is often used to assign an ethnic or cultural identity to the makers of observed material remains, through the process of tracing back a historically documented group in time and space to the target society (see Lyman and O'Brien 2001). This approach thus uses historical and archaeological evidence that is not synchronic for the entire time span under study. The main problem of the direct historical approach is that it assumes a close correlation between artifact styles and sociocultural identities—an assumption that is often unwarranted (see Shennan 1989).

Following implicitly the direct historical approach, Brockington assumed that Chontal immigrants had founded the Late Classic/Early Postclassic occupations in the eastern Oaxaca coast, perhaps around 750 CE (Brockington 1987). Without the detection of any rupture in the settlement continuity, one would naturally see the historically documented Chontal communities as direct successors of the Late Classic builders of the ballgame courts and monumental civic-ceremonial compounds. This idea circulated in later publications by Winter (1986), Camacho (1993), and Zárate Morán (1995).

The Construction of Hypotheses for Archaeological Testing

This approach stems from a common assumption in archaeology that historical sources frequently misrepresent the past, whereas, in contrast, the material record is value-free and therefore more objective, and can therefore test the validity of a source's statement (see Brown 1983; Carmack and Weeks 1981; Charlton 1981).

Balkansky (2001:176) suggested in a short review of my interpretation of the LTT (Kroefges 1998) that each place sign had to be "checked archaeologically." But how does one actually check the validity of interpreting specific place glyphs on an indigenous map through archaeological fieldwork? Would the presence of sites and features, being spatially arranged in the field as depicted on the map, be confirmation enough? Or would one require finding emblem glyphs or toponymic inscriptions at these sites that concord with the names on the map? Would the absence of such remains be regarded as an objective contradiction, when we actually have to consider innumerous factors that may lead us to miss a physical manifestation of a proclaimed historical statement? During survey, we could consult local informants on the names of specific topographic features and landscape portions for their local names and see if they match with the glyphs—but would that constitute an archaeological "test"?

Similar questions have led Brown, in his critical review of Carmack's approach, to argue that a "true" test has not been provided in either study under review (Brown 1983:67). He postulated that archaeological testing requires a specifically planned research design analogous to the Binfordian model of hypothesis testing through ethnographic analogies (Binford 1962), and concludes that "much of this type of data may not be, strictly speaking, of much anthropological importance" (Brown 1983:66). I would rather argue that such particularistic historical information provides important insights on aspects of past cultures whether testable through archaeology or not. Under these conditions, archaeological and historical information on a given topic simply constitute complementary strands of evidence.

LOCALIZATION OF HISTORICAL ASTATA AND HUAMELULA

The modern village of Santiago Astata is located due south of El Boquerón, but its inhabitants remember that the old village was at the archaeological site of Hualakgoce down the river. As Gerhard (1972) and Camacho (1993) noted, the original village was abandoned in the 1680s after a series of pirate attacks. The original location of Astata can thus be identified with the one depicted and described in documents antedating the 1680s. In the course of expanding land grants for Spanish cattle and horse farms (*sitios de estancia de ganado mayor*), the geographic situation near the Río Huamelula has been repeatedly inspected by Spanish administrators.

A detailed painting mapped the location of these ranches west of Astata (figure 13.2) and was attached to an inspection report (*diligencia*) from 1579 (AGN Tierras, vol. 2579, exp. 14, fs. 15). This illustration shows the location of sixteenth-century Astata near the seashore and between a large lagoon to the west and the mouth of the Río Huamelula to the east. Across the river, further east, a portion of the plain is covered with agricultural fields (*sementeras*). A path or road with native-style footprint elements runs from west to east of the map, just north of the lagoons and the town of Astata.

In 1682, the English pirate Basil Ringrose produced copies of early seventeenth-century Spanish nautical charts of the Pacific coast of New Spain, which had fallen into his hands after an assault on a Spanish ship a year before (Howse and Thrower 1992). Currently located at the National Maritime Museum in London, England, one chart includes the coast of eastern Oaxaca and shows the early seventeenth-century

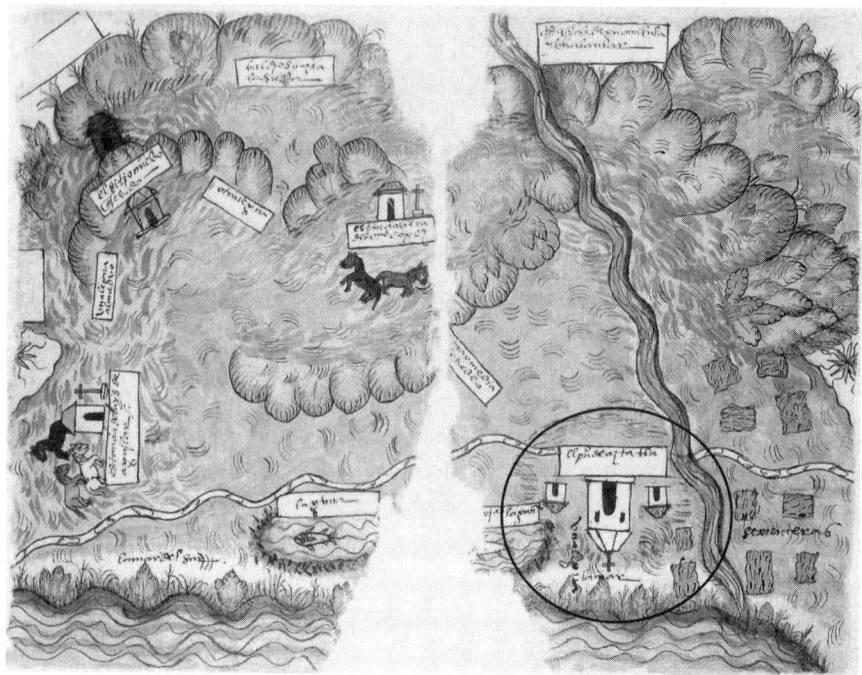

FIGURE 13.2. Location of Astata (circled) in the *diligencias* of 1579. The town lies near the Pacific coast, between a lagoon to the west and the Río Huamelula to the east. Archivo General de la Nación (Ramo Tierras, vol. 2579, exp. 14, f. 15), Mexico City.

location of Astata and Huamelula. Astata ("Estata") has its center on the right bank (east) of the Río Huamelula (called "Río Estata" on the chart), but a building on the opposite side of the river apparently pertains to the community (figure 13.3).

Looking at the archaeological record in the southern half of the PARH study area, we find three concentrations of Postclassic/Early Colonial occupation (figure 13.4), at RH09 Hualampamo, RH08 Hualakgoce, and at RH07 El Huapote. With only 1.5 kilometers of floodplain between them, they probably are two sectors of a Postclassic community, likely the one that was later recorded as Astata in the Colonial records.

The archaeological evidence for the location of Early Colonial Astata is even sketchier, because PARH visited merely a few parts of sites. At RH07 El Huapote we did not find a single sherd with diagnostic European attributes, but we did find some pieces at a site sector of Hualampamo (RH09–2) and at Hualakgoce. Again, much of the Late Postclassic pottery types may in fact have continued to be used by postconquest dwellers, particularly the red-slipped coarseware that was so

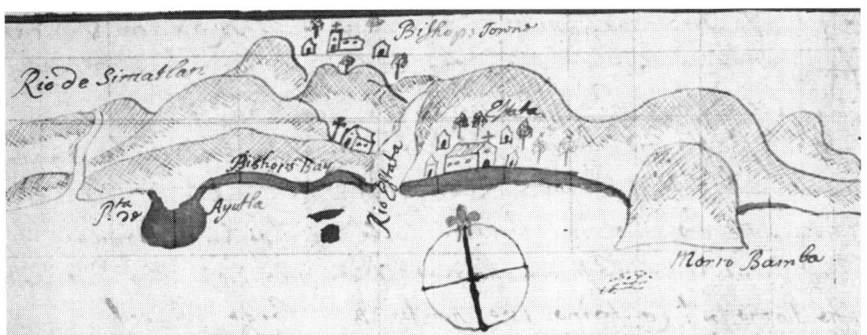

FIGURE 13.3. Location of Astata and Huamelula in Ringrose's 1682 copy of a Spanish *derrotero* (Howse and Thrower 1992). Astata still lies along the Río Huamelula ("Río Estata" here) but, due to pirate attacks, has relocated farther inland from its original site on the coast. Original in the National Maritime Museum (P/32[15]), London.

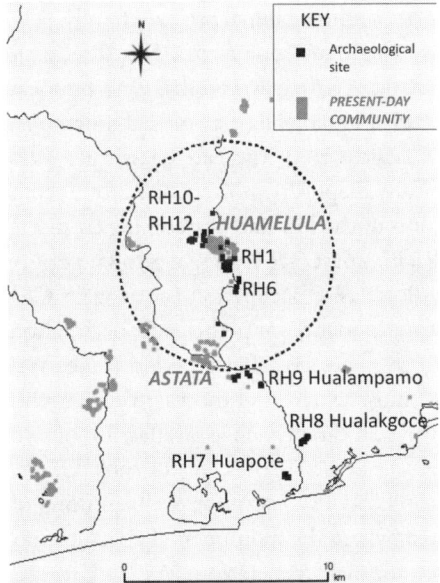

FIGURE 13.4. Site distribution along the Río Huamelula and Huamelula's perimeter of eight leagues.

abundantly found at RH07 El Huapote. According to the historical documentation, Astata must have been located in this area until circa 1680 CE, but this is poorly reflected in the archaeological record. That settlement possibly extended between Hualampamo and El Huapote, with its center near Hualakgoce and El Huapote, while other wards were dispersed in the foothills along the river. The present-day village of Santiago Astata features a Late Colonial church. It is the only physical evidence manifesting Astata's relocation from the seashore to its present location further inland, around the turn from the seventeenth to the eighteenth century.

ETHNOLINGUISTIC IDENTITY

No known document tells us when the Chontal arrived in the eastern part of the Oaxaca coast. Nevertheless, if the chronological estimate of the rulers' lineage in the LTT (c. 180 years) is accepted, it might be taken as an indirect indicator for this matter. And if the earliest depicted ruler actually represents the founder of the central place's community, which according to my previous argument was either the Chontal community of Huamelula or Astata, one could then argue that the Chontal as an ethnic group had possibly arrived to this part of the Oaxacan coast at the beginning of the fourteenth century. Alternatively, the Chontal may have dwelled in the area even a long time before, and the LTT's dynastic list can be read merely as an attempt to demonstrate the political authority of the Colonial *cacique*'s family.

Stylistic attributes of some few pottery fragments point to a Late Preclassic occupation at sites near Huamelula and Astata (Kroefges 2006b). One radiocarbon date associated with a stucco floor at RH01 Huamelula-La Soledad hints to an occupation around 400 CE, or the Early Classic period. The Late Classic period is represented by the presence of chronologically diagnostic pottery and stone sculptures related to the ballgame tradition found in the lowlands, stretching from the Mexican Gulf Coast to the Guatemalan Pacific coast (see Kroefges 2006a, 2006b; Parsons 1978; Zeitlin 1993). For an Early Postclassic occupation (900–1200 CE), however, we lack any clear material indicators. Evidence for prehispanic occupation picks up again with diagnostic pottery of the Late Postclassic period (1250–1521 CE) and postconquest ceramics, scattered most widely and most densely around the sites along the Río Huamelula. This situation can be seen as a reflection of two episodes of population along the eastern Oaxaca coast; the historically known Chontal may have arrived at the end of the Early Postclassic or the beginning of the Late Postclassic period in the study area, where the monumental civic-ceremonial compounds may have been abandoned for many generations. As the Chontal were speakers of an isolated language in Oaxaca and Mesoamerica, their origin and course of immigration are still unknown (O'Connor and Kroefges 2008).

POPULATION SIZE AND DISTRIBUTION

The LTT is silent on the matters of population size and distribution for the central community. According to the *Suma de Visitas de Pueblos* (SVP), Astata and its subject villages had 160 *"yndios"* in 1548, roughly equaling the same amount of households, whereas the *cabecera* of Huamelula counted 220 houses at that time. The population number may be just a fraction of the preconquest population, which probably suffered heavily from epidemic diseases.

The archaeological record for any period is too fragmentary, but it seems that Postclassic communities were larger than preceding and posterior occupations. However, Classic-period evidence may be less visible for being covered by posterior remains, and Early Colonial material may be indistinguishable from Late Postclassic remains. Postclassic settlement distribution may have been quite dense on the hill site of RH07 (Astata residential ward), and beneath today's Huamelula town center, but more dispersed at the northern fringe of Huamelula. Overall, Late Postclassic Huamelula (c. 2 km²) was larger but more compact than its neighbor Astata, which was divided into two separate clusters on both sides of the river (RH–08 and RH–07), just as Ringrose's 1682 map mentioned above demonstrates.

The surface distribution of Postclassic diagnostics covers all sites at the Río Huamelula and almost all site sectors. Especially to the north and east of Huamelula, the prehispanic surface record of RH11 and RH13 indicates solely Postclassic and/or Early Colonial occupations. Despite sampling limitations and classificatory problems mentioned above, this suggests that the Postclassic settlements at the Río Huamelula were much larger than those in earlier periods. If this distribution roughly indicates the settlement pattern at the time of the Spanish conquest, we can identify the large settlement of Huamelula, divided into several wards. The central part (RH12) is covered by the modern village's center. The Colonial population eventually concentrated at the site RH12, the site where two Colonial churches, San Pedro and San Sebastián, were erected. It is likely that many of the Late Postclassic ceramics attributes, which continue to be found on Early Colonial pottery, and an unknown portion of what I have classified as Late Postclassic pottery, may in fact be from postconquest occupations.

In sum, archaeological and historical sources are not suitable to confirm or contradict each other on this issue, because their temporal scopes and resolutions are not easy to synchronize. A drastic contradiction is in any case not perceivable, and thus we can regard them as complementary strands of evidence.

TERRITORIAL DIVISIONS (SIZE OF COMMUNITIES AND POLITIES)

The LTT does not illustrate the central community's territorial extent. It does, however, show an entire *señorío*'s territorial extent, which stretches from the coast up north into the highlands, including the four subject towns of Ayutla, Piltzintepec, Zapotitlán, and Mecaltepec. Ayutla is archaeologically visible in the remains recorded by Brockington et al. (1974), and Postclassic sites near Zapotitlán and Mecaltepec in the Sierra Madre del Sur have been investigated by Zborover (2007). Direct archaeological indicators for the geopolitical relationship between these communities and the central place of the LTT have not been identified, and the question of the central place's identity remains unsolved.

From an archaeological perspective, the Late Postclassic settlement distribution coincides with the Early Colonial boundary between Astata and Huamelula. With respect to the community sizes circa 1548 CE, the village of Astata is described in the SVP as having five subject villages, but no names or area indications are given. No subject villages are mentioned for Huamelula, but the size of the *cabecera* community is given: eight Spanish leagues *de boxo* (or about 42.56 kilometers of circumference, using 5.32 kilometer per league). This included apparently not only urban but also agricultural areas. Interestingly, this territorial buffer around Huamelula's center is still recognizable in modern-day settlement distribution. Figure 13.4 shows that modern-day subject villages of the *cabecera* are situated along the perimeter. Only the neighboring *cabecera* of Astata intrudes on the perimeter. As eighteenth-century court records show, this was exactly the reason for rising land disputes between Astata and Huamelula, after Astata's relocation in the seventeenth century to that spot, which, according to Huamelultecos, was "only lent" to their neighbors (Kroefges, personal field notes, 2004).

Social Differentiation

Documentary sources in the form of court testimonies and vice royal grants demonstrate the existence of a division between commoners and nobles (*caciques*, *gobernadores*, *principales*, and *yndios*) in Astata as well as in Huamelula. The LTT shows this distinction in the varying form of attires between the elaborately dressed ruling dynasty of the central town and the loincloth-wearing leaders of subject communities. Wealth differences are indicated as well in the archaeological record, visible in the surface remains of residences. Especially in Astata, more elaborate house remains and decorated pottery are concentrated in site RH08 Hualakgoce, while site RH07 Huapote featured very simple and uniform heavy-duty pottery. The central sections of the archeological site in Huamelula lie buried underneath the modern village, but the occasional ceramic fragments are more elaborate here than in the northern residential section of RH11 La Mishi. However, no burials were discovered that would have permitted more systematic investigation of wealth and status differences.

Thus, historical and archaeological sources mutually confirm each other in their rebuttal of the traditional stereotype that the Chontal people were barbarians lacking a complex sociopolitical organization or fixed settlements—as they had been portrayed by Burgoa and later historiographers.

Resource Exploitation, Production, and Exchange

The SVP report on Huamelula provides some details on the ecological and economic characteristics of Huamelula: cotton was a local product that might either have been traded directly or served to produce high-value textiles. Various artifact types confirm the brief description in the SVP (figure 13.5); for example, spindle whorls (*malacates*) to produce cotton yarn were found throughout the sites in Huamelula. The reference to the manufacture of paper, probably the fig-tree *amate* paper, is archaeologically illustrated by the presence of bark beaters made of stone. Fishing seems to have been an intensive activity as well, and it is archaeologically reflected in the distribution of fishing-net sinkers made of clay. Finally, the presence of an irrigation system provided plentiful agricultural productivity. Maize seems to have been the major crop as the SVP report suggests, and *manos* and *metates* are abundantly found in the survey area. In addition, some mineral artifacts and ecofacts were found during PARH, which point to some other economic activities: cutting tools and arrow projectile points were mainly made of obsidian from the Zaragoza and the Pico de Orizaba sources in Puebla.

Belief Systems

The consulted documentary sources are not explicit on Chontal religion or world view before the conquest; these topics were irrelevant for the largely land-dispute-related records of the mid-sixteenth century. One indirect hint, however, is given by the name of the father of Gaspar de Guzmán, Chontal *cacique* of Astata. The father appeared at witness hearings in 1554 in Tehuantepec (AGI Escribanía 160 bis. [1571]; see Machuca Gallegos 2007; Oudijk 2000; Zeitlin 2005). His name, *Chicomematate*, probably refers to "Seven Deer" (*chicome mazatl*), the Nahuatl version of a calendrical name derived from the pan-Mesoamerican 260-day calendar. That father of Gaspar de Guzmán was thus apparently born before the Spanish conquest and no further information about his origin or ethnic affiliation is provided. Nevertheless, it seems reasonable to take this name as an indicator that the coastal Chontal not only shared pan-Mesoamerican calendrical systems but also included the religious implications for their spiritual life.

Archaeological evidence for Late Postclassic belief systems is very limited. The Cueva del Diablo is on the western side of the river and, together with El Boquerón, it constitutes a significant element in the symbolic and mythical landscape of the

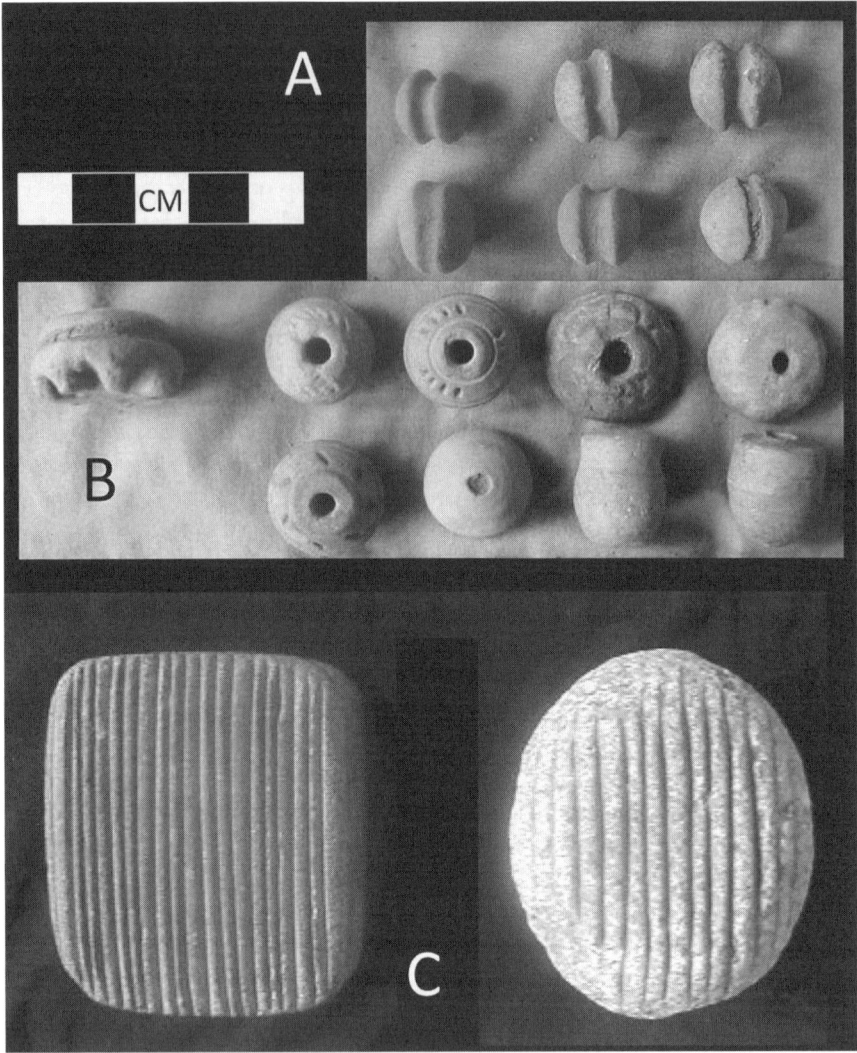

FIGURE 13.5. Artifacts reflecting resource exploitation and production, found at site RH01/Huamelula-La Soledad: (A) ceramic fishing-net sinkers, (B) ceramic spinning whorls, (C) bark beaters made of stone.

Huamelula territory, as various statements and stories by local informants reveal. Accordingly, legend has it that Huamelula was a rich, fertile village when the inhabitants were still offering goods (or their firstborns) to the devil at the cave. The devil in turn provided them with wealth and good harvests. In the 1960s, the priest of the San Pedro parish of Huamelula once entered the cave with some US seminarians and workers from Astata, to see if there were any ancient remains. Indeed, they found human skeletons and artifacts (see also Brockington 1974:27, 30). About one meter above the road level we found a rock carving of a spiral that appears ancient. The fact that Huamelultecos still practice rain petition rituals close to El Boquerón suggests that the cave at El Boquerón was indeed seen as the seat of supernatural forces responsible for rain and fertility. According to another legend, the cave was home to a giant snake, the apparition of which was associated with the beginning of the rainy season. The clouds accumulate between these cliffs, which prevent them from moving up north at the end of the dry season (see also Oseguera 2003).

This site can be understood as a locus of ritual activity. The local lore and removed burials indicate that in prehispanic times the cave was considered the seat of a serpent-shaped fertility and rain deity, where it received offerings and sacrifice victims. The petroglyph may have been a representation of this deity. After the Christian missionaries declared that the cave and the ritual belonged to the devil, Huamelultecos used another—secret—spot for their rain petition rituals, while the local lore still remembers the significance of the cave.

Civic-Ceremonial Institutions and Rulership

The political authority of Late Postclassic Astata is not well documented. The only reference so far found on the Early Colonial period is a testimony document (AGI Escribanía bis. 160 [1571]) in which native nobles from southeastern Oaxaca were to testify concerning the heritage of Tehuantepec's estates. The document includes the testimony of the *cacique* of Astata, Don Gaspar de Guzmán, a son of the abovementioned last ruler of prehispanic Astata, Chicomematatle. He was married to a daughter of Cosijopii, who was in turn later baptized Don Juan Cortéz. When the testimony was recorded in 1554, Don Gaspar de Guzmán was about forty years old. Therefore, this marriage cannot be taken as a prehispanic marital alliance between Tehuantepec and Astata.

Previously I have argued that authors from Astata were responsible for the modifications on the LTT, which was reportedly kept in the village until the mid-twentieth century (Kroefges 1998, 2009). The time when the LTT was modified by adding place-name glyphs cannot be determined with any certainty. It may have been as early as the latter half of the sixteenth century, when the Astatans reportedly used a pictorial map to provide evidence for a land dispute (see Odena Güemes 1997). Another, later scenario was the relocation of Astata at the turn of the seventeenth to the eighteenth century, when boundary conflicts with neighboring Huamelula newly arose. This situation may have been the background for the addition of place glyphs in the LTT, in which scenario the authors of the LTT's modification did not place much importance on the depicted dynasties but, rather, emphasized territorial issues.

POLITICAL DOMINANCE AND ALLIANCES

Closing this discussion, we return to the issue that opened it at the beginning: the political constellations in southern Oaxaca on the eve of Spanish conquest and the incomplete source coverage for the coastal Chontal. The corresponding *Relaciones Geográficas* are lost, and the chroniclers said little on that topic. According to the Codex Ramírez (1979: 86–89), Axayacatl once undertook a military expedition against "Tehuantepec and his allies," which took him all the way along the coast until reaching Huatulco. This brief statement suggests that the coastal Chontalpa, set between Tehuantepec and Huatulco, was part of this political configuration.

The LTT, on the other hand, does depict an Aztec intrusion in the north of the Chontal region led by "Xocotlatoani," probably Motecuhzoma II Xocoyotzin, as well as a Zapotec engagement with the central place of the LTT. As most studies on the LTT have emphasized, the exact political constellations are not easy to interpret. Are the central place and its subjects siding with Motecuhzoma against the Zapotecs, as suggested by Zborover (2002, 2006), or are they allied to the Zapotecs and shown capturing warriors that fought for Motecuhzoma, as proposed by the present author (Kroefges 1998, 2009)?

From an archaeological perspective, confirming or contradicting evidence is difficult to identify. Nevertheless, Brockington (1982) has made an instructive observation on the relationship between Tututepec's dominance over numerous communities along the Oaxacan coast, and the presence of Mixteca-Puebla style pottery remains at their corresponding archaeological sites. The use of such pottery was probably related to an elite ideology and served to link subjected local elites to the paramount Mixtec rulers in Tututepec, a common phenomenon in imperial political organizations (see Smith and Montiel 2001). It is frequent at the centers in the western half of the coast, but, as Brockington observed, very scarce or absent at sites to the east of Huatulco—that is, in the present study area. The PARH ceramic collections along the Río Huamelula did not detect more than a single fragment of Mixteca-Puebla polychrome vessels (Kroefges 2006a, 2000b). On the other hand, Late Postclassic grayware vessels typical for the Zapotec Isthmus region were abundant (Wallrath 1967; Zeitlin and Zeitlin 1990; see also Kroefges 2006a, 2006b).

The archaeological record at the Río Huamelula did not provide adequate data for determining whether Huamelula and Astata were under Tututepec's imperial dominion; such historical episodes may not be traceable in the material remains. However, the pottery data provided by Brockington's project and by PARH would suggest that there was only a comparatively loose or sporadic integration of the coastal Chontalpa within the imperial exchange networks of Tututepec, especially when compared to the communities at the Huatulco bays to the west. These were historically documented as a province of tribute-paying vassals, and they yielded codex-style polychrome pottery in quite large quantities which appears to have been imported there under unclear social, political, or economic terms (Brockington 1982; Fernández Dávila and Gómez Serafín 1988; see also Joyce et al. 2004, 2009).

Meanwhile, cultural, economic, and probably sociopolitical ties appear to have been stronger between the coastal Chontal communities and the Isthmian Zapotec power over the long run; this is not only indicated through the material culture of the prehispanic period, but continued during the Colonial period and is still noticeable today in terms of social interaction, adoption of clothing styles, and economic exchange.

CONCLUSIONS

Ethnohistorical and archaeological sources for the culture history of the eastern portion of the Oaxaca coast are—taken individually—sparse and ambiguous. Sociopolitical and economic organizations of the Postclassic period are only hypothetically inferable through hermeneutic inferences based on Colonial-period indigenous pictographic manuscripts and administrative accounts. Archaeological "testing" of these interpretations seems, in the strict sense, not possible. However, several strands of material evidence found during regional and local-scale archaeological survey can be interpreted to support one or another hypothesis, and help in judging whether these meet our expectations about the presence, quality, quantity, and distribution of materials that would reflect constellations and behavior interpreted from documentary sources. The challenge is to identify the most plausible among the several thinkable factors that may have produced the observed patterns of artifact distribution. Therefore, I suspect that the conjunctive study of archaeological and historical sources presented here (and in many other cases) constitutes a hermeneutic approach of understanding different sources through dialectical reasoning (see discussion in Hodder 1991), rather than hypothesis-testing. The presented results remain subject to reconsideration, which would involve assessing the plausibility of given interpretations and confronting them with additional relevant data of archaeological and historical nature.

REFERENCES

Acuña, Rene, ed. 1984a. *Relaciones Geograficas del Siglo XVI: Antequera*. vol. 1. Mexico City: Universidad Nacional Autónoma de Mexico.

Acuña, Rene, ed. 1984b. *Relaciones Geograficas del Siglo XVI: Antequera*. vol. 2. Mexico City: Universidad Nacional Autónoma de Mexico.

Andrén, Anders. 1998. *Between Artifacts and Texts: Historical Archaeology in Global Perspective*. New York: Plenum Press. http://dx.doi.org/10.1007/978-1-4757-9409-0.

Balkansky, Andrew K. 2001. "Review of 'The Shadow of Monte Albán: Politics and Historiography in Postclassic Oaxaca, Mexico,'" ed. Maarten Jansen, Peter Kroefges, and Michel Oudijk. *The Journal of the Royal Anthropological Institute* 7(1):175–177.

Basauri, Carlos. 1940. *Tribu: Chontales de Oaxaca. Secretaría de Educación Pública*. vol. 3. Mexico City: Secretaría de Educación.

Binford, Lewis R. 1962. "Archaeology as Anthropology." *American Antiquity* 28 (2):217–225. http://dx.doi.org/10.2307/278380.

Bintliff, John L., and C. F. Gaffney, eds. 1986. *Archaeology at the Interface: Studies in Archaeology's Relationships with History, Geography, Biology and Physical Science*. Oxford: BAR.

Bradomín, José M. 1987. *Historia Antigua de Oaxaca*. Oaxaca: Published by the author.

Braudel, Fernand. 1972. *The Mediterranean and the Mediterranean World in the Age of Philip II*. New York: Harper and Row.

Brockington, Donald L. 1974. "Reconnaissance from the Río Tonameca to Salina Cruz." In *The Oaxaca Coast Project Reports: Part II*, ed. Donald L. Brockington, and J. Robert Long, 3–33. Nashville: Vanderbilt University Publications in Anthropology, No. 9.

Brockington, Donald L. 1982. "Spatial and Temporal Variations of the Mixtec-Style Ceramics in Southern Oaxaca." In *Aspects of the Mixteca-Puebla Style and Mixtec and Central Mexican Culture in Southern Mesoamerica*, ed. Jennifer S. H. Brown and E. Wyllys Andrews V., 7–13. Middle American Research Institute, Occasional Paper No. 4. New Orleans: Tulane University.

Brockington, Donald L. 1987. "El Clásico en la Costa de Oaxaca." In *El Auge y la Caída del Clásico en el México Central*, ed. Joseph B. Mountjoy and Donald L. Brockington, 225–236. Mexico City: Instituto de Investigaciones Antropológicas, Universidad Nacional Autónoma de México.

Brockington, Donald L., María Jorrín, and Robert Long, eds. 1974. *The Oaxaca Coast Project Reports, Part I*. Nashville: Vanderbilt University Publications in Anthropology, No. 8.

Brockington, Donald L., and J. Robert Long, eds. 1974. *The Oaxaca Coast Project Reports. Part II*. Nashville: Vanderbilt University Publications in Anthropology, No. 9.

Brown, Kenneth L. 1983. "Some Comments on Ethnohistory and Archaeology: Have We Attained (Are We Even Approaching) a Truly Conjunctive Approach?" *Revista de Antropologia* 10 (2):53–72.

Burgoa, Fray Francisco de. (1674) 1989. *Geográfica Descripción de la Parte Septentrional del Polo Árctico de la América y Nueva Iglesia de las Indias Occidentales, y Sitio Astronómico de esta Provincia de Predicadores de Antequera, Valle de Oaxaca,* 2 vols. Mexico City: Editorial Porrúa.

Byland, Bruce E., and John M.D. Pohl. 1994a. *In the Realm of 8 Deer: The Archaeology of the Mixtec Codices.* Norman: University of Oklahoma Press.

Byland, Bruce E., and John M.D. Pohl. 1994b. "Political Factions in the Transition from Classic to Postclassic in the Mixteca Alta." In *Factional Competition and Political Development in the New World,* ed. Elizabeth M. Brumfiel and John W. Fox, 117–126. Cambridge: Cambridge University Press. http://dx.doi.org/10.1017/CBO9780511598401.012.

Camacho, Juan P. 1993. "La Chontalpa Oaxaqueña." *Guchachi' reza* 29:8–18.

Carmack, Robert M., and John M. Weeks. 1981. "The Archaeology and Ethnohistory of Utatlán: A Conjunctive Approach." *American Antiquity* 46 (2):323–341. http://dx.doi.org/10.2307/280211.

Charlton, Thomas. 1981. "Archaeology, Ethnohistory, and Ethnography: Interpretative Interfaces." In *Advances in Archaeological Method and Theory,* vol. 4. ed. Michael B. Schiffer, 129–176. New York: Academic Press.

Cline, Howard F. 1972. "The Relaciones Geográficas of the Spanish Indies, 1577–1648." In *Handbook of Middle American Indians,* vol. 12. ed. Robert Wauchope, 183–369. Austin: University of Texas Press.

Códice Ramírez. 1979. *Relación del Origen de los Indios que Habitan esta Nueva España Según sus Historias. Manuscrito del Siglo XVI Intitulado.* Mexico: Editorial Innovación.

Dávila Padilla, Fray Agustín de. (Original work published 1596) 1955. *Historia de la Fundación y Discurso de la Provincia de Santiago de México, de la Orden de Predicadores.* Mexico City: Editorial Academia Literaria.

de la Cruz, Víctor. 2008. *Mapas Genealógicos del Istmo Oaxaqueño.* Mexico City: CONACULTA, Gobierno del Estado de Oaxaca, CIESAS.

de León Chávez, Sara, ed. 1995. *Lo que Cuentan los Abuelos, 3.* Oaxaca: Instituto Nacional Indigenista.

Esparza, Manuel. 1994. *Relaciones Geográficas de Oaxaca, 1777–1778.* Mexico City: CIESAS.

Feinman, Gary M. 1997. "Thoughts on New Approaches to Combining the Archaeological and Historical Records." *Journal of Archaeological Method and Theory* 4 (3–4):367–377. http://dx.doi.org/10.1007/BF02428069.

Fernández Dávila, Enrique, and Susana Gómez Serafín. 1988. *Arqueología de Huatulco, Oaxaca: Memoria de la Primera Temporada de Campo del Proyecto Arqueológico Bahías de Huatulco*. Mexico City: Instituto Nacional de Antropología e Historia.

Fernández Dávila, Enrique, and Susana Gómez Serafín. 1990. "Arqueología de Huatulco." In *Lecturas Históricas del Estado de Oaxaca*, ed. Marcus C. Winter, 489–508. Vol. 1: Época Prehispánica. Mexico City: Instituto Nacional de Antropología e Historia.

García Pimentel, Luis, ed. 1904. *Relación de los Obispados de Tlaxcala, Michoacán, Oaxaca y Otros Lugares en el Siglo XVI*. Mexico City: Published by the author.

Gerhard, Peter. 1972. *A Guide to the Political Geography of New Spain*. Cambridge: Cambridge University Press.

Gerhard, Peter. 1995. *Síntesis e Índice de los Mandamientos Virreinales 1548–1553*. Mexico City: Universidad Nacional Autónoma de México.

Glass, John B. 1964. *Catálogo de la Colección de Códices*. Mexico: Museo Nacional de Antropología.

González, Alicia M. 2002. *The Edge of Enchantment: Sovereignty and Ceremony in Huatulco, Mexico*. Washington, DC: National Museum of the American Indian-Smithsonian Institution.

González de Cossío, Francisco, ed. 1952. *Libro de las Tasaciones de Pueblos de la Nueva España, Siglo XVI*. Mexico City: Archivo General de la Nación.

Hodder, Ian. 1991. "Interpretive Archaeology and its Role." *American Antiquity* 56 (1): 7–18. http://dx.doi.org/10.2307/280968.

Howse, Derek, and Norman J.W. Thrower. 1992. *A Buccaneer's Atlas: Basil Ringrose's South Sea Waggoner: A Sea Atlas and Sailing Directions of the Pacific Coast of the Americas 1682*. Berkeley: University of California Press.

Joyce, Arthur A., Andrew B. Workinger, Byron Hamann, Peter C. Kroefges, Maxine Oland, and Stacie M. King. 2004. "Lord 8 Deer 'Jaguar Claw' and the Land of the Sky: The Archaeology and History of Tututepec." *Latin American Antiquity* 15 (3):273–297. http://dx.doi.org/10.2307/4141575.

Joyce, Arthur A., Peter C. Kroefges, and Maxine Oland. 2009. "Recorrido Regional de Superficie." In *El Proyecto Río Verde: Informe Final Entregado al Consejo de Arqueología y el Centro INAH Oaxaca del Instituto Nacional de Antropología e Historia*, ed. Arthur A. Joyce and Marc N. Levine, 322–353. Unpublished report on file at the Centro INAH Oaxaca, Mexico.

Knapp, A. Bernard, ed. 1992. *Archaeology, Annales, and Ethnohistory*. Cambridge: Cambridge University Press.

Kroefges, Peter C. 1998. "El Lienzo de Tecciztlan y Tequatepec: Un Documento Historico-Cartográfico de la Chontalpa de Oaxaca." In *The Shadow of Monte Albán:*

Politics and Historiography in Postclassic Oaxaca, Mexico, ed. Maarten Jansen, Peter C. Kroefges, and Michel R. Oudijk, 45–66. Leiden: Research School CNWS.

Kroefges, Peter C. 2004. "Sociopolitical Organization in the Prehispanic Chontalpa de Oaxaca, Mexico: Ethnohistorical and Archaeological Perspectives." Unpublished PhD diss., Department of Anthropology, University at Albany-SUNY.

Kroefges, Peter C. 2006a. "¿Arqueología de los Chontales o arqueología de la Chontalpa?" In *Historia y Etnografía entre los Chontales de Oaxaca*, ed. Andrés Oseguera, 41–60. Mexico City: Instituto Nacional de Antropología e Historia.

Kroefges, Peter C. 2006b. *Archaeological Investigations at the Río Huamelula. Prehispanic Settlement, Material Culture, and Chronology in Southeastern Oaxaca, Mexico*. Oxford: BAR International Series, Archaeopress.

Kroefges, Peter C. 2009. *En Tierras Desconocidas: La Chontalpa de Oaxaca, México, Según Documentos Indígenas y Españoles Coloniales*. Cologne, Germany: Lambert Academic Publishing.

Lyman, R. Lee, and Michael J. O'Brien. 2001. "The Direct Historical Approach, Analogical Reasoning, and Theory in Americanist Archaeology." *Journal of Archaeological Method and Theory* 8 (4):303–342. http://dx.doi.org/10.1023/A:1013736416067.

Machuca Gallegos, Laura. 2007. *Comercio de Sal y Redes de Poder en Tehuantepec en la Época Colonial*. Mexico City: CIESAS.

Marcus, Joyce, and Kent V. Flannery. 1983. "An Introduction to the Late Postclassic." In *The Cloud People: Divergent Evolution of the Zapotec and Mixtec Civilizations*, ed. Kent V. Flannery and Joyce Marcus, 217–226. New York: Academic Press.

Méndez Martínez, Enrique, ed. 1979. *Índice de Documentos Relativos a los Pueblos del Estado de Oaxaca: Ramo Tierras del Archivo General de la Nación*. Mexico City: SEP-INAH.

O'Connor, Loretta, and Peter C. Kroefges. 2008. "The Land Remembers: Landscape Terms and Place Names in Lowland Chontal of Oaxaca, Mexico." *Language Sciences* 30 (2–3):291–315. http://dx.doi.org/10.1016/j.langsci.2006.12.007.

Odena Güemes, Lina. 1997. "El Lienzo de Astata: Una Nueva Posibilidad de Interpretación." In *Códices y Documentos Sobre México: Segundo Simposio*, ed. Salvador Rueda Smithers, Constanza Vega Sosa, and Rodrigo Martínez Baracs, 305–318. Colección Científica, vol. 1. Mexico City: Instituto Nacional de Antropología e Historia.

Oseguera, Andrés. 2003. "Los Signos de un Territorio Oculto: Geografía Social de la Región Chontal Oaxaqueña." In *Diálogos con el Territorio: Simbolizaciones Sobre el Espacio en las Culturas Indígenas de México*, ed. Alicia M. Barabas, 225–248. Mexico City: INAH.

Oudijk, Michel R. 2000. *Historiography of the Bènizàa: The Postclassic and Early Colonial Periods (A.D. 1000–1600)*. Leiden: CNWS.

Parsons, Lee A. 1978. "The Peripheral Coastal Lowlands and the Middle Classic Period." In *Middle Classic Mesoamerica: A.D. 400–700*, ed. Esther Pasztory, 25–34. New York: Columbia University Press.

Paso y Troncoso, Francisco del, ed. 1905. *Papeles de la Nueva España.* Segunda Série: Geografía e Estadística, vol. 1. Madrid: Sucesor de Rivadeneyra.

Paso y Troncoso, Francisco del, ed. 1939–1942. *Epistolario de Nueva España 1505–1818*, 16 vols. Biblioteca Histórica Mexicana de Obras Inéditas, Segunda Série. Mexico City: Antigua Librería Robredo.

Ramenofsky, Ann F. 1991a. "Beyond Disciplinary Bias: Future Directions in Contact Period Studies." In *Columbian Consequences,* vol. 3: *The Spanish Borderlands in Pan-American Perspective*, ed. David H. Thomas, 431–436. Washington, DC: Smithsonian Institution Press.

Ramenofsky, Ann F. 1991b. "Historical Science and Contact Period Studies." In *Columbian Consequences,* vol. 3: *The Spanish Borderlands in Pan-American Perspective*, ed. David H. Thomas, 437–452. Washington, DC: Smithsonian Institution Press.

Shennan, Stephen. 1989. "Introduction: Archaeological Approaches to Cultural Identity." In *Archaeological Approaches to Cultural Identity*, ed. Stephen Shennan, 1–32. London: Unwin Hyman.

Smith, Michael E. 1992. "Rhythms of Change in Postclassic Central Mexico: Archaeology, Ethnohistory, and the Braudelian Model." In *Archaeology, Annales, and Ethnohistory*, ed. A. Bernard Knapp, 51–74. Cambridge: Cambridge University Press. http://dx.doi.org/10.1017/CBO9780511759949.005.

Smith, Michael E., and Lisa Montiel. 2001. "The Archaeological Study of Empires and Imperialism in Prehispanic Central Mexico." *Journal of Anthropological Archaeology* 20 (3):245–284. http://dx.doi.org/10.1006/jaar.2000.0372.

Spores, Ronald, and Miguel Saldaña, eds. 1973. *Documentos para la Etnohistoria del Estado de Oaxaca: Índice del Ramo de Mercedes del Archivo General de la Nación, México.* Vanderbilt University Publications in Anthropology 5. Nashville: Vanderbilt University.

Spores, Ronald, and Miguel Saldaña, eds. 1975. *Documentos para la Etnohistoria del Estado de Oaxaca: Índice del Ramo de Mercedes del Archivo General de la Nación, México*. Vanderbilt University Publications in Anthropology 13. Nashville: Vanderbilt University.

Spores, Ronald, and Miguel Saldaña, eds. 1976. *Documentos para la Etnohistoria del Estado de Oaxaca: Índice del Ramo de Mercedes del Archivo General de la Nación, México.* Vanderbilt University Publications in Anthropology 17. Nashville: Vanderbilt University.

Taracena, Angel. 1941. *Apuntes Históricos de Oaxaca (Desde los Tiempos Precortesianos hasta la Época Actual).* Oaxaca.

Wallrath, Matthew. 1967. *Excavations in the Tehuantepec Region, Mexico.* Transactions of The American Philosophical Society, New Series 57(2). Philadelphia: The American Philosophical Society.

Wilson, Samuel M. 1993. "Structure and History: Combining Archaeology and Ethnohistory in the Contact Period Caribbean." In *Ethnohistory and Archaeology: Approaches to Postcontact Change in the Americas*, ed. J. Daniel Rogers and Samuel M. Wilson, 19–30. New York: Plenum Press.

Winter, Marcus C. 1986. "La Dinámica Étnica en Oaxaca Prehispánica." In *Etnicidad y Pluralismo Cultural: La Dinámica Étnica en Oaxaca*, ed. Miguel Bartolomé and Alicia Barabas, 106–136. Mexico City: Instituto Nacional de Antropología e Historia.

Zárate Morán, Roberto. 1995. "Los Chontales y el Patrimonio Cultural." In *El Patrimonio Sitiado: El Punto de Vista de los Trabajadores*, ed. Trabajadores Académicos del Instituto Nacional de Antropología e Historia, Delegación D-II-I-A–1, Sección X, 311–322. Mexico City: INAH.

Zborover, Danny. 2002. "Kingdom on Cloth: Cartographic-Histories and the Curious Case of the Lienzo de Tecciztlan y Tequatepec." Unpublished Masters thesis, Faculty of Archaeology, Leiden University, Leiden.

Zborover, Danny. 2006. "Narrativas Históricas y Territoriales de la Chontalpa Oaxaqueña." In *Historia y Etnografía Entre los Chontales de Oaxaca*, ed. Andrés Oseguera, 61–108. Mexico City: INAH.

Zborover, Danny. 2007. *The Chontalpa Historical Archaeology Project, Oaxaca.* Report submitted to FAMSI, http://www.famsi.org/reports/05038/index.html; accessed Dec 2010.

Zborover, Danny. 2008. "Identidades Faccionales en 'Narrativas Territoriales' de la Oaxaca Colonial: Un Enfoque Desde las Montañas Chontales." In *Pictografía y Escritura Alfabética en Oaxaca*, ed. Sebastian van Doesburg, 233–70. Oaxaca: IEEPO.

Zeitlin, Judith F. 1978. "Community Distribution and Local Economy on the Southern Isthmus of Tehuantepec: Archaeological and Ethnohistorical Investigation." PhD diss., Department of Anthropology, Yale University. Ann Arbor: University Microfilms.

Zeitlin, Judith F. 1993. "The Politics of Classic-Period Ritual Interaction: Iconography of the Ballgame Cult in Coastal Oaxaca." *Ancient Mesoamerica* 4 (1):121–140. http://dx.doi.org/10.1017/S0956536100000821.

Zeitlin, Judith F. 2005. *Cultural Politics in Colonial Tehuantepec: Community and State among the Isthmus Zapotec, 1500–1750*. Stanford: Stanford University Press.

Zeitlin, Judith F., and Robert N. Zeitlin. 1990. "Arqueología y Época Prehispánica en el Sur del Istmo de Tehuantepec." In *Lecturas Históricas del Estado de Oaxaca*, ed. Marcus C. Winter, 393–454. Colección Regiones de México, vol. 1: Época Prehispánica. Mexico City: Instituto Nacional de Antropología e Historia/Gobierno del Estado de Oaxaca.

14

Locating the Hidden Transcripts of Colonialism

Archaeological and Historical Evidence from the Isthmus of Tehuantepec

JUDITH FRANCIS ZEITLIN

Archaeologists who work with written documents may feel emboldened by the layers of detail the historical record adds to the architectural and artifactual residue we are trained to decipher. The anonymous past becomes populated with individuals whose voices and actions can be fixed with chronological precision, rather than depending on the broad phases to which ceramics styles are assigned. Moreover, their testimonies enlighten our understandings of motivation and meaning, offering an antidote to processualist claims and giving substance to the emphasis on human agency that so many of us espouse. But if we are to make full value of the partnership between archaeology and history, we must also be more fully aware of the nature of the written record available to us.

Too often archaeologists have used that record uncritically, assuming a transparency to the documents that would surprise historians, who are trained to question authenticity and authority in their sources. Modern social historians and ethnohistorians of Latin America, moreover, pay close attention to the Colonial context in which written documents emerged, recognizing the legalistic purpose of the vast majority of materials preserved in archives and the limited, often self-serving perspective of their Spanish-speaking authors. For that reason a new generation of Mesoamerican historians, collectively referred to as the New Philologists (Restall 2003), draws primarily if not exclusively on alphabetic documents composed by indigenous authors in their own languages to reconstruct the Colonial-period world of native Mesoamericans.

DOI: 10.5876/9781607323297.c014

Even where indigenous-language sources are abundant, the same issues of author-ship, agenda, and audience need to be examined in the interpretation of historical texts. From this more hermeneutical perspective, we must be mindful of the ways in which the realities of Spanish Colonial domination structured and constrained what could be written, if we wish to know what native people experienced and thought. As the political scientist James C. Scott has generalized in his influen-tial book, *Domination and the Arts of Resistance*, such situations produce a public discourse in which both powerful and subordinated actors appear to reflect the hegemonic values of the dominant group:

> The theatrical imperatives that normally prevail in situations of domination produce a public transcript in close conformity with how the dominant group would wish to have things appear. The dominant never control the stage absolutely, but their wishes normally prevail. In the short run, it is in the interest of the subordinate to produce a more or less credible performance, speaking the lines and making the gestures he knows are expected of him. The result is that the public transcript is—barring a cri-sis—systematically skewed in the direction of the libretto, the discourse, represented by the dominant. (Scott 1990:4)

To illustrate my concerns about using Colonial-era records to characterize Oaxaca's indigenous communities, their lifestyles, and their values, I examine two published texts dating to the second half of the seventeenth century that report on Zapotec-speaking people of the Isthmus of Tehuantepec. I also draw upon contem-porary archaeological data I recovered from Rancho Santa Cruz, a rural site located on the Isthmus near the piedmont community of Chihuitán (figure 14.1).

In the course of this analysis, I make use of Scott's framework to characterize these "texts" either as *public transcripts*, in the sense conveyed above, or as *hidden transcripts*, Scott's term for the kinds of discourses and commentaries on the domi-nant society that subordinated people engage in among their familiar peers. Such sentiments typically are communicated orally through jokes and gossip and, less frequently for the ethnohistorian, through private papers, letters, and diaries. One of the published texts discussed here provides a telling example of the "rupture of the political *cordon sanitaire* between the hidden and the public transcript" that Scott (1990:19) finds especially revealing of political dynamics in situations of great social and economic inequality.

My purpose in this analysis lies beyond the cautionary example it offers other Oaxaca archaeologists about the reliability of favored Colonial authors as reporters of indigenous values and behavior. What I hope to do is present a more nuanced integration of late-seventeenth-century historical and archaeological data. My read-ing of these three written and archaeological texts illuminates everyday forms of

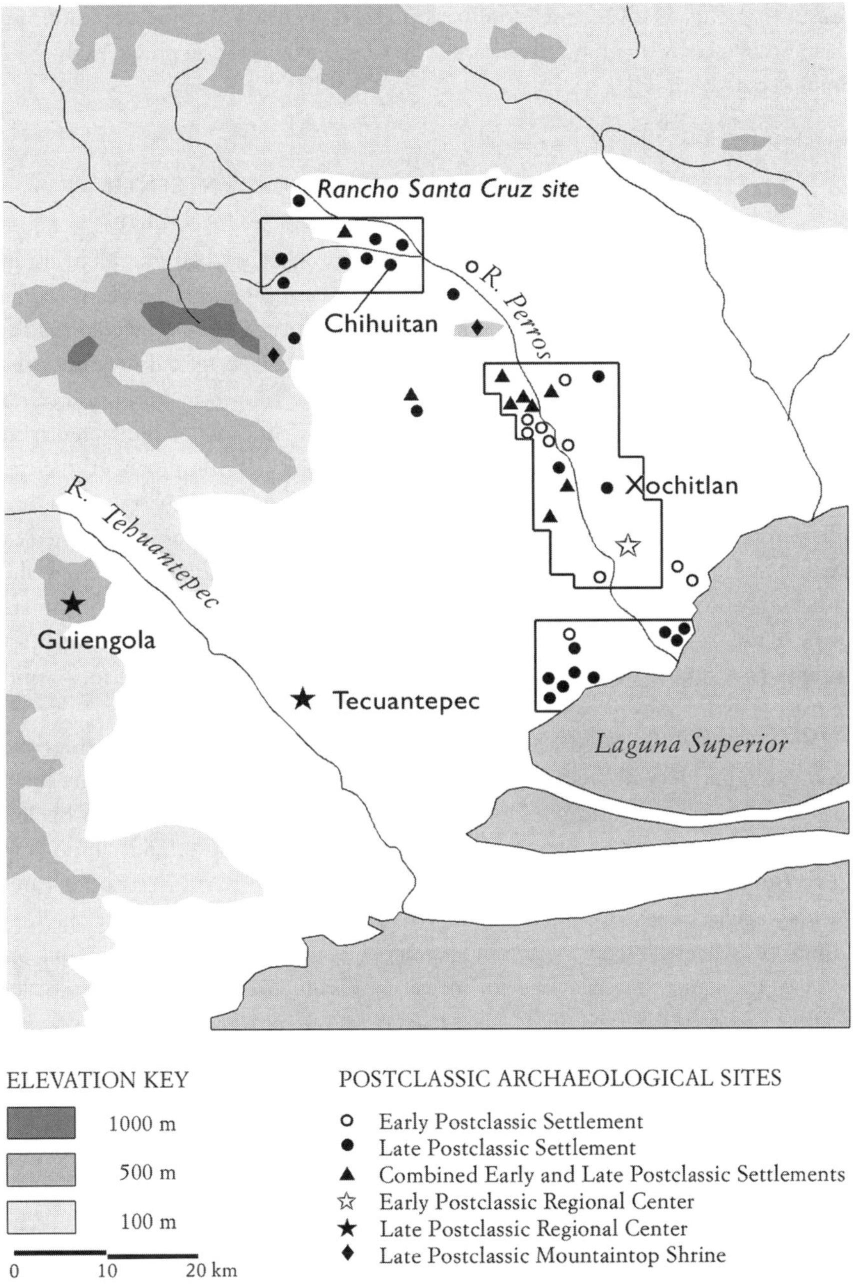

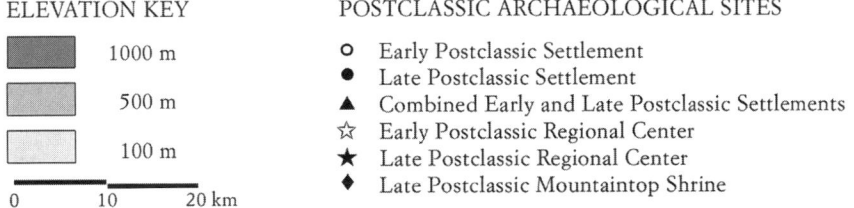

FIGURE 14.1. Postclassic settlement patterns along the Río de los Perros and the location of selected places mentioned in the text.

resistance to Spanish Colonial domination among Isthmus Zapotec communities that are masked by the tranquil picture of Colonial acculturation presented by Fray Francisco de Burgoa.

THE TEHUANTEPEC REGION IN THE MID-SEVENTEENTH CENTURY: REREADING BURGOA AS PUBLIC TRANSCRIPT

The Tehuantepec region, like most parts of Oaxaca, had absorbed the full brunt of Spanish conquest by the mid-seventeenth century and achieved a stable, if fragile, balance between traditional ways of life and novel forms imposed by colonialism. It was a balance struck in many facets of life, between *milpa* agriculture and introduced livestock pasturage, between local community autonomy and the interference of Spanish administrators, between indigenous concepts of the sacred landscape and the obligatory manifestations of Catholic piety. The dominant ethnicities that shaped late prehispanic community life on the southern coastal plain and adjacent *sierra*—Zapotec, Huave, Zoque, Chontal, and Mixe—now were joined by smaller numbers of Spaniards, Africans, and mixed-race individuals. Although the indigenous population shrank to as little as 10 percent of its preconquest estimate by 1620, the worst demographic impact of introduced diseases had passed and most Isthmus communities were making small but significant gains in population at mid-century (Zeitlin 2005).

Fray Francisco de Burgoa's (1989) massive *Geográfica Descripción* provides the most extended view of seventeenth-century life in Tehuantepec. Born in Antequera in 1606 and accepted into the Dominican order in 1629, Burgoa devoted his life to preaching among the native communities of the bishopric and supporting the ecclesiastical mission of the Province of San Hipólito Martír. Historians and anthropologists know him best for his two published works, which are the first substantial historical texts written in Spanish by a resident of Oaxaca. Drawing on some of the same materials used for his earlier chronicle of the Dominican order, *Palestra Histórial* (Burgoa 1670), Burgoa's 1674 geographical survey of Oaxaca intersperses missionary history with native oral histories and firsthand observations of the major Oaxaca Christian doctrines. Despite his frustrating penchant for turgid pious digressions, Burgoa is an unrivalled font of information about Oaxaca's native communities in the seventeenth century and about native history as it was transmitted and understood 150 years after the Spanish conquest. For, although he claimed to have seen many now-lost *pinturas* that documented this history, such manuscripts depended on a living narrator's interpretation.

Elsewhere I have focused on the Zapotec narrative accounts of their colonization of the Isthmus as presented in the *Geográfica Descripción* (Zeitlin 2003; 2005). Here my interest lies primarily in Burgoa's observations of seventeenth-century native life, which I presume are a mix of his own experiences and those reported to him by Dominican missionaries and other Spanish-speaking contemporaries. Scattered among his observations are both incidents of continued idolatry unmasked by zealous missionaries and examples of pious converts demonstrating true Christian zeal. Having served twice as Provincial for the Oaxaca Dominicans, and more briefly as Vicar General for the Order in New Spain and a member of the Inquisition, Burgoa would have had access to the scores of missionary reports and ecclesiastical judgments in which such incidents were transcribed. The historical narrative into which Burgoa placed these incidents has all the hallmarks that exemplify its status as a public transcript of colonialism. Not only would we expect this narrative to reflect the dominant colonial discourse as understood by the author, a highly respected member of the religious establishment, but the fact that it passed the inspection and approval of eight ecclesiastical censors before publication further evidences its conformity with the hegemonic values of the Colonial power elite.

Although the seemingly random structure of each chapter makes it difficult to talk about patterns, Burgoa's scattered ethnographic description revolves around the major themes of economic activities, community organization, and religious practices in the two Isthmus Zapotec *doctrinas,* Jalapa (today Jalapa del Marqués) and Tehuantepec, which are the focus of his chapters 71–74. Both sections have an early introduction to the landscape, from Jalapa's location in the floodplain between two converging rivers to the fertile coastal plain of Tehuantepec that made it such a target of prehispanic colonization. Between the two *doctrinas,* we learn of the variety of hunted game animals, fish, and birds found in the Isthmus, along with the pesky insects and scorpions that annoy humans and the dangerous caimans in local rivers. Burgoa provides a lengthy list of cultivated fruits that includes introduced species from oranges to tamarinds. That list is partially repeated near the end of chapter 74, with additional reference to the important trade commodities of cacao, vanilla, *achiote, patlaste,* and cotton. Cultivation of maize and beans must have been taken for granted, for it is not specifically mentioned for the Zapotecs, though its scarcity is referred to in a later chapter on the Huave. The residents of Tehuantepec are said to grow melons, watermelons, papaya, sugar cane, and other delectables in their gardens.

Spanish cattle and mule haciendas are discussed, mostly in the context of the disrepair of the once productive Marquesado estates, but Burgoa leaves his primary reference to native engagement with livestock until his chapters on Huave and Mixe (Zoque) practices. In discussing the industrious, able, and hispanicized Zapotec population of Tehuantepec, he points to those individuals who keep teams of forty to fifty mules with which they regularly make long trading journeys to distant parts of New Spain. Concrete examples of this commerce are the trade for cacao from Soconusco and for assorted manufactured goods from Puebla, in which he specifically mentions various kinds of cloth, soap, and metal tools like machetes, axes, plows, wrought iron work, and horse tackle. Admiring their tidy and acculturated appearance, Burgoa remarks that "todos visten muy aseado y de camino como españoles de pies a cabeza con muy buenas mulas y sillas" (Burgoa 1989:389). Slightly later he remarks on the busy market held for two hours each morning in Tehuantepec, where all manner of foods needed to sustain the community are provided, making special note of the salted meat, fresh fish, birds, iguana and sea turtle eggs, fruit, and shrimp sold there.

The approximate size of both *cabeceras* is given, with four hundred families in Jalapa's thirteen barrios and fifteen hundred in Tehuantepec, where eighteen barrios were spread on both sides of the Tehuantepec River. He notes that some Tehuantepec barrios held fifty families or more, but any further elaboration of the social forms in these barrios is limited to religious topics. Burgoa comments on how each barrio has its own chapel and that barrio members form enthusiastic choirs whose playing of instruments and exquisite singing, particularly that of young maidens, was a delight, if lasting a bit too late at night on festive occasions. On particular festivals devoted to the Holy Rosary, groups set out from each barrio chapel singing en route to Tehuantepec's town center and the church of San Pedro, where they all assembled to cacophonous effect (Burgoa 1989:390).

Not surprisingly, Burgoa devotes more space to discussions of religious belief and practice in these chapters than to any other theme, but he presents topics that challenge neither the prevailing hegemony of Catholicism nor the Dominicans' monopoly on religious affairs in these *doctrinas*. Aspects of prehispanic ritual practice are described freely, but in contexts that serve either to explain some prognostication of the eventual Spanish conquest of the Zapotecs and the appearance of friars in their midst, or to provide background on discovered acts of idolatry by nominally Christian Indians.

Both Jalapa and Tehuantepec church histories provided important examples of this religious backsliding. Burgoa's lengthy description of the idolatrous acts of the last Tehuantepec king, Don Juan Cortés, who was discovered in 1562 performing ritual sacrifices in his palace with the assistance of aged Mitla priests, gives us important insights on native resistance to Christianity's exclusivity. That the moral lesson Burgoa (1989:356) draws from this story concerns the poor example set by greedy Spaniards rather than the weakness or inferiority of the Indians is itself interesting. In the early seventeenth-century Jalapa incident, a landscape shrine devoted to Pinopiaa was discovered by chance and linked to a broader conspiracy of natives who equated the deified Zapotec royal ancestor with Santa Catarina. There Burgoa spared no condemnation of the cult and particularly of its young leader, who betrayed the trust of the friars who raised him (Burgoa 1989:331).

This difference of tone may reflect the deep affection the Oaxaca Dominicans felt for Don Juan, who was responsible for constructing Tehuantepec's massive church and convent. Alternatively, it may reflect the nature of the original Dominican reports of the idolatry, upon which Burgoa's account clearly depended. Fray Bernardo de Santa María, who was vicar of the Tehuantepec convent in the early 1560s and initially examined the *cacique*, remained a close friend and supporter of Don Juan Cortés's widow (Zeitlin 2005). Although an ecclesiastical tribunal consisting of the esteemed Provincial friars Juan de Córdova and Juan de Mata was dispatched from Oaxaca, Don Juan refused to be tried by any court other than that of the Audiencia in Mexico. We learn what judgment befell him in Mexico and of his death in Nexapa en route home, but the details of the punishment awaiting his co-conspirators in Tehuantepec are described only cursorily as a parading of the guilty parties through the streets, attired in the standard costume of the idolator, with public whipping providing the final humiliation (Burgoa 1989:358, 363).

After the Jalapa idolatry was discovered in 1706, the Provincial sent Fray Alonso de Espinosa to conduct the trial and mete out punishments at a Sunday *auto de fé* to which the communities of both Jalapa and Tehuantepec came. With the eight defendants naked to the waist, ropes tied around their throats and crowns of thorns on their heads, and each holding a black candle, they provided a spectacular backdrop to Fray Alonso's sermon in Zapotec on the dangers of idolatry. Burgoa suggests that Fray Alonso was one of those preachers able to bring people to the true faith by dint of their spirit, despite the conclusion drawn by others concerning the "incapacidad de los indios" (Burgoa 1989:332).

Fray Alonso served as vicar of Tehuantepec in those years, and Burgoa relates another incident concerning his efforts to curb pagan practices observed in the shadow of the Catholic calendar's Day of the Dead, which I will describe in more detail because of its relevance to household customs. Burgoa (1989:391) notes that the November holiday coincides seasonally with a similar feast observed during the eighteen-month prehispanic solar year. In seventeenth-century Tehuantepec, families prepared special dishes for which many turkeys were slaughtered, including *moles* and special *tamales* covered with avocado leaves (the sauce ingredient details provided by Burgoa reveal his personal familiarity with and fondness for these feast dishes). Plates with food offerings were left on tables or small altars in the house at nightfall on the Day of the Dead, awaiting the return of deceased members of the family, who, thus honored, could be expected to intercede with the gods they served in the underworld on behalf of their living descendants. To assure the success of this petition, family members had to keep vigil all night long, but with their arms folded and faces pointing downward so as not to disturb the deceased with their gaze. The next morning, the family might distribute the food among strangers and the poor but could not consume it themselves.

Knowing of this custom and hearing from spies that one noble family had just killed many birds before the Day of the Dead, Fray Alonso quietly entered their house with a Spanish resident of the town late at night to find the occupants all seated with their eyes closed and absorbed with crying about their misfortunes. When the friar confronted the *principal* with Catholic teachings about the souls of the deceased appearing before God for judgment and not needing any material sustenance, he responded that the deceased did not physically eat these offerings but that they sucked the vital force from the food, leaving behind things that had been depleted of this essence (*virtud*). Moreover, he questioned why, if this were not true, he had seen Spaniards leaving offerings of bread, wine, and mutton at tombs in the churches, to which Fray Alonso responded that this was different, that the Spanish offerings were gifts to the priests so that they would pray for them. After forcing the surprised family to eat the offerings on their table, the Dominican resolved to be more vigorous in explaining the nature of the soul and its qualities at death in his sermons (Burgoa 1989:392f.).

One last example of persistent Zapotec customs is Burgoa's passing mention of the attribution of birth names to individuals based on the Mesoamerican ritual calendar, with accompanying predispositions that the friar likened to the influence of the twelve signs of the zodiac. In a previous chapter dealing with the Chontal *doctrina* of Tequisistlán, the author related an incident in which one of the friars was nearly killed in an encounter with a caiman that turned out to have been the animal alter-ego (known in Nahuatl as *nahual*) of an Indian with a grudge against the friar (Burgoa 1989:316f.). These animal spirits were associated with specific day signs conferred at birth on the individual, a practice and belief Burgoa lamented for the vulnerability it gave individuals to the machinations of the devil. When Burgoa briefly referred to the practice in Tehuantepec, he did so to account for the poor taste of the wild meat procured in the bush, given the widespread presence of *nahuales* (Burgoa 1989:396). Although it is surprising to see the friar's acceptance of animal alter-egos, Burgoa was not alone in his broader interest in Mesoamerican astrology and its parallels with European astrology, for Fray Juan de Córdova had studied Zapotec calendrics before him. Burgoa explained that such an eminent church theologian as Thomas Aquinas had come to grips with astrology, ruling that the stars might have influence on the body but that the soul was implanted in each individual separately by God.

What kind of vision of mid-seventeenth-century Isthmus Zapotec society do we get from Burgoa's officially sanctioned account? His portrait is that of an economically prosperous and industrious people, who have readily incorporated agricultural commodities and manufactured goods appealing to Spanish tastes into their domestic lives, even as locally favored products like iguana and sea turtle eggs are noted. Indeed, his familiarity with the preparation of particular festive dishes suggests how far Spanish settler tastes like his had adapted to native cuisine. He represents the Zapotecs of Jalapa and Tehuantepec as orderly and pious, using the barrio organization, the barrio chapels, and their coordinated observances of important Catholic festivals to underscore the dominant role of the Church in maintaining a peaceful order among the subordinated people. That there had been challenges to Catholic hegemony is clear from the two earlier instances of pagan idolatry, but their recounting here serves to illuminate the Dominicans' watchful supervision and their prompt and effective handling of any backsliding. On the other hand, traditional ideas about the dead or about *nahuales* seem to be taken by Burgoa as unthreatening, if misguided beliefs, the persistence of which among individuals in the Isthmus Zapotec communities required further spiritual guidance but no physical punishment of the sort meted out to idolators.

VIEWING THE ARCHAEOLOGICAL RECORD AS HIDDEN TRANSCRIPT

Apart from his anecdote regarding Fray Alonso's stealth entrance into a *principal*'s home, Burgoa tells us nothing about Isthmus Zapotec life that could not be observed from public spaces. That shortcoming is typical of Spanish Colonial sources for Oaxaca and the reason why historical archaeology holds so much promise for completing the Colonial portrait of indigenous society in the absence of many archived letters, testaments, and other intracommunity documents composed by native authors. To illustrate that potential, I review here the findings from my 1990 excavations at Rancho Santa Cruz.

Rancho Santa Cruz is located on the Río de los Perros floodplain near the piedmont slopes of the Sierra Atravesada (figure 14.2). During the Late Postclassic, this productive agricultural zone near Chihuitán hosted a large number of scattered small sites featuring the unpainted grayware pottery introduced by Zapotec colonists (figure 14.1). Small spring-fed streams were tapped for irrigation, and Colonial-period sources including Burgoa indicate that the Zapotec nobility kept valuable fruit orchards on some of these well-watered lands. In the late sixteenth and early seventeenth centuries, individuals connected to the Tehuantepec royal family petitioned the Crown to keep sheep and goats on their Chihuitán lands (Machuca Gallegos 2007; Zeitlin 2005). The combined agricultural wealth and social prominence of its community leaders doubtlessly account for the unusually large late-sixteenth/early-seventeenth-century church in a village that today numbers only about twelve hundred inhabitants.

FIGURE 14.2. Excavation at the Rancho Santa Cruz site, Chihuitán.

The Rancho Santa Cruz site was located after a fortuitous encounter with a former resident of the hacienda. Señor Fernando Lavín Mier's family discovered in the ranch house rafters the original 1801 document petitioning the royal authorities to construct a sugar refinery (now in ruins). Responding to the standard question as to whether or not this construction would affect any indigenous community, the petitioner responded that "antes había un pueblo pero hace tiempo que se desapareció." Although the site might have been abandoned decades earlier, I use 1750 as a reasonable *terminus ante quem* for the occupation. Common-grade majolica pottery typical of that manufactured in Mexico City in the late sixteenth and seventeenth centuries was found at the site in all stratigraphic levels, albeit in small numbers and in fragmentary states. Because the site represents a new habitation area, one to which the residents moved from a nearby but less easily reached Late Postclassic site, I suspect that its occupation coincides with the late-sixteenth-century *congregación* that affected many Isthmus communities. Thus various lines of evidence bracket the site temporally between the seventeenth and early eighteenth centuries.

Despite the widespread surface presence of Colonial-era pottery at this approximately five-hectares site, extensive plowing of most level areas has left little undisturbed ground. However, two zones yielded more promising results in test excavations, one of which, referred to as Domicilio 1, had deeper deposition and more abundant contextual information (figure 14.3). My discussion of the archaeological evidence draws primarily on data from that zone, which represents a single household or household compound during two depositional phases of occupation. Two recovered post molds from the earlier deposit are associated with a tamped-earth occupational surface. This may be either the interior floor of a wattle-and-daub or adobe house or the floor of a protected outdoor work space associated with a more substantial residence. We identified just one collapsed stone wall in the Domicilio 1 excavations, but occasional fragments of fired brick, like the roof tile and brick fragments found at the second habitation area, suggest that more durable building materials were used for house construction in this community. Their intrinsic value may have led to their removal after the site was abandoned. Among the handful of iron artifacts found were cotter-pin hinges and broad-headed, short nails of the sort used in constructing wooden house doors (figure 14.4). Altogether these fragmentary remains are easily associated with a range of village house forms still in use among the Isthmus Zapotec. Only tamped-earth floors were recovered from either house area, even in proximity to stone wall features, a fact that supports my assumption that these residences were occupied by commoner families, although it remains possible that they were located on a Zapotec nobleman's rural estate. Late Postclassic elite houses located in the urban barrios of Tehuantepec had plastered floors and adobe walls, whereas surrounding commoner residences did not (see Zeitlin 2005 for a discussion of Zapotec class differences in housing).

Apart from a fishhook, few other metal tools were found, so it is not surprising that stone tools—which were primarily made from local quartzite and chert—continued in use. Small numbers of imported obsidian blades were scattered about both occupation levels, but few formal tool types were discerned among those made from local materials. Without more serious analysis, it is not possible to suggest the uses to which these tools were put. At least some of the flaked tools, like the three fragments of ovoid *manos* found in excavation, would have been used in food preparation. Although no macrobotanical remains were recovered, the Domicilio 1 excavations yielded some three thousand animal bones and bone fragments, representing waste from meals and food preparation. These materials have been thoroughly analyzed by Elizabeth T. Newman (2007), whose findings are briefly discussed in table 14.1.

A large number of animal classes are represented in the identifiable portion of the faunal assemblage. They include introduced domesticates like cow, sheep, or goat, and probably pig (not distinguishable from wild peccary), and a wide range of indigenous domesticates and wild animals, including dog, turkey, white-tailed deer, rabbit, armadillo, raccoon, agouti, iguana, turtle, snake, and both marine and freshwater fish. Indigenous species predominated, with 72.7 percent of the sample

FIGURE 14.3. A stone wall excavated at household Domicilio 1.

that could be identified at the genus or species level belonging to a wild animal or native domesticate. By contrast, 98.4 percent of the much smaller sample of identified bones from the Colonial-era Dominican convent in Tehuantepec pertained to domesticated species (Newman 2007).

It is not at all surprising that hunting, fishing, and trapping continued to be important subsistence strategies for native communities during the seventeenth century, because Burgoa listed some of these animals among those sold in the daily Tehuantepec market. Indeed, many wild species have a distinctive place in the local cuisine to this day, especially iguana and armadillo. A more subtle question is how much the diet might have changed with the introduction of European domesticates. Among mammalian groups distinguishable only by size because of the fragmented nature of the specimens, only the class "large animal" can unequivocally be identified with an introduced domesticate like cow or (perhaps less likely) horse or mule, because "medium animal" could include deer as well as sheep or goats, not to mention the indistinct pig/peccary category. Newman's biomass calculations suggest that large European domesticates contributed about 27 percent of the meat consumed at Rancho Santa Cruz. Although nearly 40 percent of the meat came from medium-sized mammals, it cannot be determined how much of that group represents wild animals, like deer, whose identifiable

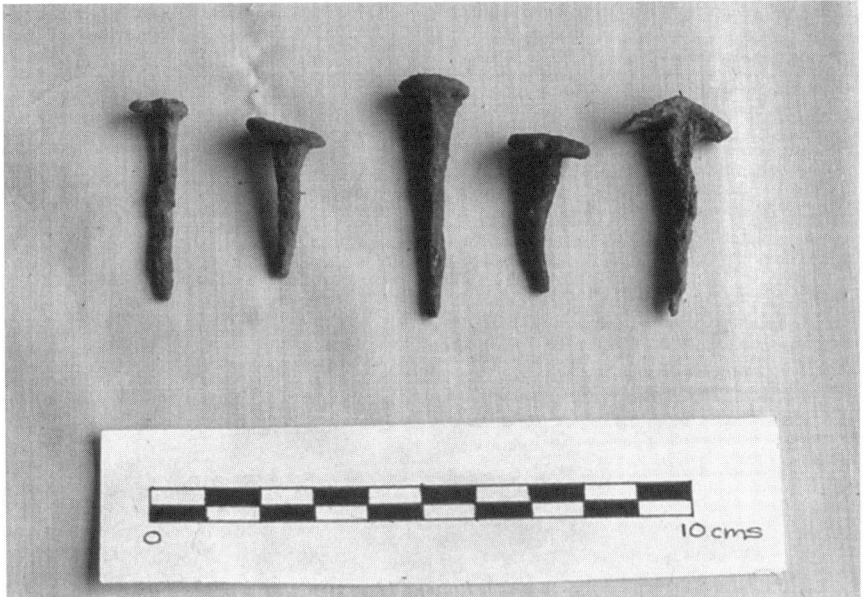

FIGURE 14.4. Broad-headed, short iron nails found at the Rancho Santa Cruz site.

remains accounted for 6.9 percent of the mammal meat, or introduced sheep and goats, whose identifiable remains represent just 1.1 percent of the sample (Newman 2007).

Reviewing these numbers, it is apparent that European domesticates did make a substantial dietary contribution to the Rancho Santa Cruz community, with minimally 28 percent of the meat represented by excavated mammal remains associated with some introduced livestock species. Because we know that salted meat was sold in Tehuantepec, these domesticates may have had an even greater dietary role in rural communities than their bony remains alone can predict. At the same time it is clear that rural villagers never lost their taste for wild animals, with the archaeological materials greatly expanding the inventory of edible species from those identified by the Dominican observer.

The most abundant artifactual material retrieved in excavation at Rancho Santa Cruz was pottery. Approximately fourteen thousand potsherds were collected and classified from excavation units or intensive surface survey. As might be expected, the Late Postclassic fine grayware tradition continued into the seventeenth century, although the once-popular serpent heads, eagles, and other effigies added to vessel supports disappeared, apparently because of ecclesiastical disapproval (cf. Lind

TABLE 14.1 Rancho Santa Cruz faunal summary (based on data presented in Newman 2007).

Identifiable by Faunal Class	MNI	Total NISP	Biomass (kg.)
OLD WORLD DOMESTICATES			
Cattle or other large mammals	2	90	6.46
Caprines (goats and sheep)	2	5	0.26
Pigs (or, less likely, peccaries)	2	8	0.17
Total	6	103	6.83
MESOAMERICAN DOMESTICATES			
Dogs	1	6	0.05
Turkeys (or other birds)	4	68	0.74
Total	5	74	0.79
TERRESTRIAL GAME AND REPTILES			
Deer	4	35	2.03
Rabbits	2	7	11
Raccoons	1	4	0.16
Armadillos	5	103	0.85
Rodents	1	1	0
Iguanas	7	55	*
Turtles and tortoises (various)	5	14	*
Snakes	1	1	*
Total	26	220	*
FISH			
Catfish	2	2	0.03
Atlantic croaker	2	6	0.13
Misc. bony fish	2	11	0.03
Unidentified fish	0	8	0.08
Total	6	27	0.28

*Not calculated for this animal class

1987:27). Buff-to-orange coarseware continued to be preferred for cooking and other utilitarian purposes, with *ollas* and *comales* the dominant forms.

Two new additions to the Colonial-period ceramic assemblage previously described in Zeitlin and Thomas (1997) merit further discussion here. Nonlocal glazed pottery, particularly tin-enameled majolicas, was found at Rancho Santa Cruz. Because Gasco (1987, 1992) also reported majolica wares in her excavations at the Soconusco site of Ocelocalco, it is clear that some Colonial-period native communities in southeastern Mesoamerica acquired these European-style wares, even if the means by which they were traded long-distance from their sources in Mexico City or Antigua (a source for some of the Ocelocalco majolica) is not well documented. Given the lively mule train traffic across Mesoamerica, it seems reasonable that both Spanish and native merchants might have carried these attractive wares. We have documentary evidence for one such early seventeenth-century Oaxaca merchant, Gerónimo López, who traveled to the native markets or *tianguis* of the bishopric, where he specialized in Spanish and Chinese merchandise, along with salvaged cochineal (1619 AGN Tierras 2968, exp. 74). Among the imported pottery found at Rancho Santa Cruz were a few fragments of Chinese porcelain.

It is a new ceramic ware of local origin, however, that is of special interest here with regard to the question of locating hidden transcripts of colonialism. Tablón Orange ware represents a novel pottery in the Isthmus ceramic sequence, with no ties to regional Late Postclassic ceramics. This orange-firing, self- or red-slipped fine ware was shaped by hand into flat-bottomed hemispherical or outslanting-wall bowls, strainers, *comales*, and other forms, most of which would fit easily within a Mesoamerican prehispanic ceramic assemblage (figure 14.5). So, too, would the painted decorations typical of the first occupation phase at Rancho Santa Cruz, with their geometric patterns of horizontal bands, spirals, and stepped-frets (*xicalcoliuhqui*), executed in combinations of orange, black, and white paint. In the second phase of occupation at Rancho Santa Cruz, painted decoration tended to be executed in a thinner line of mostly white paint, which was applied more simply across the vessel surface rather than in broad horizontal bands. Although apparently produced locally from Isthmus clays, Tablón Orange pottery was traded outside the region as well, for it appears in a small sample at Ocelocalco on the Chiapas coast (Gasco 1987:292; personal communication).

Ceramic innovation, of course, has a long history in Mesoamerica, although archaeologists most commonly focus their interest on questions of chronology and trade relations. Certainly Tablón Orange is a strong marker for the Colonial period in the Isthmus, where it may have undergone a third phase of development after Rancho Santa Cruz was abandoned, as suggested by the presence of undecorated wheel-made versions of the pottery on the surface of eighteenth- to nineteenth-century occupation zones in Tehuantepec's urban barrios. What I suggest here is that the exuberant new pottery style represents a local indigenous response to the brightly decorated majolicas that were entering Isthmus markets. Although the refined grayware of the Oaxaca Valley tradition continued to be produced (using the complicated reduction-firing techniques today maintained in the famous "black pottery" of San Bartolo Coyotepec, Oaxaca), I propose that Isthmus potters

FIGURE 14.5. Tablón Orange outslanting-wall bowl.

innovated the more colorfully decorated, oxidized pottery because they were inspired to create an indigenous alternative to the imported majolica.

The majolica pottery categories identified at Rancho Santa Cruz include a few better-quality, polychrome-painted examples of types associated with major manufacturing centers in New Spain such as Puebla. More than 80 percent of the sample, however, conforms to the styles and manufacturing techniques associated with "common-grade wares" produced in Mexico City (Lister and Lister 1987:225), wares that were executed with low tin-level glazes and painted with haphazard decorations in green or blue, based on inexpensive copper compounds (figure 14.6). These short-cut measures yielded lower-cost pottery destined for the poorer creole residents of the capital, but to what degree these price differences were still significant variables among the samples that reached distant native communities of the Tehuantepec province is not known. Presumably higher cost and less availability accounts in part for the lower frequency of all imported pottery at Rancho Santa Cruz. My proposal goes beyond a simple equation of cost with consumption patterns, however. Rather than continue to purchase traditional gray tablewares, I suggest that native consumers sought out the painted Tablón Orange forms as a

FIGURE 14.6. Sample of Rancho Santa Cruz majolica sherds.

conscious effort to display pottery in their homes that stood up to the aesthetic challenge represented by the painted majolica.

Changes in historical pottery production and consumption among Mesoamerican groups are not necessarily related to competition with introduced Colonial wares, of course. In the Mixteca Alta of Oaxaca, imported majolica and other European wares are confined archaeologically to royal household contexts in the sixteenth and seventeenth centuries and are not part of rural assemblages such as that of Rancho Santa Cruz (Lind 1987:93f.), even in deposits that include European faunal remains and metal goods. Nonetheless, Lind observes marked changes in Colonial-period vessel forms and decoration modes among the Convento-phase pottery at Chachoapan and Yucuita, where two rural noble sites subject to Yanhuitlán were excavated. Plates without tripod supports predominate in the Iglesia complex of Mixteca polychrome (although tripod-supported *cajetes* were more common during the Late Postclassic), and design motifs were limited to simple geometric and floral shapes, with no realistic representations of images with traditional religious significance (Lind 1987:23–27). In the Isthmus, where polychrome painted pottery is virtually absent from Late Postclassic urban barrios and rural communities, the geometric designs of Tablón Orange appear as a novel introduction, not a diminishing of past practices. There is a similar trend toward the increased use of flat-bottomed shallow bowls, with tripod supports preserved primarily among unpainted fine graywares.

That the local production of all varieties of fine tablewares would continue to be important both on the Isthmus and in the Mixteca Alta makes sense, given the likely continuities in cuisine preparation and household organization. Although the utilitarian function of these dishes may be clear, Lind (1987:105) sees a marked decline in their frequency during the Colonial period, as the elite households he sampled experienced a diminished role hosting community feasts and reduced access to commoner labor services in food preparation. Within the domestic space in which food was presented, we should keep in mind pottery's multiple social and dietary roles. Burgoa's colorful anecdote concerning Day of the Dead food offerings in Tehuantepec points to the continued religious purpose of household pottery, even when divorced from its more transparent symbolism or deprived of special-purpose ritual forms like censers.

From the snippets of Isthmus Zapotec life portrayed by Burgoa, it appears that most of the customary household activities evidenced archaeologically at Rancho Santa Cruz, from hunting game to using traditional tools, were not considered problematic by the dominant society. Conversely, participation in Spanish-style activities, from running mule train caravans to raising livestock, was encouraged and, in the case of the consumption of certain goods of Spanish manufacture, was forced upon communities through the corrupt *repartimientos de mercancías* to be discussed shortly (Zeitlin 2005). Taken in this context, the Rancho Santa Cruz archaeological context displays the kind of cultural hybridity we have come to expect of Colonial-era sites in the Americas. But as older acculturation models have lost their credibility in historical archaeology (Cusick 1998; Lightfoot 1995), finding the material evidence to support interpretations of indigenous agency and counter-hegemonic meaning can be challenging (but see Silliman 2001; Turgeon 1997).

The abrupt appearance of Tablón Orange among indigenous communities in the southern Isthmus appears as an anomaly inviting explanation. My proposed explanation is informed by more recent Isthmus Zapotec cultural history and the population's well-known propensity for using items of dress and personal ornament, along with local forms of music and dance, to create new markers of ethnic identity, even when these markers include elements drawn from imported fashions. Although there is no necessary reason why pottery should serve similarly as a marker of ethnicity in the earlier Colonial context, its central place in both everyday and ceremonial interactions of social life make it a potential vehicle.

Given the contextual association with attractive Colonial pottery alternatives and the broad temporal conjuncture with a period of slow recovery, I think it plausible that Tablón Orange was one of many markers of a newly emerging ethnic identity and pride among the Isthmus Zapotec. For the Isthmus Zapotec populations just beginning to rebound from the depredations of earlier demographic loss, an enthusiastic embrace of newly developed local material forms would have been a powerful symbol of regional cultural pride and an "everyday form" of covert resistance (Scott 1985) to Colonial domination rarely evidenced in the public transcript.

What makes some everyday forms of material culture or practices "resistant" and others not? Sherry Ortner points to the heuristic value of Scott's terminology, despite the elusiveness of its definition, "because it highlights the presence and play of power in most forms of relationship and activity" (Ortner 1995: 175). At the same time Ortner urges us to deepen the ethnographic context in which these power relationships play out. In the case of indigenous pottery production in Colonial Oaxaca, we know that imposed religious values inhibited the continued execution of traditional decorative styles. When Isthmus potters created Tablón Orange serving ware, they complied with the ban on zoomorphic forms with "pagan" associations, but they deliberately employed a traditional decorative motif that by virtue of its abstract nature would pass ecclesiastical scrutiny.

What specific meaning the *xicalcoliuhqui* motif may have had for Isthmus populations in the seventeenth century is unclear. Its Precolumbian usage ranged from architecture to textiles and from featherwork to ceramics. The motif's ubiquity and contextual associations have prompted various interpretations over time, including more recently as a marker of nobility and noble lineages (Hernández Sánchez 2010) or an association with movement and cycles of time (Brumfiel 2007). Robert Markens (2012), however, makes a persuasive case that both prehispanic and early Colonial representations of the *xicalcoliuhqui* in Mesoamerica are tied to water, the water serpent, and the serpent's associations with the bringing of rain. We cannot be certain that similar iconic meanings registered with the users of Tablón Orange ware throughout the Colonial period, although the association between the serpent and the sources of water persists among Oaxaca's native communities today, as Markens notes. But the fact that this motif was selected at the outset, rather than the crude geometric designs and haphazard brush lines found on the common-ware *mayólicas* that may have inspired the new pottery's invention, suggests minimally a deliberate resistance to new models and perhaps a material expression of indigenous religious concerns.[1] I argue that the new pottery style and other, less archaeologically visible, practices of seventeenth-century Isthmus communities were signs of a broadly based response to their Colonial subordination. How deeply this subordination was resented among the populace is evidenced by my third text.

RUPTURING THE LINE BETWEEN PUBLIC AND HIDDEN TRANSCRIPTS

The final seventeenth-century text discussed here is an account of the native rebellion that took place in Tehuantepec in 1660. Rushed into print in 1661 with Don Cristóbal Manso de Contreras named as its author, the *relación* was approved by a single censor. The rector of the influential Jesuit order in Mexico City, Diego de Monroy, proclaimed the value of publicizing the atrocity that had been committed in March of the previous year, the punishment dealt to the miscreants, and the "prudence, mild hand, and skill" with which the province had been returned to its former peace (Manso de Contreras 1661). The secular and nearly journalistic quality of this account (and that of the related rebellions in nearby Oaxaca provinces that was published the following year) was unusual in Early Colonial Mexico where pious chronicles like those of Burgoa were far more the norm. As I have pointed out elsewhere (Zeitlin 2005), both publications are intimately linked to the self-promoting agenda of their true author, Don Juan Francisco de Montemayor, a Spanish *oidor* not long resident in New Spain. Montemayor took it upon himself to quash what was a not-uncommon incident of native rebellion against the authority and person of a particularly abusive Colonial administrator, Don Juan de Avellán.

Because the Manso de Contreras account has been reprinted several times and because the account itself provides testimony from native and Spanish actors often at odds with the intent of the author, the 1660 Tehuantepec rebellion has been a much-studied example of native resistance to Colonial rule (e.g., Barabas 1986; Carmagnani 1992; Díaz-Polanco 1992). Many of these published studies, including my own, focus on whether or not the insurrection was indeed a revolutionary movement against Colonial authority (a mutiny, as Montemayor claimed) or a more limited "reformist" effort to reestablish the prevailing social order. While I have allied my own views with the reformist model, based on the actions of the rebellion's leadership in the aftermath of the dramatic incident that precipitated this crisis, here I will revisit that conclusion in light of the "public transcript" issues raised by Scott (1990).

Briefly, the events of the rebellion can be summarized as follows. As *alcalde mayor* of the Tehuantepec province, Juan de Avellán instituted some particularly harsh practices involving the Colonial institution of *repartimiento*, or redistribution. This eminently corrupt institution gave provincial administrators like Avellán and the financiers who backed them a monopoly on the forced sale of merchandise (at inflated prices) to native communities in their jurisdiction and the forced production of goods by these communities for sale to the *alcalde mayor* at below-market value. Avellán had required certain Isthmus communities to produce large quantities of cotton cloth for him, punishing with the whip any officials who delivered material of insufficient length or poor quality. Such punishments had resulted in the death of the *cacique* of Tequisistlán and the whipping of an Indian official from La Mixtequilla. No adjustments were made to the quotas based on illness, death, or flight from the tribute rolls, a burden that weighed particularly heavily on Isthmus women, whose labor and skills were needed to meet the quotas.

In the late morning of March 22, 1660, a large group from La Mixtequilla joined "co-conspirators" from the Santa María barrio of Tehuantepec and others to launch an assault on the Casas Reales. In the ensuing melee, Avellán and three of his underlings were killed by the angry mob as they fled the burning building, forcing numerous other Spaniards and the sitting officers of Tehuantepec's native *cabildo* to seek refuge in the Dominican church. Quickly the rebels enlisted several members of the Zapotec nobility to form a new government, one that was claimed to have greater legitimacy than the group that Avellán had installed through his habitual interference with native elections. The new *cabildo* officers immediately wrote to the outgoing viceroy, the Duke of Alburquerque, explaining their situation, denying that they were in a state of revolt, and linking the uprising to the excessive demands and cruelty of Avellán, whose death they claimed to feel bad about, even more so because it left them without a representative of the king to govern them (Manso de Contreras 1661:9v–10).

Alburquerque asked the bishop of Oaxaca to travel to the province to calm the situation and report on native grievances. Gathering the province's population together in Tehuantepec on April 19, the bishop, Fray Alonso de Cuevas Dávalos, treated the province's population with great gentility and compassion, eventually recovering arms and other goods taken from the Casas Reales on the fateful night. Alburquerque then installed as replacement *alcalde mayor* an experienced man known for his evenhandedness with the native population. Things seemed to be returning to normal, despite grumbling from a few Spaniards in Oaxaca, including the purported author of the *relación*, Cristóbal Manso de Contreras, that the Indians were getting too uppity and were even demanding that they be given seats in church at Christmas. Seizing the opportunity provided by the arrival of a new viceroy, the *oidor* Francisco de Montemayor concocted a plan to at last punish the rebellion's leaders and reinstall the previous *cabildo* officers, a plan he personally carried out the following year, sentencing thirty-seven people, including eight women, to a range of punishments ranging from death to whippings, hard labor, and perpetual exile.

Evidence is sparse that the Tehuantepec leaders were actively stoking the flames of a broadly based revolt against Spanish authority, as Montemayor sought to portray the rebellion through his surrogate. In other correspondence not included in the selection published in Manso's *relación*, the Council of the Indies requested concrete evidence to support these machinations, such as the letters purportedly sent by the rebellion leaders to other native communities or verification that the rebel governor had been referred to as "king." Montemayor never complied with this request, nor did he heed the Council's admonition to move slowly and with sensitivity to native grievances (Zeitlin 2005). Thus there is little to corroborate the revolutionary intentions of the rebellion, as I and other scholars have concluded, although Montemayor and his cronies were great political and financial beneficiaries of this show of force. From the documentation at hand, however, it is still possible to understand some of the contradictory actions taken by Zapotec actors in light of the contrast between public and hidden transcripts that Scott (1990) draws.

In the rebel *cabildo*'s letter to Viceroy Alburquerque, the leaders were quick to assert that what took place did not represent a negation of their subordinated position; indeed, they reiterated that they were good and faithful vassals of the king of Spain. Clearly these men were aware of the political and personal risks that appearing to challenge Colonial rule entailed. As Scott (1990) reminds us, the public transcript is replete with examples of peasants praising kings and similar instances of subordinated groups speaking in terms that appear on the surface to incorporate the dominant hegemony. But rather than take these as examples of "false consciousness," he suggests we look beyond the formalities of address to understand how such language is used by subordinated people to appeal to the elite's own self-justification for their power. The polite or even subservient discourse can be seen as part of a strategy to alleviate their duress (what Scott refers to as "laying it on thick"). And so the Tehuantepec rebel *cabildo* members sought to reestablish themselves as faithful vassals whose primary desire was to return to the principle of good government and prudent administration embodied in royal authority.

The very fact of the revolt shows how weakly this principle of good government was observed in practice, especially in the context of the corrupt sale of Colonial offices by a cash-strapped Crown. Two previous administrators of the Tehuantepec province had similarly incurred the wrath of the population, with one losing his life and the other being driven out of town. There were peaceful but unsuccessful attempts to stop the abuses of Avellán before the events of Holy Week 1660 through petition to the viceroy, the Duke of Alburquerque, in whose entourage Avellán first arrived in New Spain. Understandably, the rebel government was reluctant to trust his replacement. In December 1660 a delegation from Tehuantepec traveled all the way to Mexico City to have the results of recent elections confirmed by the new viceroy. Sadly, that journey itself set off the conspiratorial interpretation of the revolt fostered by Montemayor, leading to the exact obverse of their intended goals (Zeitlin 2005).

In Tehuantepec such use of the institutions and procedures of the Spanish Colonial state to preserve a tolerable sphere of political and economic autonomy was expected of elected Zapotec officials. When those efforts failed, violence frequently ensued, not just in 1660 but on several occasions in the seventeenth and eighteenth centuries (Zeitlin 2005). The actions of the angry mob that killed Avellán on March 22, 1660, represented a boiling-over of emotions and attitudes that must have been frequent topics of conversation among members of the Zapotec community, conversations that took place in private homes, in the marketplace, and in those autonomous political spaces that were so zealously defended under Colonial law.

The public transcript of 1660 hints at the emotional depth of this disgruntlement with both Avellán as an individual and Colonial authority in general. One of the Tehuantepec women, Magdalena María la Minera, was convicted for sitting on the corpse of Avellán, hitting it with a rock, and uttering abusive remarks. If his initial death was an accidental result of a stone-throwing melee, crowd vengeance was purposefully directed toward the others. Avellán's *criado* was given a few minutes for prayer before he was executed with a machete blow to his head. The torching of the Casas Reales (also instigated by a female participant in the riot) was followed by the confiscation of armaments and "treasures" in an effort to appropriate the symbols and instruments of Colonial power. Outside Tehuantepec, the report of a surly native population was supported with just a few incidents. Although hardly constituting sufficient evidence for the contention by Montemayor and Manso de Contreras that Oaxaca was on the verge of widespread insurrection, these anecdotes do hint at a broad native displeasure with the reality of their subordination that was largely hidden from public view.

COMPARING PUBLIC AND HIDDEN TRANSCRIPTS

In this comparison of three different sources of evidence for the seventeenth-century Isthmus Zapotec, distinct perspectives on native society are provided by the archaeological and historical "texts." Given the nature of the archaeological record, with its primary data drawn from the recovered remnants of daily activities, our view of life at Rancho Santa Cruz emphasizes long-term patterning in domestic activities, particularly the consumption of food and the use of material goods for household purposes. We see in those remains economic choices barely noted in the descriptions of Isthmus life provided by a familiar Spanish observer like Burgoa. Burgoa mentioned the hunting of wild animals but gave no indication of how significant they might be for subsistence. Similarly, he mentioned native long-distance traders but gave no hint as to which traded goods entered into the domestic lives of the Isthmus Zapotecs. He made reference to individuals of the nobility but paid little attention to the socioeconomic divisions within native society or the contrast between urban and rural communities. On the other hand, the historical glimpses Burgoa offers us of traditional religious practices are notoriously difficult to document archaeologically, although it is my hope that a planned research program may yet illuminate this aspect of Colonial-period native society.

What is perhaps most remarkable about all this is how different the two documentary portrayals of native society are. Although the purposes of Burgoa's chronicle and the Manso de Contreras texts are quite distinct, it may seem puzzling that the Dominican made no reference to the dramatic incidents of 1660 in a work he published just fourteen years later. Here, I would suggest, we must take into consideration the broader purpose of Burgoa's life work, which was to emphasize the great effort and success achieved by his missionary order in the salvation of Oaxaca's native souls. It was a success under challenge in seventeenth-century ecclesiastical politics, which already had seen influential reformists like Juan de Palafox y Mendoza gain sway with the Council of the Indies. Palafox argued that the religious orders, with their elaborate infrastructure, exacted too great a burden from the native populations that supported them. Removing Indian *doctrinas* from the supervision of religious orders to that of parish priests, as Palafox attempted, was an ongoing struggle for New Spain's bishops, who resented the autonomy the missionaries enjoyed (Canterla y Martín de Tovar 1982; García 1918).

In Oaxaca the Dominicans managed to stave off most efforts at ecclesiastical reorganization earlier in the century (cf. Ybañes 1630), but they must have been particularly wary of the appointment of the Carmelite Fray Alonso de Cuevas Dávalos as bishop, because he had been a close friend of Palafox when both men were in Puebla (Robles 1757). In this context, Cuevas Dávalos's trip to Tehuantepec, his success at the restoration of civil order and the return of Crown property, and his sympathetic report on the terrible suffering of the Indians would have been a telling indictment of the failings of the Dominicans, whose duty it was to protect their native parishioners. Not surprisingly then, Burgoa's sanitized portrait of the orderly nature of Isthmus Zapotec civil and religious society offers no commentary on the dramatic events that transpired just a few years earlier.

The flawed public transcript of the 1660 rebellion tells us how deeply many native actors in Tehuantepec resented their subordinate status, even as formal appeals to the Crown by the native leaders used a discourse of submission. Can we see similar counter-hegemonic practices in the material patterns illuminated by archaeology? It is my proposition that the emergence of a vibrant local pottery style during a period in which native society was slowly emerging from the devastation of depopulation and the incumbent economic and ecological challenges of new agricultural practices represents a reassertion of Zapotec cultural values.

That it appears during a period in which indigenous political leaders were struggling to maintain an autonomous sphere of interaction for their communities is, I find, no coincidence. Indeed, such conflict-laden situations in more recent times are exactly those that anthropologists find likely to generate new articulations of ethnicity among dominated groups, as both old and new practices are invested with meanings attributed to a group's distinct identity (Eriksen 2002). Thus we might expect that the archaeological record will reveal additional signs of cultural reconfiguration beyond this new ceramic marker, were we to investigate more seventeenth-century sites and look for other patterned associations among the material remains. Archaeology's potential to recover a hidden transcript of cultural values and practices intended to counter the dominant discourse of colonialism is strong, but it is also dependent on understanding the historical pressure points that the written record illuminates.

Finally, the two published documents reviewed here remind us that the supposed unity of values and ideals among the dominant sector of society that Scott finds reflected in the public transcript is itself an artificial construct. That there were disparate interest groups among the colonists with different political and economic agendas is well known to historians of New Spain, and the Dominican struggle to retain the order's position in Oaxaca reflects that division. On the level of individual actors, starkly different attitudes toward the Isthmus Zapotec are apparent in the words of the creole Burgoa and the Spanish-born Montemayor, with the former praising the hispanicized appearance of the Tehuantepec muleteers and the latter complaining to the viceroy about natives adopting Spanish patterns of dress that transgressed what he thought should be clear social boundaries (Zeitlin 2005). As Nicholas Thomas (1994:51) emphasizes, "colonialism is not a unitary project but a fractured one, riddled with contradictions and exhausted as much by its own internal debates as by the resistance of the colonized."

NOTE

1. I am grateful to Robert Markens (personal communication, October 2012) for his suggestion that the choice of motif had specific religious meaning.

REFERENCES

Barabas, Alicia M. 1986. "Rebeliones e Insurrecciones Indígenas en Oaxaca: La Trayectoria Histórica de la Resistencia Étnica." In *Etnicidad y pluralismo cultural: La Dinámica*

Étnica en Oaxaca, ed. Alicia M. Barabas and Miguel A. Bartolomé, 213–56. Mexico: CONACULTA/INAH.

Brumfiel, Elizabeth. 2007. "Solar Disks and Solar Cycles: Spindle Whorls and the Dawn of Solar Art in Postclassic Mesoamerica." *Treballs d'Arqueologia* 13:91–113.

Burgoa, Fr. Francisco de. 1670. *Palestra Historial*. Mexico: Juan Ruíz.

Burgoa, Fr. Francisco de. (1674) 1989. *Geográfica Descripción*, vol. 2. Mexico: Editorial Porrúa.

Canterla y Martín de Tovar, Francisco. 1982. *La Iglesia de Oaxaca en el Siglo XVIII*. Seville: Escuela de Estudios Hispano-Americanos.

Carmagnani, Marcello. 1992. "Un Movimiento Político Indio: La 'Rebelión' de Tehuantepec, 1660–1661." In *Patterns of Contention in Mexican History*, ed. Jaime E. Rodríguez O., 17–35. Wilmington, NC: S. R. Books.

Cusick, James. 1998. "Historiography of Acculturation: An Evaluation of Concepts and their Application in Archaeology." In *Studies in Culture Contact: Interaction, Culture Change and Archaeology*, ed. James Cusick, 23–43. Center for Archaeological Investigations, Occasional Paper no. 25. Carbondale: Southern Illinois University.

Díaz-Polanco, Héctor, ed. 1992. *El Fuego de la Inobediencia: Autonomía y Rebelión India en el Obispado de Oaxaca*. Oaxaca City: CIESAS.

Eriksen, Thomas Hylland. 2002. *Ethnicity and Nationalism*. London: Pluto Press.

García, Genaro. 1918. *Don Juan Palafox y Mendoza, Obispo de Puebla y Osma, Visitador y Virrey de la Nueva España*. Mexico: Librería de Bouret.

Gasco, Janine. 1987. "Cacao and the Economic Integration of Native Society in Colonial Soconusco, New Spain." Unpublished PhD diss., Department of Anthropology, University of California at Santa Barbara, Santa Barbara.

Gasco, Janine. 1992. "Material Culture and Colonial Indian Society in Southern Mesoamerica: The View from Coastal Chiapas, Mexico." *Historical Archaeology* 26 (1):67–74.

Hernández Sánchez, Gilda. 2010. "Vessels for Ceremony: The Pictography of Codex-Style Mixteca-Puebla Vessels from Central and South Mexico." *Latin American Antiquity* 21 (3):252–273. http://dx.doi.org/10.7183/1045-6635.21.3.252.

Lightfoot, Kent G. 1995. "Culture Contact Studies: Redefining the Relationship between Prehistoric and Historical Archaeology." *American Antiquity* 60 (2):199–217. http://dx.doi.org/10.2307/282137.

Lind, Michael. 1987. *The Sociocultural Dimensions of Mixtec Ceramics*. Nashville: Vanderbilt University Publications in Anthropology, No. 33.

Lister, Florence C., and Robert H. Lister. 1987. *Andalusian Ceramics in New Spain: A Cultural Register from the Third Century B.C. to 1700*. Tucson: University of Arizona Press.

Machuca Gallegos, Laura. 2007. *Comercio de Sal y Redes de Poder en Tehuantepec durante la Época Colonial*. Mexico: CIESAS.

Manso de Contreras, Cristóbal. 1661. *Relación Cierta, y Verdadera de lo que Sucedió y a Sucedido en esta Villa de Guadalcaçar Provincia de Tehuantepeque desde los 22 de Março de 1660, Hasta los Quatro de Iulio de 1661*. Mexico: Iuan Ruyz.

Markens, Robert. 2012. *"La Greca Escalonada en la Imaginaría Prehispánica de Oaxaca: Una Aproximación de su Significado, Contexto de Uso, y su Relación al Ejercicio de Poder Político."* Presentation given at the XXXVI Coloquio Internacional de Historia del Arte, Instituto de Investigaciones Estéticas. Mexico: UNAM.

Newman, Elizabeth Terese. 2007. *Report on Isthmus Faunal Materials: Rancho Santa Cruz, Panteón Antiguo, and Convento*. Manuscript in the possession of the author.

Ortner, Sherry B. 1995. "Resistance and the Problem of Ethnographic Refusal." *Comparative Studies in Society and History* 37 (1):173–193. http://dx.doi.org/10.1017/S001041750001 9587.

Restall, Matthew. 2003. "A History of the New Philology and the New Philology in History." *Latin American Research Review* 38 (1):113–134. http://dx.doi.org/10.1353/lar.2003.0012.

Robles, Antonio de. 1757. *Resguardo Contra el Olvido, en el Breve Compendio de la Vida Admirable y Virtudes Heroycas del Illmo: Sr. Dr. D. Alonso de Cuevas Davalos, Obispo Electo de Nicaragua, Consagrado de Oaxaca, Arcobispo de esta Imperial Cuidad de México, su Patria*. Mexico: Herederos de la Viuda de D. Joseph Bernardo de Hogal.

Scott, James C. 1985. *Weapons of the Weak: Everyday Forms of Peasant Resistance*. New Haven: Yale University Press.

Scott, James C. 1990. *Domination and the Arts of Resistance: Hidden Transcripts*. New Haven: Yale University Press.

Silliman, Stephen. 2001. "Agency, Practical Politics, and the Archaeology of Culture Contact." *Journal of Social Archaeology* 1 (2):190–209. http://dx.doi.org/10.1177 /14696053010100203.

Thomas, Nicholas. 1994. *Colonialism's Culture: Anthropology, Travel, and Government*. Princeton: Princeton University Press.

Turgeon, Laurier. 1997. "The Tale of the Kettle: Odyssey of an Intercultural Object." *Ethnohistory* 44 (1):1–29. http://dx.doi.org/10.2307/482899.

Ybañes, Fr. Diego. 1630. *El Juez Conservador de los Religiosos de Santo Domingo de la Provincia de Guaxaca: En Defense de la Jurisdicción que le Niega el Obispo de Aquel Obispado*. Pamphlet assumed to have been published in Mexico. Collection of the John Carter Brown Library.

Zeitlin, Judith Francis. 2003. "Recordando a los Reyes: El Lienzo de Guevea y el Discurso Histórico de la Época Colonial." In *Escritura Zapoteca: 2500 Años de Historia*, ed. María del los Ángeles Romero Frizzi, 265–304. Mexico City: CIESAS/INAH.

Zeitlin, Judith Francis. 2005. *Cultural Politics in Colonial Tehuantepec: Community and State among the Isthmus Zapotec, 1500–1750*. Stanford: Stanford University Press.

Zeitlin, Judith Francis, and Lillian Thomas. 1997. "Indian Consumers on the Periphery of the Colonial Market System: Tracing Domestic Economic Behavior in a Tehuantepec Hamlet." In *Approaches to the Historical Archaeology of Middle, Central and South America*, ed. Janine Gasco, Greg Charles Smith, and Patricia Fournier-García, 5–16. Los Angeles: Institute of Archaeology, University of California.

15

Using Nineteenth-Century Data in Contemporary Archaeological Studies

The View from Oaxaca and Germany

Viola König and Adam T. Sellen

When we think about museum collections from Mesoamerica, especially those that are now part of institutions in Europe and in North America, an image of glass cases and dusty storerooms comes to mind, full to the brim with three-dimensional objects—most notably ceramics—that were excavated long ago by individuals who had little regard for the rigors of current archaeological practice.[1] Although it is generally true that the older archaeological collections from Mexico were not systematically excavated, we tend to overlook the wealth of associated information that documented, often in surprising detail, how and where these troves of objects were retrieved. Moreover, we might think that these collections are only composed of three-dimensional objects, but a cultural artifact can have many forms: it can be a native painting on deerskin, *amate*, or European paper; or it can be a photo, drawing, diary, or newspaper clipping; or an audio artifact containing an oral history or music. The modern term *multimedia* aptly defines many of the artifact types that we discuss here.

The purpose of this chapter is to call attention to, and suggest ways of analyzing, a wide range of multimedia artifacts generated by nineteenth-century travelers and collectors that today constitutes a rich source of information on Oaxaca's archaeological past. The record is fragmentary, but when stitched together it composes a kind of multidimensional scrapbook that can be used to reconstruct early excavations, archaeological collections, and object provenience, as well as function as a unique look into the mindset of our intellectual predecessors. We believe, therefore,

DOI: 10.5876/9781607323297.c015

that these data can greatly contribute to our current knowledge of Oaxaca's ancient cultures. In this limited space we look at some examples of collectors and their collections by comparing views from Mexico—and Oaxaca in particular—and from Germany. We also discuss some of the methods used to assemble and process nineteenth-century archaeological data, the limitations encountered, and the possibilities for future studies.

PREHISPANIC OAXACA IN MUSEUM COLLECTIONS

The interest in collecting ethnographic and archaeological specimens from Oaxaca began at the beginning of the nineteenth century, and by the end of the era known as the *Porfiriato* (1880–1910), large sections in Mexico's National Museum of Anthropology were dedicated to the region's many cultures, a well-stocked museum existed in the state's capital, and thousands of objects from local private cabinets had been acquired by foreign museums. The philosophical force behind the frenzy in collecting was *positivism*, an intellectual movement that swept the world in the middle of the nineteenth century and arrived in Mexico with the restoration of the Benito Juárez government. For the collectors and for Mexican archaeological practice in general, the crucial contribution of positivism was the scientific empiricism that it enshrined. Evidence about past societies was to be found in objects and monuments that were not studied in situ, but were rather carted off either to private collections or public museums. So conceived, these cabinets, consisting of a wide variety of objects, were not meant to articulate different kinds of cultural and social messages—as we think of museum collections today—rather, they were seen as laboratories where debate and classification could take place. Typically, these collections were housed in ethnological museums that covered a broad range of disciplines from anthropology and archaeology to visual arts and theater, and that broadly defined their holdings as "cultural artifacts."

An example of one of these mixed ethnographic-archaeological collections was a result of the efforts of Cecilie and Eduard Seler, who in the late nineteenth and early twentieth century assembled for Berlin's Ethnographic Museum one of the largest holdings of Mesoamerican artifacts ever known (Seler 1902, 1904, 1908; Seler-Sachs 1925) (figure 15.1). Their diaries and personal letters illustrate how the couple employed a clear division of work: Eduard described, commented, and drew, while Cecilie took pictures and negotiated with local dealers (König 1999, 2001, 2003, 2007; Sellen 2006). These personal papers also paint a picture of how the collections were obtained from a wide range of sources and, when analyzed in light of other information such as photographs and drawings, or their correspondence to and from the museum, constitute an excellent record—although at times

FIGURE 15.1. Gold pendant in the form of a monkey, from Tlaxiaco, thirteenth–sixteenth centuries CE. Cecilie and Eduard Seler collection before 1897. © Preußischer Kulturbesitz, Ethnologisches Museum IV Ca 26080. Photo by Claudia Obrocki.

fragmentary—of how Oaxacan artifacts were removed from their country of origin and reincorporated into a foreign, implicitly public, context.

In this new museum context, many cultural artifacts have been stored and sporadically exhibited for over a century, and in the process they acquire a life history, that is to say, a distinct identity that developed during their time in the museum. Scholars have used the term *second life* to refer to this trajectory that begins upon its discovery, distinguishing it from a *first life*, the story of an object before it is deposited in the ground, the time period that tends to be the intellectual focus of most traditional archaeologists. This issue has been extensively discussed in a number of recent works (Gosden and Marshall 1999; Holtorf 2002; Schiffer and Miller 1999). Accepting that artifacts have biographies as people have, we can come to understand how their stories can connect different periods, from pre-Columbian times to the Colonial and Postcolonial periods, and up to the present. The Codex Tulane, for example, with its complex history and adventurous journey through different collector's hands in Mexico, Germany, and the United States, illustrates how an artifact can link time, place, and culture (König 2005; Smith and Parmenter 1991).

When considering an artifact in a museum context, then, a series of questions need to be asked (though the answers may be elusive) in order to complete the picture of an object's biography:

- Where did the artifact come from and when was it collected? What was its final destination? When did it leave the country? When did it arrive in the museum?
- Who made and/or used the object? Who excavated it? Who acquired, collected, or purchased it? Who owned it? Who sold it? Who gave it to the museum?
- What does the artifact represent? How was it used? Did it change its function? What was the context of its find? What happened to it before entering into the museum? What happened to it in the museum? Is it an original, a copy, a fake, or a reconstruction?

Furthermore, we need to be cognizant that we do not understand these diverse collections in the same way as the collectors and contemporaries understood them.

The research that has been carried out for over a century has broadened our horizons, expanded our knowledge and, from the overall view of the past, we are in a better position to identify the collectors' backgrounds and networks. Still, when we find unknown or lost collectors' "files," new insights are gained. In the best cases we can link the sources of different media from different persons and places, and there are a few notable examples, such as the Selers, where the documentation is quite complete though some questions remain. Generally speaking, documents written in German before the 1940s are in an outdated script that today can be read by only a few specialists or an older generation. For these collections a transcription into Latin alphabetic script is badly needed.

Photographs and sound recordings are also common in these files, but they are a delicate medium. Although the old glass photographic plates can be restored, more contemporary film, audio tapes, prints, and slides have been deteriorating to the point of being unusable; some images can fade away in a researcher's lifetime. In light of this situation, public and private institutions in Oaxaca have begun to register, evaluate, and document the state's photographic legacy. One hopes they will extend their net because a rich corpus of images showing people, sites, and artifacts from Oaxaca, and dating back to the very invention of the technique, remains scattered in European institutions.

COLLECTOR'S BIOGRAPHIES

Another way to understand objects is by reconstructing the lives of those who collected them. Recently there has been a wealth of scholarly interest in collector's biographies. *Baessler-Archiv*, the academic journal of the Ethnological Museum in Berlin, Germany, for example, has seen a notable increase in the number of articles dealing with the theme. In many cases the focus is placed on the collectors' personal backgrounds, such as education, participation in social movements and networks, work, and family life. Traditionally historians have provided this information, but today anthropologists, ethnologists, and archaeologists are active biographers as well. In this regard the blurring of the disciplines is welcome, because in the end we learn something new about the collector's artifacts and the respective culture they represent. However, many biographers fall short and fail to establish a relationship between a collector's biography, collections, and methods, and to the collections' sources. Family backgrounds or political engagements (such as a scholar with a Nazi background) are of vital interest to historians, but anthropologists and archaeologists generally examine other types of questions. They look for biographical data that will help in their analysis of the collection and interpret sources within the context of the cultures that produced those artifacts.

A VIEW FROM GERMANY: THE MULTIMEDIA LEGACY OF SIX GERMAN COLLECTORS IN MEXICO

The following selection of six personalities, who traveled, studied, and collected in Oaxaca or in the neighboring interethnic areas, exemplifies the multimedia character of their output. They collected and left physical remains such as archaeological and ethnographical objects, including written documents such as codices and *lienzos*, but also a legacy of intangible heritage in the form of tape recordings of songs, prayers, music, and interviews that are often linked to the physical paraphernalia.

Germans started to travel to Mexico at the end of the eighteenth century. From that period the best-known explorer is undoubtedly Baron Alexander von Humboldt, who inspired like-minded academics such as geographers and mineralogists as well as German businessmen, traders, miners, and manufacturers, instigating a voracious appetite for collecting not only Mexico's material culture but that of the whole world (Penny 2002:2). Twenty years after Humboldt's stay in Mexico, Carl Adolf Uhde (1792–1856) began to retrace his steps. During his time in Mexico City in the 1820s and 1830s, Berlin-born merchant and German consul Uhde assembled a huge archaeological collection that, through his family museum in Heidelberg, eventually ended up in the Ethnological Museum in Berlin. Uhde spent a fortune incorporating precious and rare artifacts into his collection. He kept a field staff of young, intelligent employees who were sent all over the country to excavate or buy antiquities, and in the German community of Mexico City, Uhde and his staff were called *Götzenreiter*, or "idol hunters" (Pferdekamp 1958:201). Their collections have little explicative documentation, and perhaps these men did not take notes on purpose, hoping to keep the sites they pilfered secret from the competition. As a result, in many cases we do not know the precise origin of the artifacts they collected, although a number of objects are reported to be from Oaxaca (Schuler-Schöming 1970) (figures 15.2 and 15.3).

FIGURE 15.2. Polychrome bowl from the Mixteca, Oaxaca, fifteenth–sixteenth centuries CE. Carl Uhde collection before 1850; © Preußischer Kulturbesitz, Ethnologisches Museum IV Ca 1933. Photo by Claudia Obrocki.

Fortunately, two of Uhde's contemporaries, the German mining engineers Eduard Mühlenpfordt and Eduard Harkort, would not only collect but also record what they saw and experienced with native peoples. Both men arrived in Mexico in 1827, hired by a British mining company. They stayed in the country for seven years but, strangely enough, never mention having met each other. Accompanied by his wife, Mühlenpfordt (1801–1853) worked as a director of road construction in Oaxaca, and the couple spent seven years traveling the state. He left three important works: *Los Palacios de los Zapotecas en Mitla* (Mühlenpfordt 1984), an album he completed between 1830 and 1831, and his two tomes *Versuch Einer Getreuen Schilderung der Republik Mexiko of 1884*[2] (Mühlenpfordt 1969), and *Mejicanische Bilder: Reiseabenteuer, Gegenden, Menschen und Sitten 1827–1835*,[3] a manuscript that was recently transcribed and published by Corinna Raddatz (2000). She found this last work, a document of 434 pages, in the library of the Hamburg Museum of Ethnology (Museum für Völkerkunde Hamburg). Even though parts of this text are partially published in his two-volume work, the reader will find detailed descriptions he did not publish elsewhere. For example, he provides data on archaeological sites that were less known than Mitla, such as the mounds and terraces of Soyula in the Cuicatec region, and he also includes a Cuicatec vocabulary. Mühlenpfordt paints colorful vignettes of the native Mexicans: we learn how

FIGURE 15.3. Effigy vessel with an image of Xipe, Oaxaca? Eighth–tenth centuries CE? Carl Uhde collection before 1850; © Preußischer Kulturbesitz, Ethnologisches Museum IV Ca 2641.

the Mixtecs desired to make money from the cochineal and other trade but, rather than spending their savings, they buried them in secret places, refusing to tell even their children where it was hidden. Accordingly, foreign idol hunters armed with shovels must have appeared a very suspicious lot to the hoarding Mixtec (Raddatz 2000:121).

The other miner, Eduard Harkort (1797–1836), quit the company that hired him to become instead a freelance cartographer, surveyor, and mineralogist under contract to the state government in Oaxaca. He left a diary that was translated into English with the bleak title of *In Mexican Prisons* (Harkort 1858, 1986), and his legacy also includes sketches and two copies of a Chinantec and Mixe *lienzo* that Viola König found in the Hamburg Museum (König 1989) (figure 15.4). Pérez García (1998:127) later published a different version of the Chinantec *lienzo* that had been signed by Harkort.

Harkort no doubt came across these documents because he was commissioned by the Chamber of Justice to prepare an accurate map of the state and was also involved in native lawsuits (König 1993:28–29). These incidents, as well as "nocturnal Indian ceremonies," are described in his diary (Harkort 1986:34–37). Today the whereabouts of the originals of the *lienzos* are unknown, and a source in common

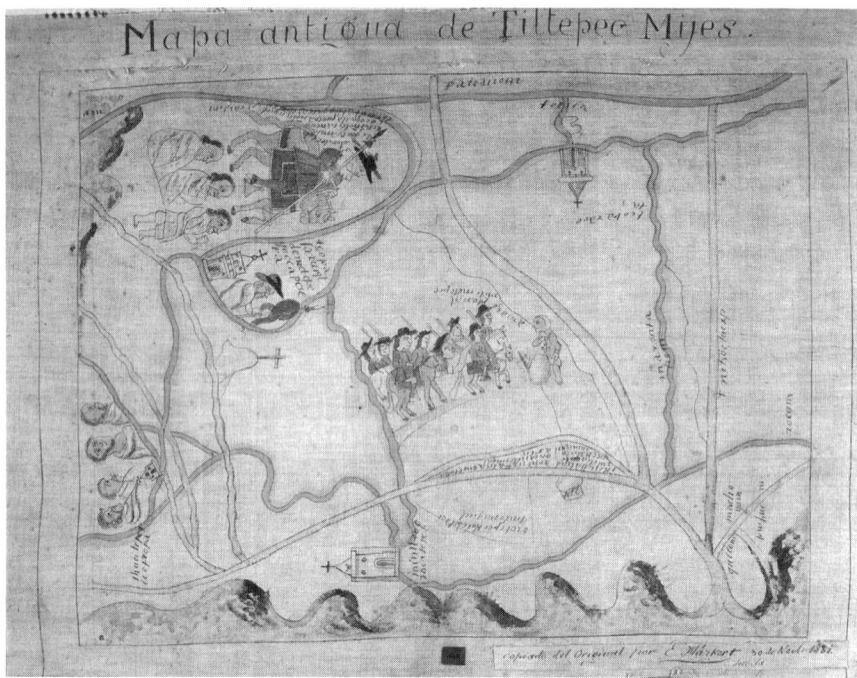

FIGURE 15.4. *Mapa de Santa María Tiltepec Mijes*, Mixe region. Copy made by Eduard Harkort at Zaachila on November 30, 1831. © Museum für Völkerkunde, Hamburg. Photograph by Burkhard Brinker.

for both the Mühlenpfordt diary and Harkort's copies of the *lienzos*, all found in the Hamburg museum, could not be traced (König 1989). Other written records and a few sketches made by Harkort are kept in his family archive (Westfälisches Wirtschaftsarchiv Dortmund).

At the beginning of the twentieth century, another trio of German collectors arrived in Mexico: the dealer and amateur ethnographer Wilhelm Bauer-Thoma (figure 15.5); his more famous compatriot, the geographer Oscar Schmieder (1891–1980); and the ethnographer and philologist Leonhard Schultze-Jena (1872–1955). Schmieder's 1929 research in Oaxaca was published in German and English, but Bauer-Thoma's and Schultze-Jena's works exist in German only. For any research focusing on native Oaxaca and especially the Sierra Zapotecs, Chinantec, and Mixe, Schmieder's (1930, 1934) work is still one of the most useful sources for this area, but it has been tainted because of his collaboration with the Nazis.

Among European and North American ethnographic museums, the name of Wilhelm Bauer is well known, in part because he flooded these institutions with

FIGURE 15.5. Wilhelm Bauer-Thoma on his horse in Monte Albán, 1902. © The Seler Archive, Ibero-American Institute, Berlin.

his photographs to stimulate interest in the purchase of collections, such as the fine holding of Dr. Fernando Sologuren (Gyarmati 2004; König and Kroefges 2001). The Ethnological Museum in Berlin probably holds the largest Bauer collection from Mexico, including some four hundred objects from Oaxaca (figures 15.6 and Figure 15.7). Although he never managed to get hired at the Berlin Museum, he used the rumor of his association to the institution to create an air of respectability, but later his reputation became seriously damaged because he had sold fakes to the museum's curator, Eduard Seler (Goedicke et al. 1992; Sellen 2005a). Nonetheless, in comparison to Uhde's band of pot-hunters, Bauer was careful to record the exact provenience of the objects he collected. Furthermore, he left interesting documents such as a Mixe vocabulary by Fray Agustín de Quintana, and published the results of his 1902 field trip to a region inhabited by the Mixe and Sierra Zapotecs (Bauer-Thoma 1916).

Although most photographs published by Bauer and Schmieder are of poor quality, Leonhard Schultze-Jena (1938), in his volume *Indiana III*, provides high-quality plates that are in some cases augmented by drawings (figure 15.8). He also left a large archaeological collection from Central Mexico that is housed today at the Ethnologisches Museum Berlin (figure 15.9). For the study of the Mixteca and the

FIGURE 15.6. Vessel with lid, found in a cave near Villa Alta. Wilhelm Bauer collection, before 1902; © Preußischer Kulturbesitz, Ethnologisches Museum IV Ca 24183.

areas of Puebla-Tlaxcala-Veracruz, his linguistic records of the Nahua, Tlapanec, and Mixtec languages are of great value, including prayers and ritual texts. The instructions and procedures he recorded for hunting deer, for example, are reproduced faithfully in the Codex Cospi and to this day are remembered in the oral traditions of the Mixteca Alta (Penth 1996/1997). Indeed, Schultze-Jena was well aware that people in remote communities who could not be understood by Christian priests and Mexican functionaries constituted a "refuge of pagan tradition" and native knowledge. His examples also show that we need to cross state borders in order to find our sources and make more efficient use of them.

A VIEW FROM MEXICO: FOUR OAXACAN COLLECTORS

A parallel view on nineteenth-century collections is also available from the perspective of the Mexican collectors who early in the twentieth century divested the bulk of their private cabinets to public museums. Four of them in particular stand out because they worked together to build their collections: Fernando Sologuren (1850–1918), Manuel Martínez Gracida (1847–1924), Francisco Belmar (1859–1926), and Abraham Castellanos (1868–1918). The colossal amounts of archaeological material they collected contributed greatly to the formation of museum collections in Mexico and overseas, but few have studied this aspect of their lives. We know quite a few biographical details about Belmar, Martínez Gracida, and Castellanos, in

FIGURE 15.7. Fragment of effigy vessel with an image of a human face and serpent maws, from Zimatlán. Wilhelm Bauer collection before 1903; © Preußischer Kulturbesitz, Ethnologisches Museum IV Ca 24875.

part because they also studied and collected indigenous pictographic documents such as *lienzos*, and we cite with admiration Maarten Jansen and a generation of his students who have compiled valuable information on many of these collectors (Doesburg 1998; Jansen and Pérez Jiménez 2000; Oudijk 2000; Van Meer 2008). On the other hand, their archaeological collections have received little scholarly attention. Until recently, for example, accurate biographical data about Sologuren—Mexico's preeminent collector—was almost unknown (Sellen 2005b, 2006; Urcid and Sellen 2009). Studying this collection has been challenging because the documentary sources for it are in three different countries and at least eight different archives (figure 15.10), a situation that is similar for other Oaxacan collectors. These data, in the form of physical collections, photographs, notes, and inventory lists, are fundamental for understanding the breadth of their work. Furthermore, we can argue that their legacy has a direct bearing on archaeological studies. Caso

FIGURE 15.8. Mixtec man praying and sacrificing a turkey to the stone image of the rain god inside the "House of Rain" at Cahuatachi, January 1930 (Schultze-Jena 1938: table XVI).

and Bernal (1952) illustrated a total of 527 artifacts in their seminal work *Urnas de Oaxaca*: two-thirds of the material came from their excavations while one-third was from the older collections in the National Museum of Anthropology. Over 100 objects came from Sologuren's collection, representing 25 percent of all the artifacts illustrated and, after excavated materials, the primary source of data. Thus one can conclude that a careful consideration of the background information about this holding is warranted.

We cannot fully understand the foreign collectors (such as the Germans discussed above) without delving into the story of the Mexicans who generated many of the collections they purchased. The relationship between the two has not been well studied and, ironically, if we wish to learn more about the local collectors we must examine the travelers because they were the ones who most extensively documented these collections. For example, Eduard and Cecilie Seler made copious notes on Sologuren's collection and were keenly interested in purchasing it. Eduard made watercolor sketches of many of the objects and interviewed the doctor on where he had made his discoveries; together they visited Monte Albán, Mitla, and Xoxocotlán. At this last site, Seler made a revealing map of the area, with notes regarding the excavations carried out by Sologuren in 1886 and those

FIGURE 15.9. Images of old Mixtec idols found buried on tops of hills or hanging from roof beams (Schultze-Jena 1938: table XVII).

by Saville in 1899. He also makes references to objects that were found in each location (figure 15.11).

The foreign buyers were particularly interested in purchasing collections that were well organized and classified. The positivist Mexican collectors, many of whom were doctors, took their inspiration from the natural sciences, so their approach to organizing archaeological material was similar to that of botanical or medical collections. They meticulously organized and labeled objects, classifying them by type and cultural affiliation. Now yellowed and peeling, many of these nineteenth-century tags still miraculously adhere to the artifacts, confirming photographic evidence—where we can see the labels but not read their content—that everything in these collections had been classified. The printed labels show that each piece was assigned a cultural affiliation, such as Zapotec, Mixtec, or Cuicatec, and in the collectors' mind these were considered "civilizations"; other lines were added for a description of the object, the district in the state where it was located, and a more specific provenience such as "found in a tomb"; and in many cases the find was also dated. Unfortunately, much of this information has been lost. For the Belmar, Sologuren, and Castellanos collections purchased by Mexico's National Museum of Anthropology, many of the objects subsequently had their labels removed, undoing decades of careful classification. Curiously, the objects from Martínez Gracida's collection that made it to Europe or to the United States still have many of their labels intact (figure 15.12).

The object labels had an important function because when the collections were transferred into public hands, inventory lists were required to document the masses of material, and the collectors would prepare these by copying the information directly off the artifact tags. In some cases it is evident—and quite logical—that an inventory's order followed the same arrangement of the objects as they appeared on the shelves, where the objects were classified by size and type. Furthermore, we have discovered that many of the Oaxacan collectors used the *same* printed labels, so we can deduce that they were trying to create a standard for classification. Thus an important conclusion from analyzing these sources is that the collectors were not solely interested in acquiring objects for possession's sake but were active in compiling and processing information about them. Systematic classification being a major tenet of archaeology, we can venture to say that these collectors participated in initiating modern archaeological practice.

THE TRANSMISSION OF KNOWLEDGE

When large amounts of artifacts and associated documentation are moved from one place to another, there is inevitably the possibility that data will be lost. As we have already discussed, four Oaxacan collectors had carefully recorded the

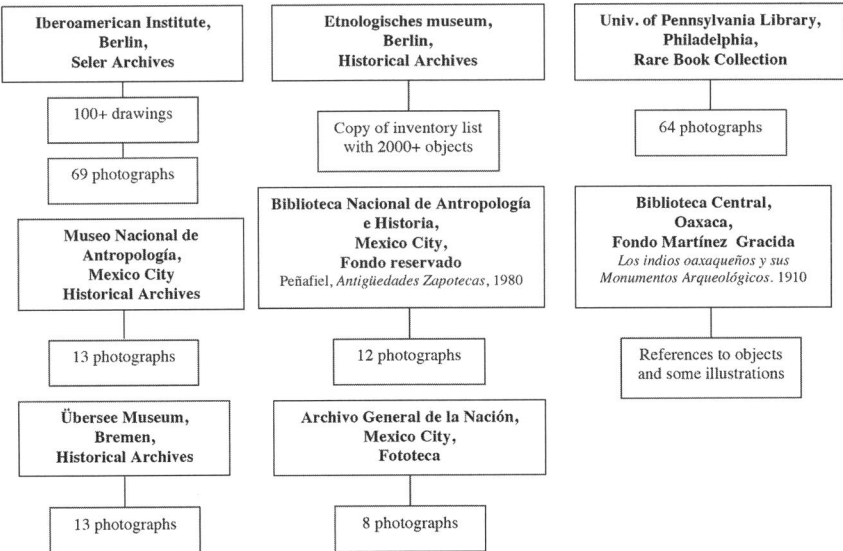

FIGURE 15.10. Location of documents that refer to the Sologuren collection.

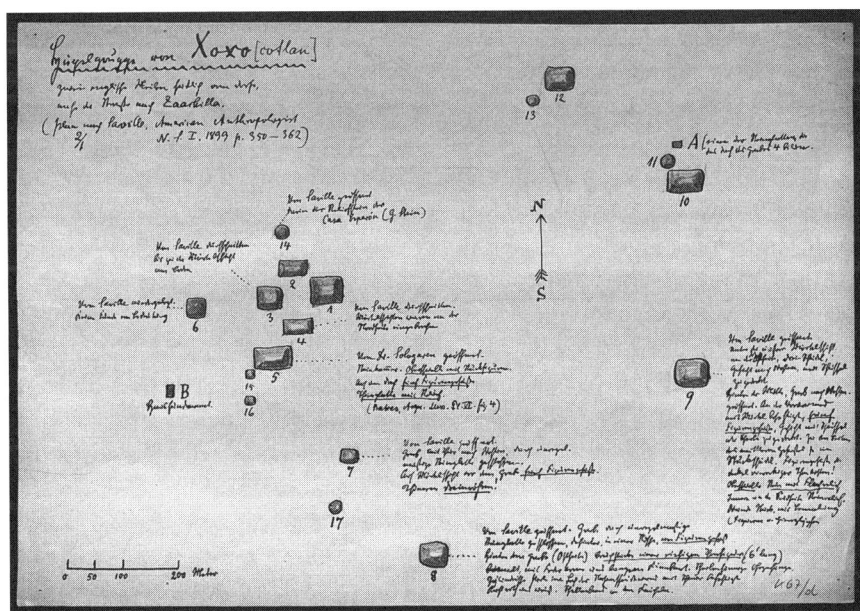

FIGURE 15.11. Seler's rendition of mounds in Xoxocotlán, circa 1900. © The Seler Archive, Ibero-American Institute, Berlin.

FIGURE 15.12. Zapotec urn with label written by Manuel Martínez Gracida. Museum of World Cultures, Göteburg, Sweden, Ca 29011. Photo by Adam Sellen.

objects in their collections using a variety of strategies but, with the onslaught of the Mexican Revolution in 1910, their scientific legacy was expunged in the wake of the chaos and social upheaval that ensued. Knowledge that was produced by those who were close to the Porfirian regime was disparaged because these scientists belonged to a different political time. Classifications were undone and much material was divorced from its associated records—labels were even stripped off the objects by careless museum workers—and over time the debates and conversations about the material they had collected were also forgotten. There are many examples, but one of the clearest is what happened to the legacy of the Inspector of Archaeological Monuments, Leopoldo Batres. Not only did the new stewards of culture take away his power, but they also had his classifications and displays in the National Museum of Anthropology dismantled. One of his exhibits was banished to the servants' bathroom in the museum. As a result, a large portion of Oaxaca's archaeological record, meticulously documented (by nineteenth-century standards), was dispersed, muddled, and lost. The disruption in the transmission of knowledge caused by the new museum administrators, in their efforts to bring a "pre-Revolutionary" institution into conformity with the new ideology, affords a dramatic example of the potentially devastating (and long-lived) effects of politically motivated management of academic and cultural institutions.

FINAL THOUGHTS ON OAXACAN COLLECTIONS

Comprised of a myriad of cultures, Oaxaca is a large state with an extensive border. If we want to make an integrated use of sources and collections, we need to keep in mind that this information might be found in areas that are in the periphery and not necessarily within the confines of the state's borders.

When researching a collection we should also be mindful of other types of media—not just the ceramic objects—because these can complement and add value to our study. For example, a photograph showing a cave, a collection comprising idols from that place, a text describing a ceremony in that cave, a transcript of the ritual prayer recited, and a tape providing the sounds of performance are seemingly unconnected fragments, but when taken together give more sense to the whole.

Local networks of collectors in Oaxaca need to be reconstructed in order to examine their relationship to contemporary collectors, dealers, and researchers. In addition, external connections may also be of significance, such as when collections and files end up in foreign institutions or as private family property.

Although new excavations in Oaxacan soil are always welcome, we think it is imperative to fully understand what has already been accomplished. Stitching together the legacy of the collectors to date has taken many years of careful historical work—visiting archives and combing museums shelves—and the results for contemporary studies are tangible. We are just beginning to weave the story of the Mexican collectors into the wider narrative of Mexico's archaeological history, filling in a gap that for years has gone ignored, and we are just beginning to understand the complex relationships they forged with their foreign counterparts. Our hope is that the sum of these data will give a boost to current archaeological studies and prompt us to reflect more on the development of our own discipline. As a note of caution, omitting the type of historical inquiry we have outlined here can lead to a distorted picture of the archaeological record we wish to understand. Finally, before we begin using this material we have to seriously update the catalogs and museum information compiled to date, because a great deal of these data are erroneous and lack verification. We conclude, then, that the reconstruction of the many multimedia collections spread across Mexico, the United States, and Europe, involving a diversity of materials and including the rigorous documentation of collectors' biographies, is a vital step in integrating Oaxaca's archaeology with its history.

NOTES

1. This article is the combination of two conference papers, Viola König's "Oaxacan Studies in German Museums: Artifacts, Images and Written Documents" and Adam Sellen's "Expeditionary Fragments: Using Nineteenth Century Archaeological Data in Contemporary Oaxacan Studies," which were presented at the SAA's 72nd Annual Meeting in the

session "Integrating Archaeology and History in Oaxaca." After we heard each other's paper, we decided that it would be more interesting to present our work as a joint effort.

2. "*Essay on the accurate description of the Republic of Mexico with a special reference to its geography, ethnography, and statistics*" (our translation).

3. "*Mexican vignettes, travel adventures, landscapes, human beings, and customs 1827–1835*" (our translation).

REFERENCES

Bauer-Thoma, Wilhelm. 1916. "Unter den Zapoteken und Mijes des Staates Oaxaca der Republik Mexico, Ethnographische Notizen." *Baessler-Archiv* 5:75–97.

Caso, Alfonso, and Ignacio Bernal. 1952. *Urnas de Oaxaca*. Mexico City: INAH.

Doesburg, Sebastian van. 1998. "Los Lienzos Pictográficos de Don Francisco Belmar." *Mexicon* 20:52–54.

Goedicke, Christian, Sabine Henschel, and Ursel Wagner. 1992. "Thermolumineszenzdatierung und Neutronenaktivierungsanalyse von Urnengefässen aus Oaxaca." *Baessler-Archiv* 40:65–86.

Gosden, Chris, and Yvonne Marshall. 1999. "The Cultural Biography of Objects." *World Archaeology* 31 (2):169–178. http://dx.doi.org/10.1080/00438243.1999.9980439.

Gyarmati, János. 2004. "Wilhelm Bauer, a German Collector and his Mexican Collections in the Museum of Ethnography, Budapest and in other Museums." *Baessler-Archiv* 52:47–53.

Harkort, Eduard. 1858. *Aus Mejikanischen Gefängnissen. Bruchstück aus Eduard Harkorts hinterlassenen Papieren*, ed. F. Gustav Kühne. Leipzig, Germany: Carl B. Lorck.

Harkort, Eduard. 1986. *Mexican Prisons: The Journal of Eduard Harkort, 1832–1834*. Ed. and trans. Louis E. Brister. College Station: Texas A & M University Press.

Holtorf, Cornelius. 2002. "Notes on the Life History of a Pot Sherd." *Journal of Material Culture* 7 (1): 49–71. http://dx.doi.org/10.1177/1359183502007001305.

Jansen, Maarten, and Aurora Pérez Jiménez. 2000. *La Dinastía de Añute: Historia Literatura e Ideología de un Rino Mixteco*. Leiden: CNWS.

König, Viola. 1989. "Zwei Lienzos aus Oaxaca, Mexiko im Hamburgischen Museum für Völkerkunde." *Mitteilungen aus dem Hamburgischen Museum für Völkerkunde* 19:175–205.

König, Viola. 1993. *Die Schlacht bei Sieben Blume:Konquistadoren, Kaziken und Konflikte auf alten Landkarten der Indianer Südmexikos*. Bremen, Germany: Edition Temmen.

König, Viola. 1999. "Auf alten Wegen in Oaxaca, Mexiko: Eduard Selers und Caecilie Seler-Sachs' Reisen, Sammlungen und wissenschaftliche 'Ausbeute' in den Jahre 1887/88 und 1895." *TenDenZen* 7:205–220.

König, Viola. 2001. "Tres Alemanes en Oaxaca." *Acervos* 6 (23):44–52.

König, Viola. 2003. "Eduard Seler y Caecilie Seler-Sachs en Oaxaca." In *Eduard y Caecilie Seler: Sistematización de los Estudios Americanistas y sus Repercusiones*, ed. Renata von Hanffstengel and Cecília Tercero Vascondes, 329–340. Mexico City: UNAM/INAH.

König, Viola. 2005. "Mary E. Smith's Interpretation of the Codex Tulane, the Codex López Ruíz, and Other Documents: Some Conclusions of the Role of Tlaxiao in the Western Part of the Mixteca Alta." *Mexicon* 27 (6):112–115.

König, Viola. 2007. "Los Eduardos y Otros: Investigadores, Viajeros y Coleccionistas Alemanes en el Estado de Oaxaca, Mexico, y sus Contribuciones para la Exploración Científica (1800–2000)." In *Culturas en Movimiento: Contribuciones a la Transformación de Identidades Étnicas y Culturas en América*, ed. Wiltrud Dresler, Bernd Fahmel, and Karoline Noack, 35–48. Mexico: UNAM/IAI/IIA.

König, Viola, and Peter C. Kroefges. 2001. "Archaeological and Ethnographic Collections from Oaxaca, Mexico, at the Übersee-Museum Bremen." *TenDenZen* 9:95–134.

Mühlenpfordt, Eduard. (Original work published 1844) 1969. *Versuch Einer Getreuen Schilderung der Republik Mexico*. Austria: Akademische Druck- und Verlagsanstalt Graz.

Mühlenpfordt, Eduard. 1984. *Los Palacios de los Zapotecas en Mitla, 1830–1*. Mexico City: UNAM.

Oudijk, Michel. 2000. *Historiography of the Bènizàa: The Postclassic and Early Colonial periods (1000-1600 A.D.)*. Leiden: CNWS.

Penny, Glenn H. 2002. *Objects of Culture: Ethnology and Ethnographic Museum in Imperial Germany*. Chapel Hill: The University of North Carolina Press.

Penth, Boris. 1996/1997. *Mit den Füßen im Himmel: Maler in Oaxaca/ Pisando en el Cielo: Pintores de Oaxaca* (documentary film). Mexico: Fundación Cultural Rodolfo Morales, A. C.

Pérez García, Rosendo. (1956) 1998. *La Sierra Juárez*, vol. 1. Mexico: CNCA/CND, Instituto Oaxaqueño de las Culturas.

Pferdekamp, Wilhelm. 1958. *Auf Humboldts Spuren: Deutsche im Jungen Mexiko*. Munich: Huebner.

Raddatz, Corinna. 2000. *Mejicanische Bilder: Reiseabenteuer, Gegenden, Menschen und Sitten geschildert von Eduard Mühlenpfordt*. Heidelberg, Germany: Universitätsverlag C. Winter.

Schiffer, Michael Brian, and Andrea R. Miller. 1999. *The Material Life of Human Beings: Artifacts, Behavior, and Communication*. New York: Routledge.

Schmieder, Oscar. 1930. *The Settlements of the Tzapotec and Mije Indians, State of Oaxaca, Mexico*. Berkeley: University of California Press.

Schmieder, Oscar. 1934. "Der Einfluss des Agrarsystems der Tzapoteken, Azteken und Mije auf die Kulturentwicklung dieser Völker." In *erhandlungen des XXIV Internationalen Amerikanisten-Kongresses Hamburg 1930*, ed. Rudolf Grossmann and Gustav Wilhelm Otto Antze, 109–111. Hamburg: Friederichsen, Walter de Gruyter, Hamburg.

Schuler-Schöming, Immina von. 1970. *Figurengefässe aus Oaxaca. Mexiko*. Berlin: Veröffentlichungen des Museums für Völkerkunde Berlin.

Schultze Jena, Leonhard. 1938. *Bei den Azteken, Mixteken und Tlapaneken der Sierra Madre del Sur von Mexiko*. Published under the auspices of El Sociedad México-Alemana Alejandro de Humboldt.

Seler, Eduard. 1902. *Gesammelte Abhandlungen zur amerikanischen Sprach-und Altertums-kunde, Sprachliches, Bilderschriften, Kalender und Hieroglyphenentzifferung*. vol. I. Berlin: Asher & Co.

Seler, Eduard. 1904. *Gesammelte Abhandlungen zur amerikanischen Sprach-und Altertumskunde, Zur Geschichte und Volkskunde México's, Reisewege und Ruinen, Archäologisches aus México, Die religiösen Gesänge der alten Mexikaner*. vol. II. Berlin: Asher & Co.

Seler, Eduard. 1908. "Les Ruines de Mitla." In *Gesammelte Abhandlungen zur Amerikanischen Sprach- und Alterthumskunde*, vol. 3, 470–486. Berlin: Asher & Co.

Seler-Sachs, Caecilie. 1925. *Auf alten Wegen in Mexiko und Guatemala: Reiseerinnerungen aus den Jahren 1895 bis 1897*. Stuttgart, Germany: Strecker und Schröder Verlag.

Sellen, Adam. 2005a. "The Lost Drummer of Ejutla: The Provenance, Iconography and Mysterious Disappearance of a Polychrome Zapotec Urn." *Baessler-Archiv* 51:115–138.

Sellen, Adam. 2005b. "La Colección Arqueológica del Dr. Fernando Sologuren." *Acervos* 7 (29):4–15.

Sellen, Adam. 2006. *Re-evaluation of the Early Archaeological Collections from Oaxaca: A Trip to the Seler Archives in Berlin*. Report submitted to FAMSI. http://www.famsi.org /reports/05016/index.html, accessed Sep 2009.

Smith, Mary Elizabeth, and Ross Parmenter. 1991. *The Codex Tulane*. New Orleans: Tulane University Middle American Research Institute.

Urcid, Javier, and Adam Sellen. 2009. "A Forgotten House of Ancestors from Ancient Xoxocotlán." *Baessler-Archiv* 56(2008):177–224.

Van Meer, Ron. 2008. "La *Genealogía de Macuilxóchitl* y la Colección Privada del Doctor Ortega Reyes." In *Pictografía y escritura alfabética en Oaxaca*, ed. Sebastián van Doesburg, 117–150. Oaxaca, Mexico: IEEPO.

Contributors

BRUCE E. BYLAND

BAS VAN DOESBURG
Biblioteca Francisco de Burgoa, Oaxaca City, Mexico

LIANA I. JIMÉNEZ OSORIO
Faculty of Archaeology, University of Leiden, The Netherlands

VIOLA KÖNIG
Ethnologisches Museum, Berlin, Germany

PETER C. KROEFGES
Department of Archaeology, Coordinación de Ciencias Sociales y Humanidades, Universidad Autónoma de San Luis Potosí, Mexico

MICHAEL D. LIND
Santa Ana Unified School District (Retired), Santa Ana, USA

GEOFFREY G. McCAFFERTY
Department of Archaeology, University of Calgary, Canada

SHARISSE D. MCCAFFERTY
Department of Archaeology, University of Calgary, Canada

JOHN M.D. POHL
Department of Art History, University of California, Los Angeles, USA

EMMANUEL POSSELT SANTOYO
Faculty of Archaeology, University of Leiden, The Netherlands

CARLOS RINCÓN MAUTNER
Department of Human Behavior, College of Southern Nevada, Las Vegas, USA

ADAM T. SELLEN
Centro Peninsular en Humanidades y Ciencias Sociales, UNAM Mérida, Mexico

RONALD SPORES
Department of Anthropology, Vanderbilt University (Emeritus), Nashville, USA

STEPHEN L. WHITTINGTON
Museum of Anthropology, Wake Forest University, Winston-Salem, USA

ANDREW WORKINGER
Department of Sociology, Anthropology and Geography; University of Tennessee, Chattanooga, USA

DANNY ZBOROVER
Center for U.S.-Mexican Studies, University of California, San Diego, USA

JUDITH FRANCIS ZEITLIN
Department of Anthropology, University of Massachusetts, Boston, USA

Index

Page numbers in italics indicate illustrations.

abandonment, during Classic-Postclassic transition, 176–77
Acatlán, 87, 89, 151, 189, 248
Acatlán polychrome, 131, 133, 152(n4), 153(n11)
Achiutla (Ñuu Ndecu; Burning Town), 122, 125
Acolhua, 179
agriculture, 267, 351; Coixtlahuaca Basin, 168–69; Zapotec, 367, 371
Aguilar, Juan de, 234
Alburquerque, Duke of, 383, 384
alliances, 29, 113, 189, 238, 354; Chontal-Aztec, 302–3; marriage, 13, 180, 184, 216–17
Almoloya, 273
altepetl (*yuhuitayu*), Coixtlahuaca, 182
Alvarado, Francisco de, 21, 55
amaranth dough paste (*tzoalli*), 106
amate, 20; paper made from, 232, 351
ancestor veneration, carved mandibles in, 107–8
animals, Zapotec use of, 373–75, 376(table)
animal spirits, Zapotec, 370
Annales school, 30
Aparicio, Felipe, 269
Aparicio Acuña, Isidro, 269
Apoala, 137
archaeological zones, 24
archaeology, 3, 4, 22, 23, 30, 31, 33, 39(n27), 55, *115*, 162, 225, 309(n2), 310(n8); Chontal region, 349, 351–53, 354–55; Coixtlahuaca Basin, 168–73; collaborative projects and, 28–29; and documentation, 26–27, *291*–92; and ethnohistory, 56–57, 64; historical events and, 341–44; and history, 32, 39(n29); Late Postclassic period, 349–50; of *Lienzo de Tecciztlan y Tequatepec*, 344–45; oral tradition and, 264–65; Rancho Santa Cruz, 371–82; Río Huamelula, 337–40; salt production, 245–50; San Miguel el Grande, 267–*69*; survey, 76–77, 80–82, 97–100; Tehuantepec, 385–87; Yucundaa, 64, 65; Zapotitlán, 296–99, 300. *See also* historical archaeology
archaeomagnetic dates, from Chachoapan, 136
Archivo General de la Nación de México, 63
Archivo Histórico del Poder Judicial del Estado de Oaxaca, 63
Archivo Histórico General del Estado de Oaxaca, 63
artifacts. *See* material culture
Astata, 333, 334, 335, 350, 351; historical locations of, 345–48; political institutions and rulership, 353–55; population size and distribution, 348–49
Atoyac, 231, 236, 238, 254(n25), 255(n28, n30); map representations of, 240–41
autos de fé, in Tehuantepec, 369

Avellán, Juan de, 382–83, 384, 385

Axayacatl, 354

Ayoxochiquilazala (Suchiquilazala), 235, 254(n25)

Ayuquila, 248

Ayutla, 349–50

Aztatlan (Santiago Astata), 334

Aztecs, Aztec Empire, 38(n22), 141, 166, 235, 354; Cihuacóatl and, 100–101; in Coixtlahuaca, 189–90; colonialism, 210, 214–16, 225; conquests by, 15–16; migrations, 185, 196(n9); in Zapotitlán, 302–3

Baessler-Archiv (journal), collector biographies, 394–95

ballcourts: at Yucundaa, 58; near Zapotitlán, 301

Balsas Basin, as tributary province, 235

Bancroft, Hubert H., 56

bark beaters, *352*

basins, Cholula polychrome, 147–48, *149*

Batres, Leopoldo, 406

battens, 105; as goddess attribute, 100, *101*, 103

Bauer-Thoma, Wilhelm, 398–*99*; collections of, *400, 401*

Belmar, Francisco, collections by, 400, 404

"Bent Hill," 127

Bernal, Ignacio, 26; Coixtlahuaca Basin excavations, 169, 171; *Urnas de Oaxaca,* 401–2

birds, on Cholula tripod bowls, 144

birth and death cycle, 100

black-on-orange wares, 190

bloodletting instruments, on Cholula polychrome vessels, 145, 146

blood sacrifice, Quetzalcoatl religion, 187

bone tools, in burials, 104–5

Borgia Group codices, 15; provenience of, 149–50; vessels depicted in, 150–51(table)

boundary conflicts, Astata-Huamelula, 350, 353–54

boundary markers, boundaries, 350; on *Mapa de San Vicente del Palmer,* 234, 235–36, 240

Bourbon reforms, 22

bowls, *133,* 141, 152(n2), 190; Cholula polychrome, *143,* 144–48; codex depictions of, 137, *139*; hemispherical, 142, *143*

bows and arrows: as Chichimec weapon, 181, 182, 196(n10); depictions of, 118–19

brine springs/wells, 231, 236, 240, 244, 257(n49)

British Museum, and Codex Egerton, 89–90

buccal masks, 107, 109; as Cihuacóatl attribute, 100–*101, 102,* 104; from Tomb 7, 105–*6*

Building J (Monte Albán), 9, 300

Burgoa, Francisco de, 21, 55, 287; on Chontal highlands, 335–36; *Geográfica Descripción,* 366–71; on Tehuantepec region, 385–86

burials, 12; with earth/fertility deity complex items, 105–8; Yucundaa historic, 59–60

Byland, Bruce, *35*–36, 75, *78,* 83, 85–86; archaeological survey by, *76*–77, 97, *98, 99*; career of, 77, 79–80

cacao, 368; ceramics and, 137, 139, 142, 151

Cacaxtla, 12

cacaxtli, 120, 121, 122

Cacaxtli Hill, 126; interpretations of, 120–24

cacicazgos, 17, 272. *See also* city-states

caciques, 17, 20; Chontalpa, 336–37; intermarriages of, 88, 89; Mixtec, 84. *See also* elites; rulership

Cahuatachi, "House of Rain" at, 402

cajetes, 190

calendars, 21; Mixtec, 102; Zapotec, 7, 8, 12, 370

Calihuala, 235, 254(n22, n25)

calpolli (calpollaque), 196(n9); recruitment of, 183–84

captives, of Lady 6 Monkey, 124

Caso, Alfonso, 26, 115; *Urnas de Oaxaca,* 401–2

Castellanos, Abraham, collections by, 400, 404

Catalina polychrome, *133*–34, 137, 196(n12); depictions and use of, *142*–*48;* distribution of, 131–32

Catarina, Santa, as Pinopiaa, 368

Catholic Church: Day of the Dead, 369–70; and Zapotec resistance, 368–69

caves: associated with salt works, 246–47; Formative period use, 221–22; Nduavee Valley, 267; ritual use of, 176, 177, 351–53

Caxiyztapa, 238

celestial movement, symbolism of, 103

censer bowls, Cholula, *147*

Central Mexican Highlands, Classic-Postclassic transition in, 176

Central Mixteca Alta Settlement Pattern Project, 223

ceramics, 12, 14, 36–37(n7), 77, 99, 177, *19,* 224, 302; Aztec, 190, 216; and blood sacrifice, 187–88; Chontal, 296, 314(n37); dates and distribution of, 135–36; depicted in codices, 137–48; as ethnic markers, 164–68; Formative period, 221–22, 223; at Iglesia Vieja salt works, 246, 247–48; Late Postclassic, 14, 190, 354; from Ngüiteri, 171–72; Oaxacan-style, *174*–75; polychrome, 131, 135–47; at Rancho Santa

Cruz, 372, 375–81, 386–87; from Santiago Tamazola, 248–50. *See also* Mixteca-Puebla polychromes; *by type*

Cerro Amole, archaeological sites on, 220–21, *222*

Cerro Chile, 300–301

Cerro Conduche (Xicotlan), material culture, *174*

Cerro de la Campana, 10

Cerro de la Paloma (Coixtlahuaca Basin), *170*

Cerro de las Minas, Ñuiñe inscriptions, 11

Cerro del Fortín, 224, 225; age of, 222–23

Cerro de Tortilla, 236, *237*

Cerro Estibo, 300–301

Cerro Maguey, 298

Cerro Ñiaxugue, 175

Cerro Verde (Coixtlahuaca Basin), sites on, 169–*70*

Cerro Zapote, 297, 298, 301

Chachoapan, 136, 379

Chalcatongo (Ñuu Ndaya), 101, 272, 273; Lady 6 Monkey at, 123–24; topography, 266–67

Chalcatongo Viejo (Mogote), 267

Chantico, 146

CHAP. *See* Chontalpa Historical Archaeology Project

Chatino speakers, 12

check dams, 171, 176–77

Chiapas, 7, 11, 13

Chiautla, 244

Chichimeca, Chichimecs, 158, 180, 196(n10); at Coixtlahuaca, 181–84; in Coixtlahuaca Basin, 165, 184–85, 188; migrations of, 178–79

Chicomemamatate (Seven Deer), 351, 353

Chicomoztoc, 165

Chilac (Tr 216), 167

Chilacatla, 178

Chiltepec, 300, 312(n27)

Chinantec, 19, 398

Chinantla, 151, 152(n4)

Chinantla polychrome, 131, 133, 153(n11)

Chocho-Popoloca, 177, 179, 188, 195(n3), 196(n8)

Chochos, Cocholtecos, 19, 165, 176, 196(n8); in Coixtlahuaca Basin, 173, 178–79

chocolate, ceramics and, 137, 139, 142, 151

Cholula, 15, 179, 195(n3); ceramic markers in, 166, 172; *pulque* ceremony in, 142–44; radiocarbon dates from, 152(n6), 153(n9, n12, n13); Quetzalcoatl and, 146, 187

Cholula Inciso, 172

Cholula polychrome, *133*, 134, 149; depictions and uses of, 142–48; distribution of, 131–*32. See also* Catalina polychrome

Chontal, 301, 311(n16), 313(n32), 313(n30), 366; belief systems, 351–3; documentary and oral sources, 295–96; on Oaxaca Coast, 333, 344, 348; social differentiation, 350–51; and Triple Alliance, 302–3

Chontal highlands, 19, 287, 313–14(n35, n37); archaeology of, 296–99, 341–44; Colonial period, 304–6, 314(n36); Postclassic period, 301–4

Chontalpa, 333; archaeological chronology, 339–40; documentary/historical sources, 334–37; historical-archaeological correlation, 341–44; population size and distribution, 348–49

Chontalpa Historical Archaeology Project (CHAP), 281, 286, 311(n18–n20); community-based participation, 307–*8*; corroborations in, 293–94; descriptive grids in, 292–93; documentary strata used in, *290, 291*–92; exhibits, *308*–9; methodology, 287–88, *289*; and Santa María Zapotitlán, 295–99

Chontecomatlan *titulos primordiales* (CTP), 301, 313(n29)

Chorotega, 179

Christianity, 87–88, 21–22

chronology, 6(table), 125; Chontalpa, *338*, 339–40

church-convents, in Yucundaa, 58–60

churches, native iconography in, 191, *192*

Cihuacóatl: attributes of, 100–*101*, 103, 105, 146

Cihuatecpan, 216

Cintéotl, 146

city-states, 11, 13, 116, 174, 272

civic/ceremonial centers, at Yucundaa, 57–*58*

Classic period, 11, 12, 33, 178, 232, 267, 291; Astata and Huamelula, 348–49; Coixtlahuaca Basin, 173–75; Mixteca Alta, 125, 161–62

Classic-Postclassic transition, 14; in Coixtlahuaca Basin, 176–79

Coatepec (Snake Mountain), 179, 185

Coatlan/Miahuatlan, 302

cochineal production, 18, 22

Codex Aubin, 185

Codex Becker, Tilantongo in, 77

Codex Bodley, 38(n19), 77; Lady 6 Monkey in, 123–24; place names in, 115, 120

Codex Borbonicus, Cihuacóatl in, 100

Codex Borgia, 80; vessels illustrated in, *141*, 142, *143*, 144, 147, *148*, *149*

Codex Boturini, 185

Codex Colombino, Tilantongo in, 38(n19), 77

Codex Cospi, 92, 400; provenience of, 149, 151

Codex Egerton, 38(n19), 92; "Jaguar town," *87*, 88; and Santa María Cuquila, 86–90

Codex Fejérváry-Mayer, 149, 151

Codex Laud: provenience of, 149, 151; *pulque* ceremony depicted in, 138, *139*

Codex López Ruiz, 87

Codex Magliabechiano, Cihuacóatl in, 100, *101*

Codex Mendoza, 254(n22, n24); on Aztec colonialism, 214–15; land tenure, 254–55(n25)

Codex Nuttall, 38(n19), 58, 312–13(n28); Lady 3 Flint in, 103–*4*; Lady 9 Grass in, 101; Lady 13 Flower in, 105; Monte Albán in, 127; Pilitas polychrome in, 137, *138, 139*; "Place of the Red and White Bundle" in, *115*; skull idols, 107; Tilantongo in, 77, 218; Zaachila-Teozacoalco interactions, 217

Codex Ramírez, 354

Codex Sanchez Solis, 87–88

Codex Selden, 38(n19), 165, 179; Lady 6 Monkey in, 101, 123, 124; place names in, 120, 121, 122

Codex Tulane, 87

Codex Vaticanus B, provenience of, 149, 151

Codex Vindobonensis, Mixtec rituals in, 137–39, 141, *142*

Codex Vindobonensis Mexicanus, 103

codices, 38(n19), 125, 169, 176; Borgia group, 150–51(table); interpretation of, 116–18; land tenure and, 19–20; meaning in, 113–14; Mixtec, 14, 15, 26, 29, 77, 84, 152(n5), 153(n14); Mixteca Pilitas polychrome vessels in, 137, *138*; pictorial, 16, 19–20; place names/signs in, 114–16, 118–28. *See also by name*

cognitive psychology, and codical interpretation, 116–17

Coixtlahuaca, 13, 57, *158,* 180, 187, 192, 256(n40); Aztecs in, 15, 189–90, 216; Chichimeca at, 181–84; creation traditions, 185, 186; as Mixtec, 173, 188

Coixtlahuaca Basin, *160, 161,* 166, 180; archaeology in, 168–73; Classic period, 173–75; Classic-Postclassic transition, 176–79; Early Colonial period, 191–92; ethnicity in, 164–65; Late Postclassic, 187–88; Nahua speakers in, 189–90; pluri-ethnic sociopolitical organization in, 185–86; Postclassic in, 194–95; Toltec Chichimeca place-name, 184–85

collections: historical, 391–92; museum, 392–94, 404; researching, 406–7

collectors: biographies of, 394–95; German, 395–400; Oaxacan, 400–402, 407; records kept by, 404–6

colonialism, 209–10; Aztec, 225, 302–3; indigenous, 299–300; Spanish, 304–6; at Teozacoalco, 211, 213–16

Colonial period, 21, 34, 99, 134, 161, 163, 273, 284; Chontal highlands, 304–6, 314(n36); codices, 38(n19), 88; documentary records, 16–17, 29; indigenous language documents, 363–64; Isthmus of Tehuantepec, 366–71; Mixteca Baja maps, 233–34; salt production and use, 243–44, 258(n53); social reorganization during, 17–19; southern Oaxaca, 286–87; Teozacoalco, 213–16; territorial disputes, 19, 313(n32); Yucundaa, 58–60

colonial towns, Spanish, 211

colonization, 214, 225

Colossal Bridge cave-tunnel, glyphs in, 172, 175, 177

commoners, 58, 131, 373; literacy of, 20, 37(n11)

communication technologies, 22–23

computers, 30

confirmation bias, 117

congregación, 17, 211, 273

Consejo de Indias, 64

Convento phase pottery, 379

Copalita River, 302

Córdova, Juan de, 21, 55, 369, *370*

Córdova-Castellanos, 87

"Corn Plants or Weeds," 126

Coronel Sánchez, Camilo, on place names, 92, *93*

Corral phase ceramics, 177

Cortés, Hernán, 19

Cortés (Cortéz), Juan (Cosijopii), 353; Burgoa's description of, 368, *369*

Cosijo, 127

Cosijopii I, 15

Cosijopii II (Juan Cortéz; Cortés), 17, 353

cosmos, Mixtec, 103

Council of the Indies, on Tehuantepec rebellion, 384, 386

court cases: land rights and salt production, 238–40; social differentiation in, 350–51

Coxcatlán, 189, 244

Coxcatlán Brushed ware, 166

Coxcatlán Gray ware, 166

Coyolapan, as tributary province, 215

Coyotlatelco horizon ceramics, 177, *178*

creation stories: Chontal, 301; Coixtlahuaca, 177, 185, 186; landscape and weaving in, 103

Cruz Cruz, Alfredo, 269

Cruz de Llegalán, *219*

Cruz phase occupations, settlement hierarchy, 223–24

CTP. *See* Chontecomatlan *titulos primordiales*

Cuauhtinchan, 179

Cuauhtla, 183

Cuautulco, 334. *See also* Huatulco

Cuetzpalin, Catalina, 88

Cueva del Diablo (Oaxaca Coast), 351–53

Cuevas Dávalos, Alonso de, 386

Cuicatec Cañada, 151

Cuicatec region, collections from, 396–97

Cuicatlán Cañada, 133, 158, 194(table)

Cuilapan, 13, 15, 98, 120, 179, 184

cults, 15, 100, 268; earth/fertility deity, 104–5;
    Pinopiaa/Santa Catarina, 368–69

cultural memory, 265

culture change, 30; environmental and geological
    processes, 162, 163–64

culture contact, 209–10, 225; at Teozacoalco,
    216–18

culture history paradigm, documents and archae-
    ology, 26–27

Cuquila, 92; and Codex Egerton, 89–90, *91*; as
    jaguar town, 86–*87*, 88

Cuthá (Tr319), 167

Cuyotepeji, 87–88, 89

Dainzú, 9

danzante monoliths, 8, 37(n10)

Dávila Padilla, Agustín, 335

Day of the Dead, in Tehuantepec, 369–70

deities: on Cholula polychrome vessels, 142–44;
    in Coixtlahuaca stories, 185. *See also by name*

descriptive grids, in historical archaeology
    research, 292–94

Díaz, Porfirio, 22–23

Díaz del Castillo, Bernal, 132

digital media, 30

diseases, European, 18–19

documentary ethnology, 56, 62–64

documentary record, 281

documents, documentation, 4, 11, 15, 29, 31, 34,
    159, 255(n30), 284, 313(n33); and archaeol-
    ogy, 26–27, 341–44; on Chontalpa, 334–37;
    of Coixtlahuaca ruling lineage, 164–65; of
    collections, 404–6; Colonial pictorial, 19,
    163; critical use of, 63–64; and ethnology,
    56, 62–63; historical, 23, 24, 163; indigenous,
    32, 159, 363–64; Isthmus of Tehuantepec,
    382–85; of salt production and land rights,
    238–40, 255–56(n39, n40); on Santa María
    Zapotitlán, 295–96, 308–9; Spanish, 16–17;
    Tehuantepec, 385–87; territorial narratives,

288, *290, 291*–92; Tonalá land tenure, 250–51.
    See also codices

Dominicans, 18, 21, 58, 369, 386; in Chontal
    highlands, 335–36

dowries, 137, 184

drinking vessels, 148; Cholula polychrome,
    142–44; codex depictions of, 137–41

Duañusa'a, 272

Durán, Diego, 55

Durán Codex, Cihuacóatl in, 101

Dutch, 18

dynasties, 88; Chontal, 336–37, 348; Mixtec,
    14–15; Teozacoalco, 216–17

eagle on a tree, place name, 120, 121

eagles, as Cholula polychrome motif, 146

Early Classic period, 10

Early Colonial period, 11, 19, 136, 302; Astata and
    Huamelula, 346–49, 350, 353; Chontal high-
    lands, 297–98, 304, 305; Coixtlahuaca Basin,
    191–92; southern Oaxaca, 286–87

Early Formative period, 7, 224; at Teozacoalco,
    222–23

Early Postclassic period, 13, 20, 107, 165, 178, 180,
    187, 348; Ngüiteri as, 171–72

Early Ventana Salada phase ceramics, 166, 167

ear spools, obsidian, 105

earth/fertility deity complex, archaeological
    evidence of, 104–8

Earth Goddess, 185

Echeverría government, 98

ecology, Huamelula, 351

effigies, amaranth dough, 100

effigy vessels, 11, *397*; Cholula polychrome, 141,
    142, 147; Coixtlahuaca Basin, *174*; Pilitas
    polychrome, 139, *140*; Zapotec, *406*; from
    Zimatlán, *401*

Ehecatl-Quetzalcoatl, 185, 187

ejidos, 23–24

Ejutla Valley, 11

El Boquerón, 351, 353

El Huapote, site RH07, 346, *347*, 350

elites, 8, 9, 17, 20, 137, 188, 379; literacy of, 10–11,
    37(n11); Mixtec, 14–15

Eloxochitlan, carved mandible from, 107

Encinas, Diego, 64

"Enclosure," 126

encomiendas, 17, 64, 254–55(n25)

English, 18

environment: Classic-Postclassic transition, 176–
    77; Coixtlahuaca Basin, 168–69; Huamelula, 351

environmental processes, cultural adaptations to, 162, 163–64, 195(n4)
Epiclassic period, 12, 178, 187
Escudo de Armas de Cuilapan, place names in, 120–21
Espinosa, Alonso de, on indigenous idolatry, 369–70
Espinosa, Filiberto, 245
estancias, 213
ethnic enclaves, 184
ethnic identity, 159; ceramics and, 164–68, 380–81; Zapotec, 175, 386–87
ethnicity, ethnicities, 174, 188, 313(n33), 366; in Coixtlahuaca Basin, 164–65; Tehuacán Valley, 167–68
ethnoarchaeology, Chontal pottery making, 296
Ethnographic Museum (Berlin), Seler collection in, 392–93
Ethnological Museum (Berlin), 394, 395, 396, 399
ethnology, 55; documentary, 56, 62–64
ethnohistory, 32, 163, 281; and archaeology, 56–57; document use, 60–64
ethnonyms, 19
Etlatongo, 224

Fane Kantsini (3 Hummingbird), 304
feast networks, 188
feasts, 380; Day of the Dead, 369–70
female earth/fertility cults, 100
fertility, spinning and weaving and, 102
figurines, Postclassic, 190, *191*
fishing, Huamelula, 351, *352*
Florentine Codex, Cihuacóatl in, 100
Formative period, 33, 224, 291; indigenous colonialism in, 299–300; Teozocoalco, 221–22
Four Jaguar, 58
Fragmento Gómez de Orozco, 164
Franciscans, 21
French, 18, 22, 30

García Pimentel, Luis, 56
garrisons (*guarnición*), Aztec, 216
Gay, José Antonio, 56
Genealogía de Igualtepec, 235
genealogies, 88–89, 113; elite, 10–11; Ihualtepec rulers, 234, *235*; Spanish-era use of, 20–21
Genealogy of Tlazultepec, 87
geoarchaeology, and cultural change, 163–64
Geográfica Descripción (Burgoa), on Isthmus Zapotecs, 366–71
geological processes, 162, 163

Germans, as collectors, 392–93, 395–400
Germany, collections in, 392–93
goblets, 152(n2); Catalina polychrome, 142, *143*
goddesses: attributes of, 100–102; weaving and, 103–4
gold, 105, 313(n30), *393*
gold mines, Teozacoalco, 213
Gómez, Francisco, 238, *239*, 240, 256(n42, n44)
Gómez, Inés, 239, 257(n47)
Gómez, María, 239, 240, 251, 257(n48)
grecas (*xicalcoliuhquis*), on ceramics, 146, 377, 381
green color, and Coixtlahuaca Basin people, 164–65
Guerrero, Classic period, 11
Guitzo Ystatapan, 238
Guzmán, Gaspar de, 351, 353
Guzmán, Miguel de, I, 256(n42), 257(n48)

hacienda system, 19
hallucinogenic mushroom ceremony, Mixtec, 141
Harkort, Eduard: collections of, 396, 397–98
heddle bars, as ritual landscape symbols, 103
Henestrosa, Andrés, 24
hero cults, 14
hidden transcripts, 364; archaeology as, 371–82
hide rolls, 20
"Hill of the Bee," 115
"Hill of the Chile Plant," 300
"Hill of the Insect," 120, 121, 123, 124, 125, 126
"Hill of the Jaguar," 119, 120, 121
"Hill of the Jewels and Gold," 119
"Hill of the Lord," Monte Albán as, 119
"Hill of the Moon," 119–20, 121, 123, 124, 125, 126
"Hill of the Raven," 312–13(n28)
"Hill of the Reed," 119–20
"Hill of the Rope," 119
"Hill of the Round Quetzal Feather," 119
"Hill of the *Teponoztli* Drum," 119
hill signs, Zapotec, 9
hilltop sites: Cerro del Fortín, 222–23; Chontal, 297–98; Formative period, 300–301
Historia Tolteca-Chichimeca, 180
historical archaeology, 29, 57–58, 279–80, 309(n1, n4), 310(n11, n13), 311(n14); Chontal region, 307–8; of indigenous colonialism, 299–300; indigenous cultures and, 306–7; integrative research in, 292–95; and Mesoamerican societies, 281–83; in Mexico, 283–85; reconfiguring, 285–86
historical events, archaeological evidence of, 341–44

historical record, 4, 162–63; of Astata, 345–48; Zapotec script and, 27–28

historiography, 5, 29

history, histories, 3, 4, 14, 32, 33, 55, 281, 299; and archaeology, 28–29, 32, 39(n29), 283; Chontalpa, 334–37; in Mixtec codices, 114–15; and social memory, 1–2. *See also* historical archaeology

Honduras, Mangue speakers, 179

Huachino, as "Place of the Red and White Bundle," *115*, 124–25, 127

Huajuapan de León, Pilitas polychrome in, 132–33

Hualakgoce, 345; site RH08, 346, *347*, 350

Hualampamo, 339; site RH09, 346, *347*

Huamelula, 333, 335, 350; cave rituals, 351–53; political institutions and rulership, 353–55; population size and distribution, 348–49

Huamelula, Río, 345; archaeology on, 337–40, 354–55

Huamelula-La Soledad, site RH01, 348, *352*

Huamelulpan: Cruz phase sites around, 223; Zapotec script at, 9–10

Huatulco, 302, 312–13(n28), 334

Huatulco, Bay of, 18

Huaves, 366, 367

Huaxyacac, 15, 17

Huichol cosmology, 103

Humboldt, Alexander von, 395

hunter-gatherers, 180, 196(n10)

iconography, 7, 8, 11; of Cholula Catalina polychromes, 144–*46*; in Coixtlahuaca church, 191, *192*; of earth/fertility deity, 100–108

identity, 11, 23. *See also* ethnic identity

idolatry, idols, 21, 107, *403*; in Jalapa, 368–69

Iglesia complex, 379

Iglesia Gentil, 220, 221, *222*

Iglesia polychrome, 134, 135, 136, 153(n7, n8)

Iglesia Vieja (San Bartolo Salinas), salt production at, 245–50

Ihualtepec (Yoaltepec), 231, 254(n25), 257(n47); salt production, 236–38; in sixteenth century, 234–35

INAH. *See* Instituto Nacional de Antropología e Historia

incense burners: human skull, 106–7; Mixteca polychrome, 141

Independence/Republican period, 34

indigenismo, 23

indigenous archaeology, 12, 23

indigenous peoples, 23–24, 34; Colonial period documents, 363–65; and historical archaeology, 306–7

industrialization, 24

inheritance, 107, 353; land and salt works, 239–40

Inquisition, Yanhuitlan, 59

inscriptions, spatial context of, 29

Instituto Nacional de Antropología e Historia (INAH), 27, 57, 98

interaction spheres, in Chontalpa Historical Archaeology Project, 291

intermarriages: of caciques, 88, 89; Teozacoalco-Zaachila, 216–17

irrigation systems, Huamelula, 351

Iscatoyac, 235

Itun Yuku Ndaku. *See* San Miguel el Grande

Itzpapalotl, 185

Ixcatec, 177–78

Ix Chel, 100

Ixlilxochitl, 235

jade, and Coixtlahuaca Basin, 164–65

jaguar pelt, as motif, 191–*92*

jaguars: on Cholula polychrome vessels, *145*, *146*, *147*; in place signs, 120, 121

jaguar-serpent, 192

"jaguar town": in Codex Egerton, 86, *87*; Cuquila as, 88–89

Jalapa (Jalapa del Marqués): Burgoa's description of, 367, 368, 371; idolatry in, 368–69

Jalieza, 10, 127

Jaliztapa, 239

Jaltepec, 101, 123, 125, 127, 128

Jaltepec Valley, 84

Jansen, Maarten, 84

jaws. *See* mandibles

Jicayán de Tovar, 235, 254(n24)

Jilotepequillo Manuscript (*JM*), 295, 301, 311(n16)

Juárez, Benito, 22, 308

Juxtlahuaca, 235

kinship, Teozacoalco-Zaachila, 216–17

knotting, and Mixtec cosmology, 103

knowledge: local/native, 84, 89–92, 93–94; oral, 4–5, 29–30, 295–96

laborers, recruitment of, 183–84

labrets, obsidian, 165

ladle censers, *141*, *147*

Lady 2 Flower (Xochiquetzal), 151

Lady 3 Flint (Shell Quechquemitl), 103–*4*, 106

Lady 3 Ocelot, 172
Lady 4 Rabbit, 217
Lady 6-Monkey, 15, 120, 125, 128; in codices, 123–24; at Jaltepec, 101, 121
Lady 6 Reed, 216–17
Lady 9 Grass, 101–2, 103, 105, 123–24
Lady 9 Monkey, 107
Lady 9 Reed, 105
Lady 13 Flower, 100, 105
Lambityeco, 107, 258(n52)
La Mishi, RH 11, 350
La Mixtequilla, 383
Landa, Diego de, 55
landscape, 84–85, 275(n5); codical place names and, 118–28; Coixtlahuaca Basin, 184–85; and lineages, 102–3; in Mixtec codices, 114–16; Teozocoalco's, 219–21; as woven, 103–4
landscape archaeology, 28
landscape of resistance, at Teozacoalco, 219–21
land tenure, 350; communal, 23–24; pictorial codices and, 19–20; salt production and, 238–40, 257(n47); Tonalá, 250–51
Las Flores (Tepelmeme), material culture from, 174
Las Flores phase, 125, 175, 267
Late Classic period, 11–12, 157, 175, 194, 298, 301; archaeology, 27, 107; Chontalpa, 340, 348; salt production, 246, 247
Late Colonial period, 20, 305
Late Formative period, 9, 267; indigenous colonialism in, 300–301
Late Palo Blanco phase, 167
Late Postclassic period, 13–14, 157, 163, 165, 177, 178; archaeology, 27, 349–50; Astata, 346–48, 353; Chontal during, 337, 348, 354; codices, 38(n19), 125; Coixtlahuaca Basin, 175, 187–88; Mixteca Alta, 161–62; Zapotitlán, 297, 298, 303–4
Late Natividad phase ceramics, 166
Late Ventana Salada ware, 166
Lavín Mier, Fernando, 372
Libro de las Tasaciones de Pueblos de la Nueva España, El, 16, 211, 314(n36)
Lienzo de Astata. See Lienzo de Tecciztlan y Tequatepec
Lienzo de Coixtlahuaca I (Seler II), 172, 181, 183, 256(n40)
Lienzo de Coixtlahuaca II (Ixtlan), 181, 183; Aztecs in, 189, 197(n13)
Lienzo de Coixtlahuaca III (Miexuiero), Aztecs depicted in, 189, 197(n13)
Lienzo de Córdova-Castellanos, 87

Lienzo de Ihuitlan, 180, 189, 190
Lienzo de Jilotepequillo (LJ), 295, 311(n18)
Lienzo de Nativitas, 170, 181
Lienzo de Ocotepec, 87
Lienzo de Otla, 181, 182; archaeological sites in, 169–70
Lienzo de San Jerónimo Otla, 181
Lienzo de San Juan Comaltepec, 85
Lienzo de Tecciztlan y Tequatepec (LTT), 290, 295, 311(n16); archaeological testing of, 344–45; place glyphs on, 334–35, 353–54; ruling lineages in, 336–37, 348; territorial divisions in, 349–50; Zapotitlán in, 297, 298, 300, 302
Lienzo de Tequixtepec I, lineages portrayed on, 164, 180
Lienzo de Tlalpitepec, 170, 181, 182
Lienzo de Zacatepec, 122
Lienzo Mixteco III, 240, 243
lienzos, 20, 163, 397; Coixtlahuaca Basin, 161, 169, 176, 179
Línea de Transmisión Tlaxiaco-Itundujia, 267
lineages: Aztec, 115, 179, 180, 190; Chontal, 336–37, 348; at Coixtlahuaca, 181–82; Coixtlahuaca Basin, 161, 164–65, 172, 177; integration of, 188, 189; landscape and, 102–3; Teozacoalco-Zaachila, 216–17
linguistics, 55, 157, 400; Otomanguean family divergence, 161–62
Liobaa phase, 107
lip-plugs, obsidian, 165
literacy, 3, 20, 23; of elites, 10–11
literary traditions: Mexican-era, 23; Oaxacan, 5, 26–27, 311(n15)
literate societies: archaeological study of, 280–83, 284, 309(n4, n6); characteristics of, 3–4
livestock: at Rancho Santa Cruz, 373–74, 376(table); Zapotec management of, 367–68, 371, 373
LJ. See Lienzo de Jilotepequillo
loom, in Huichol cosmology, 103
looting, 24
López, Gerónimo, 377
Lord 2 Dog, 180, 216–17
Lord 4 Ocelot (Lord Ocelotzin; "Tiger Claw"), 170, 181; in Coixtlahuaca, 182–84
Lord 4 Reed (Francisco de Mendoza), 88
Lord 5 Jaguar, 10
Lord 6 Monkey, 190
Lord 6 Water, 190
Lord 7 Flower (Xochipilli), 151; and pulque ritual, 139, 142–44

Lord 7 Reed; in Coixtlahuaca Basin, 164, 172
Lord 8 Deer (Eight Deer) (Yya Nacuaa), 15, 58, 77, 101, 183
Lord 8 Deer "Jaguar Claw," 115, 126
Lord 8 Water, *181*, 183
Lord 8 Wind, 128
Lord 9 Alligator, 180
Lord 9 Movement, 217
Lord 9 Wind, 101, 103
Lord 10 Movement, 124
Lord 10 Serpent, 189
Lord 11 Flower, 181–82
Lord 11 Vulture ("Smoking Eye Squirrel"), 190
Lord 11 Wind, 123, 124
Lord 12 Lizard, 172, 180, 181–82
Lord 13 Night, 10
Lord 13 Rain, 180
LTT. *See Lienzo de Tecciztlan y Tequatepec*

macana, documentary depiction of, 119
macehual settlements, tribute from, 240
Macuilxóchitl, 13, 123, 127; carved human mandible from, 107–*8*
maize, 146, 168, 169, 176
majolica, at Rancho Santa Cruz, 376–77, 378, *379*
Mama 1, 222
mandibles: carved human, *107–8*; in earth/fertility deity complex, 100–*101*, *102*, 104; in Tomb 7, 105–7
Mangue speakers, 179
Manila Galleon, 18
Manso de Contreras, Cristóbal, on rebellion in Tehuantepec, 382, 383, 386
Mapa de Santa María Tiltepec Mijes, 398
Mapa de San Vicente del Palmar, 240; description and provenience of, 232–*33*; Ihualtepec on, 234–35; salt production on, 236–38
Mapa de Teozacoalco, 26, 210–11, *213, 214, 215, 219, 220, 221,* 252–53(n9); topographs on, 233–36; Zapotec-Teozacoalco intermarriage on, 216–17
Mapa de Xoxocotlán: Monte Albán depicted on, 118–19, 121; place names on, 126–27
Mapa Número 36, 240–41, *242,* 257(n51)
mapas, 20; Harkort's copy of, 397, *397*
maps: Astata-Huamelula area, 345–48; Chontalpa, 335; Colonial period, 233–34; Mixteca Baja, 87, 231, 232
market systems, 18, 187, 189, 190
Marquesado del Valle, 19
marriages, 88, 184, 238; of Lady 6 Monkey, 123, 124, 128; Teozacoalco-Zaachila, 216–17

Marta polychrome, 131
Martínez Gracida, Manuel, 25, 56; collections by, 400, 404, *406*
Mata, Juan de, 369
material culture, 4, 34, 164, 210, 305; Chontal highlands, 303–4; Coixtlahuaca Basin, *174*; historical events and, 341–44
Matos Moctezuma, Eduardo, 79
Matrícula de Tributos, 215–16, 235
Maya, 7, 12
Mayauel, depictions of, 138, 151
Mazatec, 19, 195(n3)
Mecaltepec, 349, 350
Mejicanische Bilder: Reiseabenteuer, Gegenden, Menschen und Sitten 1827–1835 (Mühlenpfordt), 396
Mendoza, Antonio de, 64
Mendoza, Francisco de (Lord 4 Reed), and Cuyotepeji, 88
merchants, 175, 188
mestizaje, 23
mestizos, historical chronicles, 335–36
metal, in Late Postclassic, 13
Mexica, 179
Mexican Prisons, In (Harkort), 397
Mexican Revolution, 23
Mexico, 22–23
Mexico, Valley/Basin of, 13, *158,* 190, 193(table); historical archaeology, 283–84
Miahuatlán, 302
Middle Classic period, salt production, 246, 247
Middle Formative period, 5, 7–8
migrations, 25, 184, 185, 196(n9); into Mixteca, 177–78; Nahua speakers, 178–79, 194; Nonoalco, 157–58, 159; Toltec, 167
Mimich, 185
Mimixcoa, 185
Minas, Río, 213
Minera, Magdalena María la, 385
missionaries, missions: Dominican, 335–36; Spanish, 21
Mit den Füßen im Himmel, 92
Mitla, 13, 23, 104, 123, 127, 402; story of Sus Ley from, 102–3
Mixcóatl, 139
Mixcoatl-Tezcatlipoca, 177, 185
Mixe speakers, 9, 18, 19, 33, 167–68, 366, 367, 398
Mixteca, 11, 12, 13, 15, 19, 23, 28, *158,* 189, 194(table); archaeology in, 26, 29, 33; historic studies of, 399–400; intrusive groups in, 177–78; tripod *ollas,* 151–52; urban centers, 7, 9–10

Mixteca Alta, 11, 12, 84, 90, 133, *158,* 162, 176, 216, 225; archaeological survey, 76–77; Classic period in, 125, 173–75; "feline places" in, 86–87; Formative period in, 223–24; Ixcatec in, 177–78; Mixteca Pilitas polychrome from, 135–36; Ñuiñe style in, 88–89. *See also various places*; sites

Mixteca Baja, 84, 87, 92, 175, 235; Colonial period maps, 233–34; Ñuiñe style and, 88–89; pictographic maps from, 231, 232–33; Pilitas polychrome in, 132–33; salt production in, 244–50

Mixteca de la Costa, 133

Mixteca polychrome, 131, 134, *135,* 149, 152(n2), 379; distribution of, *132–33. See also* Pilitas polychrome

Mixteca-Puebla polychromes, 188; characteristics of, 131–35; locations of, 135–36

Mixteca-Puebla style (Religious Style), 157, 187, 195(n1); maps in, 232–33

Mixteca Valley, 11

Mixtec Gateway, 85–86, 94

Mixtec language, 164, 165, 179

Mixtecs, 13, 57, 103, 116, 133, 141, 167, 184, 188, 195(n3), 210, 217, 252(n8), 302, 312–13(n28), 400; codices, 14, 84; in Coixtlahuaca Basin, 173, 182, 183, 186; elite dynasties, 14–15; local knowledge, 89–92, 93–94; *pulque ritual,* 137–39

Mixtepec, 235

"Mogote del Cacique," as "Hill of Flints," 127

molcajetes de fondo sellado, 166

molds, ceramic, 187, 188, 190, *191*

monoliths: *danzante,* 8; at San José Mogote, 7

Monroy, Diego de, 382

Monte Albán, 7, 10, 12, 15, 38(n16, n22), 175, 291, 402; colonialism, 300–301; documentary depictions of, 118–19, 121; excavations of, 23, 26; place names near/for, 126–27; political power of, 120, 122–23; as sacred space, 8–9; Tomb 7, 105–7

Montemayor, Juan Francisco de, 382, 383, 384

Monte Negro, 9

monuments, 9, 12, 13, 26, 37(n12), 88–89, 310(n9); at Monte Albán, 8, 10; at Yucundaa, 58, *59, 60*

mortuary bundles, at Coatepec, 185

Motecuhzoma I, 235

Motecuhzoma II (Xocoyotzin), 214, 302, 354

Motolinía, Fernando de (Toribio de Benavente), 55

Mountain of Sand, in Codex Nuttall, 103–*4*

Mountain of War (Ñuu Yecu), 88

"Mountain That Is Opened/Hill of the Wasp," 114, *115*; location of, 126–27

mountaintop sites, in Coixtlahuaca Basin, 169, *171–72,* 175

Mühlenpfordt, Eduard, as collector, 396–97

murals, Late Postclassic, 14

Museo Comunitario (Cuquila), 90, *90*

Museo Nacional de Antropología, 63

Museo Rufino Tamayo, carved human mandible in, *107*

museums, Prehispanic collections in, 392–94

musical instruments, skull effigies as, 141

mythistorical events, 14, 21, 185

Nahua iconography, 15

Nahua speakers, 188, 195(n3); Cholula polychrome and, 132, 142; in Coixtlahuaca Basin, 178, 183, 189–90; migrations, 178–79, 194

Nahuatl, 15, 183, 400

naming, Zapotec ritual calendar and, 370

Nanacoatipec (San Antonio Nanauatipac), 178

Nanahuatipan, salt production in, 244

nationalism, Mexican, 23

National Museum of Anthropology (Mexico), collections in, 392, 402, 404

Natividad phase, 125, 175, 267; Nduavee Valley, 272–73

nautical charts, Oaxaca Coast, 345–46, *347*

Ndaxagua, 165

ndoso (toho ndoso), 273

Nduavee Valley: archaeological sites, 267, *269*; Natividad phase, 272–73

Nejapa Valley, 11

New Archaeology, 27

New Philologists, 363

New Tollan (Tulancingo), 184; rulers at, 180, 181, 189

Nextepec, 178, 244

Nezahualcoyotl, 235

Ngüiteri, 169, *171–72,* 190

Ñiatexa-Tlalpitepec, stone glyph from, *174*

Ñiaxugue, 175

Nicaragua, Mangue speakers in, 179

Nila polychrome, 131

nobility, 8, 19, 58, 122; legitimization of, 10–11

Nochixtlán, Cruz phase, 223

Nochixtlán, Valley of, 136; place signs for, 127–28; survey of, 98–99, 115–16

Nochixtlán Vase, 128

Noexcaxaiztapan, 238

Nonoalco, *158*

Nonoalca, 189
nopal, in place signs, 120, 121
Ñucuiñe, jaguar monument as, 88
Nudo Mixteco, 169–70
Ñudzahui (Mixteco), 164, 165
Ñuiñe, 250
Ñuiñe script, 11, 12, 88, 89, 175, 232
Ñujatu (Shinicuno), 267
Ñurusio, 267
Ñusa'a, 267
Nutanda'a, 267, 272
Nuttall, Zelia, 56
Ñuu Ñaña, dynasty of, 87–88
Ñuusii, 267, 272
Nuvixi, 267, 272

Oaxaca, 6(table), 38(n22, n23), 157; Middle
    Formative in, 5, 7; multiethnicity of, 34–35;
    subregions and state boundaries of, 2–3, 38(n23)
Oaxaca, Valley of, 7, 11, 12, 13, 127, 133, 184, 224;
    archaeology in, 26, 27, 29, 33
Oaxaca City, 17, 27
Oaxaca Coast, 7, 10, 13, 18, 33, 92, 312(n28), 333;
    archaeology, 29, 339–40; Chontal arrival, 344,
    348; Late Classic period, 11–12
Oaxaca Coast Project (OCP), 339
obsidian, 165, 224, 351, 373; processing sites, 99;
    sources of, 303, 313(n31)
Ocelocalco, majolica from, 377
ocelot pelts, motifs of, 191–92
Ocotepec, 87
Ocotlán, 182, 183
OCP. See Oaxaca Coast Project
offerings: Day of the Dead, 370; vessels used for,
    144–46, 152(n2)
ollas: Mixteca Pilitas polychrome, 137–42; tripod,
    135, 149, 151–52
Olmec horizon, 224, 225
Olmecs, 7, 37(n8), 224
1-Eye, 7, 37(n9)
opossums, on Cholula polychrome vessels, 145,
    146–47
oral history, 4–5, 36(n5)
oral knowledge, 4–5, 29–30; of place names,
    89–90, 92–94; on Santa María Zapotitlán,
    295–96
oral traditions, 4–5, 24, 34, 36(n5), 92, 263,
    309(n1), 335, 400; and archaeology, 264–65;
    cultural memory, 265, 274–75; of San Miguel
    el Grande, 269–74; on Zapotitlán, 303, 308–9,
    311(n18, n19, n20)

orange ware, Isthmus Zapotec, 377–80
Orizaba obsidian source, 224, 313(n31), 351
Orozco y Berra, Manuel, 56
Ortiz, Germán, 90
Ortíz, Nicodemo, 269
Otla, 182
Otomanguean languages, 157; divergence in,
    161–62
Otomí, obsidian ornaments, 165
Oyameles-Zaragoza obsidian source, 303, 351
Ozolotepec (Ocelotepec), 302
Ozomatzin from Camotlan, 88

Pacheco de Alvarado, Francisco, 234,
    253–54(n18)
Pachuca obsidian source, 303, 313(n30)
palaces, Yucundaa, 58
Palacios de los Zapotecas en Mitla, Los
    (Mühlenpfordt), 396
Palafox y Mendoza, Juan de, 386
paleoclimate reconstruction, 163
Palo Blanco phase, 166–67
Papaloapan, 33
paper, manufacture of, 232, 351, 352
paper rolls, 20
Paredón, 224
PARH. See Proyecto Arqueológico Río Huam-
    elula
Patlanala, 235
Patrimonio Real, 64
penate (crown), as symbol of royalty, 181, 183
Penth, Boris, 92
Pérez, Rafael, 270
Perros, Río de los, 365; archaeology of, 371–82
petroglyphs, at El Boquerón, 353
photographs, in museum collections, 394,
    399–400, 402
Piaxtla, 244
Pico de Orizaba, 224, 313(n31), 351
Pilitas polychrome, 132–34, 135–36, 148, 153(n10),
    196(n12); depictions in codices, 137–42
Piltzintepec, 349
Pinopiaa, shrines to, 368
pirates, 18; records of Astata, 345–46
Pisando en el Cielo: Pintores de Oaxaca, 92
pitchers, Mixteca polychrome, 139, 140
Place of Creation and Mountain of Sustenance,
    185. See also Coatepec
"Place of Reeds," 114, 120, 124
"Place of Reeds, Breasts, and Crossed Legs," 124
"Place of the Rain Deity Vessel," 114

place signs/names, 192; archaeological testing of, 344–45; in *Lienzo de Tecciztlan y Tequatepec,* 334–35, 353–54; Mixtec, 84, 114–16, 118–28; pictographic, 77, 88–89, 311(n16); San Miguel el Grande, 270–72; Santa María Cuquila as, 86–87

plates, Cholula polychrome, 145–*46*

plumed serpents, on Cholula polychrome vessels, 146

pluri-ethnicity, 174, 193–94(table)

Pochutla, 179

political power, 102; of Monte Albán, 122–23

politics: Astata-Huamelula, 353–55; Mixtec, 116; pluri-ethnic, 159

Popolocas (*Nguiwa*), 167 177, 178, 179, 188, 189, 196(n8)

population decline, Classic-Postclassic transition, 176–77, 180

porcelain, Chinese, 377

Porfiriato, 22–23

Postclassic period, 11, 33, 125, 158, 167, 194–95, 267, 298, 365; Chontal region, 301–4; Oaxaca Coast, 346, 349. *See also* Early Postclassic period; Late Postclassic period

postprocessual archaeology, 30

pottery. *See* ceramics

poverty, 24–25

prehispanic-Colonial boundary, 34

premature closure, 117

priests, *Selden Roll* depictions of, 180, *181*

Primeros Memoriales, Cihuacóatl, 100, 105

printing presses, 21

Proto-Nahuatl speakers, 178

Proyecto Arqueológico Río Huamelula (PARH), 339, 354–55

public transcripts, 364

Puebla, 189, 368; obsidian sources, 313(n31), 351

Puebla Basin, 29, *158*, 179, 180, 183, 193(table), 195(n3), 196(n7, n8)

Puebla-Tlaxcala Valley/Basin, 157, 400; Cholula polychrome in, 131, 151

Pueblo Viejo Nochixtlán, 136

Pueblo Viejo de Teposcolula. *See* Yucundaa-Pueblo Viejo de Teposcolula

Puente Colosal Ndaxagua, *Ñuiñe* inscriptions in, 11

Puga, Vasco de, 64

pulque ritual: in Codex Vindobonensis, 137–39; depictions of, 151–52; Xochipilli and, 142–44

punishments, of Tehuantepec rebels, 382, 383

Quamimilollan (San Pedro Huamelula), 334

Quauhtochco, 216

Querétaro, 176

questionnaires, *Relaciones Geográficas,* 16–17

Quetzalcoatl, 38(n20), 146, 177, 185; religion of, 187–88

Quintana, Agustín de, 399

radiocarbon dates, 153(n7), 224, 348; Cerro del Fortín, 222–23; from Cholula, 152(n6), 153(n9, n12, n13); Mixteca Alta, 161–62; from Yucuita, 136, 153(n10)

railroads, 22, 23

"Rain Deity Vessel," 126

rain petition rituals, and caves, 352–53

Ramos phase, 175, 267

Rancho Santa Cruz, 364; archaeology of, 371–82

rebellions, 18, 235; in Tehuantepec, 382–85, 386–87

"Red and White Bundle," 114, *115*, 123; destruction of, 125–26; location of, 124–25, 127

Reform War, 308

Relación de Guatulco, 179

Relaciones Geográficas, 16–17, 20, 26, 99, 183, 184; on Oaxaca Coast, 333–34; for Teozacoalco and Amoltepeque, 210–11, *212*, 218, 219

Relación Geográfica de Acatlán, 240, 244

Relación Geográfica de Teozapotlan (Zaachila), 119

Relación Geográfica de Tilantongo, 79

religion, 380; Chontal, 351–53; Christian, 21–22; Quetzalcoatl, 187–88; Zapotec, 368–69

repartimiento, in Isthmus of Tehuantepec, 382–83

reproduction, spinning and weaving and, 102

Republican period, 17, 284, 305

residential areas: San Miguel el Grande, 267; Tejupan, 99; Yucundaa, *58*

residential-ceremonial complexes, at Yucundaa, 57–58

resistance, 382; Chontal, 305–6; Zapotec, 366, 368–69, 381

Revolution, Mexican, 308–9

Reyes, Antonio de los, 21, 55, 137, 254(n20), 255(n28)

Reyes, Gloria, 245

Rinconada site, 167

Ringrose, Basil, nautical charts of, 345, *347*

Río Viejo, 11–12, 13

rituals, 380; cave, 176, 177, 351–53

Rivera Guzmán, Iván, 88–89

road infrastructure, 24

"Rocky Cave with the *Yahui,*" 127

Romero, Juana Catarina, 23
royal houses, feast networks, 188
Ruiz Medrano, Ethelia, 89–90
rulership, 8, 10, 304: Astata-Huamelula, 353–55; Coixtlahuaca Basin, 161, 169, 189; Ihualtepec, 234, *235*

sacrifice: animal, *402*; blood, 187–88; human, 7, 147, *148*
sal de grano, 245, 258(n60)
salt production/salt works, 232, 255(n32), 256(n45), 258(n53, n60); archaeological evidence of, 245–50; documentation of, 251, 255–56(n39, n40); and land rights, 238–40, 257(n47); on *Mapa de San Vicente del Palmar,* 236–38; maps showing, 231, 240–41, 257(n49); in Mesoamerica, 241–44; in Mixteca Baja, 244–45
salt springs. *See* brine springs/wells
San Antonio Nanahuatipac (Nanacoatipac), 178
San Bartolo(me) (Ihualtepec), salt production, 236, 238, 244, 245, 255–56(n39)
San Bartolo Salinas, Iglesia Vieja site, 245–50
Sánchez, Eleut, *297*
Sánchez Ramírez, Felipe, 269
Sánchez Solís, Felipe, 89
San Gabriel Casa Blanca (Nextepec), 178, 244
San Gabriel Chilac (Chilacatla), 167, 178
San Ildefonso (Ihualtepec), 238, 256(n41); salt production, 236, 240, 244
San Jerónimo *estancia*, 213, *215*
San José Chiltepec, 300, 312(n27)
San José Mogote, 7, 27, 224
San José Sosola, 92
San Juan Atzingo, 167
San Juan Comaltepec, *86*
San Juan *estancia*, 213, *215*
San Miguel el Grande (Itun Yuku Ndaku), *264*; archaeology of, 267–*69*; founding of, 269–70; oral tradition in, 263–64, 265, 271–74; place names, 270–71; topography, 266–67
San Miguel Tequixtepec, 180, 181; material culture from, *174*
San Pedro Atoyac, 236, 255(n28). *See also* Atoyac
San Pedro Huamelula museum, 338
San Pedro (Ihualtepec), salt production, 236, 238, 244
San Pedro/San Pablo Tequixtepec, monuments from, 89
San Pedro Teozacoalco, 211, *214*; *mapa* of, 211, *213*. *See also* Teozacoalco

Santa Catarina Yosonotu, 268
Santa Cruz Irundujia, 273
Santa María, Bernardo de, 369
Santa María Cuquila. *See* Cuquila
Santa María Salinas (Ihualtepec), 238, 256(n41); salt production, 236, *237*, 240, 244, 248, 255–56(n39)
Santa María Zapotitlán. *See* Zapotitlán
Santiago, Filemón, 92
Santiago, Juan de (Juan of Atoyac), 241, 256(n44); land rights and salt production, 238–40
Santiago Astata, 348. *See also* Astata
Santiago Tamazola, 258(n60); ceramic production at, 248–50
Santiago Yosondúa, 274
San Vicente del Palmar, pictographic map in, 231, 232–33
Schmieder, Oscar, 398
scholarship/research: archaeological, 25–26; collaborative/synthetic, 26–30
Schultze-Jena, Leonhard, 398; photographs of, 399–400, *402*
Selden Roll, 180, 185
Seler, Cecilie: collecting and photography, 392–93; on Sologuren's collection, 402, 404
Seler, Eduard, 56, 399; collections by, 392–93; maps by, *405*; and Sologuren's collections, 402, 404
Señor de la Columna cult, at Yukuyu'u, 268
sexual intercourse, spinning and weaving as symbols of, 102
Shell Quechquemitl, 103–*4*, 106
Shinicuno (Ñujatu), 267
Shinitikiki, 267
shrines, 221, 296, 368, *402*
Sierra de Zongolica, 158
Sierra Norte, 15, 33
Sierra Sur, 15
Silacayoapan, 235, 254(n23)
Silacayoapilla, 248
silver mining, salt use in, 243, 258(n53)
skeletons, human, depicted on Cholula polychrome vessels, 147, *148*
skulls: ceramic effigy, 141–*42*, 147; incense burners, 106–7
Smith, Mary Elizabeth, and Mixtec codices, 83–84, 87
social hierarchy, 225; Chontal, 350–51
social memory, 1–2, 24
social organization, 3, 159; Spanish era, 17–19
Society for Historical Archaeology, 283

Soconusco, 179, 368

Sola Valley, 11

Sologuren, Fernando, 136, 400; collections by, 401, 402, 404, *405*

Soria Cuevas, Tereso, Sr., 269

Soyula, 396

Spanish, 23, 38(n22), 211, 225, 235, 270, 345, 364; and Chontal, 287, 304–6, 314(n36); documentary records, 16–17; historical chronicles, 335–36; and Isthmus of Tehuantepec, 366–71; social restructuring by, 17–18

Spanish Crown, 17

Spanish language, 20, 23

spider, as weaving symbol, 105

spinning and weaving tools, 102, 105, *106*, 109, *352*

stamps, ceramic, 187, 188, 190, *191*

subsistence, Isthmus Zapotec, 373–75

Suchiquilazala (Ayoxochiquilazala), 235, 254(n25)

Suchixtlán, 128; as Chiyo Yuhu, 127

Suma de Visitas de Pueblos (SVP) census, 16; for Astata and Huamelula, 348–49, 350, 351

supra-identity, 159

Sus Ley, 102–3

Tablón Orange: ethnic identity through, 380–81, 386–87; manufacture and trade of, 377–79

Talun Carved ceramics, 12

Tamayo, Rufino, 24

Tamazola. *See* Santiago Tamazola

Tamazulapan, 57, 76–77

Tamazulapan Valley, 176, 189; archaeological survey of, 97–100

Tayata, 224

Tecamachalco, 180

Tecomaxtlahuaca, 235

tecpan, at Yucundaa, 57

Tehuacán tradition, 157

Tehuacán Valley, *158*, 166, 167, 168, 169, 172, 176, 179, 183, 189, 196(n8); pluri-ethnicity of, 193–94(table)

Tehuantepec, 17, 23, 242, 333, 352, 353, 354; Burgoa's descriptions of, 367, 371; Catholic Church in, 368, 369; native rebellion in, 382–85; Postclassic, 302, 303; public and hidden transcripts in, 385–87

Tehuantepec, Isthmus of, 7, 9, 11, 12, 13, 15, 33, 364; Aztecs in, 16, 302; rebellions in, 18, 382–85; Spanish Colonial era, 366–71

Tejupan, 57, 76–77, 99

Tejupan Valley, 176

Temple of Skull, Lady 9 Grass at, 101, *102*

Temple of the Ascending Serpent, Lady 3 Flint at, 103–4

Templo Mayor, effigy skulls in, 141, *142*

Tenayuca, 164

Tenochtitlán, 120, 176

Teotihuacan, 10, 195(n3); Oaxacans at, 174–75

Teotitlán del Valle, 13

Teozacoalco (Teotzacualco; Chiyo Cahnu), 209, 226; colonialism in, 211, 213–16; culture contact, 216–18; indigenous culture at, 218–25; and Zaachila, 216–17

Teozacoalco Archaeological Project, 210–11

Teozapotlan, 184. *See also* Zaachila

Tepeaca region, 131

Tepelmeme (Tepenenec), 184; material culture from, *174*

Tepelmeme de Morelos, 184–85

Tepelmeme cave (Puente Colosal Ndaxagua), *Ñuiñe* inscriptions in, 11

Tepenenec, 184

Tepexic, 179

Teposcolula, 57, 64–65, 223. *See also* Yucundaa-Pueblo Viejo de Teposcolula

Tequisistlán, 383

Tequixtepec, 180, 181; material culture from, *174*

Tequixtepec del Rey, 87

Terminal Formative period, 9, 300

terraces, 162; in Coixtlahuaca Basin, 175; salt production, 244–45, *246*; at San Miguel el Grande, 267

Terrazas, Carlos de, 234; land rights and salt production case, 238–40, 253–54(n18), 257(n47)

Terrazas, Diego de, 234, 253–54(n18)

Terrazas, Felipe de, 234, 251, 253–54(n18)

Terrazas, Juan de, 251

territorial narratives, 288, *290*, *291*–92, 299, 303, 304

tesquisquite, 242–43

Texcala, 244

Texupan ceramics, 166

Texupan Valley, 189

Tezcatlipoca, 146

Tilantongo, 57, 88, 115, 127, 128, 210, 225; archaeological survey, 77, 80–81, 84; Temple of Heaven at, *78*, 79; and Teozacoalco, 217, 218, *219*

Tilantongo Valley, survey of, *76*, 77

titulos primordiales, 20

Tlacaelel, 101

Tlapanec, 168, 400

tlatoani, and Cihuacóatl, 101

Tlaxcala, pluri-ethnicity of, 193(table)

Tlaxcalans, labrets used by, 165

Tlaxiaco, 57, 87; gold pendant from, *393*

tocujñuhu (*tocuijñudzavui*), 165

Toledo, Francisco, 24

Tollan (Tula Xicocotitla), 164

Tollan de Tamazolac (Tenayuca), 164

Tollantzinco (Tulancingo; New Tollan), 184; rulers at, 180, 181, 189

Tolteca-Chichimeca, 13, 186

Toltecs, 12, 38(n24), 163, 167, 189; in Coixtlahuaca, 180, 182

Toluca Valley, 175

Tolula, 15

tombs, 11, 27; with earth/fertility deity complex items, 104–9; at Ngüiteri, 171–72

Tomb 7 (Monte Albán), 26, 104; earth/fertility deity complex items in, 105–7

Tonalá, 231, 236, 252(n6), 254(n23, n25), 257(n48); land tenure documentation, 250–51, 253–54(n18); salt works in, 239–40

topoglyphs, topographs, 297, 311(n16); on *Mapa de San Vicente del Palmar,* 233–36

toponyms, 16, 312(n22, n27); Coixtlahuaca Basin, 184–85; Mixtec, 26, 84, 312–13(n28); Teozacoalco, 219, *220;* Tilantongo, *218*

Totonac, 12

tourism, 24

trade networks, 18, 23, 162, 224, 225, 269, 377; in Coixtlahuaca Basin, 172, 174, 190; Late Postclassic, 13, 187–88; salt, 238, 241–44, 258(n60); sites associated with, 300–301; Zapotec, 175, 368; Zapotitlán, 303, 313(n30)

Treading in Heaven: Painters of Oaxaca, 92

Tres Picos, 9

tributary capitals, 235

tribute: Aztec, 190, 215–16, 218, 235, 313(n30); records of, 16, 21, 211, 240

Triple Alliance, in Chontal highlands, 302–3

Tula, 38(n24), 166, 176, 177, 184, 187

Tula Xicocotitla, 164

Tulancingo (Tollantzinco), 184; rulers at, 180, 181, 189

turquoise, 13, 105

Tututepec, 13, 15, 16, 17, 215, 333, 354; Chontal region and, 301–2, 303, 313(n30)

tzoalli, 100, 106

Ucareo, 224

Uhde, Carl Adolf, 395; collections of, *396, 397*

United States, Oaxacan migrants in, 25

urban centers, 7, 9, 12, 24; Yucundaa as, 58, 65; Zapotec script at, 9–10

Urnas de Oaxaca (Caso and Bernal), 401–2

usos y costumbres governance, 34

Valderrama, Jerónimo de, 64

Vasconcelos, José, 23

vases, Cholula polychrome, 147, *148*

Vázquez de Tapia, Bernardino, 235

Vehe Andehui. *See* Tilantongo

Venta Salada phase ceramics, 172

Versuch Einer Getreuen Schilderung der Republik Mexiko of 1884 (Mühlenpfordt), 396

Virreinato and Audiencia de Nueva España, 64

warfare, 163, 304, 354; Chichimeca participation in, 181–82; Coixtlahuaca Basin, 179, 182–83, 189; depictions in Mixtec codices, 113, 114–15, 119

"War of Heaven," 101, 114, 176

warriors: recruitment of, 183–84; *Selden Roll* depictions of, 180, *181*

weaving: goddesses and, 103–4; and sexual intercourse, 102

weaving tools: bone, 104–5; symbolism of, 103–4, 109

wedding ceremonies: Mixteca polychrome vessels in, 137, 139, 151–52; Nahua, 142

"White Hill of Flints," 127

writing, 4, 9, 11, 37(n8), 38(n25)

writing systems, 20, 38(n20, n25); Late Postclassic, 13–14; Mixteca-Puebla pictographic, 158–59; Nahuatl, 15–16; *Ñuiñe* script, 12, 175; at San José Mogote, 7, 27; Zapotec, 8–10, 11, 27–28, 38(n14), 175

Xaliyztapa, 238

Xayacatzin (Lord "Mask"), 190

xicalcoliuhqui motif, on ceramics, 146, 377, 381

Xicotlan, material culture from, *174*

"Xipe Bundle," 115, 124. *See also* "Red and White Bundle"

xiucoatl (fire serpent), 177

Xochicalco, 12

Xochipilli (Lord 7 Flower), 151; and *pulque* ritual, 139, 142–44

Xochiquetzal, 100, 151

Xochitepec, 182, 183

Xoconotzin (Lord "Prickly-Pear-Fruit War Legs"), 190

Xocotlatoani, 354

Xocoyotzin (Motecuhzoma II), 214, 302, 354

Xoo phase, 107, 123, 127, 175
Xoxocotlán, 126, 184, 402, *405*
Xoxouqui Yztapan, 238

Yagul, 13, 123, 139, 153(n7)
Yanhuitlan, 57, 59, 184, 223
Yatachio, 99
Yautepec Codex, 15
Yosondúa, 273, 274
Yucuchicano, 99
Yucuita, 379; Cruz A phase settlement, 223–24;
    radiocarbon date, 136, 153(n10); Zapotec script
    at, 9–10
Yucuita phase, 175
Yucundaa-Pueblo Viejo de Teposcolula, 13, 57,
    64–65; historic burials in, 59–60; Spanish
    changes to, 58–59; survey of, 98, *99*
Yucundacua (Ocotlán), 182, 183
Yucuñudahui, 11
Yucuyaha, Lord 4 Ocelot in, 183
yuhuitayu (altepetl), Coixtlahuaca, 182
Yukuyu'u, as ceremonial site, 267–68
Yuyao, 267

Zaachila (Teozapotlan), 15, 16, 27, 104, 123, 127, 139,
    142, 184; as *Cacaxtli* Hill, 120, 126; place names

associated with, 121, 122; and Teozacoalco,
    216–17
Zacahuilotlan, 180
Zacatlán, royal house of, 189
Zapotecs, 19, 23, 26, 29, 175, 184, 188, 210, 225, 302,
    354, 398, 406; animal use by, 373–75; archaeol-
    ogy of, 371–72; Burgoa's description of, 366–71;
    ceramic manufacture and, use, 375–82; on
    Isthmus of Tehuantepec, 15, 364; rebellion by,
    382–87; ritual calendar, 7, 8, 12, 370; Spanish
    Colonial era, 366–71; in Teozacoalco, 216–17;
    writing system, 8–10, 27–28, 38(n14)
Zapotitlán (Santa María), 167, 179, 244, 313(n32),
    349, 350; archaeological data, 296–*97*; Colonial
    period, 304–6; community museum in, 307–9;
    documentary and oral sources, 295–96, 308–9;
    integrative data, 297–99; Postclassic period,
    301–4; toponyms of, 300, 312(n22)
Zapotitlán del Río, 213, *215*, 222
Zapotitlán Manuscript (ZM), 295, 301
Zapotitlán Salinas, 244
Zapotitlán-Village site, 301
Zaragoza obsidian source, 303, 351
Zimatlán, effigy vessel from, *401*
ZM. *See Zapotitlán Manuscript*
Zoque, 33, 366, 367